CONTENTS

INTRODUCTION v

LIST OF PRINCIPAL DATES xv

EDITORIAL NOTE xvii

THE DIARY 1

    Part I: OXFORD AND THE SOMERSET CURACIES,
      1758–76 1

    Part II: WESTON LONGEVILLE, NORFOLK,
      1776–1803 122

APPENDIX 620

TO
LORD FITZMAURICE
OF LEIGH

In Memory of many
Good Talks of
HISTORY, BOOKS, *and* MEN
in a Wiltshire Garden

INTRODUCTION

THE first volume of Parson Woodforde's Diary was published in the spring of 1924. The welcome accorded to this obscure Country Parson, the existence of whose diaries had hitherto been completely unknown, even to the Historical Manuscripts Commission, was immediate and widespread. The consequence was that the extracts from the Diary which grew even more interesting as the forty-four years—1758–1802—of its period advanced could not be contained in less than five volumes, the last of which appeared in 1931.[1]

Meanwhile it has been suggested more than once that five volumes, while well enough for students, for libraries, and for Woodforde disciples, are a trifle daunting to the ordinary person, particularly if the reading of books is not his principal occupation in life. Moreover, now that Woodforde has established himself, not merely as one of the greater Diarists, but as an authority on certain aspects of the social scene of his time, there is much to be said for a quintessence of him for Everyman. It is the object of the present volume to supply this need. Within the compass of this book is contained about a third of the published Diary, composed of extracts from all five volumes.

Diary writing at its best is an extremely rare and difficult art. Three names stand out, Samuel Pepys, John Evelyn, and John Wesley. All three were men well known in their lives who moved much in the crowded world. Their diaries have become historical

---

[1] This five-volume edition, edited by John Beresford, was published by the Oxford University Press, and is out of print. The manuscript of the Diary—apart from one volume which has been lost—is now in the Bodleian Library, Oxford.

documents largely on this account. The barest summary of their lives would show at once at how many points they touched the life of their times, life, that is to say, as one has been accustomed to think of it in terms of history. A bare summary of Parson Woodforde's life—and the reader will find a list of principal dates at the end of the Introduction—brings out vividly how tranquil and obscure his career was. It is, in the case of Woodforde, just because his life was so tranquil and so obscure that the Diary is uniquely interesting. The ordinary life of ordinary men passes away like a shadow.

But by means of Parson Woodforde's Diary we are able, for the second half of the eighteenth century, to meet and to know individually and personally the very men and women who lived in country villages and country towns in that period—farmers, farm labourers, shopkeepers, attorneys, menservants, maid-servants, country squires, clergy, doctors, blacksmiths, pedlars, parish clerks, publicans, merchants, and travellers by many a coach. Since life in the country, in the immemorial villages of England was—unlike our own urban day—the experience of the vast majority of Woodforde's contemporaries, the record is all the more significant.

In reading it, however, it is necessary constantly to remember the prodigious difference in the setting of the whole scene. The following is a bird's-eye view, taken at random during almost any part of the period 1750–1800.

England is governed by the Aristocracy and the King. The Rotten Boroughs return members at their bidding. Only the County Members are rather more free, and even their return is largely dependent on the support of the great lords; moreover, in any case, the county franchise is limited to forty shillings a year freeholders. The Prime Minister is the actual nominee of the King, not of the Party. Only members of the Anglican Church are legally eligible for national or municipal office, or for admittance to the universities; a certain number of Dissenters, however, manage to scrape in through the loophole of occasional conformity or the Indemnity Acts. The criminal law is immensely rigorous, and thefts of the value of 40*s.* or over are punished by death. There are 160 capital offences. Small-pox carries off the thirteenth or fourteenth part of each generation. The Slave Trade is regarded as a legitimate commercial enterprise, and slavery itself as a respectable institution. The Society for the Propagation of the Gospel owns slaves in Barbadoes, and Whitefield has slaves in Georgia. Men are 'impressed' when necessary for the navy, and, by a variety of means, not seldom forced into the army. France is regarded as the age-long enemy of England. Though the Jacobites cease, after the suppression of the dangerous outbreak of 1745–6, to be a serious political menace, the Catholics are hated or feared by the people, and subject to outbursts of mob violence, as in the Gordon Riots in 1780. The theory of Free Trade is but just born, and high Protection— with the consequent smuggling—is practised universally. There is no system of public health or public education. In the civil service promotion depends on patronage, and in the army on purchase. There are, of course, no railroads, and the roads, such as they are, are controlled by a net-work of turnpikes. Travelling is by horseback, coach, or post-chaise. The existence of highwaymen adds a certain excitement to long journeys.

Within this context, the main interest of the Diary

is its country interest. There is hardly a whisper of the Industrial Revolution now starting on its course through the discoveries and inventions of Kay, Hargreaves, Crompton, Cartwright, Cort, Arkwright, and Watt. If there is a whisper it is in the obscure visits of Alldridge, the pedlar, and Bagshaw, the Derbyshire man, to the Parsonage door, bringing with them cotton and thread and ribbons, or in the unemployment of a poor Weaver in Norwich, or in the establishment of the new Iron Foundry in that city.

Similarly, such years as 1782 to 1787 see immense events: America emerges, the Ancien Régime in France is tottering to its fall, Blake is beginning the Songs of Innocence, the first step has been taken in the exploration of the air. Inevitably spectacles so tremendous in their influence upon posterity appear to occupy wholly the historic stage. But such spectacles do not engross the attention of contemporary men. If so famous a politician and person as Fox, while visiting the treasures of the Louvre, found his mind anxiously speculating as to the condition of his turnips at St. Anne's, it is obvious that less important persons will be concerned in such matters to an even greater extent.

It is therefore essential to perspective to bear in mind that at the same time that vast events were in the making, Parson Woodforde was coursing fine, large hares with his grey-hounds Dutchess, Hector, and Reach'em; that he was sending pork, baskets of apples, and veal broth to his poor parishioners, giving alms to an old man playing on the dulcimer, bestowing pence upon all the village children on St. Valentine's day; that he was finding dinner in the company of a Bishop and a Baronet rather a strain, but on the other hand, rejoicing in the society of his farmers at the tithe-frolic, or in the more cultured society of the poet Cowper's cousins, the Bodhams and the Donnes; that despite the supposed immobility of the country gentry of the eighteenth century, Parson Woodforde thought nothing of journeying by coach all the way to Somerset—stopping in London on the way to see the sights, and fairly 'trimming it' down the Bath Road in the Balloon coach; that the American War had to be paid for in heavy taxes, and that nevertheless it was possible to maintain open house, keep two maid-servants, two menservants, and a boy, and three horses, and be very generous to one's niece and nephews on a little over £400 a year; that wood-peckers could do dreadful damage to a thatched roof; that small-pox haunted even the dreams of the eighteenth century; and how magnificently the pageant of Peace, and of the Patron Saint of Wool-combers—Bishop Blaise—paraded the streets of Norwich in 1783.

Again, how does the French Revolution affect Parson Woodforde? At first hardly a ripple of the wave reaches him. It took ten days for the news of the fall of the Bastille (July 14, 1789) to reach Parson Woodforde. On July 24th he was staying in Somerset with Sister Pounsett and having 'breakfasted, dined, &c. again at Cole', he bought an extra large crab from a travelling fisherman. Then the Bath paper arrived with news of a 'very great Rebellion in France:' exciting information, of course, but not worthy of special comment. Far worthier of comment was that 'Dies Memorabilis' of August 4th following, when George III and the Queen and the Royal Princesses visited Lord Digby at Sherborne Park. It is a wonderful description. When all France is in ferment, thousands of peaceful Dorset and Somerset folk pay charming homage in Lord Digby's park to George III, who has now become one of the most popular Kings of England.

On October 16, 1789, Parson Woodforde is back at Weston Parsonage: it is ten days since the march of the Paris mob to Versailles, followed by the enforced removal of Louis XVI and Marie Antoinette to the French capital. Parson Woodforde reads the news, and begins to realize its significance—'all anarchy and confusion.'

But though Parson Woodforde is inevitably affected by these world events, the tenor of his way is essentially the same. The tranquillity of Weston Parsonage is really disturbed by these things very little indeed.

But naturally the name of Nelson emerges most triumphantly from these quiet pages—'that great commander' as Pitt described him in the House of Commons on December 3, 1798, 'whose services fill every bosom with rapturous emotion, and who will never cease to derive from the gratitude of his country-men the tribute of his worth.' For Nelson was a Norfolk man to the backbone, and his grandfather, his father, and his brother were Norfolk country parsons.

The official day of thanksgiving in England for the Battle of the Nile was November 29, 1798, and so in the evening 'I gave my Servants after Supper some strong Beer and some Punch to drink Admiral Lord Nelson's Health on his late grand Victory and also all the other Officers with him and all the brave Sailors with them, and also all those brave Admirals, Officers and Sailors that have gained such great & noble Victories of late over the French &c., &c.'

INTRODUCTION

The nearest we get to Nelson himself is through his clerical first cousins, the elegant and agreeable Sucklings, who visit Parson Woodforde quite often; indeed Horace Suckling was on the point of becoming curate at Weston in succession to Mr. Corbould had not 'a very good Piece of Preferment and an excellent House' been bestowed on him near Beccles.

As a diarist, Parson Woodforde has a rare combination of faculties—a peculiar interest in life itself, a sense of proportion, an innate understanding of the fundamental importance of little things in the make-up of life, a deep sense of truth and the power to convey its impression in compendious phrase. It is Friday, June 28th, 1793: 'We got up about 4 o'clock this morning and at 5 got into the Bath Coach from the Angel and set off for Bath. Briton on the top of the Coach. The Coach carries only 4 inside Passengers. We had a very fat Woman with a Dog and many band boxes, which much incommoded us, and also a poor sickly good kind of a Man that went with us.' Or on April 2nd, 1788, you can see 'Mary Brand an old Woman of 80 . . . spinning by the fire tho' she almost is blind. I gave her to buy Tobacco as she smokes 0. 1. 0.' Or on October 4th, 1787, you will be held up at the Inn at Hindon for lack of horses—'N.B. At the same Inn at Hindon was Mr. Pitt, the prime Minister, in the same dilemma as we were, all the Horses being engaged—He was going to Burton Pynsent.' And on Christmas Day 1776 and for many a Christmas Day to come, you can dine at Weston Parsonage on a fine sirloin of beef roasted and plum puddings with 'old Richard Bates, old Richard Buck, old Thos. Cushion, old Harry Andrews, old Thos. Carr, old Robin Buck Mrs. Dunnell's man, and James Smith the clerk.'

At the same time you can experience the intense cold of the Winters, specially that terrible Winter, which kept on coming back, of 1794-5. Ah! how bitter it was—the snow, the frost, the cutting winds outside, the shuddering sharpness of the air within— milk frozen solid in the milk pans in the Dairy, the chill Study, the ice-cold bed-rooms. We see many birds lying dead and 'the Rooks and Crows so tame that they come up to the Kitchen door where I feed my Poultry'. Fortunately for the Poor the fount of eighteenth-century Charity seems to have flowed with generous freedom, and bread and coal are given for many months—Squire Custance and Parson Wood- forde each subscribing £10 to the general collection. So free indeed is the charitable stream on all and every occasion of distress that Widow Greaves Junior gains greatly through losing her cow: she gets £6 from her petition and buys a new cow for £4.

For students of the social scene and of social development the Diary is a mine of information supplied so naturally and so vividly that one is apt to forget how important historically it is. Among so many points it is only possible here to refer to a few— the good fellowship between different classes and sections of society and the relative absence of that snobbishness which was the least attractive aspect of the following century; the continuous and rapid improvements in the means of travel which, in fact, distinguishes the second half of the eighteenth century from all the centuries which went before; the great number of servants employed by the comfortable classes and the constant entertaining and hospitality: the heavy drinking and drunkenness; the terrible toll taken by small-pox and by consumption; the wide- spread existence of pluralism in the Church and the relatively low standard of ecclesiastical duty; the high purchasing power of money; the low prices of many articles of food—notably meat and the great consumption of it; finally the continual fount of charity and the policy of liberal Parish relief which alleviated the sufferings of the poor in hard times.

The peace which breathes from Parson Woodforde's pages is a permanent possession. In them is enshrined an illumination of village life in England at a time when the country was the familiar scene for the great majority of people. The Weston Purse Club no longer perambulates the Parish every Whit-Tuesday 'with Fife and Drum and Flag streaming', nor the children come for their pennies on Valentine's Day, nor the farmers attend the tithe-audit, nor the Parsonage servants and the Weston House servants sup together on occasion—for Weston House has been pulled down, and the Parsonage was rebuilt in 1840. Nor can you meet John Springle carrying on his head a skep of bees tied up in cloth, walking all the way from Sparham, nor watch Briton, the Diarist's servant, giving Bread to the Poor at Church 'from Money which he had received for that Purpose from some Person who desired that it may not be known from whom it came.'

Nevertheless these things have not passed away, for Parson Woodforde has kept them for ever.

JOHN BERESFORD[1]

[1] For this paperback reissue of passages from *The Diary of a Country Parson*, the opportunity has been taken to revise John Beresford's introduction by incorporating extracts from his introductions to the five-volume edition published between 1924 and 1931 and now out of print. The selection has been made by Rosemary Beresford, his elder daughter. Apart from linking phrases, amounting to some twenty words in all, the text is exclusively that of John Beresford.

PRINCIPAL DATES IN
PARSON WOODFORDE'S LIFE

JUNE 27 (June 16 O.S.) 1740 born at Ansford, Somerset, baptized three days later, 'being very ill', by his father who was Rector of Ansford and Vicar of Castle Cary.

1752 elected scholar of Winchester College.

JULY 21, 1759 elected scholar of New College, Oxford.

JULY 21, 1761 elected fellow of New College.

MAY 29, 1763 ordained deacon at Oxford.

JUNE 1, 1763 B.A. degree.

SEPTEMBER 12, 1763 leaves Oxford for Somerset.

OCTOBER 8, 1763 Curate of Thurloxton, Somerset.

JANUARY 12, 1764 Curate of Babcary, Somerset.

SEPTEMBER 29, 1764 ordained Priest at Wells.

MAY 26, 1765 Curate of Castle Cary (gives up Babcary in October).

OCTOBER 1765 takes up residence in the Lower House, Ansford.

MAY 23, 1767 M.A. degree.

JUNE 4, 1771 takes up residence in Ansford Parsonage, on his father's death, and continues as Curate of Castle Cary and Ansford till 1773.

DECEMBER 1773 leaves Ansford to take up residence at New College, Oxford, of which he becomes Sub-Warden.

APRIL 13, 1774 Pro-Proctor.

DECEMBER 15, 1774 presented to the living (Rectory) of Weston Longeville, Norfolk, but continues to reside at New College till February 15, 1776, when he goes home to Ansford.

NOVEMBER 24, 1775 B.D. degree.

MAY 9, 1776 leaves Ansford with his nephew Bill for Weston Longeville, which they reach on May 24.

MAY 24, 1776 to January 1, 1803 lives at Weston Longeville Parsonage, where he died on the latter date. In December 1778 his nephew Bill leaves Weston, and in October 1779 Nancy, his niece, arrives and lives with him for the rest of his life. Parson Woodforde never married. He proposed to a Miss Betsy White, of Shepton Mallet, on May 28, 1774, but she jilted him later for a rich Mr. Webster, of Devonshire, whom she married on September 6, 1775.

NOTE ON
EDITORIAL METHOD

IN *preparing the present single-volume edition of Parson Woodforde's Diary I have tried to keep before me one primary object, namely, to give the ordinary reader who has not leisure to read all five volumes as compendious an impression as possible of the Diarist's character, life, and times. I have not merely attempted to select as many as possible of the most interesting passages, but to choose also those—or some of those—which convey the day-to-day atmosphere and the continuity of normal life. Extracts are given from the Diary for each year of the long period covered—forty-four years— so that the reader will find himself following Parson Woodforde's career from the age of eighteen to the age of sixty-two, indeed to within two and a half months of his death.*

In the Prefatory Note to the first volume and in the Note on Editorial Method in the second volume I explained the general principles on which I had worked: the student, who may be expected to take an interest in such things, as distinct from the ordinary reader, should refer to those volumes and to the complete work.

In the present edition I have omitted a large number of footnotes or explanatory observations, and greatly curtailed others. On the other hand, references in the Diary to historical events become much more interesting if one briefly recalls their setting and circumstance, and so those footnotes which have been retained, even in shortened form, attempt to illuminate fleeting and forgotten time. The various authorities on which the footnotes have been carefully based are given so fully in the five-volume edition, that, except in one or two particular instances, I thought they might be omitted in the present edition, in the interest of brevity and space. Phrases or words used by the Diarist which, on occasion, may at first puzzle the reader, will usually surrender their meaning either in the context in which they occur or in a later context. In any event, it is part of my editorial creed that it is better to err on the side of too few, rather than too many footnotes.

1935   J. B.

THE DIARY

PART I
OXFORD AND THE SOMERSET
CURACIES, 1758–76

THE Diary begins with some entries of account at Oxford, dated October 1758. Here are a few purchases of an eighteenth-century undergraduate.

1758–9

1758.	OCT. 19.	A pair of Curling Tongs £0.		2.	8
	OCT. 20.	Two Logick Books	0.	6.	0
	OCT. 25.	Two Bottles of Port Wine	0.	3.	4
	NOV. 6.	A Sack of Coal	0.	4.	9
	NOV. 7.	A Musick Book	0.	1.	6
1759.	MAY 25.	A New Wigg	1.	1.	0
	JUNE 16.	Had of my Father	1.	1.	0
	JUNE 18.	Nosegays	0.	0.	1
	JULY 4.	Ester Oratorio	0.	5.	0
	JULY 5.	Messiah	0.	5.	0
	JULY 6.	2 White Waistcoats	1.	16.	0

He also notes that he has a 'superfine blue suit of cloathes, very good cloth' which cost £4 10s. and a chocolate suit 'bad' which cost £3.

The detailed Diary begins on July 21, 1759, with the laconic entry: 'Made a Scholar of New College'. In August and September of this year he is at home at Ansford. The early entries in the Diary are very short, thus:

1759. Aug. 28. We [his Papa and he][1] lodged at the King's Arms in Evershot, where we had exceeding good Port Wine.

Sept. 5. I went to the Bear-baiting in Ansford.

Sept. 16. One Mr. Russ of Shepton Mallett who brought Miss Payne [a friend] came after her again, but he being so very drunk, and very late, we would not let her go.

On October 1st, he sets out on horseback with his father's man for Oxford, the route being through Deptford, Yearnbury Castle, Maddington, Netherhaven, Everly (where he lodged that night at the Rose and Crown; Everly is about fifty miles from Ansford, a pretty long day's stretch on horseback); then the next day through Sharvord, Winterburn, Hungerford, Newtown, Shapwick, Farnborough, Abbey Milton, Abbington, to Oxford, which they reached on the evening of October 2nd.

The Diary continues:

1759. Oct. 6. Geree, Peckham and myself had a hogshead of Port from Mr. Cropp of Southampton.

Oct. 8. Had of Mr. Prince the Bookseller in New College Lane, a standish with sand, Ink, Wafers, and half a Hundred of Pens.

Oct. 14. Mr. Turner Junr. of this College died this afternoon about 3 o'clock in a deep consumption. [He is buried Oct. 17th at 10 o'clock at night in the Cloisters 'in a very plain and decent manner'.]

---

[1] Any words interpolated into the text of the Diary itself for explanation are shown in square brackets [ ]; ordinary brackets ( ) are the Diarist's own.

OCT. 18. Very great rejoycings this night on the taking of Quebec.

OCT. 30. Went with Masters a shooting to Stanton Woods.

NOV. 10. John Atwell brought me up a Bed, 3 Blanketts, a Quilt, Bolster and Pillow, and a letter from my Sister Jenny, together with a Hare which Esq. Newman sent me up, which I think is very kind.
    Had another bottle of Hadley's Wine.

NOV. 16. Gave away my snuff-box to a Particular Friend.

NOV. 29. . . . Mr. Messiter, Mr. Philip Hays, and Mr. Holton of Mag. Coll. spent the evening with me, and sat up till 2 o'clock in the morning. . . . Had 6 bottles of my wine.

DEC. 3. I first began on the Spinnet, Mr. Philip Hays, my Tutor.

DEC. 8. . . . Had a Half-Crown Bowl of Punch from Kennerslys. I laid in Mr. Nicolls rooms with Mr. Hearst, who turned me out of Bed, and locked me out of the room naked.

DEC. 10. I went with Mr. Bertie, Gen. Comm. [Gentleman Commoner] of this House, to see the man ride upon three Horses.

DEC. 22. My great Aunt Ann Woodforde died of the small-pox at Bicester this morning.

DEC. 25. I received the Sacrament being Xmas Day. The Warden dined in Hall with us. The Bursars give us Scholars 8 Bottles of Port Wine to drink at dinner time. They likewise give us a qutr of a Cheshire

Cheese. We have 2 large Grace Cups between courses.
We have rabbits for supper, 1 Rabbit between three
at the expense of the Domus. Sent a letter to my
Father.

1760

JAN. 21. Went and heard Doctor Blackstone's Lecture on the Crown being Hereditary.

JAN. 30. Mr. Pye the Subwarden set me Part of the
1st Lesson for this morning service to translate into
Sapphic Metre, for not being at Prayers this morning.

MAR. 3. Gave my imposition to Mr. Pye, upon
David's Lamentation over Saul and Jonathan made
by Nicolls in Sapphic Metre. Had a Bottle of my
Wine.

MAR. 22. Breakfasted at Tahourdin's. Dined at the
Cross Inn with Mr. Ben. Bathurst, Ensign of the first
Regiment of Foot Guards, who is come out to recruit.
... N.B. We had Clarett, Madeira and Port to drink.

.   .   .   .

AP. 29. Went and play'd Crikett, being the first time
of our Clubb's playing. N.B. we play'd in Port
Meadow.

MAY 14. Plaid at Crikett in Port Meadow, the Winchester against the Eaton, and we Winton: beat them.

MAY 20. Hooke, Boteler and myself went to Welch's
of Wadham College, where we designed to sup and
spend the evening, but our entertainment was thus,
one Lobster of a Pound, a half-pennyworth of Bread,

and the same of Cheese, half of an Old Bottle of Ale, Half a Bottle of Wine, and a Bottle of Lisbon, and then we were desired to retreat, which was immediately obeyed. . . . N.B. A Wadamite.

JUNE 20. I declaimed in Chapel upon—An sapiens mutet sententiam . . . affirmatur.

On July 18th, he leaves Oxford to spend the Long Vacation at home, travelling on horseback. Nothing notable happens during the vacation—much visiting of cousins, a little coursing of hares, and so on. Then, on October 10th, he sets out for Oxford, the journey on horseback taking the usual two days. What with meals, the night's lodging, tips to hostlers and maids, and turnpikes, the two days' journey costs him 17s. 9d. for himself and his horse.

OCT. 25. N.B. King George the 2nd died this morning at nine o'clock, there being an Express just arrived from London here this evening at five o'clock.

OCT. 31. Went and saw King George the third proclaimed King of England in High Street.

NOV. 1. Had a Suit of Mourning for the King brought home this very night.

NOV. 7. I declaimed in Chapel upon—Utrum immensas opes possidere alicujus periculo, vel securitati magis fere conducat. . . . Periculo.

This term he becomes acquainted with two Oxford girls, Nancy Bignell and her sister Betsy, with whom he takes numerous walks. The friendship appears to have been extremely innocent; he gives Nancy six white handkerchiefs to make for him, and later gives her and her sister Betsy each a silver thimble.

1761

JAN. 2. For Ale in a House in Holinwell, where I took some verses from a Man, made upon Nancy Bignell and myself, pd. o. o. 4*d*. At cards with Brewer, Peckham and Williams, lost, o. 5. 6.

JAN. 7. Peckham, Loggin and Webber went with me to Halse's the Sadler, where I threshed his apprentice Crozier for making verses on me.

JAN. 25. We went into second mourning for his late Majesty, King George the second. Drank tea this afternoon at Tahourdin's with George Weller.

FEB. 2. . . . Went and saw Dumas alias Darking, a famous Highwayman, in the Castle. Gave a girl there, in for stealing a Shift o. o. 2*d*.

FEB. 13. A Publick Fast for our Fleets and Armies . . .

MAR. 6. Went up into the Hall this afternoon after the Judge was in, and I could not get a tolerable Place some time, but at last I jumped from two men's shoulders and leaped upon the Heads of several men and then scrambled into the Prisoners Place where the Judge said I must not stay, so one of the Counsellors [i.e. Barristers] desired me not to make a noise, and he would let me have his Place, which was immediately under the Prisoners and opposite the Judge, where I sat and heard three or four tryalls, and likewise condemnation passed on Dumas, alias Darking, alias Hamilton, alias Harris. Was up there from 5 till 9, and then the Judge had finished everything. 1 condemned to die, 4 transported for seven years, 1 burnt in the hand and acquitted.

MAR. 11. . . . Baker and Croucher both of Merton Coll: spent their evening in the B.C.R. [Bachelors' Common Room]. Croucher was devilish drunk indeed, and made great noise there, but we carried him away to Peckham's Bed in Triumph. Baker laid with me.

MAR. 22. Being Easter Day received this morning the Holy Sacrament . . . took a walk this evening with Nancy Bignell.

MAR. 23. Mr. Darking alias Dumas etc., was hanged this morning about a quarter before eight, and after he was cut down he was carried by the Bargemen to St. Thomas Church to be buried. All the College gates was shut from ten o'clock last night till nine this morning by an Order of the Vice-Chancellor and Procters.

JUNE 14. . . . Hearst, Bell and myself, being in Beer, went under Whitmore's window, and abused him very much, as being Dean, he came down, and sent us to our Proper Rooms, and then we Huzza'd him again and again. We are to wait on him to-morrow.

JUNE 15. We waited on Whitmore this morning and he read to us a Statute or two and says he shall not mention again provided the Senr. People do not. I am to read the three first Books of Hutchinson's Moral Philosophy, and I am to give a summary account of them when I am examined for my Degree. . . .

On July 21st, 1761, he is made a Fellow of New College, and treats the Bachelors' Common Room 'all the evening with Wine and Punch'. The quantity of drink consumed by the eighteenth-century undergraduate appears to have been very considerable. The entries 'Had a bottle of my Wine' are frequent. On July 26th he notes that out of a half-hogshead of port 'I have 12 dozen and six bottles'. On July 22nd he makes an expedition to London with three other friends. They go by stage coach—'in Bews Machine'—starting at five o'clock in the morning, and arriving about tea-time at Hyde Park Corner. They go down the river and sup at Vauxhall—that centre of eighteenth-century gaiety which readers of *Tom Jones*, to say nothing of *Vanity Fair*, will remember. Next day they see the Duke of Cumberland, who finally smashed the Jacobite cause at Culloden in 1746, 'ride in his coach and six through ye Park'; they continue the countryman's usual London round—Westminster Abbey, the Tower, &c., and see a play, *All in the Wrong*, at the Theatre Royal, Drury Lane, in the evening. Next day they return to Oxford. On August 26th (1761) he is back at Ansford.

Aug. 26. ... I gave Jenny 3 yards of Riband. I gave an Ivory Thimble to her. I gave her some Court Plaister: dined, supp'd and laid at Home.

Septem. 5. Had a Letter from young Tom Rooke, from London for which I paid 0. 0. 7*d.* For reading the news at Ansford Inn 0. 0. 7*d.* ...

Septem. 27. ... George Snooke, my Tenant at Sanforde, brought me over a fine large Hare.

Septem. 28. I paid Mr. Willmott for a Spinnett £3. 3. 0 which Mama gave me.

Oct. 3. I changed my Paper Snuff Box with Miss Nancy Rooke for one of hers by way of a Remembrance of her.

On October 6th he sets out for Oxford.

Octob. 17. . . . I gave some verses on the King's Marriage for Dean Whitmore. For Oysters this evening pd o. o. 2*d*. I have been extremely well all day. I was at five o'clock Prayers this afternoon, where one Jones, a Famous Methodist was.

Nov. 4. . . . Dyer laid Williams 2*s*. 6*d*. that he drank 3 Pints of Wine in 3 Hours, and that he wrote 5 verses out of the Bible right, but he lost. He did it in the B.C.R., he drank all the Wine, but could not write right for his Life. He was immensely drunk about 5 Minutes afterwards.

Nov. 19. . . . Went this evening to Haw's (a famous Methodist) Lecture in St. Giles's Church . . . very stupid, low and bad stuff.

Nov. 27. . . . I declaimed this morning in Chapel with Reynell, upon—An omnes artes habeant inter se quoddam commune vinculum? I had Affirmatur.

Decem. 18. I was dunn'd this morning for half a Hogshead of Port, by Cropp's Agent, Howard, call'd Lord Howard. It was not in my Power to pay it at present.

1762

March 5. Judge Willmott condemned one Shadrach Smith, a gypsy, for robbing a girl of 2 shillings and beating her in a very cruel manner; this man's son was the most principal Witness against his Father, and he it was that had him hanged, or condemned to be hanged, he insisted upon his son's witnessing against, though the Judge was much against it.

Between April and June of this year (1762) he is in the country, and the following entries are made at Ansford:

AP. 20. I began the Epistles of the G[reek] Testament to learn and read for Orders. Gave a Poor Man . . . 0. 0. 2.

AP. 24. I made a Contract with Mr. Owens to shave me and dress 2 Wiggs each time, twice a week, not reckoning my being from Home, at three shillings per Quarter per annum 0. 12. 0. . . .

JUNE 12. I have been studying in my tent [He had put one up in the garden] all the day long the G. Testament. Sister Jenny and myself were invited this evening to Mr. White's Sheep-sheering, but we could not go being Saturday night, which is a very improper time to spend the evening out anywhere.

JUNE 15. Went this morning early to Berkeley, where old Mrs. Prowse lives, about two miles beyond Froom, and about sixteen miles from hence: I carried over with me three Mourning Rings that my Father gave me last night; to deliver one to old Mrs. Prowse, one to her son the Major, and one to ye Major's wife, in Remembrance of my late Uncle, the Treasurer, which were left them by a Particular Desire of my late Uncle the Treasurer [his Great Uncle Robert Woodforde, 1675–1762, for many years a country parson in Cornwall and Somerset, and later Canon and Treasurer of Wells]. . . . N.B. Old Mrs. Prowse of Berkeley, and my late Uncle the Treasurer, were very Intimate, and corresponded, when my good Uncle was living. Major Prowse is son to old Mrs. Prowse.

JUNE 28. Went upon the grey horse this morning for Oxford by myself.

> The stay at Oxford was short, and on July 20 he is back at Ansford Parsonage again: the journey from Oxford on horseback cost exactly £1; it would not have cost quite as much had he not 'treated' some friends at 'the Bear in Dropping Lane', the last stage before he reached home.

JULY 28. . . . Went with Papa and Jenny to Mr. William Melliar's this morning, where we dined with a number of other friends upon half a Buck. . . . We had a Minuet or two this afternoon by Holton, Couns[ellor] Melliar, Will: Melliar, and myself. . . .

JULY 29. . . . Papa had a letter from Cousin James Lewis at Nottingham, wherein he informs that he keeps a little school at Nottingham, and likewise that he is in great want of money. He was a Private Soldier in the Army, and being wounded in the leg rendered him unserviceable, and therefore has a Pension of five Pounds per Annum from the Government: he has been rather wild in his time, which wildness has brought him to this.

AUGUST 1. . . . Went this afternoon to Cary Church where Jerry Holton read prayers and preached for Mr. Penny. Holton preached concerning Private Interest giving way to Publick Good in regard to our having an Water Engine to prevent Fire spreading. . . .

AUG. 2. ·. . . Archdeacon Potter of Wells, and Brother-in-Law to Daniel Prince my bookseller in Oxford, called here this afternoon, but Papa was gone down to the Lower House, and Mama was walking in the Garden, and Jenny was gone to Castle Cary, and I was up in my room reading, so he did not stay long here.

Aug. 7. . . . Papa gave me a manuscript of Arch-Bishop Laud's, concerning the Old and New Testaments, being some of his own Remarks concerning them.

Aug. 12. . . . Went with Mr. Clarke over to Ansford Inn to read the News, where I pd 0. 0. 4½ . . . . There was a wedding dinner at Ansford Inn to-day, for some Shepton Mallett People. The Bride and Bridegroom's names are these, the Bride was Miss Aimes, the Brideg: Cary. The whole set all are rank Presbyterians.

Aug. 26. . . . We drank tea this afternoon at Mrs. Chiche's with . . . [and] Mr. Whithead of Bristol, a man of great Fortune, near 15000£. . . .

> On August 30th he rides over to Bristol to see his brother John, who is apprenticed there. Next day they 'took a ride down to King-Road, Sea-Mills and saw the Tyger that Captain Reed took lately, we saw the Captain. We went a board the Tyger, and the King George, and I pd 0. 1. 0.'
> Between September 13th and 19th he is at Winchester with his uncle Tom and cousin Frank, who is up for election as a Scholar: they see him safely settled there and return on September 19th.

Sep. 28. . . . Painter Clarke gave me a ticket to go to Miss Chich's Play (the Beggars Opera) this evening at Bruton, at her House and accordingly I went this evening to Miss Chich's at Bruton, and saw the Play acted and it was done pretty well. Lady Ilchester,

and her daughter Fanny a little girl, were there.
Their house was quite full. . . .

OCT. 3. . . . We had news to-day of the Havannah,
the Principal Port in the Island of Cuba in the West
Indies, being taken by the English.

OCT. 9. . . . I packed up my things for Oxford, this
afternoon and they were these—9 Shirts—9 Stocks—
2 Cravats—7 pr of Stockings, 2 White Handkerchiefs
—5 Coloured Handkerchiefs—2 Night Caps—1
Towel—2 Pr of Breeches—besides the things that I
wear, wch are 1 Pr of Leather Breeches—1 White
Coat—1 Buff Waistcoat—1 Great Coat.

NOV. 26. . . . I began this very day to take upon me
the Stewardship of the College, viz: to see the Meat
of the College weighed every day in Kitchen for one
week and for which I receive of the Manciple at the
end of the week 0. 6s. 6d. All Fellows of this College
above three years standing, and that here in College
are, take the Stewardship by turns every week from
Year's end to Year's end, and so on ad infinitum.
Had a dunning Letter from Robinson & Hartley for
the payment of £8. 15. 0 for half a Hogshead of old
Port, that I had from Southampton last year.

DEC. 24. . . . I paid Mr. Pryer this morning our
College Steward, for Mr. Hartley & Robinson of
Southampton Wine Merchants, for half a Hogshead
of Port Wine £8. 15. 0. . . .

1763

JAN. 4. Went a skating this morning upon the River
Thames. . . .

[With an interval of a thaw from 7th to 10th he skates on the Thames till January 27th, on]

JAN. 24. We skated down to Abington where we dined and for our dinners there etc. each of us pd. 2*s*. 6*d*. We were going down about an hour and half; N.B. We walked above 2 miles out of it. It is about 10 miles by water.

JAN. 8. Pd. Rice for mending my Gown and a little rip in my Coat 0. 1. 0 which is very exorbitant indeed and for the future will have nothing ever done by him any more in the World.

FEB. 17. I dined at the Chaplain's table with Pickering and Waring, upon a roasted Tongue and Udder, and we went on each of us for it 0. 1. 9. N.B. I shall not dine on a roasted Tongue and Udder again very soon.

FEB. 28. . . . Went with Dyer, Russell and Master after dinner down to the Castle to see the Prisoners; where we drank two Bottles of Port and for Wine etc., pd 0. 1. 6. William Cartwright, a young, good-looking Fellow, who is in the Castle for a High Way Robbery, drank with us the last Bottle, and smoaked a Pipe with us, and seemed very sorry for what he had committed. We gave him between us 0. 2. 0. . . .

MAR. 29. . . . Went and saw Peace proclaimed in High Street at twelve o'clock.

This was the Peace of Paris, which concluded the Seven Years War. The French gave up Canada to us and abandoned all claims to India. We had become a great Imperial Power.

– 14 –

MAY 2. Sale spoke to me this morning concerning the Curacy of Newton-Purcell, which I have promised him to take and serve the Sunday after Trinity Sunday; it is about 20 miles from Oxford; and I am to receive per annum for serving it, besides Surplice fees £28. 0. 0. I am only to serve it during Mr. Sale's Proctorship.

MAY 5. . . . This is the Thanksgiving day for the late Peace between France, Spain and England.

MAY 11. . . . I was offer'd this afternoon by Fitch of Queen's Coll: a Curacy worth £40 per annum, and to be enterd upon at Michaelmas—It is in Somersett, near Taunton, the name of the Place is Thurloxton, in the Gift of Fitch's Father. I shall write to my Father concerning it to-morrow morning; I have got to the 20th of this month to consider of it.

MAY 23. . . . I went this afternoon at five o'clock to C.C.C. to Mr. Hewish the Bishop of Oxford's Chaplain, before whom I was examined for deacon's Orders, and I came of very well. I was set over in the middle of the fifth Chapter of St. Paul to the Romans and construed that Chapter quite to the end. I was quite half an hour examining. He asked a good many hard and deep questions. I had not one question that Yes, or No, would answer. . . . Mr. Hewish is a very fair Examiner, and will see whether a Man be read or not soon. . . .

MAY 24. Breakfasted in my own Rooms again. Took a ride this morning towards Elsfield and round by Staunton upon the Grey. For half a pint of ale at Boys Water pd. 0. 0. 1. Gave Jackson's other man for taking care of the Grey and saddle etc. 0. 0. 6. For fruit pd 0. 0. 1. For wine on the green pd 0. 2. 0. The reason of my paying so much was the Impudence of two Gentlemanlike Persons (whose names were Messrs. Mercer and Loyd) pushed themselves into the Temple in our Garden while Hooke and myself were drinking there, and drank two Bottles of Wine with us. Mercer's wife and 2 more Ladies were with us. Mercer (who wore a gold-laced Hat) was very drunk and very abusive to us and Mr. Loyd: Loyd is a Schoolmaster at Abington, and Mercer's son went to School to him. Mercer's son was with us. Mercer went away about ten o'clock this evening, and made a great noise going through College. Mr. Mercer behaved very much unlike a Gentleman. Loyd came into the B.C.R. afterwards with Hooke and myself; Mr. Loyd was drunk. Mercer broke two glasses in the Temple for which Hooke and myself pd. 0. 1. 0. I went to bed at eleven and left Mr. Loyd in the B.C.R. with Hooke and some more Gentlemen. . . .

MAY 27. For an ounce of Green Tea pd 0. 0. 8. For an ounce of Bohea Tea pd. 0. 0. 4*d*.

MAY 28. Went to Dr. Hunt's of Christ Church, with Nicholls, Geree and Pitters, and subscribed to the 39 Articles before the Bishop. We paid Pope Beaver for our Letters of Orders, which we receive Monday next, in Doctor Hunt's rooms; each of us 0. 10. 0. . . . Oglander Senr. gave a very handsome glazed Lanthorne for the use of the Bowlers to light their Pipes with, this afternoon in the Temple in the Green. . . .

MAY 29. At nine o'clock, this morning went to Christ Church with Hooke, and Pitters, to be ordained Deacon; and was ordained Deacon there by Hume Bishop of Oxford. There were 25 Ordained Deacons and 13 Priests. We all received the Sacrament. . . . We were in C. Church Cathedral from nine o'clock this morning till after twelve. For wine this afternoon in the B.C.R. pd. o. o. 6.

JUNE 1. I took my B.A. Degree this morning. . . . Reynels, myself, Lucas, Peckham and Webber treated (as is usual) the B.C.R. after dinner with Wine, and after Supper with Wine and Punch all the evening. We had 27 People in the B.C.R. this evening. . . . I sat up in the B.C.R. this evening till after twelve o'clock, and then went to bed, and at three in the morning, had my outward doors broken open, my glass door broke, and pulled out of bed, and brought into the B.C.R. where I was obliged to drink and smoak, but not without a good many words. Peckham broke my doors, being very drunk, although they were open, which I do not relish of Peckham much.

JUNE 2. Several of our Fellows went at four o'clock in the morning, for Stow, and all drunk; some in a Phaeton, some in a Buggy, and some on Horse back. I went as far as Weston on the Green with them upon my Grey, and then returned home, and was home by nine o'clock this morning, and breakfasted in my room.

JUNE 4. Dined in Hall; and after dinner went with Cotton to Newton-Purcell, my Curacy, and which I am to serve to-morrow. Supp'd and spent the evening, at Cotton's Mother's, with Cotton and his Brother, and his Mother and his four Sisters. Cotton's Sisters are very agreeable Ladies. Laid at Cotton's Mother's at Newton-Purcell. Cotton's Mother's House and Furniture is rather bad; they are going out of the House soon.

JUNE 5. Breakfasted at Cotton's Mother's, with Cotton and his Brother and his four Sisters. At eleven o'clock went to my Church, and read Prayers and preached my first Sermon. Cotton's Family and about twenty more People were all that were at Church. Did Duty again at two o'clock; and then dined at Cotton's Mother's with Mrs. Cotton, and her four Daughters, and her youngest son; the eldest son was out preaching and reading prayers. Set out this afternoon for Oxford, and got home about eight o'clock. . . . Gave Cotton's maid being the only Servant o. 1. o.

JUNE 6. Had a Letter from Fitch, with a Promise from his Father of my taking the Curacy of his at Thurloxton near Taunton.

JUNE 25th. . . . Oglander Junr. and myself tryed this evening some of our Strong Beer in the B.C.R. and it is pretty good, but I am afraid it will never be better. It is some of Whitmore's brewing when he was Bursar. . . .

JUNE 29. . . . For a Pocket Pistol alias a dram bottle to carry in one's pocket, it being necessary on a Journey or so, at Nicholl's pd o. 1. o.

JULY 3. Went this morning to Ardington by Wantage in Berks for Mr. Sheffield, who desired me to change Churches with him for this Sunday, it is about twelve miles of Oxford: I preached and read Prayers there in the morning and Churched a woman; and read Prayers there in the afternoon. Coming out of Church in the morning a woman that I had Churched gave me in the middle of the Church o. o. 6. which I received and pocketed. I dined at the

Squire's whose name was Clarke, who behaved extreamly civil and genteel indeed. For going thro' three Turnpikes this morning between Oxford and Ardington pd. o. o. 5.

. . . My horse fell down on a Trot as I was going, and threw me over his head but (I thank God Almighty) I received no hurt. . . .

JULY 16. . . . For throwing some Wine last night in Bedford's face in the B.C.R. I was sconced a Bottle of Wine, which I pd. this evening to the B.C.R.

JULY 26. Paid Baggs at the Coff. House (a very impudent Fellow) a little Bill of o. 6. 7. N.B. I do not intend dealing with him again very soon for his Impudence to me yesterday morning.

AUG. 3. Spent the evening at Rice's, my quondam Taylor, with himself and wife, in High Street. They had provided a handsome supper for me (viz) a neck of Lamb and tarts, but I had supp'd at College. I smoaked a Pipe with Mr. Rice, and finished a Bottle of Wine between us, and his Wife, and then I departed. . . .

AUG. 17. Dined in Hall at the High Table upon a neck of Venison and a Breast made into Pasty, a Ham and Fowls and two Pies. It is a Venison Feast which we have once a year about this time . . . 2 Bucks one year, and 1 Buck another year is always sent from Whaddon Chase and divided between the Wardens, the Senr Fellows, and us. For an ounce of Indian Bark to put into my Pipe when smoking pd. o. o. 6d. It gives the tobacco a pretty smell and taste.

AUG. 21. Went to Chesterton again this morning and did the Duty of the day there. Dined at Mr. Pryor's again, and with him, his brother the Lawyer, his Sister and Niece and Mr. and Mrs. Weaver, Miss Goff, Mr. Payne a Baker at Brackley, an everlasting Spunger, but a droll Fellow, and Mr. Banks of our College. . . .

SEPTEM. 3. Went this morning to Draton (two little miles beyond Abingdon) and talked with Mrs. Bacon about serving that Church to-morrow. She says that she will give me half a guinea, a dinner, and stabling for my horse, therefore I promised her that I would serve it to-morrow and the next Sunday. Mrs. Bacon behaved very handsome to me; she has a school of twenty-two young Ladies. After drinking a glass of Mountain and eating a bit of crust of bread, I returned to Oxford, and dined at New Coll: in ye Hall. Mrs. Bacon pressed me to dine with her, but I had ordered in Hall, and I could not. . . . Besides our Common Dinner we had a brace of birds called Graus, that came from Williams Junr. out of Wales, as a present to Webber for reading for him during his absence in Chapel.

SEPTEM. 7. . . . Had three bottles of Wine out of my room in ye B.C.R. this afternoon and Waring had another, out of his room. Waring was very drunk and Bedford was but little better. N.B. I was very sober, as I had made a resolution never to get drunk again, when at Geree's rooms in April last, when I fell down dead, and cut my Occiput[1] very bad indeed.

On September 12th he leaves Oxford, having completed his course. He spends the rest of the month quietly at home with one or two excursions to Sherborne and Bristol. He preaches for his father

---

[1] i.e. the back of his head.

now and again at Ansford, does a little shooting, training a new dog given him by his tenant's brother, whose name is Snooke, and with his family visits 'Mr. Hoare, the Banker's gardens at Stourton'. . . . 'The Temple of Hercules in the gardens must cost Mr. Hoare £10,000, it is excessively grand. The grotto where the sleeping Nymph laid struck me much more than anything there.'

He gives his sister, Jenny (October 1st) a present of four hundred needles, four papers of pins, and two steel-top thimbles which he had bought at Oxford for her for 4s. 4d. On October 7th he sets out for Thurloxton, near Taunton, to take up his curacy: he arrives on the 8th, and after various vain attempts to find lodgings, he goes to the squire of the parish, 'whose name is Cross, and he took me at the very first word, and likewise my Horse'. He arranges to stop there on these terms: 'that I should live as he does (which is very well I am sure) that I should have my linnen washed by him, and that he should keep my horse (corn excepted) £21. 0. 0 and that for every day that I was absent, I should be allowed for each day 0. 1. 1½ which per year is £21.' He notes that 'Mr. Cross has a noble house, good enough for any Nobleman'. Mr. Cross is married and has three children and another is coming. He spends his time partly at Thurloxton with the Cross's and partly at Ansford, riding to and fro. On October 27th 'a hare being found near here, Mr. Cross and myself went out and coursed it before breakfast and killed it, with Mr. Cross's dogs, and a good course it was. Gave the man that found her 0. 0. 6 as is always customary.' He notes on November 4th that he has to return to Thurloxton from Ansford 'to-morrow being the fifth of November, to read Prayers there'. The congregation was small. 'The Ringers desired me to give them something to drink, it being customary, therefore I sent them, it being a custom, o. 1. o.'

Nov. 6. Breakfasted, dined, supp'd and laid at Mr. Cross's. Read Prayers and preached this morning at my Church of Thurloxton, it being Sunday. I likewise read Prayers there this afternoon. After the afternoon service, I privately baptised Mrs. Cross's late [i.e. lately born] child, which was a boy, and by the name of Richard, in Mrs. Cross's bedroom in this house. One Farmer Major, of this Parish, spent the afternoon and evening here, drinking with Mr. Cross all the time, neither of them eat any supper, and I left them drinking when I went to bed, which was about 10.

Nov. 16. ... I lent Doctor Clarke a pamphlet called a sure Guide to Hell this evening, and a very good moral book it is, taken properly.

On November 29th he arranges with the old Rector of Babcary for the curacy of that place—it being only six miles from Ansford—at £5 a quarter, the surplice fees, Easter offerings, and free use of Parsonage, gardens and stables, &c. He is to give up Thurloxton curacy on January 9th next. On December 5th he receives seven letters applying for his vote in connexion with the election of a new Warden of Winchester College, 'as all Wardens of Winton College are elected by the Fellows of New College'. The election was to be at New College on the 10th December. Accordingly he sets out for Oxford on the 7th. He is much solicited at Oxford for his vote by the three candidates, Hayward, Lea, and Sale, all of New College. He decides to vote for Sale and secondly for Mr. Lea. He gives an elaborate description of the election on December 10th in New College Chapel; 54 Fellows were present, and, after morning service, received the Sacrament before proceeding to elect. The Sub-Warden then read the Statute 'de Electione Custodis Collegii prope Winton'. Then five scrutators were chosen and 'went up to the Altar to a table within the rails and then began the Scrutiny and we all in turns voted for a Warden'. Finally, Lea was elected. He returns to Ansford on December 14th.

DEC. 26. . . . Two of Mr. Cross's Tenants (one a Farmer and the other a Taylor and Miller) . . . supped and spent the evening with us—they lay at Mr. Cross's this night.

On December 30th he rides over to Babcary to see his new cure. He sees Farmer Bower, apparently the principal parishioner, who is much vexed to hear there is only to be one service on Sunday. Woodforde agrees to have two if his salary is increased to £30 per annum.

1764

JAN. 2. . . . One Farmer John Major dined and spent the afternoon here; Mr. Cross sat drinking with him from 10 in the morning till 8 at night. . . .

JAN. 8. . . . I dined at Mr. Sanford's [a Parson] at Walford with Mr. and Mrs. Sanford and about ten of Mr. Sanford's children. We had a very elegant dinner, and in a very noble, spacious Parlour. . . .

JAN. 9. Breakfasted at Mr. Cross's. After Breakfast Mr. Cross and me settled matters, and I paid him for my Board 59 days at the rate of 1. 1½*d.* per day. . . .

JAN. 12. . . . After breakfast I rode upon Cream to my Curacy at Babcary about six miles from hence, where I dined upon a Sheep's heart that I carried there in my pocket, at the Parsonage house, where I am to be when I go to Babcary on any occasion.

JAN. 15. . . . After Breakfast I went upon Cream to my Curacy at Babcary, where I read Prayers and Preached, read Prayers in the morning and preached in the afternoon. This is the first Sunday I ever officiated at Babcary Church; and I like it very well. . . . I was rung into the Parish by Mr. John Bower's order, who gave the Ringers a pail of Cyder on purpose to ring me into the Parish. They gave me another ring this afternoon after Service, and for which I gave them 2. 6. . . .

JAN. 21. Breakfasted and dined at home. After dinner I set forth for Babcary, where I supped and laid in the Parsonage House. I hired Ned Dyke and his horse this morning to carry some cyder etc., to Babcary for me. I carried three dozen and nine bottles of cyder, and eight bottles of strong beer, with a little jar of pickled oysters, some cheese, and some cold tongue to Babcary, all which were given by my Father.

FEB. 4. . . . Went this afternoon from Babcary to East Charlton which is about one mile, to Parson Gapper's to thank him for serving my Church at Babcary for me last Sunday and there I drank tea this afternoon with Mr. and Mrs. Gapper. They pressed me very much to sup there and spend the evening and lay there but I could not.

FEB. 20. . . . I have been very busy all this day in planting my Peas and Beans and Radishes, and Spanish Onions, in my garden at Babcary. . . . I was sent this afternoon to a Poor Woman that lives by the Church, to come and pray by her—which I did. . .

He goes to Oxford on February 27th to 'determine' for his degree: meanwhile Parson Gapper carries on at Babcary.

MAR. 26. I churched a poor woman at Babcary yesterday and she gave me sixpence, which I sent to her again. Mr. Gapper has been so good to serve my Church for me during my absence, and I sent him yesterday a genteel note to thank him. . . .

APRIL 14. . . . Went to Parson Gapper's this afternoon at East Charlton, about one mile from Babcary, to desire him to administer the Sacrament for me next Friday being Good Friday, which he promised me he would. I am to serve Keenton for him, about a mile. I spent a good part of the afternoon with him and his wife and children, and one Miss Curtiss of Shepton Mallett their relation, a fine Lady.

APRIL 16. . . . I brewed a quarter barrel of ale to-day. . . . I gave Mary Creech [the old woman who looked after him at Babcary Parsonage] and her daughter a pair of garters each which I bought of an Irish Traveller that came to the door and for them I paid 0. 0. 6.

APRIL 30. . . . I got up this morning at two o'clock to get or make a sermon for Farmer Bertelet's funeral this afternoon, and by twelve o'clock I had finished almost all of it. . . . I buried Farmer John Bertelet this evening at six O'clock and preached a Funeral Sermon, the Church was exceedingly thronged with people. . . .

He receives 10s. 6d. for this sermon on May 6th from Mrs. Bertelet, the widow.

MAY 9. . . . One Miss Moore (a very giddy, merry, but very pretty girl, who was lately inoculated) dined with us [at Ansford].

On June 14th there is a small dispute about payments for Babcary curacy, and one, the Reverend Mr. Hopkins, proves to the Diarist that for certain early weeks in 1763–4 the payments are due to him (Hopkins). Everything is settled amicably, and the Diarist notes, 'I never saw so bold a man in my life as Mr. Hopkins is, and very droll he is. I thought I must have burst my sides by laughing in hearing him talk.' On June 18th the Diarist and his sister Jenny sup at Mr. William Melliar's, 'Counsellor [Barrister] Gapper of Wincanton', among others, being of the company. On June 22nd he gives a bachelor's supper party at Babcary, and his guests 'plaid at Fives in Babcary Churchyard this evening, and I lost there with Mr. Lewis Bower at betting with him 0. 1. 6. The gentlemen pleased me much by seeing them so well pleased with the homely entertainment.'

On July 28th he inducts Mr. Richard Cheese, who 'seems a very good kind of man, and much approved of by the Parish', into the Rectory of Babcary. Mr. Hill, the old Rector, had died: hence the change. 'Mr. John Bower is to rent his tythes etc., and is to give him per annum 100. 0. 0.

I am to be his curate, and to have per annum, besides the house and stable, gardens and Easter offerings, the sum of 30. 0. 0.' Mr. Cheese's home was at Bentley near Alton in Hampshire, where he returns on July 31st.

AUG. 18. ... I have made a promise to-day concerning a certain thing (in eating); which every time I break that promise I pay—1—0.

AUG. 19. ... After the Afternoon Service [Babcary] I went with the Captain [Rooke] to Parson Gapper's at East Charlton, where we spent the remaining part of the afternoon, with him and his wife. The Captain went afterwards to Somerton, and I returned to Ansford—and the first news I heard was, that poor Miss Milly Chiche (a niece of Mrs. Chiche's) was dead; and she died about 11 o'clock this morning. I hope to God that she (poor dear creature) is happy. I believe verily that she was good to everyone, but herself, and I am afraid that drinking was her death. . . .

SEP. 11. ... After dinner I went to East Charlton to have my Testimonium, for Priest's Orders, signed by Mr. Gapper, who did it: and at the same time I desired him to serve my Church for me on the Ordination Sunday which is the 23 of this month, and which he promised me. I spent this afternoon at Mr. Gapper's, with him, his wife, and his brother from Shepton Mallett, Doctor Gapper, who is an Apothecary there. . . . Mr. William Melliar and his wife sent their compts to-day to all our family, and desired that we should dine with them to-morrow upon a fine haunch of venison.

The Diarist is becoming increasingly anxious about his mother's health during October, and on October 30th she and his father set out for London to see a specialist there. On October 29th he enters this simple prayer: 'O Almighty Lord God, let it be thy good pleasure to restore my dear Mother to her former health: but if thou hast otherwise decreed it, not my will but thine be done.' He is left in charge of the house (October 20th) 'with all the keys, and I will take great care to be faithful in the trust committed to me'.

On December 4th he marries his first couple (at Ansford), an old farmer widower of eighty and a widow of seventy.

DEC. 8. ... Had a very satisfactory letter from Papa this morning, to inform me that all the danger is over with Mama. ... Thanks, do I return, most unfeigned to Almighty God for it.

DEC. 24. ... the new Singers came very late this evening, and they sung a Christmas Carol and an Anthem and they had cyder as usual and 0. 2. 0. The old Singers did not come at all, and I have heard that they have given it over.

DEC. 25. ... Fifteen poor old People dined here as usual being Xmas Day. We had for dinner to-day a large Rump of Beef of thirty pound roasted, and three large plum puddings. Fine beef it was.

1765

JAN. 9. ... Mr. Bridges Priest Vicar of the Cathedral at Wells called upon me this afternoon, and laid at our house all night. I took him with me up to Mr.

Clarke's where we supped and spent the evening. . . .
Mr. Bridges made himself very disagreeable to all the
Company, and exposed himself much. We had great
part of Cato[1] performed this evening, and done
tolerably well.

JAN. 10. . . . Mr. Bridges breakfasted with me, and
afterward he went home to Wells. I am not sorry
for it.

JAN. 16. . . . Papa and Mama returned this afternoon
with their maid Elizabeth Clothier, from London,
perfectly well and easy! Blessed be God for all great
mercies bestowed upon me a miserable and sinful
creature. . . .

JAN. 29. . . . Mr. John Penny sent me a small plumb
cake and a pair of w[hite] gloves this morning,
I buried his little maid this afternoon at Cary
Church. . . .

FEB. 5. Breakfasted, dined, supped, and laid at
Babcary again. I have been busy to-day in pruning
the apple trees in my garden there. . . .

FEB. 11. Breakfasted and dined at Babcary.
. . . For things that my old Woman at Babcary has
bought me this last week—paid her . o. o. 7½
Viz. for half a pound of Butter . . o. o. 4
For one pound of beef Stakes . . o. o. 3
For some Cream . . . . o. o. 0½
Gave Mary for her trouble . . o. o. 4½
For laying a wager with Betty Crich my old Woman's
daughter concerning frosty weather last Thursday,
and losing with her paid . . . o. o. 6

---

[1] Addison's tragedy.

FEB. 12. ... I went to enquire when Mr. Burge went to London (but he went last Sunday) as my Father and Uncle wanted to send five guineas to Cousin Bob Woodforde, who was last Thursday appointed Surgeon's first Mate to the Hussar Frigate 28 Guns, now cruising on the Coasts of Ireland, and as he must go to her, he begs a little money of them to go.

MARCH 4. ... After dinner I returned to Ansford where I supped, spent the evening and laid. On my return home I called upon Mr. Andrew Russ at Clanville, and spent the remaining part of the afternoon with him, Mr. Dod a Baker and a Roman Catholick, Mr. Thomas and Seth Burge. Mr. Dod and myself touched a little upon Religion, which I own was not right at all.

For going thro' Avord Turnpike paid   0.   0.   1

MARCH 25. ... I received this morning of Elizabeth Clothier my mother's maid, the sum of ten pounds, to keep for her, and I shall give her ten shillings per annum, which is at the rate of five per centum for the use of it; I do it purely to encourage her to be careful, and to make her saving. . . .

MARCH 27. ... I christened two children (Twins) of Robin Francis's this afternoon at Ansford Church for my Father by the names of Joseph and Mary, being born on Lady Day last. . . .

APRIL 4. ... Gave Betty Crich my old woman's daughter 0. 0. 6 to get her spinning work done in proper time, as I had hindered her.

APRIL 7. ... My Clarke Sam. Hutchins sat up all last night drinking therefore he did not attend at the Holy Sacrament [it was Easter Day]—for which I gave him a severe lecture, and he promised me never to be guilty of the same again, which I hope he will not. I had a piece of roast beef for dinner to-day, and I had my Clarke Sam. Hutchins, and his cousin Thomas Hutchins my gardener to dine here to-day....

APRIL 18. ... Mr. Penny is presented to the Living of Evercreech, to hold it for a minor (Justice Robbard's son of 12 years old), and is therefore going to quit my Father's curacy at C. Cary, which I am to undertake for him, and Babcary too, but I cannot serve Babcary but once a Sunday. . . .

On April 29th he goes to Oxford, and stays there till May 23rd, reading his 'Wall Lectures' for his M.A. degree.

MAY 23. I got up this morning at 3 o'clock and went to the Star Inn in the Corn Market where I took Coach and set forth for Bath, which goes there to-day. Gave our Porter for calling me this morning 0. 0. 6. Gave a Porter for carrying my Portmanteau to the Star 1. 0. There were only two more in the Machine beside me. One was (I believe) a dissenting Minister, and the other an Oxford old Lady who is going to Cirencester. We breakfasted at Burford, for which as we treated the Lady cost each of us 0. 1. 6. We took up at Burford two more passengers, one was a servant man of Major Hargrove who is at Bristol and his man is going to him; the other was a stranger of Burford a young woman going to Cirencester. Both the women left us at Cirencester, and then there was only myself, the Major's Servant, and the dissenting Minister, a very well behaved man. I paid my remaining part of the fare at Burford [He had paid 9s. on the 13th in advance] and for my portmanteau the overweight 0. 10. 6. We dined at Tetbury with a stranger, a tradesman. For my dinner and drinking afterwards paid 0. 2. 0. We got into Bath this evening about seven o'clock, and we put up at the King's Arms in Broad Street, where I supped and spent the evening and laid. My Father's man met me here this evening with horses.

MAY 24. . . . We got home to Ansford to dinner, where I dined, supped and laid at my Father's house. Blessed be Almighty God for sending me safe home to my dear Parents again. . . .

On May 26th he begins his curacy at C. Cary, and gets £20. 0. 0 a year from his father for it: this means he can only take one service at Babcary on Sunday.

MAY 27. Breakfasted, dined, and laid at home again. Brother John dined, breakfasted, and laid here again. After dinner Jack went to Wincanton to a Pony Race, and he did not return till after ten this evening. I am greatly afraid Jack is rather wild, but I hope not.

MAY 28. . . . Brother John spent the evening at the Fair [at Castle Cary].

MAY 29. . . . I read Prayers this morning at C. Cary, it being the commemorating the Restoration of King Charles the Second. . . .

JUNE 6. . . . Gave my old woman's daughter a Fairing as she goes to Camel Fair to-day, which was 0. 1. 0. Gave my Clark there [Babcary] and one Thom. Hutchins 0. 1. 0. to lay out at Camel Fair.

JUNE 23. . . . I buried poor Will. Burge this evening at Ansford Church for my Father. I hope he is happy. Poor Will. went with me the very last time that I went to Oxford, and I liked him much. . . .

JUNE 24. ... I read Prayers this morning at C. Cary it being St. John's Day. Coming from Church I called in at Stephen Gibb's at C. Cary, and I prayed by his wife who is very ill. I gave poor Stephen Gibbs, to buy something for her 1. 0.

JULY 8. ... Brother John breakfasted, dined, supped and laid here again. Brother John is very indifferent by his being too busy with Girls. ...

On July 11th he gives a dinner party at Babcary to fourteen C. Cary gentlemen, 'one of whom', he observes, 'was not invited'.

We all spent the greatest part of the afternoon in the Churchyard at Babcary, where we were diverted by some of the Gentlemen playing at Ball,[1] at which I won a betting 0. 2. 9. The Gentlemen seemed well pleased at the Entertainment, which gave me infinite satisfaction. A terrible accident happened whilst we were at dinner, which many of us went to see the Body; viz. a Poor Boy was dragged and killed by a Horse about half a mile from us on the Ilchester Road. The boy was about fourteen years old. I hope to God the Poor Boy is happy. There was no bone broken, neither was his skull fractured, but he is dead. We all came home singing, and I thank God well. My Brother John was indisposed, therefore he could not go. ...

JULY 23. ... Dined and spent the afternoon at Mr. Clarke's. ... One Farmer Tottle of Avord, a Clergyman's son, a very hearty man and within one year of fourscore, spent the afternoon at Mr. Clarke's as did another Farmer.

[1] 'Fives', I fear, against the church wall.

JULY 26. . . . For three framed pictures for my Tent of a Boy, paid 3. 0. N.B. They are new fashioned pictures of their Majesties, Mr. Pitt and Mr. Legge, Prince Ferdinand and the Marquiss of Granby.

JULY 30. . . . Jack made Papa this evening very angry and uneasy by his defending suicide and talking so saucy to him. Jack is much altered indeed within these two years. I am afraid he will be ever miserable, but God forbid!

SEP. 20. . . . Papa and Brother John had some words this evening, but it ended very well between them at last.

SEP. 26. . . . Spent the afternoon at the Lower House[1] with Brother John and one Cass Thomas of Ever-creech of whom my brother John bought a mare this afternoon and saddle and bridle for the sum of 8. 8. 0. . . .

SEP. 28. . . . Dr. Clarke's cook maid, Mary, was this morning found out in concealing a dead child in her box of which she had delivered herself yesterday morning, whether she murdered it or not is not yet known, but will be tried by the Coroner and Jury next Monday. . . .

SEP. 30. The Coroner, Mr. Norton with the Jury took inquest this afternoon upon the deceased child (a boy) of Dr. Clarke's maid, Mary, and brought her in not guilty.

---

[1] The Lower House in Ansford was part of his mother's estate; she was a local heiress, and he lived here with his brother John until his father's death. This house, of which the present owner of the diary has a pleasant picture, no longer exists.

On October 6th he takes service at Babcary for the last time, being succeeded by a Mr. Colmer. Most of October is spent in getting into the Lower House. Carpenters at work, &c.

On November 5th he enters that he reads prayers at Castle Cary Church ('being Gunpowder Treason Plot').

DEC. 1. . . . I read Prayers and preached this afternoon at C. Cary Church. Mrs. White, Mrs. Sam White, Mr. Andrew Russ, Mr. James and Richard Clarke and Brother Heighes, supped and spent the evening with us at the Parsonage. My father did not come downstairs all the evening on account of the Company and Mama being ill. It vexed my Father and Mother greatly to have company brought to the house by Jack on a Sunday, and especially as my Mother is so bad.

DEC. 4. . . . Brother John went out early this morning and did not return all day and night. He is gone a Courting. . . .

DEC. 19. . . . Jack kept me up very late this evening at the Lower House by not coming home till past 12 o'clock.

1766

JAN. 25. . . . I had a letter from Mr. Rice, my taylor in Oxford, to whom I am greatly in debt, it was a very civil letter. [He had written to explain he couldn't pay him yet.]

JAN. 30. . . . I read prayers this morning at C. Cary, it being K. Charles' Martyrdom. Papa gave me a large cheese for the Lower House this morning. I dined, supped and spent the evening at Parsonage.

FEB. 4. ... Our dear Mama is much worse and daily taking her leave of all of us.

> On February 6th he enters: 'Poor Mama grows weaker and worse daily. The Parsonage is a very melancholy house now indeed.'

FEB. 7. ... Poor Mama sent for me and Jack this afternoon up into her room and very solemnly took her leave of us; therefore I do not believe she can exist very long in this world. ...

FEB. 8. It pleased Almighty God of his great goodness to take unto himself my dear good Mother this morning, about 9 o'clock, out of this sinful world, and to deliver her out of her miseries. She went out of this world as easy as it was possible for anyone. I hope she is now eternally happy in everlasting glory. ...

O Lord God Almighty send help from Thy Holy Place to my dear Father, and to all my dear Mother's relations, to withstand so great a shock, and to live and dye so easy as she did. ...

> On February 12th his mother is buried in the vault in the chancel of Ansford Church, 'very decently and well. ... We had all Crepe Hatbands and Cloaks' and the pall bearers likewise.
>
> She left her whole estate between the Diarist, 'Sister Jane, and Brother John'.

FEB. 14. ... Papa gave me this afternoon my money box that Poor Mama kept for me from a Boy in which was half a guinea, two half crown pieces, a sixpence, two small silver coins and ½d.

Feb. 17. ... One Robert Galpine, an old School Fellow of mine at Winton College, who was expelled genteely from it, and whom I have not seen this ten years, called upon me this evening at Parsonage and spent the former part of the evening with us there. ...

Feb. 20. ... Galpine (I believe) is in the capacity of a servant to Mr. Meach of Serne in Dorset an Apothecary.

Feb. 22. ... I dined, supped and spent the evening at Parsonage. Mr. Richard Clarke, Junr and one Mr. Strong a Butcher at Pool, an acquaintance of his supped and spent the evening with us. Mr. Richard Clarke makes too free (I think) with our house.

> On March 25th he enters that Elizabeth Clothier gives him another £10 to keep for her at 5 per cent. Also Elizabeth Crich gives him £20 to keep for her at 5 per cent. He is to have half a year's notice before repayment of principal.

April 11. Gave the Bath Newsman for Mr. Pitt's speech 0. 1. 0.

June 23. ... I went this evening with Miss Rooke and Jenny to see a Play (the Orphan or Unhappy marriage) to the Court House at C. Cary, performed by some strollers, and they did it pretty well. ...

July 4. I dined and spent the afternoon at Justice Creeds, with him, his Father, one Farmer Clarke of Lovington, Tenant to the Justice, Miss Molly Pew, and Sister Jane, we went in the evening to a play called Love in a Village. I paid there 0. 1. 6. The Justice treated the Ladies at the Play. ...

July 18. ... I went to a Play at the Court House at

C. Cary (called the Provoked Husband or a Journey to London) this evening with Aunt Tom, Jenny and Mrs. Clarke and Brother Heighes and his little boy, Billy, with little Sam. Clarke. I paid for going in, being Mrs. Midnight's benefit, o. 2. o. For cherries for myself and many others there paid o. 2. o. The Company was greatly disturbed at the Play by the noise of an insolent, saucy mobb on the outside of the Play House.

Aug. 25. . . . After breakfast I went with Brother John to Wells to have Counsellor Andrew's opinion of my Mother's appointment to me, Brother John and Sister Jane, which we had satisfactorily. We paid the Counsellor for his opinion in writing 1. 1. o.[1]

Between September 1st and September 4th they (he and his brother John) go to Winchester 'to the Election', and on September 4th he notes, 'I gave Brother John this afternoon o. 5. o his money being all gone. N.B. High time to decamp.'

Sept. 12. . . . I spent the afternoon at Dr. Clarke's. . . . Brother Heighes came in at the latter part of the afternoon to us, rather merry and exposed himself greatly by his talk to me. . . .

Sep. 14. . . . Mr. James Clarke who went to Kingsgate in Kent to my Lord Holland after Mr. Melliar on Mr. Chiche's account, which is 180 miles, returned this afternoon (Sunday) about one o'clock with Mr. Melliar. Mr. James set out from Ansford last Thursday 10 o'clock in the forenoon, there and back again is near 400 miles. . . . I was taken extremely bad this

---

[1] Counsellor is an old-fashioned title for a barrister. Now instead of employing 'counsellors', we employ 'counsel'.

evening just after I was in bed in a fainting fit, but, I thank God (through Jack's assistance etc.), I soon got better. If my brother had not laid in the same room, I do believe I must have expired this evening.

SEPT. 29. [At dinner with the Creeds.]—N.B. We had a Pine Apple after dinner, the first I ever saw or tasted.

OCT. 5. . . . Mrs. Grant of Henbridge spent this afternoon at Parsonage, she came to talk with my Father about Jack and her daughter, Nancy, which I hope now will soon be settled to their satisfaction.

OCT. 18. . . . I entirely forgot that this was St. Luke's Day, and therefore did not read Prayers at C. Cary which I should have done otherwise. As it was not done willfully, I hope God will forgive it.

On October 31st, he borrows £250 of Mr. Robin White to pay for 'Oxford Debts'. He tries to get Mr. Leach of Avord and Mr. Gapper of Yarlington to take his services during his absence in Oxford, and other parsons too, but fails for a variety of reasons: Mr. Gapper because he already preaches three times on Sunday, Mr. Leach because his mother has just died; so he has to defer his journey to Oxford.

DEC. 2. Luke Barnard came to live with me as a servant this day. I am to give him per annum three pounds, a coat and waistcoat and hat besides victuals and drink, washing and lodging. . . .

DEC. 22. . . . I paid Mr. White for my half Pig— 85 p^d weight 1. 3. 0. . . .

DEC. 29. ... Jack did not come home till after one o'clock in the morning, and therefore kept me awake almost all night. He was at Farmer Cocks of Grove a dancing there.

1767

JANUARY 1. I read Prayers this morning at C. Cary Church being New Year's Day. I dined, supped and spent the evening till 10 o'clock at Parsonage, and after ten I went over to Mr. Clarke's new Hospital where I spent the whole night and part of the morning till 4 o'clock a dancing, on account of Mr. James Clarke's apprenticeship being expired. A great deal of company was there indeed, viz., etc. ... We had a very good band of musick, 2 Violins and a Base Viol. We were excessive merry and gay there indeed. [He observes that Brother Heighes 'exposed himself greatly'.]

FEB. 3. ... I spent the evening and supped at Ansford Inn, there being a Masquerade Ball there this evening, and very elegant it was, much beyond my expectation in all respects. ... Parson Penny, Gapper, Baily, Witwick and Overton and myself were the Clergymen that were there. ... Brother John [was in the character of] a Counsellor, Brother Heighes, King Richard the Third; John Burge, Othello; Sister Jane, Shepherdess; Sally Clarke, Diana Trapes[1] ... cum multis aliis, all in very rich dresses but in no particular characters. ... I did not dance the whole evening. We had good musick viz., four Violins, a Bass Viol, a Taber and Pipe, a Hautboy and French horn played by Mr. Ford.

[1] Who will be remembered as a character in Gay's *Beggar's Opera*.

FEB. 9. . . . I got up at 3 o'clock this morning to brew
a hogshead of strong beer. . . . I was busy all day at
the Lower House, and therefore stayed there the
whole day, and did not go to bed this night as we
could not tun our liquor till near two in the morning.

FEB. 12. I got up before one this morning and brewed
a 3 quarter barrel of strong beer and some small beer
and had it all cool and tunned by four o'clock in the
afternoon. . . .

> On February 16th he takes Miss Jordan to Win-
> canton—the Bear, to a concert and ball, 'a very
> genteel ball'; he danced every dance with Miss
> Jordan from 10 to 4 in the morning '(the best
> dancer in the room)'.

MARCH 7. . . . I have taken for these last three
mornings one hour before breakfast, the second rind
of Alder stick steeped in water, and I do really think
that I have gained great benefit from it, half a pint
each morning; it must be near the colour of Claret
wine. N.B. Very good to take every Spring and
Fall.

> Under date March 15th and 18th he refers to the
> 'ungenerous' action of his uncle who had been to
> see Mrs. Powell at Harding near St. Albans, Herts.,
> patron of Ansford and Castle Cary livings, to try
> and get them for his son, thus supplanting the
> Diarist. He refers bitterly to his uncle.

MARCH 24. I was bleeded this morning by Mr.
James Clarke, and had two ounces of blood taken
from me, for which I gave him 2. 6.

N.B. My blood was very rich and, therefore, proper
to be bled.

APRIL 9. Mrs. Grant of Hambridge came early this

morning on horse back to the Lower House and gave it to Jack for breaking of the Love Affair with her daughter. Mrs. Grant is too selfish.

Jack does not appear to have been perturbed as he dined at Ansford Inn with friends and then went with them to Yeovil, 'where he remained all night'.

APRIL 10. ... Jack did not please at Parsonage this evening being very much disguised in Beer, but it is but seldom and I hope will be more seldom, the more so the better.

APRIL 14. I read prayers this morning again at C. Cary Church. I prayed for poor James Burge this morning, out of my own head, hearing he was just gone off almost in a consumption. It occasioned a great tremulation in my voice at the time. I went after prayers and saw him, and he was but just alive. He was a very good sort of a young man and much respected. It was the evil which was stopped and then fell upon his lungs. Grant O Almighty God that he may be eternally happy hereafter. ...

On April 20th his father with Jane and John set out for London; his Father is going to see Mrs. Powell at Harding, Herts., about the Livings. The Diarist himself sets out for Oxford on April 21st. On May 3rd he had a new wig and his 'Tupee' cut off and head shaved. He parted reluctantly with his tupee.

On May 23rd he took his M.A. degree and stood the usual wine, Rum Punch, &c., to the M.C.R. and B.C.R. [Masters' and Bachelors' Common Room]. On June 2nd he returns by coach and postchaise via Bath to Ansford, which he reaches on June 3rd.

JULY 6. ... I sent a letter this morning to Mr. Millachip, Brazier in High Street Oxford, to send me a dozen spitting boxes. . . .

He buries a number of people during these months as a fever rages in Castle Cary.

JULY 24. . . . Aunt Anne, my Father, Sister Jane and Brother John dined and spent the whole afternoon with me at Lower House and indeed they did me great honour by doing so.

N.B. My father sent me down a couple of fowls ready roasted, and I gave them a fine ham, some beans, some greens, and a good rich raisin pudding. . . .

OCT. 10. . . . My Father let Jack have this morning 60. 0. 0 to equip himself for the [Somerset] Militia, he being an Ensign in it.

OCT. 11. . . . Mr. Will Melliar sent me a note this morning, to desire me to be at the meeting of the Gentlemen etc., of this County, at Bridgwater to-morrow, to put in nomination two proper Persons to represent this County in Parliament, the ensuing Parliament; and it was so civil a note that I could not refuse him. . . .

OCT. 12. . . . After breakfast, about six o'clock, I set forth for Bridgwater in Ansford Inn Post-chaise, in which I went to Piper's Inn, where I took another, and went to Catcott to Mrs. Wm. Melliars there, where I made another breakfast, with Mr. Wm. Melliar, his wife and daughter, Agatha Clarke and Counsellor Melliar.

. . . After breakfasting at Catcott, I went to Bridgwater in Pipers Inn Chaise, Mr. Wm. Melliar and his brother went with me in Counsellor Melliar's Chaise.

. . . There was scarce ever seen so numerous an

assembly on such an occasion. We put up our horses at the Globe Inn in Bridgwater. We dined at the Swan, with near fourscore gentlemen of the first rank in the Country. For our ordinary we each paid 0. 3. 0, for wine, fruit and servants, pd 0. 1. 6.

At 2 o'clock we all went to the Town Hall, and Sir Charles Tynte and Mr. Cox, Lieutenant Colonel of the Somerset Militia, were the two Persons put in nomination, they having by much the majority. Mr. Trevilian opposed them, and is determined to stand the Poll at the Election, though desired by his friends to relinquish it then. Mr. Mildmay, Sergeant Burland, Sir Abraham Elton, the Sheriff, Mr. Proviss Junr of Shepton Mallett and Peter Taylor spoke in the Hall for Sir Charles and Mr. Cox. Sir Wm. Haugh (a very mean Fellow) and Major Putt and Mr. Allen, both very cleaver men, for Trevilian. We were all handsomely squeezed in the Hall. Sir Charles Tynte spoke and cleared himself from the imputation he laid under concerning the Cyder Tax. Mr. Cox spoke and most elegantly and genteelly. Old Mr. Cox spoke very well with regard to his son. At the Globe Inn in Bridgwater, Barber etc., pd 0. 2. 6.

I returned in the evening in Piper's Inn Post-chaise which I kept there, with Mr. Melliar and his brother to Catcott, where I supped and slept at Mr. Melliar's.

I gave Pipers Inn Post-chaise man 0. 2. 6.

At Whist this evening at Catcott with Counsellor Melliar against his brother and his wife, won 0. 2. 6.

Nov. 7. Brother John returned this morning from Taunton, and he dined supped etc., at Parsonage and slept at the Lower House. Jack becomes his regimentals very well. . . .

NOV. 24. ... For five gallons of Rum, being part of a Puncheon, divided among several gentlemen at Dr. Clarke's this morning at 8. 9 per gallon pd 2. 3. 9. ... Colonel Cox's brother and Mr. Wm. Melliar waited on me this morning at the Lower House, and desired my vote for Sir Charles Tynte and his brother, Colonel Cox, which I promised him. They stayed with me but a little time.

NOV. 28. ... I lent Mrs. Melliar the 3 last volumes of the Conniseur, this morning, and she lent me the six volumes of Tom Jones.

DEC. 3. My man Luke Barnard, acquainted me this morning that he did not like his wages, and unless I would raise them, he must leave me, which he is to do at Lady Day next, and his year being up yesterday, I am to give him at the rate of five pounds a year till Lady Day without any new cloathes etc. I am not very sorry. He is a willing fellow but indolent and too fond of Cyder. He is going to farm, that is the reason of his leaving me. . . . Mrs. Melliar was *fashionably* frightened into a fit by a cat after supper at the Doctor's [where there was a party], but soon well. . . .

DEC. 11. I dined, supped and spent the evening at Justice Creeds, with him, his father, Mrs. Betty Baker, her three nieces of Bridgwater, that is, Miss Baker rather ordinary, Miss Betsy very pretty, and Miss Sukey very middling, rather pretty than otherwise, all very sensible and agreable, and quite fine ladies, both in Behaviour and Dress and Fortunes. . . .

DEC. 22. ... Great Bandying at Ansford Inn to-day on account of Mr. Trevelyan's (Candidate for the County of Somersett at the coming Election) giving a dinner to his friends, which were the lower sort of People. . . .

DEC. 26. . . . Jack supped and spent his evening at the Catherine Wheel and was out late. It is very disagreeable, his way of life.

1768

JAN. 4. . . . Jack did not come home till near four in the morning. He was much in liquor and quite unhappy. The Devil has had great power over him today. O Lord, grant him strength from Thy Holy Place, to withstand him better pro futuro.

JAN. 6. I read prayers this morning at C. Cary Church being Epiphany. I had a small congregation, it being excessive cold, as cold and severe weather on all accounts as in the year 1740. . . .

On January 12th he enters that he buried a man found dead in the snow.

FEB. 3. . . . One Sarah Gore, came to me this morning and brought me an instrument from the Court of Wells, to perform publick Pennance next Sunday at C. Cary Church for having a child, which I am to administer to her publickly next Sunday after Divine Service [which accordingly was done after the sermon on Sunday Feb. 7th].

FEB. 17. . . . As I returned from Church [it was Ash Wednesday] I went into Ansford Inn and read the Commendatory Prayer to poor Mrs. Perry, who was just departing this life and who died just as I had finished. She went off extremely easy, without any visible emotion at all. I hope she is gone to unspeakable joys of Eternity. Lord, make us wise to consider our latter end and live good lives. . . .

FEB. 25. . . . I sent two spitting Basons to Counsellor Melliar this morning at Gallhampton, as a present. . . .

FEB. 28. I read prayers and preached this morning at Ansford Church. . . . Brother John spent his whole day with Mr. Wright at Ansford Inn. My father and Doctor Clarke had a few words coming out of Ansford Church this morning, but all things were made up before they parted and the Dr. came and smoked a pipe with my Father at Parsonage in the afternoon, with his wife. . . .

MARCH 1. . . . Great dinners etc., given to-day at the George Inn and the Angel by Sir Charles Tynte's and Mr. Cox's friends, viz. by Lord Ilchester, Lord Berkeley of Bruton and Mr. Mildmay, but neither were there. There were a great multitude of all sorts, gentle and simple. Mr. Cox himself was there. Bells ringing etc., and a great procession through Town with Musick playing and guns firing. They all came up in the afternoon as far as Justice Creeds, and Mr. Cox himself being there, we [the Diarist was dining with Justice Creed] both went out and spoke to him, and we both went back with him, with the Procession down to the George Inn, where we drank success to him, and was there for an hour in the large room with the multitude till Mr. Cox made a very handsome, sensible and genteel speech, and then he withdrew as did we immediately. Brother John dined and spent the evening with the multitude.

MARCH 2. . . . Esq. Farr went and drank one bottle of Port with me at the Lower House this afternoon.

He has got £1000 per annum and lives in a very handsome manner in Dorsetshire. . . .

MARCH 4. . . . I lent Brother John this afternoon at Lower House, to pay his expenses at Ansford Inn last Wednesday night, 1. 1. 0.

N.B. It was the last guinea I had, but it was proper so to do, that he might by no means appear shabby. . . .

MARCH 15. Justice Creed made me a visit this morning, and my Brother gave him a song, whilst James Clarke performed on his Base Viol. . . .

MARCH 17. . . . Great rejoicings this day at C. Cary, on account of Mr. Trevylyan's declining standing the Poll for this County of Somersett after so much hurry and disturbance. So that Sir Charles Tynte and Mr. Cox are to be our members. May they make great and worthy Representatives. . . .

MARCH 21. I got up very early this morning and after breakfast I set out for Oxford for the University Election.

> He got safely to Oxford on Mr. Francis's horse, lent for the occasion, and Sir Roger Newdigate is elected, much to his satisfaction. He returns to Ansford on March 26th.

MARCH 29. . . . My Father would not play cards, it being Passion Week and the Justice [Creed, who was visiting there] was not very pleased.

N.B. No cards this week at Parsonage which I think is not amiss, though there might be no harm.

APRIL 5. . . . My tenants from Sandford Orcas came to me this morning and paid me their rents in all

4. 17. 0. . . . I gave them all a dinner; a loin of veal roasted and a good plumb pudding for their prompt pay. . . .

APRIL 6. . . . My new Boy . . . [George Hutchins] came home this morning. . . . I settled as underneath with his Father for wages.—To give him per annum 2. 2. 0. To let him have (that is, only to lend it him during the time he lives with me) a coat, a waistcoat and hat etc. He is to find himself in shoes, breeches and shirts and if I buy them for him to deduct it out of his wages. He is a likely boy and bears a good character. . . .

APRIL 14. I made a visit this morning to old Mr. Creed in South Cary. I made two dinners this day, one at the Lower House by myself to teach my new Boy to wait at table and another at Parsonage. . . .

I went over to C. Cary this night after eleven o'clock and privately baptised a child born this day and very dangerously ill in convulsions, by name George, of Perry's a Mason and a poor man in South Cary.

Mem: Never did I any ecclesiastical duty with more pleasure as it gave such great satisfaction to its Parents, and that they were so good and charitably disposed to have it done. The poor innocent Babe was taken with a violent fit, immediately after I had named it, and I really thought was dead, but it pleased God to restore it again, which was undoubtedly a blessing from Heaven for their goodness. Blessed is the man whose strength is in thee, in whose heart are thy ways! Great is Thy Mercy O Lord God of Hosts!

APRIL 15. . . . The poor little Infant which I privately baptized last night departed this world this afternoon. . . .

APRIL 17. . . . After Cary Service I buried that little Infant which I privately named two days ago,—2 days old, a very happy turn for the dear Innocent.

APRIL 19. . . . We had some Country Dancing and Minuets at Lower House [where he was giving a party]. I danced Country dances with Mrs. Farr and Miss Payne. I danced one Minuet with Mrs. Farr at last. I gave Stephen Bennett the Fidler 0. 2. 6. We were very merry and no breaking up till 2 in morning. I gave Mrs. Farr a roasted Shoulder of Mutton and a plum Pudding for dinner—Veal Cutlets, Frill'd Potatoes, cold Tongue, Ham and cold roast Beef, and eggs in their shells. Punch, Wine, Beer and Cyder for drinking.

MAY 9. . . . I never saw a Peacock spread his tail before this day at Justice Creeds and most Noble it is. —How wonderful are Thy Works O God in every Being.

MAY 13. . . . Terrible Riots in London[1] by the Paper have been and likely to be.

MAY 22. . . . My Poor Father and Jack had a dispute this evening. O that Jack was but well settled in Life, what pleasure would it give us all. . . .

MAY 23. I rec^d a note from my Father this morning by Sister Jane and wherein he insists on Jack's not coming to this house again for some time, as he disturbed him so much last night that he could not sleep.

On May 26th a 'very fine Tench (above a pound) which Jack also caught [a brace of Tench had been sent to Justice Creed] was sent up to my Father'. The Father sends £20 to the Diarist to give Jack.

These were the Wilkes Riots on May 10th in St. George's Fields.

JULY 18. . . . The Church Wardens of C. Cary (Mr. Seth Burge and Dav^d Maby) waited on my father this afternoon for leave to dig up the Fives-Place in Cary Churchyard, and it was granted. . . .

On July 23rd his great aunt arrives to stay at the Parsonage from Bath; she beats him greatly at Back Gammon. He says, later, 'My great Aunt is an extreme sensible old Lady.' On July 29th he dines and spends the afternoon with Justice Creed, his, the justice's, father, and Parson Gapper of Yarlington. Constant hospitality is interchanged with the neighbours in all these years.

On August 17th he sets out for Oxford with his boy, George Hutchins, 'my George'—for the election of a Warden of New College: Oglander elected, not his friend Sale. He notes on August 21st that they dine in College 'now at three o'clock every day, Sundays excepted, which is half after three then'. He reaches Ansford again on August 24th.

SEP. 14. . . . Mr. Hindley and Justice Creed called at Parsonage this evening in their Chair to ask me to dinner to-morrow to talk about going to Wells with them Friday, concerning the Gallery work, to wait on the Bishop, but I shall not go (I believe) nor interfere at all concerning it, but to live peaceably with all men. He is a little unreasonable to desire it, as I must then fly in the face of allmost all my Parishioners. Great and many are the divisions in C. Cary, and some almost irreconcilable. Send us Peace O Lord! With Thee O Lord all things are possible.

Squire Creed's man, for some reason, had been kept out of the gallery by the singers and the Squire wanted to have the gallery taken down.

SEP. 17. . . . I dined, supped and spent the evening at Justice Creed's with him, his father and Mr. Hindley. Nothing transpired of what they did at Wells. They behaved very respectively towards me. . . .

SEP. 23. . . . Russell of New Coll: dined and spent the afternoon with me at Lower House. He has lately been presented to three Livings worth £500 per annum by Portman. I gave him for dinner a roasted neck of Pork and some hashed Mutton. . . .

SEP. 24. . . . My father had a letter from Brother John at Taunton this evening, and in it one to Jenny, he sent home for five guineas.

N.B. My father was very angry indeed with him, as he had twenty pound of him when he went down to Taunton. Such extravagant demands cannot but hurt him greatly. I wish with all my heart he would but consider.

SEP. 29. . . . I buried Thos Roach of Bruton, who died in the Small Pox there, a poor wild creature he has been, this afternoon at C. Cary. I had a black silk hat band and a pr of black gloves sent me for burying him by his good brother, who was at the expense in burying him handsomely. He died not worth a shilling, his brother supported him for some time. His brother has behaved surprisingly kind to all his relations, and is worth a good deal of money by his diligence, goodness and benevolence.

Mrs. Carr and Miss Chambers [guests of Squire Creed's where the Diarist and his sister were dining] did not behave quite so genteel to Jenny this evening as I expected. . . .

Oct. 9. ... David Maby [also Church Warden] the Clerk dined with us, being Sacrament Sunday.

Oct. 12. ... I walked this afternoon to Yarlington and christened a child for Parson Gapper, by name Lucy. I drank tea this afternoon with Mrs. Gapper, and her mother-in-law, old Mrs. Gapper aged 83 and a fine old lady she is indeed of her age.

Oct. 26. I had a poor little cat, that had one of her ribs broke and that laid across her belly, and we could not tell what it was, and she was in great pain. I therefore with a small pen knife this morning, opened one side of her and took it out, and performed the operation very well, and afterwards sewed it up and put Friars Balsam to it, and she was much better after, the incision was half an inch. It grieved me much to see the poor creature in such pain before, and therefore made me undertake the above, which I hope will preserve the life of the poor creature.

Nov. 5. I read Prayers this morning at Cary being the 5 of Novem. the day on which the Papists had contrived an hellish plot in the reign of King James the first, but by the Divine hand of Providence was fortunately discovered.

I dined supped and spent the evening at Parsonage. The effigy of Justice Creed was had through the streets of C. Cary this evening upon the [Fire] Engine, and then had into the Park and burnt in a bonfire immediately before the Justice's House, for his putting the Church Wardens of Cary into Wells Court, for not presenting James Clarke for making a Riot in the Gallery at Cary Church some few Sundays back. The whole Parish are against the Justice, and they intend to assist the Church Wardens in carrying on the cause at Wells. The Justice is now at Lord Pawletts at Hinton.

Nov. 11. . . . At Whist this evening with James Clarke, Brother John and Brother Heighes, at which we laughed exceedingly, I lost with them in the whole 0. 0. 6. . . .

Nov. 22. I married Tom Burge of Ansford to Charity Andrews of C. Cary by License this morning. The Parish of Cary made him marry her, and he came handbolted to Church for fear of running away, and the Parish of Cary was at all the expense of bringing of them to, I rec^d of Mr. Andrew Russ the overseer of the Poor of Cary for it 0. 10. 6. . . .

Dec. 24. . . . It being Christmas Eve we had the New Singers of C. Cary this evening at Parsonage, and they having been at great expenses in learning to sing, my Father and myself gave them double what we used to do, and therefore instead of one shilling we each gave 0. 2. 0.

Dec. 26. I was very bad in my throat all night, but towards the morning was rather better, only extremely hoarse. . . . I could not go to read Prayers this morning at Cary though it was St. Stephen, which I hope will be forgiven. . . . Sister Jane visited me this morning, and she being deaf and I not able to speak, was good company. . . .

1769

Jan. 1. . . . My ring which I had lost, was unaccountably found in little Sam: Clarke's breeches, he knowing nothing of it. I gave him 0. 1. 0.

JAN. 2. We had the fine Mummers this evening at Parsonage. . . .

He had been visiting a lot—the usual round of parties, and on January 11th enters—'I am heartily weary of visiting so much as I have, but if did not it would be taken amiss in some'.

On January 13th his mother's estate, all in land and house property at Ansford, is divided into three lots and he and Sister Jane and Brother John draw the lots out of a hat.

On January 23rd he goes to Bath on horseback with his boy George. They stay at the Bear Inn till January 27th when they return to Ansford via Radstock. At Bath he sees his great aunt, and his friends Squire Farr, his wife, and daughter. He does the usual Bath round—the Pump Room, a ball at Simpson's Rooms 'very elegant indeed', makes various visits to old friends of his Father in a 'Chair'. He sees 'The Clandestine Marriage' at the Play House. He visits the Octagon Church in Milsom Street and does not approve; 'It is a handsome building, but not like a place of worship, there being fire-places in it, especially on each side of the Altar, which I cannot think at all decent, it is not liked.'

On February 3rd he gives a large supper party at the Lower House followed by a dance. The music was a bass viol and a violin; those ladies who did not dance played at quadrille. 'I danced a Minuet with Mrs. and Miss Melliar, and a few Country Dances with Miss Aggy Clarke and Miss Plummer.'

The company were well pleased with their entertainment: he gave them an excellent supper which included Veal Cutlets, Oysters, 'a very fine large Ham', Tarts, &c., Punch, Wine, Beer, and Cyder.

FEB. 5. From henceforth O Lord give me grace to walk in thy ways more circumspectly than I have done lately.

On February 9th a meeting at the George Inn of some of the leading Cary parishioners including the Diarist composes the approaching Law Suit between Justice Creed and the Church Wardens, the agreement (this proposal had been rejected two days before) being 'that as the Gallery at Cary Church was large enough to contain between 3 & 4 score people, and the Singers being not above 30 in number that there should be a partition made in the gallery for the Singers, and the other part open to any body and also for Mr. Creed to pay his own costs and the Parish the other'.

FEB. 11. ... Jack and I had a few words this evening at Lower House and indeed I was more to blame than him, being passionate. Keep me O Lord from Passions of every kind pro futuro.

Jack refuses to breakfast at the Lower House on account of this. On February 19th he enters 'Jack's stomach is not come down yet to breakfast at L.H. He breakfasts now at Parsonage.' However, he returns to breakfast at L.H. on February 22nd.

FEB. 26. ... The 36 Psalm was sung this afternoon in Cary Church by the Singers. Done out of Pique to old

Willm. Burge.[1] Old Mr. Burge concerns himself too much with the Singers.

On February 19th old Burge had annoyed the singers by sending some persons into the singing part of the gallery contrary to the recent agreement.

MARCH 7. . . . Poor Mrs. Pearce (Miss Rooke that was) is no more, she died yesterday, she met I am afraid with a bad husband.

MARCH 10. One Farmer Wittys of Butly whom I never saw but once before called upon me this morning, and desired me to lend him thirty Pound, but it was not convenient—Very odd indeed. . . .

On March 11th Brother John is advanced £100 all in cash, 95 guineas and 5 shillings, by his father to enable him to stock his share of his mother's estate, which he is going to manage himself.

MARCH 12. I read Prayers and preached this morning at Ansford Church. I read prayers and preached this afternoon at C. Cary Church.

Mem: As I was going to shave myself this morning as usual on Sundays, my razor broke in my hand as I was setting it on the strop without any violence. May it be always a warning to me not to shave on the Lord's Day or do any other work to profane it pro futuro.

I dined, supped and spent the evening at Parsonage.

On April 5th he notes that a serving boy is not

---

[1] 'My heart sheweth me the wickedness of the ungodly: that there is no fear of God before his eyes. . . . He imagineth mischief upon his bed, and hath set himself in no good way; neither doth he abhor any thing that is evil' (Psalm xxxvi, Prayer Book version).

enough, now Brother John is taking his share of
the estate, so George Green becomes their new
servant; John pays his wages and the Diarist
keeps him.

MAY 29. . . . I read Prayers this morning at C. Cary,
being 29 of May the Restoration of King Charles II
from Popish Tyranny. . . . Jack brought home with
him from Ansford Inn [where there had been 'great
cock fighting'], after 10 o'clock this evening. . . .
Dr. John Graunt, Mr. James Graunt, Joseph Wilmot,
and Janes, all of Ditchet, which supped and stayed
till 3 in yᵉ morning, quite low life sort of people, much
beneath Jack. I really wonder Jack keeps such mean
company. . . .

Between June 9th and 16th the Diarist is ill with a
violent rash on his face, hands, breast, arms, &c.,
and all the symptoms, as he describes them, of
scarlet fever or measles: sore throat, headache,
weak eyes, fever. Dr. Clarke, however, merely tells
him to keep warm indoors and eat as much as he
likes, 'not to live low, but encourage the rash'. All
this time he sees relations and friends constantly,
and after some strong purges he is well again and
out on the 16th.

JUNE 17. . . . Jack made a terrible noise at Lower
House with all the folks there. I got up out of my bed
and came down at twelve at night and found the
house in an uproar, Jack abusing of them all in a
terrible manner. Very bad work indeed of a Saturday
night in a Parson's House, it disturbed me all night.
N.B. We must part.

On June 19th he notes that Jack 'made a riot' at
the Parsonage 'being in want of money'.

JUNE 21. . . . I played with Mr. James Clarke at Battledor and Shuttlecock, and we kept the cock up once upwards of 500 times.

On June 27th he goes to Oxford to be 'sworn in Poser to Winton Coll. next Elect'. He is duly sworn on June 29th. He goes back via Stonehenge 'to show my man the great Stones there' and arrives at home on the 1st July. On July 4th he sups with Justice Creed, whom he had not seen since the gallery trouble, except by accidental meeting, and was 'very graciously received by them'.

JULY 18. . . . For two three Pound and twelve shilling Pieces of Miss Rooke this morning at Lower House, gave her Seven new guineas of George the Third, the present King of England.

He and his sister and Miss Rooke (who is staying at the Parsonage) went all the way to Stock in Dorsetshire, 18 miles away by post-chaise, to see little Jenny White because her mother was anxious about her. She was staying with the Farrs and they found 'the little maid very hearty and well'. They went unknown to Sister White 'who was greatly rejoiced at our excursion when she knew it'.

SEP. 22. . . . Great rejoicings at Cary to-day being the Coronation Day. Bells ringing all day, Cudgell playing at Crokers, a very large bonfire on the top of the hill and very grand fireworks in the evening with firing of many guns. All at Mr. Creed's, Mr. Hindley and Mr. Potts and Duck's expense. I was at all. At the Cudgell Playing I gave 0. 4. 5. The fireworks were sent from London and were Sky-Rocketts, Mines, Trees, Crackers, Wheels and divers Indian Fireworks. Old Mrs. Burge and daughter etc., etc.,

etc., drank tea and coffee, supped and spent the evening at Justice Creed's. We did not break up till near two in the morning. Everything extremely handsome and polite indeed. . . .

Sep. 23. Great doings again to-day at Cary in the Park. At one o'clock there was a shift run for by women. There were five that started for it, and won by Willm. Francis's daughter Nan of Ansford—her sister Pegg was second and therefore had ribbands. I never saw the Park so full of people in my life. The Women were to run the best of three half mile Heats: Nan Francis run a Heat in three minutes. . . .

Oct. 1. . . . I read Prayers, churched a woman [and] read the Act of Parliament against profane swearing as directed by Law. . . .

Oct. 18. After breakfast went with Mr. Creed in his Chair to Wells with a great possy from Cary to attend at the County Meeting to consider of a proper Petition [concerning the late violation of the freedom of Election—the famous Wilkes case] to his Majesty in the present crisis of Affairs. We went to the Swan, where we dined with upwards of a hundred Gentlemen of the first rank in the County. We had a very respectable meeting on this occasion. Mr. Coxe, Mr. Smith, Members for Bath, Mr. Allen, Member for Bridgwater, Mr. Seymour, Mr. Creed and Mr. Sansom and Revd. Mr. Wainhouse spoke on the occasion upon the Petitions that were presented to the Publick. Mr. Coxe's Petition with some alteration was approved of most, and agreed in the Town Hall to be presented to his Majesty by proper Persons. . . .

Britons never will be slaves was played during dinner. . . .

Nov. 12. I read Prayers and preached this morning at C. Cary Church. I was disturbed this morning at Cary Church by the Singers. I sent my Clerk some time back to the Cary Singers, to desire that they would not sing the Responses in the Communion Service, which they complied with for several Sundays, but this morning after the first Commandment they had the Impudence to sing the Response, and therefore I spoke to them out of my desk, to say and not sing the Responses which they did after, and at other places they sang as usual. The Singers in the Gallery were, John Coleman, the Baker, Jonathan Croker, Willm Pew Junr., Thos Penny, Willm Ashford, Hooper the Singing Master, James Lucas, Peter, Mr. Francis's man, Mr. Melliar's man James, Farmer Hix's son, Robert Sweete and the two young Durn-fords. . . .

Nov. 13. . . . We had news this morning of Mr. Wilkes gaining his point against Lord Halifax and 4000 pound damages given him. Cary and Ansford bells rung most part of the day on the occasion. Miss Rooke, Jenny, Mr. Richard Clarke Junr., Brother Heighes and Brother John dined, supped and spent the evening with me. I gave them for dinner a couple of rabbits smothered with onions, a roasted leg of mutton and some mince pies.

The reference 'to Mr. Wilkes gaining his point against Lord Halifax' is to the conclusion of the long-drawn-out action—it had been dragging on with deliberate ministerial postponements for six years—in which Wilkes had sued Lord Halifax for the seizure of his papers in 1763.

Nov. 20. . . . Brother Heighes and John dined etc.,

at Lower House again, and they kept me up till 2 in the morning being very quarrelsome especially my brother John.

N.B. It is too much indeed for me.

Nov. 21. . . . My brother spent the evening at the Angel at Cary and returned very much disguised in liquor, and stayed up late.

Nov. 26. I read Prayers and Preached this morning at C. Cary Church. N.B. No singing this morning, the Singers not being at Church, they being highly affronted with me at what I lately had done. . . .

> On November 28th he makes Miss Rooke a present of 'a roll of Pigtail Tobacco'—about one-quarter of a pound, and on November 30th on her departure from the Parsonage for her home, she leaves behind for him 'half a cheese for toasting'.

Dec. 5. . . . A strange man was found this evening in my father's little house. N.B. A Farmer's daughter near Bristol who was to sleep at my Father's to-night had occasion to go to the Necessary House and there was a man there, but he got clear of. He was upon no good there.

Dec. 12. . . . A poor young Fellow that drove a waggon of Mr. Lockyer's was about the middle of the night killed by the waggon going over him as he was going down our hill with other waggons in a great hurry. Mr. James Clarke and my brother John was with him when he died at the Turnpike Road. The Half Moon Inn would not take the poor Fellow in.

> On December 13th he notes that. . . . 'The poor Fellow who was killed was about 25 years of age. . . . James Clarke and Jack sat up with the poor soul till he

died and then they came and slept at Lower House.
They did all they could, I believe, to save the poor
Fellow, but he died in an hour or two after the
accident'. On December 14th he adds the additional note that 'the poor Fellow was to have been
married at Christmas'.

Under date December 13th he notes that 'a Pipe
of Port' and 'a Butt of Mountain Wine were
divided this morning at Dr. Clarke's among the
neighbouring Gentlemen'. The Diarist had some
of the port at 5*s*. 8¾*d*. per gallon. He thought it very
good but the others including 'Parson Leache' all
pronounced it to be bad.

DEC. 17. . . . The Singers at Cary did not please me
this afternoon by singing the 12 Psalm, New Version,[1]
reflecting upon some People. . . . Some people have
been about my Father's house again this evening,
about 8 o'clock. Jenny and the maid being at the
Little House, some person or another came to the
door of it and rapped against it three times with a
stick. What it means I know not. Brother Heighes,
Jack and myself all armed, took a walk at twelve this
evening round the Parish to see if we could meet any
idle Folks but we did not, and therefore came home
about two. We waited at my Father's some considerable time, till Brother Heighes was very uneasy,
being cold in his feet.

---

[1] 'Help me, Lord, for there is not one godly man left: for the faithful
are minished from among the children of men.

'They talk of vanity every one with his neighbour: they do but flatter
with their lips, and dissemble in their double heart.

. . . .

'The ungodly walk on every side: when they are exalted, the children
of men are put to rebuke.'—Psalm xii (Prayer Book version).

DEC. 23. To a fatted Goose at 5 Pence per Pound pd.—0. 2. 9.

DEC. 24. To Cary Singers this evening being Xmas Eve at Parsonage after giving them a Lecture concerning their late behaviour in Church, on promise of amendment gave 0. 2. 0.

1770

JAN. 14. . . . Mrs. Melliar sent a note to my Sister Jane this afternoon to desire her and my Brother John to spend the evening with her to-morrow.[1] Brother Heighes and myself were both excepted out of it.

JAN. 19. . . . I dined upon a roasted Pigg and spent the afternoon at Mr. Creed's with him and his Father. It was very kind of him to send to me. To Mr. Creed's servant maids, Sarah and Unity, gave 0. 2. 0.

JAN. 22. . . . For a Summons Warrant against Robt. Biggin and his brother Nathaniel . . . for shrowding an Ash Tree of my Sister Jane Woodforde's last Thursday night, to appear before the Justice, next Friday at 2 aft. pd. 0. 0. 6. . . .

JAN. 23. . . . I sent the Summons Warrant this afternoon by Wm. Corpe to the Tithing man, Thos Taylor and it was served this evening.

JAN. 24. I was sent for just at dinner time to Sutton about a mile of to go and read Prayers by a poor young woman, Sally Bond that was, and who married Farmer Wittick of Sutton, being very ill ever since she laid in, and now more likely to die than live. She was quite light headed and therefore very melancholy

[1] Very rude *written in margin.*

to behold. I also privately named her Infant by name, Sarah. . . .

JAN. 26. At two o'clock this afternoon I went up to Justice Creed's and heard my Wood Stealers examined before the Justice. Robert Biggin was found guilty and his brother Nath[1] was acquitted, therefore Robert was ordered to pay me six shillings by the 9 of February, if he does not he is to be whipped from Cary Cross to Ansford Inn. . . .

FEB. 12. . . . I went to Mr. Will[m] Melliar's and Mr. Creed's and Mr. Clarke's to desire all three of them to drink a dish of coffee with me this afternoon at Lower House and if possible to reconcile all animosities in Cary and to stop and put an end to all Law Suits now subsisting. It was agreeable to all Parties for Mr. Creed and Mr. Melliar to settle all matters and to make Peace. Mr. Creed and Mr. Melliar agreed to meet each other this afternoon at my house. I dined and spent part of the afternoon at Mr. Creed's with him and his Father, and after the Justice took a walk with me to my house and drank a dish of coffee with me. Mr. Will[m] Melliar and Dr. Clarke also drank a dish of coffee with me and after coffee we talked over the Parish Affairs. After much altercation it was settled for Peace. The terms were these as underwritten. . . .

  That all Prosecutions between the contending parties in the Parish of Castle Cary, and all animosities between the Houses of Creed and Melliar, should from that time cease, and be buried in the Gulf of Oblivion. . . . After the above [numerous technical details of settlement of Prosecution costs etc., etc.] was agreed to by all four and Mr. Melliar had made a

Memorandum of it in writing, Mr. Creed and Mr. Melliar hobbed and nobbed in a glass of Wine and drank success to Peace. . . .

Jack came home a little merry this evening and he laid me a wager of one guinea that he would not from this night get drunk all the year 1770, that is, as not to be able to tread a Scratch. . . .

FEB. 13. . . . To a wager with Brother Heighes that he could not walk the Scratch this night at 10 o'clock, lost 0. 0. 6.

FEB. 28. . . . I buried poor Thos Barnes this afternoon [who had been 'a long time killing himself by Liquor'] at Cary, aged 48. A great many people attended him to his grave. He was, I believe, no man's enemy, but to himself a great one. . . .

MARCH 8. . . . Very unsuspected news from Miss Rooke from Somerton this evening.

APRIL 18. . . . I dined at old Mr. Willm Burge's being the day of Mr. Wilkes's enlargement, and spent the afternoon and former part of this evening there with old Mr. Willm Burge etc., etc. . . . Cary bells ring all day upon the occasion. Two British Flaggs also displayed, one at Cary Cross and another on Cary Tower. A hogshead of Cyder given to the Populace at the Cross. Many loyal toasts and worthy men drank upon the occasion, and Mr. Burge's house handsomely illuminated in the evening. The Flagg on the Tower had on it Liberty and Property, the small one had on it Mr. Wilkes's Head and Liberty. Everything was conducted with great decorum and broke up in good time. We had for dinner [apparently for 15 people] a boiled Rump Beef 45 pd. weight, a Ham and half a dozen Fowls, a roasted Saddle of Mutton,

two very rich puddings, and a good Sallet with a fine
cucumber. . . .

MAY 19. . . . Something very agreable and with
which I was greatly pleased happened this evening.
It gave me much secret pleasure and satisfaction.
[The Diarist does not anywhere reveal what this was.]

MAY 26. . . . Brother John spent his evening at Cary,
came home merry, and kept me up very late and also
made me very uneasy. Brother Heighes was also
quite happy again this evening. It is at present a very
disagreeable way of living for me.

> Between May 14th and June 6th Cary enjoyed the
> presence of a theatrical company who acted in the
> Court House and attracted large audiences.
> Amongst the plays performed were *The Beggars'*
> *Opera*, *Hamlet*, *Richard the Third*, and various other
> plays and 'Entertainments'.

JUNE 27. . . . This very day I am thirty years of
age.—'Lord make me truly thankful for thy great
goodness as on this day shewed me by bringing me
into this world, and for preserving me to this day from
the many and great dangers which frail mortality is
every day exposed to; grant me O Lord the continuance of thy divine goodness to me, that thy Holy
Spirit may direct me in all my doings and that the
remaining part of my days may be more spent to thy
Honour and Glory than those already past.' . . .

JULY 4. After breakfast walked up to Justice Creed's
and about 8 o'clock went with the Justice in his Chair
to Horsington and made Mr. and Mrs. Spencer there
a morning visit who were both at home with their two
sons and five daughters, the two eldest Miss Spencers

are very fine young Ladies about 15 years old. The eldest entertained us upon the Guitar and sang charmingly with it. Mr. Spencer has a noble house and everything in the neatest manner. . . .

JULY 12. . . . Took a walk in the evening with Sister Clarke, Jenny Clarke, Sam: Clarke, Nancy Clarke, Sister Jane and Brother Heighes. I gave them all a peep through my fine spying glass, to see King Alfred's Tower, now erecting by Mr. Hoare on the very highest part of Kingsettle Hill about 7 miles of.

JULY 15. I read Prayers and preached at Cary Church and whilst I was preaching one Thos Speed of Gallhampton came into the Church quite drunk and crazy and made a noise in the Church, called the Singers a Pack of Whoresbirds and gave me a nod or two in the pulpit. The Constable Roger Coles Senr took him into custody after and will have him before a Magistrate to-morrow. . . .

AUG. 1. . . . I dined and spent the afternoon at Justice Creed's with him, his Father, Lord and Lady Paulett, and their two sons, Lord Hinton and Master Vere Paulett, who are both going to Twyford School in Buckinghamshire kept by Mr. Cleaver.

Lord and Lady and sons are very affable, good natured People. . . .

AUG. 28. For Pope's Works, 10 volumes of Brother Heighes this evening, I gave him, and they were second hand and third 1. 1. 0. . . .

SEP. 5. . . . The Duke and Duchess of Beaufort in a coach and six went through the Parish this afternoon in their road to Weymouth. Parson Penny [their chaplain] was with them and went with them. . .

On September 9th he notes that he goes with his sister Jane in their father's chaise to drink coffee with Justice Creed, the Diarist being dressed 'in my Gown and Cassock'.—It was Sunday.

OCTOB. 4. . . . The Duke and Dutchess of Beaufort and children whom Mr. Penny is with most part of his time, are all to sleep at Ansford Inn to-night, it being their road from Weymouth to Badminton. . . .

OCT. 12. . . . Mrs. Carr, Miss Chambers, Mr. Hindley, Mr. Carr, and Sister Jane dined, supped and spent the evening with me, and we were very merry. I gave them for dinner a dish of fine Tench which I caught out of my brother's Pond in Pond Close this morning, Ham, and 3 Fowls boiled, a Plumb Pudding; a couple of Ducks rosted, a roasted neck of Pork, a Plumb Tart and an Apple Tart, Pears, Apples and Nutts after dinner; White Wine and red, Beer and Cyder. Coffee and Tea in the evening at six o'clock. Hashed Fowl and Duck and Eggs and Potatoes etc. for supper. We did not dine till four o'clock—nor supped till ten. Mr. Rice, a Welshman who is lately come to Cary and plays very well on the Triple Harp, played to us after coffee for an hour or two . . . the Company did not go away till near twelve o'clock. . . . My Father's maid Betty dressed my dinner etc. with my People. The dinner and supper were extremely well done and well set of.

On October 23rd he and his brothers take a party to a dance at Ansford Inn, the music being Mr. Rice's Harp. . . . 'My partner was the eldest Miss Francis, she dances but poorly and says but little'; however they spent a 'very agreeable afternoon and evening', and did not return home till 'near two o'clock'. On December 27th he gave his usual Xmas dinner to some poor Parishioners ... 'to dine with me' and gave them his usual shilling, and a sixpenny loaf apiece. His Father is now far from well, and on December 30th he administers the Sacrament to him at the Parsonage as he is not well enough to go to church.

He gives a dinner and supper party on January 5th at the Lower House followed by a dance ... 'the Company seemed very well pleased with their entertainment. I treated them with my large wax Candle.' On January 8th he and his brothers organized a ball at Ansford Inn, 'where we had a very genteel Hop and did not break up till three in the morning'. The company, besides 'myself and Mrs. Farr who opened the Ball', consisted of three other Parsons, Squire Creed, and the usual Cary celebrities.

1771

JAN. 10. ... Brother John was greatly astonished by a light this evening as he came thro' Orchards, a field by Ansford Church, which light seemed to follow him close behind all the way through that field, and which he could not account for. I hope it is no Omen of death in the Family. N.B. The Reflection of the snow I apprehend occasioned the light that my Brother saw.

JAN. 16. ... Extreme hard frost with a cutting wind. It was allowed by my Father and Aunt Anne this afternoon that the weather now is as severe as it was in the year 1740. ...

JAN. 20. ... My Poor Father rather worse than

better. He wastes very fast. . . . Brother John is I am afraid coming into his old complaint the Stone, having some bad symptoms of it today. If it is I pray God that he may bear it with Christian Patience and Resignation. He has not been I am afraid so thankful as he should have been to Almighty God for his former deliverance from the same. Things in our Family at present look but melancholy, pray God have mercy on us all and forgive us our sins. . . .

On January 22 he (on horseback) accompanies his Father to Bath, who goes in the Ansford Inn Chaise with his faithful old maid: they hoped the Bath waters would do the old man good.

FEB. 10 (SUNDAY). . . . Brother John and Andrew Russ stayed at Parsonage this evening till after 12 o'clock, then came to the Lower House, and after Andrew Russ went home, Brother John being very full in Liquor at two o'clock in the morning, made such an intolerable noise by swearing in so terrible a manner and so loud, that it disturbed me out of sound sleep being gone to bed, and was so shocked at it that I was obliged to get up to desire him to go to bed, but all my arguments and persuasions were in vain, and he kept me up till five in the morning and then I went to bed and he went on Horseback for Bath. It was an exceeding cold night and very hard frost, and at seven o'clock in the morning snowed very hard. O that Jack was in some way of business, and that his life was something better and more religious, for in the morning whilst I was at Church, he was shooting.

On February 14th his father returns from Bath with Brother John, 'but very little better for the waters'.

Feb. 19. . . . My Father was brave and in good
spirits this morning, but in the evening was as bad as
ever and talked very moving to Sister Jane and me
about his Funeral and that he wanted to alter his
Will, and mentioned the underwritten to me and my
Sister Jane, 'that he desired that his maid [Eliz.
Clothier] should have that house where Grace
Stephens lives at present during her life, and after her
life to go to my sister Jane, as well as all the other
Poor Houses and Mrs. Parr's House and the Field
called Four Acres to her my Sister Jane. That Sister
White has one Hundred Pounds to make her equal to
her Sister Clarke in Fortune. That I have all his
Books and Book-case in his Study. And that he would
have no people invited to his funeral to make a show,
but that he is carried to Ansford Church by six of his
poor neighbours, Robin Francis and his Brother
Thomas were mentioned and that they have half a
crown a-piece.—To be laid in the vault where my
Mother is, by her side. And that a little monument
be erected in the side wall near the vault in memory
of him and his wife.' My poor Father is I think much
in the same way as my poor Mother was. Pray God
to bless him and keep him, and give us all strength to
bear so sore an affliction as such a separation must
occasion, if it be thy Divine will to remove him
from us—O God whenever such an event happens
take him to thyself, and give us grace to follow his
good examples, that with him we may deserve to be
Partakers of thy Heavenly Kingdom. Grant him O
Lord an easy and happy exit. Better Parents no
children ever had than we have been blessed with—
blessed be God for it—and make us more worthy than
we are, for all thy goodness to us. Praise the Lord O
my Soul, and forget not all his Benefits—Thou hast

not dealt with us after our sins, nor rewarded us
according to our wickedness—Praise thou the Lord
O my Soul.

I played at Back Gammon with my Father in the
evening, it takes him in some degree off from thinking
of his Pain. I won—o: 6. . . .

On March 13th he writes to Mrs. Powel at Harding,
near St. Albans, Herts, to apply for the livings of
Cary and Ansford in case his Father should die.
March 18th he had another disturbed night,
Brothers John and Heighes sat up drinking with
Captain Pompier and Mr. Goldsborough, a Midshipman, all drunk: 'They drank 3 bottles of Wine
and near 20 quarts of Cyder.' March 23rd Dr.
Dixon of Taunton who 'seems a mighty sensible
affable man' comes to see his father and receives a
fee of £5 5s.: he 'does not doubt he shall do my
Father great good'. March 28 Mrs. Powel replies
to his letter promising him Cary living but saying
nothing of Ansford.

March 31st Brother John again came home
drunk and greatly disturbed him; he enters: 'It is
most unhappy the life that I am obliged at present
to lead.' Again on April 4th 'Jack bullied and behaved to me as usual, when so very few I believe
would bear half which I do. I hope one day or
another it will be something better.'

On April 9th his Father is 'much worse than ever,
he groans very loud indeed. Pray God release him
from his Pains which are acute.' Dr. Clarke gives
him liquid laudanum to compose him. April 11th
he notes the extreme cold 'never such weather
known by any person living at present'. April 14th
his brothers are again drunk, 'Most intolerable

noises all night, it was almost impossible to sleep. . . .
Such a Sunday night again may I never feel or see.
Our house at Lower House is the worst in the
Parish or any other Parish. It grieves me to see it.'
And again on April 26th 'Jack was worse tonight
than ever I knew him. . . . I never heard a man
swear like him and for so long together. Pray
God to turn his heart soon, for I dread the conse-
quences.'

On April 30th. 'My poor dear Father very bad
this afternoon, almost choked with Phlegm in his
stomach, which I am afraid is the Rattles and a
foreboding of his speedy departure hence, which if
it is, O God receive his soul into thy everlasting
Kingdom.' On the same day he enters that his
cousin Tom Woodforde sends a basket to the
Parsonage with these presents, 'a couple of
Pidgeons, some electuary for Aunt Parr, some spirit
of Lavender for Aunt Anne, and a Pot of Confectio
Cardiaca for my Father'. On May 9th a two days'
Cock fight between Somerset and Wilts at Ansford
Inn ended in the victory of Somerset—'Wilts was
beat shamefully. I believe my Brother John won
a good deal of money at it.' On May 15th his
Aunt Parr dies. 'No woman ever could like a
Person more than she did my good Father; and
she daily prayed to depart this life before him,
and it pleased God to hear her prayers and take
her.'

MAY 16. . . . My Poor Father worse than ever a
great deal, and altered greatly after 12 at night, and
in great agonies all the morning; and it pleased the
Almighty Creator to deliver him out of all his Pain
and Trouble in this world about ½ an hour after one

o'clock at noon, by taking him to himself—blessed therefore be the name of the Lord.—It is the Lord, let him do what seemeth him good. The Lord gave and the Lord hath taken away, blessed be the name of the Lord. Have mercy upon us O Lord, miserable sinners—and send us comfort from above.

> The Diarist was left sole executor of all his Father's real and personal property left between him, Brother John, and Sister Jane.

MAY 17. . . . My Brother John, myself and Sister Jane, examined this morning, my poor Father's Bureau etc. at Parsonage and we found in Cash in all the places the sum of 518:9:6; Mortgages, Bonds and Notes of Hand 533:16:0. . . . I sent poor old Alice Stacy by her daughter this morning to cheer up her spirits a little, 0–1–0. The poor creature begged most heartily to sit up with my Poor Father, all night, which she did with Christian Speed.

> On May 22nd his Father is buried in much state. The Pall Bearers all had 'black silk Hatbands and shammy gloves'. The Under-Bearers had 'black Lamb gloves and each 0–2–6'. William Corpe (the servant) had 'a black crape Hatband and buckles and a black broad cloth Coat and waistcoat given him by us'. The Clerk—'a black silk Hatband common, and a pair of mock shammy gloves'. The sextons of Ansford and Cary had 'Lamb gloves'. The women relations, though they did not attend, 'had or are to have all black shammy gloves'. The six women 'Wakers' who sat up all night with the corpse after death—each a pair of 'Black Lamb gloves'. . . . 'Cary Bell as well as Ansford Bell tolled from 12 at noon till 8 in the evening. Everything I

hope was done decently, handsome and well—and nothing omitted but want of speaking to the Gentlemen to return to the Parsonage to pull of their cloaks at the House, which, however, most of them did—and drank a glass of wine and went.'

JUNE 4. ... After today I am to keep the Parsonage House. ...

JUNE 5. ... This morning between James Woodforde, Jane Woodforde, and John Woodforde, Housekeeping was settled as follows: that I should keep house at Parsonage, Jack at Lower House and that Sister Jane should board with me for sixteen pounds per annum, Tea, Sugar and Wine excepted. ...

JUNE 24. I read Prayers this morning at Cary being Midsummer Day. After Prayers I made a little visit to Mrs. Melliar where I met Mr. Frank Woodforde and told him, before Mrs. Melliar, Miss Melliar and Miss Barton what great obligations I was under to him for his not offering me to hold his Livings for him instead of Mr. Dolton and Mr. Gatehouse. From such base actions and dishonest men O Lord, deliver me.

On June 25th he rides over to see his cousin Mr. Dolton, Parson of Cucklington, who is to hold the living of Ansford for Frank Woodforde, and on July 9th he duly inducts him to Ansford Rectory where the Diarist and his sister Jane are to live; Mr. Dolton promising not to turn them out. On July 30th he enters: 'Busy this morning making a Pot of Medicines for Horses.' From numerous entries of fees, from this time on, it appears that he treated quite a number of horses; in one case a horse was sent him to be treated all the way from Wiltshire—Mr. Goldney of Chippenham.

On September 22nd he dines and spends the evening with the Creeds, and they 'went to the Cudgell-Playing (alias Back-Sword) at Crockers, where was good sport and a vast concourse of people'. On the same day a Mr. Wickham informs him that the Bishop of Bath and Wells had given him the Vicarage of Castle Cary. He wants to know if the Diarist can serve it for him, who replies, 'I could not serve but till he was provided.' September 25th he goes over to dine with Mr. Wickham at Shepton Mallett, and brings back with him in the chaise Miss Betsy White of Shepton, to whom he refers as follows: 'She is a sweet tempered girl indeed, and I like her much, and I think would make a good wife, I do not know but I shall make a bold stroke that way.' He sees a good deal of her.

On October 14th he and his boy go to Oxford, returning home on October 23rd.

OCT. 19. . . . The Streets of Oxford are much improved, all the Signs are taken down and put against the Houses, the Streets widened, East-Gate and Brocards taken down and a new Bridge going to be built where Magdalen Bridge now stands, and temporary Bridges during the building of it now making by Christchurch Broad-Walk, for to go up the Hill, etc.

DEC. 23. . . . Mr. Thomas Woodforde of Taunton (who is lately married to a Miss Waters of Blandford) with his new wife came to my house in a Post Chaise just at dinner time, and they both dined, supped and slept at Parsonage. His wife appears to be a very aggreable as well as a handsome young Lady and has £800 for her Fortune. I really think my cousin has made a very good choice. . . . Mr. Leache of Alford and Mr. James Clarke supped and spent the evening at Parsonage. Mr. Leache came to me to see Ecton's Liber Valorum to see whether he can hold two Livings without a Dispensation. . . . Mrs. Burton has given his eldest son the Living of Sutton. . . .

1772

FEB. 29. This morning after Breakfast I went down to Henbridge, when I saw and spent the morning with Mrs. Grant and her two daughters, Miss Jenny Wason and Miss Nancy Wason. [She and Brother John had made up their quarrel.] They all seemed to be very uneasy, particularly Mrs. Grant, who said, that my Brother seemed too gay to be able to make a good Husband to her daughter, kept too much Company for his circumstances etc. etc. I told her that he had some failings as other young men, but I thought his good ones overbalanced them as I never saw anything tending to any very bad. I staid at Henbridge till after one and then returned and dined, supped, and slept again at Parsonage. Brother John went home well pleased at my going down. . . .

On March 7th he sends Mr. Ford, the Bath 'Statuary', the inscription for his father's monument: the latter will cost £14 14*s.* The Diarist does not tell us the inscription on this monument, but Phelps,[1] who succeeded Collinson as the historian of Somerset, gives it in full. Phelps says: 'Against the north wall of the chancel [Ansford Church] is a neat monument of white marble, having inscribed on it:

H.S.E. Samuel Woodforde, A.M. ecclesiæ de

---

[1] Phelps, *History of Somersetshire*, vol. i, p. 375 (1836).

Castle Cary Vicarius; hujus item parochiæ annos
magis quinquaginta rector indefessus, et honora-
tissimo comiti de Tankerville à sacris domesticus.
Vir erat antiquis moribus, virtute, fide; pauperi-
bus erogator largus: pater prudens ac providus:
amicus certus, cordatus, fidus. Eodem tumulo
quiescunt cineres uxoris amatæ æquè ac amantis-
simæ Janæ Woodforde, quæ per quadraginta fere
annos in domesticis vitæ muneribus obeundis
plurimis antecellere, nulli forsan secunda vide-
batur. Amabiles in vita, nec in morte divisi
sunt.

Illa prius Feb. 8, 1766.   { Ætatis }   60
Ille secutus Maii 16, 1771.   { anno }   76
Valete suaves animæ, sed non æternum!
Filii mœrentes posuerunt.

On March 31st he enters into an agreement with
Mr. Wickham to serve the curacy of Castle Cary
for £30 per annum, in addition to surplice fees.
The tithes of Cary are to be farmed by the Burges,
who will pay Mr. Wickham £130 per annum for
three years, and afterwards £140 for the remainder
of his period as Vicar.

APRIL 21. .... Whilst we were at dinner they [Parson
and Mrs. Wickham] came to us to the Parsonage and
caught my Sister Jane at table with her hair up in
papers, as she is going this evening to Shepton
Assembly, but they excused it very kindly.

MAY 1. .... In the evening Mr. Creed, myself and the
Counsellor [Melliar] walked down into Cary and saw
the Fair, it being Cary Fair to-day. I saw Miss
Hannah Pew in the Fair and I gave her some Sugar
Plumbs, half a pound of them and they cost me 0. 1. 4.

. . . Brother John supped and spent the evening at Parsonage, was very much in liquor and behaved like a madman. N.B. He has received a letter from Nancy Wason, which I saw and I think she has used Jack very ill, she declares of [off] entirely, and will answer no more letters of his. It is I believe her Mother's and Sister's doing all this. . . .

JUNE 1. . . . Brother John set forth this morning for Bath to a Cock Match.

JUNE 6. . . . Brother John returned this evening and supped etc. at Parsonage; he says that he has won fifty Pounds at Bath.

JUNE 7. . . . Mr. Creed called upon me in the evening and we took a walk—after I had buried a child of Giles Francis's by name J. Francis—aged 5 years. The child died at Bath owing to a kick in the groin by another lad. Giles works at Bath, and he and his son brought the child in a coffin upon their heads from Bath, they set out from Bath last night at 12. . . .

On June 18th he goes to Wells with Mr. Wickham, sees the Bishop, who promises his support as to the Diarist's continuing in the Ansford curacy, and has tea with the Dean, Lord Francis Seymour, his wife, son and daughters. 'Lord Francis and Lady and the whole family behaved exceeding complaisant and civil to me. His Lordship told me that I had now found the way to the Deanery he would be glad to see me at all times and often. . . . It is indeed as good a family as ever I was in. . . . The Soldiers in the Town were exercising in the C. Yard whilst we were drinking tea. It was really very pretty. I don't know when I ever spent such an afternoon or day. . . .'

Again on July 31st he goes to Wells and visits the Bishop and Dean, who are very cordial to him. It has been arranged that he is to remain Curate at Ansford. 'The Dean asked me to dine with him to-morrow upon a Haunch of Venison, but I told his Lordship that I was afraid I could not.'

On August 31st he sets out for Winton with his boy—for his Poser's duties there with Bathurst. He returns on September 5th, and on October 1st he goes to Oxford to vote for a new Chancellor, the candidates being Lord North, then Prime Minister, and the Earl of Radnor. The Diarist intended to vote for Lord Radnor, but as they could not muster more than 73 votes, they abandoned his candidature, and Lord North was unanimously elected on October 3rd. He reaches Ansford again on October 6th.

1773

JAN. 6. . . . Painter Clarke's family is under great distress concerning his son Charles, who went to London on Xmas day and have heard nothing of him since, and also that a horse and bridle was found on Hounslow Heath on Monday Dec. 28 with a man genteely dressed, booted and spurred was found under a hedge near the horse shot thro' the head as mentioned in the Salisbury Paper Monday last. No one knew of his going to London but John Burge, and to whom he promised to write when he got to town, and he has received no letter at all from him.

FEB. 10. . . . I went in the evening to the Play with the Justice [Creed]. The Play was Hamlet and the entertainment—Hob in the Well.

MARCH 1. . . . Brother John spent the evening at Parsonage but was noisy, being merry, and his seeing Nancy Wason ride by our house this aft. and is reported to be married to And^w Russ this morning. Parson Rawkins and another Person with her. . . .

MARCH 28. . . . Mr. John Pouncett of Cole spent the afternoon, supped and spent the evening at Parsonage. He has an inclination for my Sister Jane. I think it would do well. . . .

APRIL 14. . . . To Eliz. Chrich this morning one year's wages due Lady Day last past paid her . . . 3. 3. 0. . . .

APRIL 17. . . . Sister Clarke, James and Richard Clarke, Jenny Clarke and Sam spent the major part of the morning with me, and agreed pretty well upon some matters relating to their affairs. The old Doctor I find is not worth much less than 16000 p^d. . . . [He had destroyed his will and the Diarist induces him to make another in the interests of his family, as the money would be divided up unfairly if he died intestate.]

APRIL 22. . . . I went up to Dr. Clarke's this morning by the desire of Sister Clarke and James, and desired him to make a Will agreeable to his Family and himself and he agreed so to do which I am very glad of.— The poor Doctor cried a little. . . .

MAY 21. . . . A grey owl was found in my back-kitchen this morning. He came down the chimney. I gave him his Liberty again. . . .

MAY 22. . . . Very busy all the morning in trimming up my Geraniums. . . .

On June 13th he takes duty at Batcombe by arrangement with Mr. Wickham, who was to take the Diarist's services at Cary and Ansford. But as soon as he got out of church at Batcombe a message is brought him that Mr. Wickham 'was not come to serve my Churches'. After a hasty dinner he rides back post-haste just in time to take a late service at Cary Church. But naturally there was grumbling over the incident. He notes 'Mr. Coward's[1] Family of Spargrove was at Batcombe Church, with many other good families'.

JULY 8. ... We all went from Sister Clarke's up into South Cary to the Royal Oak to see Mr. Nevil's grand machinery, being the whole of the woolen manufactory, from one end of it to the other, and all in motion at once. It is very curious indeed—three thousand movements at once going—composed by Mr. Nevil himself, and which took him ny thirty years in completing it. ...

JULY 19. ... Mr. Frank Woodforde was this morning inducted into the Living of Ansford, and he immediately sent me a Line that he intends serving Ansford next Sunday himself, which notice of my leaving the Curacy is I think not only unkind but very ungentlemanlike. I must be content. Far be it from me to expect any favour at all from that House. All their actions towards me are bad. ... I intend to quit the Parsonage House when my year is up, which will be Lady Day next, and to take up my residence once more at New College. ...

JULY 28. ... Sister Clarke came to let me know that Frank dines with them tomorrow [by Richard's

---

[1] Thomas Coward, Esq., Sheriff of Somerset in 1771.

invitation] upon the Goose that Sister Clarke invited
me to dine upon as tomorrow. Therefore shall not go.
This is the second time of being disappointed to dine
there.—First upon a Fawn and now a Goose.

1. *Mem:* Jˢ Clarke invited me to dine at his house
upon part [of] a Fawn last week but did not mention
any particular day.—However they had it last week
and never let me know it.

2. *Mem:* Sister Clarke invited me yesterday to come
and dine upon a goose as to-morrow, and now I cannot
go as Frank is to dine there and whom I don't choose
to associate with.—The next time I am invited there
I shall take care how I promise them. . . .

Aug. 24. . . . I called at Mrs. White's and stayed
with her and her daughter Betsy till 8 o'clock this
evening. . . . Betsy White came from London only last
Saturday. She is greatly improved and handsomer
than ever. . . .

Aug. 30. . . . As I was coming from 4 Acres down the
Lane this morning between 7 and 8 I met my Uncle
Tom on Horseback with his servant going to Mrs.
Powel's in Hertfordshire. He said to me Good morrow
to you and I made him a Bow and said your Servant
Sir! . . .

Sep. 1. . . . [He hears of a vacancy in the Mastership
of Bedford School.]—the third best thing in the gift of
New College,—a new built house with an exceeding
handsome garden—50 guineas paid the Master every
quarter—Fuel, Candles and all kinds of expenses
about the house and gardens paid for the Master and
no taxes whatsoever. An Ussher also found and paid
by the Charity—About 12 boys to teach by the

Master and Ussher. The only bad thing belonging to it, is, being a Borough Town, and there is no such thing as being neuter. Upon the whole I like it very well, and I believe shall accept of it, if it comes to me.

On September 6th he hands Mr. Wickham notice of his giving up Cary curacy at Michaelmas, and visits 'my dear Betsy White', and on September 13th he enters that Andrew Russ and Nancy Wason are married that day. On September 16th 'I carried my dear Maid of Shepton some Peaches etc., etc.' On October 4th he sets out with his boy for Oxford on horseback 'to hear about Bedford'. Unfortunately, one Hooke is nominated by New College for Bedford on October 14th, and next day the Diarist starts home for Ansford.

DEC. 14. ... [He leaves Ansford to take up his residence at Oxford:] I left my whole family rather dejected this morning. Pray God preserve them and make my journey of good to them.

DEC. 16. ... Exceeding disagreeable to me yet Oxford seems being so contrary to my old way of living.

DEC. 17. ... Things seem something better to day, and I hope will more so daily, when I get to College. [He is at present at the Blue Boar.]

DEC. 24. (Mem:) I dreamt very much of poor old Alice Stacy of Ansford and my man Willm Corpe last night—the former that she had a vast discharge of matter from her Breast—the latter that he was very drunk and almost killed by a fall from a Horse—both which I thought I saw very plainly.

DEC. 25. I breakfasted, and slept again in my Rooms

—I went to Chapel this morning at 9 o'clock being Christmas Day, and rec^d the Holy Sacrament from the Hands of our Warden who was present. The Warden was on one side of the Altar and myself being Sub-Warden on the other side—I read the Epistle for the day at the Altar and assisted the Warden in going round with the Wine.

For an Offering at the Altar, gave . . . o. 1. o. The Dean of Christchurch who is Bishop of Chester preached this morning at Christchurch, but I did not attend at it. . . . N.B. The Dean of Christchurch always preaches this day in the morning at Christchurch Cathedral. I dined in the Hall and 14 Senr Fellows with me. I invited the Warden to dine with us as is usual on this day, but his Sister being here, could not. We had a very handsome dinner of my ordering, as I order dinner every day being Sub-Warden.

We had for dinner, two fine Codds boiled with fryed Souls round them and oyster sauce, a fine sirloin of Beef roasted, some peas soup and an orange Pudding for the first course, for the second, we had a lease of Wild Ducks rosted, a fore Qu: of Lamb and sallad and mince Pies. We had a grace cup before the second course brought by the Butler to the Steward of the Hall who was Mr. Adams a Senior Fellow, who got out of his place and came to my chair and there drank to me out of it, wishing me a merry Xmas. I then took it of him and drank wishing him the same, and then it went round, three standing up all the time. From the high Table the grace Cup goes to the Batchelors and Scholars. After the second course there was a fine plumb cake brought to the sen^r Table as is usual on this day, which also goes to the Batchelors after. After Grace is said there is another Grace-Cup to drink

omnibus Wiccamisis, which is drunk as the first, only
the Steward of the Hall does not attend the second
Grace Cup. . . . We dined at 3 o'clock and were an
Hour and ½ at it. We all then went into the Senr
Com: Room, where the Warden came to us and sat
with us till Prayers. The Wine drunk by the Senr
Fellows, domus pays for. Prayers this evening did not
begin till 6 o'clock, at which I attended as did the
Warden. . . . I supped etc., in the Chequer, we had
Rabbits for supper rosted as is usual on this day. . . .
The Sub-Warden has one to himself; The Bursars
each one apiece, the Senr Fellows ½ a one each. The
Junr Fellows a rabbit between three.

N.B. Put on this Day a new Coat and Waistcoat for
the first time.

1774

JAN. 14. . . . Had a new Wigg brought home this
morning, which I put on before I went to dinner, it is
a more fashionable one than my old ones are, a one
curled wigg with two curls of the sides. I like it, and
it was liked by most People at dinner. I gave the
Barber's man, Jonathan 0. 1. 0. At Back-Gammon
this evening with Milton only one gammon, and I
lost to him by bad luck 0. 10. 6. I supped in the
Chequer and went to bed soon after.

JAN. 31. I got up this morning at half past six in
order to go in the Machine to Bath. The Porter's man
called me at six, for which and carrying my Portmanteau to the Cross Inn I gave him . . . 0. 1. 0. To
Frank Paynes Boy this morning gave 0. 6. I went to
the Cross Inn at a little after seven and the Machine
was gone, however I took a Post-Chaise immediately

from the Cross Inn and overtook the Machine at Enson about 5 miles from Oxon, and there got into it.

For the Post Chaise pd   .   .   . o. 4. o
Gave the Driver   .   .   .   . o. 1. o

There was one Passenger in it a Gentleman of Exeter College, we stopped and breakfasted at Witney at the Bridge, and then I left the Gentleman as he came there only to meet some Company.

For my Breakfast at Witney pd   . o. 1. o

At Witney the Machine took up a Poor Player, a young man who is in a consumption and going to his Friends at Bath—he looked dreadful bad.

I dined at Burford by myself, pd there   o. 4. o

At Burford pd the remaining part of the
   Fare   .   .   .   .   .   . o. 10. 6

Dr. Bosworth of Oriel and a young Lady came into the same room where I dined at Burford soon after I dined, as they were going to London in the Strand Water Machine thro' Oxford. I was not long with them at the Inn at Burford as our Machine was just setting off. At Burford we took up a young Farmer who was lame and going to try Bath Waters, and the Farmer's Sister a young Woman. The Farmer thinks his disorder to be Rheumatic. We got to Circencester about 5 this afternoon where we supped and slept. I supped in a Room by myself and spent the evening.

FEB. 1st. I got up this morning at half past five, got into the Machine about 6 and set of before breakfast for Bath, at Circencester pd .   .   . o. 3. 6
Gave the Chamber maid and Waiter   . o. 1. 6
At Tedbury we breakfasted pd there   . o. 1. o
We got to Petty France about 11, where the Machine stays two or three Hours. And as I wanted to reach

Ansford this evening, I took a Post-Chaise immediately at Petty France, and set forth for Bath. It snowed prodigiously all the way to Bath.

Gave the Bath Coachman at Petty France 0. 1. 0
For some Rum and Water at Petty France 0. 0. 3
At Petty France for a Chaise to Bath pd . 0.11. 3
Gave a Poor Boy at Petty France . . 0. 0. 6

I got to Bath about 1 o'clock, there I took a fresh Chaise for Old Downe.

Gave Petty France Driver . . . 0. 1. 6

besides a dram upon the Road. I got to Old Downe between 3 and 4 this afternoon where I stayed about a Quarter of an Hour, eat some cold rost Beef, drank a pint of Ale, and then got into a fresh Chaise for Ansford. It snowed all the way very thick from Bath to Old Downe. At Bath for chaise pd . 0.10. 6
Gave the Bath driver besides a dram . 0. 1. 6
For a chaise at Old Downe to Ansford pd 0.10. 6
Eating etc., at Old Downe pd . . 0. 1. 0

I got to Ansford, I thank God safe and well this evening about 6 o'clock. It snowed all the way from Old Downe to Ansford and the wind blowed very rough and it was very cold indeed. Gave the old Downe driver a dram at Gannard's Grave and another at home, and gave him also 0. 1. 6. I found Mr. Pouncett and my sister Jane at home by themselves, and I supped and slept at Parsonage. Brother John supped and spent the evening with us. All Friends pretty well but poor Dr. Clarke, who is worse than I left him, his legs swell and he talks but very little, and looks very ill indeed. Mr. Pouncett supped and slept at Parsonage.

MARCH 13. I breakfasted, dined, supped and slept again at Parsonage. . . . Mr. Pouncett slept at

Parsonage. I talked with him pretty home about matters being so long doing—[i.e. the marriage arranged between Mr. Pouncett and Sister Jane being so long delayed].

MARCH 16. I breakfasted, dined, supped and slept again at Parsonage. I took a ride this morning to Shepton Mallett and went thro' Evercreech and made a short visit to Mrs. Millard and her daughter Betsy who were glad to see me. I wanted to see Jack's Flame but could not. When I came to Shepton I got of at Mr. White's and there I spent most of my time with Mrs. White and my dear Betsy White. They wondered not to see me before. My Boy went with me on Mr. Pouncett's Mare. . . .

MARCH 23. I breakfasted at Parsonage this morning as did Mr. Pouncett, who after breakfast went home and returned about 12 to take his leave of me. I got up very early this morning, packed up my things, settled all accounts with my People, dined at 12 and at one set of in Ansford Inn Chaise with a very heavy Heart for Oxford thro' Bath. I left with Mr. Pouncett two guineas to be given to the Poor of Ansford, as directed by me in writing. I left with him also one guinea to be given to the Poor of Cary as also directed by me in writing. Mr. White called upon me this morning and took his leave. Robin Coleman called upon me this morning on the same. I gave my man William a good deal of my old Cloathes. I gave my maid Betty Chrich an old prunella gown.
Paid Eliz: Crich this morning a year's
   wages 3. 3. 0
Paid her one year's Interest of 20 Pound . 1. 0. 0
Paid her for her Mother do.   .   . 1. 0. 0
Paid Willm for washing 1 year .   .   10. 6

Paid Eliz: Crich for Housekeeping to this day	.	.	.	.	.	0. 2. 9
Paid Will: and Boy and Poor to this day		0. 3. 6
I gave each of my Servants going away		0. 2. 6

I left all my House in Tears and I could not refrain myself from the same. Pray God bless them all. This day left of all House-keeping to Mr. Pouncett. We had some Trout for dinner to-day, but my Heart was so full that I could eat but little. I gave Mr. Owens my Barber this morning 0. 5. 0. I called at Shepton and took my leave of my dear Betsy. I got to Old Downe about 3 this afternoon and to Bath at 5. I did not pay for the Ansford Chaise therefore am in debt to Perry for it, the sum of . . 0. 10. 6
Gave Tom Smith, the Ansford Driver . 0. 1. 6
For Old Downe Chaise to the White Lion at Bath pd 0. 10. 6
For Wine at Old Downe pd. . . 0. 0. 6
To the Old Downe Driver—gave . . 0. 10. 6
To the Turnpikes for Bath pd . . 0. 2. 0

I met Harry Rodbard this evening at the White Lion at Bath, and we supped and spent the evening together. There was a gentleman by name Pitcairn with Harry, a Wiltshire clergyman but he did not sup with us. I called at Dr. Dunn's this evening at Bath, I saw Mrs. Dunn and one Miss Chambers, but I did not see Dr. Dunn. Mrs. Dunn very much expected my sister and Mr. Pouncett. She had got the Brides Bed etc., all ready for them. I called also on Mr. Creed's Friend, Dr. Anderton and Wife. I went and called upon Dr. Ballard at the Bear Inn at Bath. My aunt Tom and her son, Frank, and Jenny Clarke are all at my Aunt's at Bath, but I did not call on them. I slept at the White Lion at Brookmans.

Next day he reaches Oxford in the evening, safe and well. On April 13th he and his colleague Cooke are sworn in as Pro-Proctors before the Vice-Chancellor, Webber—the Senior Proctor with Berkeley—nominating them as his Pro-Proctors.

APRIL 20. I breakfasted and slept again at New College. Master Senior and Blisse breakfasted with me. I went to Chapel this morning at 11 o'clock it being Term Time and Wednesday. There should have been Declamations to-day but there was none: Cooth and Trotman should have declaimed, therefore I shall punish them. . . .

AP: 21. I breakfasted and slept again at New College. For a new Pr of Gloves the other day pd 0. 2. 0. I went with Holmes to-day to the Free-Masons Lodge held this day at the New Inn, was there admitted a Member of the same and dined and spent the afternoon with them. The Form and Ceremony on the occasion I must beg leave to omit putting down. Paid on admission for fees etc. £3. 5. 0. It is a very honourable as well as charitable Institution and much more than I could conceive it was. Am very glad on being a Member of it. I supped and spent the evening in the Chequer. Mr. Stinton one of our Lodge supped etc., with Holmes in the Chequer he is a very worthy man. At 11 this night was called out of the Chequer by Webber to go with him and quell a riot in George Lane, but when we came it was quiet, however, we went to the Swan in George Lane, and unfortunately met with a Gownsman above stairs carousing with some low-life people. We conducted him to his College. He belongs to University College, is a scholar there, and his name is Hawkins, he was terribly frightened and cried almost all the way to his Coll, and was upon his knees very often in the street, and bareheaded all the way. He is to appear again to-morrow before Webber. We returned to New College by 12 o'clock.

There is no further note as to this unfortunate young man's fate at the hands of Webber: it is a pity he did not appear before the kindly Diarist: we should then have known his punishment, which would not have been a harsh one.

MAY 12. I breakfasted and slept again at New College. Lent Blisse this morning 8 of my MSS Sermons. Holmes and myself went to Exeter College about 2 o'clock and dined with Mr. Stinton, a Senior Fellow of Ex: Coll: We dined in the publick Hall at Exeter Coll: at the High Table. The Rector, Dr. Bray etc., dined with us. We had but an indifferent dinner and served up slovingly. Nothing near so neat or genteel as at New College. We spent the afternoon in their Senr Com: Room and the Rector did the same and smoked a Pipe with us. We came away before five o'clock. I went to Prayers this evening at 5 o'clock. I supped and spent the evening in the Chequer. Whilst I was at supper I was sent for to quell a riot in Hollinwell. I left my supper and went with Holmes and Oakely into Hollinwell, but it was pretty quiet. However I met with two gentlemen going into a House and I accosted them, and I believe they were the same that made the disturbance. I asked them to go to their Colleges directly and wait on me to-morrow morning at New College. Their names were Taylor of Worcester Coll: and Duprie of Exeter College. I received a letter this evening from my Sister Jane, who acquainted me that my poor old servant man William Corpe dropped down in an Apoplectic Fit May 2, and expired directly. He was that morning married to his old Sweet-heart, and this happened in the evening in the street. I am exceedingly sorry for him indeed and her also. I hope he is everlastingly happy in a better state: Pray God make us all wise to consider our latter end, for Death comes upon us we see at an hour when we little think upon it, and sometimes very sudden. My Sister also acquainted me that poor Dr. Clarke is very bad, much worse than he was.

> As to poor old William Corpe, it will be remembered that the Diarist had a curious dream about him on Christmas Eve. (See under date, December 24th, 1773.)

MAY 20. . . . I got home to Ansford this evening about 8 o'clock and I thank God safe and well, to the Old House, but found none but the maid at home, they were gone to Sister White's. . . . I supped and spent the evening at Mr. White's with him, Sister White, Sister Jane and Mr. Pouncett. I slept at the Old Parsonage House once more. N.B. the first time I ever came in one day from Oxford [he had started at 5.30 from there] to Ansford, I suppose it must be near 100 miles.

> The journey all the way by Post Chaise cost him, with meals, tips, and turnpikes, the large sum of £4. 8s.

MAY 22. . . . Have been very naughty to-day, did not go to either Ansford or Cary Church. . . . Have mercy on me O Lord a miserable, vile sinner, and pardon my failings.

MAY 24. I breakfasted, dined, supped and slept again

at Parsonage. Mr. Pouncett breakfasted, dined, supped, and slept at Parsonage. After breakfast I went down to Ansford Church and married my Sister Jane and Mr. Pouncett by license. Pray God send Thy Blessing upon them both, and may they be long happy in each other. I would not have anything for marrying them but Mr. Pouncett gave Mr. Frank Woodford 1. 1. 0. Mr. White was Father and Sister White only present.

Mr. Pouncett gave the Clerk, Dav Maby .   o. 10. 6
He gave also to Ansford Ringers   .   .   o. 10. 6
He gave also to Cary Ringers   .   .   o. 10. 6
Sister White, Brother Heighes and Son Bill dined at Parsonage. Cary Fair to-day being White Tuesday. Brother Heighes and Son Sam supped etc. at Parsonage. Brother John supped and spent the evening with us, he was rather merry, and at last noisy and not very decent. Mr. Pouncett and myself took a walk in the evening over to Cole and saw Mrs. Pouncett and Mrs. Coleman. I made a visit in the morning to Mr. Clarke's and saw the poor Doctor, who is greatly altered for the worse and am afraid he will be but a few days here. He was up gasping for breath, knew nobody and said never a word. He walked about but not without a Person to support him, being so very weak. Mr. Frank Woodforde and Mr. Overton of Pill came to the Doctor's whilst I was there, but I did not stay at all there after they came. They came to dine there.

MAY 28. I supped and spent the evening at Brother John's with him, Nancy, Sister White and Betsy White, Sister Jane and Mrs. Pouncett. . . . Mrs. Pouncett, Sister White and Betsy dined at Jack's. I went home with Betsy White and had some talk with her concerning my making her mine when an opportunity offered and she was not averse to it at all.

MAY 30. I breakfasted at Parsonage and about 9 set forth on my bay Mare for the University of Oxford. I had my boy Will: Coleman with me to carry my Portmanteau. I hired a horse for him of Crocker the carrier at Cary, am to give him for him o. 10. 6. Mr. Pouncett went with me as far as Alfred's Tower. I left my Sister Jane very low on my going away. . . .

JUNE 5. I breakfasted, dined, supped and slept again at Coll: Lent Masters Senr my Mare this morning to go to his curacy at Gadington about 6 miles from Oxon. I went to St. Mary's in the afternoon and heard an indifferent discourse by Cooke of Christchurch. For Wine this afternoon in M.C.R. pd. . o. o. 6 I went to Chapel this evening, much company there. I took a walk with Webber after 11 this evening over the University. Holmes went with us. A common Strumpet we met with, and if it was not for me would have been sent to Bridewell. It was one o'clock before I got to bed to-night.

JULY 5th. I breakfasted, dined, supped and slept again at College. . . . A little after 4 this aft: went to the Theatre and heard the oratorio of Hercules, for a ticket pd o. 5. o. There was a good deal of Company present. The Music was very fine—A Miss Davies from the Opera House sung most delightfully, Miss Molly Linley sung very well. A Mr. Gosdall gave us a fine Solo on the Violincello as did Mr. Fisher on the Hautboy. Miss Davies is to have they say sixty guineas. . . . Mr. Woodhouse a gent: Com: of University College was very drunk at the Theatre and cascaded in the middle of the theatre. Mr. Highway

one of the nominal Proctors for this week desired him
to withdraw very civilly but he was desired by one
Mr. Peddle a gent: com: of St. Mary Hall not to mind
him, my seeing Highway in that distress I went to
them myself and insisted upon Woodhouse going
away immediately from the Theatre, and then Peddle
behaved very impertinently to me, at which I insisted
upon his coming to me to-morrow morning. Mr.
Woodhouse after some little time retired, but Peddle
remained and behaved very impertinently, I therefore
intend putting him in the black Book. We did not
come out of the Theatre till near 9. For Wine this
evening in M.C.R. pd o. o. 6. Webber, myself and
Thorpe took a walk between 11 and 12 this evening
and returned a little after 12. I met with one Mr.
Broome, this evening of Brasenose College very much
in liquor and who talked rather saucily to me, but I
saw him to his Coll: and desired his company to-
morrow morning.

July 7th. I breakfasted, dined, supped and slept
again at College. Mr. Broome waited on me this
morning with an epistle and I set him one of Swifts
Sermons to translate into Latin for the offence he was
guilty of. There was nothing done this morning at the
Theatre. We dined again at 2 o'cl: to day.
For Wine this afternoon in the M.C.R. pd.   o. o. 6
Went to the Theatre this afternoon and heard a
miscellaneous concert performed there pd   o. 1. o
For Tea at Dick's Coff: H: between the acts
pd   .   .   .   . o. o. 8
The Theatre yesterday and to-day very orderly.
For Books of performance each day pd   . o. o. 6
After the Music took a walk in Merton Gardens which
was exceedingly crowded indeed. I spoke to two

gentlemen in the garden for wearing green capes to their coats.

For Wine this evening in M.C.R. . . . o. o. 6

JULY 8. I breakfasted, dined, supped and slept again at New College. . . . Put Mr. Peddle into the Black Book in these Words 'Johannes Peddle Superioris Ordinis Commensalis ex aulâ beatae Mariae Virginis, quod publice in Theatro Procuratoris deputatum in officio exequendo obstitit, summaque contumaciâ et contemptû academicae authoritatis se gesserit ab omni gradu suspendatur donec ad plenum satisficiet. Mensis Julii 7 1774 Jac: Woodforde Proc: Jun: Dep:' Mr. Broome brought the sermon I set him.

JULY 27. I breakfasted, dined, supped and slept again at College. Cooke Senr and Master Senr break-fasted with me. I sent a note to Mr. Bowerbank of Queen's this morning to desire him to dine with me to-day, which he will.

Gave Bull's Boy Gooby, this morning . o. o. 6

Mr. Hindley, Dr. Thurlowe, Master of the Temple, Dr. Burrows, Dr. Birchenden, and Mr. Bowerbank dined and spent the afternoon with me at New College. I borrowed the Chequer Room of the Bursars for my company to dine in. We were very merry and pushed the Bottle on very briskly. I gave my Company for dinner, some green Pea Soup, a chine of Mutton, some New College Puddings, a goose, some Peas and a Codlin Tart with Cream. Madeira and Port Wine to drink after and at dinner some strong Beer, Cyder, Ale and small Beer. Dr. West spent part of the after-noon and supped and spent the evening with me. I had a handsome dish of fruit after dinner. At 7 o'clock we all went from the Chequer to my Room where we had Coffee and Tea. Dr. Birchenden went

from us soon after coffee and did not return again. . . .
Mr. Hindley, Dr. Thurlowe, Dr. West, Dr. Burrows
and Mr. Bowerbank, supped and stayed with me till
after one. Mr. Hindley, Dr. Burrows, Mr. Bowerbank
and myself got to Cards after coffee. At whist I won

1. 0. 6

out of which, Mr. Hindley owes me . o. 5. o
I gave my company only for supper cold mutton.
After supper I gave them to drink some Arrac Punch
with Jellies in it and some Port wine. I made all my
Company but Dr. West quite merry. We drank 8
bottles of Port one Bottle of Madeira besides Arrac
Punch, Beer and Cyder. I carried of my drinking
exceedingly well indeed.

> On September 6th he sets out for Ansford for a brief
> visit, returning to Oxford a month later.

OCT. 13. I breakfasted, dined and slept again at
College. Coker, Master Senr and Grantham breakfasted with me this morning upon cocoa. Very low
to-day having a great purging upon me. . . . I went
to Chapel this evening at 5 o'clock. Had a letter from
Brother Heighes to let me know that our Brother John
was married to Miss Clarke of Evercreech Monday
last. Pray God they may be happy. At Back Gammon
this evening with Blisse won o. 5. o. I took some
Rhubarb this evening about 10, and went to bed.

OCT. 15. . . . I caught a remarkable large Spider in
my Wash Place this morning and put him in a small
glass decanter and fed him with some bread and
intend keeping him. . . .

Nov. 5. I breakfasted, dined and slept again at
College. Master Senr and Cooke breakfasted with

me. Paid Miss Hall my Sempstress this
morning 1. 3. 0
For Wine this afternoon in M.C.R. pd. . 0. 0. 6
For Tobacco in M.C.R. at divers times pd 0. 0. 6
I went to Prayers this evening at 5 o'clock in our
Chapel. There was a Sermon preached in our Chapel
by Mr. Crow this evening, being the 5 of November.
The Sermon was immediately before the Anthem.
The Warden received an account of the Death of
Dr. Ridley, Rector of one of our Livings in Norfolk,
by name Weston Longeville worth it is said £300 per
annum. I went to bed at 10 o'clock to-night.

> This is the first reference to the Norfolk parish in
> which he was to spend twenty-seven years of his
> life, from 1776 to his death in 1803.

DEC. 6. . . . Master Senr publickly declared this
afternoon in M.C.R. his intention of not taking the
living of Weston. I therefore immediately being the
next Senior in Orders canvassed the Senior Common
Room, and then went with Master into the Junr
Common Room and canvassed that. The Junr
Common Room pretty full. . . .

DEC. 15. . . . We had a meeting of the whole House
in the Hall at 12 o'clock, to present a Person to the
Living of Weston Longeville and to seal the remaining
Leases. The former came on first. Hooke and myself
were the two candidates proposed. Many learned and
warm arguments started and disputed, and after 2
hours debate the House divided and it was put to the
Vote, when there appeared for me 21 votes, and for
Mr. Hooke 15 only, on which I was declared and
presented with the Presentation of the Rectory. The
chief speakers for me were the Warden, Mr. Holmes,

Mr. Webber, Mr. Gauntlett, and Dr. Wall. The chief
speakers for Mr. Hooke were Mr. Caldecott, Mr.
Coker Senr, Mr. Adams, Mr. Thorpe and Mr.
Milton, the latter talked nothing but nonsense. The
Members present were as under-written. [Note that
the Diarist very sensibly votes for himself.]

For Mr. Woodforde	*For Mr. Hooke*
The Warden	Caldecot
Master Senr	Milton
Webber	Thorpe
Woodforde	Adams
Lucas	Swanton
Bathurst Senr	King
Oglander	Coker Senr
Cooke	Eaton
Gauntlett	Trotman
Wall	Gratton
Townshend	Sandford
Blisse	Bingham
Holmes	Bathurst Junr
Oakeley	Awberry
Williams Junr	Coker Junr
Cummin Senr	
Coothe	
Bragge	
Lowthe	
Cummin Junr	
Busby	
No. 21	No. 15

. . . I treated the Senr Com: Room with Wine and
Fruit in the afternoon and in the evening with Arrac
Punch and Wine. I treated the Junr Com: Room with
one dozen of Wine afternoon and in the evening with

Arrac Punch and Wine. I gave the Chaplains half a dozen of Wine, the clerks 2 bottles and the Steward one bottle. I smoked a pipe in the afternoon with Coker's Father. A little after 11 o'clock this evening I went down into the Junr Common Room attended with Master Senr, Cooke, Adams, Townshend and Holmes to thank them for the favour conferred on me. We stayed there till after 12 and returned then to the Senr Common Room and stayed till near 4 o'clock. We were exceeding merry in the Junr Common Room and had many good songs sung by Swanton, Williams Junr and Wight. And also a very droll one by Busby, which occasioned great laughter. The Junr Common Room was exceeding full and so was the Senr both after dinner and supper. Hooke dined with us Bursars and spent the afternoon in M.C.R. In the evening he and Milton set off in a Post Chaise for Wallingford.

1775

JAN. 2. I got up this morning between 5 and 7, breakfasted in my rooms upon Cocoa and afterwards went to the Cross Inn in the Corn Market, where I got into the Bath Machine to go into the West Country. Dr. Wall breakfasted with me and went with me in the Bath Machine, it being a Frost so far as Burford. Mr. Fisher of University Coll: went with us in the Machine as did one Sally Kirby, a servant maid of one Mrs. Horwood of Holton near Ansford who is now at Bath and bad in the gout. We stayed at Whitney and made a second breakfast, we treated the maid at Whitney, I pd 0. 1. 6; gave the porter at the Cross Inn Oxford 0. 1. 0. We then went on to

Burford where we stayed to change horses. Dr. Wall left us at Burford and went to his Brother's in a Chaise about 13 miles from Burford. We took up another servant maid at Whitney who went with us to Cirencester. Mr. Fisher, myself and Mrs. Horwood's maid all go to Bath together. We dined at Bibury and we treated the two maids. Fisher and myself pd at Bibury 0. 4. 6. We got to Cirencester about 6 o'clock where we supped and slept at the Bull there. The two maids supped and spent the evening with us. Fisher and myself went to an auction of Books this evening at Cirencester, the Auctioneer very saucy. I met with Brother Small [Free Mason] at the Auction. Fisher and myself treated the two maids pd 0. 6. 0 apiece this evening as we might not be hindered to-morrow.

He stops a night in Bath, and therefore does not reach Ansford till the 4th. He remains at Ansford till February 1st. Nothing very eventful happens. He is much pleased with Brother John's newly wed wife, though Brother John himself continues to cause him anxiety on account of his rather excessive regard for the bottle. Squire Creed, the younger, dies, and there is a great funeral at which the Diarist was a principal Mourner: 'The Mourners had only sattin Hatbands and gloves', still 'it was a handsome Funeral and Church full'. The Diarist is a little disappointed in the will, as no mention is made of the Ansford estate which his, the Diarist's, Aunt Collins, had left away from her family by giving it to Squire Creed, and which the latter had promised 'should revert to her family again'. He finds a new sort of Social Club started in Cary, the gentlemen and the ladies meeting separately at each others' houses every Thursday. There is the usual constant round of mutual visiting and entertainment which is so marked and pleasant a feature of country life at this period. On January 28th he rides over to Shepton Mallett and calls on 'Mr. White at Shepton, but Betsy White was not at home, she being in Devonshire at Mr. Troit's and is to remain there till Easter—was told'. Of the unfortunate results of this Devonshire visit of Betsy's—unfortunate for our faithful Diarist—we shall hear anon. He returns to Oxford on Feb. 1st.

FEB. 17. ... Mr. Peddle gent: Com: St. Mary Hall whose name is in the black Book put in by me in July last, waited on me this morning to desire me to take his name out of the same, which I promised to do upon his bringing me a Declamation on—Nemo omnibus horis sapit, and asking pardon of Highway of Baliol....

FEB. 20. ... Mr. Peddle brought me his Declamation this morning. I went to Highway of Baliol about him, and he is satisfied, therefore this aft: I sent to the Senr Proctor for the black Book and erased his name, and put satisfecit.

FEB. 28. ... I supped and spent the evening at Braze-Nose Coll: with Brother Wood, we supped in the Hall and spent the evening in the Senr Com: Room. ... It being Shrove Tuesday we had Lambs Wool to drink, a composition of Ale, sugar etc., Lobsters, Pancakes etc., to eat at Supper, and the Butler there gives a Plumb Cake with a copy of Verses of his own making upon it. ...

On April 9th he enters that he is very busy packing up for 'my Norfolk Expedition'—an expedition to take possession of his living at Weston. This is a temporary visit, as he does not go into residence till over a year later.

APRIL 10. I breakfasted in my room this morning at 7 o'clock upon some chocolate as did Cooke with me. After breakfast about 8 o'clock I set of in Jones's Post Coach for the City of London. Cooke went with me in the same, and I promised to frank him all the way to Norfolk as he goes to oblige me. Mrs. Prince and Osborn Wight of our Coll: went with us to London in the Machine or Post-Chaise. We all dined together at Maidenhead Bridge and then proceeded on to London. For Cooke and myself at Maidenhead pd 0. 8. 0. For the remaining fare for Cooke and myself pd 0. 15. 0. We got to London about six o'clock. Cooke and myself then took a Hackney Coach and went to the Turk's Head Coffee House in the Strand opposite Catherine Street, kept by one Mrs. Smith, a Widow and a good motherly kind of a woman, her person and talking very much like Mrs. Carr of Twickenham and there we supped and slept. To the Oxford coachman gave 0. 2. 0. For an Hackney Coach to the Turk's Head pd 0. 3. 0. We went in the evening to Mr. Burns in Duke Street, Westminster, Secretary to the Bishop of Norwich to leave my papers with him and to desire the Bishop to give me Institution to-morrow, but he told me that he thought the Bishop wd not so soon. Trenchard and Lovel late of the University supped and spent the evening with us at the Turk's Head. Mrs. Prince was a very agreable and merry Traveller.

APRIL 13. Cooke, myself, Mrs. Prince and one Mrs. Millard who has a Brother at Norwich, a Minor Canon, set of this morning early in an hired Post Chaise and four for Norwich over Epping Forest. At the Turk's Head Coffee House for myself and Cooke paid and gave to servants etc., £3. 3. 0. We changed Horses and Coach at the bull faced Stagg, on Epping

Forest, and went on to Harlowe where we were obliged to take chaises. From Harlowe we went on to Stanstead, where we had some Wine and Egg, and fresh Chaises. From Stanstead we went on to Bourne Bridge, took fresh Chaises and went on to New Markett where we dined and then went on in fresh Chaises to Barton Mills where we changed again and then on again to Thetford where we drank coffee and then went on to Attleborough, and then on to Norwich where we got, I thank God safe and well about 11 at night. We all supped and spent the evening together at the King's Head[1] in the Market Place, Norwich. It being after 10 when we got to Norwich we found the City Gates shut. We did not get to bed till after 2 in the morning. . . . From London to Norwich, 109 miles, and the best of roads I ever travelled.

APRIL 14. We breakfasted, dined, supped and slept at Norwich. We took a walk over the City in the morning, and we both agreed that it was the finest City in England by far, in the center of it is a high Hill and on that a prodigious large old Castle almost perfect and forms a compleat square, round it is a fine Terrass Walk which commands the whole City. There are in the City 36 noble Churches mostly built with Flint, besides many meeting Houses of divers sorts. A noble River runs almost thro the Center of the City. The City walls are also very perfect and all round the City but where the River is. On the Hills round the City stand many Wind Mills about a dozen, to be seen from Castle Mount. We drank Tea and Coffee in the afternoon with Mr. Millard and his

---

[1] We shall hear of the King's Head constantly hereafter, as the Diarist always stayed there when he went into Norwich from Weston. Alas, it is no longer in existence. I searched the Market Place in Norwich for it in vain.

Wife, Dr. Salter's daughter, in the Lower Close.
Mrs. Prince and Mr. Millard there also. After tea
we got to Quadrille—lost o. 1. o. Mrs. Millard is a
very impolite lady, rather rude. We supped and
spent the evening and slept at our Inn. Our journey
from London to Norwich cost £11. 14. 4 which I paid,
half of which I recd this afternoon from Mrs. Prince
and Mr. Millard's brother—£5. 17. 0.

APRIL 15. We breakfasted at our Inn at Norwich
and about 12 we set forth for my Living at Weston in
a Chaise. At Norwich at my Inn this morning pd
2. 2. 0 Chaise etc to Weston included. We got to
Weston which is about 9 miles from Norwich by
2 o'clock in the afternoon where we dined, supped
and slept at the Parsonage House. To Turnpike and
Driver from Norwich to Weston pd 2. 0. My curate
Mr. Howes came to us in the afternoon. Bed etc., all
in readiness for us when we came. We carried with us
some Wine and Cyder from Norwich.

APRIL 16. We breakfasted, supped and slept at
Weston Parsonage. A man and his wife, by name
Dunnell live at the Parsonage House and are good
kind of people. We went to Church this morning at
Weston, and Cooke read Prayers and preached for
Mr. Howes. I also administered the H: Sacrament
this morning at Weston Church being Easter Day—
I had near 40 Communicants. N.B. No money collected at the Sacrament, it not being usual at Weston.
My clerk is a shocking Hand. The worst singing I
ever heard in a Church, only the Clerk and one man,
and both intolerably bad. Mrs. Howes and her niece
Mrs. Davy were at Church and they would make us
get into their Chaise after Church and go with them
to Hockering to Mr. Howes, where we dined and spent

the afternoon and came back to Weston in the evening in Mr. Howes's Chaise about 8 o'clock—Gave his driver 1. 0. Mr. Howes' is about 2 miles West of Weston. Cooke likes my House and Living very much. For my part I think it a very good one indeed. I sleep in the Garrett at Weston as I would not let Cooke sleep there, but immediately under in the New Building which is very good. Cooke is mightily pleased with his Scheme [i.e. the whole expedition].

The Diarist and his friend Cooke remain together at Weston till April 26th. The time is taken up in viewing the glebe, making expeditions, interchanging visits with the Howes's, transacting on the Diarist's part a variety of ecclesiastical business, such as being inducted by Mr. Howes, taking the Oath of Abjuration[1] before the Justices at Norwich, reading the 39 Articles in Weston Church before a crowded congregation, and 'declaring my assent and consent to the Liturgy'.

On April 26th they go to Norwich for two days, see a Play one night, and the sights of Yarmouth the next.

On April 28th Cooke leaves him to go to stay with his brother-in-law, a Captain Uvedale, at Boxmoor House, near Needham in Suffolk, where the Diarist is to rejoin him in about ten days' time. Meanwhile he returns to Weston, and is busy making arrangements for receiving his tithes and letting his glebe.

On May 9th the Diarist joins his friend Cooke at

[1] The Oath of Abjuration was imposed by the Abjuration Act of 1702, and is a reminder of the Jacobite nightmare which haunted the eighteenth century, though but feebly in the latter part of it. The oath abjuring the descendants of James II was by the Act of 1702 made a necessary qualification for every employment in Church or State.

Boxmoor, about thirty-seven miles from Norwich. Cooke met him and 'conducted me to Boxmoor House to his Brother-in-Law's, Captain Saml Uvedale, who has a most noble House and a very fine Estate round the same. . . . I dined, supped and slept at Captain Uvedale's, with him, his wife and Mr. Cooke. Everything very elegant. Captain Uvedale and Lady behaved exceedingly civil and polite to me indeed . . . very agreeable People. . . .' Here he spends a most pleasant week, visiting Ipswich and going out in the Captain's 'Chariot' to call on various neighbours and relatives of the Captain's. On Sunday he hears 'a very indifferent sermon' from the Curate at Needham, but next day is compensated as 'Capt. Uvedale, myself and Cooke took a walk to Needham in the evening and smoked a Pipe there with a Shop-keeper by name Marriott a very hearty man'.

MAY 16. We got up at 5 o'clock and at 6 Cooke and myself went in the Captain's Chariot for Ipswich to go in the Ipswich Post Coach for London to-day. The Captain was up as soon as us to give orders. We took our leave of Mrs. Uvedale last night. I left in my Bed Chamber on the Table 0. 10. 6 for the Captain's Chambermaid. We got to Ipswich by 7 o'clock. Gave the Coachman and Servant Boy 0. 10. 0. For the Captain he took a ride a different way. I never met with more civility anywhere than I have done at Captain Uvedale's, his Lady very agreeable. At 7 this morning we got into the Ipswich Post Coach for London. . . .

He and Cooke stay two nights in London at the Turk's Head. On the 18th whilst walking in St. James's Park, 'the King and Queen with their guards went by us in Sedan Chairs from the Queen's Palace to St. James's Palace, there being a Levee at St. James's to-day at 1 o'clock. The King did not look pleasant but the Queen did.' They went to Covent Garden Theatre and saw the *Merchant of Venice*. 'We separated coming out of the Play House and Cooke went home by himself and I by myself. I met many fine women (Common Prostitutes) in my return home, and very impudent indeed. The Turk's Head very full after the Play. Thorpe etc., etc., there this evening.'

Next day they return to Oxford, and so ends this very pleasant six weeks' jaunt.

JUNE 13. . . . A Chinese man about 25 years of age attended by a multitude of People came to see our College and Gardens this morning, I was in the garden with him. He talks English very well. He had on his head a Cap like a Bell covered with a red Feather and tyed under his Chin, a kind of a Close Coat on his back of pink Silk quilted, over that a loose Gown of pink silk quilted also, which came down to his heels, and over that a black Gauze or Crape in imitation of a long Cloak, a pr of Breeches or drawers of pink silk also and quilted, and a kind of silk Boots of the same colour and quilted also, and a pr of red Morocco Slippers. His hands were also covered with some thin silk of pink. He had a Fan tyed to a Sash before him. He was of a moderate stature, a tawny complexion, black hair tyed in a kind of tail, small eyes, short nose, no beard, in short as to his whole Face, it was uncommonly ugly, not unlike one of the runabout gipsies. . . . After prayers I went with Acton one of our Gent: Com: to have my Profile taken of by a Lady who is come to town and who takes of

great likenesses. I was not above a minute sitting
for the same. . . .

JUNE 23. . . . This morning about 6 o'clock it pleased
God to take to himself my worthy friend young Seymour [the son of the Dean of Wells, Lord Francis
Seymour, whom we met at the Deanery some time
back] and I hope he is now eternally happy in Thy
Kingdom O Lord. Everybody that knew him, respected him much, and therefore is as greatly lamented
by his friends. He was an amiable young man indeed,
and a very good and dutiful son. Pray God comfort
his distressed Parents and Friends for so great and
valuable a loss in him. He took his Batchelor's degree
but Thursday Sennight. . . .

JUNE 29. . . . Whilst Dr. Wall and self were at the
[Freemasons'] Lodge, it was proposed in the Senr
Com. Room by Daubenny and Jeffries and carried by
a great majority, that Mr. Masters and Mr. Bathurst,
should not treat this evening for their Livings as usual,
but give five guineas or so, to the Library or for plate.
I cannot say but I was much displeased at it. . . . In
the night there was a great riot in College by the
Junior People who broke down Daubenny's doors and
broke Jeffries windows. . . .

JUNE 30. . . . A complaint being made to the Warden
of the Riot last night in College,—the Deans were
summoned to the Warden's lodgings this morning to
consider of the same, but none of the young gentlemen
that were concerned in the same, not being to be met
with, the meeting was put off till to-morrow morn. . . .

Next day the meeting was accordingly held—the
Diarist being present as one of the Deans—and the
principal offenders in the affair of the riot were

punished by confinement for varying periods, and impositions. The Diarist observes: 'For my part, I must own it did not deserve so serious a determination or attention to the same. . . .'

JULY 17. At 5 o'clock this morning went to the Cross Inn, and got into the Bath coach for the West . . . a Mr. Crocker of Wadham College, a Mrs. Tompkins wife of Mr. Tompkins the grocer in the Corn-Markett, Oxford, and her little girl by name Sukey, a very pretty little girl about 11 years old, were all the passengers. Mrs. Tompkins and her little Maid are going into Cornwall to Bodmin to see her sister who married Mr. Pickering formerly a Chaplain of New Coll: I knew him. We breakfasted at Burford, dined at Cirencester, and drank tea in the afternoon at the Cross Hands, and got into Bath about 8 o'clock in the evening. For breakfast, dinner, and tea in the afternoon I paid 0. 8. 0. as I treated Mrs. Tompkins' little girl all the way. Crocker took his leave of us at the Cross Hands—he went from thence for Bristol—he is a strange genius. For the remaining part of the Fare [he had paid already 10s. 6d. half fare in advance] and Luggage pd. 0. 14. 0., gave to the coachmen as we had two 0. 2. 0. I supped and slept at the Angel in Westgate Street—Bath. Mrs. Tompkins and little Maid did the same—both much tired.

JULY 18. I breakfasted at the Angel with Mrs. Tompkins and daughter. After breakfast I took a chaise for Ansford, Mrs. Tompkins and daughter took another chaise for Wells. We travelled together so far as Old Downe and then we parted—Mrs. Tompkins is a very good kind of woman. . . .

The period of nearly three months at Ansford

which follows is, but for one very important episode, uneventful. Brother John continues to cause him anxiety, and there is an additional cause of feeling in that the patient Diarist, having received no rent from Brother John for three years in respect of the estate left him by his Mother, not unnaturally decides that he must seek another tenant. Mr. Pounsett recovers from his illness and during convalescence wheels himself about in the garden in a bath chair, one of the kind with a little wheel fitted in to turn by hand. I confess I did not realize that this convenient contrivance was as old, or older than, 1775. On August 25th a neighbour was tried at Wells Assizes on the charge of murdering his wife, and was condemned to be hung by the judge, who did not leave the hall during the whole ten hours of the trial. The Diarist was summoned as a witness to testify to the prisoner's character, but his name being called while he was having some dinner—his endurance not equalling the judge's—he failed to appear. As, however, he thought the prisoner guilty, his absence did not, presumably, affect the issue. The poor wretch protested his innocence to the last—he was hung on August 28th —the Diarist commenting 'if he is [innocent] I doubt not he will be amply rewarded, if he is not— Lord be merciful unto his Soul'.

We come now to the main episode of this time, the conclusion of the Diarist's one and only love affair told in a few lines with characteristic brevity:

AUGUST 10. . . . Jenny Clarke returned from Devonshire last night. Betsy White of Shepton is to be married in a fortnight to a Gentleman of Devonshire by name Webster, a man reported to have 500 P^d per annum, 10,000 P^d in the Stocks, beside expectations from his Father. He has settled 300 P^d per annum on Betsy.

SEP: 13. . . . Jenny Clarke told me that she was at Shepton Mallett yesterday, and that Miss White was Married to Mr. Webster this day sennight the 6 Instant.

SEP: 16. . . . Mr. and Mrs. Webster (late Betsy White) came to Sister White's on Horseback this morning, and they dined, spent the afternoon there, and returned to Shepton in the Even^g. I did not go to Mrs. White's today tho much pressed in the aft:. Brother Heighes and myself took a walk in the evening down to Allhampton Field, and in our return back we met Mr. and Mrs. Webster in the Turnpike Road. Mrs. Webster spoke as usual to me, but I said little to her, being shy, as she has proved herself to me a mere Jilt. Lawyer White at Mrs. White's—quite drunk this evening. . . .

The following are one or two homely, and more cheerful entries before the Diarist returns to Oxford.

SEP: 27. . . . Gave a poor old man at Rachel Pounsett's by name Curtis, who is now in his 95 year, and walks strong, sees tolerable, and hears quick, and who has thatched some Hayricks this year tho' so old . . . 0. 1. 0. . . .

SEP: 29. I breakfasted, dined, supped and slept again at Parsonage. My Sister's little Maid was publicly christened this morning at Ansford Church, Mrs. Donne and Mrs. Pounsett of Cole were her Godmothers, and myself the only Godfather. Mr. and Mrs. Donne, Mr. Guppey, Mrs. Pounsett, Sister

White, Sam Pounsett, all dined & spent the aft: at
Parsonage. Frank Woodforde christened the little
Maid, and was asked to dine with us, but he declined.
Being Godfather I gave to the Midwife 0. 5. 0., to the
Nurse gave 0. 5. 0. To four Servants—1/0 each—
gave 0. 4. 0. Brother Heighes and son Sam[1] supped
etc. at Parsonage.

On October 3rd he sets out for Oxford, which he
reaches after an uneventful journey next day. On
October 26th we get the first direct reference in the
Diary to the revolt of the American colonies. . . .
'I went to the Convocation House and heard an
Address to His Majesty on American affairs read
and unanimously approved of the second time of
its being proposed. The first time there were about
three Non Placets—none the second time. The
House was pretty full on the occasion. . . .'

Oct: 30. . . . Very busy again in the Audit House
[doing the College Accounts] from 10 till 2 o'clock.
Betting with Cooke and Boys this morning in the
Audit House about casting up a sum won 0. 10. 6.
which they owe me at present. . . .

Nov: 7. . . . Very busy to-day in preparing things for
Divinity Disputations for my Bachelor of Divinity's
Degree. Harry Oglander and myself go up very soon.

On November 24th he took his Bachelor's Degree
in Divinity, paying at the same time a fee of
£12. 18. 6. For the next day or two he is 'very bad
indeed in the Influenza', but after dosing himself
with Brimstone, cream of tartar, and treacle, living
'very low', and going to bed early, he rapidly
recovers.

Nov. 28. . . . The warden sent down a note to the Junr C. Room to acquaint the young gentlemen that if any of them should make any future noise in the College, they would suffer the greatest rigour of the Statutes. We have of many nights past had very great Hallowing etc. in the Courts, what is facetiously called the upright—the He . . . Up. Lee, Warton, Alcock, Bingham, Awbery and Busby the principal gentlemen, but Lee is far the worst. They are called in the University the black Guards of New College for their noises in the street. I have been disturbed two or three nights lately by their great disturbance in the Court. The Junr Com: Room Chimney Piece was pulled down Saturday night by the above Rioters.

1776

JAN. 14, 1776. . . . The Post which should have come in last night, did not come till 10 this morning on account of the snow. Scarce ever was known so deep a snow as at present. Many carriages obliged to be dug out near Oxon. No Curates could go to their Churches to-day,—Not one from our College went today on account of ye snow. . . .

JAN. 18. . . . Williams Senr and Jeffries played at all fours this evening in M.C.R. They had very high words at last and Williams threw the cards in Jeffries's face, the whole pack, being in a very violent passion. They were both to blame, but Williams much more so. Jeffries went to his room soon after and their [there] stayed. . . .

On February 15th he sets out for Ansford, which he reached next day; the journey by post-chaise, including stopping the night at Tetbury, and all expenses on the way cost him the very large sum of £5. 9. 5. The journey was uneventful, though he spent a bad night at Tetbury owing to an officer turning up very late and making a great noise. Just outside Bath he met Mr. Holmes 'of our College' returning on horseback who had been staying at Bath and he 'told me he never spent such a six weeks in his life—highly pleased'.

The next three months at Ansford, the last he was to spend at the Old Parsonage House, passed in the usual quiet country way, except for a scare of fire on March 5th. The Diarist on that day was congratulating himself on feeling 'brave' again after a disorder which had 'proceeded from eating great quantities of water-cresses', when 'at one o'clock . . . as a leg of mutton was rosting by the Kitchen fire, a very dreadful fire happened in the chimney'. Cary and Ansford friends rushed to the rescue. Pails of water were thrown down the chimney as well as wet rugs and blankets, and in two hours the fire was extinguished. 'My Uncle sent down some Cyder in Pails to the people and we gave them more. I offered a guinea to the people upon the house but they would not take it, Mr. Burge would not suffer it.' The fire was all due to the chimney's not having been swept 'for above twelve months. . . . It is amazing that Mr. Pounsett should neglect it so long, very wrong indeed of him only to save sixpence.'

The subsequent weeks are spent—apart from the almost daily round of mutual hospitality—largely in settling things up prior to his final departure from Somerset in May. He lets his little estate of some thirty acres in Ansford to Farmer Corpe on March 11th for seven years for a rent of £35. 0. 0.

per annum, the farmer to pay all taxes except the Land Tax. He gives presents to various relations, particularly to Brother Heighes, who is presented with 'a very handsome piece that I had by me for a waistcoat, a buff-coloured with sprigs in it', also he buys some broad cloth 'for a coat and breeches for Brother Heighes . . . to wear with the waistcoat'.

Under March 26th and 27th there is an interesting reference in the Diary to various cures for the King's Evil, from which his niece Nancy (daughter of Heighes) is suffering, which will prevent her for the time being from coming with him to Norfolk. Alford Well water is said to have 'done great things in complaints of the King's Evil'. On April 14th he enters 'very much frightened and hurried this morning by hearing that my brother John had a fall from his horse in the night coming from Evercreech and was found senseless about 1 in the morning'. He is greatly relieved to find him comparatively uninjured. 'I hope this will caution him from riding when merry—he has had many falls before but none so bad as this.' On April 15th he mortgages his Ansford estate for the sum of £400, which he receives from his lawyer, Mr. Martin of Bruton, at 4 per cent. per annum. This considerable sum he expends partly on buying 'an house and orchard' for £100, partly in paying off various debts of his own and his Brother John, partly in paying back the principal and interest to various persons for whom he had acted as a sort of banker, and partly in purchasing two horses for £27. 17s. 6d. (inclusive) on which he and his nephew Bill (son of Heighes) are shortly to set forth for Norfolk. The rest is available for other expenses connected with getting into his Norfolk living. On May 6th he sends off '7 large Boxes to Mr. Willm Burge Junior, this afternoon for him to send them by the London Waggon tomorrow for Norfolk'. May 8th is spent in packing and taking leave of friends and relatives —'after supper I went down to my Brother John's and took leave'.

MAY 9. ... This morning at 9 o'clock took my final leave of the old Parsonage House at Ansford and went up to Mr. White's and there I breakfasted with him, Sister White, Mr. Pounsett and Jenny, Brother Heighes, his son Willm and Sam and James Clarke. ... After breakfasting at Mr. White's about 10 o'clock I took my leave of my Friends at Ansford and set forth on my mare for Norfolk, and Bill Woodforde and my boy Will. Coleman went with me. I left my friends very low on the occasion.

The Diarist and his nephew Bill, the boy servant, William Coleman, and the dog proceeded to Norfolk via Oxford. From the 12th to the 20th of May they stay in Oxford as the Diarist has to settle up accounts—his Fellowship had lapsed as from April 12th—and pack up those of his goods which he does not sell, for Weston. Also nephew Bill, of course, is shown the chief sights of Oxford.

MAY 20. We breakfasted at College and about 10 took my final leave of my Rooms at College and we set forth for Norfolk, myself, Bill Woodforde and my serv: Will: Coleman. . . . We got to Tame about 12 o'clock about 13 miles from Oxon: and there we dined at the red Lion kept by one Powel. When we got to Tame was very uneasy on account of my leaving at Oxford this Book and my Baldwins Journal. I sent a man immediately from Tame with a letter to

Master Senr to send back the same, and in about
three hours he returned and brought me back both
very safe. I was then quite happy—p^d him for going
o. 2. 6. . . .

A peculiar thrill of excitement and pleasure passed
through me as I read this passage, holding in my
hand the precise volume of the Diary, which had
been left behind, and retrieved thus a hundred and
fifty years ago. The party set on and slept the night
at Tring 'about 17 miles from Tame', at the Rose
and Crown. They started off at seven o'clock the
next morning and breakfasted at Dunstable 'about
10 miles from Tring. . . .'

MAY 21. . . . From Dunstable we went to Baldock
thro' Hitchin about 20 miles from Dunstable and
there we dined at the White Horse kept by one
Kendall. . . . A great many soldiers, Dragoons at
Baldock today. From Baldock we went on to Royston
about 10 miles, there we baited our Horses and
selves a little time at the Crown kept by one James. . . .
From Royston we went on to Cambridge about 13
miles from Royston and there we supped and slept at
the White Bear kept by one Garford, a very good Inn
and very reasonable. We got there about 9 o'clock,
very fine road and very pleasant indeed all the day.

MAY 22. We breakfasted at Cambridge and then set
forward. Bill and myself went after Breakfast and saw
Kings Chapel, the finest I ever saw, all fine carved
Stone, the Roof of the same—most capital piece of
Architecture indeed, gave a man that shewed it to
us o. 1. o. The gentlemen Commoners were [wear]
black Gowns and gold trimmings made slight upon
the sleeves of the same and very small gold Tossills

to their square Caps of cloth. The members of Trinity Coll: undergraduates all wear Purple Gowns— gentlemen Commoners were purple Gowns trimmed with silver instead of gold and silver tossills. The Buildings are grand at Cambridge but few of them. . . .'

Their route from Cambridge was through Newmarket (13 miles from Cambridge), Barton Mills (10 miles from Newmarket), and Thetford (10 miles from Barton Mills). They baited their horses at the Bull at Newmarket, dined at the Bull at Barton Mills, and supped and slept at the George at Thetford. 'A great many soldiers at Thetford going on to Norwich. Prodigious fine road from Cambridge to Thetford.'

Next day, May 23rd, they went from Thetford to Attleborough (15 miles from Thetford) where they dined at the Cock and from Attleborough to Norwich—another 15 miles, where they supped and slept at the King's Head. 'Our great dog'—for whom a brass collar had been purchased at Oxford for 5s. 6d.—'performed the journey very well'. Next day they reached their journey's end at Weston, 10 miles from Norwich, but finding nothing to eat they rode on to Lenwade Bridge—a mile away—and dined there. 'My servant Will: supped and slept there. Myself and Bill supped and slept at Weston at my House.'

PART II

WESTON LONGEVILLE, NORFOLK

May 24th, 1776, to January 1st, 1803

As Weston Longeville will become as familiar as
Ansford or Castle Cary, little need be said here.
It owed its second name to the priory of Longeville
in Normandy, to which its tithes were transferred
at the end of the eleventh or the beginning of the
twelfth century—a common mediaeval practice—
by its then Norman Lord of the Manor. The
population in 1776 probably did not exceed 360—
its population in 1801 was 365, in 1901, 367, and at
the last (1931) census 308. The church, exception-
ally spacious and beautiful, is of the perpendicular
period, and dedicated to All Saints. The living is
still in the gift of New College, Oxford, and still
relatively a good one. The rectory is not, alas, as
known by the Diarist, but on the same site, about
half a mile from the church. Fish continue to
flourish in the River Wensum, a lovely stream
which flows through Lenwade Bridge a mile and a
half away.

For the first few days the Diarist and Bill were
very busy and rather uncomfortable settling in.
The Oxford and Ansford boxes arrived from
Norwich, another survey of dilapidations is taken
on the Diarist's behalf, a rat catcher is set on to
catch and destroy all the rats for 10s. 6d., a labourer
is engaged for four days at 1s. 6d. a day for grubbing
up furze. They spend two days in Norwich—from
May 30th to June 1st—buying household goods,
furniture, silver and so on, also cloth for a coat for

Bill, to be made by a tailor—'an old Prussian' called Murray.

JUNE 3. I breakfasted, dined, supped and slept again at Weston. My nephew breakfasted, dined, supped and slept at Weston. Two servant maids came to me this morning and offered their services to me. I agreed with them both and they are to come to me here Midsummer day next. One of them is to be an upper servant and she lived very lately with Mr. Howes. A very pretty woman she is and understands cookery and working at her needle well. I am to give her per annum and tea twice a day—5. 5. 0. She was well recommended to me by Mrs. Howes and the reason she was turned away from Mrs. Howes's was her not getting up early enough, as Mrs. Howes told me. The other maid was recommended to me by Mrs. Howes, she is a Tenant's daughter of Mr. Howes's, she is wooled. I agreed to give her per annum— 3. 10. 0. She is to come at Midsummer also. She is to milk, etc.

Very bad all day in the toothache. The tooth is faulty. Mr. Hardy and his Boy Mason at work for me all day. Gave a man this morning for bringing home our dog 0. 1. 0. Dunnell the carpenter at work for me all day.

JUNE 4. I breakfasted, dined, supped and slept again at Weston. My tooth pained me all night, got up a little after 5 this morning, & sent for one Reeves a man who draws teeth in this parish, and about 7 he came and drew my tooth, but shockingly bad indeed, he broke away a great piece of my gum and broke one of the fangs of the tooth, it gave me exquisite pain all the day after, and my Face was swelled prodigiously in the evening and much pain. Very bad and in much pain the whole day long. Gave the old man that drew it however 0. 2. 6. He is too old, I think, to draw teeth, can't see very well.

June 5. I breakfasted, dined, supped and slept again at Weston. Very much disturbed in the night by our dog which was kept within doors tonight, was obliged to get out of bed naked twice or thrice to make him quiet, had him into my room, and there he emptied himself all over the room. Was obliged then to order him to be turned out which Bill did. My face much swelled but rather easier than yesterday tho' now very tender and painful, kept in today mostly. Paid and gave Will my servant this evening 0. 5. 0. Paid Mr. Dunnell this evening part of a bill due to him from me, for 2 cows, 3 Piggs, 3 p^r. Shoes, Flower, Tea, Sugar, News Papers, Pipes, Candles, Pan, Tobacco, Beer, Mustard, Salt, Washing, Halters, Comb and Brush, Crabs, Bread and Porterage of £14. 9. 3. the sum of a Bank Note—of—£10. 0. 0.

July 19th. I breakfasted, dined, supped and slept again at Weston. Bill breakfasted, dined, supped and slept again at Weston. Bill and myself took a ride in the afternoon to Mr. Howes at Hockering where we spent the remaining part of the afternoon with Mr. Howes and his Wife. Mr. Howes went to bury a corpse for Mr. du Quesne, and when he was gone Mrs. Howes told us that she lived very unhappy with her Husband, as he wants her to make her Will and give everything to his Family. I advised her to the contrary, and to give to her own. We were wet coming back as it rained.

Sep. 12th. . . . Largess given today to Farmers Harvest Men 0. 2. 0

A custom in this County when Harvest is in to give the Farmer's Men who call upon you, each set

0. 1. 0

SEP. 14th. ... Very busy all day with my Barley, did not dine till near 5 in the afternoon, my Harvest Men dined here to-day, gave them some Beef and some plumb Pudding and as much liquor as they would drink. This evening finished my Harvest and all carried into the Bárn—8 acres. I had Mrs. Dunnell's Cart and Horses, and 2 men, yesterday and to-day. The men were her son Thomas and Robin Buck. ...

SEP. 17th. I breakfasted at Weston and afterwards set of to Yarmouth. Bill breakfasted at Weston and he went with me. ... We got to Yarmouth about 4 o'clock, and there we dined, supped and slept at the Wrestlers in Church Square kept by one Orton. A very good house. After we dined we took a walk on the Quay and viewed the Dutch vessells, about 70 sail which came in last night, to go a-fishing soon for Herrings. The Dutch are very droll fellows to look at, strange, heavy, bad dressed People with monstrous large Trousers, and many with large wooden shoes. To turnpikes today from Weston to Yarmouth pd

0. 1. 6

My nephew is highly pleased with the Town of Yarmouth.

SEP. 19th. We breakfasted, dined, supped and slept again at Yarmouth. After breakfast we each took a Yarmouth coach and drove down upon the coast, and called again at the Fort. Will walked down there, at the Fort to-day pd. . . 0. 2. 0

It was very pleasant and delightful indeed. Nothing can beat what we saw to-day—immense sea Room,

Shipps and Boats passing and repassing—the Wind being rather high, the Waves like Mountains coming into the Shore. We rode close to the Ocean, the Waves sometimes coming into our Carriages. We returned about 3 o'clock. We had some fine smelts, shoulder of Mutton rosted and Tarts. In the evening we took a walk on the Quay, as fine a one as ever was seen. A great deal of company walking backward and forward. We got on board an English vessel, and were treated with Wine, Gin, etc. The sailors behaved very civil indeed to us, had a difficult Matter to make them take anything, but at last I did, and all the silver I had, being only   .   .   .   .   0. 1. 0 She was a Collier and going soon back to Sunderland.

Oct. 4th. ... A Mr. Roop a young Man and is a Brother of Mrs. Davy's called on me this morning, he drank a glass of Wine and decamped. I never saw him before in my Life—he is a Prig.

Nov. 3rd. ... This morning about 11 o'clock Dr. Thorne of Mattishall came to my House and inoculated my two servants Ben Legate and little Jack Warton. [A very elaborate description follows of Dr. Thorne's method of inoculation—in the arm— and the Diet and Physics to be taken during the period of inoculation.] ... Pray God my People and all others in the Small Pox may do well, several Houses have got the Small Pox at present in Weston. O Lord send thy Blessing of Health on them all.

Nov. 10th. ... I read Prayers, Preached, Churched a Woman, and christened two children by name Christopher and John this afternoon at Weston Church. A large congregation at Church, Mr. and Mrs. Carr there. All People well pleased with the

Alteration at the Church. This afternoon was the first time of my using the reading Desk and Pulpit, since its being removed, and also of a new Common Prayer Book in my Desk. I can be heard much better than where it was, and easier. . . .

Nov. 22nd. . . . Had a fine calf fall this morning from my flaked cow. My neighbour Downing, the Father of the Children that were lately inoculated has got the small pox in the natural way and likely to have it very bad—therefore I sent over Harry Dunnell this evening to Dr. Thorne's, to desire him to come to-morrow and see him, which he promised.

Nov. 23rd. . . . Dr. Thorne came this morning to poor Downing and I went to meet him there and saw him there. He has a great Quantity and I think will have a difficult matter to get over it. But by the blessing of God upon him, hope that he will do well. He is a poor labouring Man and has a Wife and seven small children. I told the Dr. that I would see him paid, if he would assist him etc. . . .

Dec. 3rd. . . . My Frolic for my People to pay Tithe to me was this day. I gave them a good dinner, surloin of Beef rosted, a Leg of Mutton boiled and plumb Puddings in plenty. Recd. to-day only for Tithe and Glebe of them . . 236. 2. 0 Mr. Browne called on me this morning and he and myself agreed and he paid me for Tithe only 55. 0. 0 included in the above, he could not stay to dinner. They all broke up about 10 at night. Dinner at 2. Every Person well pleased, and were very happy indeed. They had to drink Wine, Punch, and Ale as much as they pleased; they drank of wine 6 Bottles, of Rum 1 gallon and half, and I know not what ale.

Old Harry Andrews, my clerk, Harry Dunnell and Harry Andrews at the Heart all dined etc. in Kitchen. Some dined in the Parlour, and some in the Kitchen. 17 dined etc. that paid my Tithe, that is to say, Stepn. Andrews, Baker, Burton, Cary, Man, Pegg, Norton, Bowles, Dade, Case, Pratt, Legate Senr. and son of Ringland, Bidewell, Michael Andrews, Burrows and Legate Junr. at the Horse. Mr. Peachment came just at dinner time, but he had dined; he spent the afternoon and evening however. There was no supper at all provided for them. We had many droll songs from some of them. I made use of about 13 lemons and about 2 Pds of sugar. Bill and myself both well tired when we went to bed.

DEC. 10th. ... Mr. Chambers the Schoolmaster who is lately come here called on me this morning to let me know that he would teach my Servants Ben and Will to write and read at 4/6*d*. a quarter each—which I agreed for.

DEC. 13th. ... This day being appointed a Fast on our Majesty's arms against the rebel Americans, I went to Church this morning and read the Prayers appointed for the same. I had as full a congregation present as I have in an afternoon on a Sunday, very few that did not come. ...

DEC. 25th. I breakfasted, dined, supped and slept again at home. Bill breakfasted, dined supped, and slept again at Weston. Mr. Brooks my Upholsterer sent over a Man on purpose from Norwich this morning, with a fine Hind Quarter of London Lamb, prodigious fine it was indeed. I gave the man some victuals and drink and 0. 1. 0. The undermentioned poor old People dined at my House to-day being

Christmas Day and went to Church with me in the
afternoon, to each of them gave 0. 1. 0.

Old Richard Bates	0.	1.	0
Old Richard Buck	0.	1.	0
Old Thos. Cushion	0.	1.	0
Old Harry Andrews	0.	1.	0
Old Thos. Carr	0.	1.	0
Old Robin Buck Mrs. Dunnell's man .	0.	1.	0
James Smith the clerk	0.	1.	0

By God's Blessing I intend doing the same next
Christmas Day. Gave old Richard Bates an old black
coat and waistcoat. I had a fine surloin of Beef rosted
and Plumb Puddings. It was very dark at Church
this aft. I could scarce see. I read Prayers and
Preached this afternoon at Weston Church.

1777

JAN. 13th. . . . Went on my Mare, and my servant
Will: with me to Mr. Du Quesne's where I dined
spent the afternoon and stayed till 8 at night with
him, Mr. and Mrs. Howes and Mr. Donne. We had
for dinner a Leg of Mutton boiled, a batter Pudding,
and a couple of Ducks. It is a Clubb meeting and
goes by the name of Rotation. I became a Member of
it to-day and they all dine with me on Monday next.
Every Monday is the day. At Quadrille this afternoon—lost 0. 1. 3. I gave nothing at all to Servants.

As there was no Moon to come home by, it was
very disagreeable to come home thro' the Wood that
I did, but I thank God I got safe and well back tho'
very dark. When there is no Moon for the future will
get back before it is dark.

JAN. 16th. . . . To one Richard Andrews a Smuggler for a Pound of 9/0 Tea, and 3 silk India Handkerchiefs at 5/6 . . . . . 1. 5. 6
Tom Dunnell begun making a Pr of handsome large deal Gates for the Barton this afternoon. . . .

FEB. 14th. . . . To 36 children being Valentine's day and what is customary for them to go about in these parts this day gave 0. 3. 0 being one penny apiece to each of them.

MARCH 18. . . . My Servants Will and Suky went to a Puppett Show this evening at Morton and kept me up till after 1 o'clock.

MARCH 23. . . . I read Prayers and preached this morning at Weston. I gave notice this morning at Church that there would be Prayers on Friday night being Good Friday—there used to be none that day, which I think was very wrong.

MARCH 25. . . . My great Pond full of large toads, I never saw such a quantity in my life and so large, was most of the morning in killing of them, I daresay I killed one hundred, which made no shew of being missed, in the evening more again than there were, I suppose there are thousands of them there, and no froggs. . . .

MARCH 26. . . . Went a fishing with Nets down to the river to-day, but had little or no sport, caught 2 brace of Pike, one fine Perch, some Gudgeons and a few flat Fish—I sent the men before I went, and I found them at Attlebridge, and it made me quite angry to find them there, so angry that I left them immediately and ordered them of, and then my nephew and self took a ride to Witchingham and saw the Parsonage House there and Church. The Church is a very neat one and in good repair, the House not bad, tho' better than I thought it to be.

As we returned we found the Fishers at Leonard Bridge trying there for fish, and there we stayed with them till 5 o'clock and then returned home to dinner. For some Beer for them at the Inn there pd.   o. 1. o Harry Dunnell, Ben, Will, Allen and Barney and Tom Carr were the Fishermen and they all returned and dined at my House . . . gave them   . o. 2. o I let the Fishermen have a Bottle of Rum to carry with them. We returned quite tired and hungry and much fatigued. . . .

MARCH 29. . . . Andrews the Smuggler brought me this night about 11 o'clock a bagg of Hyson Tea 6 Pd weight. He frightened us a little by whistling under the Parlour Window just as we were going to bed. I gave him some Geneva and paid him for the tea at 10/6 per Pd.   .   .   .   .   . 3. 3. o

APRIL 17. . . . Sent my servants Will: and Ben with a cart this morn' to Norwich after some Wine from Mr. Priest and some dishes and plates etc. from Mr. Beloe's—China Merchant. Sent by them a note to Mr. Priest and one to Mr. Beloe. They did not return till 7 in the evening. They might have come home much sooner I think. The things came home very safe however as well as wine. I have now a compleat Table service of the cream coloured ware, with some other useful things. . . . My servants were both rather in liquor, and as for Will, he behaved very surly and went to bed before I supped, a pretty return for giving him half a guinea last week.

MAY 15. . . . Mr. Custance [the Squire's brother]

called on me this morning to go a fishing. We rode down to the river. Mr. Custance's mistress a Miss Sherman and one Sandall an oldish man a broken gentleman and who keeps a Mistress also tho he has a Wife living, went with us on horseback. I returned home to dinner tho' very much pressed to dine with Mr. Custance. We had but middling sport—a lease of trout, 1 pike and some flat fish. Mr. Custance behaved exceedingly civil to me. He sent me the finest trout and the pike this evening by his man Phillips. Gave the servant o. 1. o.

JUNE 4. . . . Recd. of Mr. Legate Ben's Father this morning for 2 small piggs which Sukey sold him o. 15. o. Gave Sukey out of it for selling them o. 1. o. . . . The toads in my great Pond made an extraordinary loud noise for this last week past. This being his Majesty's Birth Day had my Blunderbuss fired of by Bill above 2 hands high three times in honour of the day, and with powder only. We had the fine Pike that Mr. Custance sent me rosted for dinner with a Pudding in his Belly, and very good it was indeed, we dined on it chiefly, tho' we had a fine piece of Beef boiled besides. The Pike was more than 2 foot long after being rosted. . . .

JUNE 17. . . . Bill made me very uneasy and very angry with him at breakfast by contradicting me in a very saucy manner. I therefore told him that I was determined that he should not return with me to Weston but that I would leave him in the West. This being my Rotation Day, the following Company dined and spent the afternoon with me. Mr. and Mrs. Howes and with them Mrs. Priest and daughter from Norwich, Mr. Bottom, Mr. Donne and Sister with one Miss Church a Lady rather deformed but dressed exceedingly well with a prodigious high Head indeed, but very sensible and the Rev. Mr. Du Quesne, Chancellor of St. David's. I gave for dinner a bad Leg of Mutton boiled scarce fit to be eat by being kept too long, and capers, some green Pease and a Pigg's face, a Neck of Pork rosted with gooseberries, a plumb Pudding, with Carrots, Turnips, etc. for Roots. Miss Church and Miss Donne came and went back in a common market cart. Most of the Company were wet by coming to-day as it rained much about 2 o'clock. They all returned about 9. At Quadrille this afternoon after Tea, with Miss Church, Miss Donne, and Mr. Du Quesne, at 2d per Fish lost— o. 4. o. We were very merry with Mrs. Howes today. I gave them a plumb cake with their tea.

> On June 23rd he and his nephew, and the servant, Will Coleman, started on their journey to Somerset to visit our old friend 'Sister Jane', Mrs. Pounsett. They went on horseback, and the journey, which was uneventful, took six days.

JULY 3. I breakfasted, dined, supped and slept again at Mr. Pounsetts. Brother John being at the Christening last night being merry disturbed the whole Company so much that they were obliged to break up about 11 o'clock. Js. Clarke and Jack were going to fight. He made terrible work there I heard this morning. He is the worst Company I ever was in in my Life when he is got merry. Nothing pleases him then but making the whole Company uneasy. . . .

JULY 5th. I breakfasted, dined, supped and slept again at Mr. Pounsetts. Brother Heighes and his son Sam dined etc. with us. Sam brought his violin with him and played several tunes to us—he is amazingly improved both in Painting and in Musick—he is a very clever youth. Gave Sam this afternoon o. 2. 6. ...[1]

JULY 22. I breakfasted and slept again at Ansford. We were rather disturbed about an Hour after we got to bed, and Jenny came to my door and waked me, and asked me if something did not fall down in my Room, and that she had heard something walk in the Passage to my door, and also thought that I was ill— but it all ended in nothing. Mr. Pounsett, myself and Sister dined, spent the afternoon, supped and spent the evening at Richd Clarkes at Cary with him, Mr. Thomas, Brother Heighes and Sam Clarke. Dr. Clarke, Sister White and Sam: Woodforde supped etc with us. In the afternoon I walked down to Charles Clarke's and bought me 20 yds of Huccaback Cloth for kitchen Table Cloths in Norfolk ¾ wide at 1/1 per yd 1. 1. 6. To Richd. Clarke's servants coming away gave o. 2. o. Cousin Lewis and Son went of this morning for Nottingham. . . . I was much better to-day and more easy in my Mind. Robert Biggen for stealing Potatoes was this afternoon whipp'd thro' the streets of Cary by the Hangman at the end of a Cart. He was whipped from the George Inn to the Angel, from thence back thro' the street to the Royal Oak in South Cary and so back to the George Inn. He being an old offender there was a Collection of

[1] Samuel Woodforde, the Diarist's nephew (1763–1817), was a considerable artist in his day, and was elected an associate of the Royal Academy in 1800, and an academician in 1807. He was the most distinguished of the sons of brother Heighes. He contributed no less than 133 pictures to the Royal Academy. He was enabled to visit Italy and study there through the liberality of the banker, Henry Hoare of Stourhead, of whom the Diarist speaks more than once. Farington mentions Samuel Woodforde in his diary. His 'Dorinda wounded by Silvio' is in the Diploma Gallery at Burlington House.

o. 17. 6 given to the Hangman to do him justice. But it was not much for all that—the Hangman was an old Man and a most villainous looking Fellow indeed. For my Part I would not contribute one Farthing to it.

> The Diarist's stay at Ansford lasted for another month—the days are spent in much visiting of old friends, in fishing, and so on—and then on August 21st they set out for Norfolk, returning via Bath and Oxford. At Oxford they stayed two nights at the Blue Boar, while the Diarist visited his friends at New College. They reached Weston safely on the 29th, and found 'things in decent order'.

SEPT. 16. . . . Very busy with the engine [for pumping out the pond] this morning. Mr. du Quesne, Mr. Donne and Sister, Mr. Bodham, Mr. and Mrs. Howes and Mrs. Davy came to my House about 12 upon account of seeing some fishing before dinner as my great Pond was near empty. We were obliged to sink the engine lower, and in doing of the same in raising the engine one of the triangular Poles broke and very near killed my man Will Coleman, he was knocked down by the Pole falling on his Head, but it only stunned him for some time. I then gave him a dram and he was soon pretty well. It frightened us all very much. We caught a number of small Tench with the casting net, but could not get all the water out to-day for the Mud. The Ladies and Gentlemen all dined and spent the afternoon with us. I gave them for dinner half a dozen of my own fine Tench (taken out of my Pond in the yard) stewed, a Rump of Beef boiled, and a Goose rosted, and a Pudding. Mrs. Howes found great fault with many things especially about stewing the Fish—she could not eat a bit of them with such sauce etc. Mrs. Davy fell downstairs but did not hurt herself. Miss Donne swallowed a Barley corn with its stalk. Many accidents happened but none very bad. . . . The company went away about 9 o'clock: They all admired my plated candlesticks and snuffers. . . .

SEPT. 21. We breakfasted, dined, supped and slept again at Weston. I read prayers and preached this morning at Weston. Harry Dunnell dined with our folks today. In the afternoon my dog Pompey came home shot terribly, so bad that I had her hanged directly out of her Misery. My greyhound Minx who was with her did not come and we suppose she has met with the same fate. It is supposed that Mr. Townshend's gamekeeper who goes by the name of black Jack, shot Pompey. My nephew and self took a walk in the afternoon.

SEPT. 27. . . . I took a walk about 5 o'clock this evening by myself to Mr. Townshend's at Honingham according to a promise from me to Mr. du Quesne, and was very politely received, and drank Tea there with him, his Lady and Mr. du Quesne. The Hon: Charles Townshend[1] handsomely apologised for my

---

[1] This Mr. Charles Townshend (1728–1810) is not the celebrated Charles Townshend (1725–67), the Chancellor of the Exchequer, who perhaps more than any one man was responsible for making war with the American colonies inevitable—by his imposition of duties, tea and other, in 1767. Our Mr. Townshend was cousin of the Chancellor of the Exchequer, and was nicknamed 'Spanish Charles' (to distinguish him from his cousin)—on the ground that he was Secretary to the British Embassy at Madrid from 1751-6. From 1761–84 he represented Great Yarmouth in Parliament, and during this period held various minor offices in various administrations: Lord of the Admiralty (1765), Commissioner of the Treasury (1770), Vice-Treasurer of Ireland (1777), Vice-Treasurer of the Navy (1783). He was made a Peer in 1797, taking the title of Baron Bayning of Foxley. His wife (married August 1777) was Annabella, daughter of the Rev. Richard Smith, and an heiress.

dogs being shot by his gamekeeper, and told me moreover that whenever I had an Inclination for a Hare
I was very welcome to take a Course with Mr. du
Quesne upon his Lands: Mr. Townshend's Lady is a
most agreeable Lady indeed, very handsome and exquisitely genteel. She has been married but very
lately and is about 22. I returned to Weston before
8 o'clock. . . .

Sept. 30. . . . Harry Dunnell found an old silver
spoon this morn in levelling parts in the Pond to make
it more even. It weighed one ounce and marked with
M.E. and I apprehended it belonged formerly of the
Family of the Englands, one of which was Rector in
1575. . . .

Oct. 1. We breakfasted, dined, supped and slept
again at home. Harry Dunnell behaved very im-
pertinent this morning to me because I would not
privately name his child for him, he having one Child
before named privately by me and never had it
brought to Church afterwards. He had the Impudence to tell me that he would send it to some Meeting
House to be named etc.—very saucy indeed—To
2 Peck more of Pears of Js. Taylor, paid 0. 1. 0. Gave
to his little maid for bringing them 0. 0. 6. My servant
Will has a bad Leg owing to its being scalded two
days ago. My Folks say he has the Ague in it. I put
to it some Family Plaister and a Poultice over it.

1778

Jan. 6. We breakfasted, dined, supped and slept
again at home. Sukey's sister breakfasted here and
then went home. I did not speak one word to her, as

she came unasked. Bill went out a shooting again this morning and he brought home only 4 Blackbirds. Gave Bill this evening for powder and shot 2/6.

JAN. 19. . . . This being the day for the Queen's Birth Day to be kept Bill fired my Blunderbuss 3 Times, each charge three Caps of Powder with a good deal of Paper and Tow on it. I fired him of in the evening with 3 Caps of Powder also. . . .

JAN. 27. . . . Mr. du Quesne called on me [at Weston] this morning and stayed with me some time, he told me that a Meeting of the Nobility, Gentry and Clergy of the county of Norfolk would be held to-morrow Morn' at the Maid's Head at Norwich for opening a Subscription to advance a Regiment in these critical Times for the King. He asked me if I should be there, which I promised. . . .

[Accordingly he and Bill set forth for Norwich.]

JAN. 28. We breakfasted, supped and slept at the King's Head. To my Barber this morning gave 0. 1. 0. After dressing myself I walked by myself down to the Maid's Head to the Meeting of the Nobility, Clergy, etc. Lord Townshend, Mr. Townshend, Sir John Woodhouse, Sir Wm. Jernegan, Mr. de Grey the Lord Chief Justice's Son, a Mr Masham, Colonel Dickens etc. present. Sir John Woodhouse was Chairman and opened the business of the Meeting and he was answered by one Mr. Windham who spoke exceeding well with great Fluency and Oratory, but on the wrong side. Lord Townshend spoke after him, but is no Orator at all. Mr. de Grey then spoke very well and after him Mr. Townshend. The Question was then proposed by the Chairman that all those gentlemen that were against the subscription would retire, and many there were that retired. The subscription then was opened and Lord Townshend subscribed £500; Sir John Woodhouse also I believe did the same and some others. Mr. du Quesne was there and he subscribed 20 guineas: towards the end of the second sheet—I subscribed 5 guineas, there were many others that followed my example. N.B. I did not pay my subscription as many did not. The money is to be advanced as it is wanted. I dined and spent the afternoon at the Maid's Head with the rest of the Nobility, & Clergy & Gentry. We had about 40 that sat down to dinner. Sir John Woodhouse, Lord Townshend, Mr. Masham, Mr. Townshend, Sir Wm. Jernegan, Colonel Dickens, Mr. de Grey, Mr. du Quesne etc. etc. dined there. I sat between Colonel Dickens and Mr. du Quesne, the Colonel was at Christchurch in Oxford a Student there, therefore he and myself had a long Conference. The Colonel lives at Dereham and asked me to his House. The subscription amounted to near £5,000. The subscription is to be kept open at Kerrisons. There was also a Meeting of the opposite party at the White Swan to-day, to protest against it. The above Mr. Windham was one of them. Most People admired the manner of Windham's speaking, so much Elegance, Fluency and Action in it. For my ordinary paid 3s/0d. Extraordinary 1s/0d—o. 4. o. My nephew dined and spent the day at the King's Head. Mr. du Quesne and myself went from the meeting about 6 o'clock and drank Tea with Mr. Priest and his Wife. After tea Mr. du Quesne went home with Mr. Townshend. I then called on my Nephew, and we went to the Play. As we went in after the 3rd Act I only paid o. 3. o. The Play was the provoked Husband & Bon

Ton the Farce. We sat in the centre Box which was quite full. Sir Wm. Jernegan was in the same box and spoke to me as he came out; a very good House tonight. We slept in our own Beds at the King's Head tonight.

The Mr. Windham 'who spoke exceeding well' is the celebrated William Windham (1750–1810), friend of Dr. Johnson, scholar, diarist, and states-man. He was educated at Eton and Oxford. His first appearance in public life was the occasion here referred to by the Diarist. His liberal opinions, however, changed under the influence of the French Revolution. From 1784–1802 he represented Norwich in Parliament, and in 1794 he joined Pitt's administration as Secretary for War, a posi-tion he held till 1801. He was again War Sec-retary in the Ministry of All the Talents, 1806–7. He was a very remarkable man, a good Greek and Latin scholar, fluent in French and Italian, and a student of mathematics. His *Diary* (1784–1810) is of very considerable interest—edited in 1866 by Mrs. Henry Baring. It is in his *Diary* (pages 30–4) that occurs the memorable description of Dr. Johnson's last hours, and the words addressed to Windham, ' "God bless you, my dear Windham, through Jesus Christ," and concluding with a wish that we might meet in some humble portion of that happiness which God might finally vouchsafe to repentant sinners.'

MAR. 1. ... Read Prayers and Preached this morn-ing at Weston. Neighbour Gooch's Father was taken very ill today and thought to be dying. I sent him Tent Wine and in the afternoon went and saw him and read Prayers by him. He desired to have the Sacrament administered to him which I told him I would do it to Morrow morning. Poor Gooch has been an invalid for many years. His Pulse I thought was pretty regular, he had been convulsed in one of his hands, but talked pretty cheerful and well. My Clerks' Wife Jane Smith got immensely drunk I hear to-day.

MAR: 2. . . . Poor Neighbour Gooch died this morning about 7 o'clock. I was quite surprised to hear of it indeed, as he did not appear to me yesterday near his latter end. I hope that as his Intention was to receive the Sacrament this morning, that his Will will be, to the Supreme Being, taken as if the Deed had been done. . . .

APRIL 15. . . . We breakfasted, dined, supped and slept again at home. Brewed a vessell of strong Beer today. My two large Piggs, by drinking some Beer grounds taking out of one of my Barrels today, got so amazingly drunk by it, that they were not able to stand and appeared like dead things almost, and so remained all night from dinner time today. I never saw Piggs so drunk in my life, I slit their ears for them without feeling.

APRIL 16. We breakfasted, dined supped and slept again at home. My 2 Piggs are still unable to walk yet, but they are better than they were yesterday. They tumble about the yard and can by no means stand at all steady yet. In the afternoon my 2 Piggs were tolerably sober.

APRIL 18. . . . Between 5 and 6 in the evening I took a ride to Honingham and buried one Willen late a schoolmaster there and who died very sudden being taken as he came from Durham. His son and Daughter attended him to the grave and were much concerned for their Father. Pray God comfort them. None but those that have lost their Parents can feel that sorrow which such an event generally produces. . . .

APRIL 24. . . . Who should come to my House about 2 o'clock this day but my cousin Js. Lewis from Nottinghamshire and on foot and only a dog (by name Careless) with him. He was most miserably clothed indeed in every respect. He dined and supped and slept at my House. He slept with my Nephew in the yellow Chamber. He looked much better than when we saw him in Somersett last, in Health. . . .

APRIL 25. . . . Cousin Lewis breakfasted, dined, supped and slept again at Weston. I gave Lewis a Tobacco Box this morning, a Pr of Shoes, a Pr of Stockings, a Pr of Breeches and Shirt and Stock, and an old Coat and Waistcoat. . . .

MAY 16. . . . About 7 o'clock this evening who should arrive at my House in a Post-Chaise and Pair, but Mr. Pounsett and sister Pounsett. [He had been expecting them but did not know exactly when they would arrive.] They had come that day 100 miles. They set out from Ansford on Wednesday morn' last, and they came by way of London and in a Post Chaise all the way from London. They were much tired especially my Sister, but she was pretty tolerable. They supped and slept at my House. I was exceeding glad to see them, but did not expect them so soon. They slept in my yellow Chamber, and Cousin Lewis and Bill slept in the garrett over my Chamber.

MAY 18. We all breakfasted, dined, supped and slept again at Weston. This morning I had my great Pond drawn to show Mr. Pounsett and Jenny some diversion. And we had the largest Pike we caught for dinner and it weighed 7 Pounds. Mr. Pounsett and Jenny said they never eat so fine a Fish in all their lives—it was prodigious nice indeed. In the evening I took a walk and showed Mr. Pounsett and Jenny my Church etc., they being not at Church on Sunday as it rained much that day in the afternoon.

MAY 21. We all breakfasted, dined and slept again at Weston. I walked up to the White Hart with Mr. Lewis and Bill to see a famous Woman in Men's Cloaths, by name Hannah Snell,[1] who was 21 years as a common soldier in the Army, and not discovered by any as a woman. Cousin Lewis has mounted guard with her abroad. She went in the Army by the name of John Gray. She has a Pension from the Crown now of 18. 5. 0 per annum and the liberty of wearing Men's Cloaths and also a Cockade in her Hat, which she still wears. She has laid in a room with 70 Soldiers and not discovered by any of them. The forefinger of her right hand was cut by a Sword at the taking of Pondicherry. She is now about 60 yrs of age and talks very sensible and well, and travels the country with a Basket at her back, selling Buttons, Garters, laces etc. I took 4 Pr of 4d Buttons and gave her 0. 2. 6. At 10 o'clock we all went down to the River with our Nets a-fishing. . . . At Lenswade Bridge we caught a Prodigious fine Pike which weighed 8 Pound and half and it had in his Belly

[1] Hannah Snell (1723–92) had enlisted in 1745, after being deserted by her husband, a Dutch seaman. It was not till 1750 that she revealed her military adventures, a book of them being published under the title *The Female Soldier: the surprising Adventures of Hannah Snell*, which the author of the notice of her in the *D.N.B.* considers much embroidered. She married a second and third time. An account of her extraordinary career will also be found in Fortescue's monumental *History of the British Army*.

another Pike, of above a Pound. We caught also there the finest Trout I ever saw which weighed 3 Pound and two ounces. Good Pike and Trout we also caught besides.

JUNE 5. . . . Mr. Custance Senr of Ringland called on me this morn' caught me in a very great disabelle, and long beard. He stayed with me about half an Hour. Talked exceedingly civil and obliging and behaved very polite. . . .

This is Mr. John Custance, 'my Squire', of whom and of whose wife we shall hear frequently hereafter. He was born in 1749, the son of Hambleton Custance, and grandson of John Custance who had purchased the Weston property in 1726. Mr. Custance's wife was the second daughter of Sir William Beauchamp-Proctor—created a baronet in 1745—and she was, therefore, sister-in-law of Sir Edmund Bacon, kinsman of the owner of Earlham, a name which now conjures up charming pictures of later Gurneys through the pious art of Mr. Percy Lubbock. The Custances, as will appear from the Diary, had numerous children, seven of whom survived. Squire Custance's pleasant character and the charm of his wife are revealed as the Diary proceeds. The Squire, it is amusing to know, maintained some touch with the great world of London as being a Gentleman of the Privy Chamber.

JULY 6. . . . In the afternoon about 5 o'clock Mr. Pounsett and Sister took leave of Weston and set of in Lenswade Chaise for Norwich, in which I went with them to Norwich and had my Mare led there by Will.

Bill also rode the little Mare with us to Norwich. We
saw Mr. du Quesne as soon as we got there. He had
bespoke 2 Places in the Coach for Jenny and Mr. P.
Jenny, Mr. Pounsett and Bill drank Coffee at the
King's Head this evening, and afterwards went to
Mr. Baker's shop, Haberdasher in the Market Place
and bought some trifling things—for what I bought
pd 0. 5. 0. Mr. du Quesne, myself, Mr. Pounsett,
Jenny and Bill went to the Angel Inn in the Market
Place from whence the Coach goes out, and there we
all supped and stayed till 12 o'clock (the time the
Coach sets forth for London) and then Mr. du
Quesne, Jenny and Mr. Pounsett got into the Coach
after taking leave, and went of for London. Pray God
they might all have a good and safe journey. Bill and
myself being rather low after, took a walk for about an
Hour over the city and then went to the King's Head
and went to bed there. At the Angel for Bill and
myself I pd 0. 5. 0. My poor dear Sister shook like an
aspin leave going away, she never went in a stage
Coach before in her Life.

Aug. 26. . . . Mr. Baldwin called on us this morning,
and talked with us concerning a Midshipman's Place
for Bill and desired us to drink a Dish of Tea with him
in the afternoon which we promised him. . . . In the
afternoon took a walk with Bill to Mr. Baldwin's at
Ling and there drank a dish of Tea with him, Miss
Vertue Baldwin, Mr. Hammerton, Dr. Neale. Had a
good deal of Chat with Mr. Hammerton about Bill.
Bill is to go to London when Mr. Hammerton goes
which will be very soon, to show himself to a Captain
of a ship and that Mr. Hammerton will use all his
Interest for him. I have been most uneasy and most
unhappy all day about one thing or another. When

Bill goes away I shall have no one to converse with—
quite without a Friend.

> The entry for this day has been much crossed out—
> I suspect by some early Victorian great-niece of the
> Diarist—but from such parts as are decipherable,
> taken in conjunction with later entries, I gather
> that the Diarist's maid, Sukey, confesses to him that
> she is with child by one Humphrey. Bill also had
> been causing him anxiety for some time—again the
> entries have been deleted, but portions are just
> decipherable—apparently by paying too great
> attentions to the fair sex. The combination of
> anxieties, and it is clear the Diarist was much
> attached to his nephew—sufficiently accounts for
> the depressed conclusion of this day's entry.

Aug. 28. . . . [The Diarist and Bill visit Mr. Hammerton.] We sat and talked a good deal about Bill's
proceeding with regard to the Navy. Mr. Hammerton
said that he would do what he could, and would
advance him money to rig himself out, if he succeeds,
upon my promise of paying him again soon. It was so
friendly in Mr. Hammerton that I could not but
comply in so critical an affair. Bill is therefore to go
in the London Coach on Sunday evening and wait at
the Swan and two Necks in Lads Lane London till
Mr. Hammerton calls on him, which he says will be
either Monday evening or Tuesday morning early—
Mr. Hammerton rides. Very low and ill withal
especially going to bed. Sukey went before Justice
Buxton today with her [Information?] to swear to the
Father of the Child she is big with. I had a note from
Mr. Buxton which Sukey brought to desire the Parish
Officer the Overseer to come with her, and then he
would take her Information.

AUG. 29. . . . My Maid Sukey went with Mr. Palmer to Mr. Justice Buxton and he granted a Warrant to take up Humphrey.

AUG. 30. . . . I read Prayers and Preached this afternoon at Weston. Gave my Nephew to go to London this morning 5. 5. 0. About 8 in the evening I took a ride with Bill to Norwich and there took a Place in the Coach for him. We drank Coffee at the King's Head this evening. We supped at the Angel Inn, as the London Machine set out from thence at 12 at night. I stayed with Bill till 12, saw him safe into the Machine and then I went to the King's Head where I slept but very little. . . . At the Angel this evening I paid and gave 0. 7. 0. I was very restless and uneasy all night.

SEPT. 3. I breakfasted, dined, supped and slept again at home. I told Sukey this morning my Opinion of her respecting the late affair that has happened to her.

SEPT. 9. I breakfasted and slept again at home. Sent a Letter this morning by Mr. Burton to Mr. Priests at Reepham respecting my servant Boy whom I take out of Charity, whether I am to pay for him according to the late Act relating to Servants.[1] Mr. Priest is one of the Commissioners and there is a Meeting this day at Reepham, concerning that and the duty on Houses. To Mr. Burrow's Harvest Men gave 0. 1. 0. I took a ride to Ringland about 2 o'clock and there dined, spent the afternoon and supped and

---

[1] The tax on menservants was imposed in 1777 by Lord North when compelled to find fresh revenue of nearly £250,000. He borrowed the idea from Adam Smith's *Wealth of Nations*, and Adam Smith had borrowed it from Holland, where the tax was in vogue. In 1785 Pitt extended the tax to maidservants, despite 'many jokes of a free description', as Stephen Dowell observes.

spent the evening at Mr. Custance's with him, his
Wife and an old maiden Lady by name Miss Rush.
I spent a most agreeable day there and was very
merry. Mrs. Custance and self played at Back
Gammon together. Mr. and Mrs. Custance are very
agreeable people indeed, and both behaved exceedingly polite and civil to me. I there saw an Instrument which Mrs. Custance played on that I never
saw or heard of before. It is called Sticcardo pastorale.
It is very soft Music indeed. It is several long pieces
of glass laid in order in a case, resting on each end of
every piece of glass, and is played in the middle parts
of the glasses by two little sticks with Nobbs at the end of
them stricking the glass. It is a very small Instrument
and looks when covered like a working Box for Ladies.
I also saw the prettiest working Box with all sorts of
things in it for the Ladies to carry with them when
they go abroad, about as big again as a Tea Chest,
that ever I saw in my Life. It could not cost less than
five guineas. We had for dinner some common Fish,
a Leg of Mutton rosted and a baked Pudding the
first Course; and a rost Duck, a Meat Pye, Eggs and
Tarts the second. For supper we had a brace of
Partridges rosted, some cold Tongue, Potatoes in
Shells and Tarts. I returned to Weston about ½ past
ten o'clock. To Servants at Ringland—2.—gave
0. 2. 0. Mr. Custance also gave me to carry Home a
brace of Partridges, which my servant Will brought
home. They keep 6 Men Servants and 4 Maids.

OCT. 14. . . . Paid my Servant Maid Sukey Boxly
this morning a yrs wages due Oct. 10. The sum of
4. 0. 0. Gave to her besides her Wages, as going away
0. 4. 0. I sent Cary's Cart with one of my Horses by
Ben to Little Melton about 4 Miles beyond Easton

after my new Maid this afternoon, and she returned about 6 o'clock. Her name is Eliz: Claxton about 40 yrs of age, but how she will do I know not as yet but her Wages are 5. 15. 6 per annum, but out of that she is to find herself in Tea and Sugar. She is not the most engaging I must confess by her first appearance that she makes. My other Maid came to me also this evening. Her name is Anne Lillistone of Lenswade Bridge about 18 years of age but very plain, however I like her better than the other at the first sight, I am to give her 2. 0. 0. per annum and to make her an allowance to find herself in Tea and Sugar. Sukey this evening left us, but in Tears, most sad.

Nov. 21. ... I told my Maid Betty this morning that the other maid Nanny looked so big about the Waist that I was afraid she was with Child, but Betty told me she thought not, but would soon inform me if it is so.

Dec. 23. ... Mr. du Quesne, Mr. and Mrs. Howes, Mr. Bodham, Mrs. Davy and children Betsy and Nunn, Mr. and Miss Donne, and their cousin a little boy by name Charles Donne of London dined and spent the afternoon with me being my Rotation and all but Mr. du Quesne supped, and spent the whole night with me being very dark and some falling rain. Mr. Bodham, myself and Mr. Donne sat up the whole night and played at cards till 6 in the morning. Mr. and Mrs. Howes went to bed in my Bedroom about 2 in the Morning. Miss Donne, Betsy and Nunn Davis slept together in the Yellow Room. Mr. Donnes Nephew slept in Will's Room with Mr. Donne's Man Charles. All my Folks sat up. About 6 in the Morning we serenaded the folks that were a bed with our best on the Hautboy. Mr. du Quesne went home about

10 o'clock. I did all I could to prevail on him to stay, but could not. I gave them for dinner 3 Fowls boiled, part of a Ham, the major part of which Ham was entirely eat out by the Flies getting into it, a tongue boiled, a Leg of Mutton rosted, and an excellent currant Pudding. I gave them for Supper a couple of Rabbitts smothered in onions, some Hash Mutton, and some rosted Potatoes. We were exceeding merry indeed all the night. I believe at cards that I lost about 0. 2. 6.

1779

JAN. 1st. I breakfasted, dined, supped and slept again at home. This morning very early about 1 o'clock a most dreadful storm of wind with Hail and Snow happened here and the Wind did not quite abate till the evening. A little before 2 o'clock I got up, my bedsted rocking under me, and never in my life that I know of, did I remember the Wind so high or of so long continuance. I expected every Moment that some part or other of my House must have been blown down, but blessed be God the whole stood, only a few Tiles displaced. My Servants also perceived their Bedsteds to shake. Thanks be to God that none of my People or self were hurt. My Chancel received great damage as did my Barn. The Leads from my Chancel were almost all blown of with some Parts of the Roof. The North West Window blown in and smashed all to pieces. The East Window also damaged but not greatly. The North W: Leads on the top of the Church also, some of them blown up and ruffled, besides 2 windows injured. The Clay on the North end of my Barn blown in and the West side of the Roof the Thatch, most all blown away, leaving many holes in it. The damage sustained by me will amount I suppose to 50 Pounds if not more. However I thank God no lives were lost that I hear of and I hope not. Mr. Shaddlelows Barn, Michael Andrews's, with many others all blown down. Numbers of Trees torn up by the Roots in many Places. In the evening the Wind abated and was quite calm when I went to bed about 11 o'clock. Since what happened this morning, I prolonged the Letter that I designed to send to my sister Pounsett to relate what had happened here by the storm. And this evening sent it to her by Mr. Cary. A smart frost this evening. As the year begins rather unfortunate to me, hope the other Parts of it will be as propitious to me.

It appears from subsequent entries that so badly had the church been damaged by the storm that no services could be held till February 19th, by which date the necessary repairs to the chancel roof had been completed.

JAN. 25. . . . Busy this morning in cleaning my Jack, and did it completely. My stomach rather sick this evening—Mince Pye rose oft.

JAN. 26. [Rotation Day at Mr. Howes.] . . . Just as the Company was gone Mrs. Howes attacked Mr. Howes about putting down the chaise and she talked very roughly to him and strutted about the Room. It was rather too much in her. I did not stay long to hear it, but soon decamped and was at home before 10.

FEB. 27. . . . Never known scarce such fine weather at this season of the year, and of so long Continuance ever since almost the storm of the 1. of Jan. It was like June to-day. Thanks to God for such glorious weather.

MAR. 23. I breakfasted, and slept again at home. Memorandum. In shaving my face this morning I happened to cut one of my moles which bled much, and happening also to kill a small moth that was flying about, I applied it to my mole and it instantaneously stopped the bleeding.

APRIL 11. ... Between 11 and 12 o'clock this morning I went to Church and publickly christned Mr. Custance's child of Ringland, it had been privately named before, and the name of it was Hambleton Thomas. The Gossips were Sir Edmund Bacon Proxy for Sir Thomas Beauchamp, Mr. Press Custance and Lady Bacon. Mr. and Mrs. Custance also present at the ceremony. There were Coaches at Church. Mr. Custance immediately after the Ceremony came to me and desired me to accept a small Present; it was wrapped up in a Piece of white Paper very neat, and on opening of it, I found it contained nothing less than the sum of 4. 4. 0. He gave the Clerk also 0. 10. 6.

APRIL 15. I breakfasted, and supped again at home. About 2 o'clock took a ride to Mr. Custance's at Ringland and there dined, spent the afternoon supped and spent the evening with him and Mrs. Custance, and Lady Bacon. Sir Edmund Bacon came to us just at supper time and he supped etc there. Sir Edmund was rather merry, and was very cheerful. He is quite a young man and personable, but has an odd cast with his eyes,—rather cross sighted. I spent a very agreeable day at Ringland. We had for dinner a Breast of Veal ragouted, a fine Piece of boiled beef, a Pidgeon Pye, Custards, Puffs, and some Lemon Cream. For Supper, a young Chicken, cold tongue etc. At Whist this evening, Mrs. Custance and myself against Lady Bacon and Mr. Custance—and I lost

o. 2. o. It was astonishing hot and sultry most part of the day, and in the evening a good deal of lightening. Most uncommon weather for the time of the year. The Thermometer as high as at any time last summer. I got home about 11 at night.

APRIL 28. I . . . took a ride . . . to Sparham and made a visit to the Revd. Mr. Attle who behaved very complaisant and civil tho' a visit so long due to him from me. I drank a dish of Coffee, and one dish of Tea there and returned home. He has a noble House and his fields about him look exceeding neat and well. He built the House himself and it cost him 1000 Pound.

Between May 4th and May 8th, the Diarist and Mr. Hall of Winborough 'put into execution a Scheme upon the Northern Coast of Norfolk which had been some time talked of'. Servant Will went with them. First they went to Cromer, 'famous for catching of Crabbs and Lobsters'. Next they went to Cley and thence to Wells. At Wells they spent the night at 'the Royal Standard kept by one Smith, a civil and obliging man', and the day following 'got into a small boat, and went to sea in it'. The Diarist, however, did not enjoy himself, though they went out but a little way, as he was very 'near sick as was Will—and the waves so large that frightened me, as I thought it dangerous'. From Wells they went to Houghton Hall, Lord Orford's[1] seat, 'the House and Furniture the grandest I ever saw and the Pictures are supposed to be the best collection in Europe'. After

---

[1] George Walpole, third Earl of Orford, 1730–91; he was grandson of the Prime Minister, Sir Robert Walpole.

visiting Lynn Regis, Swaffam, and Dereham the party returned to their respective homes on May 8th, Mr. Hall to Winborough, and the Diarist and Will to Weston.

MAY 15. . . . Bled my three Horses this morning, 2 quarts each. . . .

MAY 18. . . . Mr. Howes and Wife and Mrs. Davy, Mr. Bodham and his Brother, and Mr. du Quesne all dined and spent the afternoon and part of the evening with us to-day. I gave them for dinner a dish of Maccarel, 3 young Chicken boiled and some Bacon, a neck of Pork rosted and a Gooseberry Pye hot. We laughed immoderately after dinner on Mrs. Howes's being sent to Coventry by us for an Hour. What with laughing and eating hot Gooseberry Pye brought on me the Hickupps with a violent pain in my stomach which lasted till I went to bed. At Cards Quadrille this evening—lost 0. 2. 6.

MAY 21. . . . Sent a letter this evening by Cary to Dr. Oglander Warden of New Coll: with a bill of the expenses on the repairing of my Church—in all 73. 10. 11½.

MAY 22. . . . My Boy Jack had another touch of the Ague about noon. I gave him a dram of gin at the beginning of the fit and pushed him headlong into one of my Ponds and ordered him to bed immediately and he was better after it and had nothing of the cold fit after, but was very hot. . . .

MAY 27. . . . My Maid Nanny was taken very ill this evening with a dizziness in the Head and a desire to vomit, but could not. Her straining to vomit brought on the Hickups which continued very violent till after

she got to bed. I gave her a dose of rhubarb going to
bed. Ben was also very ill and in the same complaint
about noon, but he vomited and was soon better.
I gave Ben a good dose of Rhubarb also going to bed.

MAY 31. I breakfasted at home, and at 6 this morning set forth on my Mare for the West-Country, and
took my man Will: Coleman with me, who rode my
great Horse. . . .

The journey occupied six days and was uneventful.
On the 31st they slept at Barton Mills at the Bull;
on June 1st at Royston at the Talbot—as they
passed through Newmarket in the morning they
saw Lord Orford, 'just going out a-hawking'—on
June 2nd at Aylesbury at the George Inn; on June
3rd at Newbury at the Pelican; on June 4th at
Amesbury at the New Inn; and on June 5th they
arrived at eight in the evening at Ansford, 'and I
thank God found all my Friends there hearty and
well, and exceeding glad to see me. I supped and
slept at Mr. Pounsett's—my Horses there also. My
man Will: Coleman supped and slept there also. . . .'
The six days' journey cost the Diarist in all
£6 3s. 3½d., including the horses.

For more than three months the Diarist and Will
stayed at Ansford—Mr. du Quesne taking the duty
meanwhile at Weston. At Ansford we immediately
get back into the old Somerset atmosphere, the
days spent in a constant interchange of generous
hospitality between the numerous relations and
friends, in frequent fishing expeditions, occasional
visiting of feasts and fairs, and jaunts farther afield.
Needless to say the Lewis's, father and son, very
shabby as usual, turn up, having walked from
Nottinghamshire, and live on their hospitable

relations for some weeks. On leaving his sister's house on Sept. 6th (to return to Weston) the Diarist notes—'to Nancy Hossy late my Sister's Maid for making some Handkerchiefs for me etc—gave her—0. 2. 6. I gave her coming away being a pretty Girl one Kiss.'

SEP. 18: I breakfasted, dined, supped and slept again at home. Soon after breakfast my Friend Mr. Hall called on me and dined and spent the afternoon with me. Poor Mr. Hall was very uneasy concerning an affair that happened at Walton about 3 weeks ago, where he was insulted in public Company by one Nelthorpe and endeavouring to come at him to lick him had greatly hurt his leg between a door and its lintel. Mr. Hall could not get at him or else would have licked him handsomely, I wish that he had done it. I gave him for dinner some rost Beef and an Apple Pudding. I sent Will: this morn' to Mr. Custance's at Ringland and Mr. Du Quesne's at Tuddenham to enquire after them.

OCT. 2. . . . As I was out in my Garden this morning in my Ermine old Hat and Wigg, Beard long and a dirty shirt on, who should walk by at the end of the garden but my Squire and Mr. Beauchamp with him, Mrs. Custance's Brother. They walked into my Garden and went over it, they liked it exceedingly. They would not walk into my House. . . .

OCT. 9. . . . Had a letter this evening from my Sister Pounsett in which she tells me that Sister Clarke and Sam, and Nancy Woodforde are coming to Weston and were to set of from Ansford on last Wednesday, to stay three or four days in London and then of for Weston. Two boxes with their cloaths were already sent.

OCT. 12. . . . About 8 this evening my Sister Clarke, Nancy Woodforde and my Nephew Saml. Clarke arrived at Norwich [where the Diarist was meeting them] in the London Machine from the West greatly fatigued by being up all last night. They drank some tea immediately and soon decamped to bed—they slept at the King's Head.

OCT. 21. . . . Mr. and Mrs. Kerr sent over to us this morning to desire that we would dine with them, we sent word back that we could not having no carriage to go there, he then sent back word that he would send his one Horse Chair after the Ladies—which we could not refuse complying with,—therefore at about 1 o'clock Sister Clarke and Nancy went in the Chair and myself walked to Mr. Kerr's, and there dined, spent the aft: supped and spent the evening, with Mr. and Mrs. Kerr, Mr. Bodham of Mattishall. We had for dinner a Leg of Pork boiled, a Turkey rosted and a couple of Ducks. We had for Supper a couple of Fowls boiled, a fine Pheasant rosted and some cold things. Dinner and Supper served up in China, Dishes and Plates. Melons, Apples and Pears, Walnuts and small Nutts for a desert. We played at Quadrille after tea, at which I won 0. 0. 6. My Servants Will and Ben went out a coursing this morn' by my order and did not return till after we were gone. They coursed a brace of Hares but killed never a one. We returned as we went and got home about 11 o'clock. Mr. Kerr would make me accept of a Hare also. To Mr. Kerr's servants gave 0. 1. 6. Sister Clarke gave the Servants 0. 3. 0. We spent a very agreeable day indeed at Mr. Kerr's.

OCT. 23. . . . Had a letter this evening from Bill Woodforde from on board the Fortune Sloop of War, and now at Spithead performing Quarantine, being lately arrived from the Barbary Coast, had been out about 2 months. He informs me that he had suffered many hardships, and he seems to be tired of the Sea already. He now sincerely repents of his late behaviour at my House at Weston, and of his not taking my advice to him. He also tells me that he has bought some curious things for me and desires me to accept of them—one of them is a large Moorish sword—also a curious Purse with some pieces of money in it. . . .

> Between October 26th and 30th the Diarist, Sister Clarke, Sam Clarke, and Nancy Woodforde enjoyed the now familiar 'Scheme' to Yarmouth, the Diarist's guests being 'highly delighted with the sea, having never seen it before'. They were away— spending a night or two at Norwich, four nights in all: 'we got home to Weston about 3 o'clock and there we dined, supped and slept at the old House. We all seemed very glad of our getting home.'

DECEM. 4. . . . This evening by Mr. Cary came Bill's present to me, viz: a large Moorish sword and a curious Moor's purse made of Morocco leather with some coins in it. He also sent me two curious shells and a quill that came from Falklands Island. It is some gratitude in him I must confess—but he expects something in return as he complains in his letter to me of being very low in pocket. . . .

1780

JAN. 28. . . . I breakfasted, supped and slept again at home. Sister Clarke, Nancy and Sam breakfasted etc. here again. I went to Church this morning a little before 12 and publickly presented Mr. Custance's child in the Church. Sir Edmund Bacon and Lady, and Mr. Press Custance assisted as Sponsors. Mr. Custance was also at Church with the others. After the ceremony Mr. Custance came up to me and presented me with a Norwich Bank Note of five Guineas, wrapped up in some writing Paper. He asked me to dine with the Company at Ringland at 2 o'clock, therefore I walked by myself there and dined and spent the afternoon and stayed till after 7 in the evening and then walked back home. The Company present were Sir Edmund Bacon and Lady, Mr. and Mrs. Custance and Mr. Press Custance. Coming away gave George the servant 0. 2. 6. We had for dinner a Calf's Head, boiled Fowl and Tongue, a Saddle of Mutton rosted on the Side Table, and a fine Swan rosted with Currant Jelly Sauce for the first Course. The Second Course a couple of Wild Fowl called Dun Fowls, Larks, Blamange, Tarts etc. etc. and a good Desert of Fruit after amongst which was a Damson Cheese. I never eat a bit of a Swan before, and I think it good eating with sweet sauce. The Swan was killed 3 weeks before it was eat and yet not the lest bad taste in it.

JAN. 31st. . . . A very comical dull day with us all. Sister Clarke very low. In the evening Sam spoke in favour of the Methodists rather too much I think. We did not play Cards this evening as usual.

FEB. 4. . . . This being a Day [it was a Friday] for a general Fast to be observed thro' the Kingdom, to beg of Almighty God his Assistance in our present troubles being at open rupture with America, France and Spain, and a Blessing on our Fleets and Armies; I therefore went to Weston Church about 11 o'clock and read the proper Prayers on the Occasion, but there was no Sermon preached. My Squire and Lady at Church, and there was a very respectable Congregation that attended at it. Most of my Family went and Sister Clarke and 3 Servants. We did not dine till 4 o'clock this afternoon. Sent a long Letter to my Sister Pounsett this evening. Sister Clarke, Nancy, Sam, and myself, all took it in our heads to take a good dose of Rhubarb going to bed.

MAR. 8. I breakfasted, dined, supped and slept again at home. Sister Clarke breakfasted, etc here again, as did Nancy and Sam. We were very quere after dinner today, having but a plain dinner, viz. some hash Mutton, a plain sewet Pudding and a couple of Rabbits rosted. Sam made me rather angry at dinner when I asked Sister Clarke if she would have the outside of the Pudding or the first cut of it, upon which Sam said I hope you will not Madam, for you know that I always give the outside to the Dogs. . . .

APRIL 17. . . . About 5 o'clock my Sister and Sam went of in Lenewade Chaise for Norwich, to take Coach for London this night. I sent my Man Will with them to Norwich. Will returned about 10 at night and informed us that they got safe to Norwich, but could not go from thence till to-morrow night, the Coach being full. I lent my Sister towards bearing her expenses—5. 5. 0. I gave Sam my little book of Mapps—Atlas Minimus. . . . We were all very low at parting with each other, poor Nancy very low indeed. I gave to Nancy this evening 0. 5. 0. . . . My Head Maid slept with Nancy and is so to do.

APRIL 26. . . . Busy in painting some boarding in my Wall Garden which was put up to prevent people in the Kitchen seeing those who had occasion to go to Jericho.

MAY 3. I breakfasted, dined, supped and slept again at home. About ½ past 9 o'clock this morning my Squire called on me, and I took my Mare and went with him to the Hart[1] just by the Church where most of the Parish were assembled to go the Bounds of the Parish, and at 10 we all set of for the same about 30 in number. Went towards Ringland first; then to the breaks near Mr. Townshend's Clumps, from thence to Attertons on France Green, where the People had some Liquor, and which I paid, being usual for the Rector—o. 4. 6. Mr. Press Custance was with us also. From France Green we went away to Mr. Dades, from thence towards Risings, from thence down to Mr. Gallands, then to the old Hall of my Squire's, thence to the old Bridge at Lenewade, then close to the River till we came near Morton, then by Mr. Le Grisse's Clumps, then by Bakers and so back till we came to the place where we first set of. Mr. Custance Senr then called the six following old men (that is) Richd. Bates, Thos. Cary, Thos Dicker, Richd Buck, Thos Cushion and Thos Carr, and gave each of them half a guinea—To George Wharton, who carried a Hook and marked the Trees, my Squire gave also five shillings. To Robin Hubbard also who carried a Spade he gave 5 shillings, and sent all the rest of the People to the Hart to eat and drink as much as they would at his expense. The Squire behaved most generously on the occasion. He asked me to go home and dine with him but I begged to be excused being

[1] The Hart survives as an inn at Weston, looking precisely the same, I imagine, as it has looked for some centuries: it is a charming little old inn, with the cosiest of kitchens.

tired, as I walked most of the way. Our Bounds are supposed to be about 12 miles round. We were going of them full five hours. We set of at 10 in the morning and got back a little after 3 in the afternoon. Nancy was got to dinner when I returned. Ben, Will and Jack all went the Bounds. Ben's Father Wm. Legate in crossing the River on horseback was thrown of and was over head and ears in the River. My Squire's man John was likely to have had a very bad accident in leading the Squire's horse over a boggy place, both horses were stuck fast up to their Bellies, and by plunging threw him of in the mire and was very near being hurt by the horses plunging to get out, but by great and providential means escaped free from any mischief. The horses also were not injured at all. The man had his new suit of Livery on and new hat, which were made very dirty. Where there were no Trees to mark, Holes were made and Stones cast in.

JUNE 5. ... Mr. Mann's Boy who was taking care of some Horses in a Field, where there was a large Clay Pitt full of water, by accident fell in and was drowned and found about Noon Time quite dead. He was a Child of one Spincks by the Church—a sad misfortune indeed, but hope the poor Lad is much happier than if he had stayed longer here. Mr. Mann very uneasy.

JUNE 9. ... About 2 o'clock who should make his appearance at my House but Nancy's Brother William, who is a Midshipman aboard the Ariadne of 20 Guns. He came from Yarmouth on horseback this morning. He wore his Uniform, and he dined, supped and slept at my House. Nancy was very happy to see him indeed.

June 11. . . . Bill breakfasted, dined and drank Tea this afternoon and about 5 o'clock this evening he went for Yarmouth to go on board the Ariadne— Nancy very low at parting. I made Bill a Present this afternoon of 5. 5. 0.

June 13. . . . I dined and spent the afternoon at Mr. Du Quesne's being his Rotation, with him, Mr. Howes and Mr. Bodham. We had for dinner a Leg of Mutton boiled and Capers, three nice Spring Chicken rosted and a Piggs Face and a Pudding. . . . I returned home about 9 o'clock and who should I see but Nancy's Brother returned from Yarmouth his Ship being sailed but will return e'er long. . . .

June 16. . . . Bill painted our Coat of Arms today on the front of the Temple [just erected] in my garden. . . .

June 17. . . . Bill breakfasted and spent the morning at Weston and about 1 o'clock set of for Yarmouth. He had my little [Mare] to ride some of the way and my Servt Will went with him on the great Horse. Will did not return till near 11 at night. I began to be very uneasy on his not returning—but he told me that there was no Coach set out for Yarmouth all this day from Norwich and therefore he went with Bill as far as Accle 11 miles beyond Norwich. A confirmation of the news of yesterday on the Papers—and the disturbances in London quite over. Charles Town [in Carolina] taken and 8,000 of the Rebels killed and taken.[1]

June 18. . . . I read Prayers and Preached this after-

[1] This success and subsequent victories by Lord Cornwallis roused hopes which were shattered on October 19, 1781, by the surrender of Yorktown, into which Cornwallis had been hemmed by Washington and the French.

noon at Weston. My Squire and Lady at Church and a Brother of hers. Press Custance's Woman at Church and in my Seat also.

JUNE 19. . . . My Squire called on me this morn' and talked to me a good deal about his Brother's Mistress sitting in my Seat yesterday and whether she had leave, and also that she strutted by them in a very impudent manner coming out of Church—and stared at Mrs. Custance.

JULY 24. . . . The Press Gang from Norwich came to Weston last night and carried of a man from Oddnam Green about 9 o'clock.

SEP. 22. . . . My Squire called on me this morning to desire me to come over in the afternoon and privately name his new born son. I married one John Wont and Rose Branton this morning by License at Weston Church—a compelled marriage. N.B. am owed by Mr. Mann the Church Warden for marrying them, as I could not change a Guinea—o. 10. 6. I took a ride in the afternoon to Mr. Custance's of Ringland and privately named his child by name Edward. I stayed and drank a dish of Coffee with the Squire and one Mr. Martineau of Norwich, a Doctor and Man Midwife.[1] Recd. a printed Letter from the Bishop to

[1] Doubtless an ancestor—possibly grandfather, certainly a kinsman of the famous nineteenth-century Martineaus, Harriet and her brother James. The Martineaus were of Huguenot origin, Gaston Martineau of Dieppe settling as a surgeon in Norwich after the revocation of the Edict of Nantes. In the biography of James Martineau by James Drummond and C. B. Upton (1902), it is stated (pp. 2–3): 'The profession of this founder of the English branch of the Martineaus became to some extent hereditary. In the records of the French Church at Norwich we twice meet with the name of David Martineau entered as that of an eminent surgeon. Philip Meadows Martineau, the uncle of James, was also distinguished; and within the family in Magdalen Street the eldest son devoted himself to the ancestral calling.'

send him an account of the Roman Catholicks in my Parish—but I don't know of one in it.

SEP. 23. . . . Had another Letter from my Sister Pounsett this evening to inform me that my Niece Sophy Clarke, and my Nephew Robt White were set of together to be married. Js. and Richd Clarke, Frank Woodforde and his Wife were all confounded angry about it—as they think Robt too much of the Clown. Their Pride is hurt much—for my part I think it a good Match on both sides and if they marry I wish them happy—they are both good natured.

OCT. 13. . . . Mr. Cary's daughter (the Widow Pratt) is we hear with child by her Servant that lived with her last year, but she pretends to say that she was ravished one night coming from her Father's by a man whom she does not know.

OCT. 15. . . . Will came home drunk this evening after Supper from Barnard Dunnell's at Morton and he and my head Maid had words and got to fighting. Will behaved very saucy and impudent and very bold in his talk to me. Shall give it to him to-morrow for the same. . . .

OCT. 16. . . . I gave Will a Lecture this morning concerning last night's work.

NOV. 12. . . . I read Prayers and Preached this morning at Weston. Neither my Squire nor Lady at Church this morning. As I was returning from Church this morning Mr. Press Custance overtook me and acquainted me that Mr. Custance had lost his last [i.e. latest] Child this morning—it had been ill some time. I walked with Mr. Press Custance back to Church and fixed on a Place in the Church where the Child is to be buried. We heard this morning by

Mr. Press Custance, that many people were robbed yesterday between Norwich and Mattishall by two Highwaymen. They are both known and were very near being taken—One of them is a Nephew of one Parferoy (a gardner at Ringland) and his name is Huson. My Man Ben knows him very well. These two Fellows slept at Ben's Father's on Friday Night and were in the Parish of Weston most of the day yesterday. Nancy was much alarmed on hearing the above. It was lucky that I did not go to Norwich last week.

Nov. 13. . . . About 11 o'clock this morning took a ride to Norwich and my Servant Willm Coleman went with me. I carried with me upwards of 150 Pound in Bills and Cash, and got to Norwich very safe with the same. Went to Mr. Kerrison's Bank and there recd. a Bank Note of 150 Pd which I immediately inclosed in a Letter and sent it by the Post to Dr. Bathurst of Christ Church, and which I hope will get safe to him there. [This was tithe the Diarist had collected for his friend, Dr. Bathurst, the non-resident Parson of the neighbouring parish of Witchingham.] Kerrison the Banker asked me to dine with him but cd not. . . . At 4 o'clock this afternoon I set of for Weston, and got home safe and well thank God about 6 in the evening. . . .

Nov. 21. . . . The two Highwaymen that lately infested these Roads were taken at Swaffam last night or this morning.

Dec. 15. . . . Nancy and myself being rather out of spirits and ill last night, took a dose of Rhubarb each last night and this morning we were both brave. Mr. Hall dined and spent the afternoon with us. He

also dined here the day that I went to Norwich, with
Nancy—Nancy was not well pleased with him, and
about leaving a dog here behind him, which however
he did not, as Nancy was against it. I gave him for
dinner some Fish and a Shoulder of Mutton rosted—
he left us about 4 o'clock. Mrs. Davie called here this
aft. in Mr. Howes's Chaise with her daughter Betsy,
who is just returned from School and is to spend a few
days with Nancy, therefore Mrs. Davie left her with
us. . . . Betsy slept with my Niece Nancy Woodforde.

DEC. 16. . . . Nancy had a letter from her Brother
Will this evening wherein he mentions that all matters
between him and his Captain are made up—dated
from Sheerness. Little Betsie Davie cried a good deal
this evening after Supper, but about what I know not.
She is of a very meek Spirit, poor little maid.

DEC. 31. . . . This being the last day of the year we
sat up till after 12 o'clock, then drank a Happy New
Year to all our Friends and went to bed. We were
very merry indeed after Supper till 12. Nancy and
Betsie Davie locked me into the great Parlour, and
both fell on me and pulled my Wigg almost to Pieces.
—I paid them for it however.

1781

FEB. 3. . . . Had but an indifferent night of Sleep,
Mrs. Davie and Nancy made me up an Apple Pye
Bed last night. . . .

FEB. 12. . . . We did not go to bed till after 12 this
night, the Wind being still very high. We were as
merry as we could be, I took of Mrs. Davie's Garter

tonight and kept it. I gave her my Pair of Garters and I am to have her other tomorrow. . . .

Next day Mrs. Davie, who had been staying at the Rectory on and off since January 30th, went to Parson Howes's of Hockering, taking Betsy with her, who had been at the hospitable Diarist's since December 15th.

MAR. 20. . . . About 12 o'clock I took a ride to Dereham and Will went with me. Got there about 2 o'clock, put up my Horses at the King's Arms kept by one Girling and there I supped and slept, had a very good Bed. Soon after I got to Dereham I walked to Mr. Hall's Rooms, he lodges at a Barbers by name Field, and there I dined and spent the afternoon with him by appointment. We had for dinner a fine Lobster hot and some Mutton Stakes, had from the King's Arms. Before dinner Mr. Hall and myself took a Walk about Dereham, went and saw a whimsical Building called Quebec. We dined at 3 o'clock and after we had smoked a Pipe etc., we took a ride to the House of Industry about 2 miles West of Dereham, and a very large building at present tho' there wants another Wing. About 380 Poor in it now, but they don't look either healthy or cheerful, a great Number die there, 27 have died since Christmas last. We returned from thence to the King's Arms and then we supped and spent the evening together. To Mr. Hall's Clerk of Garvaston who came to give him notice of a Burial on Friday, being very poor, gave, 0. 1. 0.

MAR. 21. I breakfasted with Mr. Hall at his lodgings. . . .

MAR. 24. ... The four Highwaymen that infested these roads last Winter, were all tried at the Assizes held last week at Thetford, found guilty and all condemned. Since that they made an attempt to get out of the Castle and very near completed an escape.

MAY 4. ... We [Mrs. Davie is again staying at the Rectory] were very merry this morning with Nancy, making her believe that she took a bad half Guinea at Norwich and which I took of her again, but gave her only 9/6. I soon after sent it to Cary's and got 10/6 for it which greatly heightened our Mirth. She had the 1/0 after.

MAY 16. ... Between 7 and 8 o'clock this morning went down to the River a fishing with my Nets. Ben, Will, Jack, Harry Dunnell and Willm Legate (Ben's Brother) were my Fishermen. We begun at Lenewade Mill and fished down to Morton. And we had the best day of Fishing we ever had. We caught at one draught only ten full Pails of Fish, Pike, Trout and flat fish. The largest Fish we caught was a Pike, which was a Yard long and weighed upwards of thirteen pound after he was brought home. We caught about 20 brace of Pike, but threw back all the small ones—also we caught abt 15 brace of Trout, the largest not more than a Pound and half—all the smallest we threw back—3 brace also of Perch—one tolerable Tench and I dare say near if not quite five hundred Brace of Roach and Dace. Prodigious sport indeed we had today tho' cold and wet. As we were fishing by Coplin's, he came out and ordered my men of from his land, and behaved quite contrary to the opinion I had of him. After talking with him some little time he said I might fish, but then I would not, at which he seemed rather uneasy. We eat some cold

meat which we carried about one o'clock and re-
turned home to dinner at 4. For Beer at Barnard
Dunnells of Morton, pd. o. 1. o. Gave Beeston,
Cantrell, Palmer of Morton and Barnard Dunnell
some Pike, and most of the flat Fish to the Poor at
Lenewade and Morton and of my own Parish. Harry
Dunnell and Will Legate dined etc. with our Folks.
Paid them also for their labour today o. 3. o. I was
rather fatigued this evening by Fishing.

MAY 17. . . . Mr. Priest of Norwich came to my
house about 1 o'clock and he stayed and dined with
us and spent the afternoon and in the evening returned to Norwich. I was very glad to see him, as he
and wife behaved very civil to Nancy. Mr. and Mrs.
Howes, Mrs. Davie, and Mr. du Quesne dined and
spent the afternoon with us also. I gave my Company
for dinner my great Pike which was rosted and a
Pudding in his Belly, some boiled Trout, Perch, and
Tench, Eel and Gudgeon fryed, a Neck of Mutton
boiled and a plain Pudding for Mrs. Howes. All my
Company were quite astonished at the sight of the
great Pike on the table. Was obliged to lay him on
two of the largest dishes, and was laid on part of the
Kitchen Window shutters, covered with a cloth.
I never saw a nobler Fish at any table, it was very well
cooked, and tho' so large was declared by all the
Company to be prodigious fine eating, being so moist.
At Quadrille after tea, neither won or lost. At about
9 they all left us. I put a large Pike into the Boot of
Mr. Howes' Chaise before he went.

MAY 30. . . . Nancy scarce eat any thing for dinner
today, I desired her not to eat too much, and therefore
she would not eat after, neither would she eat any
supper.

JUNE 3. . . . I read prayers and administered the Holy Sacrament this morning at Weston Church being Whitsunday. It rained very heavy in the Night a Thunder storm, with little Thunder or Lightning, but much Rain. All Nature seemed this morning greatly refreshed by the Rain, as it was so much wanted. Thanks be to the Lord for so blessed and gracious a Rain. My Squire and Lady at Church and at the H. Sacrament. Nancy also was at Church and at the H. Sacrament by my desire, and was the first time of her ever receiving it. My Clerk Js Smith dined with our Folks today.

JUNE 8. . . . Mr. and Mrs. Custance and Mr. du Quesne dined and spent the afternoon with us and stayed till 8 o'clock in the evening. Mr. and Mrs. Custance were dressed very neat. We put their Coach in my Barn. I gave them for dinner, a Couple of Chicken boiled and a Tongue, a Leg of Mutton boiled and Capers and Batter Pudding for the first Course, Second, a couple of Ducks rosted and green Peas, some Artichokes, Tarts and Blancmange. After dinner, Almonds and Raisins, Oranges and Strawberries. Mountain and Port Wines. Peas and Strawberries the first gathered this year by me. We spent a very agreeable day, and all well pleased and merry.

JUNE 30. . . . Nancy by being with Mrs. Davy had learnt some of her extravagant Notions, and talked very high all day. I talked with her against such foolish Notions which made her almost angry with me, but when we went to bed we were very good Friends and she was convinced.

JULY 1. . . . Poor Robert England Mr. du Quesne's old servant died this afternoon in the Fever that rages so much. He drove Mr. du Quesne's Chaise to Norwich and back again with Mr. Priest and Wife in it, only Wednesday last. Mr. du Quesne is sorely grieved about him.

JULY 24. . . . I read a good deal of the History of England today to Nancy whilst she was netting her Apron. Very dry again. I feed my Geese with Cabbage now.

JULY 30. . . . Nancy and myself get up every morning before 7 o'clock under the penalty of forfeiting sixpence each day—Sundays only excepted.

AUG. 2. . . . Mr. and Mrs. Custance got into their new House for the first time to sleep there. But Mrs. Custance was taken ill before she got there. Supposed to be in labour.

AUG. 6. . . . Nancy took a walk this morning to Mr. Custance's new House and there stayed and dined and spent the afternoon there. I walked in the afternoon there and drank Tea, and about 8 walked back to our House with Nancy. Begun shearing Wheat today. Harvest very forward. Gave Mrs. Davie a very genteel steel Cork Screw this afternoon. Gave Nancy some Muslin to make a shawl.

AUG. 18. . . . Mr. du Quesne returned home Wednesday last. The Arch Bishop of Canterbury and his Lady Mrs. Cornwallis are come also to Mr. Townshends at Honingham.[1]

---

[1] Frederick Cornwallis, D.D. (1713–83). He succeeded Dr. Secker as Archbishop of Canterbury in 1768. Though apparently a popular man, he was a prelate very much of the world, and altogether inferior to his predecessor in talents. He married in 1759 Caroline Townshend, a sister to Mr. Charles Townshend of Honingham: hence his visit there.

AUG. 21. . . . Nancy and myself dined and spent the afternoon at Mr. Jn. Custance's at the New Hall with him and Mrs. Custance. They sent their Coach after us and carried us back home in it. We had for dinner Ham and 2 Fowls boiled, some young Beans, Veal Collops and hash Mutton for the first course. A rost Duck, baked Puddings, Apple Tart etc. second. They behaved very civil and very friendly to us. Mrs. Custance gave Nancy a Pearl necklace and Pearl Chain to hang from the Necklace, a Pr of Pearl Earrings and another Pr of Ear-rings. Mrs. Custance is exceedingly kind to my Niece indeed. We returned home about 8 o'clock in the evening. After spending a very agreeable day.

AUG. 22. . . . I took a ride to du Quesnes this morning, stayed with him about an Hour, found him rather low still, and fretting himself about being so tyed by the leg, in dancing backward and forward to Townshends with his great Company. The Archbishop of Canterbury and Lady are there etc. The Archbishop and Lady go from Townshends Saturday next. Du Quesne is then determined to visit his Neighbours, tho' Townshend be ever so much affronted at it. . . .

SEP. 19. . . . Weston Bells rung yesterday and again to-day, on Mrs. Custance being brought to bed and in the New House.

OCT. 25. . . . Mr. Hall called on us about noon but did not dine with us, tho' I asked him, as I dine at 3 o'clock. He is not looked upon in this neighbourhood so much as he used to be, as his visits are merely interested for himself, and that he never makes any kind of return for the same, not even the smallest Present to any Person.

Octob. 26. I breakfasted, dined, supped and slept again at home. Nancy breakfasted, dined etc here again. Took a ride about noon to Mr. Custance's, saw him, his Wife and Lady Bacon, they were all full dressed and just going to Earlham to Mr. Bacon's to dinner. Took a ride from thence to Lenewade Bridge and so home. Beckham the Net-Maker called here at dinner and he dined with our Folks. He fights cunning. He came to mend my dragg Net but I would not have him mend it at my House as I know him to be an expensive Boarder. If he has it to his House to mend it will cost me 1. 2. 9 which is very dear indeed. I told him that I would send it to his House, if it was to be mended by him. I saw Mr. Custance's new Brewhouse when there to-day. Everything on a very large scale, so large as to brew eight Barrels at a brewing, every article most convenient.

Oct. 29. . . . Mr. Cary and Mr. Hardy dined with our Folks to-day. Clerk Hewitt of Mattishall Burgh called on me this even' by desire of Mrs. Davy to taste some smuggled gin which I liked and he is to bring me a Tub this week.

Nov. 1. . . . Mrs. Custance with her little Boys made us a short visit this morning. I gave her eldest Boy Hamilton an Humming Top. I gave George also a silent Top, wch I bought for them some time ago.

Nov. 15. I breakfasted and spent the morning at Norwich. After breakfast took a Walk to Bakers and bought a smelling Bottle of burnt salts for which I pd 0. 1. 0. For a Comb also at Bakers pd. 0. 0. 6. For a silent Top also at Bakers pd 0. 0. 6. At Mr. Beatniffe's, Lady's Pocket Book for 1782 pd 0. 1. 0. At Mr. Tolls for a Pr of Cotton Stockings for Nancy pd 0. 7. 6.

Called on Mr. Hall about 11 o'clock and we took a walk to Mr. Landy's in the Market Place a Chymist and Druggist and bought of him 1 oz of Rhubarb o. 3. o., of ditto for a small vial of Goulard's Extract pd o. o. 3. The above Mr. Landy was of Winchester and his Mother whom I knew very well and often ticked with her lived in a House in College Street and kept a Huckster's Shop there, and she had many a shilling of me. Mr. Landy is married and came from London to Norwich about 3 years ago. He has a very good shop and House. I did not see his Wife. I invited him over to Weston. I returned to the King's Head about noon, paid my Reckoning and set of for Weston to dinner. I asked Hall to take a ride with me and dine at Weston but he begged to be excused. Pd. and gave at the King's Head etc. o. 13. 10. I made Mr. Hall pay his share at the King's Head. I got home to Weston about 3 o'clock and dined, supped and slept at the Parsonage House. Nancy breakfasted, dined etc. at Weston. I was rather tired and fatigued by being out. Will informed me to-night of his being ill in the venereal way.

DEC. 1. I breakfasted, dined, supped and slept again at home. Nancy breakfasted, dined, etc. here again. It is very true that L. Cornwallis and his whole army and 40 Ships 160 Cannon etc. are all taken by the Americans and French in Virginia. My People went out a coursing this morning and they brought home a brace of Hares, a Rabbit and a Partridge, which they found in a Trap. They saw a great many Hares to-day and had fine sport. I could not go out with them being busy.

DEC. 7. . . . Immediately after breakfast I rode to Honingham and married a very odd Couple, a fine

young Man about 22 years of age, by name Robert
Martin and an old, infirm, weak Widow about 50
years of age, by name Jane Price, by License, and for
du Quesne, as he was not returned home yet. I recd.
for marrying them, the usual Fee there 5. 0. We had
for dinner to-day a Neck of Mutton boiled and a
Goose. At Quadrille with dummy this evening won
0. 6.

DEC. 25. I breakfasted, dined, supped and slept
again at home. Nancy breakfasted, dined etc. here
again. I read Prayers and administered the H. Sacrament this morning at Weston being Christmas Day.
My Squire's Lady at Church and at the Sacrament.
The Squire was not well enough to attend. Richd.
Bates, Richd Buck, (Tom Cary), Tom Carr, Tom
Dicker, Tom Cushion and Js Smith my Clerk all
dined at my House. I gave each of the poor old Men
1/0, being 0. 7. 0. We had a good piece of rost Beef
for dinner and plenty of plumb Puddings. Poor old
Tom Cary could not dine here being ill, but he is
another day and have 1/0. Gave Nancy this evening for Card Mony etc. as she is going to spend a few
days at Mattishall with Mr. and Mrs. Bodham 1. 1. 0.
   To Spragg's lame son for a Christmas Carol gave
0. 0. 6.

DEC. 31. I breakfasted, dined, supped and slept
again at home. Nancy breakfasted, dined etc. here
again. To my Malster's Man a Xmas Box gave 0. 1. 0.
To Mr. Cary for things from Norwich etc. pd 0. 6. 2.
Walked out a coursing this morning with my dogs
for four Hours; had a very fine course with one Hare
and which we at last killed; saw no other Hare. Betsy
Davy was brought this morning on horseback from
Hockering to spend a day or two with Nancy. She

dined, supped and slept here. Being the last day of the year we sat up this night till after 12 o'clock; drank our Friends health everywhere with many returns of the present season and went to bed.

1782

JAN. 4. . . . Busy all the morning in my garden, having enlarged my Pleasure Ground a Trifle by taking in part of the small Field near Goochs House. Nancy sent a Letter to her Father this Evening.

JAN. 7. I breakfasted, dined, supped, and slept again at home. Nancy breakfasted, dined &c. here again. To Mr. Cary for things from Norwich &c. pd. 0. 11. 6. To my Servant Man Ben. Legatt paid this morning a Years Wages due to him the 6 Instant 10. 0. 0. To my Senior Maid Elizabeth Claxton paid also this morning a Years Wages due the 6 Instant 5. 15. 6. To My Servant Man Will: Coleman paid this morning a Years Wages due to him the 6 Instant 4. 4. 0. To Ditto also for 20 Coomb of Grains pd. 1. 0. 0. To Ditto also for dressing my Wiggs a year 0. 10. 0. To my under Servant Maid Lizzy Greaves paid this morning also a Years Wages due 6th Instant 2. 0. 6. To my Boy, Jack Warton, gave this morning 0. 10. 6. Mr. Cary dined with our Folks to-day. My Taste very indifferent and so it was yesterday at Dinner. Everything tastes very disagreeable to me—I don't know what occasions it unless it is my having taken some Brimstone and Treakle—or having made use of some strong sage Tea every Day about 11. in the Morn' lately, I have also a small Cold, which might be the cause.

JAN. 21. . . . By one and another, hurried all the day long—almost.

JAN. 25. . . . My lower Maid Lizzy went to her Mothers this evening to sleep there, as she has my leave to go with her Mother to-morrow to Norwich to get a pair of Stays for herself.

JAN. 29. I breakfasted, supped and slept again at home. Nancy breakfasted, dined &c. here again. At 12 took a ride to Mr. Custances, stayed and chatted with them near an Hour. From Mr. Custances rode to Hockering to Mr. Howes's being his Rotation to-day and there dined, spent the afternoon and stayed till 9 at Night, with Mr. and Mrs. Howes, Mrs. Davy, the Widow Paine, relict of the late unfortunate Alexander Paine, Mr. Du Quesne, Mr. Bodham and Mr. Smith. We had for Dinner, some Salt Fish, a Piece of boiled Beef, a Turkey and Mince Pies. At Quadrille this evening lost 0. 1. 0. I did not get home till after 10 o'clock, and bitter cold riding home it was, being a hard Frost and Snow on the ground and windy. Nancy could not go being still indifferent, therefore she sent a Note early this morning to Mrs. Davy, to desire them not send the Chaise after her, as they promised. The four Breasts and Hands of my two Piggs, with one of the Loins I sent to my poor Neighbours, viz. to Gooch, to Clarke, to Downing, to Norton, and to Nat Heavers. Nancy a good deal better this evening.

JAN. 30. . . . Nancy very busy all the morning in making Cakes, Tarts, Custards and Jellies for to Morrow. Nancy brave to-day and pretty well exercised all day. Fair today but bitter cold indeed.

FEB. 4. . . . To a poor old Man that plays on the Dulcimer gave 0. 0. 6.

FEB. 8. . . . This Day being appointed to be observed as a Fast on the present Troubles and Wars abroad,[1] I went to Weston Church this morning at 11 o'clock and there read Prayers proper on the occasion—but there was no Sermon after. I had a large Congregation—Mr. Custance was at Church—Mrs. Custance not, being so cold. After divine Service I walked with Mr. Custance to his New Hall, and there spent an Hour or better with them. We sent over after Church to Hockering to enquire after Mrs. Howes, and about 3 my Servant Boy returned and greatly surprized us by acquainting us that poor Mrs. Howes was no more —she died at one o'clock this morning—Pray God, she may be happy, and the Family comforted under so sore an affliction—She will be greatly missed by all the Rotation &c. Nancy and myself were greatly concern'd to hear of it and more so, as it was so unexpectedly. . . .

FEB. 12. I breakfasted, dined, supped and slept again at home. Nancy breakfasted, dined &c. here again. At 10 o'clock this morning took a walk to Hockering to attend poor Mrs. Howes's Funeral there to-day. The Snow was very deep in some Places as I went. My Man Will went with me—We got to Mrs. Howes's before 11 and there met Mr. Shelford senr., Mr. Du Quesne, Mr. Priest senr of Reepham, Mr. Potter of Scarning, Mr. Bodham, Mr. Smith, Dr. Thorne and Mr. Priest of Norwich. I found all the Clergy in gowns and some in Cassocks also—I did not carry my

[1] We were fighting at this time with our backs to the wall against the rebel Americans, the French, the Spaniards, and the Dutch, to say nothing of Hyder Ali in India: we had lost nearly all the American Colonies, a considerable portion of the West Indies, and Minorca. On the other hand we had captured various French settlements in India and in Africa, and Dutch settlements in India.

gown, as I did not know whether or not the Clergy appeared in them—I borrowed one however, of Mr. Howes and likewise a Band. Before we went to Church there was Chocolate and Toast and Cake with red Wine and white. At half past 11 o'clock we went to Church with the Corpse in the following Procession. The Corpse first in an Hearse and Pair of Horses, then followed six Chaises, in the first which was Du Quesnes went Du Quesne and Dr. Thorne, in the second which was Mr. Shelfords went Mr. Shelford and Mr. Smith, in the third which was Mr. Priests, went Mr. Priest and myself, in the fourth which was one from Dereham, went Mr. Potter and Mr. Bodham, in the fifth which was from Norwich went Mr. Priest of Norwich and a Mr. Forster the Undertaker, in the sixth which was Mr. Howes's, went Mrs. Howes's two Servant Maids in deep mourning. The Underbearers and Servants all in Hatbands black closed the Procession and an handsome appearance the whole Procession made—we returned to Mr. Howes's in the same manner as we went from it to Church—Mr. Du Quesne buried her —The Pall-Bearers were Mr. Shelford, Mr. Priest, Mr. Potter, Mr. Bodham, Mr. Smith and myself— we had all black Hatbands and Gloves, but they were white. Poor Mrs. Howes if she had lived till to Morrow wch was her birth Day—she would have been 69 Years. It was as decent, neat, handsome Funeral as I ever saw and everything conducted in the best manner—and by its being so I conclude that it was Mrs. Davy's good management. Mr. Howes, Mrs. Davy &c. kept above stairs all the Time—They desired me to walk up to them which I did after the Funeral, but did not stay long with them—found them low and left them so. After our return from Church we had Cake and Wine and Chocolate and dried Toast carried round. My Servant and all Servants that attended and all the drivers all had Hatbands and gloves given to them. We walked back again and got home about half past 2 o'clock—and a bitter cold walk we had back, the Wind in our Faces and it snowed most of the way, which was beat in our Faces. We walked over France Green and by Hockering Park House.

FEB. 14. . . . This being Valentine Day gave to 52 Children of this Parish, as usual 1 penny each 0. 4. 4. Gave Nancy this morning 1. 1. 0.

FEB. 28. . . . Was rather uneasy to-day on Account of being afraid that I have got the Piles coming or something else—unless it is owing to my eating a good deal of Peas Pudding two or three days ago with a Leg of Pork.

MAR. 14. . . . Nancy complained much of her knee this afternoon and was very low upon it, being afraid that it is getting bad again—but pray God! prevent that. I was very low also this evening on her account & c.

MAR. 17. . . . A great deal of Snow fell in the Night, and many heavy Storms of Snow, Hail &c. most of this Day. I read Prayers and Preached this afternoon at Weston. Had a small congregation, owing to the Weather. None of Mr. Custances Family at Church. Having heard that Thos. Thurston's Wife (who is and has been ill a long while) longed for some rost Veal from my House, having therefore a Loin rosted for Dinner, I sent her a good Plate of it.

MAR. 20. . . . I got up rather early this morning

being disturbed by a noise in my Study, in cleaning of it, at which I was rather angry and scolded a little.

MAR. 21. . . . The poor Woman whom I sent some Veal to Sunday died yesterday morning—She eat nothing afterwards till she died, But she eat hearty of the Veal I sent her.

MAR. 22. . . . I buried Eliz: Thurston Wife of Thos. Thurston this afternoon at Weston, aged 45 Yrs. It snowed all the whole Day with very cold high Wind.

APL. 1. . . . Mr. Custance sent after Nancy this morning to spend the Day with Mrs. Custance and to have her Hair dressed by one Brown, the best Ladies-Frisseur in Norwich. About Noon the Weather turned out very wet and the Wind very high and so continued till 9 at Night. The Barometer sunk from this morning at 10 o'clock to 10 at Night 13 Degrees from No. 28–17 to 28–4. Nancy returned home about ½ past 9 o'clock this Even', with her head finely dressed of but very becoming her. Mrs. Custance would not let Nancy pay the Barber, but she paid for her and it cost no less than half a guinea. Mrs. Custance gave the Barber for dressing her Hair and Nancys the enormous sum of one guinea—He came on purpose from Norwich to dress them. Mrs. Custance (God bless her) is the best Lady I ever knew.

APL. 11. . . . It being a very fine morning I took a ride by myself to Mr. Custance's—but neither of them at home—Then went to Witchingham and saw Bathurst's[1] Parsonage House, the Roof of which is

---

[1] Dr. Henry Bathurst, the non-resident Rector of Witchingham: he was later (1805) to become Bishop of Norwich. There is a fine statue of him in Norwich Cathedral.

very bad towards the North and some of it down and more falling—I found Harrison the Tenant very luckily there, as he does not now live in the House—as it is so bad—but he lives at a Brother in Laws (Wright) at Attlebridge. I returned home to Dinner by 3 o'clock.

APL. 16. . . . One Mr. Aldridge who carries about Cottons, Linens, Muslins, Lace, Holland, &c. in a Cart and comes round regularly this way once in ten Weeks, called at my House this morning, and I bought of him a Piece of Holland (alias Irish Cloth) for Shirts, 25 Yards at 3*s*/–*d* per Yard—for which I pd. him 3. 15. 0. For half a Yard of Cambrich for Chitterlons 0. 5. 0. For 7 Yards of Lace Edging for Nancy p^d 0. 5. 0. For 4 Yards of Ribband for my 2 Maids p^d 0. 2. 0. Nancy also bought of him 4 Yards of Pink Ribband 0. 2. 0. Also she bought 1 Y^rd and ¼ of Lace for Mrs Davy 0. 3. 0. It rained incessantly all the Day long, and in the Afternoon very heavy Rains fell, the Wind also very high, and so continued till we went to bed—Wind ENE—I intended to have rode to Norwich to Day, if no Rain.

MAY 14. . . . I bled my 3 Horses this morning. It being my Rotation Day, Mr. and Mrs. Bodham, Mrs. Davy, Mr. Howes and Mr. Du Quesne dined and spent the Afternoon with us—Mrs. Davy supped and slept here as she is to spend a Day or two with Nancy. I gave my Company for Dinner, 4 Spring Chickens boiled and a Ham, part of a Rump of Beef boiled, a Leg of Mutton rosted with sweet Sauce and a boiled Plumb Pudding. At Quadrille this Evening lost 0. 1. 0.

MAY 29. . . . Very busy all the Morning, packing up our things for to go into the Country, as we set out in the Evening. Mr. Du Quesne, who goes to London with us dined and spent the Afternoon with us—and about 5 o'clock this Evening Nancy and myself went in Lenewade Bridge Chaise, and Mr. Du Quesne in his own Chaise, for Norwich and there we drank Tea at the Angel where the London Coach puts up and in which we are to go in to Night. To the Driver of the Lenewade Chaise gave 0. 1. 6. Paid and gave at the Angel for eating &c. 0. 2. 6. My Servant Will Coleman went with us and is to go into the Country with us. We met Mr. Priest of Reepham and his Son S^t. John at Norwich—The latter is going to Bury in the outside of the London Coach. No inside Place vacant. For 2 inside Places in the London Coach p^d at Norwich 1. 16. 0. For 1 outside Place in Do. p^d at Do. 0. 10. 6. To extraordinary weight of Luggage at 1$\frac{1}{2}$ per P^d p^d 0. 8. 6. At 9 o'clock this Evening we all set of for London.

MAY 30. We travelled all night long and I thank God safe and well. We breakfasted at Sudbury—and I paid there 0. 2. 6. Our Coach was quite full having six in it—4 gentlemen and 2 young Ladies. We got to London about 2 o'clock in the Afternoon all safe and well, thank God for it. To Coachmen from Norwich gave 0. 4. 0. We did not like the Inn where the Coach put up (which was the Swan and 2 Necks in Lad-Lane.) therefore we got into a Hackney Coach and drove to the Bell Savage on Ludgate Hill and there dined, supped, and slept. Mr. Du Quesne went with us there and dined and spent the Afternoon with us— In the Evening he went to the Arch-Bishops at Lambeth where he supped and slept. Nancy bore her

Journey very well as did Will and myself. We were all very glad to get to bed to night, being tired.

MAY 31. We breakfasted, dined and spent the Afternoon at our Inn. Before we breakfasted, I hired a Coach and we went in it to St. James Park. Will also went with us. From the Horse Guards we all walked up the Park to St. James's Palace and saw the Guards relieved at 9 o'clock—a very pretty sight. We also saw most of the State Rooms in the Palace. Gave to People at St. James's Palace 0. 3. 6. From thence we walked up the Park to the Queens Palace but did not go into that—the Royal Family being there. After that we walked down the Park back to the Horse-Guards and there took a Hackney Coach and returned to our Inn to breakfast. Mr. Du Quesne came to us at breakfast—and after breakfast, Nancy, myself and Will took a Coach and went to the Tower and saw the Horse Armory, the small Armory, the Artillery, the Regalia, and the wild Beasts.[1] Mr. Du Quesne went with us in the Coach as far as the Royal Exchange and there he took his Leave of us. At the Tower gave in the whole 0. 9. 0. From Breakfast to Dinner we were taken up in seeing the Tower, and did not dine till 5 o'clock at our Inn. For Coach hire to Day p^d 0. 5. 6. After Dinner we walked to a Milleners Shop and I bought 3 dressed Caps for Nancy, for my Sister Pounsett and her little girl, with about 10 Yards of Ribband besides—p^d there 1. 10. 6. To a small Paper Caravan for the above p^d 0. 1. 6. I went by myself and gave a Peep into St. Pauls Church this aft: To a

[1] Zoological gardens were as yet non-existent, and one went to the Tower to see the wild beasts, specially the lions. 'The lions of the Tower are the origin of that application of the term "lion" to any conspicuous spectacle or personage, which has long since become universal.' Lecky, *England in the Eighteenth Century*, vol. ii, p. 216.

Barber this Afternoon for shaving &c. gave 0. 1. 0.
For 2 inside Places in the Salisbury Coach p^d 2. 2. 0.
For 1 outside Place Do. p^d 0. 10. 6. Paid and gave at
the Bell Savage for all of us abt. 1. 15. 0. They were
very civil People at the Bell Savage Inn by name
Barton and a very good House it is. About 10 o'clock
at Night we set of in the Salisbury Coach from the
same Inn for Salisbury, and the Coach guarded. I
was bit terribly by the Buggs last Night, but did not
wake me.

JUNE 1. We travelled again all night long and I
thank God got safe and well to Salisbury between
2 and 3 o'clock in the Afternoon—The Coach was
full also. Gave the Coachman that drove us 0. 4. 0.
We breakfasted at Whitchurch for which I pd. 0. 2. 6.
Paid at Salisbury for extraordinary Luggage 0. 6. 6.
At Salisbury we made a running Dinner and between
3 and 4 in the Afternoon we got into a Post Chaise for
Hindon—and Will went on an hired Horse thither.
Pd. and gave at Salisbury for Chaise, Horse &c. abt.
1. 1. 0. We got to Hindon abt. 6 o'clock—then took a
fresh Chaise and set of for Stourton and Will on a
fresh Horse. Pd. and gave at Hindon for Chaise &c.
abt. 0. 12. 6. We got to Stourton abt. 8 o'clock, then
we took a fresh Chaise and set of for Cole—and Will
on a fresh Horse. Paid and gave at Stourton for
Chaise &c. abt. 0. 12. 6. We got to Cole about 10
o'clock and I thank God safe and well and found my
good Friends there all well—blessed be God for all
things—and accept my most sincere and unfeigned
thanks for thy great goodness to us in preserving us
from all the Dangers of so long a Journey that we have
taken. My good Friends were very happy to see us
and waiting impatiently for our arrival. Sister White

and her Daughter were at Cole expecting us and they supped and slept at Cole. Nancy, myself and Will all supped and slept at Cole. I was terribly swelled in the face and hands by the Buggs. Mr. Pounsett with my Sister and little Maid very glad to see us.

JUNE 18. I breakfasted, supped and slept again at Cole. Very violent Storm of Thunder and Lightning with heavy Rains about 10 o'clock this morning—but I thank God no Damage was done by it at Cole, and I hope no where else, either by Land or Water. The Thunder was the most rumbling I ever heard. About 1 o'clock Mr. and Mrs. Pounsett and self went to Ansford and dined and spent the Afternoon at James Clarkes, with him Mrs Richd Clarke, my Brother John his Wife and Nancy, Sister White, Brother Heighes and Mr Thomas. We had for Dinner, 3 Fowls boiled, a bit of Pork boiled, a Leg of Mutton boiled and Capers, a green Goose rosted and asparagus and a baked plumb Pudding. We spent a very merry day there—Brother Heighes's Dr [daughter] Juliana spent the Afternoon there with us. After Dinner Brother Heighes talked very angry to Nancy. We got home to Cole between 9 and 10 at Night and as we went—Jenny on Horseback and we on foot. We heard at Ansford that there were 3 Men struck down in Pilton Church by the Lightning this morning.[1] One of them killed instantly—but the others like to recover. The Man that was Struck dead was tolling a Bell for a Person lately dead, the other two were near him. Pray God have mercy on the poor Man.

JUNE 20. ... I took a Walk by Myself about Noon to Ansford and there dined and spent part of the After-

---

[1] Benjamin Franklin had invented the lightning-conductor in 1752, but evidently this church was not yet fitted with one.

noon at my Brother John's, with him, his Wife, Nancy and Mr Thomas. Mr Pounsett came to us in the Afternoon and then my Brother John, Mr Pounsett, Mr Thomas and self took a walk to Cary and drank Tea and smoked a Pipe at Mr. Thomas's. We had for Dinner to day at my Brother's a Leg of Lamb boiled and Spinnage, a couple of Fowls rosted and Asparagus and a nice Batter Pudding with Currant Jelly. Sister Pounsett and her little Maid went to Ansford in one of the Bruton Chaises (which I hired to bring back Nancy to Cole) this Afternoon and drank Tea at Mrs Whites. Mrs J^n Woodforde and Nancy met them at Mr Whites. We all returned to Cole about 9 o'clock at Night. Mr Pounsett and myself walked back again to Cole. Had a very long Letter whilst I was at my Brother Johns, from M^r Du Quesne dated the 18 Instant from Lambeth Palace— wherein he acquaints me that in Norfolk the 31 of May there happened at Weston and adjacent Villages a most terrible Tempest of Thunder, Lightning and Hail there which did great Damage to Mr Custances new House and likewise broke many of my Windows —The Corn in Weston Field almost all destroyed by the Hail which were as big as Bulletts and were 12 Inches deep in Weston Field—Thank God! no lives are said to be lost. Nancy supped and slept at Cole. My Letter from Du Quesne was franked by Mr. Townshend. Very sickly in London in the Influenza. Very few escape—Mr. Du Quesne has been confined to his Room in it—Mrs. Townshend was very dangerously ill in it. Called on old Mrs Penny, Mr Francis Senr, Dr Viggarr, old Mr Maby, John Burges, but he was not at home, and Sam Burge this Even'. We met Mrs Melliar and Sally Francis in a Chair as we were walking back to Cole and we had some Chat

together—Mrs Melliar asked me to her House very
genteely. J^s Clarke was with them—we met them
at Mr Thorntons at Honywicke. We did not go into
Mr Thorntons being late.

JULY 20. ... Mr. Thomas spent the Morning with us
Yesterday, he came to ask me to preach for him on
Sunday but I could not, as I brought no Sermon
with me—The last Time I was in the Country I had
some Sermons with me and was never asked to preach
therefore I thought it of no Use to bring any now.
Sister Pounsett rode to Ansford behind Ellis this
morning and there stayed and dined and spent the
Afternoon at Mr Whites.—Mr Pounsett rode in the
Evening to Ansford after her.—They did not return
home till near 10 at night—I went out in the Evening
afishing by myself and caught 1 Trout and 1 Eel.

The entries for nearly two months are now missing,
from August 6th to October 2nd, 1782. It seems
probable that the Diarist made the entries during
this period in some temporary booklet, as there is
no gap in the neat, numbered volumes—the present
volume ending on August 6th, and the next one
beginning on October 2nd. Sometime in the interval he returned to Weston, where we rejoin him.

OCT. 19. ... Busy in readg Evelina a Novel, lent
Nancy by Mrs. Custance—there are 3. Volumes of it
—wrote by a Miss Burney—they are very cleaver and
sensible.[1]

OCT. 24. ... Nancy came home about 12 o'clock and

---

[1] Miss Burney's (1752–1840) *Evelina* had appeared in January 1778,
and her *Cecilia* in the summer of 1782. Horace Walpole was naturally
at this moment criticizing *Cecilia*: it is equally natural that Parson
Woodforde in the country should only now be reading *Evelina*.

Mrs. Davy and another Lady (a Mrs. Church) with her. Mrs. Davy and the other Lady did not stay long —Nancy stayed and dined, supped and slept here. Mr. Hall, just returned from Andover in Hants, came here about Noon and he dined, supped and sat up all Night at my House, having no bed but mine which I offered to him, but he would not accept of it, therefore obliged me to sit up with him all Night. We had for Dinner a Piece of boiled Beef, some Herrings which Mrs. Davy brought here and a Couple of Ducks. Mr. Pyle dined with our Folks—his men at work here.

OCT. 25. I breakfasted, dined, supped and slept again at home. Hall went away about 10 o'clock. I was quite ill all day by setting up last night and will not do it again for any Hall in the Kingdom—He might have as well went to Lenewade and slept as he used to do—but he minds nothing but self and his Money. I slept about noon for 2 Hours and tolerably well. Nancy breakfasted, dined, &c. &c. again at home. Nancy sent a Letter this Evening to her Aunt Woodforde.

NOV. 9. . . . Mr. Smith of Mattishall made us a morning visit, but could not dine with us, his Rotation next Thursday, he very kindly invited Nancy. I offered to pay Mr. Smith this morning for his serving Weston for me in my late long absence but I could not prevail on him to accept of anything.

NOV. 16. . . . Had a Letter this Evening from my Sister Pounsett—all well. Another Letter came also for Nancy, and I believe from her B^r Sam. Cobb of Mattishall a Rat-Catcher and whom I formerly employed came to my House this morning by Order, and I engaged with him for to kill all my Rats at one

Guinea Per Annum and likewise to kill all my Mice. And the first Guinea is to be paid the first of Decem^br 1783—I gave him for Entrance Mony 11. 0. He is to come as often as there is Occasion for him—And is to be kept in Victuals and drink.

Nov. 20. ... Mr. Custance made me a Morning Visit, and desired that we would dine with him Monday next. Mrs. Custance soon after Mr. Custance was gone made me a Visit and stayed with me till near 2 o'clock. Very soon after Mrs. Custance was gone Mr. Howes with Mrs. Davy and Nancy came here and they stayed and dined and spent the afternoon with me—and Mr. Howes with Mrs. Davy prevailed on me after many Entreaties and at last with great reluctance on my Part, to let Nancy return with them to Hockering as they are going to Norwich to-Morrow, which I did, tho' much against me. Poor Mr. Howes and Mrs. Davy had set their hearts so much on it, that they were made very uneasy at my refusing them at first, and they almost cried and said that they would never be friendly with me if I did not admit of it. Mr. Howes said he would never enter my Doors more. The chief and principal Reason I gave, was, I did not approve or ever could that my Niece should make so free at Mr. Priest's—Mrs. Davy having sent a note this morning before they came here, that she with Nancy intended dining with them to Morrow at Norwich. It made me rather uneasy after they were gone back as I cannot by any means approve of it on any Account neither should I at last, unless to make old Mr. Howes easy. Mr. Custance told me this morning that he had a few Days ago about 80 Turkies, geese, Ducks, and Fowls stolen from [him] in one night—many of them that were fatting. This is the time of the year that many idle Fellows from Norwich go about the Country stealing Poultry to send them to London to make a Penny of them. I never had any stolen yet, but daily expect it. Burrows of Morton had but a few Days ago also taken from him Poultry to the Amount of 3 or 4 P^{ds} value. We had for Dinner to day one Fowl boiled and Piggs face, a Couple of Rabbitts smothered with Onions, a Piece of rost Beef and some Grape Tarts.

Nov. 30. .... Nancy had a brown Silk gown trimmed with Furr brought home this Evening by Cary from her Mantua Maker Miss Bell. It was a very good rich silk that I gave her which formerly belonged to my poor Aunt Parr, whose Effects came to me.

Dec. 3. .... This being the Day for my Tithe Auditt, the following Farmers paid me their Tithes, Girling, Peachman, Howlett, Rising, Forster, Herring, Dade, Mann, J$^{n}_{o}$ Pegg, Page, Andrews, Wm. Bidewell, Case, Ringgar, J$^{n}_{o}$ Pegg, Norton, Buck, Rush, Silvie, Cary, Burroughs, Baker, Thos. Leggatt, Wm. Leggatt, Rose Bean for the Widow Pratt, red^{d} in all to day 265. 3. 0. They all dined here, but J$^{n}_{o}$ Pegg and Mr. Mann and stayed till near 11 at night. Forster behaved so insolent towards me that I dont intend to have him ever again at my Frolick. Poor J$^{n}_{o}$ Buck broke one of my Decanters. I gave them for Dinner, some Salt Fish, a Leg of Mutton boiled and Capers, a Knuckle of Veal, a Piggs Face, a fine Surloin of Beef rosted, and plenty of plumb Puddings. J^{s} Smith, my Clerk, dined with our Folks in Kitchen. I dined with the Farmers in the great Parlour, Nancy dined by herself in the Study. Wine drank 6 Bottles. Rum drank 5 Bottles besides Quantities of strong Beer and Ale.

DEC. 24. ... To Widow Horner for Hulver [Holly] agains[t] Xmas Day gave 1. 0. The same as I used to give to her late Husband. Paid Will for things from Norwich &c. 0. 8. 7.

DEC. 25. ... This being Christmas Day I went to Church this Morn' and then read Prayers and administred the Holy Sacrament. Mr. and Mrs. Custance both at Church and both received the Sacrament from my Hands. The following poor old Men dined at my House to day, as usual, Js. Smith, Clerk, Richd Bates, Richd Buck; Thos. Cary; Thos. Dicker; Thos. Cushing; Thos. Carr—to each besides gave 1/0—in all 0. 7. 0. I gave them for Dinner a Surloin of Beef rosted and plenty of plumb-Pudding. We had mince Pies for the first Time to-day.

DEC. 26. ... To Weston Ringers gave this morning 0. 2. 6. To my Butchers Boy, Billy Stouton gave 0. 1. 0. To my Blacksmiths Boy, Charles Spaule gave 0. 1. 0. To my Malsters Man, J^s Barrett gave 0. 1. 0.

DEC. 27. ... About 12 went out a coursing, ran two good Courses and killed one of the Hares which Jack found sitting and for which I gave him as usual 0. 1. 0. My young Greyhound Hector performed incomparably.

1783

Jan. 4. . . . To poor old Joe Adcocks Wife who very lately fell down and broke her Thigh—sent her by Will o. 1. o.

Jan. 7. I breakfasted, and spent most of the Morn' at home. Nancy breakfasted, and spent part of the Morn' at home. Betsy Davy breakfasted, and spent part of the Morn' here. Mrs. Davy breakfasted with us this morning. As soon as the Ladies had breakfasted, they set of for Norwich and Nancy with them. I stayed till near 12 before I set forth for Norwich and my Servant Will: went with me—We all went by appointment to Mr. Priests and there dined, supped and spent the Evening. Mrs. Davy and Nancy slept at Mr. Priests. I slept at my old Inn the Kings Head. Mr. Du Quesne dined, supped and slept at Mr. Priests. We had for Dinner some fresh Salmon and Oyster Sauce, a boiled Turkey and Oyster Sauce, a fore Qr. of London Lamb, mince Pyes, &c. Mrs. Cooper, Miss Blomfield, Mr. and Mrs. Fearman, Mr. Reeves, Mr. Starkey, and Mr. Mully drank Tea this Afternoon with us at Mr. Priests and all stayed to Supper but Mrs. Cooper and Miss Blomfield. After Tea we had a vocal and instrumental Concert— Nancy sung. Mr. Du Quesne, Mr. Reeves, Mr. Starkey and Mr. John Priest played on their violins. Mr. Fearman on the Base-Viol and Mr. Mulley on the Organ—a very good Concert. We did not sup till near 10 at night—and then we had a very handsome supper—A Couple of boiled Fowls and Oyster Sauce, a rosted Hare wch I sent them—one Duck rosted, a hot Tongue, Tarts, Italian Flummery— Blamanche black Caps and sweet-Meats. I did not

get to bed till after 12 to-night. Gave Mr. Priests
Maid coming away 0. 1. 0. Sent Dr. Bathurst a
Letter to day and in it Bills to the amount of forty
Pounds.

JAN. 11. ... But very poorly all day—no Appetite at
all. Expected much a Letter from my Sister Pounsett
this Even' but had none—It was a great disappointment to me.

JAN. 13. ... This Evening paid all my Servants their
Years Wages—due January 6, 1783.

To my Head Maid, Betty Claxton p^d			5.	15.	6
„ „ Lower „ Lizzy Greaves p^d .			2.	0.	6
„ „ Man Will: Coleman p^d .		.	4.	4.	0
To Ditto for Grains p^d .	.	.		17.	0
To Ditto for dressing my Wiggs p^d	.			10.	0
To Ditto what he owed me I gave	.	1.	1.	0
To my Farming Man Ben Leggatt p^d.	10.	0.	0
To my Boy, Jack Warton	.	.		10.	6
Gave to him besides as a free gift	.			2.	6

JAN. 24. ... Nancy was low at Dinner owing to me
—Was sorry for it.

JAN. 25. ... This Evening the Ipswich News brought
us the joyful News of Peace being signed at Versailles
the 20 of this month and recd. at London the 25.
No mention of the same in either of the Norwich
Papers. The above Peace is with America, France and
Spain, but not with the Dutch—Tho' daily expected
by them.[1]

[1] The provisional articles of peace between England, France, and
Spain were signed on 20 January 1783, the similar articles with the
United States having been signed on 30 November 1782. The preliminary treaty of peace between Great Britain and Holland was not signed
till 2 September 1783, but long before this a truce had put an end to

JAN. 26. . . . Thos. Carr dined with our Folks to day. I read Prayers and Preached this Afternoon at Weston. Mr. Custance and a Mrs. Collier, an elderly Lady, at Church. Sent old Mary Adcock at Noon—a hot rosted Fowl, a fourpenny Loaf and a Bottle of Beer.

FEB. 5. . . . To a poor old Man with a Dulcimer gave 0. 0. 6.

FEB. 7. . . . Sent a very long Letter to my Sister Pounsett. Very wet Season indeed, every Day Rain, my Garden almost covered with Water—every Ditch brim full.

FEB. 10. . . . To Ben this Evening for a Horse which he bought this morning for me of John Norton, a short dark Punchy Horse with a Hog main and dock'd Tail aged 10 Years next Midsummer, and one that bears a very good Character in the draft Way and one that is very hardy and always kept so p^d Ben 4. 4. 0.

FEB. 11. . . . Mrs. Custance with her 3 little Boys and Hetty Yollop their Nurse made us an early morning visit and stayed with us till after 12 o'clock.

MARCH 5. . . . Much colder than yesterday—Wind much higher and Frost more severe—The coldest Day for some years. I was very low and indifferent all day long. The Barometer very low, and the Wind

hostilities between English and Dutch. Thanks to Lord Rodney's victory, to differences between the Americans and the French, to the skilful diplomacy of the Prime Minister, Lord Shelburne, in London, and of his representative in Paris—Mr. Alleyne FitzHerbert (afterwards Lord St. Helens)—the peace was better than it might have been. We lost America and Minorca; we gave up Florida; we restored various conquests in Africa to France, and in India to France and the Dutch. On the other hand, we recovered six West Indian islands, and we retained Canada and Gibraltar—both, at one time during the negotiations, in jeopardy.

being very rough when I went up to my Chamber to go to bed, being not the lest sleepy, I lighted my Fire, and sat down and read the Life of Lewis 14 of France till after 2 o'clock in the morning and then went to bed, the Wind still high. I heard some Noise between one and two but it did [not] last.

MARCH 6. . . . The first thing I was informed of when I came down stairs, was, that my Stable had been broken up, in the Night and that there was stolen out of it, a Hatchet, a Hook, a Bridle, and a pair of hedging Gloves of Bens. There was seen Yesterday a Couple of idle Fellows passing and re-passing my House, I saw them once go by, one of them was in a long blue Coat, the other in a brown one. They came in at the back Window of the Stable, which they cut away, to wrench it open with a large stick wch was found just by, they left behind them a P^r of Sheep Sheers broke directly in the middle— They also took Bens Cart Whip, which they left on the Muck-heap. I think myself well of, in having so few things stolen as there were so many in the Stable and in the Corn Room. I sent for Harry Dunnell to mend the Window and to John Spaule to make some new iron work for the same, all which were done by the Evening and all right again. Harry Dunnell dined with our Folks and for his work to day I gave him 0. 1. 0. There were several Stables in the Parish broke into besides mine last night, Peachmans, Bucks, Widow Pratts, Manns and Forsters—and several things stolen. Nancy was very much alarmed on hearing the above. I did not go to bed to Night till after 12 o'clock.

MAR: 8. . . . To a poor Boy by Name Allison of Lyng, turned out of doors by his Parents as he says—

gave this Even' 0. 0. 6. A change of the Ministry will soon take place as mentioned on the Papers—Ld North and Charles Fox have shook hands—O North, how low art thou fallen.

MAR: 23. . . . I read Prayers and Preached this Afternoon at Weston. I buried this Evening at Weston poor old Thos Reeves commonly called Dr Reeves— aged 71 years. Mrs. Davy came here about 7 in the Evening in Mr Howes's Chaise and she supped and slept here as did the Driver and the Horses—She came here by appointment this Evening to carry Nancy with her to Norwich early in the Morning to see the Grand Procession of Bishop Blaize &c. It was very kind of her indeed. No Person besides ever gave her the most distant offer. And if Mrs Davy had not been so kind, she could not have gone, as I could not by myself have made it agreeable to Nancy without some Lady being with her.

MAR: 24. . . . About 6 o'clock this Morning we all got up to go to Norwich and after breakfast we set forth at 8 o'clock, Mrs Davy and Nancy in the Chaise, myself on Horseback, Will, Ben and Lizzy on horse-back, Jack went behind the Chaise as I was willing that all sh^d go that could. Betty, my Upper Maid stayed at home being Washing Week. We all got to Norwich about 10 o'clock—The Road we went was filled with People on Horseback and foot, going to see the fine Sight—Ben carried Lizzy behind him on Phyllis and the first Time she ever carried any one, double, and she carried her very well and safe, to Norwich and back again. I put up my Horses at the Kings Head—Mrs Davy and Nancy were at Mr Priests. The grand Procession began about 11 o'clock this morning—I saw them first beyond Black Friars

Bridge near St. Saviours Church and a very pretty
and grand Sight it was. The Order of the Procession
was as follows.

Four Trumpeters
Marshal-Man
Peace
Orator
Banner of Brittania
Plenty
Drums and Fifes
20 Argonauts
Hercules

Lynceus {	The Golden Fleece borne on a grand Palanquin by four Men	} Tiphy[s] Calais
Zetes {		
Castor {	Jason drawn in a Phaeton by four Horses	} Pollux

Standard of the Argonauts
20 Argonauts
Militia Band
Standard of the City
Two Vergers
Orator

{	Bishop's Chaplain in a Phaeton and Pair }

{	Bishop Blaize in a Phaeton drawn by 6 Horses }

Standard of the City

The book-keepers, Shepherds and Shepherdesses belonging to the different Societies of Combers 12
Companies—Seven Companies on foot—Five Companies on Horseback.

Mr. and Mrs. Custance, Sr Edmund Bacon and
Lady at the Kings Head, I called on them about

11 o'clock, and gave them an Account of the grand
Sight and left with them a Paper of the Procession.
I never saw so great a Multitude of People in my Life
collected together, the Market-Place was as full as it
could be, both in the area, at the Windows and on the
Tops of the Houses—and every Street besides full of
People from all Parts of the County. The Procession
proceeded thro' every principal Street of the City and
it lasted till 4 in the Afternoon. We eat some cold
Ham and Veal at Mr Priests about 2. A Mrs Goddard
an old Maid, Du Quesne's Maid Betty and a Miss
High with her in Du Quesne's Chaise were at Mr.
Priests, as was Miss Priest of Reepham. About ½ past
4 we all set forth for Weston and got home about
7 o'clock, rather fatigued. Mem: Just without the
Gates Mr Howes's Chaise broke down, one of the
Axle-Trees being broke, which my Servant Boy Jack,
behind the Chaise, found out—but luckily for it we
were near Mr Howes's Coach Maker, a Mr Baldwin,
who lent them a carriage leaving the old Shatterdan
behind to be mended. Paid and gave to day at Norwich abt. 2. 6. We were all highly delighted indeed
with this Days Sight—it far exceeded every Idea I c^d
have of it. Hercules, Jason, and Bishop Blaize, were
exceedingly well kept up and very superbly dressed.
All the Combers were in white ruffled Shirts with
Cross-Belts of Wool of divers Colours—with Mitred
Caps on their heads—The Shepherds and Shepherdesses were little Boys and Girls on horseback, very
handsomely and [with] great Propriety dressed.
Orations spoke in most of the principal Streets. I
never saw a Procession so grand and well conducted.[1]

---

[1] This grand procession was a combined celebration of the conclusion
of peace, and of the patron saint of the Norwich woollen trade—
Bishop Blaise. The legend of Bishop Blaise is this. He was Bishop of
Sebaste in Armenia, and perished sometime between A.D. 289 and

April 10 ... Mr Howes was this Day married to his 4th Wife, a Mrs Brown.

April 11. ... Mrs. Davy sent us some bride-Cake this morning from Hockering and with a Note to Nancy.

April 14. ... Mrs. Davy drank Tea this Afternoon with us, and about 7 o'clock in the Evening returned to Hockering and Nancy went with her to spend a day or 2 there.

April 30. ... About 1 o'clock took a ride to Mr Smiths at Mattishall and there dined and spent the Afternoon, it being his Rotation Day, with him, Mr. and Mrs Bodham, Miss Bodham, a Miss Kitty John-

316 in one of the persecutions of the Christians. He had fled to a cave. There he was fed by the birds whom he healed of any illness, and was adored by all the wild beasts, lions and tigers, who always waited quietly till the saint had finished his devotions before asking his benediction. Soon he was dragged from his cave by the persecutors. On his way to his trial he performed two miracles. He extracted a fishbone from the throat of a child who was choking to death, and he caused a wolf to restore a poor woman's only pig. He perished after frightful tortures, among them his flesh being torn with iron combs, 'such as are used to card wool'. He became one of the 'Fourteen Holy Helpers' invoked by the faithful—his feast day was 3 February—and enjoyed a remarkable popularity in the Middle Ages in England, France, Germany, and Italy. He was the patron saint of woolcombers, whether at Norwich, at Paris, or at Rome, and he was invoked for all ailments of the throat. (See the detailed and charming account of Bishop Blaise by Miss Ella B. Edes in the *Dublin Review*, 1889, vol. xxii, pp. 340–6.)

The other characters in the grand procession—Jason, Hercules, Castor and Pollux, Lynceus, Zetes, Tiphys, Calais—are there because they went in search of the Golden Fleece together with the other Argonauts. Time was when Norwich streets had been gay on various festivals with the procession of twenty companies of different crafts with patron saints, banners and beauty. Bishop Blaise of the woolcombers, who so delighted Parson Woodforde, alone enjoyed this resurrection of medieval glory, sharing it with the wistful return of Peace. (Blomefield, *History of Norfolk*, vol. iii, p. 206, contains a list of the twenty city companies.)

son, Niece of Mrs Bodham's, Mr. and Mrs. Howes, and M^r Du Quesne.—Mrs. Davy not there but at Dereham, on account of a little Miff between her and Mr Smith—but what, we know not. We had for Dinner a Leg of Lam[b] boiled, a Piece of rosted Beef, a baked plumb Pudding, some Crabbs, Tarts, Rasberry Creams, and hung Beef, grated. I called on Dr Thorne before Dinner, saw his Wife, Garden and House—all very neat indeed but small. At Quadrille this Evening won 0. 4. 0. I played the finest Sans Prendre Vole to Night, that I ever had—Not a loosing Card in hand—It was Mattadores, 9 black Trumps in Spades and the King of Hearts—I was the last Player; after the first Card was played, I declared the Vole. I did not get home to Weston till 10 at Night.

MAY 1. ... The 2 Fellows who were suspected breaking open my Stable and many others, were tried this Day at the Sessions at Norwich and convicted of the Robbery of stealing a Sack from Mr Howlett and are to remain in Prison for three years—which I hope will do good.

MAY 6. ... To a Man who comes from Windham and carries about stuffs for Gowns &c. for 27 yards and half at 9^d per yard p^d 1. 0. 6. Gave both my Maids a Gown apiece of it and of the same Colour, something of the Pea Green. Gave Nancy also, to make a Skirt for her of a light blue 6 y^ds. Nancy much better to day tho' not quite well yet. Cobb the Rat-Catcher dined with our Folks to day. We caught and killed about 3 Dozen of Rats in the Barn before Dinner to day—3 old female Rats with their young ones—2 old dog Rats and some half grown.

MAY 15. ... At half past 6 this morning took a black

Dose of Physic in bed, then laid down till half past 7 then got up and came down to breakfast. I had a very disagreeable Night of rest, sweated a vast deal and started much in my Sleep, being in the Horrors. Mrs Custance made us a long morning Visit till after one o'clock—during the Time that Mrs Custance was here Mrs Davy from Hockering came here, having been sent for by me to spend a few Days with Nancy, and she dined supped and slept here with Nancy. Soon after Mrs Custance left us, Dr Thorne came here and stay'd abt an Hour. In the Afternoon Mr and Mrs Custance with their eldest Son Hamilton, came here, and drank Tea and stayed till 8 in the Evening with us—We dine with them Saturday. I was brave (thank God) this Evening—my Physic having oper-ated very well—Altho' hurried so much to day. I began taking going to bed some Camphire and Nitre Powders.

MAY 26. . . . I buried poor Joe Adcocks Wife this Evening aged 43. Pray God comfort the poor Man in his distress, he having buried, his Father and Mother and Wife within 6 Weeks.

JUNE 1. . . . Three of Mr Custances Servant Maids drank Tea with our Maids this Afternoon.

JUNE 5. [He had gone to Norwich the day before.] I breakfasted at the Kings Head—and after being shaved I walked to Mr Francis's—then to Priests to taste some Port Wine and there bespoke a Qr of a Pipe. Called at Beales in the Fish Markett and bought 3 Pairs of fine Soals—2 Crabbs—and a Lobster—Pd him for the above and for some Fish I had before of him 0. 8. 4. About 11 o'clock sent Will home with the Fish to have for Dinner as I have Company to dine

with me to-day. At Mr Bakers for a P^r of large
Scissars to trim Horses p^d 1. 6. At Dittos—for 2 P^d of
Pinns for Nancy and Mrs Davy p^d 4. 8. Called at
Buckles and bespoke a large Lock for my Back-Door.
At Quantrells Gardens for a Glass of Gin and Water
p^d 0. 3. Paid and gave at the Kings Head 0. 8. 9.
Called on my Sadler Allum and bespoke a Pillion for
Nancy. Called on my Upholsterer Horth and bespoke
a Bolster Tick and some Paper to paper one of my
Garretts. Gave my Barber—Milsham—this morning
0. 1. 0. About 1 o'clock I mounted my Mare and set
of for Weston and did not get home till near 4 o'clock
on Account of my poor Mare, she having filled herself
so much on dry Meat last Night—I was afraid that
she would have dropped on the road as she puffed and
blowed so terribly—I walked her most part of the
way—and I got of and walked many Times—It
vexed and fretted me much on Account of having
Company to Dinner.—It was also very hot and was
obliged to wear my great Coat, the Pockets of which
also were loaded with 2 Pounds of Pins &c., however
I did get home at last as did my Mare—And I found
Mr Smith and Mr Baldwin with my Ladies at home.
I was pretty much fatigued with the Heat and fretting.
Mr Smith and Mr Baldwin dined and spent the
Afternoon and part of the Evening with us till 9 at
Night. Nancy and Mrs Davy dined, breakfasted,
supped &c. again here. We had for Dinner 3 P^r of
fine Soals—a Leg of Mutton rosted, and some Goose-
berry Tarts. After Tea we got to Cards, at Loo, at
which I won 4. 0. I dined, supped and slept at home.

JUNE 13. . . . Mr. Custance's 3 little Boys with 2
'Nurse' Maids came here this Afternoon and stayed
here till 8 at night. I gave the little Boys for their

Supper some Strawberries and milk with which they were highly delighted. They came here on foot but went back in the Coach. Mrs. Alldis the House-keeper called here in the Afternoon and she drank Tea with the Nurse Maids and ours in Kitchen.

JUNE 16. . . . I walked to Forsters this morning between 11 and 12 and read Prayers and admini-stered the H. Sacrament to Mrs. Forster who is some-thing better to day—Her Mother was with her and received the Sacrament also with her. After I came down Stairs from Mrs. Forster I saw Forster and Herring of Ringland—Mr. Forster was very sorry for what he had said and if I would forgive him, he w^d beg my Pardon—which I did and he promised never to affront me more—so that all matters are made up.[1] To Mr. Cary for things from Norwich &c. pd. o. 6. 8. Of Ditto—for 7 Pints of Butter at 7^d rec^d o. 4. 1. To Goody Doughty for 3 Lemons p^d o. o. 6. I privately baptised a Child of Billy Bidewells this morning at my House—by name William. Mr. Custance sent us some beans and a Colliflower this Even'.

JUNE 25. . . . Very uncommon Lazy and hot Weather. The Sun very red at setting. To a poor old crazy Woman this morn' gave o. o. 6. Nancy and myself dined and spent part of the afternoon at Weston House with Mr. and Mrs. Custance—Mr. Rawlins dined also with us—whilst we were at Dinner Mrs. Custance was obliged to go from Table about 4 o'clock labour Pains coming on fast upon her. We went home soon after dinner on the Occasion—as we came in the Coach. We had for Dinner some Beans and Bacon, a Chine of Mutton rosted, Giblett Pye,

---

[1] It will be remembered that Forster had been excessively insolent to the diarist at the latter's frolic on 3 December 1782.

Hashed Goose, a Rabbit rosted and some young Peas,—Tarts, Pudding and Jellies. We got home between 5 and 6 o'clock. After Supper we sent up to Mr. Custances to enquire after Mrs. Custance who was brought to bed of a fine girl about 7 o'clock and as well as could be expected.

JUNE 27. . . . After breakfast Nancy and self dressed ourselves and walked to Hungate Lodge to make the first visit to Mr. and Mrs. Micklewaite who were both at home and appear to be tolerable agreeable People —He is very young. She is much older and appears rather high. We stayed about half an Hour with them and then returned.

JUNE 30. . . . I privately named a Child this morning of Dinah Bushell's by name Keziah One of Job's Daughters Names.[1] To Mr. Cary for things from Norwich &c. pd. o. 11. 1. Of Ditto for 6 Pints of Butter recd. o. 3. 6. To Betty for things pd. o. 1. o. I privately named a Child of Brands of East Tuddenham, by name—John—this Afternoon—Mr. Love the Painter dined with our Folks in Kitchen. He brought me the new Register from Mr. Whistlers wch. I sent by him to have Mr. Custances Name in gold letters.

JULY 15. . . . Nancy got up very Early this morning and rode behind Ben to Mr. Bodhams at South Green, she got there before they were down Stairs.

[1] 'So the Lord blessed the latter end of Job more than the beginning: for he had fourteen thousand sheep, and six thousand camels, and a thousand yoke of oxen, and a thousand she asses. He had also seven sons and three daughters. And he called the name of the first, Jemima; and the name of the second, Kezia; and the name of the third, Kerenhappuch. And in all the land were no women found so fair as the daughters of Job: and their father gave them inheritance among their brethren' (Job, chap. 42, vv. 12–15).

She went away before breakfast, and before I was up. At one o'clock I took a ride to Mattishall to Mr. Smiths it being his Rotation Day and there dined and spent the Afternoon with him, Mr. and Mrs. Bodham, Mr. Ashull, Mrs. Davy and Nancy. Mr. and Mrs. Howes not there which I think very rude, as they promised, and their going this day to Shipdam but I apprehend they intend dropping the Rotations which for my Part I am not sorry for, as Mrs. Davy is soon going to board at Mattishall in the Parsonage House. We had for Dinner 3 boiled Chicken, a Tongue, some Peas, a piece of rost Beef, Cherry Pudding and Cheese Cake. At Quadrille this Evening lost o. o. 6. Between 8 and 9 this Evening Nancy and self sat of on Horseback for home and got there I thank God safe and well before 10 o'clock—Nancy but little tired.

JULY 28. . . . This has been the hottest day this year, and I believe the hottest that ever I felt, many say the same. We fully expected a Tempest to day, but thank God had none.

JULY 29. I breakfasted, supped and slept again at home. Nancy got up very early this morning and went behind Ben to Mattishall to Mr. Bodhams being his Club Day and there she breakfasted and spent the Afternoon and in the Evening returned as she went, to Weston, where she supped and slept again at home. Mr. Custance sent us a Note this morning to invite us to Dinner on Tuesday next to meet Mr. and Mrs. Micklewaite. About 1 o'clock I took a ride to Mattishall to Mr. Bodhams and there dined and spent the Afternoon with him, Mrs. Bodham, Mr. and Mrs. Ball of Catfield, Sister to Mrs. Bodham, Mrs. Davy, Mr. Smith, Mr. and Mrs. Howes, Mr. Ashull and Nancy.—We had for Dinner a Piece of boiled Beef, some Beans and Bacon, a couple of Ducks rosted, a Veal Pye and some Apricot Dumplins. At Quadrille this Evening won 0. 2. 0. As we were coming away Mrs. Howes came to me and asked me to their House it being their Rotation next, but I entirely refused to go, as they had not only kept away from mine very lately, but would not let Miss Howes come who was very desirous of coming to Weston. I gave it to her, and most of the Company seemed pleased with my behaviour. We did not get home till after 9 in the Evening. Nancy was obliged to change Horses, the flies teazing Phyllis very much which made her kick a little.

Aug. 5. ... Nancy and self dined and spent the afternoon at Weston House with Mr. and Mrs. Custance, Sr Thomas Beauchamp and Lady,[1] and Mr. and Mrs. Micklethwaite. They sent their Coach after us and we returned home in it. We had for Dinner some fresh Water Fish, Perch and Trout, a Saddle of Mutton rosted, Beans and Bacon, a Couple of Fowls boiled, Patties and some white Soup—2nd Course— Pigeons rosted, a Duck rosted, Piggs Pettytoes— Sweetbreads—Rasberry Cream, Tarts and Pudding and Pippins. After Tea, Lady Beauchamp and self played a Rubber of Whist against Mr. Custance and Mrs. Micklethwaite and we came of Conquerors and Winners—each won 0. 4. 0. We spent a very agreeable Day and got home by abt. 9 o'clock. Mrs Micklethwaite was very stately and reserved. Mrs. C. does not much admire her I believe.

[1] Sir Thomas Beauchamp-Proctor (1736–1827) was Mrs. Custance's brother, and succeeded his father in the baronetcy September 13, 1773. He lived at Langley Park, near Norwich, and was sheriff of the county in 1780–1. He married on May 5, 1778, Mary, second daughter of Robert Palmer, of Sonning, Berks.

AUG. 14. ... I sent Will: early this morning to Hockering, after Mrs. Davy who returned here to breakfast, and she dined, supped and slept here with Nancy. My Maid Lizzy very ill today, worse than ever, and kept her Bed most part of the Day. Dr. Thorne came here whilst we were at Dinner, and he dined with us but obliged to leave us immediately after Dinner, having a great many Patients to visit. He ordered that Lizzy should begin to take the Bark[1] immediately as the fever was abated, and which I sent for to his House this Evening. She begun taking the Bark at 10. this Night and is to take it every two Hours till she has taken a Dozen Papers. If it purges her she is to have 4 Drops of Laudanum in her Bark when she takes it then 3 Drops—then 2. then 1 Drop which will take of the purging. Betty is to set up till 4. in the morning to give her the Bark and then Will: as he brews to Morrow, will give it her. We had for Dinner to day a boiled Leg of Mutton and Capers, a Duck rosted and one of Nancy's Pudding with Jelly.

AUG. 28. I breakfasted, supped and slept again at home. Nancy breakfasted, supped and slept again at home. Lizzy's Mother breakfasted, dined and spent the Afternoon here and in the Evening returned to her home. My sick Servants but indifferent again to day. About 2. o'clock Mr. and Mrs. Custance called here by appointment and took Nancy and self with them in their Coach to Mr. Townshends at Honingham where we dined and spent the After-

---

[1] The use of Peruvian bark (i.e. quinine) in medicine was greatly extended by that eminent physician, botanist, collector of manuscripts and *objets d'art*, and godfather of London streets, Sir Hans Sloane (1660–1753). Sir Hans Sloane succeeded Sir Isaac Newton as President of the Royal Society in 1727.

noon with Mr. and Mrs. Townshend, Mrs. Cornwallis,[1] Widow of the late Arch-Bishop of Canterbury's and who is also Sister to Mr. Townshend, Mr. and Mrs. Custance, and Mr. Du Quesne—The latter of whom we were glad to see, as it was so long since we saw him. Mr. and Mrs. Townshend behaved very genteel to us. The drawing Room in which we drank Tea &c. was hung with Silk. The Chairs of the same kind of Silk and all the woodwork of them gilded, as were the Settee's. The looking glass which was the finest and largest I ever saw, cost at secondhand 150. 0. 0. The Height of the Plate was seven feet and half, and the breadth of it was five feet and half, one single Plate of glass only. The frame and Ornaments to it, was carved and gilded and very handsome. There was two Courses at Dinner besides the Desert. Each course nine Dishes, but most of the things spoiled by being so frenchified in dressing. I dined on some fryed Soals, some stewed Beef with Caper Sauce and some Hare rosted, but very insipid. After Coffee and Tea we got to Cards to Loo at which I had the good Luck to win abt. 0. 1. 0. Mrs. Cornwallis and Nancy did not play Cards with us but with the Children, Miss Caroline and Miss Amelia Townshend, about 3. or 4. years old. Nancy sung one Song, then Mr. and Mrs. Custance, Nancy and self came away about half past seven o'clock, we got home about 8 o'clock. To Page's Harvest Men gave a Largess of 0. 1. 0.

Aug. 31. ... My Man Will went to bed this Evening bad. Lizzy very poorly—Jack still continues mending.

---

[1] I find the following amusing reference to Mrs. Cornwallis in a letter of Horace Walpole's to the Countess of Upper Ossory, dated December 18, 1781: 'I was diverted last night at Lady Lucan's. The moment I entered, she set me down to whist with Lady Bute—and who do you think were the other partners? The Archbishopess of Canterbury and Mr. Gibbon.'

SEP. 2. . . . After breakfast Nancy and myself took a ride to Du Quesnes and from thence to Mr. Bodhams at Mattishall where we dined and spent the Afternoon with him, Mrs. Bodham and Miss Bodham. We had for Dinner a Leg of Mutton boiled and a Couple of Ducks rosted and Apple Tarts. We returned home by 8. in the Evening. Will: very bad all the time he was out to day. Ben also complained this Evening—Jack also bad to-day. Almost all the House ill in the present Disorder and which is called the Whirligigousticon[1] by the faculty. It is almost in every House in every Village. Mr. and Mrs. Bodham have had it and not well yet. The popping of guns about to Day frightned my Mare. To Turnpike to day p^d 0. 0. 2. Gave to Children besides 0. 0. 3. Mr. Smith was at Mr. Bodhams before dinner, but could not stay and dine with us.

SEP. 4. I breakfasted, supped and slept again at home. Nancy breakfasted, dined, &c. &c. again at home. To Largesses to day gave 0. 2. 0. About 1. o'clock Mr. and Mrs. Custance called here in their Coach and took me with them to Norwich to dine with the Bishop. I was dressed in a Gown and Cassock and Scarf. We got there to the Palace abt. 3. o'clock, and there dined and spent the Afternoon with his Lordship Dr. Bagot, and his Lady Mrs. Bagot, whose Name before Marriage was Miss Hay, the two Miss Hay's her Sisters, two Mr. Hay's her Brothers, a Mr. Gooch the Bishop's Chaplain, Dr. Brook of Yarmouth, Mr. Buxton of Easton, and his Nephew the Revd. Mr. Buxton, Mr. Du Quesne,

---

[1] The 'Disorder' in fact appears to have been a bad local outburst of malaria; see the entry for March 13th, 1784, where it is referred to as the ague, and where a detailed account of Dr. Thorne's method of treatment is given.

Mr. Priest of Reepham, and 5 strange Clergymen.
There were 20 of us at the Table and a very elegant
Dinner the Bishop gave us. We had 2 Courses of 20
Dishes each Course, and a Desert after of 20 Dishes.
Madeira, red and white Wines. The first Course
amongst many other things were 2 Dishes of prodigious
fine stewed Carp and Tench, and a fine Haunch of
Venison. Amongst the second Course a fine Turkey
Poult, Partridges, Pidgeons and Sweatmeats. Desert
—amongst other things, Mulberries, Melon, Currants,
Peaches, Nectarines and Grapes. A most beautiful
Artificial Garden in the Center of the Table remained
at Dinner and afterwards, it was one of the prettiest
things I ever saw, about a Yard long, and about
18 Inches wide, in the middle of which was a high
round Temple supported on round Pillars, the Pillars
were wreathed round with artificial Flowers—on one
side was a Shepherdess on the other a Shepherd,
several handsome Urns decorated with artificial
Flowers also &c. &c. The Bishop behaved with great
affability towards me as I remembered him at Christ
Church in Oxford. He was also very affable and
polite to all the Clergy present. Mr. and Mrs.
Custance were exceedingly pleased, with both Bishop
and Mrs. Bagot, as seemed everybody else.[1] About
half past 6. o'clock we all withdrew from the dining
Room to the Library or Drawing Room, where we
had Tea and Coffee brought round to each of us.

[1] Dr. Lewis Bagot (1741–1802) was the seventh son of Sir Walter
Bagot, and was educated at Westminster and Christ Church, Oxford,
of which he became successively Canon and Dean. He was made
Bishop of Bristol on February 23rd, 1782, and translated to Norwich in
1783. In 1790 he was again translated to St. Asaph. His wife was a
niece of the Earl of Kinnoul, and sister of Dr. Hay of Christ Church.
'Amiable, gentle, benevolent, humble and laborious'—such are the
pleasing epithets applied to Bishop Bagot in the *D.N.B.* His portrait
by Hoppner is in the Hall of Christ Church.

There was a strange Lady that came to Tea with us. Abt. half past 7 Mr. and Mrs. Custance and self took our Leave as did the rest of the Company, we got home between 9 and 10. It lightned a good deal as we came home. Mr. Custance would carry me quite to the Parsonage as we returned home, tho' I desired him to put me down at the Church. I was exceedingly pleased with this Days excursion. Nancy rec^d a long Letter from her Brother William dated the 29 June from Staten Island in North America brought by Mr. Custance's Servant from Norwich this Evening. The Letter came to 0. 2. 4. He is very well and has escaped many Dangers in America. He sent inclosed in his Letter some Continental Money Paper valued there at 10 Shillings and which he desired to be given to me.

Oct. 6. ... My Folks continue better, thank God for it. I rode down to Mr. Howletts this morning and christned a Child of his, born last Night, by name William—and it being the first Child that I have christned since the Act[1] took place concerning the Duty to be raised on Christnings Burials and Marriages, and therefore recd. the Duty of 0. 0. 3. I called at Weston House on my Return and spent an Hour with Mrs. Custance—Mr. Custance was not at home.

Oct. 11. ... Mr. Custance made us a morning Visit and invited us to dine with some Company at Weston House on Monday. Recd. a disagreeable

---

[1] This Act was passed by the Coalition Government of 1783, and entitled, 'An Act for granting to His Majesty a Stamp-duty on the Registry of Burials, Marriages, Births, and Christenings'. A sum of 3*d.* had to be paid in respect of each entry in the register, the Parson being authorized to demand and receive the said sum. It was one of the new taxes to meet the burden of the American War. It was repealed by Pitt in 1794, as it 'was acknowledged to have an injurious operation as regards the morals of the people'.

Letter this Evening from my Brother Heighes concerning his being distressed for Cash.

OCT. 12. . . . Had another disagreeable Letter this morning from the Bishop's Register to preach at the Cathedral of Norwich on the Sunday Morn' Feb: 8 next. I read Prayers and Preached this Aft: at Weston Church. Neither Mr. or Mrs. Custance at Church.

OCT. 24. [He had gone to Norwich the previous evening.] I breakfasted, supped and slept again at the Kings Head. After breakfast I dressed myself in my best Coat and Waistcoat and then walked down in my Boots to the Bishops Palace and had a long Conversation with the Bishop abt. many things—but what I went to his Lordship chiefly on, was my being appointed on the Combination List to preach at the Cathedral the 8. of February next, when my Name had been inserted but a few Years back. To which his Lordship replied, that as I did not then preach in propria Persona was one Reason, and the Second was that he was willing that the Pulpit at the Cathedral should be filled properly by able and beneficed Clergy, and that it was rather a Compliment conferred by him on those that he so appointed. From the Palace walked to Mr. Morpheus and stayed with him near an Hour—from thence went to Mrs. Brewsters and bought some Needles for Nancy pd. 0. 1. 0. Gave my Barber this morning for shaving me 0. 1. 0. About 2 o'clock went to Mr. Priests and there dined and spent the Afternoon with him, his Wife and Son J$_o^n$. We had for Dinner a boiled Neck of Mutton and a brace of Partridges and some Tarts. After Dinner a Mrs. Barker a beautiful Woman whose Maiden name was Quarles made a Visit to Mrs. Priest. There is one more Sister of hers unmarried and also very hand-

some. Pd. Mr. Priest this Afternoon for 2 oz: Rhubarb
0. 5. 0. To Do. for a Q^r of a Pd. of Magnesia pd.
0. 1. 4. To Do. for a Q^r of a Pd. of Cream of Tartar
pd. 0. 0. 3. Abt. 4 this Afternoon left Mr. Priests and
went to one Studwell China Man in the Market Place
and bought 2 China Pint Basons, and half a Doz. half
Pint Tumblers, half a doz. upright Beer Glasses and a
black Tea Pot pd. 0. 13. 6. To my Fishmonger,
Beale, for Fish sometime back pd. 0. 4. 6. To divers
other things this Evening 0. 1. 0.

OCT. 26. ... I got up this Morn' exceedingly out of
Humour and continued so till Dinner. I was very
sorry for it. I read Prayers and Preached this Afternoon at Weston. Mr. and Mrs. Custance, Mrs. Davy
and Nancy at Church. We did not dine till after
4 o'clock this Afternoon.

OCT. 30. ... Ben busy in plowing for Wheat as it is
to be set.

NOV. 7. ... Mr. Custance made me a long morning
Visit and offered to send his Coach after me to dine
with him to day by appointment, but I told him that
Mr. Du Quesne who dines also at Weston House to
day would take me with him in his Chaise thither as
he promised and therefore abt 2 o'clock Du Quesne
did call on me, stayed with me abt. half an Hour and
then we both went to Weston House in our Gowns and
Cassocks (as we are to meet the Bishop of Norwich
there to day) and there we dined and spent the Afternoon with Mr. and Mrs. Custance, The Bishop and his
Lady Mrs. Bagot, his Lordships Chaplain Mr. Gooch,
and S^r. William and Lady Jernegan. Mr. and Mrs.
Branthwaite were also invited but did not come, the
former having sent word in the Morning that he had

the Gout. The Bishop was not dressed in his Gown and Cassock, but in a purple Coat and a short silk Cassock under it. The Company all broke up about half past seven o'clock. I got home by 8. Could not prevail with Du Quesne to Stay and sup with me on his return. We had for Dinner some stewed Carp, Ham and Fowls, a fine Cygnet rosted &c. &c.—the first Course—a brace of Pheasants rosted, a fine Hare rosted, Blamange, Green Peas, Jelly &c. &c. the second Course. Many Dishes of Desert afterwards but nothing extra. The Bishop took Du Quesne very genteelly in to preach a Charity Sermon the ensuing Year at Norwich towards the Support of the Charity Schools there. Sr. Willm. Jernegan is a very fine Man, very easy, affable and good natured. Lady Jernegan is a fine Woman but high and mighty.[1] They are both of the Romish Persuasion. It being Friday and a Fast Day of Course to them, they however eat Fowl, Pheasant and Swan and Sr. William eat some Ham. Upon the whole we spent an agreeable Day, but must confess that being with our equals is much more agreeable.

DEC. 2. . . . This being my Tithe Audit Day, the following People attended, and paid me every thing that was due. Howlett, Girling, Baker, Bush, Forster, Peachman, Michael Andrews for his Brother Stephen who is ill, Mann, Silvy, Js. Pegg, Jno. Pegg, Dade, Page, Buck, Ringgar, Norton, Bidewell, Burroughs, Herring, Thos. Leggatt, Willm. Leggatt, Case, Bean for Mrs. Pratt, Rising, and Tom Cary—They all dined, spent the Afternoon and Evening till 10. o'clock, and then they all went to their respective

[1] After all she was a great-great-granddaughter of Charles II and Barbara Villiers.

homes, it being my desire that they would not stay after 10 o'clock. I gave them for Dinner a Leg of Mutton boiled, and Capers, some Salt Fish, plenty of plumb Puddings and a Couple of boiled Rabbitts, with a fine large Surloin of Beef rosted. Plenty of Wine, Punch and Strong Beer after Dinner till 10 o'clock. We had this Year a very agreeable meeting here, and were very agreeable—no grumbling whatever. Total recd. this Day for Tithe 286. 15. 0. Paid out of the above to Steph: Andrews 0. 15. 0. Ditto to Mr. Dade 6. 17. 0. Ditto to Mr. Mann 4. 14. 0. Ditto to Mr. Bidewell 0. 13. 0. After the Company was all gone and we thought everything were agreeable and happy in my House, we were of a sudden alarmed by a great Noise in the kitchen, and on my immediately going out there found my Servant Man Will: Coleman beating about the Maids in a terrible manner and appeared quite frantic and mad. I seized him by the Collar and as soon as he was loose, he ran out into the Yard and jumped into the Pond there in a moment but he was soon taken up by Ben, which frightened us so much that we were obliged to sit up all night. We got him to bed however about 1 o'clock and after some time he was somewhat quiet —but it frightned us so much that Nancy and self did not go to bed till 6. in the morning. Ben and Jack did not go to bed at all. The reason of his being so, was on Lizzy's Account, as he wants to marry her and she will not, and he is very jealous. Am afraid however that it proceeds from a family complaint, his Father having been crazy some time. It is therefore now high time for him to leave me which I shall endeavour to do the first opportunity. It made me very ill almost instantly and made my niece very unhappy as well as ill also.

Dec. 25. . . . I dined today being Christmas Day at 1 o'clock and the following poor old [People] dined here also, viz. Thos. Cary, Thos. Dicker, Thos. Cushing, Ricd. Bates, Ricd. Buck, Thos. Carr, and Js. Smith my Clerk. After they had dined I gave to each one Shilling 0. 7. 0. Pray God! ever continue to me the Power of doing good. I read Prayers and Preached this Afternoon at Weston. Mr. and Mrs. Custance both at Church.

Dec. 30. . . . Mr. Custance's Servants, George, Harry, Haylett the Gardner with the Cook Maid, Betty and Sukey Chamber-Maids all supped and spent the Evening with our Folks in Kitchen. They stayed till 10. o'clock and then walked home. I gave them a Couple of rost Fowls and some good Punch. Won of Nancy at Cribbage this Evening 0. 2. 0.

1784

Jan. 21. . . . Bitter cold, very hard Frost, and much Snow in the Night. I went out with my Man this morning tracing Hares, we found one fine one which the Dogs killed. At Cribbage this Evening with Nancy won 0. 2. 0. She was very sulky and sullen on loosing it, tho' not paid. She did not scarce open her Mouth all the Even' after. Mr. and Mrs. Hardy supped and spent the Even' with our Folks.

Jan. 26. . . . Nunn Davy, Betsy's Brother, came here this morning on horseback and he stayed and dined, supped and slept here. He slept by choice with my Servt Willm. Gave Nunn this Evening to carry to School 0. 1. 0. At Cribbage this Evening with Nancy won 0. 1. 0. I rejoiced much this morning on shooting

an old Woodpecker, which had teized me a long Time
in pulling out the Reed from my House. He had been
often shot at by me and others, but never could be a
match for him till this Morn'. For this last 3. Years
in very cold Weather did he use to come here and
destroy my Thatch. Many holes he has made this
Year in the Roof, and as many before. To Goody
Doughty for 7 Lemons pd. o. o. 6.

FEB. 7. I breakfasted and spent part of the Morn' at
home. Nancy, Mrs. Davy and Betsy did the same.
Snow very deep indeed and bitter cold Weather.
About 11 o'clock this morning myself, Mrs. Davy,
Betsy and Nancy got into Lenewade Bridge [Chaise]
to go to Norwich as I am to preach to Morrow at the
Cathedral. We were obliged to have four Horses the
Snow being so very deep. We got to Norwich I thank
God safe about 2 o'clock. We were obliged to go
round by Mr. Du Quesnes to get to the Turnpike road
as soon as we could on Account of the Snow wch. was
very deep indeed especially over France Green and no
Tract of Wheels to be seen. We were very fearful
going over that Green as it was very dangerous. It
was very hard work even for the four Horses to get
over that Green. It was much better on the Turnpike.
The Snow in some Place was almost up to the Horses
Shoulders. Towards Lynn the Snow is much deeper
and the Road to it almost impassable. Will went on
horseback with us to Norwich. We all dined, spent
the Aft: supped &c. at the Kings Head. To the
Drivers of Lenewade Chaise gave o. 3. o. To 4 Box
Tickets to go to the Play this Even' pd. o. 12. o.
Norwich Streets and Market Place nothing but Ice,
very dangerous walking about, very bad also for
Carriages. At 6 o'clock we all went to the Theatre

which was unusually crowded on Account of the Money recd. to night being to be given in Charity to the poor of Norwich. The Play was, As You Like It, and Rosina the Entertainment. I never saw the Boxes so full before. There was taken this Evening at the Theatre 71 Pounds. To a Coach to the Theatre and back again for 4 pd. 0. 4. 0. I walked down to Bunns Garden before Dinner and saw his Air Balloon[1] —but it was not floating.

FEB. 8. We breakfasted and slept again at the Kings Head. At 10. o'clock this morning we all went in a Coach to the Cathedral. I went full dressed and being Preacher sat next to the Sub-Dean Dr. Hammond. Whilst the Anthem was singing I was conducted by the Virger to the Pulpit and there Preached a Sermon from these Words 'Let your light so shine before Men that they may see your good Works and glorify your Father wch. is in Heaven.' After Sermon was over I walked back to the Vestry, had my Hood taken of, and then a Person came to me and gave me for Preaching 1. 1. 0. I gave the Virger for the Use of the Hood 0. 1. 0. Neither Bishop, Dean or Mayor at the Cathedral. The Cathedral was not crowded owing to the cold. Lady Bacon was at the Cathedral and immediately after I had conveyed the Ladies back to the Inn and I had undressed myself, I waited on Lady Bacon and sat with her some Time at her Lodgings at one Hirsts. We all then went to Mr. Priests where we dined, spent part of the Afternoon, supped and spent

---

[1] Balloons had been invented by the brothers Montgolfier, and first ascended in France in June 1783. 'Do not wonder', wrote Horace Walpole to Sir H. Mann on December 2nd, 1783, 'that we do not entirely attend to things of earth: fashion has ascended to a higher element. All our views are directed to the air. *Balloons* occupy senators, philosophers, ladies, everybody. France gave us the *ton*. . . .'

the Evening with him, his Wife, and their Son John. In the Afternoon we took Coach and went to Alderman Starling Days where we drank Tea with him, his Wife, his Mother, and Sister in Law, his Son and a Capt. Poole, a very good kind of a young Man. Mr. Day behaved with great Politeness and everything very genteel. As we returned in the Coach from Mr. Days we were very near being overturned before we got to Priests. To Coaches this Day for us pd. o. 8. o.

FEB. 9. We breakfasted at the Kings Head and stayed in Town till near 2. this Afternoon and then we had a Chaise and four from the Kings Head and set of for Weston to get there by Dinner. I walked down to Mr. Frosts this morning and pd. him a Bill for things had of him in 1780, 2. 16. o. To my Barber this morning gave o. 2. o. At Chases for Books pd. o. 3. 1. At Scotts for a Pr. of Gloves pd. o. 2. 2. At Bakers for things pd. o. 4. o. Paid and gave at the Kings Head abt. 3. o. o. Called at Mr. Francis's, Priests, Buckles, Smiths my Mercer and Garland my Taylors. We got I thank God safe home to Weston about 4. this Afternoon—the Snow as deep as we went and harder work for 4 Horses than going to Norwich. Gave the Drivers as they brought us home safe o. 3. o., some strong Beer and some Victuals. We did not dine till near 5 this Afternoon. Lent to Mrs. Davy this morning at the Kings Head 2. 2. o. Mrs. Davy, Betsy, and Nancy dined, supped and slept at Weston.

FEB. 16. I breakfasted, dined, &c. &c. again at home. Nancy breakfasted, dined, &c. &c. again here. Mrs. Davy, and Betsy breakfasted, dined, &c. &c. here again. Mr. Mann and Mr. Buck Overseers of the Poor called on me this Morn' to desire me to

subscribe something to the Poor during this very severe
Weather and gave them for myself and Nancy 2. 2. o.
Mr. Custance subscribed towards the Poor 5. 5. o. To
Mr. Cary for things from Norwich &c. pd. o. 13. o.
To Will for Expenses at Norwich &c. pd. o. 13. 10.
To Betty for things pd. o. 4. 3. Paid Mrs. Davy what
I owed her being o. 2. o. Mr. Matthews Exciseman of
Mattishall, with whom Mrs. Davy boards, called here
about Noon on Mrs. Davy and he dined on some cold
Meat and then returned back. Did not get to bed till
after 1. o'clock Mrs. Davy not being very well.

MAR. 13. . . . Nancy brave to day (tho' this Day is
the Day for the intermitting Fever to visit her) but the
Bark has prevented its return—continued brave all
day. Dr. Thorne and Betsy Davy with him on a little
Hobby called on us this morning and stayed with us
about half an Hour, but could not prevail on them to
dine. Sent Ben early this morning to sell a Cow and
Calf for me which he did and returned home to
dinner. Ben sold the Cow and Calf, and which I recd.
of him 6. o. o. Dr. Thorne's Method of treating the
Ague and Fever or intermitting Fever is thus—To
take a Vomit in the Evening not to drink more than
3 half Pints of Warm Water after it as it operates.
The Morn' following a Rhubarb Draught—and then
as soon as the Fever has left the Patient about an
Hour or more, begin with the Bark taking it every two
Hours till you have taken 12 Papers which contains
one Ounce. The next oz. &c. you take it 6. Powders
the ensuing Day, 5 Powders the Day after, 4 Ditto
the Day after, then 3 Powders the Day after that till
the 3rd. oz. is all taken, then 2 Powders the Day till the
4th. oz: is all taken and then leave of. If at the beginning of taking the Bark it should happen to purge,

put ten Dropps of Laudanum into the Bark you take next, if that dont stop it put 10. drops more of Do. in the next Bark you take—then 5 Drops in the next, then 4, then 3, then 2, then 1 and so leave of by degrees. Nancy continued brave but seemed Light in her head. The Bark at first taking it, rather purged her and she took 10 Drops of Laudanum which stopped it.

APRIL 13. I breakfasted, dined, &c. &c. again at home. Nancy breakfasted, made a running dinner upon a Mutton-Stake about 1. o'clock, and then sat of in Lenewade Bridge Chaise with my Upper Maid with her, as likewise my Servant Lad, for Norwich, to be at the County Election for Members of Parliament, which begins to Morrow at the Shire-Hall on Castle Hill. It was talked that there would be a severe Contest between Sr. John Wodehouse, Sr. Edwd. Astley and Mr. Coke, but Yesterday it was the common report that Coke had declined the Poll. I am (as is Mr. Custance) for Sr. John Wodehouse only, Sr. Edwd. Astley having made an unlucky Junction with Mr. Coke—whose parliamentary Conduct has been quite opposite of late Sr. Edwd. Astley having voted for the popular Mr. Pitt and Mr. Coke for Fox, and Lord North. My Maid and Boy returned from Norwich abt. 5 o'clock. They brought me word that Nancy got very well there and is at Mr. Priest's, being invited thither by them. Very soon after Nancy went I took a ride to Weston House but both Mr. and Mrs. Custance were gone to Norwich. I stayed about an Hour with the little Folks and returned home to Dinner by 3 o'clock.

APRIL 14. I breakfasted upon some Mutton Broth about 6. o'clock and very soon after breakfast I mounted my Mare and went of [to] Norwich and Will: went with me for to be at the County Election for Members of Parliament. We got to Norwich a little after 8. o'clock—put up my Horses at the Woolpack, and then walked to Mr. Priests and there made a second breakfast on Tea and Toast. Nancy was not down Stairs. About 10 o'clock the Market Place and Streets in Norwich were lined with People and almost all with Wodehouse's Cockades in their Hats. After breakfast I went to Mrs. Brewsters and got 6 Cockades all for Wodehouse—3 of them of blue and Pink with Wodehouse wrote in Silver on the blue, the other 3 plain blue and Pink for my Servants at home. About 11 o'clock Sr. John Wodehouse preceded with a great many Flaggs and a band of Musick, made his public Entry on horseback, attended with between two and three Thousand Men on Horseback, They came thro' St. Giles's, then thro' the Market Place, then marched on to the Shire House on the Castle Hill and there Sr. John Wodehouse with Sr. Edward Astley were unanimously chosen Members for the County. After that they had dressed themselves handsomely and were chaired first round the Castle-Hill and then three times round the Market Place amidst an innumerable Number of Spectators and the loudest acclamations of Wodehouse for ever. Sr. Edwd. Astley met with little Applause, having joined Coke before. I never saw such universal Joy all over the City as was shown in behalf of Sr. John Wodehouse. I dined at Mr. Priests with him, his Wife, Son John, Mr. Priest of Reepham and Daughter Bekky and 2 strange Ladies. We had for Dinner some Whitings and a Fillett of Veal. Pd. at Studwells China Shop a small Bill of 0. 3. 0. I intended to have went out of Town to night but our Warden of New College with

Peckham the Steward, and Jeffries and Jeanes the
Outriders came to Norwich this Afternoon they being
on their Progress and went to the Swan Inn—therefore soon after Tea I went to them and there supped
and spent the Evening with them, they were very glad
indeed to see me and so was I them. They had been
to Witchingham and there heard that I was at
Norwich at the Election there. It happened very
unluckily that I could not see them at my House, as of
all Days but this, I could have contrived to be at
home. They all looked pretty well but the Warden
who looks thin and has a very bad cold and a Cough.
I sent Will home this Evening and to come again to
Morrow. I slept if I can call it so, at Mr. Priests and
very uncomfortably indeed—did not go to bed till
near 2 in the morning. Miss Priest, her Father, Mr.
Priest of Norwich and Son being at the Assembly. To
little trifling expenses at one Place and another pd.
o. 2. 6.

MAY 26. ... At 11 o'clock took a ride to Church to
attend at a Vestry there held for examining things
belonging to the Church. Mr. Howlett, Mr. Mann,
Stephen Andrews, and John Buck only attended—
From Church rode to Mr. Custance's but both Mr.
and Mrs. Custance were gone to Norwich to see their
Children now under Inoculation. I took a ride afterwards to Du Quesne's and there dined and spent the
Afternoon with him, Mr. and Mrs. Priest of Norwich
and Mr. Mrs. and Miss Priest of Reepham. We had
for Dinner some Pike and Maccarel, a fore Qr. of
Lamb rosted, Pidgeon Pye—Charter &c. &c. I
carried Mr. Du Quesne a Cucumber in my Pocket.
After Tea Mr. Du Quesne, Mr. Priest of Reepham
and myself played a Game of Bowls on his Green.

I lost o. o. 6. To some Children opening the Gate gave o. o. 6. I returned home to Weston about 9 this Evening. We had a most gracious Rain this Evening and it lasted.

MAY 31. . . . A smock Race at the Heart this Afternoon, I let all my Folks go to it but Lizzy, and all came home in good Time but Will who being merry kept me up till 11 o'clock and then went to bed without waiting any longer for him, and just as I was going to sleep he came and made a Noise under my Window and then marched of and I went to sleep.

JUNE 1. . . . I gave Will notice this morning to leave me, but Nancy hearing of it prevailed on me to try him a little longer with us—but am afraid it won't do. I married at Weston Church this Morning by Banns Willm. Hill and Hester Dunham both old People. Recd. only for marrying them having recd. 2s. 6d. before—o. 2. 6. Goody Doughty called here this morning and paid me some Mony I lent her a while ago—being o. 10. 6. . . .

JUNE 5. . . . Nancy recd a Letter from her Brother Sam this Evening which gave her great Spirits, he having lately been introduced to the Queen and presented her a Picture of his Painting being her Son Prince Frederick. Sam talks of great things, of being soon knighted. Am very glad that his Lot fell in so fortunate a Soil—And his Merit is deserving the same. Sam's News too great to be true, am afraid.[1]

---

[1] This is Samuel Woodforde, R.A. His hopes of knighthood were not realized. Prince Frederick is the Duke of York (1763–1827), who now surveys London from his column on the Steps. He was unfortunate as a commander in the field, but as an administrator and army reformer he was most efficient.

JUNE 10. .... About 3 o'clock this Afternoon Mr. and
Mrs. Custance called on us, took us into their Coach
and carried us to Mr. Micklethwaites where we dined
and spent the remaining part of the Afternoon and
part of the Evening with Mr. and Mrs. Micklethwaite, Mrs. Branthwaite Senr of Norwich, Miles
Branthwaite and Wife, a Miss Howes, and Mr. and
Mrs. Custance—we returned as we went in Mr.
Custance's Coach between 8 and 9 o'clock. We had
a very genteel Dinner, Soals and Lobster Sauce,
Spring Chicken boiled and a Tongue, a Piece of rost
Beef, Soup, a Fillet of Veal rosted with Morells and
Trufles, and Pigeon Pye for the first Course—Sweetbreads, a green Goose and Peas, Apricot Pye, Cheesecakes, Stewed Mushrooms and Trifle. The Ladies
and Gentlemen very genteely dressed. Mr. Micklethwaite had in his Shoes a Pair of Silver Buckles
which cost between 7 and 8 Pounds. Miles Branthwaite had a pair that cost 5 guineas.

JUNE 17. . . . Prodigious fine growing Weather
indeed. Very busy all the Morning in writing.

JUNE 30. .... Mr. Cantrell sent me word this morning
early that his C.[haise] was pre-engaged to Miss
Lombe unknown to him—therefore was obliged to
send Will to Mattishall to acquaint them of being
disappointed and could not send for them—Ben also
being gone to Norwich for Fish. The Rotation therefore is to be put of, and only the Priests Families and
Du Quesne to dine here to day. To Mr. Cary for
things from Norwich &c. p^d o. 5. 6. Sent by Will to
Mrs. Davy a Couple of nice Spring Chicken, half of a
plumb Cake, and Tongue and some Potatoes. Thus
far at 2 o'clock—when lo! a Market Cart arrived at
my House from Mattishall with Three Ladies in it,

Mrs. Davy, Miss Betsy Donne and Nancy who all stayed and dined, supped and slept here. Mr. and Mrs. Priest and Son Rich^d of Norwich, Mr. Du Quesne and Mr. Smith dined and spent the Afternoon here. We had for Dinner some fryed Soals—4 boiled Chicken with some Bacon—a Goose rosted—Neck of Mutton boiled and Capers—Peas—and Pudding and Tarts. Mrs. Davy brought back the Chicken I sent to her which we had for Supper—with other things. About 8 in the Evening most of the Company left us. Mrs. Davy and Miss Betsy Donne slept in Nancy's Room and Nancy in the Garrett over me. Miss Donne is a most agreeable young Lady, full of vivacity, very pretty with an excellent Voice.

July 2. [The Ladies had returned to Mattishall on the previous day.] . . . About 1 o'clock I took a ride to Mattishall and there dined, supped and spent the whole Night at Mr. Smith's, with him, Mr. and Mrs. Thorne, Mr. and Miss Pinching, Mrs. Davy, Miss Betsy Donne and our Nancy. We had for Dinner at Mr. Smith's, boiled Beef, rost and boiled Chicken, part of a fine ham, a Couple of Ducks rosted and Peas —Pudding, Tarts and Cheesecakes. For Supper a cold Collation, with Lamb-Stakes and Gooseberry Cream and green Peas &c. We were very merry the whole Day and all Night, singing all Night long by Miss Donne. She is an excellent lively girl indeed and about 17 Years Old. We broke up at 4 in the Morning. I immediately sat of for Weston—got home about 5 o'clock—and went to bed directly— Saw the Sun rise coming home. To Mr. Smith's Boy —Robin gave 0. 1. 0. I went to Mr. Hewitts in the Afternoon to desire that Miss Donne might sleep at Mr. Thornes to Night.

JULY 3. . . . I got up about 9 o'clock and soon after breakfast I took a ride to Mattishall to see Mr. and Mrs. Bodham and there dined and spent the Afternoon with them, Betsy Donne and Nancy Woodeforde. I called at Mrs. Davy's and Mrs. Thornes. Mrs. Davy gone this morning for Pulham. My Man Ben came after Nancy about noon in a Market Cart— After Tea I returned to Weston as did Nancy, but she was at home before me: I was very flat and dull on leaving my dear Miss Betsy Donne. Nancy supped and slept again at home. We are both glad that this Week is over. Nancy rec^d this Week from her Brother Sam from London a neat genteel and pretty Baloon hat. Mr. and Mrs. Custance are gone to Sr Thomas Beauchamps to spend a few Days with them at Langley Park.

JULY 5. . . . After Dinner I paid Lizzy half a Years Wages due this Day, and then dismissed her from my Service, as she is going on my recommendation to Weston House. I gave her extraordinary o. 2. 6. I paid her for Wages 1. 6. 6. In the Evening sent Ben with a Market Cart for my New Maid who lives at Mattishall and she came here about 8 at Night and she supped and slept here. Her Name is Molly Dade about 17 years of age—a very smart Girl and pretty I think. Her Friends bear great Characters of Industry &c.

JULY 15. . . . We were to have had Betsy Davy and Mary Roupe over from Mattishall to have spent this Day with us but Mrs. Davy's going to Pulham yesterday on a Love Affair with a Mr. Rand who went with her and came back with her, but Matters however could not be settled then. Mr. Rand is a Man of very good Fortune, keeps a Carriage and is an Apothecary and has great business—A very sensible Man, a Batchelor about 50 years of Age. And lives at Snetti-sham near Burnham. To a Man this morning that brought a very pretty kind of a Monkey to shew gave 1. 0^d. He called it the Mongooz from Madagascar.

JULY 16. . . . About 10 o'clock this morning Mr. Matthews with a Cart full of young Folks came to my House—viz, Betsy Davy, Hannah Thorne, Mary Roupe and Nunn Davy—they all spent the Day with us, and a pretty Day it was. Nothing but Noise the whole Day long—Between 7 and 8 sent them back to Mattishall as they came. Mr. Matthews went home before Dinner. Ben went back with them in the Cart.

JULY 17. . . . Mr. Love finished painting my Par-lours this Day at Noon. Hylett, Mr. Custance's Gardener was this morning turned out of his Place and payed of—being found out by Mr. Custance in sending Fruit &c. to Norwich by the Elsing Carrier—Mr. Custance went after the Carrier himself this morning and took from him 4 Quarts of very fine Strawberries and some Cucumbers packed up by Hylett for to be sold. Mr. Custance in a very great Passion.

JULY 19. . . . Nancy went this morning before 7 o'clock behind my Man Will to Mrs. Davy's at Matti-shall where she is to spend a few Days with her . . . .

JULY 20. . . . At 4 this Afternoon I mounted my Mare and rode to Mattishall where I drank Tea and stayed till 9 in the Evening at Mrs. Davy's with her, Mr. and Mrs. Bodham, Miss Donne, Mr. Du Quesne and Nancy Woodforde—Mr. Smith was to have been there also—but went for London this morning very suddenly and much discomposed. The Cause of it is

this, Mrs. Davy had a Letter this morning from
Mr. Rand who is distracted after her, the Contents of
which were communicated to Mr. Smith, which made
him almost frantic, he immediately made Mrs. Davy
an Offer to marry her after his Mothers Decease,
what answer was returned I know not, but he marched
from Mattishall directly. Mrs. Davy was extremely
low and uneasy about it. After one Pool of Quadrille
we had a Syllabub and some Rasberries with Cream
and Sugar—and Wine. We all broke up about
9 o'clock rather after. At Quadrille this Evening won
0. 1. 0. To Mrs. Davy's Maid gave coming away
0. 1. 0.

JULY 22. .... At 11 o'clock went to Church to attend
at a Vestry ab^t moving of the Singing Seat—Mr.
Peachman, Dade, Page, Forster, J^n_o Pegg, Stephen
Andrews, Howlett and J^n_o Buck attended also—Mr.
Peachman, with some others were for letting of it
remain where it is—but they all said that they would
agree to have it placed wherever I pleased—Accordingly I fixed to be a proper Place for it behind the
Font and so inclose the Belfry—wch was concluded on
and so the Vestry was dissolved. They all behaved
extremely obliging to their Rector. Between 2 and 3
I rode up to Weston House and there dined and spent
the Afternoon with Mr. and Mrs. Custance, and Mr.
and Mrs. Collier of Quebec near Dereham. Mr.
Charles Collier and Wife very agreeable People.
Soon after Tea they went of for Quebec—I stayed
till after 9 looking with Mr. Custance over a new Set
of Copper Plate Prints respecting Captain Cooks
Voyage to Kamskatsca—very fine they are, cost 10
Guineas.

AUG. 4. .... About 10 o'clock this Night a Clergyman

by name Cam[p]bell (Vicar of Weasingham in this
County and formerly of Oriel Coll: Oxford and afterwards Fellow of Worcester Coll: in the same University) came to my House and he supped and slept here
—himself and horse. I remember him at Oriel Coll:
but not so intimate as to expect that he would have
taken such freedom especially as he never made me
a Visit before. He slept however in the Attic Story
and I treated him as one that would be too free if
treated too kindly. It kept me up till after 12 o'clock.

SEP. 1. . . . Mr. Hardy and Boy fastened up 3
Windows with Brick for me, and having finished by
Noon I sent them both into my Wheat Field to sheer
Wheat with my three Men.—And they dined, &c.
here. A very fine Day, than[k] God, for the Harvest.
Mr. Custance sent us a brace of Partridges which was
very kind of him as it is the Day of Shooting.

SEP. 4. . . . I sent Mr. Custance about 3 doz: more
of Apricots, and he sent me back another large Piece
of fine Parmesan Cheese—It was very kind in him.
Nancy had a Letter from her Brother Sam, nothing in
it. I finished carrying Wheat this morning.

SEP. 15. . . . Went out with my Greyhounds this
morning about an Hour in Weston great Field—
found a Hare coursed her and killed her—during the
time that I was out, Mrs. Custance with Mrs. Collier
Senr called on my Niece and stayed with her near an
Hour. To Largesses to day gave 0. 4. 0.

SEP. 22. . . . About 12 o'clock took a ride to Weston
House, spent half an Hour with Mr. and Mrs.
Custance, Mrs. Collier Senr and Mr. George Beau-

champ, and came back. At 2 o'clock took a Walk to Mr. Micklethwaite's and there dined, spent the Afternoon, supped and spent the Evening with him, his Wife, his Father and Mother, old Mrs. Branthwaite, Captain Micklethwaite and Wife, Mr. Jonathan Micklethwaite and my Niece.—About 5 o'clock we dined. Before Dinner I publickly baptized their little Boy at home, which I did not much like, but could not tell how to refuse—He was privately named before at Norwich I believe—His Name is Nathaniel. Old Mrs. Branthwaite and old Mrs. Micklethwaite were the Godmothers—and old Mr. Micklethwaite and his Son Captain John Micklethwaite were Godfathers. We had a very genteel Dinner and Supper. Old Mr. and Mrs. Micklethwaite and his Son the Captain, the strangest kind of People I almost ever saw. Old Mrs. Branthwaite almost as strange and vulgar. Nancy was sent for in their Carriage and we returned home in it about 12 at night—very windy, very wet, and very dark; I thank God we got home however safe. I gave the Driver and the Man behind it each 1. 0.–0. 2. 0. After Tea and Coffee We got to Whist at which I won 0. 1. 0. Coming away this Evening Mr. Micklethwaite made me a present, for christening his Child, of 1. 1. 0. Upon the whole spent an odd disagreeable kind of a Day—as did also Nancy—we laughed much after we got home.

Sep. 28. . . . My Maid Betty has not been able to do any thing for this last Week owing to a bad Thumb and is still bad. Poor Molly Dade my other Maid very bad in a Cough and am afraid it is rather consumptive—She has increased it to day by easing the other Maid in helping her and she is so foolish to tell

Molly that she is in a Consumption—which makes the poor Girl very unhappy.

OCT. 6. . . . My Maid Molly, I think, is a good deal better. Widow Greaves here again all Day and Night.

OCT. 7. . . . Jack told me this morning that he is advised to get another Place being too old for a Skip-Jack any longer. He wants to be a Plow Boy to some Farmer to learn the farming Business as he likes that best—I told him that he was very right to try to better himself, and at Lady Day next he is to leave my House for that purpose. He has been a very good Lad ever since he has been here. Widow Greaves here again all Day and Night.

OCT. 10. . . . My New Maid (in Betty's Place) Sally Dunnell came here this Evening, which was sooner than we expected her by a Day—but we contrived for her to sleep here &c. tho' my other Maid nor Mrs. Greaves were as yet gone. They all slept here to night. I published Bettys Banns for the last time this Aft: at Church—I suppose she will marry very soon. My new Maid seems to be a mighty strapping Wench.

OCT. 11. . . . After breakfast paid my Maid Eliz: Claxton who leaves me to day, three Q^{rs} Wages—being 4. 7. 0. She breakfasted here and left us about 11 this Morn'. Paid Mrs. Greaves also for the Time she has been with us this Morning at 6^d Pr Day 0. 5. 0. She had both Victuals and Lodging here also. She left us about the same Time. Mrs. Custance with her eldest Son made us a long Morning Visit from 12 till 2 o'clock. Gave poor old Mary Dicker this Morn' 0. 1. 0. She came to pay Rent for her House belonging to the poor Widows of this Parish.

OCT. 14. . . . Finding my new Maid (who came as

Cook to us) to know nothing of her business, I therefore this Evening gave her notice that she must leave
my Service and as soon as possible—I believe her to
be a goodnatured Girl but very ignorant.

Oct. 15. ... My new Maid Sally Dunnell left my
Service this Morn'. Gave the Maid as she was going
away for the Time she had been here at 6ᵈ per Day
o. 3. o. To Mr. Dade a Poor Rate for Land in hand at
10ᵈ 1. 5. 2½. To Mr. Cary for things from Norwich
&c. for last Week 16. 4¼. To my Niece Nancy for
things pᵈ o. 8. 6. Mr. Custance made us a long
Morning Visit. Mr. Hall from Hampshire and a
Mr. Fellowes of Haviland a Gentleman of great
Fortune and Member for Andover called here on
horseback whilst Mr. Custance was with us—I went
to them and spoke with them, but they would not get
of their Horses—having not time. My poor Maid
Molly Dade, not so well to day as I could wish her,
having somewhat of a Fever on her. She is one of the
best Maids that ever we had and very much liked by
us both and would wish to keep her but am very much
afraid it will not be in our Power tho' we are both
most willing to keep her. She is one of the neatest,
most modest, pretty Girl[s] I ever had. She is very
young, but tall, only in her 17ᵗʰ year. Ben went early
this Morning beyond Dereham to buy me a Cow,
now in her full profit, but could not. It was at a Sale
of Colonel Dickens's near Dereham. Widow Greaves
came to us again this Evening to be with us till we can
get another Maid—I sent for her.

Oct. 19. ... I sent my Maid Molly Dade this morning behind Ben to Mattishall, to stay a few Days at
home, to see if change of Air would do her Cough
good. Her Sister Betty, continues in her Place. Poor

Molly is as good a Girl as ever came into a House, I never had a Servant that I liked better—Nancy also likes her very much indeed—I wish to God she might get the better of her illness. Widow Greaves still with us and at present likely so to be.

Nov. 2. ... Soon after breakfast I took my Men with [me] a coursing. Set out about 11 and stayed till after 4 in the Aft: we brought home a brace of Hares and a Rabbit, both Courses with the Hares very fine indeed. Whilst we were out, a Servant Maid came to offer her Service here, who lately lived at Mr. Eatons at Elsing and but a very little time indeed only a Quarter of a Year—Nancy could not recollect her Name or give any direct answer as I was out. By the Account that Nancy gave me, don't think she will do —she being rather high and her late Wages 8 Pounds per Annum—Her Friends live at Foxley a place I by no means approve of—as it has [been] proved that many from that Place have been guilty of many felonious Acts and but very few Years ago. She formerly lived at old Mr. Gurdons at Letton and for 9 years—She afterwards lived with his Son—N.B. Old Mr. Gurdon's House of Letton about 3 years ago was broke open and robbed of all his old family Plate, but was never discovered. The above Robbery was supposed to have hastened the death of poor old Mr. Gurdon a most worthy Man.

Nov. 3. ... Sent Will: this morning to Mr. Smiths at Mattishall with a Hare—told him to call on Molly Dade, during the Time that he was gone Molly's Father called here—he gave us a very poor Account of our worthy Maid poor Molly Dade—that he believed she cannot recover. We were extremely sorry for her. He came after her Stays that were here, the others being too large for her—so much of late has she fallen away. Mr. Dade could not stay to dine with us to day. Will on his return also told us that Mr. Thorne had given poor Molly over and that he could do no more. Pray God Almighty comfort her—and with patience wait the Almighty's Will—As good a Girl as ever lived.

Nov. 7. ... My Maid Betty Dade (in the room of her poor Sister Molly) went to see Molly this morning— My Man Ben carried her behind him. We sent her a Knuckle of Veal for Broth and a Jar of Black Currant Jamm. Betty and Ben returned about 5 this Evening —she left her sister but very poorly and very weak. I read Prayers and Preached this Aft: at Weston. Mr. and Mrs. Micklethwaite at Church. Nobody from Weston House at Church to day.

Nov. 9. ... After breakfast I rode down to Lenewade Bridge to attend Dr Bathursts Tythe Audit and there dined and stayed till after 4 o'clock in the Aftr and then returned home—All safe and snugg. I was far from being well however to day. This Evening I had a new Servant Maid come as Cook, Molly Peachman, she is to have 5 Guineas Per Annum, Tea included— Nancy prevailed on me to take her.

Nov. 17. [He had gone to Norwich the previous day to bank Dr. Bathurst's tithe at Kerrisons Bank.] I breakfasted at the Kings Head—and stayed in Norwich till 1 o'clock and then sat of for Weston. Ben returned with my Mare to Norwich this Morn'. To Studwell, China Man p^d a Bill of 0. 18. 6. To Beale, Fishmonger p^d a Bill of 0. 7. 6. I went and saw the Dwarf Man that is at Norwich by name James Harris from Coventry—He is exactly 3 Feet high, very well proportioned in every respect—But with him, was a Girl which exceeded every Thing I ever saw—she had no Hands or Arms, and yet wonderfully cleaver with her Feet. She cut out a Watch Paper for me whilst I was there with her Toes she opened My Watch and put it in after done. Her Name was Jane Hawtin, about 22 years old. She talks very sensible and appears very happy in her Situation—She uses her Toes as well as any their Fingers. I gave her for cutting the Watch Paper 0. 1. 0. To the Dwarf gave 0. 0. 6. To Mr. Priest for Sal volatile &c. p^d 0. 3. 4. Called at Brownsmith's Silk Mercer, and there paid a Bill for Nancy for Silk, for a Gown &c. 6. 1. 0. I talked to them of their Behaviour to Nancy, in trusting her. At Bakers for a small Whip &c. p^d 0. 3. 0. To $\frac{1}{2}$ P^d of netting Cord p^d 0. 1. 3. To a Pair of riding Gloves p^d 0. 2. 0. To my Barber, Mileham gave 0. 1. 0. To a very poor Weaver with a large Family and a Wife and can get no Work whatever gave last Night 0. 1. 0. At the Kings Head paid and gave 0. 7. 0. We got home safe and well (thank God) by 3 o'clock and escaped the Rain very well—but very cold it was. I found Nancy and Mrs. Davy brave and well. I dined, supped and slept again at home. Mrs. Davy, breakfasted, dined &c. &c. again here. Nancy breakfasted, dined &c. &c. again at home.

Nov. 30. . . . [He has his Tithe Audit.] They were all highly pleased with their Entertainment but few dined in the Parlour. They that dined in the Kitchen had no Punch or Wine, but strong Beer and Table Beer, and would not come into Parlour to have Punch &c. I gave them for Dinner some Salt Fish, a Leg of Mutton boiled and Capers, a fine Loin of Beef rosted, and plenty of plumb and plain Puddings.

They drank in Parlour 7. Bottles of Port Wine, and both my large Bowls of Rum Punch, each of which took 2 Bottles of Rum to make. Forster went away the most disguised of any. In the Kitchen they were all cheerfully merry but none much disguised— Howlett, J^n_o Pegg and Will: Leggatt tho' Parlour Guests were rather pretty forward. Rec^d to day for Tithe &c. from above—234. 13. 0. Paid out of the above to Mr. Mann for Coal—0. 5. 0.

DEC. 1. ... Nancy came home [from Weston House] about Dinner time and she dined, supped and slept at home again and glad so to do. Nobody came in the Coach with Nancy home but she had 4 Horses in the Coach. I was quite dull all Day after the fatigue Yesterday. Mr. Girling and Forster had a Battle last Night after they left me at Mr. Peachmans—Forster much injured for the time.

DEC. 17. ... My Man Ben went [with] Betty this morning early in a Cart of Bidewells to Mattishall to see her Sister—they did not return till 5 o'clock this Evening—Betty brought us but a very poor Account of her Sister, as she gets worse and worse daily— cannot live long. Pray God grant her a Speedy relief from her present Situation—to Life if it be thy good Pleasure, or happiness. Mr. Cary dined with our Folks in Kitchen.

DEC. 25. ... I read Prayers and administered the H: Sacrament this Morning at Weston Church, being Christmas Day. Mrs. Custance at Church and at the Sacrament. Mr. Custance not there being ill at home. J^s Smith, my Clerk, Richd Buck, Thos Cushing, Thos Carr, Richd Bates, Thos Dicker, and

Thos Cary, all dined at my House as usual on Christmas Day, I gave to each of them a Shilling to carry home to their Wives before they went away—in all—0. 7. 0. I gave them for Dinner a Piece of rost Beef and plumb Puddings—and after dinner half a Pint of strong Beer apiece. N.B. All old Men.

1785

JAN. 6. . . . Paid my Servants their Wages this morning that is to Willm Coleman a Y^rs Wages 5. 5. 0. To Ditto for dressing my Wiggs 0. 10. 0. To Ditto for 2 P^r of Shoes 0. 12. 0. To Ditto for Grains 4 Coomb 0. 4. 0. N.B. beside the above I give him his Cloaths. To Ben Leggatt a Y^rs Wages due now 10. 0. 0. To Jack Warton a Y^rs Wages due now 1. 1. 0. To Betty Dade for half a Y^rs Wages due to her and her Sister Molly between them p^d 1. 6. 6. Mem: I then told Betty Dade that from this time I intended to give her 5 Guineas per Annum as I designed the same to her poor Sister, if her health would have permitted to stay with us—but now that is all over, she daily getting worse and worse, as her Father who came over here this Morn' told us, by whom Mr. Smith sent us some Medlars. At Cribbage this Evening and cutting the cards won 0. 2. 0.

JAN. 9. . . . I read Prayers and Preached this Afternoon at Weston. None from Weston House at Church being wet. Mr. Micklethwaite was at Church. I dreamt last Night that I went to Weston Church with a Corpse after me, and just as I came to the Church Yard Gate, saw another Corpse bringing from Morton Road way, and which had died of the small Pox. The corpse that I attended on seeing the other,

I ordered to be carried into the Chancel, till the other
was buried. When I returned to the Chancel, thought
I saw a most elegant Dinner served up—particularly
fish—whether I waked then or not I cannot tell, but
could recollect nothing more of my dream besides.
My Maid Betty Dade went to see her poor Sister
Molly this morning behind Ben—they returned about
5 in the Afternoon. Poor Molly just alive and that all
being in the last stage of a Consumption—she is very
sensible of her approaching End and happily resigned
to it. Pray God Almighty bless her and grant her an
happy delivery from her present State and eternal
happiness after it.

JAN. 16. ... Mr. Custance at Church but not Mrs.
Custance. I was very dull and low this Evening,
having no company at all, now Nancy is from home
[at Mrs. Davy's]. And not used of late to be much by
myself—better soon.

JAN. 22. ... About 1 o'clock Mrs. Davy with Nancy
in Mr. Thorne's Chaise came here and Mr. Thornes
Man with them. Mrs. Davy stayed here about half an
Hour, would not dine here, and then set of back for
Mattishall, leaving Nancy with me—Very glad she is
come home. Nancy dined, supped and slept at home.
Paid Nancy this Evening for some Patty Pans &c.
o. 2. 6. and which she had paid for me to Mrs. Davy.
Mrs. Davy did not by any means behave as she used
to do towards me—was scarce civil to me.

JAN. 23. ... Very fair and fine to day, quite a
Summers Day. I read Prayers and Preached this Aft:
at Weston. Mr. Dade of Mattishall came over here
this morning to let his Daughter know, that her poor
Sister Molly died last Night! poor Soul! I doubt not

of her happiness in a future Life—She was long expected to die. Pray God bless her Spirit and comfort her Relations. Mr. Dade did not stay long here this morning. Mr. and Mrs. Custance both at Church this Aft. And they desired that we would dine with them on Friday next—and that they would send their Coach.

JAN. 24. . . . Betty's Father came over here this morning from Mattishall after her to go home and be at the Funeral of her Sister to Morrow—and to return home Wednesday Morn'. Mrs. Greaves came here this morning by my desire to assist in the House during Betty's absence.

JAN. 25. . . . One Sucker from Mattishall a little Farmer came here this morning with his Son John about 13 Years of age to desire me to take his said Son at old Lady Day next in room of Jack Warton who then leaves me on Account of his now being too old for his Place—and which after some talk with the Father I agreed to take him then being well recommended before by Mr. and Mrs. Bodham and Mr. Smith. I gave the Boy, by way of earnest Mony 0. 1. 0. I am to give him per Annum for Wages 1. 1. 0. A Coat and Waistcoat and Hat when wanted, to allow him something for being washed out and mended—And his Friends to find him in Stockings and Shoes &c. At Cribbage this Evening with Nancy lost 0. 1. 0.

JAN. 29. . . . Nancy and self had a few words this morning but soon over, poor dear, I dont wish to make her at all uneasy. At Cribbage this Evening won with Nancy 0. 1. 0. Betty Dades Father came here this morning. Had a Letter this Evening from Dr. Bathurst.

JAN. 30. ... I read Prayers and Preached this morning at Weston. None from Weston House at Church this morning. I read the Service for King Charles's Martyrdom.[1] Gave poor Joe Adcock who was at Church and lately had something of a paralytic Stroke 0. 1. 0.

FEB. 4. ... Finished reading Roderick Random this Evening.[2]

FEB. 9. ... Nancy completely finished this Evening her new spot net Apron—and very pretty it looks.

FEB. 14. ... To 62 Valentines at 1^d each this morning gave 0. 5. 2. About 4 o'clock this Afternoon Mr. and Mrs. Custance sent us word that they would drink Tea with us this Afternoon—which put us in a little hurry. In about half an Hour they came, drank Tea and Coffee played a Pool at Quadrille after and then went home again—they left us between eight and nine this Evening. At Quadrille this Evening lost 0. 1. 0.

FEB. 26. ... I dreamt a good deal about Jenny Woodforde Frank Woodforde's Wife, of her being dressed all in white, looked exceeding pale but very handsome. I hope my Dream portends no ill to her.

FEB. 27. ... Harder Frost than ever with high Wind with some falling of very small kind of Snow—colder than ever. I read Prayers and Preached this morning at Weston. Very small Congregation indeed—not 20 Persons there and only two Women amongst them —Palmers Wife of Morton and the Clerk's Wife

[1] This commemoration service was not removed from the Prayer Book till 1859.
[2] *Roderick Random* was Tobias Smollett's (1721–71) first novel: it appeared in 1748.

Jenny Smith. None from Weston House of any kind. John Norton dined with our Folks in Kitchen.

FEB. 28. ... The Frost severer than ever in the night as it even froze the Chamber Pots under the Beds. Wind very rough and tho' the Sun shone all the morning very bright yet it continued freezing every minute. Most bitter cold to day indeed, and likely to continue. ...

MARCH 8. ... Of one Aldridge who called here this Morning with a Cart with things, for ½ Yard of Cambrick p^d 0. 5. 0. Of Ditto—for corded Muslin ½ Y^rd for the Maids 0. 3. 6. and which I gave between them for Caps.

MARCH 10. ... Mr. Du Quesne made us a morning Visit on his road to Priests of Reepham—he looked mighty Well. Will: Coleman went early to Norwich this Morn' on my Mare, to Hylatts who was lately Gardener to Mr. Custance, after some Cucumber Plants which he promised him—He returned about 1 o'clock and Hylatt came with him and he dined here with our Folks. He did not come directly to my House as Mr. Custance's Coach was here with Mrs. Custance but put up his Horse at the White Hart and stayed till after. Mrs. Custance came here about Noon and staid with us till near 2 o'clock—She came very soon after Mr. Du Quesne left us—She came thro' the Kitchen to the Study, it being so very cold.

MARCH 13. . . . I read Prayers, Preached and christened a Child by Name, Tabitha Bithia, this morning at Weston Church. Mr. Custance and Mr. Micklethwaite were at Church. Mem: Bithia is a very uncommon Name, but it was the Name of

Pharoah's Daughter—See 1 Chron. iv 18.[1] It was a Child of Reeves at the Hart and a pretty Girl. Bitter cold tho' fair all day—In the Evening it froze almost as sharp as any time this Year.

MARCH 14. . . . Poor Neighbour Clarke's Wife and 4 Ch¹ldren are taken down in the small Pox—Their Neighbour Gooch, his Wife, nor any of a large Family of children belonging to them, have none of them had the Small Pox.

MARCH 15. . . . Sent poor Clarkes Family a large Bushel Basket of Apples, to make Apple Dumplins for poor Souls. Sent another basket of same to Goochs Family. To Nortons and Downings Family sent each a Basket of Apples. . . .

MARCH 16. . . . Dr. Thorne called here this morning —He has been inoculating John Gooch and whole Family. Nancy complained very much this morning of the Wind in her Stomach—I desired her to drink some strong Beer after Dinner instead of Wine, which she did and was better after it.—She was much oppressed by Hysteric wind before—She also by my desire had some Milk for breakfast and is to continue it. Neighbour Clarkes Wife and Family as well as can be expected.—It is a good kind of small Pox they have.

MARCH 19. . . . I called last night at poor Neighbour Clarkes, but did not go in, found they were as well as could be expected. I left with the Woman that nurses them, who is John's Mother, to buy some necessaries o. 2. o. Had a Note this morning from Mr. Custance to ask us to dinner on Monday next.

---

[1] 'And his wife Jehudijah bare Jered the father of Gedor, and Heber the father of Socho, and Jekuthiel the father of Zanoah. And these are the sons of Bithiah the daughter of Pharaoh, which Mered took.'

MARCH 25. . . . I read Prayers this morning at Weston being Good Friday. Mr. Custance was at Church, complained of the Cold. To Widow Gaff and Widow Grant—gave each 1ˢ/0ᵈ—0. 2. 0. Very cold again to day, dark, cloudy and damp. Sent a long Letter to my Sister Pounsett by Cary. I eat no Meat all day being Good-Friday—neither did Nancy —and we did not dine till 5 o'clock. I dined on Fritters and toasted Cheese—Nancy had Eggs. Just as we were sat down to dinner Mr. Smith's Servant Boy with a Note from his Master came here. It was to desire me to serve Mattishall for him on Sunday next in the Afternoon—he being very ill. I sent an Answer back soon as I had dined that I wᵈ.

MARCH 26. . . . At the Assizes at Thetford in this County 8 Prisoners were condemned, three of the above were reprieved.—The other five left for execution—One Jˢ Cliffen a most daring Fellow was hanged on Thursday. Jˢ Cliffen as mentioned on the last mentioned was hanged on Thursday last at Norwich on Castle-Hill and behaved most daringly audacious —His crime was robbing 2 old Men, Brothers, by names Seaman on the Yaxham Road, knocked them both down first, of which Blows one of them died soon after—the other recovered. Cliffen's Body was this Day carried to Badley Moor and there hung in Chains at one Corner of the said Moor.

MARCH 28. . . . Called this Morning at Goochs Stile and enquired how himself and Family were in the small Pox—and he told me that they were all finely— gave him 0. 2. 0. Called also at Clarkes and enquired how they were in the small Pox—they were also tolerable, gave them 0. 2. 0. Gave Gooch and Clarke another Bushell of Apples apiece—the others being

done. To my Clerk J^s Smith being Easter Monday
gave 0. 2. 6.

APRIL 4. ... After breakfast, being fine Weather, I
took a ride and Will with me, thro' Hockering, North-
Tuddenham, to Baddeley Moor where Cliffen stands
in Chains, most shocking road all around where he
stands for some way thought we should have been
mired. . . .

APRIL 9. ... To a poor deaf Man from Mattishall
gave 0. 0. 1. Mrs. Custance with her 2 Children
William and Fanny came here this Afternoon about
5 o'clock without the lest notice and stayed with us
about an Hour and then returned back to Weston
House—did not drink Tea. I had not finished my
Afternoon Pipe but put it away. I told Mrs. Custance
that I had been smoking and hoped she did not dislike
Tobacco—and she said she liked it. Nancy had a very
long Letter from her Sister Juliana.

APRIL 12. ... I buried poor old Widow Pully this
Aft: aged—80 y^rs. My Servant Willm Coleman was
out all the Evening till just 11 o'clock—came home in
Liquor behaved very rudely and most impudently to
me indeed, I told him that I was determined never
more to bear with such Behaviour, and that he sh^d
certainly go to Morr'. Mr. Peachman called here
about 7 o'clock and paid me for 4 acres of Turnips at
30^s per Acre—6. 0. 0. He did not stay long with us—
drank some fresh [?].

APRIL 13. ... I got up between 5 and 6 o'clock this
morning had Will before me as soon as possible, paid
him his Wages and dismissed him before 8 o'clock.
For a Q^rs Wages at 5 Guineas p^d him 1. 6. 3. For a

Q^{rs} dressing Wiggs at 10^s p^d him 0. 2. 6. For a Q^{rs}
Allowance for Shoes at 12^s p^d him 0. 3. 0. For brew-
ing-Grains 6 Coomb at 1^s 0^d p^d him 0. 6. 0. In all
paid him 1. 17. 9. I threw him down a Couple of
Guineas for him to have the remaining, but he would
not take one farthing more than the above 1. 17. 9.
Being so much hurried last night and this morning
made me quite ill all Day—vomited a good deal at
Night after which took a Dose of Rhubarb and was
much better.

APRIL 14. ... Had an exceeding good Night (thank
God) and much better. Will had away his Chest early
this morning and is now at work in the Garden at
Mr. Cary's. I wish he might do well and better than
he did here.

APRIL 15. ... Will: came to me to day to desire
I would give him a Character if wanted, which I
promised him. He seems to be rather cast down to
day and at no work.

APRIL 16. ... Will: Coleman I hear went of early
this morning for Norwich and in high Spirits. I had
2 yong Men offer themselves but neither w^d do as
they never waited at Table in their lives.

APRIL 18. ... Saw the first Swallow this Season this
Morning. Will: Coleman called here this morning
very early to take his Leave of his late Partners—He
was gone before I was below Stairs—He has got a
Place at Catton—at 10^s/6^d per Week and no Board or
1^s/0. Per Day and board. Mr. Du Quesne came here
about 2 o'clock in his Chaise and he dined and spent
the Afternoon here and ab^t 4 o'clock we went with
him in his Chaise to Norwich got to Kings Head about

6 o'clock—there met Mr. and Mrs. Custance, just going to the Play, we stayed after that and drank a Dish of Tea—and then we took a Coach and drove to the Theatre. Got there just as the first Act was over—We sat in the Mayors Box—The Mayor (Partridge) was there also. Lady Bacon and Mrs. Custance in the next Box to us. Sr William Jernegan came and spoke to us. The Play was the Duenna—and Farce the Divorce. Both bespoke by Sr Will and Lady Jernegan. After we came from the Theatre which was ab^t 10 we all supped at the Kings Head and there slept. Mr. and Mrs. Custance returned to Weston after the Play. The Kings Head was quite full of Company, Mr. Du Quesne and myself were obliged to sleep in one Room and down the Yard—Nancy just by us in a single Room and a very good one. We did not go to bed till after 12 o'clock.

APRIL 24. . . . Will: Coleman we heard to day was come again to Weston could not be easy at Norwich tho' he had employment.

APRIL 25. . . . Will: Coleman came to us this morning as we were walking in the Garden, and said that he could not be easy after his late bad behaviour, till he had spoke to me and asked pardon for it—I then told him that I would employ him as a Gardener and give him a shilling a Day and his Board for 2 Days in a Week—but that he must get a Lodging from my House, and if he can somewhere in the Parish. He appeared then quite happy and went directly about his work in the Garden. To Mr. Cary for things from Norwich &c. p^d o. 7. 6½. To Nancy for Butter at 10^d p^d o. 2. 6.

APRIL 26. . . . Bretingham Scurl a new Servant

came here whilst we were at Dinner, I ordered him into Parlour directly and made him wait at Table and he did pretty well. He appears to be a good-natured willing young Fellow. Will: Coleman who is gardening for me looked rather shy upon Scurl at first—We call him Briton.

APRIL 27. . . . My new Boy Jack Secker came back from Mr. Thornes after inoculation this morning to us. Clerk Hewits Son Will: brought him here behind him, gave Will: o. 6. . . .

JUNE 1. . . . Mr. and Mrs. Custance called here about 11 o'clock and took Nancy with them in their Coach to go to Norwich. They would have taken me up also but I preferred going on horseback, about 12 therefore, I went to Norwich and took Briton with me, and we got there about 2 o'clock—but was wet getting thither. About 3 o'clock this Afternoon a violent Tempest arose at Norwich in the North East, very loud Thunder with strong white Lightening with heavy Rain—which lasted about an Hour—immediately after which Mr. Deckers Balloon with Decker himself in a boat annexed to it, ascended from Quantrells Gardens and very majestically.—It was out of Sight in about 10 Minutes, but appeared again on his Descent. It went in a South East Direction— I saw it from Brecondale Hill, and it went almost over my Head. Mr. and Mrs. Custance and Nancy were at Mackay's Gardens. They saw it also very plain from thence. A vast Concourse of People were assembled to see it. It was rather unfortunate that the Weather proved so unfavourable—but added greatly to the Courage of Decker that he ascended so very soon after the Tempest. It also bursted twice before he ascended in it, upon the filling it, if it had not, a Girl about 14 was to have went with him in it—but after so much Gas had been let out—it would not carry both. Mr. Du Quesne was there and in the Gardens. Mrs. Thorne, Mrs. Davy and Captain Thorne overtook me going to Norwich just by the Turnpike—I parted with them just by St. Giles's Gate and saw nothing more of them afterwards— They were wet as well as we on the Road—I put up my Horses at the Woolpack. The Tempest happened as I was on Brecondale Hill. I went directly to a red House adjoining, and was very kindly asked to walk in to a Parlour, which I accepted—Whilst I was there I found that I was got into Mrs. Thornes Brothers, Mr. Thos Agges. I saw a very pretty Quaker there, a young Woman. After I returned from seeing the Balloon—I went to a Perfumers Shop in the Haymarket by name Amyot and bought some Essence of Jessamine, Lavender, Bergamot for all which I paid o. 2. 3. I then called at Bakers and bought a Habit Brush for Nancy with a looking Glass at the back of it p^d o. 2. o. I then called at Priests, there saw Du Quesne, but neither eat or drank there—For some Amber Grease, Oil of Time, Lavender, and Spermaceti p^d o. 2. 3. After that I mounted my Mare and sat of for Weston—got home about 8 o'clock this Evening and then dined, supped and slept in the old House—Nancy was at home about an Hour before me —very much tired. We were very wet coming home this Evening. At Norwich for 1 half Pint of Porter and gave the Maid o. 3. Mr. and Mrs. Custance, Nancy, myself, and in short all that went to see the Baloon were highly pleased. We were all sorry that the Weather was so bad for it. Decker however has gained great Credit by it.

JUNE 8. . . . I dreamt very much last Night of Mr. Smith and Mrs. Davy and that connection entirely broke of—I told Nancy of it at breakfast.—Just as we were going to sit down to dinner, Mr. Matthews brought a Note to my Niece from Mrs. Davy—to let her know that she was in great distress, having rec^d a Letter this morn' from Mr. Smith to break of any farther connection with her—his Friends being so very averse to the Match And that he was going to leave England directly. Mrs. Davy desires my Niece to come over to her directly—but she could not go.

JUNE 10. . . . Nancy made part of a breakfast at home and at 8 o'clock this morning she sat of in Mr. Bucks Market Cart and Ben with her for Mattishal[l] Burgh to Mrs. Davys where she is to spend a few Days with her, as she is very low from what has lately happened by Mr. Smith. Sent a very long Letter to my Sister Pounsett by Cary. Sent also one for Nancy to her Brother Sam.

JULY 7. . . . Busy all Day, shewing Briton the method of brewing. It made me rather cross—Ironing being also about.

JULY 13. . . . Mr. Thomas of Dereham called on us this Morn' but did not stay. Sent Ben very early to Norwich this morning after Fish, he returned about 11 o'clock and brought with him eight pair of small Soals with two Couple of Chicken. Mr. and Mrs. Thorne and their Daughter Hannah and a Miss Pinching, and Mr. Thorne's Nephew Mr. Walker an Attorney about 18 Years of Age, Captain Thorne, Mrs. Davy, Betsy and Nunn, came to our House about 3 o'clock and they all dined, supped and spent the Evening, and stayed till 3 o'clock in the Morn with us. We had for Dinner some Pyke and fryed Soals a nice Piece of boiled Beef, Ham and a Couple of Fowls, Peas and Beans, a green Goose rosted, Gooseberry Pies, Currant Tarts, the Charter, hung Beef scraped &c. For Supper fryed Soals, a Couple of Chicken rosted, cold Ham &c. &c. Artichokes, Tarts &c. Fruit after Dinner and Supper—Strawberries, Cherries, Almonds—Raisins &c. &c. Miss Pinchings Brother came to us from Norwich about 10 o'clock this Evening just as we were going to sit down to Supper and he supped &c. with us. Just as the Ladies and Gentlemen were going to drink Coffee and Tea in the Garden, I was sent for to go to Weston House to name a Child of Mrs. Custances who was brought to bed this Afternoon about 2 o'clock—I therefore walked up directly to Weston House and named the Child by name Mary Anne, the smallest Infant I think I ever had in my Arms—The Child came 10 Weeks before its Time, therefore afraid that it would not live. I soon returned to my Company but lost my Coffee and Tea. After Tea the Ladies and Gentlemen got to dancing and danced and sang till Supper Time —About 12 o'clock this night we all got to dancing again—We had many droll Songs from Mr. Walker who sings with great good humour and very well— He is a mighty lively and agreeable young man indeed—They all stayed with us till 3 o'clock in the Morning and then all returned to Mattishall but Betsy Davy who was left here to spend a few Days with us.—Upon the whole we spent a very agreeable, merry and cheerful Day, and every thing conducted and done extremely well by our Servants.

JULY 22. ... Sent a Letter to my Sister Pounsett to let her know that I had turned Will: Coleman away and that he is soon going for the West to his Friends.

JULY 25. . . . About 11 this morning Mrs. Davy, Betsy and Nunn, Colin and George Roupe, all on horseback and single made us a morning Visit for about an Hour and half and then returned back to Mattishall. They eat some cold Meat and drank some Beer here. To Mr. Cary for things from Norwich &c. p^d o. 9. 7. Colin Roupe told us that the Baloon which Major Money went up in, went 7 Leagues on the Sea, and that Major Money was 5 Hours up to his Chin in the Sea before he was taken up, and then by chance, a Boat very providentially being returning by him. He was in the Sea till 11 o'clock Saturday Night.[1] Will: Coleman dined with our Folks in Kitchen, he intends setting of for the West to Morrow. Ben and Briton were up with Will, at the Hart, this Evening, stayed there till after 10 o'clock.

JULY 26. . . . Will: Coleman called on us this morning to take his Leave, I gave him to help pay his Expences. 1. 1. 0. Gave him also for a Deal Chest which I gave him to put his Cloaths in the Sum of o. 10. 6. Will: was very low on the Occasion as was Nancy. He left us about 1 o'clock to go with the Morton Carrier to Norwich—and there to take Coach at Night. I shall be glad to hear that he is got safe

---

[1] This was one John Money (1752–1817), who as a soldier served in the American war under General Burgoyne, participating in the disaster of September–October 1777 with which that versatile general's name is associated. He is described in the *D.N.B.* as 'one of the earliest English aeronauts'. The unfortunate event chronicled by the Diarist took place after an ascent from Norwich on July 22nd, 1785. In a book published in 1803 he advocated the use of balloons in war. His career in the British Army after he went on half pay in 1784 as a major was not exciting; nevertheless he attained by steady promotion the rank of general in 1814. He died at Trowse Hall, Norwich, on March 26th, 1817.

into Somersett. To Cuppers Wife for 10 Chicken gave
0. 5. 0.

Aug. 1. . . . Coming from Mr. Custance's met with
a dumb Man almost naked—I gave him poor Creature
0. 0. 6. I sat and chatted with Mrs. Custance about
20 Minutes. Soon after we had dined, Mr. Du Quesne
came to us, smoked a Pipe with me and drank Tea
with us again.

Sep. 14. . . . Mrs. Davy and Betsy came here this
morning ab^t 8 o'clock in Clarke Hewitts Cart drove
by Billy Hewitt and they breakfasted, dined, supped
and slept here. Finished Harvest this day before
Dinner.

Sep. 15. . . . Mrs. Davy, Betsy, and my Niece, after
Tea this Afternoon about 6 o'clock went from my
House in Clark Hewitts Cart (which was left here
Yesterday) to Mattishall Parsonage where Mrs. Davy
boards with a Mr. and Mrs. Matthews (which Mr.
Matthews is an Exciseman and came from Lambourne
in Berkshire) whose House Mrs. Davy and Betsy
leaves at Michaelmas next, on Account of the Affair
being broke of between her and Mr. Smith, therefore
Nancy went with them to spend a few Days there
before they left Mattishall. They carried with them
in the Cart some cold boiled Beef, stuffed with
Parsley, some Turnips, Radishes, Colliflowers and
4 Cucumbers. My Boy Jack Secker drove them with
my Horse in it.

Sep. 22. . . . Mr. Custance sent us a brace of Partridges this Morn' which was very kind of him—
Mr. Micklethwaite has not sent us any, tho' daily out
with a Double-barrelled Gun and often in my Closes
close to my House. To Largesses to day gave 0. 1. 0.

Jⁿ Pegg called on me this Morn' on account of the new Taxes on Male and Female Servants, Horses and Waggons &c. I entered one Male Servant Briton, and two Female, Betty Dade and Molly Peachman—and two Horses. I was to have went to Mattishall to day and dine at Mrs. Davy's, but the Weather proving so very wet, prevented me—I fully intended to have went.

SEP. 26. . . . Dr. Bathurst's Curate Mr. Wilson sent me a Letter this Afternoon to desire me to advance some Money to him by Dr. Bathursts desire—I sent him an Answer that it was not in my Power, but referr'd him to some of the Doctors Tenants. Mrs. Davy likewise desired Nancy to speak to me to lend her twenty Pounds—but it is not in my Power.

SEP. 29. . . . We brewed again to day at which I assisted my Man Briton most part of the Day. To a poor distressed old Man of Mattishall by name Hudson for Oysters at 8ᵈ per Score pᵈ him o. 1. 6. He has bred up a large Family by the Blacksmiths business but since the Death of his Wife and being 60 Yʳˢ of Age and some of his Family not turning out well, obliged him to give up his business and broke, and become very poor.

OCT. 1. . . . Mrs. Davy and Betsy with Mr. Ashill, in a Dereham Post-Chaise called here this morning about 8 o'clock, breakfasted here and then took Nancy with them to a Place called Thurning about 10 Miles from Weston N.E.N. to look at a boarding Place for Mrs. Davy and Betsy—I did not like that Nancy should crowd into the Chaise with them and for no Purpose whatever—It made me rather cross. They all returned to dinner about 3 o'clock to my House. I gave them for Dinner, a fine Rump of Beef boiled and

Dumplins, a rost Fowl and a rost Duck and a large Damson Pye—Mrs. Davy, Betsy and Mr. Ashull sat of for Mattishall about an hour after Dinner. Mrs. Davy and Betsy have agreed to board at Thurning at a Mr. Elwin's, very good, creditable People and genteel. They go there at the half Quarter after Michaelmas. Mrs. Davy seemed displeased and uneasy all the Day. Nancy had a Letter from her Brother Sam in London—who tells her that he is going to Italy to finish his Studies in Painting—Mr. Richd Hoare made him the Offer and with it £100 per Annum during the Time that he is abroad.[1]

OCT. 10. . . . In the Afternoon my Maid Molly Peachman left my Service, being to be married to Morrow Morning. I paid her for 11 Months Wages at 5. 5. 0. Pr Ann. 4. 16. 6. She paid me out of it, what I lent her being 1. 1. 0.

OCT. 11. . . . I went to Church this morning and Married my late Maid, Molly Peachman to one J^s Shipley by Banns. Received for marrying them only 0. 2. 6. having had half a Crown before on publishing the Banns. Hambleton Custance, with his two Brothers George and William, with their Nurse Maid were present at the Marriage being a very fine morning.

OCT. 12. . . . I sent after my New Maid, Nanny Kaye, this Afternoon to Hockering, she returned home about 7 o'clock.

---

[1] Richard Hoare (1758–1838) was the son of Richard Hoare (1735–87) of the famous banking house who was created a baronet in 1786, in which title our Mr. Richard succeeded him in 1787. He was grandson —maternal—of the Mr. Henry Hoare mentioned earlier in the Diary, and succeeded to his property in Somerset in 1785. He was eminent as an antiquary, and historian of Wiltshire.

OCT. 22. . . . Had a Letter this Evening from my Sister Pounsett in which she mentions that Nancy's Brother Willm is coming into Norfolk to see us. My Man Briton had a new Suit of Livery brought home this Evening from Norwich, with a very good new great Coat of Brown Cloth and red Cape to it. I told Briton that I gave neither to him, but only to wear them during his Service with me.

OCT. 24. . . . The Tooth-Ach so very bad all night and the same this Morn' that I sent for John Reeves the Farrier who lives at the Hart and often draws Teeth for People, to draw one for me. He returned with my Man about 11 o'clock this Morning and he pulled it out for me the first Pull, but it was a monstrous Crash and more so, it being one of the Eye Teeth, it had but one Fang but that was very long. I gave Johnny Reeves for drawing it 0. 2. 6. A great pain in the Jaw Bone continued all Day and Night but nothing so bad as the Tooth Ach. To Mr. Cary for things from Norwich &c. p^d 0. 8. 8.

NOV. 8. . . . Went down to Lenewade Bridge this morning to attend at Dr. Bathursts Tithe Audit, dined there and stayed till near 6 o'clock this Evening —then returned home safe (thank God) with the Cash. All but one Person attended which was one Neale. Had not been home much more than an Hour before Nancy's Brother Willm came on horseback to our House from the West—he supped and slept here. He came thro' London, called on his Brother Saml who will also come to Weston in a few Days.

NOV. 10. . . . To John Pegg for Land Tax, &c., &c., pd. 5. 15. 0. About 11 o'clock this morning Mr. Press

Custance called on me in a Post Chaise, and I went
with him in it to Weston Church, clerically dressed,
and there buried in the Church Mr. Custances
youngest Daughter Mary Anne which was brought to
Church in their Coach and four with Mrs. Alldis the
Housekeeper and the Childs Nurse Hetty Yollop—
only in it besides the Corpse. The Infant was only
16 Weeks old. After interring it—I rec^d from Mr.
Press Custance 5. 5. 0. wrapped up in a clean Piece of
writing Paper. I had also a black Silk Hatband and
a P^r of white Gloves.

Nov. 19. . . . As I was dressing for Dinner, Nancy's
Brother Saml from London came here in a Chaise,
and he dined supped and slept here with his Brother—
He sat out of London, last Night at 8 o'clock, travelled
all night in the Mail Coach—came here about 3 this
Afternoon.

Nov. 20. . . . Nancy and her two Brothers, Willm and
Saml, breakfasted, dined, supped and slept again at
Weston Parsonage. I read Prayers and Preached this
morning at Weston. Mr. Micklethwaite at Church—
none from Weston House. It gave me much pleasure
to see Nancy and her two Brothers appear so happy
here—and so in each other.

Nov. 28. . . . Between 2 and 3 o'clock, Mr. Custance
sent his Coach after us to go and dine at Weston
House. Nancy my two Nephews, and self went in it,
and dined and spent the Afternoon there with Mr. and
Mrs. Custance, Mrs. Collyer Senr, and Mr. and Mrs.
Collyer of Dereham.—After Tea and Coffee we got to
Cards at Quadrille at which I lost 0. 4. 0. About 9
this Evening myself and Nephews put on our great
Coats and walked home to Supper, as there was no
Moon and too dark for a Carriage. Nancy was left

behind where she supped and slept. Rec^d of Ben this Evening for 2 Piggs sold to his Father 1. 2. 0.

DEC. 1. . . . After breakfast my Nephews and self took a ride to Mattishall, called at Mr. Thornes, Mr. Smiths and Mr. Bodhams, neither of them at home— We saw Mrs. Bodham and Miss Bodham with whom we stayed about an Hour, drunk a glass of Wine apiece and eat some Cake and returned home to dinner after a pleasant ride. About 5 o'clock this Afternoon, Mrs. Davy and Betsy came here from Norwich in a Post Chaise, and they supped and slept here with my Niece. For Mrs. Davy to the Norwich Chaise Driver p^d 0. 1. 6.

DEC. 3. . . . My Nephew Samuel drew my Picture to day in Crayon. He likewise drew his own Picture, his Brother's and Sister's, Mrs. Davy's and Betsy's.

DEC. 4. . . . I made my Nephew Saml a present this Evening of 5. 5. 0.

DEC. 5. . . . Saml set of from my House for London by way of Norwich—His Brother Willm rode with him to Norwich. And Ben carried his Trunk &c. in Carys Cart to Norwich. My Nephew Sam: rode to Norwich on my little Mare Jenny. My Boy Jack went with Ben to have back Jenny. . . .

DEC. 12. . . . To Cobb the Rat-Catcher, his annual Stipend p^d 1. 1. 0. To my Butcher, Henry Baker, his Bill for the Year p^d 41. 5. 0. Paid him before my Nephew and Niece. Poor Tom Twaites of Honingham who was beat by the Poachers at Mr. Townshends the other day is lately dead of the Wounds he then rec^d from them. His Skull was fractured in 2 Places.

DEC. 18. ... The Captain [Will] breakfasted, dined, &c. here again. I read Prayers and Preached this Morning at Weston. Mr. Custance was at Church this morning. Whilst I was at Dinner to Day, a Letter was brought me by my Butchers Lad, from the Bishop of Norwich to request me to preach the 19 of March next at St. Clements at Norwich, for the Benefit of the Charity Schools there. I did not relish it.

DEC. 19. ... The Captain and myself took a ride to Norwich and the Servant with us—We got there between 1 and 2 o'clock, put up our Horses at the Kings Head and there dined at the Ordinary on a fine piece of boiled Beef and a Saddle of Mutton &c. After Dinner the Captain and myself, went and saw the learned Pigg at the rampant Horse in St. Stephens —there was but a small Company there but soon got larger—We stayed there about an Hour—It was wonderful to see the sagacity of the Animal—It was a Boar Pigg, very thin, quite black with a magic Collar on his Neck. He would spell any word or Number from the Letters and Figures that were placed before him paid for seeing the Pigg 0. 1. 0.[1] After that went with Bill to two or three Places and then returned to the Kings Head, soon afterwards my Nephew mounted his Poney and set of for Weston and my Servant with him. It was about 6 o'clock in the

This was the learned pig to which Cowper refers in a charming letter to the Rev. John Newton on April 22nd, 1785: 'When I received your account of the great celebrity of *John Gilpin*, I felt myself both flattered and grieved. ... Your letter was followed the next post by one from Mr. Unwin. You tell me that I am rivalled by Mrs. Bellamy; and he, that I have a competitor for fame, not less formidable, in the Learned Pig. Alas! what is an author's popularity worth, in a world that can suffer a prostitute on one side, and a pig on the other, to eclipse his brightest glories? ...'

Evening that they went away, very dark and no Moon. After they went I walked about Town and paid several Bills and then walked to the Assembly-Rooms near Chapel Field and heard an excellent Lecture on Astronomy &c. spoken by one Walker, with a View of his Eidouranion of transparent Orrery —was highly pleased with it. A great deal of Company present I paid o. 2. 6. I then returned to the Kings Head and there supped, and slept. Supper being just going in for the Family I joined them, and there met with the best Supper I ever met with at an Inn.—Hashed Fowl, Veal Collopes, a fine Woodcock, a Couple of Whistling Plovers, a real Teal of the small kind and hot Apple Pye. . . .

DEC. 21. . . . This being St. Thomas's Day, had a great many poor People of the Parish to visit me, I gave to each of them that came, sixpence. Gave in all to day to the poor 1. 5. 6. About 12 o'clock Mr. Ashill of Norwich called here in his return home from Thurning, after visiting Mrs. Davy and Daughter there—The former sending for him on being taken exceeding ill about the late disagreeable Affair with Mr. Smith. Mr. Ashill says that it has almost made her distracted, she is very unhappy. Mr. Ashill eat some cold Mutton &c. and then at 2 o'clock sat of for Norwich again.

DEC. 29. . . . Had a very long Letter from Mr. Smith this morning concerning Mrs. Davy and himself, wherein he lays the whole blame on her in a late affair accusing her for her too great familiarity to one Clarkson. To my Butchers Man, Billy Stonton, Xmas Gift o. 1. 0. To Neighbour Howes's Wife for 5 Chicken p^d o. 2. 6.

1786

JAN. 7. . . . I walked with my Nephew before Dinner up to our Church, but had great difficulty to get thither for the Snow, in the Lane by Billy Bidewells the Snow was full 4 foot deep in many Places—we were pretty near half an Hour getting there. In the Lane leading from Church Street to Car-Cross was quite full of Snow and up almost to the top of the Hedge.—We returned home rather a better way by Js. Smiths and down Blacker-Field. I sent Ben to Norwich this Morning as Cary did not go, but gave him orders not to run risk or danger if he met with difficulties from the Snow. He returned home safe about 4 o'clock this Aft.

JAN. 8. . . . No Divine Service at Church this Morning, owing to the Snow having rendered the roads almost impassable from most Parts of the Parish.

JAN. 9. . . . Dr. Thorne dined and spent the Afternoon here and did not leave us till near 9 o'clock——He was obliged he said to get over hedges into the Inclosures in some Places, the Lanes being impassable.

FEB. 12. . . . I sent Nancy and Betsy Davy Yesterday Morn' to Coventry and have not as yet spoke to either of them.

FEB. 13. . . . Nancy and Betsy not sent for from Coventry as yet.

FEB. 14. . . . To 53. Valentines to Day gave o. 4. 5. Nancy and Betsy Davy called home this Aft. from Coventry. The Captain after breakfast took a ride to Thurning to see Mrs. Davy and there stayed and dined and spent the Afternoon, but returned home to Supper.

FEB. 18. . . . Mr. Smith of Mattishall sent me a note this Morn' to desire me to meet him in Weston Churchyard privately, which I accordingly did, and there I stayed with him near an Hour, talking over the Affair between him and Mrs. Davy—by which he made out that Mrs. Davy was as artful and bad as any Woman could be. It surprised me astonishingly indeed. After breakfast the Captain took a ride to Mattishall and did not return till 12 at Night, just as I was going to bed after sitting up for him till that Time—I cannot say but I was rather displeased at it especially being Saturday Night. Had another Letter from Mr. Jeanes abt. Witchingham. Sent my Man Ben with 10 Coomb of Barley to Norwich to sell for me and he sold it at 9^s o^d per Coomb in all recd. 4. 10. 0. He brought back ½ Chldrn of Coal for which he paid Lock o. 15. 2.

MAR. 10. . . . My Nephew took a ride this morning to Elmham to see an ancient Roman Lamp lately dug up there and which he saw and returned home to dinner. The Captain seemed well pleased on seeing the above it was rather small but well preserved and is of Copper. He drew a Sketch of it on Paper with his Pencil.

MAR. 11. . . . Betsy Davy breakfasted, dined, &c. &c. here again. The Captain breakfasted, dined &c. &c. here again. Mr. Custance called on us this Morning, stayed with us about half an Hour, and desired our Company at dinner on Wednesday next with our Company. This Evening about 6 o'clock Mrs. Davy came here in a Post Chaise from Norwich in her way from Pulham having been there and in Suffolk on Account of the Death of a Brother of hers at Woodbridge. Mrs. Davy drank Tea this Aft. supped and slept here.

MAR. 12. . . . I read Prayers and Preached this Morn' at Weston Church. Mr. and Mrs. Custance at Church. Neither any from my House at Church but self and 2 Servants. Mrs. Davy took on a good deal to day, and soon after Tea this Evening she took it in her head to go to bed. I had been persuading her not to go to Mattishall.

MAR. 17. . . . Mrs. Davy breakfasted, dined, supped and slept here again. Betsy Davy breakfasted here and about 12 she took leave of Weston Parsonage and went on horseback to Mr. Thorne's at Mattishall, and there she dined, supped and slept—poor dear soul— She was much hurried by her Mother on going away. Am much afraid it will be a very long time before she will be at Weston Parsonage again. The Captain took a ride to Mattishall with Betsy Davy and he dined with her there, and returned home to Supper. Dr. Thorne being from home at the assises at Thetford which begins this day.

MAR. 18. . . . Mrs. Davy breakfasted and spent part of the Morn' with us.—About 1 o'clock Mrs. Thorne of Mattishall came after Mrs. Davy to spend a few Days with her and they returned to Mattishall about 2 o'clock. Our Parting was rather cool than otherwise. . . .

MAR. 23. . . . Poor Mr. Micklethwaite is gone to Lynn, and it is thought will never return again as he declines very fast in a consumptive Complaint.

MAR. 28. . . . Nancy breakfasted and spent the

Morning with us till after 1 o'clock, then Mrs. Bodham of Mattishall came after her in her Chaise, and
she returned with her to Mattishall before Dinner
and is to stay some Days with Mr. and Mrs. Bodham
at South-Green.¹ Nancy's Brother breakfasted, dined
&c, here again. I married this morning Harry
Andrews, Widower and Mary Horner, Widow—rec^d
for it o. 5. o.

MAR. 29. . . . Brewed some strong Beer to day, in w^ch
assisted Briton.

MAR. 30. . . . Brewed again this morning some more
strong Beer. Mr. Thorne and Nephew Walker, gave
us a Call this Morning.

MAR. 31. . . . We were to have went to Mattishall to
dinner to day at Mr. Bodham's, but my Nephew's
little grey horse being taken very ill, and obliged to
send for a Farrier, prevented our going according to

¹ Mrs. Bodham requires notice, for she was the poet Cowper's 'my
dearest Cousin', or 'my dearest Rose', of his delightful letters.
She was his cousin because she was Anne Donne, the niece of
Cowper's mother, also Anne Donne, who in turn was the daughter
of Roger Donne (1673–1722), of Ludham, Norfolk, gentleman,
descended from the great Dean of St. Paul's. Cowper considered
that he himself was more of a Donne than a Cowper—see specially his
letter to Mrs. Bodham of February 27th, 1790. It was Mrs. Bodham
who sent Cowper the picture of his mother, which drew from him the
exquisite poem, 'O that those lips had language!' and it was 'to my
cousin, Anne Bodham', that in 1793 he wrote the lyric 'on receiving
from her a Network Purse, made by herself'. Mrs. Bodham was born
in 1748, and lived to be 98. She married the Rev. Thomas Bodham,
M.A., Fellow of Gonville and Caius College, Cambridge, and sometime
curate of Mattishall, and as they had no children they brought up their
niece, Miss Anne Vertue Donne, who was the daughter of the Rev.
Castres Donne. She is the diarist's 'Miss Anne Donne', and at this time
was about five years old. Mrs. Bodham was first cousin of Dr. William
Donne (1735–1803), who was a well-known Norwich surgeon; he is
mentioned more than once by the diarist. One of her nephews was the
Rev. John Johnson (1769–1833), rector of Yaxham, and Welborne,
Norfolk, who has come down to fame as Cowper's 'Johnny of Norfolk'.

promise. I sent a Note to my Niece who is there on a Visit and she sent me an Answer, that Mr. and Mrs. Bodham were very angry with us. Mr. Du Quesne was asked to meet us on purpose.

APRIL 16. . . . This being Easter Day I went to Weston Church this Morning and there read Prayers and administered the H: Sacrament to at least 30 Communicants. For an offering at the H: Sacrament gave 0. 2. 6. Mrs. Custance at Church and at the H: Sacrament, Mr. Custance not there being sent for unexpectedly to Norwich. Neither Nancy or Brother at Church. My Clerk, James Smith, dined with our Folks in Kitchen. My good tempered Cow Polly, had a Calf this Morning early.

APRIL 19. . . . Mr. Walker from Mattishall came here about 12 o'clock and he dined and spent the Afternoon with us—a very droll Young Man he is and an excellent Singer. About 1 o'clock who should come to my House but Mr. Jeanes the New Rector of the Witchinghams,[1] I mounted my Mare immediately and went with him to great Witchingham and inducted him into the Church &c. He then returned with me and dined and spent the Afternoon with us —In the Evening he returned to Norwich to his Wife and another Lady who are at Lodgings in the City— Jeanes was only married last Thursday in London, she is very young it is said. We had some Fish and a Surloin of Beef rosted &c. Betsy Davy returned with Mr. Walker in the Evening to Mattishall to Mr.

---

[1] Jeanes or Jeans, Thomas (1749–1835), son of Thomas, of Christchurch, Hants, gentleman. Merton College, Oxford, 1767; Fellow of New College, B.A. 1773, M.A. 1776, D.D. 1816, rector of Witchingham, Norfolk, and vicar of St. Johns, Maddermarket, Norwich, 1785, until his death in 1835.

Thornes. Nancy had a Letter from her Sister this Evening.

APRIL 27. . . . To J^n_o Pegg for $\frac{3}{4}$ of Years Servants Tax for Males and being a Batchelor, double p^d 1. 17. 6. To Ditto—for Female Servants Tax also for $\frac{3}{4}$ Year and being a Batchelor double p^d 0. 15. 0. To Ditto $\frac{1}{2}$ Years Horse Tax p^d 0. 10. 0. I pay for 1 Male Servant 2 Female Servants and for 2 Horses. For every Male Servant per Annum 2. 10. 0. For every Female Servant per Annum 0. 10. 0. For every Horse, for riding per Annum 0. 10. 0.

MAY 27. . . . Very fine Weather indeed for the Wheat &c. 'Lord make us more worthy thy Divine Favours.'

MAY 30. . . . We all went to Dereham this Morning to Mr. Thomas's and there dined and spent the afternoon with him, Miss Thomas, Miss Betsy and Miss Anne Thomas, and Mr. Du Quesne—It was very hot to day. Nancy went with Briton in the little Cart, and myself and Nephew went on horseback. We returned home a little after 9 this Evening, we spent a tolerable agreeable Day there—Miss Thomas is very reserved and not handsome—Miss Betsy is very agreeable and pretty—Miss Anne very still and coarse. We had for Dinner a boiled Leg of Mutton and Caper Sauce, a green Goose rosted and Gooseberries, Veal Cutlets, Lobsters, pickled Salmon, Damson Tarts and Syllabubs. . . .

JUNE 2. . . . About 1 o'clock we sat of for Mattishall to Mr. Smith's and there we dined and spent the Afternoon with him, Mr. Du Quesne, Mr. and Mrs. Bodham, Miss Anne Donne of Norwich, and a Mr. Lane a young Clergyman, whom Mr. Smith invited on my Account for me to speak to him to serve my Church during my absence from Weston, as I intend (Deo volente) spending a few Weeks with my Friends in Somersetshire soon. He seems a good kind of a young Man, and very willing to engage on it. He lives at Hingham, he is to enter on serving Weston the 25 of this Month, and to serve it from that Time for a Q^r of a Year for which I am to give him at the rate of 30 Pounds per Annum with all surplice Fees during that Time. We had for Dinner to Day some Maccarel, 3 spring Chicken and a Tongue, a Leg of Mutton rosted, Gooseberry Tarts and Custards. After Coffee and Tea we got to Quadrille lost 0. 0. 6. We returned home to Weston about ½ past 9 o'clock as we went—that is, Nancy went with Briton in the little Cart, The Captain and myself on horseback. We spent a very agreeable Day—Whilst we were at Cards we had a Syllabub carried round.

JUNE 5. . . . This being Whit Monday there was running for a Shift, plowing &c. &c. this Afternoon at the Heart.

JUNE 8. . . . Had my Garden mowed again for the 2nd time. Got a pain in my right Ear to catching Cold I believe. Had a Tub of Gin brought me this Evening from Robt Buck of Honingham, blacksmith, by my Man Ben Leggatt. I am to pay for it to Ben 1. 3. 0.

JUNE 9. . . . My Ear something better to day—took some Rhubarb last night. Bottled of my Gin this morning—19 Bottles. The Captain very busy about his Ship, as she is to be launched to Morrow, having Company to dine with us.

JUNE 10. . . . My Ear pained me very much all the Morning. Mr. Custance sent us a nice Melon this

Morning. The Captain very busy this Morning with his Ship. Sent Briton early this Morning to Norwich after Fish &c. he returned before 12 o'clock with Maccarel &c. He went in the little Cart and had the Horse Punch. Mr. and Mrs. Bodham with Miss Anne Donne from Norwich, Mr. Du Quesne, Mr. Smith, and Mr. Lane of Hingham who is to officiate for me at Weston during my Absence dined and spent the Afternoon with us. Just before Dinner the Captain launched his new Ship, before the Ladies and Gentlemen present but to his great Chagrin and the Company's disappointment it upset and went down to the starboard side almost immediately and took in Water and could not be righted. She was far too much overmasted. We were all exceedingly sorry on the Captains Account. We had for Dinner some Maccarel, a fore Q^r of Lamb, 3 boiled Chicken and a Pigs Face, Pigeons and Asparagus, Lobster, Apricot and Gooseberry Tarts and Custards. After Dinner by way of Desert—A Melon, Oranges, Almonds and Raisins. The Company left us about 8 o'clock this Evening.

JUNE 12. . . . My Ear pained me much again this morning. To Mr. Cary for things from Norwich &c. p^d 0. 8. 6. To my Man Briton for things from Norwich &c. p^d 0. 14. 8. Took a good large Dose of Rhubarb last Night, as did also Nancy, made her get up at 4 o'clock this Morn'. The Captain got up early this morning and sat of for Mattishall to my Glaziers, Hubbard, after some Lead to put on at the bottom of the Ship by way of a false Keel and returned home with it 10 o'clock, with a long piece which weighed 25 Pound—After he had breakfasted he put on the Lead to the bottom of the Vessel and then she sailed as well as our most sanguine wishes could desire.

JUNE 14. . . . Paid to Nancy this Afternoon for the little Market-Cart which she paid Mrs. Davy Yesterday and which Mrs. Davy had paid to Mrs. Elwin of Thurning for the Widow of the late Rev^d Mr. Headley of North Walsham 1. 11. 6.

JUNE 18. . . . I read Prayers and Preached this Morning at Weston Ch[urch]. Mrs. Custance with her eldest Son at Church and my Niece. Mr. Custance at home on the late Death of Mr. Morris, a Relation. Nancys Brother not at Church also, not being dressed in time. Mrs. Custance with her three Sons drank Tea with us this Afternoon—Mr. Custance not at home—Mrs. Custance &c. came to see the Ship on the Water. She admired it very much indeed.

JUNE 23. . . . Nancy and Brother breakfasted, and dined here again. After dinner we all went to Norwich in a Post Chaise which we had from thence, and carried our Baggage with us, Briton went also in my Cart with a Trunk for the Captain—We all got to Norwich about 6 o'clock and drank Tea at the Kings Head, and stayed there till half past 6 o'clock and then went to the Angel Inn and at 7 o'clock this Evening, myself, Nancy and Brother went in the heavy Coach for London with three strange Women in it also. Paid at the Kings Head at Norwich for Chaise from Weston, Tea &c. about 0. 15. 0. For 3 Peoples Fare to London I p^d 4. 10. 0. For extra Luggage—12 St. I p^d 0. 15. 0. It was very hot this Evening, especially with a Coach full.

JUNE 24. We had a very fine pleasant night of travelling we went thro' Bury &c. we breakfasted very early but where I know not—I paid for our breakfasts 0. 3. 0. To the Coachman that drove us half way gave 0. 3. 0. We all got to London (thank God) safe

and well by 3 o'clock this Afternoon—to the Swan
and 2 Necks in Lad Lane where we had some
Rum and Water. To the last Coachman gave o. 3. o.
After staying some little Time in Lad Lane we had a
Coach and went with our Luggage to our old Inn the
Bell Savage at Ludgate Hill where we supped and
slept—and kept by the same People, Burton and his
Wife. Nancy and her Brother walked out in the
Evening by themselves, giving me the Slip, and did not
return till Supper time, at which I was much displeased and gave it to them smartly, and to make it
still worse soon as Supper was removed and having
ordered a Bottle of Wine, they left me without drinking a drop and went to bed leaving me by myself—I
sat up by myself very uneasy till about 12 and then I
went.

JUNE 25. We breakfasted, supped and slept again at
the Bell Savage. Very much pestered and bit by the
Buggs in the Night. After dressing ourselves, after
breakfast we walked down to Charing Cross, and
there took a Coach and went to Kensington Gardens
and there we walked about till near 3 in the Afternoon
—and then we walked back to the 13 Cantons near
Charing Cross where we dined on Beef a la mode and
which was very good. For the Coach and Turnpike
to Kensington Gardens p^d o. 3. 2. In our walk back
we called at a House and refreshed ourselves with
some Rum and Water and then walked on. We met
the Prince of Wales's Carriage with him in it, as we
walked back to Charing Cross. For our refreshment
at the above house p^d o. 1. 6. At the 13 Cantons paid
and gave about o. 2. o. After we had dined we retired
to an adjoining House to drink Cyder where I smoked
a Pipe p^d there o. 1. 6.

JUNE 26. We breakfasted, supped and slept again at
the Bell Savage. I was bit so terribly with Buggs again
this Night that I got up at 4 o'clock this Morning and
took a long Walk by myself about the City till breakfast time. After breakfast we walked to Osborn Place.
Spital Fields to deliver a Letter for Mrs. Bodham to
Miss Eliz: Donne at that Place, but she was from
home, after leaving the Letter we immediately returned back—We went thro' a most black-guard
Place going to the above House. We took Coach part
of the way coming back and went to the 13 Cantons
again at Charing Cross where we dined again on beef
a la mode p^d there o. 2. o. For the Coach hire thither
and back p^d o. 3. o. In the Evening we took Coach
and went to the Circus in St Georges Fields and there
saw wonderful Feats of Horsemanship &c. performed
by Hughes and his Children. For Coach hire thither
p^d o. 1. o. For 3 Pit Tickets at the Circus I p^d o. 9. o
For Oranges &c. to day p^d o. 1. o. For a little red
Book of Prints p^d this Evening o. 12. o. I saw a vast
number of strange Prints at the Shop. We were
obliged to walk back this Evening from the Circus as
we could get no Coach. Andrew Russ, Mr. Russ's son
of Castle-Cary called on us this Morning, he lives as
a Journeyman to one Gould an Hatter, near St Pauls
Church Yard.

JUNE 27. We breakfasted, dined and slept again at
the Bell Savage. One George Pace, a young Man,
and Mess Mate of my Nephews called on us this
Morning and he dined supped and spent the Evening
with us at the Bell Savage. Nancy and me walked
about Town by ourselves this Morn'. The Captain
and George Pace went with themselves. I shewed
Nancy the Mews and the Kings Cream coloured

Horses, also the Kings State Coach which she sat in.
Gave to the Men that shewed us the same 0. 2. 0. For
a Silver Fruit Knife for Jenny Pounsett p^d 0. 10. 6.
At Charlesworths near Covent Garden for Gauze
Gloves, Ribband &c. for Nancy I paid 1. 1. 0. For
three Places in the Bath Coach for to Morrow Night,
for part of the Fare thither p^d 3. 3. 0. In the Evening
Nancy and Brother, George Pace, and myself went in
a Coach to the Theatre in the Hay-Market late Mr.
Footes[1]—and there saw a Play and Farce, both performed incomparably well—it begun about 7 o'clock
and not over till after 10 or very near 11 o'clock. For
4 Tickets and Coach hire back and thither I p^d
0. 15. 0. To a Barber for shaving and dressing me p^d
0. 2. 0. George Pace did not leave us till near 12 this
Evening. I did not pull of my Cloaths last Night but
sat up in a great Chair all night with my Feet on the
bed and slept very well considering and not pestered
with buggs.

June 28. We breakfasted again at the Bell Savage.
I did not pull of my Cloaths last Night again but did
as the Night before, and slept tolerably well. After
breakfast George Pace called on us and then went
out with the Captain—Nancy walked with me to one
Smiths in Surry Street, Strand, a Barber and there had
her Hair full dressed—Smith was Sam Woodfordes
Hair Dresser—I was shaved and had my Wig dressed
there. I gave him for shaving and dressing 0. 1. 6.
After that, the Captain and George Pace joined us and
we walked about Town, shopping &c. till 3 this Aft:
and then went to the 13 Cantons again and there dined
again on Beef a la mode, I p^d for all 0. 2. 6. The
Captain and George Pace then left us and Nancy and

---

[1] i.e. Samuel Foote (1719–77), the eminent actor, wit, and dramatist.

myself walked back to our Inn, packed up all our things and were ready for our Journey by 6 o'clock. I paid at the Bell Savage, our Bill 3. 14. 0. To Servants at the Inn gave 0. 10. 6. At a Q^r before 7 this Evening Nancy and self got into the Bath Coach, and were just setting out, after some time waiting for Bill, when he luckily arrived, but it was enough to make one very mad, he was at last obliged to leave some things behind him. We had four of us in the Coach and Guard on top. It carries but 4 inside, and is called the Baloon Coach on Account of its travelling so fast, making it a point to be before the Mail Coach. We trimmed it of indeed, tho' only a P^r of Horses.

JUNE 29. About 4 o'clock this morning we all breakfasted but at what place I know not—p^d for the same 0. 4. 0. To the first Coachman and Guard I gave 0. 4. 0. For the other part of our Fare to Bath p^d 1. 7. 0. For extra Luggage—p^d also at breakfast 0. 13. 0. We all got safe to Bath (thank God) this morning about 10 o'clock, to the Castle-Inn, where we made a second breakfast, and there also dined supped and slept. To the last Coachman gave 0. 1. 0. After breakfasting at Bath we took a walk over the City till dinner time to shew Nancy the public Rooms &c. she being never at Bath before—gave for seeing them 0. 1. 0. We had very good accommodation at our Inn.

JUNE 30. We breakfasted and spent all the Morning at Bath, and about Noon we got into a Post Chaise and set forth with our Luggage for Shepton Mallet about 19 Miles from Bath, got there about 5 o'clock, had some Rum and Water at the George Inn, took a fresh Chaise and sat of for Cole to Pounsetts—thro' Ansford. At the Castle Inn at Bath for Chaise to

Shepton, our own eating, Lodging &c.—paid and
gave there 2. 7. 4½. For some Fish, Soals and a Crab
to carry to Cole p^d o. 3. 2. To the Bath Driver and
for Rum and Water at Shepton p^d o. 3. o. We saw
my Nephew J^s White at Shepton Mallett. When we
got to Ansford Turnpike Gate we dropt the Captain
and his Trunk &c. there—who went to his Fathers.
Nancy and self went on to Cole, driving pretty fast
thro' Ansford, calling no where—and thank God got
to Cole to my Sister Pounsetts about 8 o'ciock this
Evening and found both my Sister and Mr. Pounsett
and Daughter brave. For the Shepton Chaise and
Driver—p^d and gave o. 10. 6. To Turnpikes to day
p^d about o. 2. o. We supped and slept at Mr. Pounsetts, very little fatigued.

JULY 15. . . . After breakfast I walked out a fishing,
had not put my Line in Water more than five Minutes
before I caught a fine Trout of one Pound and a
Quarter with a Grasshopper. It measured in length
14 Inches and in the highest Season. Mrs. Pounsett
Senr dined and spent the Aft: with us. After Tea this
Aft: walked out again with my Rod and Line up the
Bruton River and there caught another fine Trout
which weighed 1 Pound and ¼ and measured 14½
inches. Mr. Sam: Pounsett supped and spent the
Evening with us.

JULY 30. . . . Nancy's Brother Willm came over here
this Morning and he dined and spent the Afternoon
here. A Mrs. Forster (late Slade) came over here this
Morning and she dined and spent the Afternoon here.
Mr. and Mrs. Pounsett, Mrs. Forster, Sister White,
Nancy and Brother, and Jenny Pounsett all went to
Pitcomb Church this Afternoon. I stayed at home
having a little Head-Ache and thinking also that they

would be crowded at Church. Robert White and Wife, Jˢ White and Juliana Woodforde spent the Afternoon with us—a good house-full.

Aug. 7. . . . Robert Shoard who married Farmer Corps Daughter and since the Farmer died, has continued my Estate at Ansford, called on me this Morning and paid me a Years Rent due Lady Day last past the Sum of 35. 0. 0. I paid him out of it for Poor Rates and Church 1. 12. 2¼. I paid him also for a new Gate 0. 7. 0. I gave Robert a Receipt on stampt Paper, and to let him with his Mother Law continue on the Estate. Poor Farmer Corp died just before we came down. He had over-heated himself it was said and was imprudent to drink cold Water after it. Brother John and Wife and Jˢ Clarke spent the Aft: with us. Jˢ Clarke supped and spent the Evening also with us.

Aug. 10. . . . Nancy and self very busy this morning in making the Charter having some Company to dine with us—But unfortunately the Cellar Door being left open whilst it was put in there to cool, one of the Greyhounds (by name Jigg) got in and eat the whole, with a Cold Tongue &c. Sister Pounsett and Nancy mortally vexed at it. Jˢ Clarke and Wife and Jenny Ashford dined and spent the Afternoon with us—We had for Dinner some Maccarel, boiled Beef, a Couple of Ducks rosted, a brace of Pigeons rosted and a Barberry Tart. Mrs. Pounsett Senʳ dined and spent the Afternoon with us.

Aug. 29. . . . Jˢ Clarke and Wife made us a morning Visit. Nancy much better all day and eat very hearty —She recᵈ a Letter this Aft: from her Brother Samˡ at Rome. He is very well—but complains of poor

living there. The Letter was dated 9 of this Month
—only 20 Days ago. Brother John and Wife and
Mrs. Richd Clarke dined and spent the Afternoon
with us—We had for Dinner Ham and Fowls, Tripe,
green Peas, a fine Hare and Rasberry Tart. At
Quadrille this Evening lost o. 1. o. Nancy borrowed
of me last Night for Cards o. 2. o.

SEP. 1. . . . This being the first Day of Partridge
Shooting, Mr. Pounsett went out about 6 o'clock this
Morn' and returned home before 11 o'clock with four
brace of Birds. Sr Richd Hoares deputy Gamekeeper
Richd Barley went out with him—Mr. Pounsett killed
the most Birds. . . .

SEP. 12. . . . After breakfast my Sister Pounsett,
Daughter and self took a walk up to Sally Poyntings
who had a Mother 87 Years of Age, but we did not
see her, I left with her Daughter for her, to buy
Tobacco for her o. 1. o. Sister White walked over
from Ansford to Cole this Morning and she dined,
supped and slept here. Nancy's Brother Willm spent
the Aft: supped and spent the Evening with us. Sam:
Pounsett supped &c. with us. At Quadrille this
Evening with Sister White, and Mr. and Mrs. Pounsett—at 1^d per fish won o. o. 6.

SEP. 15. . . . A Miss Nancy Chiddock of Batcomb
drank Tea with us this Afternoon at Mrs. Donnes—
an agreeable well looking middle Aged Maid.

SEP. 19. . . . Gave Brother Heighes this morning a
Pair of Spectacles with a very handsome Tortoise-
shell Case and Silver mounted—they were formerly
the Treasurers I believe. Brother Heighes with his Son
Willm and Daughter Juliana dined and spent the
Afternoon with us. Robert White dined and spent the

Afternoon here. At Quadrille this Evening lost 0. 2. 6.

SEP. 21. ... Nancy, Sister Pounsett and self went to Ansford this Morn' on foot with Nancy's Brother Willm who came over to breakfast and we all dined at Castle Cary at R: Clarkes with her, my Brother John and Wife and Juliana Woodforde and her Father—We had for Dinner, a Neck of Mutton boiled and Capers and a rost Shoulder of Pork alias mock Goose and a nice plumb Pudding. J^s Clarke spent part of the Afternoon with us. My Brother John indifferent to day being merry last Night and very near being killed last Night going home from Ansford Inn to his own House on horseback and falling of—His face is cut but little however. We all drank Tea this Afternoon at Mr. John Burges with him, his Wife and her Mother Mrs. Millward. Nancy and self walked back to Cole in the Evening, Jenny rode. Mr. Pounsett went of early this Morning a hunting and he dined &c. at Mrs. Donnes at Westcomb.

SEP. 23. ... Went out a coursing this morning with Mr. Pounsett towards Godminster, killed a brace of Hares and a Rabbit. I parted with Mr. Pounsett before we returned, and walked by myself into Bruton and went to Mr. Harry Martins by appointment and borrowed of him 50. 0. 0. for which I gave him my Bond—so that I owe Mr. Martin now on Mortgage and Bond 700. 0. 0. For drawing the Bond &c. p^d him 0. 12. 6. I was very uneasy all the Morning long. Patty Davidge a Tenant of mine at Ansford called here this Afternoon and paid me only 1. 1. 0. out of 4. 4. 0.—I gave her out of that also 0. 2. 6. At Quadrille this Evening neither won or lost.

OCT. 4. I breakfasted and spent part of the Morning at Cole. Nancy breakfasted, and spent part of the

Morn' at Cole. After taking Leave of our Cole
Friends, Nancy and self set forth in a Chaise from
Bruton for Weston. Gave to my God-Daughter Jenny
Pounsett o. 2. 6. To poor little Betsy Guppey, an
Orphan gave o. 2. 6. To Mr. Pounsett's three
Servants gave 1. 1. 0. Mrs. Pounsett's Senr Maids
Sybil and Sally gave o. 5. 6. We called at Wincaunton
to see Miss Tucker, but she was gone. From Wincaunton we went on to Meer and there changed
Chaises and went on to Hindon—there we were
obliged to bait the Horses as we could get no Chaise
and then went on in the same Chaise for Sarum.
N.B. At the same Inn at Hindon was Mr. Pitt the
prime Minister, in the same Dilemma as we were all
the Horses being engaged—He was going to Burton
Pynsent.[1] We got to Salisbury to the White Hart
about 6 in the Evening and there we supped and
slept, a good Inn, kept by one Weeks—The Inn
almost full being the Salisbury Musick Meeting this
Week. For the Chaise to Meer and Driver p^d o. 14. 6.
For the Chaise to Salisbury and Driver p^d 1. 5. 6.
To Turnpikes and some refreshment for ourselves
o. 3. 6.

OCT. 5. We breakfasted, dined, supped and slept
again in Sarum. We walked about Salisbury a great
deal to day, saw the Bishops Garden—and the
Cathedral—and also the Company returning from
another Church after the grand Musick.—All the

[1] Burton Pynsent was the estate in Somerset which had been left,
together with nearly £3,000 a year, to Pitt's father, Chatham, in 1765
by Sir William Pynsent, Bt., a country gentleman quite unknown to
the great Minister, but an admirer of him. It was here that Lady
Chatham died in 1803. William Pitt the younger, when the diarist and
Nancy saw him in this travelling dilemma, was in the third year of his
seventeen years' unbroken period of premiership, and was only just
twenty-seven.

Ladies highly dressed. To the Girl that shewed us the Cathedral gave o. 1. o. For a pair of Scissars and a Penknife to day p^d o. 5. o. For 2 Places in the London Coach for to Morrow Morn early—paid half price on taking the same o. 18. o. Paid our Bill this Evening— which with Serv^ts came 1. 15. o. Nancy also bought a neat p^r of Scissars for o. 4. 6.

Oct. 6. We got up about 4 this morning and at 5 got into the London Coach and set forth for London. We had one Passenger from Salisbury with us an Officer in the Guards, an handsome young Man. At Stockbridge where we breakfasted we took up an other Gentleman, a sensible old Man. For our breakfast at Stockbridge p^d o. 2. o. We all dined together at Staines Bridge and there I paid for Nancy and self o. 5. o. For the other part of the Fare and extra Luggage 1. 4. o. We got to London (I thank God safe and tolerably well) about 6 o'clock in the Evening, there parted with our Company, and we stayed at the Inn where the Salisbury Coach, Inns, at the Angel at the back of St. Clements in the Strand—a very good Inn, and there we supped and slept and had good beds. To the Coachmen to day gave o. 4. o.

Oct. 7. We breakfasted, supped and slept again at the Angel. We dined at Bettys Chop-House on beef Stakes p^d o. 3. 6. In the Morning we walked down to St. James's Palace and saw the Guards relieved and heard the German Band. Nancy was much frightened, being hurried at the Soldiers marching quick, and we being in their way. They however soon passed us on our standing still. After Dinner we [went] in a Coach and called on Miss Pope in Newgate Street at a Mr. Whites—who is a Hatter—there stayed till near 9 in the Evening, and it being very wet, before I could get

a Coach to go back to our Inn, after walking Miles,
I was wet thro' and thro'—at last did get one and got
back to our Inn between 9 and 10 o'clock. For the
first Coach to Miss Popes p^d 0. 1. 6. For the last
Coach being very wet gave 0. 2. 6. I was pretty much
fatigued this Evening being wet &c. Nancy I thank
God pretty well, but very sorry for me.

Oct. 8. We breakfasted, dined supped and slept
again at the Angel. A Miss Stevenson, No. 33 Greek-
Street-Soho, Nancy's London Millener breakfasted
with us this Morning. I went by myself and saw the
Guard relieved again this Morning at St. James's
Palace. Miss Pope drank Tea with us in the Afternoon at the Angel—and after Tea we took Coach and
went to Magdalen Chapel in St Georges Fields being
Sunday and heard Prayers read and a Sermon. Very
excellent singing at Magdalen Chapel.[1] The Women
had a thin green Curtain before them all the Time,
one of them played the Organ. Dr. Milne preached
from these Words 'And Nathan said unto David thou
art the Man.'—Another Clergyman read Prayers—
We had a first Seat. Gave towards the Charity at going
in 0. 3. 0. We kept the Hackney Coach all the time in
waiting for us, and after Divine Service we returned
in it to the Angel, and Miss Pope supped and spent
the Evening with us—For the Coach to the Magdalen
Chapel and back again p^d 0. 4. 6. Andrew Russ spent

---

[1] The Magdalen House or Hospital, for the reformation and relief
of penitent prostitutes, was founded in 1758, among the founders being
Sir John Fielding, half-brother of the novelist. The hospital was at first
in Prescot Street, Goodman's Fields, but was moved in 1772 to St.
George's Fields—the south end of Blackfriars Road—a part which was
regarded then as relatively rural. In 1863 it was again removed to
Streatham, where accommodation was subsequently provided for 190
inmates (see Wheatley and Cunningham's *London Past and Present*, vol. ii,
p. 454).

the Evening with us. I hired a Coach and carried Miss Pope home in it and went with her—For the Coach p^d o. 2. o.

Oct. 9. We breakfasted, dined, supped and slept again at the Angel. Nancy very ill all day, and vomited much and often. Pray God send her better—and safe to Weston. I went and saw the Guards relieved again this Morn' at St James's Palace—Horse and Foot. After that returned home to Nancy stayed a little Time with her, then walked into Bishopsgate Street, to the black Bull, and there took 2 Places in the Norwich Expedition Coach which carries 4 Passengers, and sets of from London at 9 to Mor: Night. Paid there, for our half Fare or rather part 1. 1. o. To Books &c. this morning p^d o. 2. o. Andrew Russ supped and spent the Evening with us.

Oct. 10. We breakfasted dined and spent the Afternoon at the Angel—After breakfast we took a Coach and went to Charlesworths, Haberdasher in great Russel Street, Covent Garden, and there Nancy bought divers things—I lent her the same 1. 1. o. For the Coach to Russel Street paid o. 1. o. From thence we walked to Southampton Street very near the last Place, and there at a very good Linen-Drapers Shop, kept by a Mr. Jeremy, a very civil Man, bought some Table Linnen, Muslin, a piece of Holland, Cravats &c. paid there 13. 6. o. At the Angel this Afternoon paid my Bill 3. 4. 5. To the Servants at the Inn very civil People gave o. 12. 6. In the Evening about 6 o'clock we took a Coach and our Baggage with us to the Bull in Bishopsgate Street —a very good Inn—and there we drank Tea—For the Coach to the Bull p^d o. 1. 6. For Tea &c. at the Bull p^d o. 1. 9. About 9 we got into the Expedition Coach and sat of for Norwich—To the Porter gave o. o. 6. We had 2 very civil Men with us, Passengers. It was a very pleasant warm Moon light Night.

OCT. 11. After travelling all Night (thank God safe and well) We got to Newmarket to breakfast, and there stayed half an Hour—paid for our breakfasts o. 2. o. To the Coachman and Guard gave o. 3. o. Whilst we were at Newmarket and changing Coaches and Luggage, found that a small red Trunk of my Nieces was left behind in London, in which were all her principal Matters—It vexed her at first very much —but on my assuring her that I saw it safely lodged in the Warehouse, she was more composed. I would not pay the remaining part of our fare or for our Luggage till the Trunk was forthcoming. We changed Horses at Thetford and there parted with our 2 Men Passengers that came with us from London. They were very civil obliging People—We then went on to Norwich by ourselves in the Coach. Got to Norwich about 2 o'clock to the Maids Head and there dined and spent the Afternoon. To the Coachmen from Newmarket gave o. 2. o. For our Dinner &c. at the Maids Head p^d &c. o. 4. o. In the Evening went in a Hackney Coach both of us and our Luggage to the Kings Head our old Inn, and there drank Tea supped and slept. For the Coach to the Kings Head p^d o. 1. o. Nancy quite ill after she got to the Kings Head.

OCT. 12. We breakfasted, dined and slept again at the Kings Head. Mr. Priest called on us this Morning at the Kings Head. We drank Tea, supped and spent the Evening at Mr. Priests, with him, his Wife and their Son John. Mr. Barker and his Wife (a very pretty and agreeable Woman) drank Tea with us this Afternoon at Mr. Priests. After Tea we played a Pool at Quadrille won o. 2. 6. We got back to our Inn soon after 10 this Evening. Made all the enquiry I could and sent the same to London. Nancy but indifferent and thinking too much on her Trunk, as no Trunk was brought by either of the Mail Coaches.

OCT. 13. We breakfasted at the Kings Head at Norwich and about 12 set of for Weston Parsonage in a Post-Chaise of Ravens at the Kings Head and (I thank God) about 2 o'clock we got safe and tolerably well to the old Parsonage House at Weston, found all my Servants tolerably well and things tidily—Paid and gave at the Kings Head for Chaise &c. 1. 7. 6. To my Barber and his Boy at Norwich gave o. 1. 6. Paid at Beales for Fish now and time back o. 5. o. At Bakers for 2 small powder Machines o. 1. o. Lent to Nancy to buy some Flannel 1. 1. o. To the Norwich Driver besides a Dinner gave o. 1. 6. We dined, supped and slept at our old House again. My Niece seemed something better on being at home.

OCT. 17. . . . Mr. Matthew Lane of Hingham (my Curate at Weston during my Absence) came here about 2 o'clock by appointment, and he dined and spent the Afternoon with us—a very good natured Man. I paid him for serving my Church 16 Weeks 9. 4. 6. He owes me out of a ten Note I gave o. 15. 6. . . .

OCT. 23. . . . Mrs. Custance spent most of the Morning with us. Mr. Smith of Mattishall made us a Morning Visit—he brought us a brace of Partridges. Dr. Thorne called to see Nancy but did not stay long. He came whilst Mr. Smith was here, but did not

come into the same Room, there being rather a Cool-
ness between Mr. Smith and Mr. Thorne.

OCT. 24. ... Sent Mr. Custance this Morn' a Coomb
of Apples, fine Beefans, 3 Bushels, a present from me.
Very busy all the Morning in gathering our Apples.
Nancy very busy in making a black Silk Hat for
Mrs. Custance, all this Day and best part of Yesterday.
Nancy was not quite so well again to day.

OCT. 28. ... Rec^d a Letter this Evening from an old
School-Fellow no less than Mr. Thos Elbridge Rooke
who is at present at a Mr. Haymans Sadler-Street
Wells, Somersett—under great distress, having lost
both Feet, all his Family Friends dead, and humbly
hoping that I would contribute something to his
relief—What Changes have happened to that Family
—Whilst his Father Mr. Rooke of Somerton was alive
things had every appearance of success, but his un-
toward Son the Writer of the above Letter to me who
spent every thing he had and what his Father left him
after he died, which was almost of a broken heart on
seeing his Son going on so very badly. In my next
Letter to my Sister Pounsett shall desire her to make
enquiry after him, and to send him something for me
—tho' little is in my Power to do, having many very
near Relations that are in want.

NOV. 3. ... To J^n_o Pegg ½ Years Land Tax, ditto
Servants Tax—ditto House Tax—ditto Window Tax
—ditto Horse Tax in all paid him 11. 0. 0.[1] Sent Mr.

---

[1] The reader should note that Parson Woodforde's taxes have gone
up 20 per cent. since 1779. This was, of course, due to the American
War and the drastic increase in taxation which Pitt was compelled to
impose in 1784 and 1785 to meet the burden. Horace Walpole, writing
to Sir Horace Mann on July 8th, 1784, expressed himself on this subject
as follows: 'There is much noise about a variety of new taxes, yet only

and Mrs. Jeanes this Morning a large Sack of Apples (Beefans) a Couple of Pigeons and a very fine fat Duck ready for the Spit—to them at their Parsonage at Witchingham, they being very lately got in there with almost every inconvenience, they were highly pleased with the above. Had my brewing Copper new set by Mr. Hardy.

Nov. 9. ... Rec^d a Note from Mr. Custance &c. this morning, that they would drink Tea with us in the Afternoon. Mr. and Mrs. Custance with Mrs. Collyer drank Coffee and Tea with us this Afternoon and stayed till about 9 o'clock. At Cards this Evening lost 0. 5. 0. Nancy also lost at Loo confined to 15 pence 0. 2. 0. Poor Mrs. Collyer coming in at my Kitchen Door an old Nail caught hold of her Apron, a very fine Muslin one with a deal of work on it, and rent it in a most shocking manner indeed. We were all very much concerned about it.

Nov. 10. ... Went out a Coursing this morning for an Hour or so, but saw no Hare. We dined and spent the Afternoon and part of the Evening at Weston House till after 9 o'clock with Mr. and Mrs. Custance, Mrs. Collyer Senr and a Mr. Chamberlain who is a Roman Catholick Priest and lives with Sr Wm Jernegan and Family and what is most remarkable in him is, that he was bred up a Protestant, was at the University of Cambridge, had Preferment in the Church of

a few have a right to complain of them. The majority of the nation persisted in approving and calling for the American War, and ought to swallow the heavy consequences in silence. Instead of our colonies and trade, we have a debt of two hundred and fourscore millions! Half of that enormous burthen our *wise* country-gentlemen have acquired, instead of an alleviation of the land-tax, which they were such boobies as to expect from the prosecution of the war! Posterity will perhaps discover what his own age would not see, that my father's motto, *Quieta non movere*, was a golden sentence. . . .'

England to the Value of £800 per Annum all of which he has lately given up, renounced the Protestant Religion, and has been made a Monk. A very good kind of Man he appears to be and very sensible—has been in France &c. He is now Chaplain to Sr Wm Jernegan, that Family being of the Romish Persuasion. After Coffee and Tea, Mrs. Custance, Mrs. Collyer, Nancy and myself got to Cribbage at wch won 0. 2. 0. Nancy lost all that was lost being 0. 5. 0. Mr. Custance and Mr. Chamberlain did not play. It being Friday Mr. Chamberlain eat no Meat only some Fish and some Rice Pudding. Mr. Chamberlain slept at Weston House, the Evening being wet and dark—We returned as we went in Mr. Custances Coach. It made it rather late with us before we got home as we waited some time for Moonlight. It was near 12 before we got up stairs to night.

Nov. 22. ... Nancy very well when she came down Stairs this Morning, but very soon after taken very ill in an Ague, vomited very much, was laid on the bed most of the Morn', could not get up to dinner—but rather better about 5 o'clock this Afternoon and came down Stairs and was much better after Tea. I buried this Afternoon about 4 o'clock, John Plummer an Infant aged only 5 Weeks. I knew nothing of burying the above Infant till 3 o'clock this Afternoon, then on hearing the Church Bell, I sent to Church to enquire the reason, and word was brought me, that there was a Child then at the Church Gate for Interment—It being my Dinner Time, I went as soon as ever I had finished my Dinner—Some Mistake of my old Clerk or the Father of the Child—in not acquainting me.

Dec. 5. ... This being my Day for the Tithe Audit

the following Farmers dined and spent the Afternoon and Evening till after 10 o'clock at Night at my House—namely, Peachman, Howlett, Girling, Andrews, Bidewell, Ringgar, J^n Pegg, J^s Pegg, Mann's Nephew J^n_o Rose, Cary, Norton, Baker, Forster, Dade, Silvey, Reynolds, J^n_o Heavers, Willm Leggatt Senr (and Willm Leggatt Junr) and Widow Pratts Man Ross Beane, and Robt Rising. They were all pleased and went away in good Spirits.[1] J^n_o Buck paid me his Tithe but did not dine with us. Mr. Heming came in the Afternoon and spent the Afternoon and Evening with us. Nancy dined in the Study to day by herself. We had for Dinner, Salt Fish, a Leg of Mutton boiled and Capers, boiled and rost Beef and plenty of plumb and plain Puddings—Punch, Wine and Strong Beer after Dinner. There was six Bottles of Rum made into Punch, 3 Bowls, 2 Bottles of Rum in each. There was

---

[1] The Essex farmers in Cowper's excellently amusing poem, *The Yearly Distress*, written a little before this date for the shy Rev. William Unwin—who found these tithing-time dinners very trying—were apparently less jovial than Parson Woodforde's Norfolk neighbours:

. . . . .

> The punch goes round, and they are dull
>   And lumpish still as ever;
> Like barrels with their bellies full,
>   They only weigh the heavier.
>
> At length the busy time begins,
>   'Come, neighbours, we must wag.'—
> The money chinks, down drop their chins,
>   Each lugging out his bag.
>
> One talks of mildew and of frost,
>   And one of storms of hail,
> And one of pigs that he has lost
>   By maggots at the tail.
>
> Quoth one, 'A rarer man than you
>   In pulpit none shall hear;
> But yet methinks, to tell you true,
>   You sell it plaguy dear.'

. . . . .

seven Bottles of Wine—great Quantities of strong Beer—9 Lemons—1 P^d and ½ of Sugar and half a Pound of Tobacco made use of. Rec^d in all to day about 26o. o. o. Mr. Dade paid me almost all that was due to me for last Year and this present Year. It was after 1 o'clock before we got to bed to night. Rec^d of Ben for a Pigg that he sold for me to one Lane about 3 Quarters old o. 11. 6.

DEC. 7. . . . Not at all well all this Day—worse at Night. Took some Camphire and Nitre going to bed. Nancy's Pigg was killed this Morning and a nice, fine, fat White Pigg it is. It is to be weighed to Morrow Morning. We are to make some Somersett black Puddings to Morrow, if we can by our Receipt from thence.

DEC. 10. . . . I read Prayers and Preached this After-noon at Weston C[hurch], Mr. and Mrs. Custance at Church and a large Congregation besides at Church being fine, cheerful Weather. Nancy had two Letters from Mrs. Davy this Afternoon done up in a parcel, and with the same a little Lump of something, but what, I know not—as Nancy never mentioned a word of what it was, nor of a single word in either of the Letters—I care not for it, but shall take care to be as private myself in matters.

DEC. 11. . . . Nancy quite bluff and rather pert this morning. I privately named a spurious Child of one Mary Parker's this morning by name John. The Fathers Name I could not get intelligence of. The Wind was very high most part of last Night. Sent Mrs. Custance this Morning a large Baskett of my Potatoes, fresh dug, as she praised them so much.

To Ben this Evening for things from Norwich &c. p^d
10. 7. Gave him besides for my Tithe Frolick 1. 0.
To Briton for divers things p^d 6. 0. Gave him besides
for my Tithe Frolick 2. 6. To Betty for divers things
p^d 6. 9. Gave her besides for my Tithe Frolick 2. 6.
Gave to Nanny my Cook, for my Tithe Frolick 2. 6.
Gave to my Boy, Jack, for my Tithe Frolick, 1. 0.

DEC. 19. . . . Henry Baker, my Butcher, called here
this Morning by my desire, and I paid him a Bill for
Meat for the last Year, the sum of 33. 2. 6. for which
I took a stamp Receipt in full. Mr. Custance made
us a morning Visit on foot and stayed with us a full
Hour—during his being with us, Mr. and Mrs. Jeanes
came to our House and they dined, supped and slept
here by appointment. Mrs. Jeanes does not look by
far so well as she did. Has been much hurried by
change of Servants &c. We gave them for Dinner
some Soup, a boiled Neck of Pork, a fine rost Turkey,
Apple Pye and Puffs. After Coffee and Tea we got to
Cribbage lost 0. 1. 0. We did not get to bed to Night
till 12 o'clock. Mr. and Mrs. Jeanes slept in Nancys
Room and Nancy slept over my Bed Chamber. Mr.
Jeanes's Servant Lad George England about 15 Years
of Age dined supped and slept here. Mr. Jeanes's one
Horse Chaise was put into my Barn. Two of Mr.
Jeanes's Horses also were with my Horses all Night.
Mr. Jeanes's Servant Lad G. England seems fonder
of Kitchen Fire than any Work.

DEC. 21. . . . This being St Thomas Day, I gave to
the poor of my Parish that came to my House at 6^d
each 1. 7. 0.

DEC. 26. We breakfasted, dined, &c. &c. again at
home. To the Weston Ringgers, their annual Gift of

0. 2. 6. To my Malsters Man a Christmas Gift gave
0. 1. 0. To my Blacksmiths Son a Christmas Gift
0. 0. 6. Mr. Girling, Mr. Custances Steward, called
here this Afternoon and paid me Mr. Custances
Composition for Land in hand, for Tithe the Sum of
13. 12. 6. Very sharp Frost indeed last Night and this
Morning it froze the Water in my Bason this Morning
that I wash in, quite over, in half an Hour after it had
been brought up Stairs.

DEC. 29. . . . Had another Tub of Gin and another
of the best Coniac Brandy brought me this Evening
ab^t 9. We heard a thump at the Front Door about
that time, but did not know what it was, till I went
out and found the 2 Tubs—but nobody there.[1]

DEC. 31. We breakfasted, dined &c. &c. again at
home. I read Prayers and Preached this Morn' at
Weston C[hurch]. Neither Mr. or Mrs. Custance
at Church this Morn'. They sent us a wild Duck this
Morning. This being the last Day of the Year, we sat
up this Night till after 12 o'clock—then drank Health
and happy New Year to all our Somersett Friends &c.
and then went for Bedfordshire alias to bed.

[1] Where are the swains, who, daily labour done,
With rural games play'd down the setting sun;

. . . . .

Where now are these?—Beneath yon cliff they stand,
To show the freighted pinnace where to land;
To load the ready steed with guilty haste,
To fly in terror o'er the pathless waste,
Or, when detected, in their straggling course,
To foil their foes by cunning or by force;
Or yielding part (which equal knaves demand),
To gain a lawless passport through the land.

So Crabbe describes the country smuggler in his early poem *The Village*, published three years before this date, in 1783.

1787

JAN. 10. . . . Nancy a very small matter better in her left Knee. To Ben, this Morning for things pd 3. 4. 3. To Ben, also for a Years Wages—pd. him 10. 0. 0. To Betty, for things pd. 0. 5. 8½. To Betty, also for a Years Wages—pd. her 5. 5. 0. To Briton, for things pd. 0. 18. 1. To Briton, also for a Years Wages—pd. him 8. 0. 0. Briton made me uneasy being discontented. To Nanny, for a Years Wages—pd. her 5. 5. 0. Of Nanny, having lent her, recd. 1. 1. 0. To Jack, for a Years Wages pd. him 1. 1. 0. At Cribbage this Evening with Nancy neither won or lost.

JAN. 16. . . . Paid to Nancy this Morn' her Annual pay 10. 0. 0. To ditto also for a fat Pigg 2. 9. 0. Recd. of ditto for divers things pd. for her 8. 9. 6. To a Man for some Cod Fish and Oysters pd. 0. 5. 1. At Cribbage this Evening with Nancy—won 0. 0. 6.

JAN. 18. . . . Nancy very indifferent indeed all day— worse. Sent Briton to Reepham on foot this Morning with my Watch to be mended, the main Spring being broke, owing to my putting it forward by the Key. Briton did not return till 4 this Afternoon and then very wet and dirty, owing to the very sudden Thaw. It was quite a hard Frost when he set out, and I thought it more safe for him on foot than horseback but poor Fellow he had a terrible bad walk back being both very dirty and very wet. I gave him a glass of Gin on his return. Betty being gone to her Friends at Mattishall and Briton also out at dinner Time, I was with pleasure under the necessity of assisting at Dinner. Nancy complained a good deal in the Evening. We diverted ourselves at Cribbage this Evening at which neither won or lost.

JAN. 21. ... Nancy very indifferent again this morning, had her breakfast in bed, did not get up till after
One o'clock. I read Prayers and Preached this Afternoon at Weston C[hurch]. Neither Mr. or Mrs.
Custance at Church this Afternoon. Nancy was down
Stairs on my return from Church and seemed pretty
cheerful till about 10 Minutes before Dinner and then
had several Symptoms of her late Fever, could not eat
but very little indeed for Dinner and that little she
brought up soon after, and then was something better,
and better still after Tea. She had little or no sleep
all last Night.

JAN. 24. ... Nancy had rather a better Night than
last Night but breakfasted in her Chamber, came down
about Noon, and stayed down all day afterwards. At
11 o'clock this Morn' I went a coursing and did not
return till just 4 o'clock this Afternoon, had prodigious
fine Sport with 2 Hares, especially the last on France
Green, but killed neither. Another Hare also stole
away from us near Hockering Heath which none of
the Dogs saw. I was rather tired when I came home
but very little. Mr. and Mrs. Jeanes called on my
Niece during my being out as did also her Doctor
Mr. Thorne. Ben and Jack went out with me this
Morning. Nancy could not prevail on Mr. and Mrs.
Jeanes to stay and dine with us, they had been at
Weston House this morning—Mrs. Jeanes looked pale
Nancy told me, but as she is far advanced with Child,
hope 'tis nothing more than a consequence. Mrs.
Custance sent word by Mrs. Jeanes that she would
come any Morn' and sit with my Niece, when again
able.

JAN. 25. ... Nancy had a very indifferent Night and
rather worse today, being still weaker. She did not

come down Stairs till 2 o'clock this afternoon. However she made a good Dinner on a boiled Leg of Mutton and Caper Sauce and was better after. Rode to Ringland this Morning and married one Robert Astick and Elizabeth Howlett by Licence, Mr. Carter being from home, and the Man being in Custody, the Woman being with Child by him. The Man was a long time before he could be prevailed on to marry her when in the Church Yard; and at the Altar behaved very unbecoming. It is a cruel thing that any Person should be compelled by Law to marry. I recd. of the Officers for marrying them 0. 10. 6. It is very disagreeable to me to marry such Persons.[1] . . .

JAN. 28. . . . Nancy pretty well this morning and is certainly better, but breakfasted a bed, and after

---

[1] These so-called compulsory marriages, though not compulsory by law, were an inevitable effect of the law as it stood, specially of the Bastardy Act of 1733 (6 George II, c. 31). For under that Act a woman had only, upon oath before a justice, to charge any person with having gotten her with child to enable the said justice, on application of the overseers of the poor, to apprehend and imprison the man charged, unless he gave security to indemnify the parish. By another clause of the Act the marriage of the woman caused the release of the man from penalty. Hence, in numerous cases, if the man could not indemnify the parish, he preferred wedlock to imprisonment.

The same scene which Parson Woodforde here describes so graphically in prose was described by the poet Crabbe with incomparable power in verse, twenty years later, in 1807, in *The Parish Register*:

> Next at our altar stood a luckless pair,
> Brought by strong passions and a warrant there;
> By long rent cloak, hung loosely, strove the bride,
> From ev'ry eye, what all perceived, to hide.
> While the boy-bridegroom, shuffling in his pace,
> Now hid awhile and then exposed his face;
> As shame alternately with anger strove,
> The brain confused with muddy ale to move:
> In haste and stammering he perform'd his part,
> And look'd the rage that rankled in his heart;
> (So will each lover inly curse his fate,
> Too soon made happy and made wise too late.)

•   •   •   •   •

breakfast about 11 o'clock got up and came below
Stairs, where I found her on my return from Church.
I read Prayers and Preached this morning at Weston
Church neither Mr. or Mrs. Custance at Church, nor
above 20 People in all at Church—The Weather
being extremely cold and severe with much Snow on
the ground and still more falling with cutting Winds.
After Service I buried a Daughter of Harrisons an
Infant aged only 5 Weeks—I think that I never felt
the cold more severe than when I was burying the
above Infant. The Wind blowed very Strong and
Snow falling all the time and the Wind almost directly
in my Face, that it almost stopped my breath in reading the funeral Service at the Grave, tho' I had an
Umbrella[1] held over my Head during the Time.
Nancy brave all day but still very lame, she did not go
to bed till after 10 o'clock this Evening. Mr. Thorne
called again on his Patient this After: about 3 o'clock
—soon after we had dined.

FEB. 1. ... Nancy near the same as Yesterday, breakfasted, dined, and supped below Stairs. I privately
named a Child of Dinah Bushells this morning at my
House by name Robert. The Mother brought the
Child herself, though the Infant was only born the
18 of January and the Mother quite hearty and strong.
Yesterday and today were so warm and lively that it
had more appearance of Summer than Winter. May
they not be succeeded with uncommonly severe and
rough Weather—Or, as the Norfolk People commonly

[1] This is the first mention of an umbrella by Parson Woodforde.
Umbrellas did not come into general use in England before the 1780's,
and the man who first appeared with one in 1778 in London was jeered
by the mob. They were regarded as effeminate. It is significant that in
1787 Parson Woodforde only succumbed to having one held over his
head during a frightful blizzard at a funeral.

call such fine Days in Winter Weather-breeders—
producing bad Weather.

FEB. 3. . . . Nancy had but an indifferent night and
after taking her Physick this Morning was very sick
and brought up some of it, her breakfast would not
stay on her Stomach also, nor anything else but a little
Water Gruel, and that but a little Time, was extremely ill all the Day long till about 8 in the Evening
and then was a small matter easier. The Mercury she
took last Night was much too strong for her weak
frame at this present. The Physic she took this morning had little or no effect, as she brought it up almost
the whole, therefore she had violent griping pains in her
Bowels the whole Morning without much coming from
her as the Mercury only operated without the Aid of
Physick to carry it of, therefore there must be a great
deal of Mercury left behind—however when she went
to bed, she was somewhat easier. Mr. Thorne called
here this Morning accidentally having been to bleed
Mrs. Custance at Weston House. He was not pleased
on hearing that Nancy was so bad as not to be seen
by him being above Stairs. I am afraid she caught
cold, as her pain within her was so bad that she could
not get from the close-Stool for near 2 Hours together.
I went up to see her in the Evening, and she was very
low and cried a good deal—but seemed rather easier—
after she had her Tea and Toast she seemed something
better and soon after came down Stairs and stayed
the rest of the Evening. When she went to bed she
was tolerably easy. I was very uneasy indeed the
whole Day on my dear Nieces Account. 'Pray God
give her more ease.' I sent Briton to Norwich this
Morning after News, &c. in my little Cart,—he returned by dinner time. No letters from the West, or

elsewhere, as there were none from the West, I wonder much at it; as Nancy has long expected one from her Aunt and one from her Sister Juliana.

FEB. 10. . . . Nancy tolerable this morning but did not come down to breakfast, nor was below Stairs till Noon', just as she was coming down stairs Mrs. Custance came to us and stayed till near 3 o'clock. She seemed far from well, having a low nervous Fever hanging about her, and very far gone with Child. I tried to divert her as much as I could, showed her some Medals of mine &c. I was quite sorry to see her so very low and weak. Nancy dined, supped &c. below Stairs and was tolerably well and cheerful all Day.

FEB. 12. . . . Nancy breakfasted, dined, &c. below Stairs again and was better than she was Yesterday, her Spirits very good with a good Appetite, but her lameness still continues, tho' I think, not quite so bad. Mrs. Bodham sent Nancy a Note this Morning, to excuse her not coming over to see her, being ill with a cold—Nancy returned an answer to it. Mr. Thorne also called here about Noon to see his Patient, stayed here about an Hour, during that time Mrs. Custance made us a visit and stayed with us till 3 o'clock, learning of Nancy to make the Diamond-edge-netting. I wrote it out for her. Mrs. Custance much better than on Saturday last. Sent Ben this Morning with my great Cart to Mr. Du Quesnes after a large Walnut Tree to transplant into my Garden—which we did directly; it was planted well and supported with 3 Stakes. I wish it might live, but have some doubt of it, as it is so large and the Roots injured much. Mr. Thorne left no Medicine whatever for Nancy.

FEB. 19. ... Nancy I thank God a good deal better today but did not get up till 1 this Afternoon. Mrs. Custance called here this Morning with her eldest Daughter and stayed with us an Hour. Nancy was not below when she came, but was soon after. Mr. Thorne and Betsy Davy called here just as Mrs. Custance was going away and they stayed with us an Hour, I would have had them dine here but they were ordered to the contrary I suppose. Betsy Davy was grown much taller, but very shy to me, and rather affected in her way. I sold 2 acres and ½ of Turnips today to be fed of to Gould of Attlebridge for 2 guineas and half. Turnips now are very Cheap indeed in Weston as there are many to sell and Weather so very fine. Had a Note from Mr. Smith of Mattishall this Morning by Dade, to desire me to serve his Church on Sunday next, but was obliged to return for answer that it was not in my Power as I was pre-engaged to serve Witchingham for Mr. Jeanes who is gone to London with his Wife. Nancy continued brave all the Day and sat up till after 10 at Night— then took a Rhubarb Bolus and went to bed quite cheerry.

MAR. 13. ... Whilst we were at breakfast, Mrs. Davy from Thurning with a Servant with her, called here and drank a Dish of Tea with us, stayed about half an Hour afterwards and then went on to Mr. Thornes at Mattishall. I did not ask her to stay and dine with us. She talked of returning back to Thurning Thursday or Friday next—I did not ask her to call on her return. Nancy was highly pleased to see her. Mrs. Davy behaved as free as if nothing had been said respecting her Character by Mr. Smith. She is grown much fatter than she was. I never knew a Woman of much greater Effrontery. The Election for the City of Norwich comes on Thursday next, a strong Contest is expected.

MAR. 14. ... Read to my Niece to day a great many Letters of Mr. Fenns[1] new Publication of antient Letters, lately published, in the reigns of Henry the sixth, Edward the fourth, and Richd. the third.

MAR. 17. ... Sent Briton on horseback to Norwich after News &c. He returned about 4 o'clock with the same. No Letter or any Tidings whatever of Mr. and Mrs. Jeanes. Mr. Hobart had only 80 Majority of Sr. Thos. Beevor. The Election at Norwich conducted with great credit to the City. No appearance of a Riot or any disturbance whatever, but all things were carried on in the greatest Order and Peace. No Stavesman whatever on the Occasion. Sr. Thos. Beevor is said to have demanded a Scrutiny at first, but has since dropped it, is said. For Churching a Woman at Witchingham recd. o. o. 6. Briton returned home from Norwich with a Hobart Favour in his Hat, and highly pleased.

MAR. 18. ... I read Prayers, Preached and churched a Woman at Witchingham this Morn', for Mr. Jeanes.

[1] This was Sir John Fenn (1739–94), a Norfolk antiquary of note, who was the purchaser of the original manuscript and first editor of the famous *Paston Letters*. These he published in four volumes, between 1787 and 1789. A fifth volume was published by his nephew after his death. George III knighted him for his work on May 23rd, 1787. The letters were published under the title, *Original Letters written during the reigns of Henry VI, Edward IV, Richard III, and Henry VII, by various persons of rank and consequence, and by members of the Paston family* (see *D.N.B.*). Horace Walpole, writing on February 1st, 1787, to the Countess of Upper Ossory, refers to these letters: 'The Letters of Henry VI's reign, etc., are come out, and *to me* make all other letters not worth reading. I have gone through above one volume, and cannot bear to be writing when I am so eager to be reading. . . . What antiquary would be answering a letter from a living countess, when he may read one from Eleanor Mowbray, Duchess of Norfolk!'

Mr. Jeanes Man is gone to London to his Master with
Mr. Jeanes Stallion, being sent for by him. Mr.
Jeanes is expected in the ensuing Week. I read
Prayers and Preached this Afternoon at Weston
C[hurch]. Also churched 2 poor Women at Weston
Church. Mr. and Mrs. Custance at Church this
Afternoon and a very full Congregation at Church
this Aft: I gave the two poor Women the Churching
Fee. I met Mr. Custance on my return from Witch-
ingham this Morning on the little Common, and he
very genteelly desired me for the future to go thro' his
inclosures by his House whenever I wanted to go to
Witchingham or Lenewade Bridge, &c. as that way is
somewhat nearer than the other. Nancy told me this
Evening that Mrs. Davy had had an offer of marriage
made her, but not said whom—also that her Daughter
Betsy has had an offer also from young Walker who
was lately at Mr. Thornes. The above are very great
Secrets.

MAR. 21. . . . Very pleasant, cheerful Day, thank
God for it.

MAR. 26. . . . Polly my Poll-Cow had a Bull Calf this
Morning.

MAR. 27. . . . Mrs. Custance made us a morning
Visit and stayed with us an Hour—She is quite
hurried and uneasy on Account of her little Boy,
William, having got the Measles, and herself never
having them, and also that she is very near her Time
of being brought to bed, having scarce a Month to
go with Child. Am exceeding sorry for poor Mrs.
Custance indeed and likewise for Mr. Custance who
must be very much concerned. Busy brewing some
strong Beer to day.

Mar. 30. . . . Mr. Custances Coach damaged my great Gates last Night. About Noon, Mr. and Mrs. Jeanes from London came here in their road home to Witchingham, and stayed an Hour with us, and refreshed themselves with some cold rost Beef and Porter &c. and then went for home. Mrs. Jeanes looks much better. Mr. Jeanes whilst in Town bought a close Carriage and a pair of black Horses to go in the same. Mrs. Jeanes came down in it. It looks smart. Mr. Jeanes came down on his fine Stallion as he could not dispose of him for so much as he asked. For a fine Eel 2 pd. weight pd. o. o. 6.

April 5. . . . My Boy, Jack Secker, left my Service this Day and went home with his Father who came after him about Noon. I paid him for Wages due 5. 6. My new Boy, Charles Crossley, of this Parish came to my House this Evening about 5 o'clock. Mr. Custance sent us a fine Cucumber this Morn'.

April 17. . . . This being my Rotation Day Mr. and Mrs. Bodham with them Miss Kitty Johnson, Mr. Du Quesne, Mr. Smith and Mr. and Mrs. Jeanes, all dined, and spent the Afternoon with us—We had for Dinner, some Skaite and Oyster Sauce, Knuckle of Veal and a Tongue, a fine Fore Quarter of Lamb and plumb Pudding. 2nd. Course, Asparagus, Lobster, Rasberry Tartlets, black Caps set into Custard &c. We had also Cucumbers and Radishes. There were three Carriages, 5 Servants and 8 Horses. Soon after Coffee and Tea, they all left us.

May 6. . . . I read Prayers, Preached, and churched a Woman this morning at Weston Church. Mrs. N. Micklethwaite and Miss Branthwaite at Church. None from Weston House at Church. For churching

a Woman this morning recd. o. o. 6. Soon after my
return from Church, one of Mr. Custances Servants
called here to let us know that Mrs. Custance was
brought to bed of a Boy about 11 o'clock this Morn'.
She with the little stranger as well as can be expected.
I buried this Evening one Willm. Hill aged 65 yrs.
He was ill but a very little Time—was well respected
and a great many People at his burial.

MAY 21. . . . Mr. Jeanes made us a short morning
Visit. Of John Gooch for Turnips for his Cow almost
all the Winter recd. of him 1. 1. o. but I returned it to
him again immediately. Very busy all the morning
in cutting the Weeds in my Bason and cleaning the
same, and likewise in launching the Ship Anna in the
same.

MAY 28. . . . Mr. and Mrs. Jeanes with Miss Short
dined and spent the Afternoon with us. We had for
Dinner a nice boiled Leg of Lamb, a very nice small
rosting Pigg, Apricot and Gooseberry Tarts Oranges
and Nutts by way of desert. Soon after Coffee and
Tea, They returned for Witchingham and took my
Niece with them in their Carriage to spend a few
Days with them.

MAY 29. . . . It seemed a little strange to be quite
alone not being used to be so—In the Evening rather
dull. Willm. Bidewell (who has taken Collisons
Estate that John Pegg had from Michaelmas next,
and to which Estate is annexed a publick House where
Bens Father at present lives but is going out at the
above Time) called on me this morning and another
man with him, to ask my consent for the above public
House to be continued on, and one Page (lately a
Farmer and lived in this Parish, last Year and broke

here) to live in it, but I said that I would never consent to it by any Means. The above Phillip Page is an old Man, had a Bastard about 3 Years [ago] by Charlotte Dunnell.

JUNE 7. . . . Walked to Bens Fathers this Afternoon and read Prayers to his Wife, she being dangerously ill.

JUNE 9. . . . I went and read Prayers again this morning to Mrs. Leggatt and administered also the H. Sacrament to her—she was very weak indeed and but just alive. She was sensible and showed marks of great satisfaction after receiving the H. Sacrament. She never received it before. Pray God bless her. Sent Briton early to Norwich this morning with my little Cart after things from thence.

JUNE 12. . . . Our Archdeacon Mr. Younge and Morphew Junr. breakfasted with us this Morning at 9 o'clock. After breakfast I walked with them to our Church to see the same—As the Archdeacon is going round to survey the Churches of this Deanery. And there I took my leave of them for the present. We had Tea and Coffee for breakfast. Nancy likes the Archdeacon much, he is a very cheerful merry little Man and sensible, and came out of Devonshire some few Years ago. The late Bishop of Norwich was his Uncle. . . .

JUNE 24. . . . I read Prayers, Preached and Christned a Child by name John, this Morning at Weston Church. Mr. and Mrs. Custance, Mrs. Micklethwaite and her Sister Miss Branthwaite at Church. Nancy was at Church this morning and walked there and back. My Niece has not been able to go to Church since she returned from Somersett in October last.

JUNE 28. . . . We brewed some small Beer to-day. We had Peas for the first time out of our Garden.

JUNE 29. . . . Sr. Willm. Jernegan sent me by Mr. Custance a Treatise on the Plant called Scarcity Root.[1]

JULY 3. . . . Mr. and Mrs. Custance, with their Sons, Hambleton, George and William, drank Coffee and Tea with us this Afternoon and stayed till 8 o'clock. They all walked about my Garden and were well pleased, particularly the young Gentlemen with the Ship. Glorious Time now (thank God) for the Hay-sell.

JULY 5. . . . All my Hay up in Cock and very finely made thank God.

JULY 9. . . . Mr. Jeanes made us a short morning Visit, and he acquainted us that his Wife was brought to bed of a Daughter this morning about 7 o'clock, and as well as he could wish her to be in her state. She was not more than 10 hours in labour. Mrs. Jeanes's Mother, Mrs. Springer, was to have been with them at the time, but is expected to Morrow. Mrs. Custance 2 Daughters Fanny and Emily came to our House this Evening on a Walk, and they drank some Milk and Water and eat some Cakes. I walked with them and the Maid Sally good part of the way back, as far as John Bakers, and there the Rain overtook us but not much, and there another Maid Sukey, met us,

---

[1] The Scarcity Root was the mangel-wurzel, and was so called owing to confusion of the German word Mangel, meaning *want*, with the German word Mangold, meaning *beet*. Wurzel managed to retain its identity as *root*. The mangel-wurzel was first brought into notice in England in 1786 by Sir Richard Jebb, a distinguished doctor and scientist.

and there I left them. I was wet thro' on my return back to my House. The little Folks, I hope, got home without being wet. I gave to each of the little Ladies a Medal apiece in imitation of an half Guinea in kind of brass. My Folks busy in bringing our Hay home and stacking it all Day long. The Major Part of it stacked to day.

JULY 11. ... I was very busy all the Morning long in helping them in the Field, as we were busy carrying our Hay. We finished about 8 this Evening and then came Rain.

JULY 21. ... Nancy very busy this morning in making some Rasberry Jam and red Currant Jelly. She made to day about 8 Pd. of Currant Jelly and about 9 Pound of Rasberry Jamm. This Evening as we were going to Supper, a covered Cart drove into my Yard with 3 Men with it, and one of them, the principal, was a black with a french Horn, blowing it all the way up the Yard to the Kitchen Door, to know if we would [like to see] a little Woman only 33 Inches high and 31 Years of Age. As we did not give our Dissent, she was taken out of the Cart and brought into our Kitchen, where we saw her and heard her sing two Songs. I dont think she was any taller than represented, but rather deformed, seemed in good Spirits, sang exceedingly high with very little Judgment and was very talkative. She was called by the black Polly Coleshill of Glocester. The Black told me that he formerly lived with the Earl of Albermarle I gave him 0. 1. 0.[1] Ben returned from Norwich about 4 this afternoon.

[1] As a natural consequence and offshoot of the slave trade, numerous negroes were brought to England in the eighteenth century, and until the great decision of Lord Mansfield in 1772 in the case of the slave

JULY 31. . . . About 9 o'clock this Morning Mrs. Davy with her Daughter came to my House in a one Horse-Chaise and they dined and spent the Afternoon with us—In the Evening Mrs. Davy returned home to Thurning but left her Daughter to spend a few Days with Nancy, Betsy being far from well, having a violent palpitation of the heart—she is now however much better than she has been of late. We had for Dinner some Veal, Beans and Ham, a piece of boiled Beef, a Green Goose and some tarts. Betsy Davy supped and slept here.

AUG. 10. . . . About 1 o'clock this Morning there was a most violent Tempest—very much Lightning and the most vivid, strong and quick I think I ever saw before—Not so much Thunder but very loud what there was—The Rain was some time before it came but then it was very heavy, the Rain did not last long. We were much alarmed, the Maids came downstairs crying and shrieking at 1 o'clock. I got up immediately and thinking when I went up Stairs to bed last Night that there was likelihood of a Tempest being so hot, I had lighted my little Lamp, and only laid down on my Bed with most of my Cloathes on and was just dozing when I heard the Maids all of a sudden shrieking at my Door. We lighted some Candles. Nancy had one in her Room, they were much frightned. It continued incessantly lightning from before 1 till 4 this Morning—then it abated and then I went to bed and slept comfortably till 9 o'clock.

'Somerset' were treated as slaves. By Lord Mansfield's judgement every slave, by the mere fact of landing on English soil, became free. It was presumably as a consequence of that judgement that Parson Woodforde's black friend had been able to leave Lord Albemarle's service and earn a free and cheerful living with his French horn and his little dwarf show.

Thank God Almighty, for preserving us all safe from so violent a Tempest. May all others escape as well. It was most dreadful to behold the Lightning. Mr. Massingham, Dr. Thornes Apprentice, just called here in the Evening to enquire after Betsy Davy &c.

AUG. 11. . . . My Parlour and Study Chimnies finished this Day and I thank God safe and well. I gave the Men to drink on the Occasion o. 1. o. A great deal mentioned on the Papers concerning the dreadful Tempest on Friday Morn' last, but thanks be to the Lord, but very little damage done or any Lives lost. May all other Parts escape as well.

AUG. 12. . . . I read Prayers and Preached this Aft. at Weston C. Mr. and Mrs. Custance at Church this Afternoon they returned from Yarmouth last Friday. The Cossey Singers at Weston Church this Afternoon. I likewise christned two Children this Aft: at Church.

AUG. 22. I breakfasted, supped and slept again at home. Nancy breakfasted, dined &c. &c. again at home. Betsy Davy breakfasted, dined &c. here again. Soon after breakfast I walked to Church and there buried Mary Cushing Wife of poor Tom Cushing who was ill but very few Days aged 63 Years. On my return home from Church, found Mrs. Micklethwaite at my House, who came to inform us that having been disappointed of some part of the Company that we were to meet at her house to Morrow, begged to put of the Engagement to Tuesday next. As she walked to my House by herself, I walked back with her and stayed half an Hour with her, during that Time Captain Laton and Lady called there. On my return home from Mrs. Micklethwaites, whom should I find at my House but Roger Hall who dined and spent the Afternoon with Nancy and Betsy. My being engaged to Mr. Townshends could not dine with him, but shall to Morrow (deo volente) as he has engaged himself to dine with me to Morrow. Between 2 and 3 o'clock I took a ride to Honingham Hall and there dined and spent the Afternoon with Mr. and Mrs. Townshend, Mrs. Cornwallis, Mr. Du Quesne, Mr. Priest of Reepham and Mr. and Mrs. Jeanes. Mr. Jeanes was in a very frenchyfied Dress, black silk Coat, Waistcoat and Breeches with a Chappeau de brache under his left Arm.[1] After Coffee and Tea, Mrs. Cornwallis, Mr. Priest, Mr. Du Quesne and self got to Cribbage won 0. 1. 0. Returned home to Weston about 8 o'clock. Nancy and Betsy Davy were heartily tired of Halls Company, he was gone to sleep at Lenewade Bridge before I returned. To Cupper of my Parish gave 0. 0. 6.

AUG. 28. ... My Greyhounds being both very full of fleas and almost raw on their backs, I put some Oil of Turpentine on them, which soon made many of them retire and also killed many more. ...

SEP. 4. ... About 11 o'clock this Morning walked to Weston Church to christen Mr. Custance's last little Boy, but the Company not being arrived Mr. Custance sent his Coach after me to go to Weston House which I did and there stayed about half an Hour with Mr. and Mrs. Custance, Sr. Thomas and Lady Durrant, the latter is Mr. Custances own Sister and a very fine

[1] Parson Woodforde's contempt for the French extended to their language. By a *chappeau de brache* he evidently means a *chapeau-bras* which is defined in Fairholt's *Costume in England* as 'a hat made to fold, and carry beneath the arm, by beaux who feared to derange their wigs'. From Planché one learns that the hat was made of silk, was flat, and three-cornered.

Woman, there was a Daughter with them about 11
Years old, her Name as her Mothers Susannah. Mr.
and Mrs. Collyer of Wroxham then sent word that
they were waiting at Church, we all then went in two
Coaches and four to Weston Church where I publickly
presented (being privately named by me before by
name John) the young Gentleman. Sr. Thomas
Durant and Mr. Collyer, God Fathers, and Lady
Durant the only Godmother. Two Coaches and four
and a Post Chariot at Church. After the Christning
we walked about Weston Church about 20 Minutes,
then the Company went for Weston House—and I
walked home to the Parsonage. About 2 o'clock I
dressed and walked up to Weston House and there
dined and spent the Aft. with Mr. and Mrs. Custance,
Sr. Thomas and Lady Durrant and Daughter, Mr.
and Mrs. Collyer, and Mr. Press Custance—After
Coffee and Tea Sr. Thos. and Lady and Daughter set
of home to a place called Scottow—Sr. Thos. invited
me to his House.[1] After they were gone, Mrs.
Custance, Mrs. Collyer, Mr. Press Custance and self
sat down to Cribbage at Shillings, at which I won
0. 3. 0. Mrs. Collyer and Self against Mrs. Custance
and Mr. Press. About 8 this Evening I walked home.
N.B. Mr. Custance very genteelly made me a present
for christning the Child, wrapped in White Paper of
the Sum of 5. 5. 0. In the Morn' I sent a Dozen of
very fine Anson Apricots to Weston House which were
on the table after Dinner and all eat, but not a word
mentioned from whence they came, therefore suppose

---

[1] Sir Thomas Durrant (1722–90), of Scottow, Norfolk, was created a
baronet on January 22nd, 1784. He married, *circa* 1773, Susanna, first
daughter of Hambleton Custance, of Weston, Norfolk, by Susanna,
daughter and heiress of John Press (hence Mr. Press Custance), Alderman of Norwich. He was Sheriff of Norfolk in 1784–5. His wife survived him till 1833.

that neither Mr. or Mrs. Custance knew anything of
the Matter.

SEP. 28. ... I spent a good part of the Morning at
the Church and in the Church Yard, my People being
busy in laying some Gravel upon the Walks there and
making the Church Yard more decent.

OCT. 2. ... Nancy went in her little Cart with Briton,
and I on my Mare to Witchingham about 1 o'clock
and there we dined and spent the Afternoon at Mr.
Jeanes's with him, his Wife, Mr. Du Quesne, Mr. and
Mrs. Priest of Reepham with their two Daughters,
Rebeccah and Mary. We had for Dinner a Couple of
small Chicken boiled, and a Tongue, one stewed
Duck, a fine Haunch of Venison and a baked Pudding.
Mr. Du Quesne fell backward from his Chair in the
Afternoon and bruised himself much. The Ladies
were not in the Room at the time. We returned as we
went directly after Coffee. Mr. Du Quesne went with
me, he complained a good deal of his Fall when on
horseback in giving him much Pain. Mr. Du Quesne
should have went in his Carriage especially as Mr.
Jeanes desired him, and to take up my Niece with him
in the same, and which he might have done. We spent
a very agreeable Day and did due justice to the
Venison which came out of the New Forest from Mr.
Jeanes's Father.

OCT. 15. ... Very fine and fair and a Frost early in
the Morn'. I was very busy this morning in my
Garden making some new Strawberry Beds.

OCT. 17. ... St. Faiths Fair to day. I would not let
any of my Servants go to it, on Account of a very bad
Fever of the putrid kind, raging there and of which

many have died there already. To 2 Dozen fresh Herrings paid o. 1. o.

OCT. 18. . . . Nancy took an Airing in her little Cart this Morning being very fair and fine—Briton with her. Went out a Coursing this Morn with my Dogs, ran one Hare and killed it—a very fine one.

Nov. 12. . . . Soon after breakfast I walked out a Coursing and took Ben and the Boy with me, did not return till near three, afternoon, we had tolerable Sport, coursed one Hare and a Couple of Rabbitts, all of whom we killed, it was a very large Hare. I think I never knew so pleasant a day so far in November, it was more like Summer than Autumn. I was very indifferent the whole Day, could eat but very little for Dinner being over fatigued and likewise my Spirits but very bad.

Nov. 14. . . . To a poor Man of Easton having lost a Horse, o. 1. o. Poor Neighbour Downings Wife bad in a Fever.

Nov. 15. . . . Recd. this Morning of one Platt of Hockering a Pigg Jobber, for 6 small Piggs at 13ˢ 6ᵈ each—4. 1. o.

DEC. 11. . . . I took a ride this Morning to Weston House and spent half an Hour with Mrs. Custance— Mr. Custance being walked out—I went to ask them to dine with us to Morrow to meet Mr. and Mrs. Bodham. Mrs. Custance seemed much pleased with it, but could not promise till she had seen Mr. Custance. Mrs. Custance having ordered her Coach to go to my House, I desired her not to counter-order it, therefore she with 3 Children went and spent half an Hour with my Niece and then returned back again. About ½ past 2 o'clock Mr. and Mrs. Bodham with

Miss Mary Donne of Norwich came to my House to spend a day or two with us. Mr. and Mrs. Bodham with Miss Mary Donne, dined, supped and slept at my House—Miss Donne slept with my Niece in the Attic Story over me. Miss Mary Donne is a very genteel, pretty young Lady and very agreeable with a most pleasing Voice abt. 21 Yrs. very tasty and very fashionable in dress. Mr. Bodhams Coachman Js. returned home to Mattishall with his pair of Horses before Dinner and is to come again on Thursday Morning after them. Mr. Bodhams Footman Thos. dined and slept here. We had for Dinner to day a boiled Leg of Mutton with Capers, a Couple of Chicken rosted and a Tongue, a Norfolk plain batter Pudding, Tripe, Tarts and some blamange with 4 Sorts of Cheese. For Supper some Oysters, a wild Duck rosted, Potatoes rosted, and some cold Chicken &c. After Coffee and Tea we got to Quadrille, viz: Mr. and Mrs. Bodham, Miss Donne and self. I won 0. 3. 0. I did not get to bed to Night till after 12 o'clock.

DEC. 28. I breakfasted, dined, &c. again at home. Nancy breakfasted, dined, &c. again at home. To a poor Sailor with one Arm gave 0. 0. 6. Dr. Thorne made us a morning Visit. At Cribbage this Evening with Nancy lost 0. 0. 6. My Maid Betty was carried home in my little Cart with Ben to spend a Couple of Days at her Fathers at Mattishall being Christmas Holidays.

1788

JANRY. 13. . . . I read Prayers and Preached this Afternoon at Weston C. Mrs. Custance and her 2 eldest sons at Church, but not Mr. Custance, he being detained on Justice business, having had a Felon by name Wakefield of Booton brought to him this Aft. on very great suspicion of his being guilty of the Murder of one Thos. Twaites of Honingham, when a great many Poachers were at Mr. Townshends about 3 years ago, and at which time the above poor old man was murdered by having his skull fractured by a Bludgeon. The above Wakefield was impeached by an Accomplice one Beales who was of their Party, and is now in the Castle at Norwich as one of the Gang. It is also reported that he has impeached about ten more of the said gang.

JANRY. 25. ... Sent the Hare I killed yesterday to Mr. Bodham by Briton. Of Nancy for not being below Stairs for 2 Mornings before 10 o'clock, forfeit each time 6^d recd. o. 1. o. Briton returned before Dinner and informed us that Mr. Bodham continued still very indifferent.

FEB. 1. ... Mr. Carter of Ringland sent me a Note this Morn' before breakfast, to desire my Sentiments on a particular Question relating to the tolling of a Bell for a Child that died without being baptised at its decease, at any time from thence to its being interred and at the putting of it into the ground. I sent an Answer back to Mr. Carter, that as the Funeral Service could not be read over it, the tolling of the Bell at any time to be inadmissable. Recd. of Mr. Cary for 2 Pints of Butter at 10^d—o. 1. 8. Sent Briton down to Cantrells at Lenwade Bridge to send me some Wine and some Porter on Monday.

FEBRY. 6. ... Very busy all the Morning being very fine Weather in trimming up my young Scotch Firs.

FEB. 7. . . . Mr. Jeanes made us a long morning Visit, and during his being with us Mrs. Custance called on us and stayed about an Hour with us. To one Coxford of Felthorp, Yesterday, for a Dozen of Brooms—paid him as usual 0. 2. 6. To a poor Woman, disordered in mind, gave 0. 0. 6. Mr. Jeanes, told us this morning, that Mrs. Jeanes's Mother was married to one Mr. Lock, that very Day when we last dined with him at Witchingham. Mr. Lock is a Man of Fortune in Hampshire and keeps Horses.

FEB. 11. . . . Nancy not being below Stairs this morning before the clock had done striking 10 forfeited—0. 0. 6.

FEB. 14. . . . This being Valentines Day, I had a good many Children of my Parish called on me, to each of whom, gave (as usual) one penny, in all 0. 3. 1.

FEB. 18. . . . As soon as we were below stairs we heard of the Death of old Mrs. Peachman, Mr. Peachmans Mother, she died in the Night—Hope her removal is a happy one.

FEB. 20. . . . I breakfasted, dined, &c. again at home, Nancy breakfasted, dined &c. again at home. Morning mostly fair and fine tho' the Barometer was down to $28 = 17$—lower much than of late. Mr. Custance spent an Hour with us this Morning. Mr. Peachman called on me this afternoon about my burying his Mother on Friday next—He told us that his Mother was in her 83rd Year, that she went off very suddenly but with the Greatest Ease. That she had been below stairs the Day she dyed, that on her return to her Chamber she dyed directly. Poor old Mrs. Peachman had been all her life a very industrious, careful and I believe very good Woman. She never knew a Days sickness—had kept in the former Part of her life, Norwich Market twice in a week, for thirty Years together.

FEB. 29. . . . Mr. Taswell sent early to me this morning that he would take a Family Dinner with us to day and desired us to send to Mr. Custance that they might not wait dinner for him. He went from Weston House early this morning to go to Aylsham to read Prayers there to day being Friday. At 11 o'clock this Morning I sent Briton to Weston House to let them know that Mr. Taswell was to take a Family Dinner with us to day, Briton returned pretty soon and informed us that Mr. and Mrs. Custance, Lady Bacon and Son and Master Taswell would also come and partake of the Family Dinner, and they sent us some Fish, a wild Duck and a Sallad. It occasioned rather a Bustle in our House but we did as well as we could— We had not a bit of White bread in House, no Tarts whatever, and this Week gave no Order whatever to my Butcher for Meat, as I killed a Pigg this Week. We soon baked some white bread and some Tartlets and made the best shift we could on the whole. About 3 o'clock Mr. and Mrs. Custance, Lady Bacon and Son, Mr. Taswell and Nephew arrived and they dined, drank Coffee, and Tea and returned home about 7 o'clock this Evening to Weston House. Mr. Taswell with his Servant came here a little time before the other Company on horseback from Aylsham, he dressed himself at my House. We gave the Company for Dinner some Fish and Oyster Sauce, a nice Piece of Boiled Beef, a fine Neck of Pork rosted and Apple Sauce, some hashed Turkey, Mutton Stakes, Sallad &c. a wild Duck rosted, fryed Rabbits, a plumb

Pudding and some Tartlets. Desert, some Olives, Nutts, Almonds, and Raisins and Apples. The whole Company were pleased with their Dinner &c. Considering we had not above 3 Hours notice of their coming we did very well in that short time. All of us were rather hurried on the Occasion.

MARCH 11. .... Mr. Custance's Servant brought me a Letter this Evening from my Brother Heighes, he having been at Norwich to day, in which he presses us much to come into the Country this Summer, his Daughter Juliana being very ill, and apprehended to be in a decline, and is very desirous of seeing her Sister, but she is far from being able at present to take such a journey and being so lame as unable to walk without holding. Very bitter cold all the day long and severe frost tho' fair. I dont know when the cold Weather affected me more than it has this very day. My Brothers Letter affected Nancy very much, made her quite low.

MARCH 13. .... Nancy took a ride out this morning in her little Cart, for about 2 Hours and then returned home.

MARCH 15. .... Sent Ben to Norwich with a sample of Wheat to shew, and likewise to get the News Papers &c. I sent a very long letter to my Sister Pounsett by Ben and in it a Recipe from Dr. Buchan for Juliana Woodforde, Nancys Sister, for her bad Cough. Ben returned to dinner, he sold my Wheat for 23ˢ/6ᵈ per Coomb to Mr. Bloome of Trowse Mill near Norwich. I made a bet with Nancy on Wednesday last of 2ˢ/6ᵈ, that it rained before 8 o'clock this Evening which it did not till about 7 this Evening, as she lost her bet on so near gaining it, I not only omitted receiving the same, but gave her besides o. 2. 6.

MARCH 19. . . . Soon after breakfast being rather mild, Nancy took a ride in her Cart with Briton with her to Mattishall to Mr. Bodhams. Soon after she was gone, Mrs. Custance with her 2 Daughters and their Brother Willm. came to my House and after staying better than half an Hour, returned home. I gave the little Folks some Cakes whilst they stayed here. Soon after Mrs. Custance was gone, I christned a Child privately of one Wood's by name Mary Anne. Nancy returned home this Evening to Tea and in high Spirits—Mr. Bodham a good deal better; she likewise saw Mrs. Davy at Mr. Thornes and Mr. Thorne also met Nancy on the road on his return home from Norwich being sent for thither by express, his Sister (a Mrs. Walker and Mother to young Walker) being taken so ill that she died this Morning and she is to be buried at Weston as Nancy tells me.

APRIL 2. I breakfasted, supped and slept again at home. Nancy breakfasted, dined, &c. again at home. My poor Greyhound by name Hector died almost suddenly this morning in the Cover, He was running about the Cover all the Morning before breakfast. I apprehend that he broke (by furious running) some Vessel near the Heart, as he never got up after he laid down—very soon dead indeed. About 12 I took a ride to Mattishall to see Mr. and Mrs. Bodham, met them in their Carriage and Mr. Ashill with them on the Turnpike going to Honingham to put Mr. Ashill down there in his way for Norwich. They asked me to go to their House and dine with them as they would soon be back, which accordingly I did, and they returned in about half an Hour. Before they returned, I took a walk to a Cottage just by Mr. Bodhams to see one Mary Brand an old Woman of 80 who belongs to

Weston and to whom I send Mony every Year out of the Charity belonging to poor Widows of Weston. She lives with her Daughter, Wife of Jos. Bruton and a Tenant to Mr. Bodham, I found her spinning by the fire tho' she almost is blind. I gave her to buy Tobacco as she smokes 0. 1. 0. We had for dinner, a nice piece of boiled beef, Mutton stakes, mince Veal, Apple Dumplins and Pudding. I returned home about 6 o'clock to Tea. Whilst I was out Dr. Thorne called on my Niece and left with her for me, for burying his Sister Mrs. Walker last Monday Sennight 2. 2. 0 which I think was very handsome of him. Mr. Bodham is not right well yet, and looks poorly.

APRIL 19. I breakfasted, dined &c. again at home. Nancy breakfasted, dined, &c. again at home. Recd. a Letter this Evening from Mr. Du Quesne at London, intends being home to night, it was dated April 14— He talks very highly of Cole, and the many Civilities recd. from our Somersett Friends. Recd. also a very short Letter from my Brother Heighes informing me that his Daughter Juliana is entirely given over by the Faculty—poor Girl—Nancy recd. also a very melancholy Letter from her Brother Willm. concerning poor Juliana, that she was at the last stage of Life, and to desire Nancy to come down immediately into Somersett. Am afraid by this time that poor Juliana is no more. Nancy was half distracted almost on the Account. She cried incessantly the whole Evening, I sincerely pity her—no two Sisters could love one another more. Mr. Du Quesne's Head Maid, Betty, called on us this afternoon to let us know that Mr. Du Quesne would be at home this Evening.

APRIL 21. I breakfasted, dined, &c. again at home. Nancy breakfasted, dined, &c. again at home. After breakfast we took a ride to Mr. Du Quesnes, Nancy in her little Cart and myself on Horseback. We found Mr. Du Quesne at home and very well after his long Journey, stayed with him near 2 Hours. Mr. Du Quesne told us that he never met with More Civility than he received from our Somersett Friends when he was with them, particularly from my Sister Pounsett, Mr. Pounsett, and from my Brother John Woodforde and Wife and Mrs. R. Clarke. He spoke very much of my Brother Johns Genteel Behaviour towards him —and of the kind Attention of Nancy's Brother the Capt. to him. He saw Nancys poor Sister Juliana, she would go to my Brother Johns to dinner to meet Mr. Du Quesne—and she liked him very much. Mr. Du Quesne said that she was extremely weak and no hopes of her getting the better of it. He brought for Nancy a little Parcel from her poor Sister and gave it to her—which she opened on her return home. It was a small roundish red Morrocco Purse with a small silver lock to it and in it was a new half guinea of 1787 and 2 Queen Anne's Sixpences. It made her very uneasy and unhappy for a long time after, was rather more composed before she went to bed. It made my heart ache to see her so miserable. Had a note this Morning from young Mr. Quarles to desire me to appear at Reepham in his behalf on Wednesday the 30 Instant at 11. in the Morn'.

MAY 2. . . . My little Cart was brought home from being painted this Evening from Shorts of Honingham —and now looks very smart indeed—it is of a very dark green.

MAY 8. . . . Sent Briton to Norwich early this morning for things wanted from thence, he returned by dinner, and brought a Letter for Nancy from her

Brother Willm. upbraiding her for not coming to see her Sister, who is still alive and that is all—poor Girl I am sorry for her but am not pleased with Willm. for such a Letter to her Sister, as it made her very unhappy and very ill, vomited a good [deal] and could eat nothing at all for Dinner. Instead of condoling with her about her poor Sister and sorry for her not being able to go into the Country he rebukes her with want of humanity &c. It is quite cruel and unfeeling of him I think. His Letter was compcsed of a great many fine Epithets and sentimental thoughts.

MAY 12. . . . Merry doings at the Heart to day being Whit Monday plowing for a P^r of Breeches, running for a Shift, Raffling for a Gown &c.

MAY 17. I breakfasted, dined &c. again at home, Nancy breakfasted dined, &c. again at home. Sent Ben very early this Morning to Norwich with ten Coomb 2 Bshls of Wheat. He sold it to Mr. Bloome at 24^s/0^d per Coomb—I recd. for the same 12. 0. 0. He also brought me 2 Letters—One from My Sister Pounsett and the other from my Brother Heighes both which brought the disagreeable news of Nancy's Sister's Death, poor Juliana Woodforde, she died on Monday Morn' last about 11 o'clock. Poor Nancy greatly affected on hearing of the same. Nancy had a Letter by Ben from Mrs. Davy. Sent a Dozen, hollow little Cakes to Weston House. In my Sister Pounsetts Letter was a Bank Bill of the value of 10. 0. 0. To John Greaves and Brother pd. this Even' 0. 8. 0 for Carpenters work and sawing.

JUNE 6. . . . To my Man Ben for things pd. 4. 4. 8. that is, £1. 18^s. 0^d. for a Tub of Coniac Brandy of four gallons by Moonshine Buck and £2. 6^s. 0^d for two

Tubbs of Geneva of 4 Gallons each by ditto and the odd 8ᵈ for Horses Shoes removed.

JUNE 11. I breakfasted, supped and slept again at home. Nancy breakfasted supped, &c again at home. Betsy Davy breakfasted, supped, &c. here again. About 1 o'clock Mr. Du Quesne called here on horseback and I went with him on my Mare to Mr. Jeanes's, and Nancy and Betsy Davy went thither also in my little Cart, where we all dined, with Mr. and Mrs. Jeanes Junr., Mr. and Mrs. Jeanes Senr., Mr. and Mrs. Locke (who came to Mr. Jeanes's last Night) Miss Short, Mr. Charles Springger, (Brother to Mrs. Jeanes Junr.) Mr. and Mrs. Priest and Miss Mary Priest from Reepham. We had a very excellent Dinner, that is to say, a fine Piece of fresh Salmon with Tench and Eel, boiled Ham and Fowls, the best part of a Rump of Beef stewed, Carrots and Peas, a fore Qr. of Lamb rosted, Cucumbers and Mint Sauce, a Couple of Ducks rosted, plain and Currant Puddings. After Dinner 2 large Dishes of Strawberries, some Blanched Almonds with Raisins and Aples. We were much crowded at Table, rather unpleasant. Major Lloyd with his 2 eldest Daughters joined us at the Tea Table in the Evening which made the whole Company then consist of 18 in Number. After Coffee and Tea we had two or three Songs from Miss Kate Lloyd who sings delightfully indeed. It was sometime after 9 o'clock before we got back to Weston—we returned as we went. Upon the whole we spent a very agreeable Day. Mr. Jeanes Senr. is a mighty cheerful good natured plain downright Man. Mr. Locke a very neat well looking old gentleman, and Country Esq. fond of Hunting, keeps 16 fox Hounds, talks plain Hampshire and Delights also in farming. Mr. Charles

Springer a very modest young Man about 17 or 18 yrs, in some branch of Trade belonging to the India House.

JUNE 14. ... To the poor lame girl, Betty Deeker gave 0. 0. 6.

JUNE 24. ... To 6 Chicken and 5 Ducks this morning pd. 0. 6. 4 of one Dalliday of France Green. To Briton for things from Norwich last Saturday, Newspapers, Soap, Currants &c. pd. 0. 14. 8. To a poor Man of Felthorp, Sufferer by fire gave 1. 0. Recd. of Mr. Cary for Butter at 8^d 0. 1. 8.

JUNE 26. ... To some Scotch Snuff at Mr. Carys p^d 0. 0. 1.

JULY 7. ... Mr. Custance sent me a Melon and with it a Note to inform us that Mrs. Custance was this morning about 2 o'clock safely delivered of another Son and that both Mother and Child were as well as could possibly be expected in the time. Mr. C. also desired me (if perfectly convenient) to wait on him in the afternoon and name the little Stranger. After Dinner therefore about 5 o'clock I took a Walk to Weston House and named the little Infant, in Lady Bacons dressing Room by name, Neville. The Revd. Mr. Daniel Collyer of Wroxham was with Mr. Custance when I first went in but he soon went. I stayed and drank Tea with Mr. Custance and Sons and did not return home till after 8 this Evening.

JULY 18. ... Mr. Walker from London (Betsy Davy's intended) spent part of the morning with us—He came to his Uncles Mr. Thorne of Mattishall last Night. He looks ill indeed and Country Air advised for him. ....

JULY 21. ... Mr. Walker from Mattishall spent part of the Morn' here. To my Maid Betty Dade for things pd. o. 2. 4. To my Servant Man, Briton Scurl for Do. pd. o. 1. 8. Mr. Custance with his 3 eldest Sons, Hambleton, George, and William, drank Coffee and Tea with us this Afternoon—Hambleton and George go to School to Morrow to Mr. Phillips of Palgrave.

JULY 23. ... Mrs. Davy and Daughter breakfasted, and spent part of the Morn' also at Weston. Mr. Walker from Mattishall came here about 10 o'clock this Morning and stayed about an Hour. About 12 o'clock Mrs. Davy and her Driver Mr. Harris, Betsy Davy and my Niece in my little Cart with the Boy behind, and Mr. Walker and my Man Briton on horse-back, sat of from my House for Foulsham, where my Niece is to spend a few Days with Mrs. Davy and her Daughter, at a Mr. Thorne's there. Briton and my Boy returned from Foulsham this Evening about 8 o'clock—All got well there. Mr. Walker left them about Bawdeswell.

JULY 28. ... I was very low-spirited this Evening after Tea. I believe that Tea made me worse rather I think. I shot a Wood-Pecker this Morn' in my Garden.

JULY 29. I breakfasted, dined and spent the Aft. at home. In the Evening took a ride to Norwich and Briton with me, and there I supped and slept at the Kings Head. In the Evening before Supper I walked into St. Stephens and saw the Polish Dwarf, Joseph Boruwlaski and his Wife who is a middle sized Person, he is only three feet three Inches in height, quite well proportioned everyway, very polite, sensible and very sprightly, and gave us a tune upon the Guitar, and one Tune of his own composing. The common price

of admittance was one Shilling, but I gave him rather
more o. 2. 6.

JULY 30. I got up this morning about six o'clock and
before breakfast mounted my Mare and sat of for
Bungay and Briton with me, went three Miles at least
out of our Way to find out Ellingham where Mr. Hall
is Rector, called at Mr. Donnes at Brome, saw only
Mrs. Donne her Husband being gone to Bungay, did
not unlight but from thence went to a Mrs. Johnsons
where at present Mr. Hall boards (about half a Mile
from Mr. Donnes) and there I met with him and a
neighbouring Clergyman a Mr. Francis with him eat
a bit of Cake and drank a Glass of very old Madeira
and then went with Mr. Hall to his Parsonage House,
about half a Mile from Mrs. Johnsons, and there
stayed with him till he had dressed himself. Such a
Parsonage House and Garden and in so low a place,
close also to the River which often overflows, besides
Ellingham Mill so close that the Sound of it is continually heard. Such a House and Situation I think
very far from being agreeable. Mr. Hall however is
fitting of it up in a shabby Manner and at present
sleeps there of nights, no Man, Maid, Horse, Dog, or
any living Creature but himself there—The House
very small indeed. After Mr. Hall had dressed himself, He went with me to Bungay about two Miles and
half from his House, and there we dined and spent the
Aft. at the three Tunns kept by Mr. and Mrs. Utting.
Mr. Hall had Mrs. Johnsons Horse to go with me.
We got to Bungay about 3 o'clock, and glad enough
I was to get there having had no breakfast. We had
for Dinner some fish and a Leg of Mutton which was
just fit as we got thither. In the Evening about 8
o'clock Mr. Hall left me. As we were going into

Bungay to Day we met Mr. Donne and his Brother in Law Mr. Mott with him in a one horse Chaise. We had some Chit-Chat together, but not for any considerable time. I supped and slept at the three Tunns at Bungay. [He returned home next day.]

AUG. 11. ... Mr. Walker and Betsy Davy came over on single Horses this Morning from Foulsham and they breakfasted, dined, and spent the Afternoon with us. We had a good deal of singing to Day from my Niece and Mr. Walker—the latter sung many new Songs. We spent a very agreeable Day together. We had for Dinner a boiled Leg of Mutton and Capers, a Couple of rost Chicken, Apple Pye and black Currant Tarts—Apricots, Apples and black Currants for a Desert. Mr. Walker and Betsy Davy came to us about 9 o'clock this morning and stayed till half past six in the Evening. We had a Note that Mr. and Mrs. Bodham would dine here on Wedn.

AUG. 16. ... Mrs. Davy with one Harris in a Cart called here, this Evening about 5 o'clock and drank Tea here in her road from Norwich to Foulsham. Soon after Mrs. Davy came also Mr. Walker and with him another young Man by name Viol, both almost wet thro' and they drank Tea also here in their road from Norwich homewards, so that my House was more like an Inn this Evening than anything else.

AUG. 28. ... About 11 o'clock this Morning I took a walk to Weston Church and there married by Licence Jas. Herring of Norwich to Miss Peachman of this Parish, for which I recd. of Mr. Herring 2. 2 0 which I think was very handsome of him. It was a smart genteel Marriage 2 close Carriages with smart Liveries attended. Sheriff Buckle of Norwich and Mr.

John Herring who was Sheriff of Norwich the last year and his Son, old Mr. Peachman, Mrs. John Herring, Mrs. Forster of this Parish, and a very pretty young Lady very neatly dressed, and attended as a Bride Maid and whose name was Miss Wingfield were at the Ceremony. The Bells rung merry after. Mr. Buckle Mr. Herring and Son and old Mr. Peachman returned with me on foot from Church to my House and eat some Cake and drank some Cyder &c. Mr. Peachman pressed me much to dine with them but I was not well enough to go into Company tho' thank God much better than I expected to be to day.

AUG. 29. ... Finished my Wheat Harvest to day at Noon ...

SEPT. 1. ... This Evening Mrs. Siddons from London, acts for the first time on the Norwich Theatre, she is to perform only for seven Nights and then returns. [Parson Woodforde, judging by the silence of subsequent entries, made no effort to see her.]

SEPT. 25. ... Nancy, Mrs. Davy and Betsy breakfasted here and as soon as they had done breakfast, they went of for Norwich in a Norwich Chaise from the Kings Head. And at 10 o'clock I mounted my Mare and sat of for the same place and my Servant Man Ben went with me to carry my Portmanteau. My Servant Man Briton went with the Chaise and sat with the Driver before the Chaise. Going into Norwich about a Mile from it I met Mr. Smith of Mattishall coming from Norwich we just spoke to each other and that was all.[1] Ben had my Mare back

---

[1] A coldness seems to have developed in Parson Woodforde's relations with Mr. Smith, possibly connected with the latter's affair with Mrs. Davy.

to Weston in the Aft. Mr. Walker had taken Lodgings
at Norwich at a Mr. Curtis's in St. Gregory's, for
himself and Sister, my Niece and myself, and Mrs.
Davy and Betsy—for which we are to give 2 Guineas
and half—when I arrived at Norwich I found all the
Ladies Heads dressed. At 4 o'clock we all went to the
King's Head and there dined on some fresh Herrings,
a rost Turkey, a Shoulder of Mutton rosted and some
Tarts. A Mr. Townson a young Gentleman from
London and an Acquaintance of Mr. Walkers; Mr.
Colin Roupe, and his Brother George also dined with
us. Very soon after Dinner, Mrs. Davy and Betsy,
Miss Walker and my Niece went in an Hackney
Coach to St. Andrews Hall to hear the Concert this
Evening. Mr. Walker and myself walked thither.
The Tickets to the Miscellaneous Concert to Night
were 7 Shillings and 6 pence each. Mrs. Custance
being a Subscriber and having a transferable Ticket,
was so kind as to lend my Niece hers for this Evening.
Mr. Walker procured Tickets for the rest of us. He is
to pay for Tickets, Coaches, Lodgings &c. and when
finished Mr. Walker and self are to divide the expenses between us. A great deal of Company indeed
at the Hall and full dressed—911 supposed to be
present. The Concert was very fine indeed, and
Madame Mara, the famous Singer, sung delightfully.
I never heard so fine a Voice—Her Notes so high.
The Kettle Drums from Westminster Abbey sounded
charmingly, beat by a Mr. Ashbridge. Near 100 per-
formers in the Orchestra. The Concert was over
between 10 and 11 at Night but we were obliged to
wait a full Hour before we could get to our Hackney
Coach, so many Coaches before it and some an Hour
after us. I went back with the Ladies in the Coach to
our Lodgings and there we supped and slept. I dont

know what our Company would have done without my Servant Briton, being with me. Saw at St. Andrews Hall this Evening and conversed with them S^r. Willm. Jerningham, S^r. John Woodhouse, Captain Laton, Mr. Branthwaite, Major Lloyd, Mr. Press Custance, Mr. Du Quesne, Mr. Jeanes, Mr. Bodham, Harry Smith of New College, Mr. Priest of Norwich and Son—&c.

SEPT. 26. As I only laid down on the Bed last Night with some of my Cloaths, I got up pretty early (considering we did not go to bed till near 2 this morning) and I took a Walk in the City, went to Bacons and got Tickets for the Oratorio this morning at St Peters Church—went also to Browns my Barber and was shaved—paid him also for a new Wigg I had sometime back the sum of 1. 1. 0. Gave him also for dressing my Wigg &c. 0. 2. 6. Called at Beales and paid for Soals Aug. 6. 0. 3. 0. Then returned to my Lodgings to breakfast about 9, and there breakfasted with Mrs. Davy and Betsy, Miss Walker, my Niece, and Mr. Walker. Soon after breakfast, Mrs. Davy and Betsy, Miss Walker, my Niece, and Mr. Walker went in a Coach to St. Peters Church to the Oratorio of Judas Maccabeus,[1] I walked to the House of Mr. Priests and there waited for Mr. Custances Coach to return Mrs. Custance's Ticket to her, the Coach called about 11, with Mr. and Mrs. Custance in it,

---

[1] Composed by Handel in 1746 (produced in 1747) and dedicated to the Duke of Cumberland, the victor of Culloden in that year. It was the first of Handel's Oratorios to win popularity in England. Up to 1746-7 the great composer, despite the devoted patronage of George II and Queen Caroline, had had a difficult and depressing time in England, though Dublin, which he visited in 1741-2, and where the *Messiah* was first performed, received him rapturously. With *Judas Maccabeus* the tide set finally in his favour in England, and he died full of years and honour in 1759.

and I went with them to St. Peter's Church and there heard the fine Oratorio of Judas Maccabeus which was performed very capitally—Madame Mara also performed her part very well indeed. There was supposed to be present 1200 People. The Church was quite full, I got as near to my Party as I could. Mrs. Davy during the performance made some little disturbance, fainting away, but she soon came to herself again, quite a fine Air. Betsy Davy did not mind it at all, as she knows her well. The Oratorio was not over till 3 this Afternoon. We all walked back from St. Peters to our Lodgings and there I left them and went to the Wool-Packet in St. Giles's, where my Servant Ben was waiting for me with my Horses. I then mounted my Mare, and went home with Ben to Weston did not get home till 6 o'clock this Evening and there dined, supped and slept at the Parsonage House. I thank God, got home safe and well after my Hurry without being either much fatigued or heavy. I left my Party at Norwich, as they all go to the Assembly this Evening in Chapel Field. I desired Mr. Walker to settle all Accounts at Norwich and that I would reckon with him at home. Gave the Servant Girl at the Lodgings 0. 1. 0. I was highly entertained by the Musick both Days. Scarce ever seen so much Company at Norwich. Lodgings scarce to be got and some exceeding dear indeed—two Rooms it was said, was let at 10 guineas. Almost all the principal Families in the County there.

Sept. 27. ... Between 2 and 3 o'clock this Afternoon there came to my House in a Post-Chaise from Norwich Mrs. Davy, Betsy, Miss Charlotte Quarles and my Niece, and they all dined and spent the Afternoon here. After Tea Mrs. Davy with Miss Quarles went on in the Chaise to Foulsham. Betsy Davy was left at my House to spend a day or two with Nancy. Just as we had finished Dinner Mr. Walker came to us from Norwich and he dined and slept here, being very much fatigued by his late Hurry at Norw. As the Driver of the Chaise was given nothing going with them to Norwich or coming back—I gave him 3. 6. After Tea Betsy Davy and me played against Mr. Walker and Nancy at Whist at which—lost—1s/0d. We had for Dinner to day some fryed Soals a Leg of Mutton boiled and Caper Sauce, a Couple of Ducks rosted, and some Tarts &c. Mrs. Davy and Miss Quarles left us about 6 o'clock. After they were gone Mr. Walker and me settled our Norwich Accounts. The Expenses were as follows. Dinners at the Kings Head &c. 2. 12s 2. Post Chaise from Norwich to Foulsham 0. 18. 0. Ditto from Weston to Norwich 0. 10. 0. Coach Hire in Norwich 0. 16. 0. Lodgings at Curtis's in St. Gregory's 2. 12. 6. Breakfasts, Suppers, and Dinner at the Lodgings 1. 10. 2½. Tickets to the Hall at 7s/6d each 1. 17. 6. Tickets to the Church at 5/0 each 1. 5. 0. Sum total 12. 1. 4½. Paid my Moiety to Mr. Walker 6. 0. 6 that is, in Cash to him 4. 16. 0. Tickets paid by me for the Church 1. 5. 0. It was a dear Frolick but nevertheless I should have been sorry that my Niece had not went to it. It also gave me pleasure to attend at it, and would have given more to all parties if Mrs. Davy had not been so full of strange Vagaries expecting so much Court and Attention from everyone. There was not one of the Party pleased with her. We all went to bed in tolerable good time to night. Miss Charlotte Quarles is a great Beauty and exquisitely genteel without the lest affectation but very affable and very agreeable.

OCTOB. 11. Mr. Walker called here this morning but did not stay he had been out with the hounds. Sent Briton early this Morning to Norwich after News &c. He returned by dinner time. Received by him a long Letter from my Brother Heighes, who informs me that his Son Willm. is going to marry a Miss Jukes a fortune of £5000.

OCT. 17. ... Mr. Jeanes sent me this morning a large Hamper of common Apples, I sent the same Hamper back full of my Apples called Beefans with a great many Shrubs, Laurels &c. &c.

OCT. 27. ... Mr. Walker went out early this Morning a hunting and did not return the whole day. Poor Betsy Davy could eat no Supper and obliged to go to bed, her heart ached so very much. Mr. Walker sent over a Messenger from Mattishall this Evening to inform us that he sleeps at Mattishall.

OCT. 28. ... Nancy breakfasted and spent part of the Morn' at home. Betsy Davy breakfasted and spent part of the Morn' here. Mr. Walker came here this Morning between 10 and 11 o'clock, stayed about half an Hour and then went in my little Cart with Betsy Davy and my Niece to Foulsham where they are to dine, sup, and sleep for this night only and to return home to dinner to Morrow by 3 o'clock. I gave them a Chicken to carry with them for dinner. Mrs. Davy is at Pulham as yet and expected to stay there. Mr. Townshend with his eldest Daughter both on horseback called here this morning about 12 but did not get of from their horses. They went from my House to Weston House. The Widow Case waited on me this Morning and paid me the remaining money due from her late Husband to me for the last

Year 1. 5. 0. I paid her out of it for 400 green Walnuts 2. 0. Sent to each of my neighbouring Families a two Bushel Basket of Apples (called Beefans) viz. to John Clarkes, Will Richmonds, J$_0^n$ Nortons, Robt. Downings, Richd Bucks, Nath. Heavers, and John Peachmans. I caught Paul Bowden this evening lopping an Ashen Tree of mine—gave him a Lecture and told him to take care for the future.

OCT. 29. ... At Mr. Cary's Shop, for Tobacco and Snuff pd. 0. 0. 9. Recd. this morning by Mr. Custance's Servant Richd. brought by him from Norwich from the Post Office a gilt Card enclosed in a Cover from Mr. and Mrs Coke of Holkham, containing an Invitation to me and my Niece the fifth of November next to a Ball and Supper at Holkham. The Card was printed all but our Names and in these words. Mr. and Mrs Coke desire the honour of Mr. and Miss Woodford's Company the 5th of November, at eight o'clock to a Ball and Supper, in Commemoration of the glorious Revolution of 1688. Holkham, Oct. 1788. The Favour of an Answer is desired. My Servant, Briton, paid for the same 0. 0. 8. N.B. a general Invitation throughout the County. Mr. Walker with my Niece and Betsy Davy returned home to Weston about 3 o'clock this Afternoon; and they dined, supped and slept here. At Whist this Evening won 0. 1. 0.

NOV. 3. ... Mr. Walker breakfasted, and spent most of the Morn' with us, and at half past 12, went of for Norwich in one of the Kings Head Chaises as he goes for London this Afternoon in one of the Mail Coaches. Who should come in the Kings Head Chaise from Norwich but Nunn Davy Betsy's Brother who is just returned from out of Yorkshire where he has been for the last 3 Years. He looked sharp and well and went back with Mr. Walker to Norwich after staying about ½ Hour as he is going to Pulham to see his Mother. Between 9 and 10 o'clock this Evening Mr. Walker returned to us from Norwich having put of going to London till after the 5th of November, and he supped and slept here again. Grand Works to be at Norwich the 5 Instant. We made it late going to bed to night. My poor old Spaniel Bitch Mab was hung this Morn' she being very old and almost blind. I had her hanged out of Charity.

Nov. 5. ... Soon after breakfast (young Rose called here and desired me to lend him my Greyhounds, having found a Hare sitting) Mr. Walker and self took a Walk with the Greyhounds and saw the Hare coursed which gave great Sport indeed, but was killed at last. I never saw a better Course. I let Mr. Rose have the Hare for a Friend of his. After we had killed that Hare we went after another and found one in about an Hour, but we had very little Diversion with her, the Greyhounds scarcely seeing her, She soon got of. Saw never another tho' we stayed out till 3 o'clock. Mr. Walker almost knocked up by walking so long, we were out from 11 till 3 in the Afternoon. Whilst we were out again this Morning Mrs. Custance with 3 Children called at the Parsonage, and spent an Hour with my Niece and Betsy Davy. Mrs. Custance brought a brace of Partridges for us. After Tea again this Evening we got to Whist, Partners the same, Betsy mine, Nancy Mr. Walkers and we beat them again won 0. 1. 6. So that Nancy owes me now 0. 17. 0. Very fine Evening tho' cold for the Holkham Jubilee.

Nov. 6. I breakfasted, dined, &c again at home.

Nancy breakfasted, dined, &c. again at home.

Betsy Davy breakfasted, dined, &c. again here.

Mr. Walker breakfasted here and soon after he had breakfasted, he mounted his Horse and sat of for Norwich and there he dined and spent the Afternoon but returned to us in the Evening about 7 o'clock or rather after.

To Ben this Evening for things pd. . 1. 1. 4½
To Briton   ditto   do.   pd. . 0. 4. 1
To Betty   ditto   do.   pd. . 0. 11. 4

Mr. Walker supped and slept here again. He rode from Norwich here in about 3 Qrs. Hour. He went to bed long before us being tired &c.

Nov. 7. . . . About 3 o'clock Mr. Walker, Nancy, Betsy Davy, and self went to Weston House and there we dined and spent the Afternoon with Mr. and Mrs. Custance, Mr. Press Custance, Sʳ Thomas and Lady Beauchamp, Mr. George Beauchamp and Mr. Lemon a Clergyman. After Coffee and Tea this Evening we got to Cards, 2 Tables, one Table at Commerce, the other at Whist. I was at the latter and Mr. Lemon was my Partner against Sʳ Thomas and Lady Beauchamp, we played 2 Rubbers at 1ˢ/0ᵈ Whist lost 0. 8. 0. We returned home about 9 o'clock as we went in Mr. Custances Coach. We had for Dinner, Some Fish, Ham and Chicken, Giblets, Piggs Fry, Saddle Mutton roasted, boiled Beef on the side Table &c. 2nd Course Hare rosted, a Pheasant do. Snipes do. &c. Madeira, Cherry, Claret and Port Wines. Lent Mr. Walker at Cards 0. 2. 6. Sʳ Thos. and Lady Beauchamp talked a good deal to Mr. Walker being some Relation to Lady B. We did not get to bed till after 12 o'clock as it is the last Night of Mr. Walker being with us.

Nov. 8. . . . Mr. Walker breakfasted, and spent the Morning with us, and at 1 o'clock set of for Norwich to go in the Mail Coach this Afternoon at 4 for London.

Nov. 11. . . . Two Men from Hockering by names, Bugdale and Ames, called here this Morning to see 8 Piggs, Shots of mine which I have to sell, I asked 10 Pound for them, they offered me 8 Pound. I then told them that they should have them at 9 P. but they would not give that, so we parted. Brewed a Barrel of small Beer to day. Reported this Day at Norwich that our good King was dead, pray God it might not be true.[1]

Nov. 13. . . . About 2 o'clock I took a ride and Briton with me to Mr. Du Quesnes and there dined and spent the Afternoon with him, Mr. and Mrs. Custance, Mr. and Mrs. Jeanes, Miss Davy and Miss Woodforde, the 2 latter went and returned with Mr. and Mrs. Custance in their Coach. After Coffee and Tea we got to Cards. I lost 0. 1. 6. We had for Dinner Cod and Oyster Sauce, boiled Chicken and Piggs face, a Saddle of Mutton rosted and Roots—2nd Course a brace of rost Pheasants, 1 duck rosted, the Charter &c. We returned home about ½ past 9 o'clock and on our return found Mr. Walker at Weston Parsonage, who is returned from London in pursuit of his Port-manteau which is at present lost. He supped and

[1] It was on November 5th that George III's illness, insanity, declared itself beyond all possibility of question. During his illness the king resided for the most part at Kew Palace, being moved there from Windsor on November 29th. The king's physicians, Dr. Warren and Sir George Baker, took a somewhat gloomy view of the case, but a doctor of genius in the treatment of insanity, Dr. Willis (who was also a parson), predicted a rapid recovery. Dr. Willis was right: early in February 1789 the king became much better, and on February 27th bulletins were discontinued.

slept here. He came in a Post-Chaise from Norwich, which went down to Lenewade Bridge with the Driver, and to take up Mr. Walker to Morrow Morn' back to Norw. The report this Day, is, that his Majesty is better.

Nov. 14. ... After breakfast Nancy, and Betsy Davy would go to Norwich with Mr. Walker, and there they dined at the Kings Head and returned home to Tea about 6 o'clock and Mr. Walker instead of going to London as proposed returned with them. A pretty expensive and foolish Scheme indeed—I was not pleased. To Neighbour Case for Pork at 4½d pd. o. 2. 3. After Tea this Evening we got to Whist lost o. 3. o. The News relating to the Kings Health this Day at Norwich, was, that he remains near the same, by no means better—still in the greatest danger. Mr. Walker paid me what I lent him at Cards o. 2. 6.

Nov. 15. ... Mr. Walker breakfasted here and then sat of for Norwich in my little Cart and Briton with him, who is to bring back News &c. Mr. Walker goes by the Mail Coach this Aft. for London. Briton returned about 5 o'clock this Afternoon. Brought me a Letter from my Sister Pounsett to let us known that Nancys Brother William was gone of with Miss Jukes to be married, and that they were at Portland Island. Briton also said that Mr. Walker did not go to London this Day neither, and that he would return to my house again this Evening, which he did to Supper and also slept here again. It was after 12 before I got to bed this Night. Mr. Walker brought us a brace of Pheasants.

Nov. 16. ... I read Prayers and Preached this Afternoon at Weston Church—none from Weston House at Church. Nancy, Betsy Davy, and Mr. Walker also from Church. I prayed at Church for our most gracious and truly beloved Sovereign King George the third. I did it out of my own head, no prayer yet arrived.

Nov. 17. ... Mr. Walker went out a hunting this morning and did not return to us till near 6 o'clock this Evening. At Whist this Evening lost o. 1. 6. So that Nancy owes me now only o. 12. 6.

Nov. 18. ... Soon after breakfast Mr. Walker took a ride to Norwich to take a place in the Mail Coach for this Afternoon for London—but he returned to us this Evening between 7 and 8 o'clock and it being very dark, he hired a Man to come with him on another horse—Joe at the Kings Head. After Joe had refreshed himself and Horse also he returned back to Norwich. Mr. Walker said that there was no Place in the Coach but all that is nothing, his inclination was to stay. Betsy Davy's Birth Day now 18 Years of Age.

Nov. 19. ... Mr. Walker breakfasted here, and then sat of once more for Norwich to go in the Mail Coach this Afternoon for London—I still think it rather dubious where [whether?] he goes or not this Day. On his taking leave he went up to Nancy and wished her well shaking her by her hand, and then went to Betsy and did the same, but to me (altho' in the Room at the same time) he never said one word or took the lest notice of me (tho' I also helped him on with his great Coat) after he was mounted and just going out of the great Gates then he said good Morning and that was all—very slight return for my Civilities towards him of late and which I did not expect. It hurt me

very much indeed. Mr. Walker did not return however this Day to us.

Nov. 20. ... To one Platten of Hockering sold 8 fine
Piggs, littered in April last for 8. 8. 0. I gave him for
good luck out of it—0. 1. 0. Mr. Jeanes made us a
morning Visit and brought us some fine Prawns just
arrived from Hants. Miss Woodforde rather pert this
morning.

Nov. 21. ... Mr. Walkers Birth-Day now 21 Years
of Age.

Nov. 22. ... Sent Ben early this Morning to Norwich
after News and other things from thence, he returned
about Dinner time. No Letters for us. Betsy Davy had
a Letter from Mr. Walker from Thetford and with it a
Parcel in which was nothing but a Fox's Brush or Tail.

Dec. 6. ... Sent Ben to Norwich on horseback after
News &c. He returned home to dinner with the same.
Betsy Davy had a Parcel and a Letter from Mr.
Walker in Town. The Parcel contained a very hand-
some red Morocco Almanack and Pocket Book, gilt
with a silver Clasp to the same—quite new fashioned.
Nancy also had a Letter from Mr. Walker and a
Barrel of Oysters sent her by him also.

Dec. 20. ... Mrs. Custance with her two Sons
Hambleton and George who are just returned home
from School, made us a long morning Visit. They
both looked well, but George has Childblains on one
foot. Sent Briton early this morning to Norwich with
my little Cart, after News &c. he returned abt. 4.
Received a Letter by him from Mr. Walker in which
he mentions having sent me 2 Gallons of English Gin,
but he mentioned nothing of when it was sent, by
what Conveyance, or where left.

DEC. 21. ... I read Prayers and Preached this morning at Weston C. Also gave Notice of the H. Sacrament to be administered on Thursday next being Xmas Day. None from Weston House at Church this Morn' being bitter cold Frost with high Wind and Snow. Very small Congregation at Church this Morn'. It was intensely cold on my return from Church with high Wind and Snow. It was very penetrating. Betsy Davy almost lame in both feet by Childblains. Nancy also complained of something similar—they both by my desire had some white worsted Stockings of mine to put on, and to leave of their cotton ones. Betsy Davy found the first effects of it at Mr. Jeanes's when at Witchingham—so very cold there.

DEC. 22. ... Yesterday being St. Thomas, the poor People came to my House for their Xmas Gifts this Morning. To 56 poor People of my Parish at 6^d each gave 1. 8. 0. Harry Baker my Butcher called on me this Morn' and I paid him for Meat from Dec. 6, 1787 to Decem^{br} 6, 1788 the Sum of 39. 11. 0. Recd. of Ditto for a Calf &c. 1. 15. 8.

DEC. 23. ... To Mr. Ames my Cooper, paid a Bill of 0. 18. 6. Just as we were going to Dinner a Man came express from the Kings Head at Norwich, with a Letter for Betsy Davy from Mr. Walker at London to desire her to meet him at Norwich at the Kings Head on Christmas Day next Thursday and that Nancy would accompany her. He mentioned in his Letter that he had ordered a Post-Chaise from the Kings head to be at my House for them in the Morning. Very wild, unsteady, and thoughtless Work indeed.

DEC. 24. ... This being Christmas Eve I had my

Parlour Windows dressed of as usual with Hulver-
boughs well seeded with red-Berries, and likewise in
Kitchen.

DEC. 25. . . . I read Prayers and administered the
H. Sacrament this Morning at Weston Church being
Xmas Day. For an Offering at the H. Sacrament gave
0. 2. 6. Mr. and Mrs. Custance at Church and at the
H. Sacrament. Before I went to Church this Morning
Nancy and Betsy Davy went of in a Norwich Chaise
which came to my House by 7 o'clock this morning
for Norwich to meet Mr. Walker at the Kings Head,
and there they dined, but returned home to Tea in
the Afternoon and Mr. Walker with them. Mr.
Walker supped and slept here. Js. Smith, my Clerk,
Thos. Cary, Thos. Carr, Richd. Buck, John Peachman, and Nath. Heavers had their Christmas Dinner
and each $1^s/0^d$—0. 6. 0. Poor old Richd. Buck and
old John Peachman being both Lame, could not
come to my House to dinner, so I sent their Dinner to
them, &c. Sent also a Dinner to the poor Girl Betty
Deeker.

1789

JAN^{ry} 1st. . . . About 12 Mr. Walker went to Norwich
in a Chaise that he had ordered from thence. To J^n_o
Short, Wheelwright pd a Bill of 1. 18. 9. To Robt.
Buck, Blacksmith of Honingham pd. 0. 6. 9. Mr.
Walker returned to us by Tea time this Aft. At Cards
this Evening won 0. 2. 0. So that Nancy owes me now
0. 7. 0. Bitter cold this Evening and a very hard
Frost. N.B. Fox's Brush &c. made me quite sick and
tired.

JAN^ry 2. ... Mr. Custance came to us this Morning on foot and spent above an Hour with us—tho' so bitter cold. I slept but indifferent last night, so bitter cold. After Tea we got to Cards—nothing lost or won. As cold today as it has been yet. ... Mr. Walker's Cough somewhat better. Nancy, Betsy Davy, and Mr. Walker are all confederate against me and am never let into any of their Schemes or Intentions &c. Nancy I think ought not to be so to me.

JAN^ry 3. ... Did not get to bed till near 1 o'clock—being very uneasy. The treatment I meet with for my Civility this Christmas is to me abominable.

JAN^ry 4. ... Mr. Walker breakfasted, and spent the Morn' here. At 12 he went from my House in a Chaise for Norwich to go for London this Afternoon. I read Prayers and Preached this Morn' at Weston Ch. None from Weston House at Church had a very small Congregation, it being so intensely cold. I never felt the cold so much in my Life before. It froze the whole Day long within Doors and very sharp. The Barometer in my Study very high 30 = 5. The Thermometer in Ditto very low—48. The Air very clear and very piercing.

JAN. 6. ... Bitter cold day again with high wind, it froze in all parts of the House. Sent Ben round my Parish with some money to the Poor People this severe Weather, chiefly those that cannot work at this time, some 1 Shilling apiece—some at 1^s/6^d apiece. In all, Ben gave for me this Day 1. 14. 6.

JAN. 20, TUESDAY. [Note that from this date the Diarist always, or nearly always, inserts the day of the week: hitherto he has been content with the day of the month only.]

I breakfasted, dined, &c. again at home.

Nancy breakfasted, dined, &c. again at home.

Betsy Davy breakfasted, dined, &c. here again.

I could not get to sleep last Night till quite late thinking on such Variety of things and People. Mr. Howlett and Mr. Forster called here this Afternoon as they were going to a Parish Meeting at the Heart to speak to me respecting the Rent due for the Poor Cottage where Dick Buck &c live, which belongs to the Widows Charity—I told them that I expected the Parish would pay the Arrears. Mr. Howlett brought with him in a Baskett a Couple of Guinea Fowls, a Cock and a Hen, as a present from him and his Wife.

JAN. 21, WEDNESDAY. . . . Mr. Buck, Overseer of the Poor, called on me this morning to inform me that the Parish will pay part of the Rent due for the poor House.

JAN. 24, SATURDAY. . . . Sent Briton early this morning on horseback to Norwich after News &c. returned home by Dinner. Brought a Letter for Nancy from Mr. Walker. An old Man came express from Foulsham with a Letter for Betsy Davy from Mr. Walker in Town. Betsy gave the old Gentleman for coming over with it 1s/6d. I gave him some Victuals and Drink. The Wind was so high in the Night that I got up about 2 o'clock but did not come below. Went to bed before 5 o'clock.

N.B. Not a Word mentioned to me by either Betsy or Nancy concerning anything in the Letters sent by Walker. Betsy very busy all the Evening writing since she recd. Walkers Letter—but to who not one Word to me. They are both artful.

JAN. 25, SUNDAY. ... Nancy and Betsy went to bed exactly at 10 to night.

MARCH 4, WEDNESDAY. ... Mr. Du Quesne dined and spent the Aft. with us. He was not in good Spirits, owing to disagreeable things happening in his Family with regard to Servants, his Man Servant James Atterton having been too familiar with his two young Servant Maids, Lizzy Greaves, an old Servant Maid of Mine about 23 Years of Age, and another Girl by name Mary, both of which are with Child by James. The former Maid Lizzy, was married Yesterday to James, and the other discovered her Situation only last Night. James also had kept Company with Lizzy's Sister, Sukey, now Servant at Weston House for the last four Years. James never appeared to have been such a sly Fellow as he has proved to be, but much the contrary. We had for Dinner to day a boiled Chicken and a piece of bacon, some rost Beef and Tarts. Mr. Du Quesne left us before Tea.

MARCH 8, SUNDAY. ... I read Prayers and Preached this Afternoon at Weston Church—Also read with the greatest Pleasure a Prayer composed on the Occasion on the restoration of his Majesty's Health, which I received this Morning. I return also to thee O Lord my private but most unfeigned Prayer of Thanksgiving for the same, And may so good a King long live to reign over us—and pray God that his amiable and beloved Queen Charlotte may now enjoy again every happiness this World can afford, with so good a Man, and may it long, very long continue with them both here and eternal happiness hereafter. This is the ardent and most fervent Prayer of one of their most sincere subjects for the best of Kings and Queens. Neither Mr. or Mrs. Custance at Church. The Weather, I suppose, being so very Cloudy with Snow. Nancys Birth Day to day she is now entered into her 32. Year.

MARCH 17, TUESDAY. . . . This morning settled Money Matters with my Niece for the last year—paid her the balance in ready Cash—which was—4. 4. 0. The whole that I had paid for her and gave her the last Year—amounted to 31. 2. 9. Brewed some strong Beer to day. Nancy very discontented of late, and runs out against living in such a dull Place.

MARCH 18, WEDNESDAY. . . . Brewed some more strong Beer to day. It always takes us 2 Days to brew a Barrell of strong Beer. Great Rejoicings at Norwich this Evening on the happy restoration of his Majesty's Health. I gave to our People in the Kitchen on the Occasion a Bottle of Gin to drink the King's Health, this Evening after Supper, and the Queens to Morrow.

MARCH 19, THURSDAY. . . . Most part of the Day fine but Air very cold. I took a little Rharbarb this Evening going to bed being rather dull and melancholy.

MARCH 26, THURSDAY. . . . Very sharp Frosts of Nights still prevail and very cold Weather, no appearance of Spring yet to signify. The Wall fruit Trees seem to promise very well, the Apricots as full in Blossom as can be, but they are not full out, otherwise the Frost would cut them.

MARCH 28, SATURDAY. . . . I took a Walk to Weston House this Morning to see Mr. Custance who is ill in a swelled Face. I stayed with him an hour and half and returned home to dinner. Mr. Custance pressed me much to dine with him as he was alone, and Mrs. Custance at Raveningham, at Sr Edmund

Bacons, but I could not as I expected a Letter from the West by my Servant, Briton, who went to Norwich this morning after News &c. and which in all probability would be most unwelcome to me and likewise to my poor Niece—accordingly when I returned which was about 3 o'clock to my House, Briton was returned, and with him brought a Letter sealed with black Wax to me, which on opening I found to be from my Brother John, informing us, that my dear Brother Heighes died on Sunday last the 22 Instant about 11 o'clock in the Morning from a violent inflammation in the urinary passage which finally terminated in a Mortification in a very short time, pray Almighty God that he might be more happy in a future State than he has experienced in this, and all his frailties in this Life forgiven. We heard nothing of his being ill till Tuesday night last, and now gone, O Lord make us wise to think on futurity. We were both most unhappy, on hearing the fatal News, my Brothers Letter was dated on the 22 Instant the Day my poor Brother died. My Brother John rather bad in a cold but all our remaining Friends well. Pray God comfort my Nephew Willm in his great distress. My Brother mentions that he believes that my late Brother Heighes had left his Sons Willm. and Samuel executors, and that they are to pay Nancy a share of his Estate in Sussex in money.

APRIL 5, SUNDAY. ... I read Prayers and Preached this Afternoon at Weston Ch. Mr. Custance at Church this Afternoon—Mrs. C. not at home. The poor Girl Mary Deeker died this morning at the Widows Cottage, she has scarce ever been well. It is a happy change for her, I hope to God.

APRIL 11, SATURDAY. ... Sent Briton this morning

early with my little Cart to Norwich after News &c.
&c. He returned abt. 4 o'clock this Afternoon and
with him brought me a Letter from my Sister Pounsett, in which she says that our late poor Brother
Heighes had made a Will and left his Estate in Sussex
equally between his Sons Willm. and Sam[l] and their
Sister A. M. Woodforde which I think very good and
just of him. It is rather apprehended that the Widow
will have the Estate during her natural Life. Briton
also brought all our Mourning home, viz. a black
Coat and Waistcoat for me. A Black Bombasine
Gown and Coat for Nancy with long Sleeves, and also
a black stuff German Great Coat for her to wear in
common. Mr. Du Quesne sent a Servant over to our
house about 2 o'clock with a fine Trout, and that if
we were not engaged he would dine with us to day
and at 3 he came and dined and spent the Afternoon
with us. We had for Dinner the Trout, some minced
Veal, and a Neck of Mutton rosted.

APRIL 17, FRIDAY. ... To Neighbour Gooch for a
Leg of Veal at $3\frac{1}{2}$d p[d] 0. 3. 0. Mr. and Mrs. Custance
drank Tea with us this Aft. in a friendly way, stayed
till near 8 o'clock. Mr. Custance very kindly brought
us a bunch of Radishes which was a very great rarity
as the Weather has been of late uncommonly severe
for the Season. To a Calfs Head of Nann Gooch paid
0. 1. 0.

APRIL 19, SUNDAY. ... I read Prayers, Preached,
and publickly christened a Child this Afternoon at
Weston Church. Neither Mr. or Mrs. Custance at
Church this Afternoon. There was a very full Congregation at Church this Aft. Read a Royal Proclamation for a general thanksgiving day to be observed on
Thursday next upon the late great and wonderful

recovery of our most gracious and truly beloved Sovereign King George the third. If he had not recovered God only knows, what troubles England might have been involved in just at this time. Thanks be to God! Between 7 and 8 this Evening Mr. Walker and Betsy Davy came to my House they were on horseback. They stayed and drank Tea and at 8. sat of for Foulsham, as I was determined not to offer them beds. They came from Lynn this morning, in Post Chaises from Lynn to Dereham, and afterwards on horseback.

APRIL 20, MONDAY. . . . Soon after breakfast Mrs. Davy of Foulsham with a Servant Boy with her on single Horses came to our House and she stayed and dined and spent the Afternoon with us, but went away before Tea back to Foulsham. We had for dinner a Fillet of Veal rosted and a nice boiled Ham, Tartletts &c. Mrs. Davy was not well pleased with me nor I with her. She is without exception the most bold Woman I know.

APRIL 22, WEDNESDAY. . . . Very busy in sowing Barley are People now employed—it promises to be a very fine Barley Sill.[1]

APRIL 23, THURSDAY. . . . This being a Day of public thanksgiving to Almighty God for his late great mercies to our good and gracious King George the third, in restoring him to Health after so dangerous an illness, I walked to Church at 11 o'clock and there read Prayers proper for the Occasion with the other morning Prayers, a good many People at Church but neither Mr. or Mrs. Custance or any of

Barley Sill means Barley sowing.

the family. Mr. Custance went for London yesterday I heard. He is to stay a Week in Town it is reported. Mr. Custance being one of the Gentlemen of the privy Chamber to his Majesty, I apprehend is the Occasion of his going, as this Day the King goes publickly to St. Pauls to return thanks, both Houses of Parliament attend him etc. It is to be a grand Procession thither. It is to be a great day of rejoicing every where almost. We heard firing of Guns from many Quarters ab^t Noon. There was nothing at all done at Weston in that way.

APRIL 25, SATURDAY. . . . Mrs. Bodham sent my niece a Letter this morning to desire our Company next Week at Mattishall which we sent word that we would wait on them. To Neighbour Richmond for four Goslings six weeks old, at 15^d apiece, paid her 0. 5. 0. Sent Ben early this morning to Norwich with my old Cow, Polly, and her Calf with her, to sell for me on the Hill, but he returned with them both about 5 o'clock this evening, having very little or nothing bid for them.

APRIL 29, WEDNESDAY. I breakfasted, and spent most of the Morn' at home. About 1 o'clock took a ride to Mattishall and Briton with me to Mr. Bodham's, got there about 2 where I dined, supped and slept. Only Mr. and Mrs. Bodham and my Niece there. Briton slept there. As I was putting on my Boots in the Kitchen this morning to go to Mr. Bodhams, Mr. Walker and Betsy Davy called at the Kitchen Door on horseback, to whom I went out to speak to with only one boot on. I asked them to unlight and have some refreshment but they neither would. They both looked very cool on me, particularly Betsy Davy who scarce deigned to cast a look on me when I spoke to her, they

behaved with great reserve. We had for dinner today
at Mr. Bodhams some boiled Beef, a Fillet of Veal
rosted and a Tongue, a boiled Pudding and some
Tarts. Mr. and Mrs. Hewitt drank Tea and spent
part of the Evening with us. At Cards after Tea lost
0. 2. 6. We did not get to bed till near 12 o'clock
tonight.

MAY 3, SUNDAY. . . . I read Prayers and Preached
and christned a Child by name Joseph this afternoon
at Weston Church. None from Weston House to day
at Church. Mr. Custance not returned home as yet.
Rec^d a letter this Evening from my Niece at Mattishall
to let me know that she goes to Morrow to Mr.
Thorne's to spend a few days with Mrs. Thorne &c.
Betsy Davy and Mr. Walker are I believe there. I
was very much displeased at it and shall send for her
home to Morrow early. I am almost continually
vexed and tormented by her connection with the
Davy's &c. They have almost alienated my regard
for my Niece.

MAY 4, MONDAY. . . . I got up at 6 o'clock this
morning and sent of Briton after Nancy as soon as I
could. . . . Nancy returned with Briton which was
very good of her about 2 o'clock and she dined and
slept at home.

MAY 9, SATURDAY. . . . Mr. Cary brought my
Newspapers today. No Letters. Mr. Custance re-
turned home from London this Evening. I sent to
Weston House this Evening to enquire. I read the
Letter which Nancy rec^d from her Brother William
last Wednesday and which she gave me. I think
William talks at present in too high Strains rather
disrespectful both of the Living and the dead. No

Compliments from either him or his Wife to us. A very long Letter but full of egotisms. He also desires his Sister to write to her B[rother]. Sam on the disagreeable News of his Fathers Death &c.

MAY 11, MONDAY. ... We had Maccarel to day for Dinner being the first we have seen any where this Season, 5^d apiece, but the Spring is so very backward that there are no green-gooseberries to eat with them nor will there be any for some time. To Cantrells Son Rich^d for bringing me 4 Dozen of London Porter, one Bottle broke in Carriage, gave o. 6.

MAY 20, WEDNESDAY. ... Mr. Walker with Betsy Davy behind him, called here about 2 o'clock and after staying with us about half an Hour Mr. Walker mounted his horse and went of for Foulsham leaving Betsy Davy behind to spend the Day and the Night with us, and she therefore dined, supped and slept here. She looks very poorly and is very bad again in her old Complaint the palpitation of the heart and Cramp in her head. Too much raking about has been I think the cause of her being so ill again, much beyond her Strength.

MAY 21, THURSDAY. ... Betsy Davy breakfasted, dined, and spent part of the Afternoon with us. About Noon Mr. Walker came here and he dined and spent part of the Afternoon with us till 4 o'clock, and then Mr. Walker and Betsy Davy behind him went of for Foulsham. We had for Dinner some Skaite, and a nice Neck of Pork rosted and Apple Sauce, and Tarts and Tartlets. My Maid Nanny Kaye lost her poor old Father this week and is to be buried to Morrow, therefore she desires to go to the Funeral to Morrow at Foulsham. And as it is supposed that she and her

Sisters must be at the expense of burying their Father, I gave her towards defraying the same the sum of 1. 1. 0 with leave to go to Foulsham to Morrow. . . .

MAY 22, FRIDAY. . . . Nanny got up early and walked for Foulsham to attend the Funeral of her poor Father this day. I gave her leave to stay till to Morrow.[1]

MAY 27, WEDNESDAY. . . . Mr. and Mrs. Jeanes, and Mr. Du Quesne dined and spent the Afternoon with us, and stayed till 8 o'clock. After Coffee and Tea we got to Whist won 0. 2. 0. We had for Dinner 3 nice spring Chicken boiled and a Tongue, a Knuckle of Veal, a fine Piece of rost Beef and a plumb Pudding. A green Goose rosted and Asparagus and green Apricot Tarts. Mr. and Mrs. Jeanes sent us a verbal Message on Sunday last that they would dine with us this day.

MAY 28, THURSDAY. I breakfasted, dined, &c. again at home. Nancy breakfasted, dined, &c. again at home. I had a very odd Dream last Night, I dreamt that I should die the Friday before the fifth of Nov[br] next; not my Will o Lord but thine be done, if it be thy good pleasure thus to fulfil the same. And may thou O Good God forgive me all my Sins.[2]

JUNE 1st MONDAY. . . . To a decayed old Schoolmaster gave 0. 1. 0. . . .

JUNE 3, WEDNESDAY. . . . Soon after 8 this morning I got into my little Cart and Briton, with me, and

[1] Foulsham was nine or ten miles from Weston, so Nanny's walk was long as well as sad.
[2] In the margin, or rather on the blotting-paper which separates each page of the manuscript volume, opposite to this date is drawn a neat hand pointing ominously to this entry.

away I drove of for Norwich and got thither in about
2 Hours. I got out just as we got to the Gates and
walked into the City, leaving the Care of the Cart to
Briton. I chiefly went to Norwich to Day to get Fish
for Company to Morrow at Weston Parsonage, and
to bespeak Places in the Expedition Coach for London
on Tuesday Evening next, for myself, Nancy, and our
Servant Man Briton. Whilst at Norwich I called at
Buckles and he being a Trustee for settling Mr. Frosts
Accounts, he having lately failed by paying more
attention to his Bottle than business that of Master
Builder. I paid Buckle for him 1. 2. 0 which was a
Bill for Deals last Year had of him. To Allum, Sadler,
also he being in the same Predicament paid him a
small Bill of 0. 5. 6. To half a Dozen Maccarel pd
0. 1. 6. To half a Dozen sweet Oranges pd 0. 1. 0.
To a new Rasor of Critchfield warranted good and
grinding another Rasor and setting another pd
0. 3. 9. To a Glass of Rum and Water &c at Norwich
pd 0. 0. 4. To 4 small Crabbs pd 0. 0. 6. At half past
1 o'clock we sat of from Norwich for Weston and got
home safe and well thank God by half past 3. John
Priest of Norwich was married Yesterday Morn' to
a Miss Raven of Turnstead, a Farmer's Daughter.
Mr. and Mrs. Thorne sent a Note whilst I was from
home to day, that they could not dine with us to
Morrow, as they could not leave their Daughter
Hannah she being much worse in her fits than usual.
Mr. Thorne might however come I think.

Parson Woodforde and Nancy set off for Somerset
on June 9th and stayed with Sister Pounsett till
Sept. 8th. Mr. Du Quesne visited them while they
were there.

JUNE 29, MONDAY. . . . Was out a fishing almost

the whole Morning but had very little Sport, only 1 small Trout. Old Mr. Dalton and son John called on me this Morning stayed half an Hour with us. I did not know old Mr. Dalton at first as he now wears his Hair.[1] He lives at Pitcomb where old Mrs. Hunt lived. Mr. Sam Pounsett smoked a Pipe with us this Afternoon.

JULY 11, SATURDAY. I breakfasted, supped and slept again at Cole. Nancy breakfasted, supped and slept again at Cole. Mr. Du Quesne breakfasted, supped and slept again at Cole. Sister Pounsett and Daughter, my Niece Nancy and self with Mr. Du Quesne dined and spent the Afternoon at Ansford, at Mr. Frank Woodfordes with him and his Wife, at Ansford Parsonage the Place and House in which I was born and lived many Years but had not been in it before this day, for almost fifteen years, owing to a disagreement between us, which now I hope will be ever done away. The House and Garden greatly altered for the best. We had a very good Dinner, a fine Piece of fresh Salmon, a Leg of Mutton rosted, fricasseed Rabit, a Couple of Ducks rosted and Peas, a currant Pye and Syllabubs &c. A good Desert of Fruit after Dinner, Strawberries, Cherries and Currants. Mr. Frank behaved very hearty and generous to us as did his Wife, who seemed to be very attentive. Between Dinner and Tea I took a Walk by myself to my Uncle Toms and saw him and his Wife

[1] Wigs had been going out of fashion for some time now: as early as 1765 the periwig makers had petitioned the king, complaining 'that men will wear their own hair' (see Horace Walpole's letter of February 12th, 1765, to Lord Hertford: *Letters*, vol. vi, p. 188). It is significant from this entry of the Diary, that even the old were giving them up. Soon only the clergy would be faithful to a fashion which had been universal in Europe since the second half of the seventeenth century.

who were both glad to see me, both very old. We returned to Cole before 9 o'clock this Even' as we went, that is, Mr. Du Quesne, Sister Pounsett and Daughter and Nancy in Ansford Inn Chaise. I walked thither and back again with Briton. Some small Rain fell during my return back. Sister Clarke drank Tea with us at Ansford Parsonage this Afternoon.

JULY 24, FRIDAY. I breakfasted, dined &c. again at Cole. To a Fisherman for a fine Crab, 4 P^d, pd o. 1. o. Very great Rebellion in France by the Papers[1] —The Bath Paper (the only Paper taken in here) comes every Friday Morning. Mr. Robert Clarke of Castle-Cary spent the Aft. with us. He was drove in by the Rain, as he was going to Bruton, and stayed till the Evening, he did not go to Bruton.

AUG. 3, MONDAY. . . . My Brother and his Wife spent the Afternoon with us, they came over on purpose to let us know that Mrs. Melliar had sent them word that the King, Queen and some more of the Royal Family were to dine at Sherborn to Morrow at Lord Digbys,[2] and that they go to Morrow. They drank Tea with us and went away ab^t 8 o'clock.

AUG. 4, TUESDAY. Dies Memorabilis. I breakfasted, supped and slept again at Cole. I rose this morning at 6 o'clock, shaved and dressed, and at 7 I went in a Bruton Chaise and my Niece Jenny Pounsett with me, to my Brothers at C. Cary and there we made

[1] Parson Woodforde has just heard of the fall of the Bastille on July 14th.

[2] Henry Digby, seventh Baron (1731–93). Shortly after this royal visit to his ancestral seat at Sherborne he was created an Earl (1790). He was a friend of Horace Walpole's whose letters contain several references to him.

a second breakfast, after that my Brother and Wife, Mrs. Richd Clarke and Nancy, a Dr. Brodum who is a German Doctor, Mr. James Clarke and Wife and the latters Brother Mr. Willm Dawe, all sat of about 9 o'clock for Sherborne to see the Royal Family, and we went in the following manner, the German Dr. with Mrs. J^s Clarke, old Mrs. Ashford and Mr. Gardner all in Dr. Brodums Chariot, my Brother and his Wife in Mrs. R. Clarkes Chair, Mrs. R. Clarke, Nancy and Jenny Pounsett in the Bruton Chaise, Mr. James Clarke and myself in his Phaeton, and Mr. Willm Dawe on my Brother John's Horse. We got to Sherborne about 11 o'clock, had some White Wine Negus at the Antelope, and then we all went down to Lord Digby's Park, and there walked about till about 12 o'clock, at which time, the King, Queen, Princess Royal, Princess Elizabeth, and Princess Augusta arrived in the Park in three Royal Coaches with 4 Horses to each. We were very near them as they passed by. After they had taken some refreshment, they all walked upon the Terrace before the Crowd. We were all very near indeed to them, the King looked very red and is very tall and erect, The Queen and Princesses rather short but very pleasing Countenances and fair. After the Royal Family had walked round the Garden, they returned into Lord Digby's for a time. The King walked first with Lord Digby who held his hat in his hand, The Kings Hat was on, then the Queen with her Lady in waiting, then the Princess Royal and her Attendant Lady, then Princess Elizabeth and her Attendant Lady, then Princess Augusta and her attendant Lady. The King was in his Windsor Uniform, blue coat with red Cape and Cuffs to the Sleeves, with a plain round Hat with a black Ribband round it, The Queen was in a purple

Silk, and white Bonnett, The Princesses all in Pink
Silk and white Bonnetts. After they had been within
Doors about an Hour They all came into the Park,
the King on horseback, The Queen and Princesses
and their Ladies, in two open Carriages, and they all
passed thro' the Multitude, I was close to them as they
passed. They took a ride quite round the Park, and
were I suppose in performing it near 3 Hours. The
King returned to the House by Water—The Queen
and Princesses returned in their Carriages. They then
went to Dinner at Lord Digbys. It was 5 o'clock this
Afternoon before they got into Lord Digbys. Our
Company then made the best of our way to our Inn
to dine also. Nancy and the other Ladies bore the
fatigue pretty well, we were obliged often to sit on the
grass in the Park, being there almost 6 Hours. It was
a most delightful Day, thank God for it. John Goldsborough and Wife, Sam. Gatehouse and his Wife and
2 little Children, Miss Mogg Daughter of Mrs. Goldsborough by a former Husband, my Brother and Wife,
Mrs. Richd Clarke, Nancy, Jenny Pounsett, and
myself, dined all together at the Antelope, on cold
Ham and Veal, cold boiled Beef, Tarts &c. Some of
the Ladies too tired to eat much—In short we were
all tired pretty well—I eat very hearty. There were
in the Park I suppose near 5000. The two Clubbs of
Sherborne met the Royal Family at the entrance of
the Park with Musick preceding them and Colours
flying. Colours flying on the Church and Bells ringing. Lady Waldegrave and Lady Courtown, Lord
Courtown, with Colonel Gwyn, Colonel Goldsworthy
and Colonel Digby arrived with the Royal Visitors
from Weymouth to Sherborne Castle. About an
Hour after we had dined we called for the reckoning
and sat of for Castle-Cary &c. The Gentlemen paid

the Bill, each of us o. 10. o. Mr. James Clarke and his Party dined at Mrs. Dawes who lives at Sherborne and is Mother to James Clarkes Wife—Dr. Brodum boards at her House. The above Company remained at Sherborne all Night, intending to go to Weymouth to Morrow. The Royal Visitors were to return to Weymouth to sleep to night—Pray God bless them all. I returned with my Brother in his Chair. We did not reach Cary till near 11 at night, I then got into the Bruton Chaise with my Niece Jane Pounsett and we got to Cole about 12, and there I supped, smoked a Pipe and went to bed, very sleepy and much fatigued. We all I thank God returned safe and well after spending a long Day of much pleasure. Lord Digby's Park with the Water most Delightfull. I gave the Driver of the Chaise o. 1. o.

SEP. 7, MONDAY. . . . Sister Pounsett very low on the thoughts of our leaving Cole to Morrow. Pray God comfort her. Gave Willm Arnold this Evening o. 1. o.

SEP. 12, SATURDAY. I breakfasted, dined, supped and slept at the Angel at the back of St Clements, as did Nancy. We walked about the City most of the Morn'. I called on Miss Pope by myself this Morn' at one Mr. Whites, Hatter, in Newgate Street. We went to the Lyceum and saw some very curious Wax Work, paid for seeing it o. 2. o. It was just by the Exeter Change in the Strand. We also saw just by some very curious wild Beasts for which I paid o. 1. o. Walked into Lombard Street and changed two of Gurneys Bank Notes of 10 P^d each for Cash.[1] Then

---

[1] The particular Gurney—of that Norfolk Quaker family—who was at this date a great Norwich Banker was John Gurney (d. 1809), the

went to the Black Bull in Bishopsgate Street and took
2 Places in the Norwich Expedition and one outside
for Monday Afternoon. Paid in part to the Book-
keeper 1. 1. 0. To one Dozen of large Silver Table
Spoons new and half a Dozen Silver Desert Spoons at
a Shop in the Strand near Temple Bar p^d 10. 0. 0,
which I look upon as a great Bargain. To a Pound of
Sealing Wax also at another Shop near the above,
10 very large Sticks p^d 4. 6. To Fruit &c paid to day
about 0. 1. 6. To 2 Volumes of Taylors Sermons just
published in boards only paid 0. 10. 0. I was heartily
tired before I got to bed by walking. To a Sermon on
the Recovery of the King by Lancaster p^d p. 1. 0.

On Tuesday, Sept. 15th, the Diarist and his niece
reached Weston in safety—'found all our People
well and all things in very good Order and Harvest
all in'.

SEP. 17, THURSDAY. . . . Mr. and Mrs. Custance,
Mrs. Townshend and Mrs. Cornwallis, and Mr.
Jeanes made us a Morn' Visit. Mr. Jeanes was gone
before Mrs. Townshend came—We had a Levy Day
at Weston Parsonage. To one Largess to day gave
0. 1. 0.

SEP. 19, SATURDAY. . . . Mrs. Jeanes made us a
very short Morning Visit. To Largesses to day gave
0. 2. 0. Sent Briton on horseback this Morning to
Norwich after Newspapers &c. he returned home to
Dinner. Gave Nancy this Morning for well mending
a Pair of Velveret Breeches for me 0. 1. 0. Gave my

father of a numerous family, among them the famous Elizabeth (1780–
1845), who married Joseph Fry, Daniel Gurney (1791–1880), Banker
and Antiquary, and Joseph John Gurney (1788–1847), Philanthropist
and Author. John Gurney, the Banker, had leased Earlham from the
Bacons in 1786.

two Maids a Cotton Gown apiece that I bought for them in London cost me 1. 8. 0. Gave my Servant Man Ben a Waistcoat Piece 0. 6. 0. Gave my Servant Lad, John in Cash 0. 2. 6.

Sep. 25, Friday. . . . Very fine Weather indeed, and scarce ever known a more plentiful Harvest in Norfolk and elsewhere. Give us all O Lord grateful Hearts for the same. Brewed a Barrel of Table Beer to day.

Oct. 5. . . . Gave Briton Leave to go and see his Friends at Reepham to day being Reepham Petty Sessions. About 1 o'clock Mr. Walker, with Mrs. Davy and her Daughter came to my House in a one Horse Chaise and they dined and spent the Aft. here, drank Tea at 5. and returned home soon after to Foulsham. A Servant Man came with them. We had for Dinner a Loin of Veal rosted, some hashed Hare and a Damson Pye. Mr. Walker looked very unwell as did Betsy. Briton returned home about 8 this Evening.

Oct. 16, Friday. I breakfasted, dined, &c again at home. To a poor old man of Hockering by name Thomas Ram, having lost a Cow gave 0. 2. 6. Brewed another Barrell of Table Beer to day. Sad News from France all anarchy and Confusion. The King, Queen and Royal Family confined at Paris. The Soldiers joined the People, many murdered.

Oct. 24, Saturday. . . . Sent Briton early this Morning to Norwich with my little Cart after many things. Rec^d for 2 small Piggs of Tom Carr's Wife 12. 0. Briton returned from Norwich about 4 o'clock brought me a long and pleasing Letter from my Sister Pounsett, whom I thank God to find by her writing that she is better in health. She also informed us that my Brother John and Wife and Mrs. Richd Clarke, intend setting out for Norfolk in about a fortnights time to spend the Winter with us. We shall be very happy to see them. Pray God! they may have a safe and pleasant journey.

OCT. 31, SATURDAY. . . . Very high Wind with much Rain in the Night but about 5 o'clock this Morn' it was highest, it shook the House, but thank God we received no damage. It was a very strong N. N. Easterly Wind. It blew down a great many apples and split a large weeping Willow in the Rasberry Garden.

NOV. 7, SATURDAY. . . . Very melancholy News on the Papers respecting the Ships wrecked and lives lost at Yarmouth and near it by the very high Wind early in the Morn' Saturday the 31. of October. May those poor Souls lost be O Lord better of. And send thy divine Comfort to all their Relatives. Mr. Custance sent us a brace of Partridges. Billy Bidewell brought our Newspapers from Norwich to day. We had no Letters whatever. We were in great expectation of hearing from Somersett, as we now daily expect my Brother and Wife, and Mrs. Richd Clarke, to be with us.

NOV. 11, WEDNESDAY. . . . To James Pegg this morning paid 11. 2. 3 that is, half a Years Land Tax 6. 0. 0, Half a Years House and Window Tax 2. 15. 0. Male-Servant Tax, for half a Year 1. 5. 0. Female ditto, for ditto 0. 10. 0. Horse Tax, for ditto 0. 10. 0. Additional Horse Tax, for 1 Quarter, 0. 1. 3. Cart Tax, for Half a Year 0. 1. 0. Bottled of Mr. Palmers Rum this morning, it is strong, but nothing near so fine flavoured, as what we had last from Mr. Priest of Norwich. Sent Briton early this morning to Norwich with my little Cart, for many things from thence but more particularly for Letters as we are in daily expectation of seeing my Brother &c. Killed another fat Pigg this Morning, and the weight was 9 Stone and half. Briton returned home from Norwich about 4 o'clock this Afternoon, brought me a Letter from my Brother John, informing us of the Death of Mrs. James Clarke on Friday Sennight last, 'pray God she may have a happy change'. I sincerely pity the 2 infant Children that she has left, and likewise her disconsolate Husband poor Doctor Clarke I heartily pity him. My Brother also informed us that himself, Wife and Mrs. Richd Clarke intend being at Norwich Friday.

Nov. 12, Thursday. . . . Sent Ben early this Morning to Norwich to order a Chaise to be sent to my House by 11 o'clock this morning to carry us to Norwich to meet our Somersett Friends there to Morrow. The Chaise came at the time appointed and between one and two this Aft. we went in it to Norwich thank God safe and well by 4. this Afternoon to the Kings Head, and there Nancy and self dined, supped and slept. My Servant Man Briton went with us.

Nov. 13, Friday. I breakfasted, dined, supped and slept at Norwich. Nancy breakfasted dined &c at Norwich. About 11 o'clock this Morn' our Somersett Friends my Brother and Wife and Mrs. Richd Clarke arrived at Norwich from London in the Expedition Coach after travelling all night. We were very happy to see them arrived safe thanks be to God for the same, considering their great fatigue they all looked very well, they breakfasted, dined, supped and slept at the Kings Head. Bought this day of Willm Hart, Cabinet Maker on Hog Hill Norwich 2 large second hand double-flapped Mohogany Tables, also one second hand Mohogany dressing Table with Drawers, also one new Mohogany Washing-Stand, for all which paid 4. 14. 6. that is, for the 2 Tables 2. 12. 6. Dressing Table 1. 11. 6. Mohogany Wash-stand 0. 10. 6. I think the whole of it to be very cheap. To my Barber, Browne for a wig p^d 1. 1. 0. To a Quart Bottle of nice Mushrooms of Mrs. Nutter paid 0. 6. 0. To a Quart Bottle of Mushroom Catchup 0. 3. 6. To a Baskett for packing up the same 0. 0. 6. To 4 handsome Glass Salt-Cellars cut Glass at Cooks Glass Shop paid 0. 16. 0. To 12 Patty Panns &c at Studwells p^d 0. 2. 6. To 12 Yards of Diaper for Towells p^d 0. 15. 0. To 6 Yards of Huckaback for D^o p^d 0. 6. 0.

Nov. 14, Saturday. We all breakfasted and spent the Morn' at Norwich. At about 2 o'clock my Brothers Wife, Mrs. Richd Clarke and Nancy got into one of the Kings Head Chaises, and my Brother and self into another, and sat of for Weston to which Place we got safe and well 'thank God' to the Parsonage House about 4 o'clock where we dined, supped and slept. The Drivers Baited themselves and Horses for an Hour and then returned back to Norwich. To the Drivers being very wet gave 0. 4. 0. To Fish this Morning at Norwich p^d 0. 1. 0. To half a Collar of Brawn this Morning of one Present in the Market-Place 21. P^d at 1^s/4^d per Pound paid 1. 8. 0. To some second-hand Harness for my little Cart of one Chesnut in St. Giles's p^d 1. 15. 6. Called on both Mr. Priests, bespoke a Quarter of a Pipe of Port Wine and 4 Gallons of Rum of Mr. Priest Senr this Morning. Paid and gave at the Kings Head this Morning for 3 Chaises to Weston included 5. 10. 6. Saw Mr. Walker this morning at Norwich he looked very poorly, he is going to Mr. Broadbanks. My Brother and Wife slept in the Parlour Chamber, Mrs. R. Clarke and Nancy in the Attic Chamber over the Study, being lately much altered. I think my Brother is grown very fat of late.

Nov. 19, Thursday. . . . About 10 o'clock this morning my Brother and Self took a Walk to Mr. Townshends Plantations where we met Mr. and Mrs. Townshend and Mr. Du Quesne and we took the diversion of coursing all the Morn' and till near 4. in the Afternoon. Very fine Sport indeed we had, both my Greyhounds were there and they beat the whole field, I suppose there were 12 Greyhounds out and as many People on horseback to beat for us. My Greyhound Bitch, by name Patch, met with a sad accident towards the end of our Coursing in running after a Rabbit, by breaking a large Ligament in the off hind Leg in jumping over some paling, we all thought at first that she had broken her thigh. We sent her home immediately, and Dr. Thorne who by chance happened to be there, said, on examination, that she might do well, and that we should bathe it with Vinegar and Brandy. Mr. Townshend was very much concerned at it. We got home about 4 o'clock, rather tired. My Brother complained of a Pain in his Stomach was afraid that it was a gouty Pain. He was rather better before he went to bed. Mr. Townshend gave us a hare.

Nov. 20, Friday. . . . Rec^d to day for 2 small Piggs 0. 16. 0. Mr. and Mrs. Jeanes made us a morning Visit. I asked them to dine with us but they would

not, I asked them also to dine with us on Tuesday
next to meet Mr. Du Quesne, but Mrs. Jeanes said it
was inconvenient, tho' she had the assurance to invite
us the Wednesday following without once offering to
send their Carriage for the Ladies. We declined
accepting the Invitation immediately.

Nov. 27, Friday. . . . Mr. Custance very kindly
called on me this Morn to enquire how I did, he did
not stay long as he was going on to Mr. Townshends
on a Visit. I thank God had a better night of rest than
I have had the 3 last Nights. Had no Cramp at all.
My Brother recommending me last Night to carry a
small Piece of the roll Brimstone sewed up in a piece
of very thin Linnen, to bed with me and if I felt any
Symptom of the Cramp to hold it in my hand or put
it near the affected part, which I did, as I apprehended at one time it was coming into one of my legs,
and I felt no more advances of it. This I thought
deserving of notice, even in so trifling a book as this is.
My Brother and Wife, Mrs. Richd Clarke and Nancy
went to Mr. Du Quesnes to dinner. Mr. Du Quesne
sent his Chaise for the Ladies and my Brother went in
my little pleasure Cart with Briton. I privately named
a Child of John Reeves's this Afternoon at my House
by name William. I was not well enough to go with
my Company to day and therefore begged to be
excused. They returned home to Weston Parsonage
about 9 o'clock, very well pleased with their Jaunt.
I had only a little mince-Veal for Dinner and eat but
very little of that. Mr. and Mrs. Jeanes were at Mr.
Du Quesnes and dressed in high Style indeed as they
told me. Mr. Priest of Reepham was also with them.

Decem. 1, Tuesday. I breakfasted, dined, &c.
again at home. My Brother and Wife, Mrs. Rich^d

Clarke and Nancy breakfasted, dined, &c. here again.
Mrs. Custance called at our Gate this morning but
did not come in—It being my Tithe Audit. Mr. Du
Quesne also called on us this morning and stayed
about ½ an Hour with us. He is going to dine at
Mr. Jeanes's and from thence to Mr. Priests. The
following Farmers paid me for Tithe this Morning,
and dined and stayed till after 12 at Night at my
House. Stephen Andrews, J^s Pegg, John Rose, John
Norton, Henry Case, Charles Hardy, Robt Rising,
Jonas Silvey, John Buck, Thos Reynolds, John Girling,
John Peachman, Willm Howlett, Charles Cary, Robt
Emeris, Willm Bidewell, John Greaves, John Baker,
J^s Pratt and John Heavers. We had for Dinner, some
Salt Fish, a Couple of boiled Rabbitts and Onions,
a boiled Leg of Mutton, boiled Beef and rost Beef and
plumb Puddings. My Brother dined with us in the
Parlour and the Ladies by themselves in the Study.
There was drank, about half a Dozen Bottles of Port
Wine, 8 Bottles of Rum, besides as much strong Beer,
as they wished to have. I was far from well the whole
Day, having a very bad Cold and a very troublesome
Cough. Rec^d to day for Tithe about 245. 11. 0. Paid
John Buck a poors Rate at 10^d in the Pound from
Michlms 1788 to Lady Day 1789. I am rated at
£30. 5s. 0d, therefore I paid him 1. 5. 2½. We were
all very merry, and very harmonious. My Brother
sung 2 or 3 Songs.

DEC. 28, MONDAY. . . . Rec^d of Edwd Gooch this
morning for Tithe 0. 6. 0. To one Willm Mason of
Sparham who goes about at Christmas playing on
10 Bells gave him 0. 1. 6. To my Malsters Man James
Barrett Xmas Gift 0. 1. 0. I walked to Church about
2 o'clock this afternoon and buried poor John Gooch

who has left a Wife and several Children but most of them out. He was lately a near Neighbour of ours for some Y^{rs}. I thought that he had been older only 48 Y^{rs}. At Quadrille this Evening lost 0. 0. 6.

1790

JAN^{ry} 1st, 1790. Anno Domini 1790. I breakfasted, dined, &c. again at home. My Brother and Wife, Mrs. Clarke and Nancy breakfasted, dined &c. here again. To my blacksmiths Man, J$^{n}_{o}$ Spaule Senr gave 0. 1. 0. Rec^{d} for 4 small Piggs of Clarke of Easton 1. 10. 6. Mr. Jeanes called on us this morning and informed us that his Wife was brought to bed Yesterday of another Daughter and that they are both as well as can be expected in so short a time. Mrs. Jeanes's Mother is now with them at Witchingham. Mr. and Mrs. Custance with Mr. Du Quesne dined and spent the Afternoon with us, stayed till 8 with us and would have stayed longer but their eldest Daughter was very bad in the Scarlet Fever. We had for Dinner to day some Skaite and Oyster Sauce, Peas Soup, Ham and Chicken, a boiled Leg of Mutton and Capers, a rost Turkey, fryed Rabbit, Brawn, Tarts, Mince Pies &c. Put into Mr. Custances Coach as they returned home a Q^{r} of the mild Cheese that Mr. Pounsett sent us. Mr. Custance liked it very much at dinner. We had 2 Tables at Cards this Evening, Whist and Quadrille. I played at the Whist Table and lost 0. 2. 0. Mr. Du Quesne stayed about an Hour after Mr. and Mrs. Custance, and then we got to Loo. It was after 1 o'clock before I got to bed, my Brother being rather merry and very talkative.

JAN^{ry} 2, SATURDAY. ... It was very near 11 before we finished breakfast. My Brother drove Mrs. Clarke out in my little Cart this morning on Sparham Heath. Nancy was very pert and saucy at Dinner to day. About Tea time this Evening Nunn Davy from Yoxford in Suffolk called here in his road to his Mothers at Foulsham, and he drank Tea, supped and slept here, he came on a little Hobby. At Cards, Commerce, this Evening lost o. 1. o. Nancy won both Pools, 6^d each Person put in at a Pool. Miss Custance still very bad in the Scarlet Fever.

JAN. 6, WEDNESDAY. ... Paid my Servants their Years Wages this Morn'. To my Maid, Betty Dade, 5. 5. o. To my Man, Ben Leggatt 10. o. o. To my Man, Bretingham Scurl, 8. o. o. To my Boy, John Dalliday 2. 2. o. At Quadrille this Evening lost o. 1. o.

JAN^{ry} 8, FRIDAY. ... Nunn Davy called here this morning soon after breakfast in his road to Pulham but did not stay. Nancy with Mrs. Clark went over to Mr. Du Quesne's this morning in my little Cart and returned to Dinner. Mr. Walker came here about 1 o'clock in a Fakenham Chaise and he stayed and dined, supped and spent the Evening with us. About 10 o'clock this Evening he went in the same Chaise to Lenewade Bridge Inn to sleep. Mr. Walker looked very bad indeed and made us low. At Cards this Evening, Commerce, won o. 2. 6. It was after 12 o'clock before I got to bed to night.

JAN^{ry} 11, MONDAY. ... Nancy behaved very pert to me after Dinner.

JAN^{ry} 13, WEDNESDAY. ... Was taken very ill [this] morning in bed about 4 o'clock with a violent pain in my Stomach, which I apprehend proceeded from gouty Wind there and likewise from Bile. I continued ill all the whole Day, could not eat any Dinner &c. In the Afternoon was taken with a vomiting, and afterwards was some matter easier. I took a small Dose of Rhubarb and Ginger going to bed to night, as did my Brother also. Pray God! I might be better to Morrow, as it adds to my Uneasiness to make my Somersett Friends not enjoy themselves as well as I could wish. My poor old Clerk, J^s Smith is very ill, he dined with our Folks in Kitchen to day but looks very bad. It was very wet this Evening but quite warm.

Jan^ry 14, Thursday. ... Was I thank God! some small matter better this morning, tho' but an indifferent night of rest. Mem. The Season so remarkably mild and warm that my Brother gathered this morning in my Garden some full blown Primroses. Took two small Doses of Camphor and Nitre. Mrs. Custance made us a Morning Visit. At Quadrille this Evening lost o. o. 6. To a poor Man of Saham Tony, having suffered by fire, by name Winer gave o. 2. 6.

Jan^ry 27, Wednesday. ... Much Rain during last Night, very dirty indeed. To one Thomas Carpenter, a broken kind of a Farmer and first Cousin to Mr. Peachman and who lives in Mr. Howlets House (late Forsters) gave him towards purchasing a Cow which Mr. Howlet as he told me, would give him liberty to keep, and who has also a Wife and three Children, o. 5. o. As soon as I gave him the above he asked to drink. At Quadrille this Evening neither won or lost.

Jan^ry 28, Thursday. I breakfasted, supped and slept again at home. My Brother and Wife, Mrs. Clarke and Nancy breakfasted, supped and slept again here. About 2 o'clock Mr. and Mrs. Custance called here in their Coach and took up Mrs. Woodforde and Mrs. Clarke and went to Mr. Du Quesnes where they dined and spent the Afternoon. Mr. D. Quesne sent his Carriage after my Brother, self and Nancy and we also dined and spent the Afternoon at Mr. Du Quesnes with him and the above Company. We returned as we went about 9 o'clock this Even'. Mr. Custance shewed me a Letter when at Du Quesnes from Mr. Walkers Uncle of Woodstock to a Mr. Barker, Wine Merchant, at Norwich informing him that Mr. Walker was a profligate abandoned young Man, and to guard Barker from trusting him with any more Money or any one else, that he should allow him 30 P^d per Annum to keep him from starving provided he made a better Use of it than he has hitherto done, and if he did not, he should even withdraw that. Mr. Custance also told me that he had made use of his Name, Sr Thos Beauchamps and mine to get money raised for him at Norwich particularly the above Mr. Barker of whom he has had 300 P^d, besides many others. Among the others Hylett, Hostler at the Kings Head to whom he owes 50 P^d. Also Mr. Custance told me that Walker should say that he was coming over to my House for a few Days, was to be married to Betsy Davy very soon, that I was her Guardian and he was to have her fortune of me directly on the Marriage &c. I was astonished to hear such things, but not so much as I should otherwise, had I not been an eye-witness in some degree of his profligacy and extravagance. I have a long time given him up, his behaviour to me last Winter made me despise him utterly. Nancys encouraging him to come to my House after such behaviour has greatly lessened my esteem for her, as she shewed no regard

for me. After Tea and Coffee we got to Cards won
o. 1. o. The Wind being very high about 12 o'clock
I did not get to bed till after 2 o'clock in the Morn'.

JanʸY 30, SATURDAY. . . . Sent Ben to Norwich this
morning after News &c, he returned by Dinner time.
No Letters. Walker is talked of very much at Norwich, there are two Writs out against him, he is gone
of but is supposed to be at Thetford at an Inn.
Neither won or lost at Quadrille this Evening.

FEB. 4, THURSDAY. . . . My poor Cow very weak
indeed not able to get up. My poor Greyhound Patch
died in the Night in her Kennel, she had fresh strained
herself a Day or two ago, and hurt herself so much
that she could not stand at all and groaned very much.
Mr. Du Quesne made us a long Morning Visit and
brought over his Violin and played a good deal. Mr.
Priest and Son, Robert of Reepham called also on us
whilst Mr. Du Quesne was with us. Mr. Priest and
Son returned with Mr. Du Quesne to spend the Day
and night with him at Tuddenham. Dr. Thorne of
Mattishall called on us whilst we were at dinner, had
about half dined, and he sat down and eat very hearty
of a rosted Pigg, drank Tea with us and left us a little
before 8. Not a word mentioned concerning Walkers
Situation.

FEB. 5, FRIDAY. . . . My poor Cow rather better
this morning, but not able to get up as yet, she having
a Disorder which I never heard of before or any of our
Somersett Friends. It is called Tail-shot, that is, a
separation of some of the Joints of the Tail about a
foot from the tip of the Tail, or rather a slipping of one
Joint from another. It also makes all her Teeth quite
loose in her head. The Cure, is to open that part of

the Tail so slipt lengthways and put in an Onion
boiled and some Salt, and bind it up with some coarse
Tape. I took a Walk to Weston House this Morning
and after chatting with Mrs. Custance, christened a
Child of Mrs. Alldis the Housekeeper by name Betty.
My Brother complained a good deal to day of a pain
in his Stomach, which he is afraid that it proceeds
from something gouty there.

FEB. 23, TUESDAY. . . . Mrs. Custance made us a
Morning Visit. She is very near her time. Pray God!
grant her a happy minute whenever it arrives.

FEB. 24, WEDNESDAY. . . . Had little or no sleep
during the whole of last Night, being very much
troubled with Bile. Was very low-spirited, eat no
Meat the whole day and took a good dose of Rhubarb
going to bed. To a run-about Man for a Groce of
Corks p^d 0. 2. 6. At Quadrille this Evening neither
won or lost.

FEB^ry 27, SATURDAY. . . . Sent Briton early this
morning to Norwich with my little Cart after News
and many other things. He returned about 4 in the
Afternoon. No Letters. I took a Walk with my
Brother this Morning to Morton Hall, round by Attlebridge and so home. We were rather fatigued with
our Walk. At Quadrille this Evening won 0. 0. 6.
Briton heard at Norwich to day that Mr. Walker was
not in the Castle neither could he be found out. He
also said that it was reported that he was near £1500
in debt.

FEB. 28, SUNDAY. . . . I read Prayers and Preached
this Morning at Weston Church, and also churched a
Woman. None from Weston House at Church, Mrs.
Custance being in the Pains of Child-birth, 'Pray God

Almighty befriend her and grant her a happy moment' is the sincere Wish and Prayers of not only myself but of all my Friends now at Weston Parsonage. Sent up this Evening to Weston House again and to our great Joy received the good News that Mrs. Custance was safely brought to bed of a Boy and both as well as possibly could be wished.

MARCH 3, WEDNESDAY. I breakfasted, dined &c again at home. My Brother and Wife, Mrs. Clarke and Nancy breakfasted, dined &c here again. Nancy had a Letter by Mr. Cary from Mrs. Davy of Foulsham relating almost the same bad Actions that Walker had been guilty of &c. I wish now to break of every Connection with Mrs. Davy and all her long train of Acquaintance. I desired Nancy to drop her Acquaintance by all means, which if she does not (after their Characters are so well known) she will disoblige me as much as she possibly can do, and so &c. Mrs. Davy in her Letter desires her to look for a House to board at in her Neighbourhood as she intends leaving Foulsham very soon. N.B. I dont think Nancy has had a Letter from her before for the last twelvemonth. Nancy's Character (being too intimate with Miss Davy) is not talked of so well: as she used to go with Betsy Davy and Walker to Norwich &c by themselves. They all spent the Day and slept at Mrs. Davy's at Foulsham when Mrs. Davy was gone from home. Betsys Character is entirely ruined by her indiscreet ways, many times out by themselves, suffered herself to go for his Wife at public Places &c. Walker even boasts (as people say) of his behaviour to Betsy and says the worst of things of her. He now proves to be one of the most profligate, wicked, artful, ungrateful and deceiving Wretches I

ever heard of, I never liked him. I believe both
Mother Davy and Daughter also to be very cunning,
close and not without much Art. I never wish to meet
them again at my House none of the 3.

MARCH 4, THURSDAY. . . . At one o'clock took a
Walk by myself to Weston House and there privately
baptized Mrs. Custances last little Boy by name
Neville. Only three Days old this Day, a pretty Babe.
This Evening just before Tea, a Clerk of Mr. Morphew Junr of Norwich brought me a letter from his
Master, to acquaint me that my worthy Friend, Mr.
Francis my Attorney was dead, died to day and to
desire me to write to the Society of New-College in
behalf of him concerning Coll. affairs in Norfolk, of
which Mr. Francis had the care. Neither won or lost
at all at Cards to Night.

APRIL 2, FRIDAY. . . . I read Prayers this morning
at Weston Church being Good-Friday. Mr. Custance
at Church. My Brother only walked to Church with
me. It being exceeding cold and windy, the Ladies
did not go to Church from my House. Gave my
Clerk, J^s Smith, a good black striped Coat and Waist-
coat, a p^r of old Velveret Breeches and a powdered
Wig, this Afternoon at my House, and likewise a
Dinner of cold Meat. Had a Note from Mr. Du
Quesne this morning with a present of a score fine
Smelts brought with him from Ely, he returned home
Yesterday. Gave the Boy that brought the Note
0. 0. 6. We had no Meat for Dinner to day, but only
some Smelts, boiled Eggs, Fritters and toasted Cheese.
I did not play at Quadrille this Evening being Good-
Friday; but my Brother and Wife, Mrs. Clarke and
Nancy did till after 8 to night.

APRIL 27, TUESDAY. . . . Rec^d a Note this Morning from Dr. Thorne informing me of the death of his Nephew Walker, and that he should be glad to have him buried at Weston on Thursday next. I returned an answer to it.

APRIL 29, THURSDAY. . . . Between 1. and 2. o'clock this Afternoon walked to Weston Church and buried Mr. Thorne's Nephew Robert George Walker, aged 23 Years. He was brought in a Hearse with 4 Horses, but from whence I know not. Dr. Thorne was present, and a young Man Son of Mr. Thorne of Kimberly, and a short Man (at whose house) Walker was at, were all that attended. My Brother walked with me to Weston Church. I had a black silk Hatband and a pair of Beaver Gloves. And the Dr. also gave me 1. 1. 0. There was not the least Description on the Coffin or any kind of Ornament, quite plain and uncoloured. At Quadrille this Evening won 0. 1. 0.

MAY 6, THURSDAY. . . . To 18. Yards of black Ribband of [Bagshaw] pd. 0. 5. 0. Gave my Brother half my black Ribband. The Ribband is designed to put round our Necks to prevent sore throats.

MAY 10, MONDAY. . . . Between 12. and 1. o'clock we all sat of for Norwich in two of the Kings Head Chaises. Got to Norwich about 2. o'clock, partook of a cold Collation at the Kings Head and at 3 got into one of the Yarmouth Coaches and of for Yarmouth and about 7. in the Evening (thank God) got safe thither to the Angel Inn in the Market Place, kept by a Mr. and Mrs. Dark. At Norwich I paid and gave abt. 0. 5. 0. To the Yarmouth Coachman gave 0. 3. 0. At Accle for Rum and Water pd. 0. 0. 6. My

Brother and Wife and Mrs. R. Clarke, very highly pleased with Yarmouth and the Sea View. We supped and slept at the Angel at Yarmouth. My Servant Briton I took with us.

MAY 12, WEDNESDAY. I breakfasted, dined, supped and slept again at the Angel Inn at Yarmouth, as did likewise My Brother and Wife, Mrs. R. Clarke and Nancy. As soon as we had breakfasted we got into the Yarmouth Coaches again and took a ride on the Beach, called at a public House on the Coast and had some refreshment, and returned home about 2 o'clock to our Inn to dinner. Paid and gave the public House on the Beach 0. 2. 0. In the Evening I called on Lady Bacon who is in Lodgings near the New-Chapel Yarmouth. I stayed with her about half an Hour. To a small Box Compass pd. 0. 1. 0. To a small Book with some Poems of Goldsmith 0. 0. 9. At a Pot-House on the Quay with my Brother amongst some jolly Tars, for Porter 0. 0. 4. For some Cakes at a Confectioners pd. 0. 1. 0. At a Hospital for old Sailors gave 0. 1. 0.

MAY 13, THURSDAY. I breakfasted and dined at the Angel Inn at Yarmouth, as did also my Brother and Wife, Mrs. R. Clarke and Nancy. After breakfast I walked out with the Ladies to see the New-Chapel and to attend divine Service there this Morning being Holy-Thursday, but when we got thither, there was no Duty at the Chapel, however the Clerk shewed us over the Chapel. I gave to the Clerk for shewing it 0. 1. 0. We then walked down to the Quay and called at a Mr. Ramey's to see some very curious drawings of Mrs. Rameys, done by a red hot Poker on Box. They were very curious indeed and highly finished. To the Servant Man that shewed it us gave 0. 1. 0.

We then returned to our Inn and dined on some cold
Meat and Sallad and some Tarts. My Brother did not
go with us, but went out by himself and did not return
till we had almost dined; he had been out with some
Tars and had been drinking with them and was a
little merry. To the Barber this Morning gave 0. 2. 6.
For 3. Yarmouth Coaches for 2. Mornings pd 0. 12. 0.
To the Servant men that attended gave 0. 1. 0. After
Dinner I went into the Bar and paid Mrs. Dark her
Bill. Our fare at the Angel 5. 12. 10. To Servants at
the Angel, gave abt. 0. 12. 0. At 3. o'clock this Afternoon the Norwich Coach came to the Angel Inn after
us, Into which we soon got and sat of for Norwich,
stayed a very little time at Acle just to change Horses
and then of for Norwich, to which place I thank God
we got safe and well by 7. in the Evening, where we
supped and slept at the Kings Head.

MAY 19, WEDNESDAY. . . . Mr. Love the Painter
dined with our Folks to day in Kitchen, he being
painting my Weather-cock.

MAY 20, THURSDAY. . . . The Weather-cock
finished gilding to day.

MAY 26, WEDNESDAY. . . . Memorandum. Had
the Weather-Cock erected in my Garden this Morning, and a very good effect it has there, looks very well
indeed and handsome. The Pole painted a dark-
green, and the Weather-cock black and gold. It is
put in the middle of the first Clump of Firs on the
right, hand from the front Door of the House. To
John Greaves, Carpenter, for work, pd. 1. 0. 1½. At
Quadrille this Evening, won abt. 0. 1. 6.

JUNE 2, WEDNESDAY. . . . Mrs. Clarke very indifferent indeed, breakfasted in bed. Mrs. Custance

made us a short morning Visit and took leave of our Somersett Friends. Mrs. Clarke rather worse this Afternoon—her Disorder is the Mumps or swellings of the Chaps. She could eat no Solids only spoon-victuals all day. I took a Walk this Evening with my Brother to Mr. Howletts and Mr. Girlings, but none were at home, so the Compliments are paid.

June 3, Thursday. I breakfasted, dined, and spent part of the Aft. at home. My Brother and Wife, Mrs. R. Clarke and Nancy breakfasted, dined, and spent part of the Aft. here. Mrs. Clarke still poorly but rather better than Yesterday. Paid Briton for things 0. 9. 4½. Paid Betty for ditto 1. 1. 0 out of which she owes me 0. 0. 8. Two of the Kings-Head Chaises came to my House this Afternoon according to order, and at 5. o'clock we all sat of for Norwich— My Brothers Wife, Mrs. Clarke and Nancy in one Chaise, and my Brother and self in the other, we got to Norwich by Tea-time to the Kings Head where we all drank Tea, supped and slept. Gave to my Brother this Evening my Silver Cork-Screw with a five Guinea Norwich Bank Note wrapped round it— 'Pignus Amicitiæ'—St. Peter's very musical Bells rung this Evening which highly pleased our Somersett Friends as they never heard them before. We were all rather low at our leaving Weston Parsonage this Afternoon. Our Somersett Friends go of for the West to Morrow Aft. 3 o'clock.

June 4, Friday. I breakfasted, dined, supped and slept at Norwich. Nancy breakfasted, dined &c. &c. at Norwich. My Brother and Wife, and Mrs. Clarke, breakfasted and dined with us at the Kings Head, and at 3. o'clock, this Afternoon, after taking leave of us,

they went of for London in the Expedition Coach,
from the Kings Head—a double-Coach. Mrs. Clarke
but very indifferent with a swelled Face. It being the
Kings Birthday St. Peters Bells rang most part of the
Day and at 1. o'clock Lord Heathfields Light Horse
were drawn up in the Market Place and fired 3.
Vollies in honour of the Day. We also saw St.
Andrews Hall and likewise the Mayor and Aldermen
go from thence full dressed to the great Church to
Prayers and a Sermon this Morning about 11. I gave
to a Man at St. Andrews Hall 0. 1. 0. Shewed the
Ladies also Bunns Rural Gardens and the Iron-
Foundery this Morning. At parting we were all very
low on the Occasion. Pray God send them a safe
Journey into the West. Nancy and self took a Walk
in the Evening to Mr. Priests Senr. and there drank
Tea with Mr. and Mrs. Priest and their Son John.
Soon after Tea a Dr. Hooke and one Mr. Taylor
joined us, and I played one Rubber at Whist with
Mr. Priest Senr. Dr. Hooke and Mr. Taylor, I lost
0. 1. 6. At 7. o'clock I took Nancy with me in one of
the Hackney Coaches down to Bunns Gardens to hear
a Concert and see some Fireworks. We stayed there
till near 11. o'clock—the Concert was midling, the
Fireworks very good. Paid at the Gardens for 2.
Tickets 0. 2. 0. We returned as we went and in the
same Coach. Paid the Coachman there and back,
0. 3. 0. There was very little genteel Company there,
but as Nancy never saw any publick Gardens before,
she was well pleased with the sight. Lord Orfords
droll-dressed Militia Men at Norwich, red Cloth
Slops and long white Trowsers. Paid Nancy for her
Pigg that was lately killed 9 St. 1. 11. 6.

JUNE 7, MONDAY. ... To Ross Bean, losing a good

Horse, gave 0. 10. 6. Mr. Du Quesne gave him the same as did Mr. Custance.

July 5, Monday. . . . John Piper and Man, Willm. Thorogold, nailing up my Fruit Trees against the Walls. Mr. and Mrs. Custance, and their 5 Children, Miss Fanny, Miss Emily, Master Hambleton, George and William, drank Coffee and Tea with us this Afternoon, and after Tea we played one Pool of Commerce of 6. each and which Master George Custance won. It was quite a treat for the little Folks to be out. They seemed quite happy here—wch gave us much pleasure.

July 15, Thursday. . . . Paid a Qrs. Land-Tax to Js. Pegg this morning 3. 0. 0. To a poor Woman from Dereham by name Hall with a small Child with her was taken very ill with a violent Pain within her by my great Gates and was laid down in the road, I went out to her and gave her a good Glass of Gin and gave her sixpence to go to the Inn, but she did not go there but returned back towards Dereham. She is a Widow and belongs to the House of Industry near Dereham. I hope she is no Impostor. Mr. and Mrs. Custance with Mr. George Beauchamp and his new Bride drank Tea with us this Afternoon. After Coffee and Tea we got to Cards to limited Loo at one penny a Fish, at which won, about 0. 4. 0. Nancy lost at it 6^s/1^d. Nancy owes me at Cards this Even' 7^s/1^d. Mr. B[eauchamp] lost upwards of a Guinea. They left us a little before 9. o'clock. Mrs. Beauchamp much like her sister Lady Beauchamp not so handsome, but taller and larger. Thank God! something better after taking Rhubarb last night.

July 22, Thursday. . . . Nancy very pert and saucy this morning.

AUGUST 3, TUESDAY. . . . I thank God, had a tolerable good Night last Night. I drank but very little Wine Yesterday or to day only 2. or 3. Glasses. I used myself before and all last Winter to near a Pint of Port Wine every Day and I now believe did me much harm.

AUG. 22, SUNDAY. ... I read Prayers and Preached, this Afternoon at Weston Church—Mr. and Mrs. Custance at Church. Mr. and Mrs. Custance with their two young Ladies, Mr. and Mrs. Townshend with Mrs. Cornwallis and two of the Miss Townshends, and Mr. Du Quesne drank Coffee and Tea with us this Afternoon. They all came in two fullbodied Coaches with four Horses to each and each drove by two Postilions, no Coach Box to either. Mr. Du Quesne came quite unexpected it being Sunday, but was very glad to see him. He came in his one horse Chaise. He was not in high Spirits. They came about 6. and went away about 8. o'clock. It was an awkward day for visiting, but It was Mr. Townshends appointment. They all seemed well pleased as they went away. There were 7 Servants and 12 Horses with the Company.

AUG. 24, TUESDAY. ... Sent one Dozen and one very fine Apricots from my best Tree called the Anson Apricot, to Mr. and Mrs. Custance at Weston House by my Maid Betty. They sent us back some fine black Grapes which came from Mackay's Hot House, a Gardner at Norwich. Delightful Harvest Weather, blessed be God for it.

AUG. 28, SATURDAY. ... Briton went early this Morning to Norwich on horseback, after News-papers &c. I sent a long Letter to my Sister Pounsett by him.

He returned home to dinner—No Letters. In shearing Wheat this Afternoon Briton cut off part of his left hand Thumb with the Sickle, owing in a great Measure to his making too free with Liquor at Norwich to day, having met his Uncle Scurl there who treated him with Wine. It bled very much I put some Friars Balsam to it and had it bound up, he almost fainted.

AUG. 29, SUNDAY. ... I read Prayers and Preached this morning at Weston Church. Mr. and Mrs. Custance at Church. As I was coming out of the Church-Yard a very handsome Carriage with four grey Horses in it with Servants in white Liveries and I believe turned up with Green, passed by Our Churchyard Wall—supposed to be Lord Buckinghamshires. There were two Gentlemen in it, supposed to be Lord Buckinghamshire and his Brother Hen. Hobart.

SEPT. 6, MONDAY. ... Mr. Bodham sent me over this Morning early (by Willm. Ward his farming Man) a nice black greyhound Puppy, a Dog, seven Weeks old. I gave Willm. for the trouble of bringing it o. 1. o. I set the Name of Snip to it. Mr. Jeanes called on us this Morning to ask us to dinner on Saturday.

SEPT. 8, WEDNESDAY. . . . Norwich Musick Festival begun this Morning. I did not go having had enough of the last Musick Meeting in September 1788 —at which I experienced a great deal of uneasiness and for which it cost me besides about 7. o. o. It was a very good day for the Harvest.

SEPT. 9, THURSDAY. ... Mrs. Custance called on us this Morning and very good-naturedly and genteelly offered us places in her Coach to Morrow Morning to go with her to the Musick at Norwich in

the Morning at St. Peters Church—The principal
Parts of the Divine Messiah &c. being to be performed
there.

SEPT. 10, FRIDAY. . . . We breakfasted before
7 o'clock this Morning: at half past eight Mrs. Cus-
tance took us up into her Coach and carried us to
Norwich and put us down at St. Peter of Mancroft
Church before eleven o'clock and there we stayed till
three in the Afternoon highly delighted indeed with
the Musical performance. Select Pieces from the
Messiah, Joshua &c., a great Band with the Abbey
Double Drums; between 8 and 900 People present.
Tickets 5ˢ/0ᵈ each. Segniora Storace the principal
Singer, Miss Pool the second. Saw Sr. Edmᵈ and
Lady Bacon, Sr. Thos. and Lady Beauchamp, Sr.
John Woodhouse, Mr. Hobart, Mr. Windham and
our New Bishop Dr. Horne and Family &c. We
returned with Mrs. Custance to Weston House about
5 in the Afternoon and there took a Family Dinner
with her and Mr. Custance. The latter was but just
returned from Scottow having been there ever since
Monday last in adjusting the late Sr. Thos. Durrants
Affairs, he being left joint Executor with Lady Durrant. We returned home to Weston Parsonage by 8,
rather fatigued with the hurry of the Day. On our
return home found a Note on my Table from Mr.
Jeanes, to put off our dining with him, on Monday
next instead of to Morrow. As the Haunch of Venison
will be better by being kept till then as supposed by
some—Hope it will be sweet.

SEPT. 17, FRIDAY. . . . The young Woman Spincks
(who lately had a Bastard Child by one Garthon of
Norwich) called on me this morning to acquaint me
that her Child is dead, died last night, owing it is

supposed to her [having] given him a Sleeping Pill
which she had of her Neighbour Nobbs whose
Husband is very ill and had some composing Pills
from Mr. Thornes, one of which Nobbs wife advised
her to give her Child to put him to sleep whilst she
was out. The Child slept for about 5 hours, then he
waked and fell into convulsion fits wch. continued for
4 Hours and half and then died in great Agonies.
If the Child died owing to the effects of the Pill, I
believe it not intentionally given to destroy the Child
as she always had taken particular care of him and
looked remarkably healthy. I advised her to make
herself easy on that respect. Mr. Peachman and Mr.
Buck also called on me this morning soon after and
talked with me a good deal on the death of the Child.
They both think that the Childs Death was owing to
the Mothers giving the Pill to it. I had no objection
I told them of burying the Child without the Coroners
Inquest, as It was possible the Child might have died
without taking the Pill, however it ought to be well
considered on for the public good. I took a walk with
my Niece to Weston House this morning, in our way
there we met with Mr. Custance in Weston Field, and
soon after Mr. Press Custance with another gentleman by name Mitchel out of Devonshire, on a shooting party, Mr. Du Quesne also we saw in Weston
Field whilst with Mr. Custance in his return home
from Reepham. If I mistake not the above gentleman
by name Mitchel who was with Mr. Press Custance
I saw at Bruton Church when last in Somersett, and
I believe Son of Mr. Mitchel the School-master at
Bruton and a Clergyman and who came from Devonshire. He looked exactly like him I must confess.
We stayed about an Hour with Mr. and Mrs. Custance and returned home to dinner. In the Afternoon

I walked to Mr. Bucks and advised him and the Woman Spincks to inform the Father of the Child of its death and to send for Mr. Thorne to have his Opinion whether the Childs Death was owing to the Pill being given it, as Mr. Thorne made them. Mr. Buck sent immediately to Mr. Thorne. I returned home to Tea before the Dr. came. To Largesses to day gave 0. 2. 0.

SEPT. 18, SATURDAY. . . . Sent Briton early to Norwich this morning with my little Cart, returned not till 3 this Afternoon the Cart being obliged to have something done to it. No Letters at all. He brought 2 pair of Soals and half a Dozen new Maccarel the first this Season. Mr. Thorne called here about Noon having been to see the dead Child and said that its Death was owing to the Mothers giving it part of the Pill. Soon after the Doctor went, the Mother of the Child Eliz. Spincks came here to know what to do, I told her to go to the Overseer (Emery) to send for the Coroner and inspect the Body before I could bury it. To Largesses to day, gave 0. 4. 0.

SEPT. 19, SUNDAY. ... I read Prayers and Preached this Afternoon at Weston Church. Mrs. Custance with her 2 Daughters at Church. It being a fine Day Nancy was at Church. But few Farmers at Church this Afternoon on Account of an Inquest being taken by a Coroner from Norwich on the Body of Eliz. Spincks Boy. They were from 1. till near 5. on the above business. The Jury brought in their Verdict— not intentionally given by the Mother to her Child. This Evening between 6. and 7. I buried the Child (by name Garthon Spincks) in the Churchyard. As we were walking back from Church we met with Mr. Forster in his Market-Cart and with him Mr. Priest of Norwich whose intention was to have been at Weston Church this Aft. but they were too late. We saw them just by our House. I asked them to walk in but they did not. Mr. Priests Wife is at Lenewade Bridge at Forsters. Mr. Forster asked us to drink Tea to Morrow in the Afternoon to meet the Priests of Reepham there.

SEPT. 24, FRIDAY. ... Nancy was taken very ill this Afternoon with a pain within her, blown up so as if poisoned, attended with a vomiting. I supposed it proceeded in great measure from what she eat at Dinner and after. She eat for Dinner some boiled Beef rather fat and salt, a good deal of a nice rost duck, and a plenty of boiled Damson Pudding. After Dinner by way of Desert, she eat some green-gage Plumbs, some Figgs, and Rasberries and Cream. I desired her to drink a good half pint Glass of warm Rum and Water which she did and soon was a little better—for Supper she had Water-gruel with a Couple of small Table Spoonfuls of Rum in it, and going to bed I gave her a good dose of Rhubarb and Ginger. She was much better before she went to bed —And I hope will be brave to Morrow.

SEPT. 28, TUESDAY. ... As I was walking out this Morning I met with Mr. Maynard a Clergyman that lives at Attlebridge Inn and serves Attlebridge, Alderford, Morton and Ringland—most of them only served once a fortnight. It being near my House I asked him to walk in which he did, and drank a Glass of White-Wine and eat some plumb Cake, then took a Walk with me round my Garden and then left me. Nancy did not make her Appearance being dressing. Thos. Cupper of this Parish died Yesterday, I never heard that he had been worse than usual, he was at

Norwich last Week and brought home ill on Saturday last. He has left a Wife and one Child.

NOV. 13, SATURDAY. ... To one Barber (assistant to Mr. Hardy, Mason) who is very good to a poor blind Mother, gave 1. 0.

NOV. 20, SATURDAY. ... To Mr. Cantrell's Servant Lad for bringing me one Dozen of Port Wine and 2. Gallons of Rum in a small Cask, gave him 0. 0. 6. Returned by him 13. Bottles and the empty Cask. I buried about 2. o'clock this Afternoon poor Lydia Betts, Widow of the late old Richd. Betts. I did not know that she was ill, till she was dead. She was above 70. Years of Age, I was told. The Corpse was carried by my House, and what was remarkable a recruiting Party with a Drum and fife and Flag flying, passed just before all by chance—Drum beating and fife playing. They came from Lyng, Lyng fair being Yesterday in pursuit of a young Fellow who had listed Yesterday and had run away, and who shd. that young Fellow be but Barber, Mr. Hardy's the Mason's Lad, to whom I gave a Shilling to last Saturday, hearing he was a good sober Lad and particularly kind to his aged Mother. Mr. Cary brought our News from Norwich. No Letter.

NOV. 22, MONDAY. ... A right true November Day, dark, wet, windy and cold.

NOV. 25, THURSDAY. ... Nancy repeated to me this Evening seventy two Verses taken out of a Magazine of some of the Kings of England from 1066 the time that William the Conqueror began to reign till 1737 when George the 2nd succeeded his Father George the 1st. She repeated them without missing one Word. I sent Ben after breakfast round the Parish to let them know that my Tithe Audit will be Tuesday. He returned about 4. in the Aft. pretty full of Liquor. Every Farmer almost asked him to drink.

DECEM. 7, TUESDAY. . . . It pleased Almighty God this morning about 7. o'clock to release my poor suffering Parishioner Henry Nobbs from his extreme Misery. Pray God grant that his long sufferings may be succeeded by an eternal Happiness in Heaven. My poor Parishioner also Eliz. Atterton was removed from this Life and I sincerely hope to a better, this morning near the above time. Her complaint, they say, proceeded from the heart. Mr. Forster of Lenewade Bridge, called on me this morning by my desire, and I paid him a 48 Stone Bill for Flour for my House for this Year, 5. 7. 6.[1] To 7 Yards of purple Cotton for a morning Gown of Mr. Aldridge who travels with a Cart, pd. 0. 14. 0. To 7 Yards of white Cotton for a Lining, pd 0. 8. 0. To $\frac{1}{2}$ a Yard of $10^s/0^d$ Cambrick of Do. pd. 0. 5. 0.

DECEM. 8, WEDNESDAY. . . . Paid Charles Cary, Shoemaker, this Morn', 2. 8. 0. Paid Mr. Palmer my Malster this morning a Bill for Malt &c. for the last Year, 22. 18. 6. Paid Mr. Baker my Butcher this Morning a Bill for Meat for the last Year, 46. 5. 0. Paid Mr. Cantrell for Porter &c. last Year. 4. 13. 0. Poor old John Clarke departed this Life, and I hope

---

[1] Parson Woodforde's flour bill for the year is notable as indicating how much less bread was consumed in the eighteenth century in a normal middle-class household than to-day. On the other hand, the consumption of meat was enormous. The Sumner Committee on the Cost of Living in their Report, 1918, p. 11, take the pre-war consumption of bread and flour for a working-class family of 5.6 persons as 32 lb. per week. Parson Woodforde's household consisted of himself and Nancy, two maid-servants, two men-servants, and a boy, i.e. seven persons. Yet his consumption of bread (baked at the parsonage) and flour works out at only 13 lb. a week.

for a better, this Morning. I walked over this Evening to my Neighbour John Clarke's, whom, as I heard was rather worse but I found him better than I expected to find him, but still very indifferent and very low. I gave him to buy Oatmeal for Water Gruel o. 1. o and when I got home I sent him over a Bottle of white Wine to put into his Gruel and likewise part of a cold rost Loin of Veal.

DECEM. 9, THURSDAY. . . . Paid my Cooper, Mr. Ames, this Morn' his Bill, 1. 2. 10½. Brewed a Barrel of Table-Beer. About one o'clock took a Walk to Weston-Church and buried poor Henry Nobbs and Eliz. Atterton a great many People attended at their Funerals. Eliz. Atterton I buried first, the other Corpse not being brought, as soon as I had buried her, the other Corpse was brought to the Church-Yard Gate, and I went thro' the whole Service again after the first. Eliz. Atterton, was 56. Years old. Henry Nobbes, was only 25. Years old. Pray God they may be both happy in Heaven. May Almighty God everlastingly reward poor Henry Nobbes for his very, very great Sufferings here. His poor aged Mother attended at the Funeral and came to see me after with Tears in her Eyes to thank me for what I had done for him. But O Lord! not unto me but unto thy divine Goodness be ascribed all the Praise. To old Tom Carr, gave this Afternoon o. 1. o.

DECEM. 11, SATURDAY. . . . Gave Nancy this morning a green silk damask Gown, that was formerly my poor Aunt Parrs. My Newspapers brought by Billy Bidewell to day. No tidings from the West-Country.

DECEM. 13, MONDAY. . . . When I came down

Stairs this Morning could hear no tidings of Ben at all, which still made me more uneasy. I then sent for Willm Large and sent him on horseback after him. And about 2. o'clock Ben with Willm Large returned and I thank God safe and well. Ben went Yesterday in the Afternoon with a Mr. Watson Steward to Sr. John Woodhouse to Kimberly Hall, where having made too free with the Baronets strong Beer, fell of his Horse coming home and lost her, so that he walked about all the Night after her and did not find her till about Noon, she was found at Kimberly in a Stable of Mr. Hares, a boy happening to see and put her in there. I ordered Willm Large to dine here and to have 2^s/o^d. Thank God! that Matters turned out no worse. Windy and wet and my Study Chimney smoak[ed]. Nancy also had a Note from Mrs. Bodham to let us know that they with Miss Anne Donne from Norwich would dine with us on Wednesday next and sleep that Night. I was very indifferent all day long could eat but very little and not relish that, tho' we had a fine fat rost Goose for Dinner.

DECEM. 22, WEDNESDAY. . . . Had a Pigg killed this morning, Weight, 7 St. ½. Nancy gave me a blue and White Handkerchief that her Brother William took out of a Spanish Ship in the last War, when he was in the Navy.

DECEM. 25, SATURDAY and Christmas Day. I breakfasted, dined, &c. again at home. Nancy breakfasted, dined &c. again at home. I read Prayers and administered the H. Sacrament this morning at Weston Church being Christmas Day. Gave for an Offering, 0. 2. 6. Mr. and Mrs. Custance at Church and at the Sacrament. Mr. Custance's two eldest Sons were at Church and during the administration

of the H. Sacrament were in my Seat in the Chancel
to see the whole Ceremony by Mrs. Custance's desire.
My old Clerk J^s Smith, old Tom Cary, old Nat.
Heavers, old John Peachman, and old Christ.
Dunnell dined at my House on rost Beef and Plumb
Pudding. I gave also to each to carry home to their
Wives 1^s/0^d, o. 5. o. Sent old Tom Carr not being
able to come as being ill, his Dinner, and with it,
o. 1. o. I lighted my large Wax-Candle being Xmas
Day during Tea-time this Afternoon for abt. an Hour.
It was very mild thank God to day for this time of the
Year tho' wet and very dirty walking. Nancy having
herself new made the late green Silk Gown I gave her,
wore it this Day for the 1st time.

1791

JANUARY 1st 1791, SATURDAY. I breakfasted,
dined, &c. again at home. Nancy breakfasted, dined,
&c. again at home. We did not set up last Night to
usher in the New Year, as it migh[t] be as well omitted
and by the blessing of God hope that this Year may
bring more pleasant Days than the last Year to me.
Since our Somersett Friends left us in June last my
Niece hath been almost daily making me uneasy by
continually complaining of the dismal Life she leads
at Weston Parsonage for want of being more out in
Company and having more at home, tho' I enjoy no
more than herself. It was not so in 1780. Billy Bidewell brought my Papers from Norwich, and am sorry
to find by the Papers that much damage and many
Lives lost by the late violent Storm of Wind with most
terrible Thunder and Lightning on Thursday Morn'
December 23, 1790. It is thought by many that it was

attended by a slight Shock of an Earthquake. St. Mary's Church Steeple in Oxford it was mentioned is so much injured by the Lightning, that it is apprehended it must be taken down. The Royal Family at Windsor were alarmed and it is said, arose at a very early hour. Pray God we may hear no bad News from Somersett. My Nephew William's Letter to his Sister was dated Wednesday Dec^{br} 22—The very Day before.

JAN^y 8, SATURDAY. . . . Ben went early with my great Cart to Norwich. and carried in it 10. Coomb 2. Bshls. of Barley to Mr. Bloomes at the Duke's Palace. . . . The high Wind waked me about 2. o'clock this Morning and tho' I did not get up yet the Wind continued near the same, without my sleeping any more, at half past 8. got up, very much deranged for want of more sleep, the Wind still continuing the same, and is still very high at my writing this tho' past seven o'clock in the Evening. At 11. calm. Holland with his two Sons Franck and George, Chimney Sweepers, were here this Morning about four o'clock and swept my Study, Parlour, Kitchen and Back Kitchen, Study Chamber and Parlour Chamber Chimnies, and thank God recd. no hurt tho' the Wind was very high all the Time. I gave his youngest Son George a Xmas Box, 0. 1. 0. They all made a comfortable Dinner on cold Meat. Ben did not return till 5. o'clock this Evening. Mr. Bloome had my Barley upon honour, no price sent back, as he always gives me as much as any. He brought back $\frac{1}{2}$ Chldrn of Coal from Mr. Bloome. Nancy sent a long Letter by him to her Aunt J$^{n}_{o}$ Woodforde. No Letters for us. No News I hope recd. is better for us.

JANY. 22, SATURDAY. . . . I privately named a

Child of the Widow Nobbes this morning at my house by name Elizabeth. To a poor old infirm Man that came to my House this morning gave some Victuals and, o. o. 6. Sent poor Harry Clarke who is still very bad, by his Brother, some Victuals and some Money. My Cook Maid (Nanny Kaye) some few days ago gave my Niece notice of leaving her service at Lady Day next, as she intends then to enter into the marriage state. One Willm. Spraggs (Son of the Gardner whom I used to employ and who is now in Bridewell at Wyndham for stealing Wood from Mr. Brainthwaite at Taverham) not more than 20. Years of Age, is the Young Man that she is going to marry. I think she might do better. He also was with his Father in the above affair and was very near being taken at the time.

JANY. 24, MONDAY. ... I had 2 Girls come to offer themselves this Morn' the first by name Hardy a very pretty Girl of Ringland, the other one of John Bakers Daughters, both under 20. N.B. neither would do having never been out.

FEB. 14, MONDAY. ... To Children being Valentines day under 14. Years of Age and able to say 'good Morrow Valentine', in Number 40. at 1^d each, gave 3. 4. We dined and spent the Afternoon at Weston-House with Mr. and Mrs. Custance and Mr. Du Quesne. Mr. Custance sent his Coach after us and we were brought back in Mr. Du Quesne's Chaise. After Tea, we got to Loo, neither won or lost. Nancy lost about 4. or five Shillings. We had for Dinner Cod and Oyster Sauce, a Fillet of Veal rosted, boiled Tongue, stewed Beef, Peas Soup and Mutton-Stakes. 2nd Course, a rost Chicken, Cheesecakes, Jelly-Custards &c.

FEB. 16, WEDNESDAY. . . . Gave John Norton to carry home to his Wife (who is very ill by taking Mercury after the small-Pox) a very fine fat Chicken ready trussed.

FEB. 20, SUNDAY. . . . I read Prayers and Preached this Afternoon at Weston Church—Mr. and Mrs. Custance at Church. I was rather out of temper this Aft. on Account of my Maid's (Nanny Kaye) Banns being not published this Afternoon by me, as she never mentioned it to me before I went to Church. Pray God! forgive me.

FEB. 21, MONDAY. . . . To a little Boy (Edward) of one of Downings Girls by Mr. Barton late of this Parish—gave 0. 1. 0.—As he was assisting my Boy pulling Turnips. Had a Couple of Tubbs of Gin brought me this Evening about 8. o'clock—soon safely lodged.

FEB. 22, TUESDAY. . . . To one Mary Shinkin of Lenewade Bridge having lost a Cow very lately— gave 0. 2. 6. A Mary Noller of Felthorpe about 25. Years of Age and who lived with Major Lloyd one Year at Michaelmas last, came to offer here. She has a Mother and 7. or 8. Brothers and Sisters. I did not agree with her, but If I did take her I would let her know in a Week, if she did not hear from me, then I should not take her—I did not like her Appearance being of a bold Masculine Cast—Neither her home or Family. Mrs. Custances two younger Sons, John and Neville now under inoculation for the Small-Pox.

FEB. 27, SUNDAY. . . . I read Prayers and Preached this Morning at Weston Church. None from Weston House at Church—It being a very cold, windy, and wet Day, as bad a Day almost and as cold, as any during all Winter. I published the Banns for the first time between my Maid Nanny Kaye and Willm Spraggs of Attlebridge. recd. for publishing the same o. 2. 6 which I gave to my Maid (Nanny) on my return from Church, and at the same time told her that I hoped she might repent not of what she was about to do. She is about 34. and he about 20. with an indifferent Character.

MAR. 7, MONDAY. . . . Washing Week at our House and a fine Day. The small-Pox spreads much in the Parish. Abigail Roberts's Husband was very bad in it in the natural way, who was supposed to have had it before and which he thought also. His Children are inoculated by Johnny Reeve, as are also Richmonds Children near me. It is a pity that all the Poor in the Parish were not inoculated also. I am entirely for it.

MAR. 8, TUESDAY. . . . Gave poor Roberts one of my old Shirts to put on in the small-Pox—His, poor Fellow, being so extremely coarse and rough, that his having the small-Pox so very full, his coarse Shirt makes it very painful to him. I sent his Family a Basket of Apples and some black Currant Robb. There are many, many People in the Parish yet [who] have never had the Small-pox. Pray God all may do well that have it or shall have it. Went this Afternoon and saw poor old John Peachman Who is very lame, found him unable to walk and having no relief from the Parish gave him money. Called also at Tom Carys Shop and left some money for Roberts's Familys Use for such useful things as they might want and they have. Recd. for 4 Pints ½ Butter, at 9^d, o. 3. 4. Lady Durrant at Weston House.

MAR. 11, FRIDAY. . . . Mem. The Stiony on my

right Eye-lid still swelled and inflamed very much. As it is commonly said that the Eye-lid being rubbed by the tail of a black Cat would do it much good if not entirely cure it, and having a black Cat, a little before dinner I made a trial of it, and very soon after dinner I found my Eye-lid much abated of the swelling and almost free from Pain. I cannot therefore but conclude it to be of the greatest service to a Stiony on the Eye-lid. Any other Cats Tail may have the above effect in all probability—but I did my Eye-lid with my own black Tom Cat's Tail. . . .

MAR. 15, TUESDAY. . . . My right Eye again, that is, its Eye-lid much inflamed again and rather painful. I put on a plaistor to it this morning, but in the Aft. took it of again, as I perceived no good from it. I buried poor John Roberts this Afternoon about 5. o'clock, aged about 35. Yrs.

MAR. 16, WEDNESDAY. . . . My Eye-lid is I think rather better than it was, I bathed it with warm milk and Water last Night. I took a little Rhubarb going to bed to night. My Eye-lid about Noon rather worse owing perhaps to the warm Milk and Water, therefore just before Dinner I washed it well with cold Water and in the Evening appeared much better for it. Recd. for Butter this Evening at 9ᵈ per Pint 0. 2. 7¼. Mr. Custance came (walking) to my House about six o'clock this Evening, he found us walking in the Garden, he drank Tea with us and left us about 7. o'clock. He gave me a Guinea to pay for the Inoculation of Harry Dunnells Children 6. in Number, which was extremely kind and good of him—The Parish refusing to pay for the same, tho' at the same time they agreed to the inoculating Case's Family and have had it done, tho' a Farmer and better off. All

Mr. Custances Actions to the poor assimulate with the above, every one of them generous and charitable to the highest. Mrs. Custance just the same. Pray God! they may both long enjoy Health and Life, and blessings from above daily attend them. I wrote a Note this Evening to Mr. Thorne to desire that he would come to Weston to Morrow and inoculate Harry Dunnells 6. Children. I gave the Note to Harry Dunnell for one of his Children to carry it very early to Morrow Morn' to Mattishall to Mr. Thorne before he goes out.

MAR. 20, SUNDAY. . . . The first thing almost that I heard this Morn' was the Death of John Greaves, my Carpenter, a very inoffensive good-kind of a young Man as any in my Parish, married about 2. Years or more ago, to a Servant Maid of Mrs. Lombe's, a good kind of a young Woman, and lived very happy together and daily getting up in the World. Pray God comfort her and assist her in this Day of her great distress, and may thy good Providence protect her and her Fatherless Child, and likewise give her a safe and happy deliverance of another Child with which she expects to be brought to bed almost every hour. Defend her O Lord from the small-Pox in this time of her great necessity and trouble if it be thy good pleasure. The small-Pox being almost at present in every part of the Parish by inoculation etc—Poor John Greaves was very suddenly taken of. He had been ill but a few Days, but in a very dangerous Disorder, called the Peripneumony. Mr. Thorne was sent for and attended him, but I am afraid he was not sent for soon enough. I had not the most distant Idea that he was in such danger as it turned out. He was a Man well respected by all that knew him. I am sincerely sorry for him and heartily pity his poor Widow. Pray God! befriend her and support her. I read Prayers and Preached and churched a Woman this Afternoon at Weston Church. Being a poor Woman I took nothing for churching her. None from Weston House at Church to day. We had almost all Day some falling of Rain.

APRIL 6, WEDNESDAY. . . . I walked to Church this Morning and married my late Maid, Anne Kaye, and Willm. Spraggs Junr. of Attlebridge, by Banns, I gave my fee which I received of the Man, to the Woman. The Man's Brother Andrew Spraggs was Father. Brewed a Barrel of Strong Beer.

APRIL 15, FRIDAY. . . . Quite a Summer's Day to day. All Nature gay. Turnips quite a dead Load upon the Land. Many are obliged to throw them into Ditches &c. I am obliged to carry many off from Carys Close.

APRIL 16, SATURDAY. . . . Mr. Cary brought my News &c. from Norwich. A Reward of 100 Pound offered on one of the London Papers for apprehending one Richard Perry (eldest Son of John Perry that formerly kept Ansford Inn) for running away with a Miss Clarke (about 14 Years of Age) from a boarding School at Bristol. Her fortune great £6000 per Annum.

MAY 1, SUNDAY. . . . I read Prayers and Preached this Afternoon at Weston Church and also christened a Child. None from Weston House at Church, had but a small Congregation being very wet. Dinner— Breast of Veal rosted.

[As from this date Parson Woodforde almost invariably makes a brief note of the daily dinner at the Parsonage. Hitherto he has simply set down the more succulent dinners provided for guests.]

MAY 3, TUESDAY. . . . Saw the first Swallow this morning. Recd. for Butter this Morn' at 8ᵈ per Pint 0. 2. 8. Old Roberson the Apparitor dined with our Folks in the Kitchen to day, he brought me notice of the Bishops primary Visitation being to be held at Norwich the 15 June next—Dr. George Horne our present Bishop, an Oxford Man, and very lately President of Magdalen College in that University. I walked to Church this Afternoon and buried a Child of John Reeves's aged 9 Weeks. Dinner to Day, Surloin of Beef rosted.

JUNE 2, THURSDAY. . . . Mr. Hardy and Nephew Js. Hardy begun building a new Cart-Shed, for a new little Pleasure Cart that I have bespoke at Norwich.

JUNE 5, SUNDAY. . . . I read Prayers, Preached, and gave notice of a Sacrament on Sunday next being Whitsunday, this Morning at Weston Church. Mr. Custance at Church as was Nancy. We had Green Peas for Supper this Evening being the first pulled this Season by us. Also cut the first Cucumber and gathered the first Strawberries.

JUNE 27, MONDAY. . . . Mr. and Mrs. Jeanes and Mr. Springger called at the bottom of our Garden this morning abt. 10 o'clock in their Journey into Hampshire but did not stay with us above 10 Minutes and were off. Mrs. Jeanes and Mr. Springger with two Children were in Mr. Jeanes's close Chaise, and Mr. Jeanes was in his little low Cart. He had his grey Horse led by a Man. Hired Horses from Norwich to go in the Close Chaise. They were to call at Mr. Du Quesnes and have a Snap. They go to Attleborough,

Thetford &c. to London. Mrs. Custance with her two eldest Sons, Hambleton and George spent an Hour with us this Afternoon. Counter-Revolution in France, the King, Queen and Dauphin have made their escape. Dinner to day Hash-Mutton and a Suet Pudding &c.

JUNE 29, WEDNESDAY. ... The News of to day, is, that the French King and Queen &c. are retaken and carried back to Paris. I hope that it is not true, tho' on Lloyds Paper.[1]

JULY 7, THURSDAY. ... At 9 this morning I went in my little old Cart to Norwich and Briton with me, got there by 11. thank God very well. Walked then immediately to the Cathedral, and heard a very good Sermon preached by a Dr. Cobb, Rector of Carleton St. Peter, very severe on Dr. Priestly the Apostate if properly named—The Bishops primary Visitation this Day for the Deanery of Hingham &c. Mr. Du Quesne I saw there. Walked after to Adams & Bacon Coachmakers near St. Stephens Gates and paid them for a new little Curricle painted a deep Green and without Springs and in which I intend returning home, pd. 9. 9. 0. It is near the height of the old one but much lighter. Paid Beales a Bill for Fish 0. 12. 3. Paid also to the same for 5 Pr. very small Soals, 0. 0. 9. Paid Mr. Lock, Timber Merchant, for 12 Deals 2. 11. 0. Paid Mr. Studwell a Bill for China &c., 1. 19. 6. At Mr. Scotts for a Pair of Gloves, pd. 0. 2. 0. Called on the Priests, for a very small Bottle of Æther of John Priest, pd. 0. 0. 6. For a Glass of white-Wine at Mr. Aldis's, pd. 0. 0. 6. For Ginger-bread Buttons at Blacks, pd. 0. 0. 2½. For one Pint

---

[1] Parson Woodforde in these entries for June 27th and 29th is referring to the abortive flight to Varennes.

of Porter, pd. 0. 0. 2. At about 5 o'clock got into my new Curricle, and set of for Weston, and Briton with me, and got home by 7. this Evening, Cossey Road. I left my old little Cart at Norwich, shall send for it on Saturday next by Briton. My new Curricle goes very easy indeed, like it much. I dined and supped all at one time to day, after I got home. Fryed Soals and cold green Goose for Dinner.

JULY 14, THURSDAY. . . . I hope this Day will be attended with no bad Consequences, this being the Day that the French Revolution first took Place there last Year, and many Meetings advertised to be held this Day in London, Norwich &c. throughout this Kingdom to commemorate the above Revolution.[1] Pray God! continue thy Goodness to this Land and defeat all the designs of the Enemies to it. Dinner to day, Giblet Soup and Shoulder Mutton rosted. Very busy all day about painting the Doors of my Coach House &c., quite tired at Night.

JULY 21, THURSDAY. . . . Shocking Accounts on the Papers of dreadful Riots at Birmingham, Nottingham &c. on Account of commemorating the French Revolution the fourteenth of this Month. The Presbyterian and Independent Meeting Houses pulled down to the Ground and the inside furniture burnt, many of the Dissenters Houses destroyed, amongst the

---

[1] The commemoration was of the fall of the Bastille on July 14th, 1789: Parson Woodforde's memory is momentarily at fault in thinking of the Revolution as beginning 'last Year'; or perhaps he is thinking of the festivities in France, on July 14th, 1790, when the king swore fidelity to the new constitution. On the eve of that day Wordsworth —then a Cambridge undergraduate—landed at Calais with his friend Robert Jones, and saw

> How bright a face is worn when joy of one
> Is joy for tens of millions.

The poet also saw dances of liberty beneath the evening star.

rest Dr. Priestlys, both Town and Country Houses burnt.

Aug. 2, Tuesday. . . . My Servant Maid Nanny Golding had another Fit this morning, screamed out most hideously and so loud that Ben heard her in a Field beyond the Cover, where he was hoeing Turnips. I never heard so frightful a Shriek or crying out. She continued in the fit near an Hour and then went to bed with a violent headache, and there lay all Day and night. It frightned us all. I must part with her at Michaelmas. Brewed a Barrell of Beer to day. Nancy recd. a Letter this Afternoon by Mr. Custance's Servant from her Brother Saml. who is just arrived in England from Italy, it was dated from Dover July 30, last Saturday, he was very well and going for London and from thence into Somersett, says nothing of coming here. Dinner to day rost Beef and Gooseberry Pye.

Aug. 7, Sunday. . . . I read Prayers and Preached this Morning at Weston Church. Mr. Custance at Church, as was Nancy. Poor Love the Painter who lived with his Father at Norwich was buried Yesterday, he had been in a low way some time owing to his being very deaf, and one day last Week cut his Throat —pray God forgive him. He was a great Support to a very infirm and aged Father, and afraid that he might be reduced to want. He was a young Man of good Character and much respected, he used to be much at Weston House, and has painted some Rooms for me, and gilded my Weather Cock the last thing he did for me. I am sorry for him.

Aug. 9, Tuesday. . . . I measured my Oak in the Garden this morning and it has gained in one Year in Girt, one Inch. I drove Nancy in my new Curricle this morning to Mr. Townshends at Honingham Hall,

spent about an Hour there with Mrs. Townshend and
Mrs. Cornwallis and returned home to dinner. Mr.
Townshend not at home. Mrs. Townshend behaved
very genteelly to us indeed.

AUG. 14, SUNDAY. . . . I read Prayers and Preached
this Afternoon at Weston Church. Sr Edmd. Bacon
was at Church and the only Person in Mr. Custances
Seat. There was a large Congregation at Church.
Poor old Js. Smith my Clerk made a shocking hand
of it in singing this Afternoon at Church, much
laughed at. Dinner to day, Fillett of Veal rosted.

SEP. 5, MONDAY. . . . A great deal of Rain fell
during last Night. Dinner to day boiled Beef and a
Suet Pudding. Mrs. Thorne called here this Morning
in a one horse-Chaise, stayed about half an Hour and
then went on for North-Repps near Cromer to her
Cousin Barclays where she stays some Days. The
Barclays are Quakers of very great fortunes live
mostly in London, but generally at this Season of the
Year come down from Town for the Benefit of Sea-
bathing, and prefer Cromer.[1]

---

[1] The Quaker family of Barclay appears to have been identified with
Banking in London even before 1729, when their books begin. The
chief eighteenth-century Barclay seems to have been David, who 'is
recorded to have received successively on Lord Mayor's Day, at his
house in Cheapside, Queen Anne, George I, George II, and George
III'. In coming to Cromer the Barclays were following the relatively
new fashion of sea-bathing which Cowper refers to in his *Retirement*
published in 1782:

> 'Your prudent grand-mammas, ye modern belles,
> Content with Bristol, Bath and Tunbridge Wells,
> When health required it would consent to roam,
> Else more attached to pleasures found at home.
> But now alike, gay widow, virgin, wife,
> Ingenious to diversify dull life,
> In coaches, chaises, caravans, and hoys,
> Fly to the coast for daily, nightly joys,
> And all, impatient of dry land, agree
> With one consent to rush into the sea.—'

SEP. 12, MONDAY. . . . Gave my Servant-Maid, Nanny Golding, warning this Morning to leave my Service at Michaelmas next, on Account of her being subject to bad fits. I was sorry to do it, as she was or at least appeared to be, a very good Servant. I should have been glad to have kept her—if I could, but fits are dreadful, they are so very alarming and come on so suddenly. To Andrews's Men, a largess, gave, o. 1. o. To Howletts Ditto, do. gave, o. 1. o. To Pratts Ditto, do. gave, o. 1. o. Dinner to day Veal Soup, Veal Collops, and Bacon and a brace of Partridges rosted and Apple Dumplins.

SEP. 13, TUESDAY. . . . After breakfast I walked out a coursing and took Ben, Briton, and my Boy Downing with me. I took my three Greyhounds, Fly, Snip and Spring, and two Spaniels, Spring and Carlo with me. We stayed out till two o'clock and coursed only one Hare which we killed. We saw no People out either shooting or coursing, but heard some Guns at a distance. Dinner to day, Giblet-Soup, fryed Beef and Potatoes, and a fine young Hare rosted. To Baker's Men, a Largess, gave o. 1. o. To Dallydays Son (who lately lived with me) for bringing me two young live Hares, o. 1. o. Recd. for Butter this Evening at 9^d, o. 1. 1½.

SEP. 16, FRIDAY. . . . A Hare being seen near my House by Ben I went out with my Dogs, found her, had a very fine Course and killed her. Dinner to day Jugged Hare, very good.

SEP. 17, SATURDAY. . . . Betty went Early this Morning to Norwich with Ben in my little old Cart after News and many other things. Betty went to Norwich to buy my two old Washer-women Mary

Heavers and Nann Gooch a new Gown apiece which I intend giving to them. They returned home about 4 o'clock. Ben brought me home 2 pair of fine Soals. Dinner to-day a nice roasting Pigg. To Emery's Man, a largess, gave, 0. 1. 0.

OCT. 10, MONDAY. . . . I weighed a Bushell of Harts-Wheat (which I had of Mr. Jeanes's Man Willm. last Saturday for Seed) this morning, Weight 4 Stone 11 lb. I also weighed a Bushell of mine, (which this year is very fine) and that weighed 4 Stone, 9 lb. I had a Coomb of Mr. Jeanes's Wheat and my Servant Man, Ben, paid for it Saturday 1. 7. 0. It certainly is very capital, clean Wheat.

OCTOB. 12, WEDNESDAY. . . . I paid my Maid Nanny Golding this Morning her half Years Wages due Oct. 10, 2. 12. 6. And about 2. o'clock this Afternoon her Mother came after her and she returned with her to her own home. I was sorry to part with her as she was a very good Servant I believe and had it not been that she was subject to fits, should not [have] parted with her so soon. Pray God! she might get better of the fits. Since she has taken Assafœtida Drops by my desire she has not had a fit since. I gave her the remaining part of a bottle to carry home. My new Maid Winfred Budery came home this Evening about 5 o'clock. I hope she will do. Dinner to [day] a Couple of rost Chicken and Piggs Face and a broiled blade bone of Veal.

OCTOB. 28, FRIDAY. . . . Nancy had a Letter from her Aunt J$^{\text{n}}_{\text{o}}$ Woodforde this Evening by Mr. Custance's Servant George—In which is mentioned the Death of Mr. James Clarke on the 27 of September last. Mr. Franck Woodforde and Mr. Messiter Executors for his Children—Nothing mentioned of

Mrs. R. Clarke having anything. My Sister Pounsett was said to be very indifferent. Pray God! she may soon get better. Mrs. Thornton of Hatspen also dead, and Mr. Perry late of Ansford Inn died lately at Glastonbury. Mr. Willm. Ashford said to be in a decline. Sister Clarke but poorly and her Son as strange as ever.

NOV. 6, SUNDAY. . . . I privately named a spurious Child of Mary Younges by John Bridges this Morn' at my House. I read Prayers and Preached, christened a Child of John Hubbard's, and buried one James Thacker of the Parish of Lyng, this Afternoon at Weston Church. I had a very large Congregation at Church. Mr. Custance with his two Daughters at Church. I did not take any thing for burying the young Man, tho' he did not belong to the Parish, his Father being poor and willing that his Son should lie near his Mother. I would not even take the duty on Burials, but pay it myself. Neither did I take the duty for christening Hubbards Child. It was near five o'clock this Afternoon before I could get to dinner. We had for Dinner to day, Calfs Feet boiled and a Loin Veal rosted.

NOV. 12, SATURDAY. . . . Sent Ben very early to Norwich this morning with 10 Coomb 2 Bshls. of Wheat to Mr. Bloome. He returned about 4. this Afternoon with News &c. He brought no Coal, tho' ordered, there being none. He sold my Wheat at 23ˢ/0ᵈ Per Coomb and brought me home in Paper and Cash for the same, 11. 10. 0. It was 6ᵈ per Coomb more than mentioned on the Norwich Paper for this Day. It was very fine Wheat. Recd. of John Norton for 2. small Piggs, 0. 10. 6. Recd. of Ditto, for 2. larger Ditto, 1. 10. 0. . . .

Nov. 15, Tuesday. ... About Noon (being fine) I walked out a coursing taking only Briton and the Boy with me, Ben being in Weston Great Field plowing. We stayed out till near 4 o'clock, saw no Hare but coursed one Rabbit and killed it. We walked over most of the large Brakes by Ringland. Nancy very busy with the Maids all the Morning in making some black Puddings &c.

Nov. 20, Sunday. ... Mr. Forster of Lenewade Bridge sent us a string of Eels, gave his Man, o. 1. o. I read Prayers and Preached this Afternoon at Weston-Church. Mr. and Mrs. Custance with Mr. and Mrs. Willm. Beauchamp at Church. They did not come to Church till I was reading the first Lesson, owing to our Clocks being so different, Mine full half an Hour faster. Dinner, Eels, boiled Rabbit, and a rost Goose.

Dec. 5, Monday. ... Mr. Mann called on me this Morning and as he cannot wait on me to Morrow, he being going to Gressenhall Fair then, paid me his Annual Composition for Tithe the Sum of 36. 16. o. I paid him for Carriage of Coal, 2 Chldrn, o. 10. o.

Dec. 6, Tuesday. ... This being my Tithe Audit Day the following People waited on me, paid me their respective dues and dined and spent the remaining part of the day with me, they left me about 12 o'clock at night, well pleased with their entertainment. Mr. Girling and Son, Mr. Peachman, Mr. Howlett, John Baker, Jonas Silvey, Henry Case, Js. Pegg, Robt. Emeris, Stephen Andrews, Hugh Bush, Willm. Bidewell, John Buck, John Norton, Thos. Reynolds Junr., John Culley, Charles Hardy, Henry Rising, Thos. Cary, and John Heavers. Widow Pratts Son James came soon after dinner and paid me for his Mother.

He came quite drunk and behaved very impudently.
Stephen Andrews and Billy Bidewell rather full. Billy
Bidewell paid me for a Calf which he is to have of me
in a few Days, o. 10. 6. Recd. for Tithe to day about
285. o. o. I gave them for Dinner a Surloin of Beef
rosted, Sliff-Marrow-Bone of Beef boiled, a boiled Leg
of Mutton and Caper-Sauce, a Couple of Rabbits and
Onion Sauce, Some salt Fish boiled and Parsnips, and
Egg Sauce with plenty of plumb-Puddings and plain
ditto. They spoke highly in favour of my strong Beer,
they never drank any better they said. Paid Stephen
Andrews for Carr[iage] of Coal, o. 15. o. Paid Ditto,
for 1½d Rate to the Church o. 2. o. Recd. of Ditto,
my last Visitation Fee, o. 2. 6. Mr. Howlett was very
dull and dejected. There was drank, six Bottles of
Rum which made three Bowls of Punch, four Bottles
of Port Wine, besides strong-Beer. No Punch or Wine
suffered in Kitchen. Mr. Girling who had been to
Norwich this Morning brought us News of Lord
Orfords Death a Man universally respected and will
be universally lamented as he was one of the Most
Charitable, humane Men, as has been known many
a Day. His Death is supposed to be entirely owing to
the Loss of his most intimate Friend, Mrs. Park who
lived with him and had many Years. She had been a
particular Friend to him.[1]

DEC. 12, MONDAY. . . . Most piercing cold indeed
this morning and a sharper Frost if anything than
Yesterday, it froze within Doors in a very few Minutes

---

[1] Lord Orford's death meant the succession to the title, as 4th earl,
of Horace Walpole, now an old man of seventy-four. Horace Walpole
did not take up his residence at Houghton, where he had once lived
with his father, the Prime Minister; he did not, therefore, become even
a remote neighbour of Parson Woodforde who, in literature, may be
said to represent the best audit ale, as Horace Walpole represents the
best champagne of the eighteenth century.

this Morn. The Thermometer was this Morning at nine o'clock down to No. 42, tho' in my Study. Norton and Bush had some Words I heard to day at my Tithe Audit in the Kitchen, which was never mentioned to me before or known by me till Norton himself came and told me this Morn' he having applied to Mr. Custance for a Warrant against Bush for assaulting him. Mr. Custance told him to come to me. I advised him to make it up with Bush. Norton is in one of his crazy fits. It vexed me to hear of it. I thought all was harmony and Mirth that Night in the Kitchen.

DEC. 15, THURSDAY. . . . To one John Sparkes of Easton past 72 Years a Labourer, having lost his only Hobby which used to carry him to his Work at Honingham he being a Brick-Maker, gave 0. 2. 6. Frost still continues very severe.

DEC. 25, SUNDAY and Xmas Day. . . . This being Christmas I walked to Church this Morning and read Prayers and administered the Holy Sacrament to 22 Communicants. Gave for an Offering at the Altar 0. 2. 6. None from Weston House at Church this Morn' the Weather being very cold, wet and windy and extreme bad Walking, being all Ice under [foot]. My Foot extremely painful, hard Matter to get to and from Church, but thank God I went thro' it all better than I expected. The following old Men dined at my House being Christmas Day and each had a Shilling apiece to carry home to their Wives, 0. 6. 0. James Smith, Thomas Carey, Thomas Carr, Christopher Dunnell, Nathaniel Heavers, and John Peachman. Dinner to Day Surloin of Beef rosted, plumb Puddings and mince Pies. My large Wax Candle lighted up as usual for one Hour (being Christmas Day) in the

Evening. It froze again sharp this Evening. Thank God my foot was much better at Night. I laid my Foot up in a Chair almost all the Aft.

DEC. 26, MONDAY. . . . To Js. Fisher, blacksmiths Man, Xmas Gift, 1. 0. To J$^{n}_{o}$ Austin, Butchers Man, Xmas Gift, 1. 0. It froze again all last Night and this Morning which makes it worse walking than ever. Paid Mr. Cantrell of Lenewade Bridge for Porter, Wine and Rum for the Year, 3. 6. 0. To Weston Ringers, gave 0. 2. 6. To J$^{n}_{o}$ Short Junr, Wheelwrights Son Xmas Gift 1. 0. To Js. Barratt, Malster's Man, Ditto, 1. 0. Dinner to day, boiled Beef and Pork and Greens. Blessed be God for it, my foot is much better. Mrs. Custance was brought to bed of a Daughter last Night, in about half an Hour after the Dr. came. We did not hear anything of it till this Evening and then by chance. I sent up almost immediately.

1792

JANY. 1ST, 1792, SUNDAY. I breakfasted, dined, &c. again at home. Nancy breakfasted, dined, &c. again at home. I read Prayers and Preached this Afternoon at Weston Church. None from Weston-House at Church. Mrs. Custance near the same as Yesterday, poorly. Had a pretty full Congregation at Church to day. Returned to one Flood who some time back sent me the fee for publishing his Banns and was afterwards forbid by the Girl, 0. 2. 6. My Foot (blessed be God for it) is much better. I walked to Church quite trig, but have not as yet left of my great Shoe lined with bays and still sleep with a worsted gauze-Stocking on that foot, which I think have done good. Dinner to Day, Neck of Pork rosted and Apple-Sauce.

Pray God an happy Year may this be to us and to all our Friends every where, and Especially to our most worthy and particular Friend Mrs. Custance, now under very great Affliction; may thy Almighty Goodness O Lord! send thy restoring Angel to her and bless every medicine made use of for her recovery: And also send Comfort to her truly most most affectionate and loving Husband Mr. Custance in his present great distress, and to their dear Children Health.

JANY. 3, TUESDAY. . . . Gave Betty Leave to go home for a couple of days to see her Friends at Mattishall. Ben carried her in my old Cart to E. Tuddenham. Master Custance with his two Brothers, George and William made us a morning Visit, stayed about half an Hour with us, and then I took a Walk back with them to Weston House and there privately baptized Mrs. Custance's last Child (Born on Christmas Day last) by name Charlotte. I was ready dressed and just going to take a Walk to Weston-House as the young Gentlemen came. Poor Mrs. Custance still extremely ill, not able to move. Mr. Custance most unhappy abt. it tho' Mr. Martineau[1] says, he sees no danger. Pray God Almighty restore her to her former Health soon, is the earnest Prayers and Wishes of her many many Friends, particularly to her dearest Friend and deservedly so, my much ever respected Squire Mr. Custance. It is my daily, Morning and Evening Prayer, that she might get over it and that soon. Poor Lady Bacon I sincerely pity on her Sister being so ill. I never knew two Sisters in all my life testify more regard one to another more than Lady Bacon and Mrs. Custance, and I believe them to be as good Women in every respect as England ever

'Doctor and Man Midwife.'

produced. A Hare was found setting near the Church by John Baker Junr., sent Ben out with my Dogs and they soon killed her. I told Ben to give John 1ˢ/0ᵈ. It was a very large Hare its weight was 8lb ½. Dinner to day boiled Beef.

JAN. 6, FRIDAY. . . . Sent Briton to Weston House again this Morn' brought me bad News of poor Mrs. Custance, that she had had a very bad Night, and all very uneasy about her at Weston-House. 'Pray God Almighty bless the means that are made use of for her Recovery and preserve her, and likewise comfort her distressed Husband, Children, and her dear Friends allied to her.' Her present distressed Situation makes me very unhappy, as she has been so kind to us. Mr. Thorne called on me about dinner time stayed about half an hour, left Compts to my Niece and should be glad to see her at his House to meet Miss Davy in February. I made little or no Answer to him on that Account as our Connection with the Davys are at an End. I asked him to dinner but he declined it. Nancy still at Mr. Du Quesne's with Miss Priest.

JANRY. 7, SATURDAY. . . . Mrs. Custance (thank God for it) is something better. . . .

JANRY. 10, TUESDAY. . . . Mrs. Custance still mending for the better, thank God. Much better I am this morning, and had a good Night but am far from well nevertheless. Paid my Servants this morning their Wages, viz.

To Ben Leggatt a Yrs. Wages due Janry 6,		10.	0. 0
To Bret. Scurl	ditto	ditto	8. 0. 0
To Billy Downing	ditto	do.	2. 2. 0
To Eliz. Dade	ditto	do.	5. 5. 0
To Winfred Budery, a Qrs. Wages due			
Janry 6			1. 6. 6

Paid to my Servants this Day in all 26. 13. 6.
Recd. of Briton for a Calf, sold to Wm. Bidewell, 10. 6.
Paid Ben, Betty, and Briton with Norwich B[ank]
Bills. Ben and Betty took them without the lest hesita-
tion but Briton refused to take one, which hurt me,
however some time after, he complied and took it.

JANRY. 14, SATURDAY. . . . Mrs. Custance still
continues getting better. Betty also a good deal better
this Morning. The most severe Frost last Night and
this Morning as I ever felt. The Milk in the Dairy in
the Pans was one Piece of Ice and the Water above
Stairs in the Basons froze in a few Minutes after being
put there this Morn'. I don't know that I ever perceived the cold so piercing as this Morning, have kept
a Charcoal-Fire in my Celler since we brewed.
Dinner to day a boiled Chicken with Pork and Greens
and a fat Goose rosted, and Damson Tarts &c. Billy
Bidewell brought our News for us.

FEB. 3RD, FRIDAY. . . . Nancy now thinks that she
hears better to day. Took a Walk this Morning to
Weston-House stayed better than half an Hour there
and then returned home to Dinner. Mrs. Custance
still confined to her bed and as helpless as ever, quite
lame of one Side, in every other respect tolerably well.
Mr. Custance gone out. Dinner to day boiled Rabbit
and Leg Mutton rosted. At Cribbage this Evening
with Nancy, won, 0. 0. 6. I am neither well or ill,
have at times strange feeling about me, cold streams
running over my Shoulders &c. at times, and restless
Nights.

FEB. 8, WEDNESDAY. . . . Nancys hearing almost
entirely recovered. Had a Note this Evening by Js.
Atterton from Mr. Du Quesne, sent an Answer back
by him, and also sent by him a Quart Bottle of Tent

Wine and a Couple of Lemons to his Sister in Law
Sus. Greaves who is in the last Stage of a Consump-
tion. Pray God comfort her in distress and soon
release her. Dinner to day, boiled Leg of Pork and
Peas Pudding, a rost Rabbit and Damson Tarts. At
Cribbage this Evening, lost 0ˢ/6ᵈ.

FEB. 14, TUESDAY. ... This being Valentine's Day
gave this morning to 62 Children of my Parish at 1ᵈ
each 5. 2. Mrs. Custance rather better than yesterday.
At Cribbage this Evening with Nancy, lost, o. 6.

FEB. 15, WEDNESDAY. ... Mrs. Custance sent her
Coach and four after Nancy this morning to spend an
Hour with her in her Room which she did and returned about 1 o'clock. She found Mrs. Custance
better than she expected but nevertheless so bad as to
be unable to move herself in bed or likely to do so
perhaps for the next two Months, owing it is supposed
to some violent strain in the back-bone on Child-
bearing. In every other respect very well, can eat and
drink heartily and now in tolerable good Spirits.
After Nancy was gone I took a Walk with my People
a coursing and stayed out till 3 o'clock. Coursed one
Hare and one Rabbit and killed both. On my return
home I privately baptized a Child of Johnny Reeves
that was at my House by name Sarah. As I was a
coursing this morning a Gentleman smartly dressed
rode up to me and enquired whether I had seen Mr.
Peachman. His name was Jarrett Dashwood as
Briton informed me. We had just killed a fine Hare.

MARCH 11, SUNDAY. . . . I read Prayers and
Preached this Morn' at Weston Ch[urch]. Mr. Custance at Church, a small Congregation. It was fair
this Morn' but very cold. N.E. Wind Also a smart

Frost and much Snow on the ground. Dinner to Day
a Breast Veal rosted and hash Mutton. Dr. Manners
Sutton (a near Relative of the late Duke of Rutland)
is appointed Bishop of Norwich in the Room of the
late Dr. Horne. Dr. Sutton is a young Man for a
Bishop only 36 but is married and has 11 Children.
Mr. Custance says that he is a little Man, but well-
spoken of in London and elsewhere.[1]

APRIL 8, EASTER-DAY. . . . I read Prayers and
administered the H. Sacrament this morning at
Weston Church. Had a great many Communicants.
Mr. Custance one of them. Gave for an Offering at
the Sacrament 0. 2. 6. My old Clerk Js. Smith dined
with our Folks. . . .

APRIL 13, FRIDAY. . . . Quite Summer-like
Weather. Dinner a fine Pike boiled and Veal-Cutlets.
Gave my Boy Billy Downing, he having been a very
good lad and of most good natured turn and having
asked Leave to go to Norwich with his Mother to

[1] Charles Manners-Sutton (1755–1828) was a grandson of the third
Duke of Rutland, his father being Lord George Manners-Sutton. He
was educated at Charterhouse, and Emmanuel College, Cambridge,
where he took his degree as fifteenth Wrangler in 1777. He was
ordained, and after a few years as pluralist country parson in two
family livings, he was made Dean of Peterborough in 1791. His next
promotion was to the Bishopric of Norwich, to which was added the
Deanery of Windsor *in commendam* in 1794. In 1805 he became Arch-
bishop of Canterbury. He appears to have been a man of considerable
ability and exemplary piety. 'He was of imposing appearance', says
his biographer in the *D.N.B.*, 'liberal almost to a fault, very accessible
and affable to his clergy, and exemplary in his domestic life.' His chief
title to remembrance is his association with the great movement for
educating the children of the poor promoted by the National Society,
of which he may be regarded as one of the founders. A high-churchman
he consistently opposed catholic emancipation, but supported the
claims of Dissenters for relief from various legal disabilities. His wife
was Mary, daughter of Thomas Thoroton, and they had the normal
eighteenth-century family of twelve children, of whom ten were
daughters.

Morrow-Morning to buy a Pair of Breeches &c. gave him this Even' 5. 0.

APRIL 14, SATURDAY. . . . Billy Bidewell's Wife brought our News-Papers. My Boy Downing walked about 5 o'clock to Norwich with his Mother, returned ab^t 7. in the Ev[ening].

APRIL 24, TUESDAY. . . . Mr. Jeanes called here this morning in his way to Mr. Du Quesnes, but did not dismount. A most gracious and gentle Rain in the Afternoon. Had a Tub of Gin brought this Evening.

APRIL 26, THURSDAY. . . . We dined and spent the Afternoon at Weston-House with only Mr. Custance at dinner with us. We drank Coffee and Tea in the Octagon Room alias Mrs. Custances dressing Room, and Mrs. Custance being finely drank Tea with us, she looks very well considering her long Confinement. Tho' she is now able to sit up in a Chair, yet she cannot walk a step without great Assistance. This is the first time that I have seen her for the last four Months, No Gentlemen besides those of the Families have as yet been admitted to her presence, I was the first. Mr. Custance sent his Coach after us, but it being fine Weather I walked thither and back. Nancy had a long Letter from her Brother Willm. Paid Mrs. Custance this Afternoon my Subscription-Money for Penn's Sermons, 2 Vol. Octavo, 0. 12. 0.[1]

APRIL 27, FRIDAY. . . . Sent Mrs. Jeanes a Couple of fat Spring Chicken by Winfred, as she cannot get any. Sent Mr. Jeanes by the same Hand a black-Pudding. Mr. Du Quesne dined and spent the Aft.

---

[1] Presumably James Penn (1727–1800), a Church of England Divine who wrote tracts and sermons, some of which, says his biographer in the *D.N.B.*, 'show considerable humour and satirical power'.

with us He made a Visit to Weston-House before Dinner. Paid Mr. Emeris this Evening, half Years Poor-Rate at 10^d, in the Pound, 1. 5. 2½. Mr. Du Quesne looked but poorly, thin and very weak. He eat however very hearty and drank much small-Beer. . . .

MAY 21, MONDAY. . . . Sent Briton this Evening after Nancy [who had been staying a day or two with the Jeanes's] in my new little Curricle, she returned safe and well ab^t 8 o'clock, she met with a Storm on her Journey. She supped and slept at home. She gave me a worse description than ever of the bad management in Mr. Jeanes House and dirtier than ever. Had not Miss Lloyd been there Nancy would not have liked it at all. Mrs. Jeanes more affected. Miss Lloyd told Nancy that she could not endure being there, as she is treated by them like almost unto a Servant, being ordered about so—And as for Mrs. Jeanes Brother Springer she never saw or heard so poor a *Honey*.[1] Dinner to day rost Shoulder of Mutton &c.

MAY 30, WEDNESDAY. . . . Great Rejoicings at Weston House &c. Bells ringing, Guns-firing &c. on Account of Mrs. Custance coming down Stairs for the first time for the last 5 Months. I gave my People on the Occasion a bottle of Gin to drink this Evening in Kitchen. I am most heartily glad that Mrs. Custance is so much recovered, hope she wont make too free. Dinner to Day boiled Chicken and Oyster Sauce, a Pigs Face, cold Loin of Veal rosted &c.

MAY 31, THURSDAY. . . . Gave my Boy Downing

---

[1] *Honey* is a term of endearment as old as Chaucer (see *N.E.D.*). Nancy evidently had her uncle's faculty for expressing herself with mild, and compendious irony.

leave to go and see the Poney-Race at Lenewade Bridge gave him also (as he has been painting my Pales) to lay out o. 1. o. . . .

JUNE 9, SATURDAY. . . . Sent Ben this morning to Norwich with my little old Cart and Rodney in it, after News &c. Sent by him also a Letter to my Sister Pounsett, in Answer to her last, acquainting [her] that we cannot go into Somersett yet, Mrs. Custance's last Child not being as yet christned publickly. Ben returned about 4 o'clock this Aft. No Letters. Rodney went exceedingly well in the Cart. Dinner to day Calfs Fry and Leg Mutton rosted.

JUNE 15, FRIDAY. . . . Miss Rebeccah Priest alias Miss Priest of Reepham, came to us this morning before we had been down Stairs and she breakfasted, dined and spent the Afternoon with us, we expected her Yesterday but not to day. We were very glad to see her. She is a very good kind of young Woman, sensible and agreeable without any Affectation whatever. We had for Dinner boiled Calfs Head and Pigs face, a Piece of rost Beef and a Gooseberry Pudding. About 6 o'clock in Afternoon Mr. Priest with his two sons Willm. and Charles from Windham School joined us and drank Tea with us, and about 7. they all sat off with Miss Priest for Reepham. Mr. Custance sent us a Cucumber this morning.

JUNE 17, SUNDAY. . . . I read Prayers, Preached, and churched Mrs. Custance this Afternoon at Weston-Church. The first time of Mrs. Custance being at Church since December last, having been so long ill, she is still very weak, not able to go without a Stick. Mr. Custance at Church and 3 eldest Sons and both Daughters.

JUNE 25, MONDAY. . . . Rafling for a Gown this Evening at the Heart both my Maids went, but returned without Gown.

JUNE 26, TUESDAY. . . . Begun cutting my Clover being a fine Day. Mr. Du Quesne called here about 11 o'clock in his Whiskey, did not get out, as he was going to Reepham. A little before 12 I walked to Church and publickly presented Miss Charlotte Custance in the Church—present Mr. and Mrs. Custance with all their eight Children, and Lady Bacon, the Sponsors were represented by their Proxies Lady Bacon for Miss Hickman, Mrs. Custance for Mrs. George Beauchamp, and Mr. Custance for Mr. Willm Beauchamp. Immediately after the Ceremony Mr. Custance very genteelly presented me with a five Guinea Note from Gurney's Bank at Norwich. We dined and spent the Afternoon at Weston-House with Mr. and Mrs. Custance, Lady Bacon and Mrs. Press Custance. We went and returned in the Coach. Dinner boiled Tench, Peas Soup, a Couple of boiled Chicken and Pigs Face, hashed Calfs Head, Beans, and rosted Rump of Beef with New Potatoes &c. 2nd Course rosted Duck and green Peas, a very fine Leveret rosted, Strawberry Cream, Jelly, Puddings &c. Desert—Strawberries, Cherries and last Years nonpareils. About 7 o'clock after Coffee and Tea we got to Cards to limited Loo at which, lost o. 6. Sent Briton to Norwich this Morning to put a Letter into the Post-Office, an answer to my Niece Pounsetts. In his return I rec^d another from her in Town fearing that her first Letter did not arrive, still pressing us much to go to London and return with her to Cole.

JULY 9, MONDAY. . . . Mem. A Stalk of Wheat (from a field that was formerly a Furze-Cover) I measured this Morning, and it was in Length six feet seven inches and about a barley corn. Dinner to day Peas and Pork and Leg Lamb boiled.

AUG. 2, THURSDAY. I breakfasted, supped and slept again at home. After breakfast about 9 o'clock I drove Nancy to Norwich to be at the Musical Meeting at the Cathedral, for the Benefit of the publick Hospital. We got to Norwich by 11 o'clock we went immediately to the Cathedral, I gave at the entrance of the Church, 1. 1. 0 for the Charity, which is reckoned handsome but we were some time before we could get Seats, the Church being so exceedingly crowded. Nancy got a seat under the Orchestra and very little after I got a most excellent Seat along with the Stewards of the Charity. After Prayers, Our new Bishop gave us a very good Discourse on Charity, more particularly that for which we were assembled. His Text was from the 25. Matthew 35, 36 Verses 'I was a Stranger and ye took me in: Naked, and ye clothed me; I was sick, and ye visited me.' We had very select and grand Pieces of sacred Musick from Handels Compositions before and after the Sermon. All together it was not only delightful but seemed heavenly and gave us Ideas of divine Musick. It finished about half past two o'clock. For Musick Books at Bacons, pd. 1. 0. We walked, immediately as it was over, to Nosworthys where we were showed a very good room above Stairs where we had some refreshment, some Mutton Stakes and a Cucumber, Porter and Port-Wine—all very cleaver. Nosworthy, when we were going away, on my asking him what we stood indebted to him said only for the Port-Wine to be paid for, but I told him that would not do, therefore I desired or insisted on his taking, 7. 6 which after much intreaty he took. From thence we went to St. Giles's Gate, got into our Curricle about six o'clock and thank God! arrived safe and well at home about eight o'clock, not so much fatigued as Yesterday but Nancy was pretty much tired and very hot. We called at the Falcon at Cossey on our return home and had a Tankard of Porter, pd. o. 4. We had delightful Weather and we spent a very pleasant day indeed upon the whole. We never went near the Priests, they never invite us on any public Doings whatever at Norwich. Briton went with us, our Horses at the Woolpocket. The Assizes finished this morning.

SEPT. 1ST, SATURDAY. ... Mr. Custance made us a long morning Visit, he was on foot. He made us very uneasy by what he told us, which was, that they were going to leave Weston-House and reside at Bath in about a Month from this time, that their Children might be educated there, the Misses. ...

SEP. 9, SUNDAY. ... I read Prayers and Preached and churched a Woman this Afternoon at Weston Church. Mr. and Mrs. Custance and Sr Edm^d Bacon at Church. Lady Bacon not at Church, her Daughter Maria, ill. Miss Woodforde also at Church being fine Weather. Weston Singers sung this Afternoon and very well. I gave to Weston Singers towards Books 1. 1. 0. Dinner to day, rost Beef and an Apple Pudding. Poor old Mrs. Cary died about Noon, 81 Years old.

SEP. 15, SATURDAY. ... Had a Tub of Rum brought me this Evening.

SEP. 16, SUNDAY. ... We were much agitated this Evening about what I had brought me Yesterday. Bad reports about the Parish.

SEP. 17, MONDAY. ... I got up very early this

Morning and was very busy all the Morn' in very necessary business.[1] Recd. for Butter this Morn' at 10^d, 3. 4. Dinner to day boiled Beef very salt indeed, very much out of sorts—much jaded, and had [no] Appetite. Mem. J^n_o Norton is supposed to have informed against his Neighbour Buck.

Oct. 4, Thursday. ... Took a Walk with Nancy this Morning to Weston-House to take leave of Mr. and Mrs. Custance and see the little folks before they set out for Bath, They go on Sunday next. We stayed an Hour with Mrs. Custance saw the 5. youngest Children. Mr. Custance was gone to Mr. Du Quesne's, but we met him on our return home, at the bottom of the Croft (alias Field adjoining to our Garden) he having been at our House enquiring after us. He was on horseback, and stopped and talked with us some time, and then parted, we wishing him Good Health and a safe Journey to Bath &c. Mrs. Custance looked very well indeed, altho' she has been fatigued in ordering matters relating to their removal. We wished her &c. Health &c. Knights and his Wife are the only People to be at Weston-House during their absence. Mr. Custance intends being at Weston in January or February next, but will make a short stay here. We shall most severely feel the Loss of such good and very friendly Neighbours and pray God

[1] Parson Woodforde was presumably busy in hiding, perhaps even burying, his smuggled rum. We share his anxiety, for by clause xxii of 19 Geo. III, c. 69, he was liable to a forfeit of £10 for each offence of buying smuggled goods, while the village blacksmith, as supplier, was liable to a fine of £50. Moreover, the Act deliberately encouraged the odious practice of 'informing' because it provided that if the seller informed against the buyer within twenty days, and before any information had been laid against himself, he would be forgiven his own offence. Fortunately, as will be seen later (entry Oct. 12), Buck, the blacksmith, got off with a small fine, and Parson Woodforde resumes his secret purchases.

bless them and theirs wherever they go and send them a safe Journey. Dinner to Day Skaite and Veal Collops &c. Rec^d this Evening for Butter at 10^d o. 3. 4.

OCTOB. 7, SUNDAY. ... Our very good and worthy Friends Mr. and Mrs. Custance with five of their Children with two Nurses and Rising the Butler, left Weston this morning about 10 o'clock and gone for Bath. They had their own Coach and four, and a Post-Chaise. As we were walking in the Garden at the time Nancy saw them at the opening in Church Street, I heard them very plain. Their own Horses carry them to Attleborough, and there the Horses return with their Servants the drivers back to Weston House. Pray God bless them and theirs, and may every thing turn out to their most sanguine wishes. It made us quite low all the whole Day. It is a great, very great loss to us indeed. I read Prayers and Preached this Afternoon at Weston Church, churched a Woman and published Banns of Matrimony and read four Briefs. Weston Singers sung this Afternoon. Nancy walked to Church with me being fine Weather. Am very glad it was so good a Day for Mr. and Mrs. Custance &c. travelling. Dinner to day, boiled Neck of Mutton and a very fine and tender Cock-Pheasant rosted.

OCT. 12, FRIDAY. ... Mr. Jeans made us a Morning Visit, eat a Fig or two, carried some to his Wife, but could not stay to dine with us, tho' asked so to do. Mr. Jeans informed us that he had heard it rumoured about, that there would be a great Mob collected at St. Faiths Fair on Wednesday next, on Account of the dearness of Wheat and other Provisions, but I believe rather from the late long propensity of the discontented to a general Disturbance, so prevalent at present in France. The Norwich Mob to meet the Country Mob on the above day at St. Faiths. John Buck, the blacksmith, who was lately informed against for having a Tub of Gin found in his House that was smuggled, by two Excise Officers, was pretty easy fined. Dinner to day boiled Tongue and Turnips and a fine Couple of Ducks rosted.

OCT. 23, TUESDAY. . . . Had a Tub of Brandy and a Tub of Rum brought this Evening. Gave one of the Men that brought it 1/0.

OCT. 24, WEDNESDAY. . . . Very busy between 8 and 10 o'clock this Morn in bottling off Brandy and Rum. . . .

OCT. 25, THURSDAY. . . . Mr. Du Quesne called here about 2 o'clock in his way to Mr. Priests at Reepham, being so late he did not get out of his Carriage, he brought a Letter for Nancy from Mrs. Custance at Bath inclosed in one to Mrs. Townshend from Mrs. C. They all got to Bath very safe and well on the Thursday after they left Weston-House. Mrs. Custance writes in high Spirits. Bath seems to do her much good respecting health. Dinner to day boiled Skaite, boiled Chicken and Oyster Sauce and Shoulder Mutton rosted.

OCT. 27, SATURDAY. . . . To a Man of Bargewell (by name Brighton whose Father and Mother lately kept the Bell Inn at Billingford) who escaped this Morning out of Bargewell's Poor House being hardly kept alive there, the Allowance so very short, the House being farmed out at 1s/6d per Week for each poor Person—I gave him as he appeared to be a very civil spoken Man and as one that once knew better days 0. 1. 0. He was going for London he said to his

Wife who is a Housekeeper to some Person in Town.

NOV. 1, THURSDAY. . . . My right foot worse this morning than yesterday. Mr. Jeanes was here this morning before I was stirring, tho' was down Stairs before 8 o'clock. Soon after Mr. Priest from Mr. Du Quesnes came here on foot, and soon after him Mr. Priest's Chariot from Reepham with Miss Mary Priest in it, and with her Mrs. Jeans and her two Daughters Mary and Caroline with their Nurse Susan Harrison arrived at my House and they all breakfasted with us on Tea and Toast. Immediately after breakfast Mr. Jeans got on his Horse and went for Windham, where he gets into the London Expedition about 4. this Afternoon for London for a few days. Mr. Priest and Daughter went for Reepham soon after. Mrs. Jeans, two Daughters and Nurse were left at Weston Parsonage and there dined, supped and slept. Mrs. Jeans slept with Nancy in the best Chamber, with Miss Jeans on a Mattress on the floor of the same Room, and the youngest about 7. Months old with her Nurse, Susan Harrison in the Attic Story. We had for Dinner to day, some boiled Skaite, a Leg of Mutton rosted and Damson Tarts. For Supper one rosted Partridge &c. It is rather disagreeable to be so lame just at this time—but thank God! it is no worse.

NOV. 9, FRIDAY. I breakfasted, dined, &c. again at home. Nancy breakfasted, dined, &c. again at home. Mrs. Jeans, her two Daughters and Nurse breakfasted, dined, supped and slept again at Weston Parsonage. At Noon put on my common Shoe on my right foot, it being almost quite well and swelling gone. Mr. Du Quesne called here about one o'clock stayed about an Hour with us and then went home, as he came, on horseback, on old Fox. I asked him to dine with us, but there being no Moon, he could not. Dinner to day hash-Mutton and Suet Pudding—Mutton Stakes and a rost Goose &c. No tidings of Mr. Jeans as yet, how long they stay with us cannot tell, they only begged to be taken in for 3. or 4. Days and now it is more than a Week—The Children particularly the smallest very great trouble, continually a fire above Stairs, washing, &c. &c.

Nov. 10, Saturday. I breakfasted, dined &c. again at home. Nancy breakfasted, dined, &c. again at home. Mrs. Jeans, her two Daughters and Nurse breakfasted, dined and spent part of the Afternoon here. As my Servant Lad, Billy Downing, was going to Lenewade Bridge after some flour for the House, he saw Mr. Jeans with a young Lady in a Post-Chaise, going to Witchingham, and the Chaise went thro' our Parish. Mr. Jeans asked him if his Wife was gone home, to which the Boy answered, no—however they went on for Witchingham Parsonage, and about 3 o'clock or rather after a Note came to Mrs. Jeans from Mr. Jeans with a Servant Boy and a little Cart to convey Mrs. Jeans and Children home. Accordingly as soon as they had dined, Mrs. Jeans with her two Children got into the Cart and went for Witchingham. The Nurse, Susannah Harrison was sent for afterwards by the same convenience, tho' rather dark when she went. I cannot say, but it was by no means genteel in Mr. Jeans to go thro' the Parish and not call. That they are gone, neither myself or Niece much lament—as the Children gave much unnecessary trouble, and Mrs. Jeans too much affected. Sent Briton early to Norwich this morning in my little old Cart after News and many other things. Briton returned time enough to wait at dinner. He brought us some Whitings which we had for dinner, with boiled Beef, Beef-Stake Pye &c.

NOV. 28, WEDNESDAY. . . . Much talking about Mobs rising in many parts of the Kingdom especially in Norfolk and in Norwich, a great Number of Clubs about the County and City, who stile themselves Resolution-Men alias Revolution-Men. A great many rich People it is said back them. It was also rumoured that there was to be a meeting of the County Mobs this day at Norwich. That there were also great disturbances at present in London. Pray God! however we may have Peace. Dinner to day boiled Beef &c. Sent poor Frank Clarke who continues still very bad, 2ˢ/0ᵈ.

DEC. 8, SATURDAY. I breakfasted, dined, &c. again at home. Nancy breakfasted, dined, &c. again at home. Dinner to day Calfs-Fry and a rost Chicken. Our Newspapers brought by Bidewells People. Alarming Accounts on the Papers, Riots daily expected in many parts of the Kingdom, London &c. &c. A fresh Proclamation from the King on the present Affairs. The Tower of London putting in Order—Double Guard at the Tower and at the Bank ordered. Some People unknown sent to the Tower for high Treason. Meetings held in London by the Lord Mayor Aldermen and Magistrates, at Norwich the same. Militia ordered to be embodied the ensuing Week. Meeting of the Norfolk Magistrates on Tuesday next at Norwich. Norfolk Militia to meet on Monday next, One Division at Yarmouth, the other at Lynn. Every appearance at present of troublesome times being at hand, and which chiefly are set on foot by the troubles in France. Pray God! however prevent all bad designs against old England and may we enjoy Peace. Parliament meets on Thursday next.

DEC. 15, SATURDAY. . . . Billy Bidewells People brought our Newspapers. The Meeting at Norwich on Tuesday last was a very full one, almost all the Magistrates in the County attended, and very active measures taken to prevent any public disturbances from the different Societies or Clubs, respecting their late levelling behaviour. The Kings Speech in the House of Lords, a very long one, but very good one, much liked. Most parts of the Kingdom have had general Meetings respecting the present threatening and levelling Principles, and fully attended. And proper measures taken to prevent any bad conse-quences from the levelling doctrines, dispersed among the poorer sort of People, by seditious publications &c. of late so much spread abroad every where. Every thing carried on at Norwich at the above meeting without the lest appearance of Riot or Dis-order, and in other places the same, tho' it was rumoured about that it was the intention of many riotously disposed People, to have a rising of them this Week at Norwich, thank God it did not.[1]

[1] In the course of his speech to both Houses of Parliament on Dec. 13th, 1792 (an admirable example of Pitt's style, for clearly the speech was drafted by him), the king referred to 'the seditious practices . . . which have of late been more openly renewed, and with increased activity. A spirit of tumult and disorder (the natural consequence of such practices) has shown itself in acts of riot and insurrection, which required the interposition of a military force in support of the civil magistrate. The industry employed to excite discontent on various pre-texts, and in different parts of the kingdom, has appeared to proceed from a design to attempt the destruction of our happy constitution, and the subversion of all order and government; and this design has evidently been pursued in connection and concert with persons in foreign coun-tries.' So far neutrality in continental affairs has been maintained, but the French efforts to excite disturbances in other countries 'and to pursue views of conquest and aggrandizement' are causing me serious

DEC. 25, TUESDAY. . . . This being Christmas Day
I walked to Weston Church this morning and there
read Prayers and administered the Holy Sacrament
to 26. Communicants, myself included. Gave for an
Offering at the Altar o. 2. 6. Weston Singers sung the
Christmas Anthem this Morning at Church and very
well indeed. The following old Men dined at my
House to day being Christmas Day. Thos Cary, Thos
Carr, Christ. Dunnell, Nath. Heavers, John Peach-
man, and my Clerk Js. Smith. To each of whom, I
gave after Dinner 1^s/o^d, 6. o. Dinner to Day, Surloin
of Beef rosted and plumb Puddings. It pleased me
much to see the old Folks so happy as they were.

DEC. 29, SATURDAY. . . . Sent Briton to Norwich
this Morning after Newspapers &c. He went on
horse-back. Briton returned home to dinner, no
Letters. Dinner to day, boiled Pork and a rost Goose.
To my Miller's Man, Jⁿ Shorten, Xmas Gift, 1. o.
Revolution Clubbs every where much suppressed and
Constitutional Societies daily increasing all over the
Kingdom. Levelling Principles and Equality almost
discarded.[1]

uneasiness. I must therefore augment my naval and military forces for
prevention and internal defence 'being persuaded that these exertions
are necessary in the present state of affairs, and are best calculated both
to maintain internal tranquillity, and to render a firm and temperate
conduct effectual for preserving the blessings of peace'. It is melancholy
to remember that this speech, with its forlorn hope for the preservation
of peace, was made only six weeks before the great war which lasted,
with two brief intermissions, from 1793 to 1815.

[1] The trial of Louis XVI, the determination of France (decree of
Dec. 15th) to treat Belgium 'according to the rigour of war and of
conquest', and the strong measures taken by the Government roused
the country. As Parson Woodforde says, Constitutional Societies
increased daily, proffering their services against invaders from without
and 'Levellers' within. Chauvelin, the French Envoy in London,
regretfully wrote to his Government during Dec. that England was not
ripe for revolution; in a month the English had quite changed; 'merely

DEC. 31, MONDAY. I breakfasted, dined, &c. again at home. Nancy breakfasted, dined, &c. again at home. Mr. Forster of Lenewade Bridge called on me this Morning, and I paid him a Bill for Flour for the last Year, 3. 19. 6. Paid him also a Years Rent for College-Land due Michaelmas last, the Sum of 16. 0. 0. He brought us, as a present, a few red Herrings. John Piper and his Man, Thos Rudd, Gardners came to prune my Trees this Morning, and they breakfasted, dined, supped and slept here.

1793

JANry 18, FRIDAY. . . . At Cribbage this Evening with Nancy, won, 0. 6. Mem. promised Nancy a new riding Habit and Hat.

JANry 19, SATURDAY. . . . Sent Briton on horseback this morning to Norwich after News-papers &c. Briton returned to dinner. There was a mad dog ran through our Parish Yesterday and by our House, and People after him about our dinner time, we heard nothing of it, till this Afternoon by Briton. Our Dogs I hope escaped. By the public papers this day, there appears but very small hopes at present of the King of France long remaining here upon earth, his blood-thirsty Enemies being so wicked and inveterate against him. Pray God however he may escape, if not, may his earthly Crown be changed into an heavenly one.

JANry 26, SATURDAY. I breakfasted, dined, &c. again at home. Nancy breakfasted, dined, &c. again at home. Dinner to day Souse, Veal Pye and Calfs

through fear of convulsions dangerous to property, they have passed from admiration of us to hatred, and from the enthusiasm of liberty to the delirium of servitude.'

Heart rosted. Billy Bidewells People brought our Newspapers from Norwich. The King of France Louis 16 inhumanly and unjustly beheaded on Monday last by his cruel, blood-thirsty Subjects. Dreadful times I am afraid are approaching to all Europe. France the foundation of all of it. [France declared war on England on Feb. 1st.] The poor King of France bore his horrid fate with manly fortitude and resignation. Pray God he may be eternally happy in thy heavenly Kingdom. And have mercy upon his Queen, 2. Children and their Aunt Princess Elizabeth, all of whom by the Papers are very ill indeed in their confinement. Their lives are in great danger now of being taken away by the French Assassins or Ruffians.[1]

JAN^ry 28, MONDAY. . . . Nancy not over nice this Evening.

FEB. 1st, FRIDAY. . . . Poor young Tom Cary only Child of Taylor Carys about 21 Years of Age, died this Morn' of a violent Fever, very soon carried off. His Parents almost distracted about him. He was beloved by all that knew him it is said as being a very good-natured, inoffensive Man. At Cribbage this Evening wth Nancy won 0. 6.

FEB. 7, THURSDAY. . . . Mr. Custance arrived this

---

[1] Marie Antoinette was guillotined on October 16th, 1793, during the Reign of Terror; her son, Louis XVII (*de jure*), died in 1795; her daughter, Madame Royale, was released to her Austrian relatives in December of the same year, married the Duke of Angoulême in 1799, and survived till 1851. The King's sister, the Princess Elizabeth (described by Horace Walpole in a letter dated November 14th, 1793, as 'the angelic Madame Elizabeth'), was guillotined on May 10th, 1794. Of the execution of Louis XVI, Lecky observes: 'Since the massacre of St. Bartholomew no event in a foreign country had produced such a thrill of horror in England.' Fox declared it to be 'a most revolting act of cruelty and injustice'.

afternoon about 4. o'clock at Weston House from Bath, very well. . . .

FEB. 8. . . . Mr. Custance was so kind as to make us a long morning Visit tho' rainy most of the Morning. Mrs. Custance and Family he left well at Bath. Mrs. Custance sent Nancy by Mr. Custance a small present of Tunbridge Ware, a kind of Vice with a Cushion to pin work to at a Table. Also a large wooden Spoon and a four-pronged wooden Fork for dressing up a Sallad, quite fashion. Mr. Custance looked tolerably well after his Journey. My left side of my Face much swelled again.

MAR. 22, FRIDAY. . . . Got up this morning with a comical kind of a sore throat, not much pain, had something of it Yesterday, rather worse to day—made use of Port Wine Yesterday pretty freely, and some black Currant Rob. Sent poor Frank Clarke, 1. 0. Dinner to day Leg of Mutton rosted &c. Mr. Custance was so kind as to drink Tea and Coffee with us this Afternoon, and stayed till near nine in the Evening, he sets off for Bath soon. Whilst Mr. Custance was here, was seized with a violent pain in the small of my back, which continued the whole Evening, could not move from my Chair without great pain. To a poor travelling Woman going into Kent from Yorkshire gave to her to help her on 1. 0.

APRIL 4, THURSDAY. . . . About 2. o'clock this Afternoon two Men of Sudbury's at Norwich came with my Side-Board and a large New Mohogany Cellaret bought of Sudbury, brought on the Men's Shoulders all the way, and very safe. The Mens Names were Abraham Seily, and Isaac Warren. I gave them what ever they could eat and drink, and when they went away, gave them, 1. 0. to spend either on the Road or at home and sent word by them to Sudbury to pay them handsomely for their Days work. Just as we were going to set down to dinner, Dr. Thorne called on me, on my late poor Butcher's Account, as he is one of the Executors. I paid to him, due from me to Baker 9. 2. 0. I asked him to dine with us but he declined. Dinner to day, Neck of Mutton rosted &c. Poor old Mr. Cary at the Point of Death.

APRIL 5, FRIDAY. ... Mr. Peachman called on me this morning to shew me what was collected already on the Petition that I drew up for poor Peachman and his Wife on the late Fire. There was collected upwards of 7. 0. 0. Rec^d of my Butcher, Stouton, for Tallow, 1. 6. Called this morning at Mr. Carys, and found the old Gentleman almost at his last gasp. Totally senseless with rattlings in his Throat. Dinner to day boiled Beef and Rabbit rosted. Poor old Mr. Cary died this Afternoon.

APRIL 6, SATURDAY. ... Mrs. Bidewell brought our Newspapers and likewise a Letter from my Niece Jane Pounsett in which was a great deal about nothing at all. All Friends however pretty well, except Mr. P. who has very lately had a bad fit of the Gout. ...

APRIL 19, FRIDAY, Fast-Day. ... This being a Day appointed to be observed as a publick Fast in these seditious times and France (the avowed Disturbers of all Peace in Europe) having declared War against us, unprovoked, I walked to Church about 11. o'clock and read Prayers provided on the occasion at Weston Church this Morning, a large Congregation attended Divine Service which I was very glad to meet on the Occasion. Pray God our Prayers may be accepted, the Hearts of all the Enemies to Peace converted, and a happy and general restoration to Peace, good Order and Government re-established to all the different Powers of Europe concerned. I found it very cold [going] to Church and back again rough N.E. Wind with Hail and Snow &c. Dinner to day rost Loin of Pork &c.

APRIL 22, MONDAY. . . . Between eleven and twelve this Morning I drove Nancy over to Mr. Du Quesnes in my Curricle and we spent an Hour with him at Berries Hall and returned home to dinner. Mem. Not asked to Dinner, tho' we should not if so. We found Mr. Du Quesne tolerably well considering he has been ill lately. A Sale to day at the late old Mr. Cary's House. Tho' there was a good deal of Sun to day, yet the Wind from the E. was very cold.

APRIL 29, MONDAY. . . . Dinner to day Neck of Veal rosted &c. Mrs. Andrews (Stephen Andrews's Wife) who has been ill some time, and little or no Appetite was saying to Mrs. Hardy a little time ago, that she should relish she believed a bit of rost Veal from my House if sent unexpectedly, therefore I sent her a Bone of Veal to day with which she was much pleased and ate hearty of it.

MAY 2, THURSDAY. . . . Mr. Du Quesne made us a long morning Visit in his one horse Chaise, came to meet Mr. Priest of Reepham as per Note to him, and from hence Mr. Priest was to return with Mr. Du Quesne to dinner. Mr. Priest however never came and Mr. Du Quesne returned to his own home to dinner, though we asked him to dine with us more than once. He complained much of being terribly shook about in his Chaise by the badness of the roads more particularly those of his own Parish. Mr. Du Quesne is very far advanced in Years but he will not own it. He is by no means fit to drive a single Horse Chaise. His Servant Man that came on horseback with him, was afraid that he would overturn coming along, he cannot see the ruts distinctly, he will not however wear Spectacles at all. He cannot bear to appear old, but must be as young in anything as the youngest Person.

MAY 24, FRIDAY. We breakfasted, supped & slept again at home. We got up soon after six this Morning, dressed and breakfasted, and at half past seven we got into our Curricle and drove to Norwich, found the road very dusty and the Air very cold both going and coming back. We called at both the Priests, saw John Priest & Wife, his Father & Mr. Priest of Reepham. Nancy bought her a new black beaver hat with purple Cockade and band. She gave for it 1. 3. 0. She bought it of One Oxley in the Market place. I also bought a new hat of him, pd. him for it 1. 1. 0. Whilst my Niece was at Barths, Stay & Habit Maker, I walked to Bacons and paid him for Knox's Sermons lately published, one Vol. Octavo 0. 6. 6. To the Widow Studwell, at the China Shop, pd. 0. 8. 0 for Basons &c. To 4 Maccarel, pd. 0. 1. 8. Paid Sudbury for my new Cellaret &c. 4. 4. 6. To 11. Dozen of Buttons Coat & Waistcoat, some Italian, some Clay's Paper ones, all black at Bakers pd. 0. 9. 6. Sent a Letter to my Niece Jane Pounsett. Called at my Mercers, Smiths, and bespoke a Coat, Waistcoat and Breeches of him. Then went to my Taylors Forster, and told him to mak[e] a Suit of Livery for Briton. About 2. o'clock we got into a snug Room at the Wool-Pocket in St. Giles's where our Horses were, and eat some very nice pickled

Salmon which we enjoyed, had a Pint of Port Wine besides Porter, pd. for it o. 3. 6. Nancy then went to try on a new Habit & Stays at Barths, at 5. o'clock called for her, walked with her to [where] St. Bennets Gates lately stood, and at half past 5. got into our Curricle and drove back to Weston Parsonage, where we got thank God safe and well at half past 7. o'clock. It was very cold on our return, glad of our great Coats. Mr. DuQuesne & Mr. Stoughton called at my House to day whilst we were out.

JUNE 4, TUESDAY. . . . Sent Ben early to Norwich this morning after fish. Mr. DuQuesne, Mr. and Mrs. Jeans, and with them a Miss Mist about 16. Years, and Mr. Stoughton Rector of Sparham, dined & spent the Afternoon with us. We had for Dinner fryed Soals, Ham & 3 boiled Chicken, a Surloin of Beef rosted, Gooseberry Tarts &c. Mrs. Jeans very affected, & talked very consequential. Mr. DuQuesne looked very poorly, complained much, eat however pretty tolerably and was jocose. Whist played before and after Tea. I won at Whist with DuQuesne, Jeans & Stoughton 2^s/o^d. The Company did not leave us till half past 8.

JUNE 24, MONDAY. We breakfasted, and spent the morning at Weston Parsonage, after breakfast we were very busy in packing up things in our Trunks for our intended Journey into the West of England as We set off to day. About 2. o'clock this afternoon we left Weston, got into one of the Kings Head Chaises from Norwich, and went for Norwich, got thither about 4. and there dined & spent the Afternoon at the Kings Head. Briton went with us in my little old Cart. Ben went with him to have back the Cart to Weston. At 9. o'clock this Evening we got into the Angel Post

Coach for London. Briton rode on the Top of the
Coach. Paid for our Dinners, Chaise &c. at the Kings
Head 1. 0. 5. To Chaise Driver & Servants at Norwich gave 0. 4. 0. For extra Luggage, paid about
0. 9. 0.

JUNE 25, TUESDAY. After travelling all Night and
till 2. o'clock this Afternoon, we got safe & well
(thanks to Almighty God) to London, to the Angel
Inn at the back of St. Clements near the Strand,
where we dined, supped & slept. To extraordinaries
in the Night, Coachman &c. pd. 0. 5. 0. Nancy &
self bore our Journey last Night very well. Nancys
Brother Saml. supped and spent the Even' with us at
the Angel Inn, he looks thin & pale, but was in good
Spirits.

JUNE 26, WEDNESDAY. We breakfasted, dined,
supped & slept at the Angel Inn. Soon after breakfast
Mr. Saml. Woodforde joined us and being fine
Weather we all walked to Leicester Fields, and there
saw the Panorama, a fine deception in painting of the
British & Russian Fleets at Spithead in the Year [?].
It was well worth seeing indeed, only one Shilling
apiece, I pd. 0. 3. 0. We stayed about an Hour there,
Company continually going to see it. We called at
Samuel's Lodgings in Tavistock Row, Covent Garden,
and saw his Paintings—very good Picture of Carac-
tacus &c. At Reeves Hosiery Warehouse in the
Strand early this Morning for a pair of Boot Stockings,
pd. 0. 4. 6. For a brown travelling worsted Cap, pd.
0. 4. 0. For a Cotton & worsted shaving Cap, pd.
0. 2. 3. For a Silk Purse at the same Shop, pd. 0. 2. 0.
For a Caracature of Charles Fox, pd. 0. 2. 0. Mr.
Saml. Woodforde dined, supped and spent the Evening with us at the Angel. After Coffee and Tea this

Evening we walked to the Theatre in the Haymarket and there saw performed a Comedy called Ways and Means, with the Entertainment of Peeping Tom of Coventry, for 3 Tickets pd. 0. 9. 0. We sat in the Pit and had very good places. It was near 11 o'clock before it was all over.

JUNE 27, THURSDAY. We breakfasted, supped & slept again at the Angel. My Nephew Saml. breakfasted, dined, supped and spent the Evening with us at the Angel Inn. I got up very early this morning and walked into the City to Lombard-Street to Gurney's banking Shop, to change some Norwich Notes, but after staying there some time, was obliged to come away without doing it, their not doing any business till such an Hour. I then went and saw the Mansion House, gave 0. 1. 0. After breakfast We walked into the City and called on Mrs. Gudgeon in Newgate Street. I left my Niece and her Brother at Mr. Gudgeons whilst I went again to Gurneys banking Office and there changed two ten pound Notes for ready Cash—very bluff Folks. I returned from thence to Mr. Gudgeons and they behaved extremely civil & friendly to us all. After regaling ourselves with Chocolate &c. we then walked to the Shakespear Gallery filled with beautiful Paintings. We afterwards went to the Poets Gallery filled also with fine Pictures. There was a Picture of Samls. in one of the Galleries. For seeing the Galleries and for Catalogues, pd. 0. 8. 0. To 2. inside Places in the Bath Post Coach for to Morrow Morn' at 30^s/0^d each, 1. Outside 16^s/0^d, pd. 3. 16. 0. For fishing Hooks & Lines &c. near Temple Bar pd. 9. 0. In the Afternoon we were busy in packing up our things as we go so early to Morrow Morning for Bath. I also paid my Bill at the

Angel this Evening which including Servants & Beds, amounted to 3. 18. 6. To Barber and Servants at the Inn, gave abt. 13. 0.

JUNE 28, FRIDAY. We got up about 4 o'clock this morning and at 5 got into the Bath Coach from the Angel and set off for Bath. Briton on the top of the Coach. The Coach carries only 4 inside Passengers. We had a very fat Woman with a Dog and many band boxes, which much incommoded us, and also a poor sickly good kind of a Man that went with us. We breakfasted at Maidenhead on Coffee & Tea. For Strawberries at Maidenhead pd. 0. 1. 0. For our breakfasts pd. 0. 2. 0. We were very near meeting with an Accident in Reading, passing a Waggon, but thank God we got by safe and well. It was owing to the Coachman. As we went out of Reading we met a Regiment of Soldiers, some Militia going into Reading. At Reading there were two young Gentlemen by name Jolliffe that got up on the top of the Coach, being going home from School for the Vacation. I remembered their Father at Winchester School. We dined at the Pelican Inn, Speanham Land. The young Gentlemen dined with us, I franked them. Their Father lives about 10 Miles beyond Bath. For our Dinners, Coachman &c. pd. abt. 14. 0. Paid at Speenham Land for extra Luggage abt. 4. 0. About 10 o'clock this Evening, thank God, we got safe and well to Bath, to the White Hart Inn, where we supped & slept—a very noble Inn. Found our Friends Mr. and Mrs. Pounsett & Daughter at Bath, at Lodgings in the Orange-Grove, at one Roubelles, all tolerably well. Mr. Pounsett better for being at Bath. They were very glad to see us. For Extraordinaries on the road to day pd. abt. 2. 6. As soon as the young

Jolliffes got to Bath, they hired a Chaise immediately & set off for home. The fat Lady that came with us, supped with us. It was rather late before we got to bed. We were very happy to find that our friends were not gone from Bath. We are to have Lodgings to Morrow in the same house with them.

JUNE 29, SATURDAY. We breakfasted at the Hart and after breakfast paid at the Inn for our Suppers last Night &c. 0. 9. 6. To Servants at the Inn, Barber included 0. 5. 0. We then ordered our Trunks to Mr. Roubelle's in the Orange Grove where our Friends were and then we dined, supped & slept. Mr. Custance & two eldest Sons called on us about Noon & stayed ½ an Hour with us. After Nancy had dressed herself I walked with her to No. 1. Portland-Place and paid our respects to Mrs. Custance and the rest of her Family. We found Mrs. Custance very well indeed and all her eight Children. They were very glad to see us and desired us to dine with them to Morrow.

JUNE 30, SUNDAY. We breakfasted, supped & slept again at Roubelles. We dined & spent the Afternoon at Portland Place with Mr. and Mrs. Custance, & Family. Miss Custance Sister to Mr. Custance also dined with us. My Niece Jane Pounsett went also with us to Portland Place. We spent a very agreeable Day with Mr & Mrs. Custance &c. We had a very handsome Dinner.

JULY 1ST, MONDAY. We breakfasted, dined &c. again at Roubelle's. After we breakfasted Mr. and Mrs. Custance & some of their Children with them made us a morning Visit at Roubelles. Soon after they left us I walked about Bath with my Sister

Pounsett & Daughter and Nancy a shopping. At Perrival's Shop in Milsom Street for three Pieces of Muslin ten Yards each Piece and one Yard & half wide—very great bargain, I paid 3. 15. 0 which was only twenty five Shillings apiece. I gave one Piece to my Sister Pounsett, another to my Niece Pounsett and the other Nancy had.

JULY 2, TUESDAY. We breakfasted at Roubelles, supped & slept there again. Nancy & self dined & spent the Afternoon at Portland-Place with Mr. & Mrs. Custance and Family and a Miss Welcher Governess to the young Ladies. For a Small box-trunk this morning of one Maxfield on the borough walls paid 0. 10. 6. To a Mr. Jones, Mercer in the Abbey Church Yard for two Yrds. and $\frac{3}{4}$, Superfine black thin Cloth at 19^s/0^d, 2. 2. 9. To ditto, for 1 Yrd. $\frac{3}{4}$ rich florentine at 12^s/0^d, 1. 1. 0. At Perrivals Shop for another Piece of Muslin ten Yards and 1 Yrd. $\frac{1}{2}$ wide, which I intend to give Sister White, 1. 5. 0.

JULY 3, WEDNESDAY. We breakfasted at Roubelles and spent the Morning at Bath. About 1. o'clock we all set off from Bath in two Post-Chaises for Cole. Myself and 2. Nieces in the first Chaise. Mr. Pounsett & Sister in another. Gave to Servants at Bath, Barber &c. included 3. 6. We got to Frome about 3. o'clock to the George Inn where we dined. Our Chaise got to Frome very near an hour before Mr. Pounsetts. Market Day at Frome. For the Bath Chaise and Driver pd. and gave 16. 0. For our Dinners &c. at Frome, I paid abt. 13. 6. We all arrived safe and well to Cole (thanks to God) about 9. o'clock this Evening, very little fatigued, and then we supped & slept at the old House. For the Frome Chaise to Cole & Driver, pd. abt. 15. 0. To Horses from Bath to Cole for Briton pd. abt. 9. 0. Nancy's Brother Willm. & Wife we found at Mr. Pounsetts. My Brother John we also saw this Evening at Cole.

July 8, Monday. We supped and slept again at Cole. At 7. o'clock this morning I took a Walk with Nancy to Mrs. R. Clarkes at C. Cary, and there breakfasted, dined, & spent the Afternoon, with her, my Brother & Wife. Between breakfast & dinner I took a Walk to Gallhampton to Willm. Woodfordes, stayed about an hour & half with him & Wife & returned to Cary to dinner. Willm. & Wife behaved very friendly and kind. Willm. has made a very pretty place of his little Cottage. Intensely hot indeed all day, sweated amazingly. Dinner to day, Peas & Bacon, boiled Beef, a Couple of Ducks rosted, and a Gooseberry Pye. We returned to Cole in the Evening about 9. as we went.

July 16, Tuesday. We supped & slept again at Cole. Very hot to day. About 8. o'clock this morning, I walked with Nancy and my Niece Jane Pounsett to Castle-Cary, and there breakfasted at Mrs. R. Clarkes with her, my Brother & Wife, Mr. and Mrs. Gudgeon from London, Mr. Gudgeons Father from Town and old Mr. Pope of Shepton-Mallett, Father to Mrs. Gudgeon. We had a very genteel breakfast indeed, Coffee & Tea, bread & Butter, cold Tongue &c. After breakfast I walked with Nancy & Jenny Pounsett to different houses in Castle-Cary, shopping &c. At Noncullus's Shop for 2. Pair of brown thread Stockings to wear under boots &c. pd. 0. 6. 0. At Fields at the Angel at Cary for some Negus pd. 0. 1. 0. We dined & spent the Afternoon at Sister Whites at Ansford with her, her Son Robert, Mr. Fooks Attorney at Shepton-Mallett, Sister Pounsett, and a Master

Charles Webster. We had for dinner Ham & Chicken, boiled Whiting, Beans & Peas, a Couple of Ducks rosted and a Currant Pye, with a hearty welcome. Called on my old Uncle Mr. Thos. Woodforde & his wife, also on their Son Mr. Frank & Family, they all behaved very genteelly. My Uncle very hearty, 87 Years of Age, walked with us from his own house to the Parsonage without a Stick. My Aunt is 84, & pretty hearty considering. Sister Pounsett was carried to Ansford in Robt. Whites Chaise but she walked back with us, we did not get to Cole till near 10. o'clock. We were all fatigued but Nancy bore it the best of all. Very hot to day. Gave Sister [White's] Servants, Willm. Coleman & Maid 0. 2. 0. Gave Mr. Robt. Whites Children Sophia & Robt. 0. 2. 0. Saw my old running Footman J^n_o Coles, gave him 1. 0. Lord Willoughby de Broke & Lady came to Mr. Frank Woodfordes this Evening.

AUGUST 14, WEDNESDAY. . . . At Quadrille this Evening lost 0. 0. 6^d. Had an unpleasant Letter this Evening from my Maid Betty Dade at Weston Parsonage in Norfolk, informing me that my other Maid Winifred Buderoy has turned out very bad, was with Child and so near her time that she was paid her Wages & sent away from my house which was very well managed by Betty. Poor Mr. DuQuesne rather worse than better.

SEPT. 26, THURSDAY. . . . We were sorry to see on this Days Paper from Bath that our very valuable and worthy Friend the Revd. Mr. DuQuesne of Tuddenham was no more. It is a very great Loss to us, but I hope to him, Gain. Pray God he may be eternally happy. Dinner to day boiled Leg of Mutton & a rosted Rabbit. In the Afternoon Miss Webb and

Miss Hussey went in a Wincaunton Chaise (which was sent for them) to Wincaunton to spend a few days there and then for Bath and London. They left us between 4. and 5. in the Afternoon. At Cribbage this Evening with Mr. Pounsett, lost 1. 6.

OCT. 7, MONDAY. . . . Very busy all the Morning in packing up our great Trunk, which is to go by the London Waggon to Morrow from Castle Cary. . . .

OCT. 11, FRIDAY. We breakfasted at Cole & spent part of the Morn' there. To Mr. Pounsetts Servants gave 1. 1. 0. To Sybbil & Sally at the other house gave 0. 5. 0. About 11. o'clock this morning we took our leave of our Cole Friends, got into one of Bruton Chaises and went off for Frome, got to Frome by one o'clock, had some little refreshment there for which I paid about 0. 3. 6. For the Bruton Chaise, single Horse & Driver pd. 1. 2. 0. About 2. o'clock we got into a Frome Chaise for Bath, but had not gone above 500. Yards from the Inn, going up Frome Hill, when on a sudden turn up the Hill we met with a large tilted London Waggon with eight Horses in it and very heavily loaden, and it being very narrow where we met it, the Driver of the Chaise in backing his Horses to avoid being drove over overturned the Chaise, but very providentially blessed be Almighty God for it! we received very little Injury, Nancys Face was a little bruised. It was a wonder that we escaped so well, as we were afraid that the Waggon would have crushed us. Briton got off his Horse & stopped the Horses in the Waggon, The Waggoner being rather behind. The Chaise Windows & Pole were broke, we therefore walked back to the Inn, stayed about half an Hour till the Pole was mended, and then set off in the same Chaise for Bath. We got to

Bath (thank God safe & well) about six o'clock this Evening, to the White Hart Inn in Stall Street, kept by one Pickwick, where we drank Tea, supped and slept, a very good, very capital Inn, everything in stile. Sent Briton this Evening with a Basket of Game to Mr. & Mrs. Custance No. 1. Portland Place. There were in it a brace of Pheasants & a Hare. For the Frome Chaise, single Horse & Driver pd. 1. 2. 0. [They stayed at Bath till Oct. 16th.]

OCT. 16, WEDNESDAY. We got up this morning at 5 o'clock and at six sat off in the Oxford Post-Coach for Oxford. Two young Gentlemen went with us in it. Gave the Porter that called us &c. 0. 1. 0. We all breakfasted at Chippenham pd. there 0. 2. 6. We dined at Cricklade, paid there 0. 6. 0. We passed thro' Malmsbury and there staying to change Horses, we walked and saw the Ruins of Malmesbury Abbey & Church, gave the Clerk 0. 1. 0. About 8 o'clock this Evening we got safe & well to Oxford (blessed be God for it) to the Angel Inn in High Street, where we supped & slept. To Coachmen to day gave 0. 4. 0. Paid also to the Coachman the remaining fare 1. 7. 0. For Luggage also paid him 0. 4. 0. We were rather tired & jaded before we got to bed.

OCT. 17, THURSDAY. We breakfasted, dined, supped & slept at the Angel Inn. After breakfast we walked about the University by ourselves. A Meeting of the Warden & Fellows of New-College being this morning we did not call there. We went to Christ Church and called at Dr. Bathursts but he and Family were in the Country. I called at New-College about 2. o'clock this Afternoon saw Caldecot and Mr. Cook who was last Year presented to the Living of Hardwiche, and also saw Mr. Sissmore who

behaved very kindly to me. They desired me much
to dine at College to Morrow. Caldecot shewed me
the improvements making in the Chapel, which when
finished will be one of the finest Sights in the whole
University. After Dinner I took another Walk with
my Niece and shewed her more of the University.
She went with me this Evening to Magdalen College
Chapel to Prayers. We returned to our Inn to Tea,
and after Tea I walked into St. Giles's and called on
my Friend Dr. Holmes formerly of New-Coll. saw
him, Wife & Sister, desired him to give my Niece a
Dinner to Morrow at his House, as I am to dine at
New-College then—rather formal reception. I called
at Dr. Walls in St. Giles's but did not see him. In my
return to my Inn called on the Head of Exeter College
Dr. Stinton who is bad in the Gout stayed about half
an Hour and then went to my Inn. Called on my
Friend Locke the Silversmith this Morning who
behaved very obligingly and knew me at first Sight.
I changed a ten Pound Note with him, he keeps a
Bank and does great Business. Dr. Holmes's Wife is a
very agreeable Woman, and his Sister is very pleasant,
exactly like him. The high Street of Oxford greatly
improved since I last saw it all paved like London,
and I think is one of the finest Streets in the Kingdom.
[On Oct. 19th the Diarist and Nancy proceed to
London which they left on Oct. 22nd for Norwich via
Bury.]

OCT. 23, WEDNESDAY. We arrived at Bury about
3 o'clock in the Morn' and there dropped our inside
Passenger, and there took up three Ladies, one of
them, a Miss Baldwin of Reepham who went with us
to Norwich, all of them very agreeable. We breakfasted at Tivetshall Ram, pd. there 0. 2. 6. We

travelled all the Night with Lights. About 11 o'clock this Morning We got safe & well to Norwich (thanks to Almighty God for it) and but little fatigued tho' we travelled all night. To the Coachman from London, gave 0. 4. 0. For extraordinary Luggage, paid 0. 10. 6. We dined at the Kings Head, our old Inn, and could scarce get a Room to dine in, being very full. Soon after dinner we got into one of the Kings Head Chaises and went off for Weston, where we got safe and well & found all my People at Weston Parsonage very well & glad to see us, thank God! about 5 o'clock this Afternoon. Paid at the Kings Head for our Dinners Chaise &c. 1. 1. 4. Gave to poor lame Joe, the Boot Catch 0. 1. 0. Gave the Driver of the Chaise 0. 2. 0. We drank Tea, supped and slept once more at our old House, Weston Parsonage. Whilst we were at Norwich I wrote a Letter to my Sister Pounsett informing her of our safe arrival at Norwich, & put it into the Post Office myself. Accept O Almighty God! my sincere & unfeigned thanks for thy great goodness to us, in our late long Journey into the West & back again, and all the dangers we have escaped, particularly for that great & providential escape near Frome in Somersett. Lord! ever make us thankful, and may thy divine goodness ever protect us. Travelling Expenses and others from June 23, 1793 from the time we left Weston to our return back again this Evening to Weston, amounted in the whole—78. 19. 7.

OCT. 24, THURSDAY. . . . We were busy all the morning in unpacking our Trunks. Gave Betty a new Gown bought in London.

OCT. 25, FRIDAY. . . . Mr. Maynard of Morton called on me this Morn' to desire me to [sign?] his

Testimonium, being lately presented to the Living of Morton by Capn. Le Grisse which I did; he is to hold for a Minor—16 Years old. . . .

Oct. 26, Saturday. . . . Paid Briton this morning for divers things 0. 9. 3½. Paid Betty also for things in my absence 1. 13. 2½. Recd. of Betty for Butter sold in absence 2. 19. 2½. Sent Ben early this morning to Norwich after my great Trunk and to bring back some Coal for me. He returned with the above between 5. and 6 o'clock. I privately baptized a Child of John Tooley's this morning at my House, by name Elizabeth. I also privately baptized a Child of Clare Driver's this Evening being ill, by name Hannah. I nominated and appointed Thos. Thurston to being Clerk, in the room of poor old J. Smith. Dinner to day boiled Neck of Mutton & a rost fowl.

Nov. 2, Saturday. . . . Sent Briton early this morning to Norwich in my little old Cart after News & many other things. Sent by him also a Letter to put into the Post Office for the Revd. Mr. Sissmore of New-College, Oxford, and in it a Norwich Bank Note of Gurneys of ten Pounds, to be presented to the Society of New-College, towards the improvements in their Chapel, which when finished will be great and will be well worth every observer 10. 0. 0.

Nov. 4, Monday. . . . After breakfast I drove Nancy over to Witchingham being fine Morn' to Mr. Jeans's and spent the remaining part of the Morn' with him & his Wife. We met with Mr. Jeans in our Parish coming to us. Mrs. Jeans is far advanced in pregnancy. We stayed there till almost 2. o'clock, they pressed us much to dine with them, but there being no Moon and likewise some Rain falling we could not, but borrowed an Umbrella and Mr. Jeans's french Cloke for Nancy & returned home by three o'clock. It rained tho' very gently all the way. Dinner to day Knuckle of Veal boiled & Pigs face and a Neck of Pork rosted with apple Sauce. Mrs. Jeans was pressing for us to dine with them more than was agreeable. It was rather beyond the Line of being pleasing.

Nov. 19, Tuesday. . . . Got up very early this morning about half past five. Brewed a Barrel of Table Beer to day. We took a Walk this morning to Weston House, it being very pleasant, and walked over most part of it, we found it as well as could be expected but for want of fires, it feels rather cold, and some of the Paper in the Rooms, rather faded. We also walked over the Garden, which appeared in tolerable good order, kept by Knights & Son. Gave Knight's Son, bringing some Strawberry Plants to us Yesterday Morning o. 1. o. I found myself very unwell this Aft. so very low. The Gout flying about me. Very much oppressed with Wind in my Stomach. Dinner to-day Neck of Pork rosted &c. I eat but little.

Nov. 25, Monday. . . . Mr. and Mrs. Bodham made us a long Morning Visit, it gave us much pleasure to see them. Mr. Bodham looked poorly & complained much. Mrs. Bodham appeared rather thinner than usual. They were so kind as to bring us a profile Picture of our late worthy Friend Mr. DuQuesne. They eat a Biscuit with us & drank a Glass of Wine. I am much afraid that poor Mr. Bodham is not long one of this World, he is much altered. Soon after Mr. and Mrs. Bodham left us, Mr. Priest of Reepham called on us in his way to Honingham Hall where he dines and sleeps at Mr. Townshends. He is gone to settle Mr. DuQuesne's

Affairs with him. I privately baptized a Child of Hubbard's this Afternoon by name John at my House. Dinner to day, boiled beef &c. N.B. Blackbirds & Thrushes singing this Morn' in our Garden as if it was Spring, very mild. Thank God! that I continue bravely & can eat. N.B. Took 4 more of Nancy's Pills this Evening.

Nov. 27, Wednesday. ... To a poor Kentish Man who goes about the Country and plays Tunes on the Church-Bells, gave 0. 1. 0. Thank God I still continue finely and go on taking the Pills every other Night. Took four this Evening, going to bed. Sleep very well again.

Dec. 11, Wednesday. ... My poor old Spanish Dog, by name Spring, was found this morning dead and stiff, under the hay Stack, worn out with age, being 14. Years old. He has looked very thin and poor some time. ...

Dec. 25, Wednesday also Christmas Day. We breakfasted, dined, &c. again at home. This being Christmas Day I walked to Church this morning, read Prayers and administered the Holy Sacrament, gave for an Offering 0. 2. 6. Had a very respectable Appearance at the Altar to partake with me of the H. Sacrament, 2. Rails. The Singers sang the Christmas Anthem and very well, between the Litany & Communion. The following poor People dined at my House or had their Dinner sent them & one Shilling each—Widow Case, my Clerk Tom Thurston, Christopher Dunnell, John Peachman, Tom Carr and Nathaniel Heavers. Nat. Heavers & Tom Carr had their Dinners sent them being ill. Gave to the above People in all 0. 6. 0. Dinner to day, a boiled Rabbit

and Onion Sauce, Surloin of Beef rosted, plumb
Puddings and Mince Pies.

1794

JAN. 17, FRIDAY. . . . Mr. Girling called on me this
morning and paid his Composition for Tithe last Year
44. 16. 0. Dinner to day, Odds and Ends. Mr. Jeans
on horseback with his Daughter behind him, made us
a morning Visit.

JAN. 19, SUNDAY. We breakfasted, dined, &c. again
at home. I read Prayers & Preached this Morn', only
few being there. Dinner to day, Breast of Veal rosted
&c. Nancy made me very uneasy this Afternoon and
does very often, by complaining of the dismal Situation of my House, nothing to be seen, and little or
no visiting, or being visited &c. If we have of late lost
our best Friends, by the removal of Mr. Custance's
Family to Bath, and the Death of Mr. DuQuesne,
must it not be affected by me as well as her? In short
my Place has been too dull for her I am sorry to say
for many Years.—As things are so—infœlix!

JAN. 25, SATURDAY. We breakfasted, dined, &c.
again at home. About Noon very high Wind indeed
with some Snow. Barometer very low down to 28—7.
I don't know that I ever saw it lower. Sent Briton to
Norwich after News &c. he went in my little old Cart,
and returned in very good time before 4. this Afternoon. A terrible Journey he had back, so very rough
Wind, with Snow and intensely cold. He said, it
almost took away his breath. Mem.—The Barometer
about 4. o'clock this Afternoon was down to 28—4,
the lowest I ever remembered. The Wind so high that

it greatly alarmed us. Part of my Barn uncovered by it, Thatch blown off, Many Tiles from my House blown down &c. Pray God: preserve all that are exposed to it particularly all poor Souls on board Ships. Dinner to day a Couple of Rabbits boiled and Onion Sauce, some beef Steakes &c. But the Wind was so very tempestuous at dinner time, that we made a very poor dinner. The Wind rather somewhat abated towards the Evening but still very high. Glass rather rose. I sat up in my Study the whole Night.

JAN. 27, MONDAY. . . . Had but a very indifferent night of Sleep, having the Cramp in both feet great part of the Night owing I apprehend to the extreme cold Weather as it frose very sharp within doors last night. Very much indisposed all the Day, appetite very bad indeed, and Spirits greatly depressed for want of more natural rest. The last two Nights deprivation of Sleep, have much unhinged me. Dinner to day, boiled Tongue and Mashed potatoes and some rost Pork &c. Exceeding cold all day, froze within doors all the Day. The present severe cold Weather pinches me greatly. It snowed all the Morning but it was very small. Afternoon mostly clear but intensely cold indeed. Parliament met on Tuesday last January 21. Kings Speech very good and spirited one. Mr. Pitt 218—Majority in the House of Commons. I did not hear of any great damage being done by the High Wind Saturday, thanks to God for it.

JAN. 28, TUESDAY. . . . Thank God! had some tolerable Sleep last Night. Very severe frost indeed, freezes sharp within doors and bitter cold it is now. Two Women froze to death Saturday last going from Norwich Market to their home. . . .

JAN. 30, THURSDAY. . . . Had a very indifferent

Night of sleep scarce any at all. Recd. of my Butcher for Tallow at 3ᵈ per lb. 0. 2. 9. A Frost again but not so sharp as Yesterday. It did not freeze within doors last Night. Recd. for Butter this Evening at 1ˢ/0ᵈ, 0. 2. 6. It froze also in the Afternoon, and the Barometer still rising, but in the Evening it thawed and some Rain fell. I was saying before dinner that there would be alteration of Weather soon as I a long time observed one of our Cats wash over both her Ears— an old observation and now I must believe it to be a pretty true one. Dinner to day Peas Soup & rost Neck of Pork &c. Ben went out a tracing for a Hare this morning before breakfast, found one, and killed it, but the Greyhounds had eat full half of it, before Ben could get up to beat them off. After breakfast Ben & Briton went out a tracing till dinner time and they brought home a brace of fine Hares.

JAN. 31, FRIDAY. . . . A great many Rats & Mice killed in the Barn this morning by the Dogs in moving the Wheat. Thank God! slept very well last Night and got up this Morning much better than of late. It was quite mild to day to what it has been. Dinner to day rost Beef &c.

FEB. 10, MONDAY. We breakfasted, dined, &c. again at home. Between 11. and 12. o'clock this morning we took a Walk to Hungate Lodge, and paid our respects to Mr. and Mrs. Carbould, who came there to reside on Thursday last and were married that Morning at Talcolneston by Mrs. Carbould's Father the Revd. Mr. Warren, and was the first time of our ever seeing either of them. They behaved very friendly to us as well as politely and appear to be very agreeable, pleasant People. We were treated with Chocolate & Wedding Cake. Mr. Carbould is a

Clergyman and Son of a Mr. Carbould, many Years
an Hatter at Norwich of whom I have had many a
Hat. He has retired from business about 5. or 6.
Years, and with a fortune of at least 15. Thousand
Pound. He has only two Children one Son & one
Daughter. We called on Mrs. Peachman as we went
there. Paid my Butcher (Billy Stoughton) this morning his Quarterly Bill for Meat the Sum of 10. 8. 6.
The roads were very dry, but the Wind very rough
indeed as we went to Mr. Carboulds this morning and
likewise on our return home.

FEB. 11, TUESDAY. . . . To 7. Yards of Cotton a
mixed Colour of black, purple and Green, for a morning Gown for myself, this Morning of Aldridge at
2^s/2^d. per Yrd. pd. 0. 15. 2. Of Ditto for 7. Yrds of
white Cotton for a lining to the above at 1^s/0^d per
Yard, pd. 0. 7. 0. Of Ditto, for a Pr. of Castle-Cary
Stockings pd. 0. 5. 0. Dinner to day, Leg of Pork
boiled & Peas Pudding. Mr. Custance arrived at
Weston House this Aft. from Bath, after being absent
almost a whole Year. I sent to enquire for him in the
Evening. To a poor Man of N. Tuddenham out of
work and a very cleanly old Man, gave this Morn'
0. 0. 6.

FEB. 12, WEDNESDAY. . . . Mr. Custance very
kindly made us a morning Visit and stayed with us
more than an Hour. He was in high Spirits & appeared happy to be again at Weston. But he looked
very thin. . . .

FEB. 14, FRIDAY. . . . This being Valentines Day,
I gave to the Children of my Parish that came to my
House this morning under fourteen Years of Age and
could walk and talk, to each gave a penny and I gave

in all 53. of them 0. 4. 5. Mr. Carbould gave one halfpenny to each. Dinner to day boiled Pork & Greens & a Suet Pudding. There was a total Eclipse of the Moon this Evening. It begun about 8. o'clock and did not end till 12. But it being very cloudy could not see anything at all of it.

FEB. 23, SUNDAY. . . . I read Prayers & Preached this Afternoon at Weston-Church which was very full of People. Mattishall Singers were at Church and sung exceedingly well, attended with a bass-Viol and an Hautboy—Betty's Father was one of them. Mr. Custance at Church, as were also the new Bride Mrs. Carbould & her Sister in law Miss Carbould, they sat in my Seat in the Chancel, also their Servant Maid sat in my Servants Seat. Dinner to day, Shoulder of Mutton rosted &c.

FEB. 28, FRIDAY. We breakfasted, dined, &c. again at home. I read Prayers this Morning at Weston Church being a day appointed for a public Fast to be observed throughout England, to implore the Almighty's Protection from our Enemies. Mr. Custance was at Church this Morn' tho' wet. A large Congregation also attended Divine Service. There was no Sermon. Dinner to day Salt Fish & Parsnips &c.

MARCH 7, FRIDAY. . . . Paid Robert Buck of Honingham for his Father a blacksmith for Iron-Work done to Cart &c. 0. 16. 0. Nancy drove out Rodney in the new Cart this Morning by way of an airing. Briton with her. I took a walk this morning by myself to Weston House to see Mr. Custance, but he being rode out I walked on to Mr. Jeans at Witchingham, and in my walk there, I called at Mr. Fosters at Lenewade Bridge and spent about half an hour there with him, his Wife, her Mother Mrs. Chambers, and I think her Sister. Got to Mr. Jeans about 1. o'clock, stayed abt. an hour with Mr. & Mrs. Jeans, & returned back to Weston-House about half past two, saw Mr. Custance and chatted with him about half an hour and then returned home to dinner. Saw Mr. and Mrs. Copland at Mr. Jeans. At Betty Cary's Shop this Evening for things pd. o. 1. o. Had 2. Tubbs of Geneva brought me this Evening by Moonshine, 4. Gallons each Tub. Sent a Note this Evening to Mr. Carbould at Hungate Lodge to invite him, Mrs. Carbould & Miss Carbould to dinner on Wednesday next. Recd. a Note back that they would wait on us. Note shockingly bad wrote.

MARCH 8, SATURDAY. . . . Busy this morning in bottling off Moonshine. . . .

MARCH 24, MONDAY. Sent Ben, early this morning to old Mr. Gould's of Swannington, after a Horse, upon trial in my little Cart, he having lately given me a very favourable Account of him as one that would do in the place of Rodney which is gone blind. Ben returned with the Horse before breakfast; on liking the Appearance of him, after breakfast I drove him out in my Curricle and taking Nancy with me, we went to Mr. Jeans at Witchingham, stayed there upwards of an hour and then returned home, much pleased with the Horse. I am to give Gould for the Horse 15. Guineas if I liked him on trial. He is of a dark Chestnut Colour, very compact make, of the Suffolk kind, short body, handsome forehand, just the height for our little Curricle, hog mane, short dock Tail, and the only blemish in him, is a bone Spavin in the oft hind Leg, which at present is by no means bad,

he goes a little limping at first setting out. His Age
I apprehend to be about 8. Years. His Name is
Punch. Nancy likes him very much. Both Mr. &
Mrs. Jeans were at home & glad to see us. Briton
went with us on foot. I walked however some of the
way there and back again. I could not spare another
Horse being busy in plowing and Rodney gone to
Goulds to supply Punchs place. I sent Ben this
Evening after Rodney to Goulds and to let him know
that I liked his Horse very well and that he would call
on me the first Opportunity and I would pay him for
the horse. Dinner to day, boiled beef &c.

APRIL 3, THURSDAY. . . . Richmond's Goose that
we bought some Years ago brought forth 13. Goslings
from 13. Eggs.

APRIL 11, FRIDAY. . . . One of my Greyhounds,
young Fly, got to Betty Cary's this morning and ran
away with a Shoulder of Mutton undressed & eat it
all up. They made great lamentation & work about
it. I had the Greyhound hanged in the Evening. . . .

APRIL 12, SATURDAY. . . . Newspapers brought by
Bidewells People. A County Meeting held to day at
Norwich concerning voluntary contributions for the
internal defence of the Country in the present Crisis
in case of a french Invasion, or any Riots &c. I did
not go to it, neither did Mr. Custance.

APRIL 22, E. TUESDAY. . . . Hearing Yesterday
that Mr. Mellish, who succeeded Mr. DuQuesne was
come to reside at Tuddenham, I drove over to the old
House and paid my respects to him this morning,
stayed about half an Hour with him and returned
home to dinner. Mr. Mellish is quite a young Man,
fair with flaxen hair, rather short & lisps, very much

of the true Gentleman in his behaviour. There was another young Clergyman with him who was on a Visit for a few days there. In my return home I called at Mr. Corboulds and took up my Niece who was there. Dinner to day boiled beef & mince Veal &c.

APRIL 23, WEDNESDAY. . . . It being a very fine pleasant Morning I drove my Niece over to Mattishall to Mr. Bodhams and made them a long Visit, but we returned home to dinner. Mr. Bodham is I think better, but worse than ever with regard to his temper, for ever scolding & finding fault.

MAY 5, MONDAY. . . . At twelve we took a Walk to Weston House and spent an agreeable hour with him [Mr. Custance]. He walked over his Garden with us. We carried him a Couple of Dozen of our small Cakes, as he is fond of them. He walked great part of the way with us on our return.

MAY 14, WEDNESDAY. We breakfasted, and spent part of the Morning at home, about 11. o'clock I drove Nancy in my little Curricle to Norwich, and we got thither about 12 o'clock after a very pleasant ride, Briton went on horseback with us, put up ourselves and horses at the Kings-head in the Market-Place, our old Inn and there we dined supped and slept. Briton went with us on the Mare, Jenny. In the Evening we went to the Theatre and saw acted a Comedy called the School for Wives. The Entertainment, Midas, a very good house. It was for the benefit of one Jackson. The Song of God save the King was sung with great Glee. We did not return to our Inn till 11. o'clock. Dinner to day, fresh Salmon & Veal Cutlets &c. It was so hot at the Theatre, that Nancy was quite ill on her return to the Inn, could eat nothing for Supper. Soon after we got to Norwich,

I walked about the City and paid many Bills that I owed, viz. To Lock, Timber-Merchant, pd. 1. 3. 0. To Sudbury, Upholsterer, pd. 5. 7. 0. To Forster, Taylor, pd. 4. 9. 6. To Bacon, Bookseller, pd. 0. 16. 3. To Priest, Wine-Merchant, pd. 2. 4. 0. To Steward, Attorney, pd. 6. 7. 1½. To Buckle, Ironmonger, pd. 0. 9. 6. For two Box Tickets for the Play, pd. 0. 6. 0. Gave Briton also to go to the Play 0. 1. 0. To Ratifee-Cakes 2. oz., of Blacks, pd. 0. 0. 3. We called on both the Priests Families, this Morning. To Rum & Water at the White Hart, pd. 0. 0. 3.

MAY 15, THURSDAY. We breakfasted, dined, &c. at the Kings Head. I got up very early this Morning between four and 5. o'clock and saw a Regiment of Militia March out of Town, the South-Lincoln. After breakfast, I walked out with Nancy to Miss Brownes to see the Fashions. Gave Nancy a very handsome Sash &c. paid for the same, 0. 18. 0. Mr. Bloome waited on me this morning at the Kings Head and we settled Accounts together. I paid him for Coals & Oats 16. 2. 0. And I recd. of him for Corn 49. 16. 6. So that I recd. on the balance 33. 14. 6. After that I walked about by myself & pd. more Bills. To Smith, Mercer, pd. 8. 4. 0. To Frank, Barber, for a Wigg, pd. 1. 1. 0. To Mrs. Brewster, Haberdasher, pd. 3. 10. 6. To Manning, Brazier, pd. 0. 4. 6. To Willmott, Hatter, pd. 0. 19. 6. Nancy bought her a pretty Hat suitable to the Sash.

MAY 16, FRIDAY. We breakfasted & spent the Morning at Norwich. I got up again very early this morning to see some more Soldiers march out of Town. At Graham's Shop for a pr. of black Silk Stockings and changing another pair that I bought there last Year which did not fit me, pd. 0. 16. 0. To

4. pair of white worsted Gauze Do., pd. o. 7. 4. To divers trifling things & given away abt. o. 1. o. At Nosworthy's for some shaving Soap &c. pd. o. 2. o. A Regiment of the Leicester Militia we saw March into Town about Noon from Yarmouth very much fatigued indeed, being a long March. Soon after they were balloted, we ordered our Carriage and sat off for Weston. Got home thank God! safe & well & in good Spirits by four o'clock this Aft. & there dined on some cold Fore Qr. of Lamb, supped & slept at home. Paid at the Kings Head for ourselves and Horses two Nights & part of three Days, 1. 19. 11.

MAY 31, SATURDAY. ... Mr. Custance made us a Morning Visit to take his leave of us, being going to Bath very soon. He seemed very low on the thoughts of quitting Weston. I was quite sorry to see Mr. Custance so dejected. I believe he goes from Weston to Morrow Morning.

JUNE 4, WEDNESDAY. ... It being the Kings Birth-Day, I put the Ship into the Lagoon in my Garden, full dressed ...

JUNE 10, TUESDAY. ... This being Whit-Tuesday, Weston-Purse-Club, took their annual perambulation round the Parish. I gave to them as usual o. 10. 6. There are thirty of them and to that Number they confine themselves, which is very right of them. Dinner to day, Leg Lamb boiled & Loin fryed &c. In the Evening we walked to Hungate-Lodge and drank Coffee and Tea, by appointment, with Mr. and Mrs. Corbould, old Mr. Corbould and Miss, a Mrs. Bell and a Miss Perkins, a sharp Girl but not handsome. Mrs. Bell is own Sister to the late Mr. Baldwin[1]

[1] James Baldwin, Rector of Lyng with Whitwell 1757–83, and of Brandon Parva 1745–83.

of Ling. After Coffee we got to Cards, two Tables, one Quadrille the other Whist, Mr. Corbould Senr. and Miss with Mrs. Bell, played at Quadrille, Mr. & Mrs. Corbould against Miss Perkins and self—we lost, but only o. o. 6. Nancy lost at Quadrille o. 1. 6. We did not get home till very near 10 o'clock. Thank God! appeared something better to day.

JUNE 11, WEDNESDAY. . . . Sent Ben early this morning to Norwich with my great Cart, after my new Garden Roller of Cast-Iron. He returned home with it before two o'clock and brought some Maccarel which we had for dinner with a very nice small Neck of Pork rosted &c. It is a very clever Roller and is called the ballance Roller, as the handle never goes to the Ground. It is certainly very expensive but certainly also very handy. The Roller amounts in the whole to 4. o. o. viz.: Cast-Iron 2 cwt.—2 qrs.—26 lb., at $2\frac{1}{2}^{d}$ per lb. 2. 17. 6. Hammer'd-Iron, 40 lb. at $6\frac{3}{4}^{d}$, do. 1. 2. 6. Ben had leave to dine out, & to stay out all Night.

JUNE 15, SUNDAY. We breakfasted, dined, &c. again at home. I read Prayers, Preached and christened two Children this Afternoon at Weston Church. Nancy walked with me to Church being pleasant. Great News, Lord Howe has beat the French Fleet took seven Men of War with about 5,000 Men. Lord Hood also has beat the French in Corsica.[1] Dinner to day fore-Qr. of Lamb rosted &c. Between Tea and Supper Mr. and Mrs. Corbould in

---

[1] The French Fleet had gone out from Brest to safeguard a convoy of grain from America; the convoy got in, but the Fleet was utterly defeated by Lord Howe (1725–99) on June 1st, off Ushant. About the same time Lord Hood was in process of capturing Corsica with Nelson's help. It is interesting to remember that Nelson's father was a Norfolk country parson—the Rev. Edmund Nelson, Rector of Burnham Thorpe.

taking their Evening Walk called on us and stayed about an hour with us.

JUNE 18, WEDNESDAY. ... Mr. and Mrs. Carbould called on us this Evening between Tea & Supper & stayed an hour or better with us. They came home from Norwich to dinner to day. They told us a good deal about the Guild as they were at it—A great many People but very few great folks. Mrs. Corbould met with a sad Accident at the Assembly last Night during Tea-Time. A Tea Kettle of boiling Water was by some Accident or another overturned into Mrs. Corboulds lap, but providentially did not scald her, she was obliged to leave the Assembly Room directly, and did not return any more to it.

JULY 2, WEDNESDAY. ... I got up very early again this morning [he was at Norwich] and took a long walk before breakfast; bad News from the continent this morning—The French have beat the Allies.[1]

JULY 7, MONDAY. ... Exceeding hot indeed this Morning, Therm. 102. To a poor Sailor having lost his left hand, gave 1. 0. ...

JULY 17, THURSDAY. ... Soon after Eleven this Morning I drove Nancy over to Mr. Mellishs at East-Tuddenham and paid our respects to Mr. Mellishs Mother and his Sister, we stayed near an Hour with them and then returned home to dinner—They are very genteel, and fashionable Ladies—Miss Mellish

---

[1] The Allies were beaten by the Republican Army under Jourdan at the battle of Fleurus on June 26th, 1794, and on July 5th they determined to evacuate Belgium after a series of defeats which had begun with that of the Duke of York at Tourcoing on May 18th. 'The battle of Fleurus', says Lord Acton, 'established the ascendancy of the French in Europe as the 1st of June had created that of England on the ocean. They began the offensive, and retained it for twenty years.'

very handsome indeed, and seemed very sensible &
accomplished. Mrs. Mellish a fine old Lady and very
chatty—They are People of great Fortune I apprehend, and live quite in Style. We had a warm ride of
it. Miss Mellish's Name is Nancy. Miss Woodforde
likes Miss Mellish very much. Dinner to day Breast
of Mutton rosted &c.

JULY 24, THURSDAY. . . . I reprimanded Briton
this Evening for going to Bidewells and staying there
unknown to me longer than he ought and am afraid
was rather tipsy. At bed-time, which was full two
hours after, he gave me notice that he had rather
leave my Service at Michaelmas next. Such is the
gratitude of Servants. He has been with me nine
Years the 26. of April last, which I find is much too
long for any Norfolk Servant for they will then get
pert, saucy & do as they please. Such of late has been
the behaviour of Briton. To Morrow Morning, I told
him, I should speak to him.

JULY 25, FRIDAY. . . . I told Briton this Morning
that I should by no means keep him after Michaelmas
—He did not care for he could get a Place he did not
doubt, if not, he had a home to go to, his Fathers.
After breakfast, he walked into the Garden to work
singing out very loud, which was very impudent.[1]
Thank God Almighty am brave to what I was. . . .

AUG. 10, SUNDAY. . . . Cut a Cucumber in our
Garden this morning that measured in length eleven
Inches and half. I read Prayers & Preached this
afternoon at Weston Ch. Nancy walked with me to
Church this Afternoon. Had a pretty full Congrega-
tion at Church. Dinner to day, hash'd Calfs Head,

[1] Briton did not go at Michaelmas after all.

and a Piece of rost Beef &c. Mr. and Mrs. Corbould drank Coffee & Tea with us this Evening, they came about 6. and stayed till half past 8. Mrs. Corbould not at Weston Church this Afternoon as she went to Marlingford-Church with Mr. Corbould.

Aug. 11, Monday. ... Master Charles Townshend called here this Evening and eat some of our harvest Cake—He came on a little Hobby & Mr. Townshends Butler, Griffith, with him. I took a Walk this morning to see George Warton who is very ill, found him in a sad state, and to me appears to be very near his End— I could not perceive any sense in him.

Aug. 21, Thursday. . . . Finished Harvest this Evening. I cracked my Parlour Bell this Evening by giving it a very gentle Touch with my little Stick, and which I had done many times before without hurting it. It fretted me a good deal, but not at all abt. the value.

Aug. 22, Friday. . . . Going over my Turnips in my two acre Piece this Even' I started a Hare and my greyhound, Snip, being with me, had a Course with her, but she got off.

Aug. 24, Sunday. . . . I got up very indifferent this Morn' such a lowness upon my Spirits, and sinking within me. After dinner thank God! was something better. I read Prayers, Preached & christened a Child this Aft. at Weston Church. Miss Woodforde at Church. . . .

Aug. 25, Monday. . . . To Knights for fruit from Weston House gave 0. 1. 0. which fruit I sent to Mr. Corboulds at Hungate Lodge. Mr. Corbould gave us a short morning Call. About one o'clock this Aft. I

walked to Weston Church and buried poor George
Warton, aged 65. Years. At three o'clock this After-
noon we walked to Hungate Lodge, and there dined
& spent the Afternoon with Mr. and Mrs. Corbould.
Miss Corbould, Mr. & Mrs. Day of Horsford, a Mrs.
Payne, Sister to Mrs. Day, formerly Westons, and
Mr. and Mrs. Jeans of Witchingham. Mrs. Howman
of Hockering drank Tea at Mr. Corboulds. We had
a very genteel Dinner—First Course at the upper
End, stewed Tench, Veal Soup, best part of a Rump
of Beef boiled, 2 rost Chicken and a Ham, Harrico
Mutton, Custard Puddings, backed Mutton Pies,
Mashed Potatoes in 3. Scollop Shells brown'd over.
Roots 2. Dishes. Second Course. At the upper End,
Rabbitts fricasseed, at the lower End Couple of Ducks
rosted, Trifle in the Middle, blamange, Cheesecakes,
Maccaroni, and small Rasberry-Tartlets. Desert of
Fruit mostly that sent by me to them, Peaches, Nec-
tarines and three kinds of Plumbs. We got home
between 8. and 9. in the Evening. Mr. and Mrs.
Jeans drove furiously by our House as they went to
Mr. Corboulds, Mrs. Jeans took Miss Woodforde up
pretty sharply, but Nancy silenced her very soon.

AUG. 26, TUESDAY. . . . Brewed a Barrell of Table
Beer to day. To 4. Yards and 3. Quarters of Cambrick for Handkerchiefs for myself, at 6 Shillings a
Yard, paid Aldridge 1. 8. 6. which will make me five
good Handkerchiefs, and a small one for Nancy
besides. . . .

AUG. 30, SATURDAY. . . . We made some Cheesecakes to day, the first we ever made and exceeding
good they were indeed. Billy Bidewells People
brought our Newspaper for us.

SEPT. 1ST, MONDAY. We breakfasted, dined, &c.

again at home. Herring, & his Nephew, Tuttle of
Norwich & Peachman beat very early this Morning
for Partridges all round my House, before anybody
else, shot several times, and about Noon came again
& did the same, went thro' my Yard, but never sent
me a single Bird. A little before 2. Mr. Corbould, with
young Londale and John Girling Junr., Mr. Custances Gamekeeper, called on us & Girling gave us a
Leash of Partridges. Dinner to day, boiled Calfs
Head, Pork & Greens, and one Partridge rosted, &
Pigeon Pye. This being the first Day of Partridge
shooting, Guns from all Quarters of Weston were
heard, Morn' & Afternoon. Mr. & Mrs. Corbould
with Miss Corbould & young Londale gave us a call
between Tea & Supper for about ½ an Hour.

SEPT. 2, TUESDAY. ... Herring sent me this Evening a brace of Partridges.

SEPT. 14, SUNDAY. ... I read Prayers & Preached
this morning at Weston Ch. Miss Corbould with my
Niece were at Church. In the Afternoon we took a
Walk to Mr. Courboulds and drank Coffee & Tea,
with him, Mrs. Corbould, Miss Corbould, a Mr.
Hastings, Rackham & his Wife of Hockering Park
Farm, belonging to old Mr. Berney of Brecon-Ash.
... Hastings appeared to be a modest well behaved
young Farmer. Rackham & Wife very bold & high,
and but low in the World neither.

SEPT. 15, MONDAY. ... Took a ride this morning
in my little Curricle to Mr. Mellish's at E. Tuddenham, to make him a Visit after his return from London
on Friday last, after the very late melancholy Event
in his Family, the Death of his Mother, who was taken
off very soon indeed, by a very violent Fever, she is

much regretted by all that knew her. We never saw
her but twice, once at Mr. Mellish's & once at my
own house and that not above two Months ago, and
then she appeared as well & in as good Spirits as I
ever saw any Person. Pray God! she may be happier
and send Comfort to her much distressed Family—
As so good a Parent must occasion on her decease such
sorrow as is not to be described or felt but by those
that have experienced it—The Loss of my dear
Parents I feel to this Moment, and never can forget it
during Life. I stayed with Mr. Mellish about an
Hour, and then returned home to dinner. I found
him very low. Mr. Jeans had been with him this
Morning before. At Harwich all Day, having Masons
white-washing my Study Ceiling &c. &c. Dinner to
day, Neck of Pork rosted &c. Mr. Collison sent us 2.
brace of Partridges this Aft.

SEP. 25, THURSDAY. . . . My ankle very painful in
the night at times, which made me sleep but very
little, dismal dreams. My ankle having given so much
Pain last Night & having applied nothing at all to it
but our Family Plaster, soon after breakfast I sent to
John Reeves at the Heart who practises something in
the doctoring way, for some Yellow Basilicum Ointment, which I immediately applied to my ankle, &
wch. Dr. Buchan[1] recommends, pray God! it may do
good—But I have my doubts of its turning out a very
serious matter—I mean my ankle which I am afraid

[1] Doubtless Dr. William Buchan (1729–1805), whose *Domestic Medicine; or the Family Physician*, first published in 1769 went into nineteen
editions during Buchan's lifetime. It was the first work of its kind published in this country, and was translated into many languages, including Russian. Other works by Dr. Buchan concerned the *Diet of the
Common People*, the *Offices and Duties of a Mother*, and *Cautions concerning
Cold Bathing and Drinking Mineral Waters*. Dr. Buchan was buried in
Westminster Abbey.

is much worse than it appears to be—very dangerous. It makes me I must confess very low. Mr. Corbould made us a morning Visit. Dinner to day, boiled Tongue & Turnips &c.

SEPT. 26, FRIDAY. . . . Had a better night of Sleep than the last Night and my Ankle not so painful, better I believe from my applying the Basilicum Ointment Yesterday, and it appeared better this morning on being fresh dressed. My Spirits (thank God) much better to day. Very busy all the morning from breakfast to dinner in cleaning my Study Pictures thoroughly. Dinner to day, Eels fryed & boiled, and boiled Beef. I relished my Dinner very well to day & eat hearty.

SEPT. 29, MONDAY. . . . Slept very well all night & ankle very easy. Paid my Butcher, Willm. Stoughton, this Morning for Meat, for the last four Months, a Bill of 10. 17. 6. Dinner to day boiled Chicken & Pork & Veal Cutlets. I had one Person, by name Anna Harrison, come to me to day to be examined, against the Day of Confirmation at Reepham on Tuesday the seventh of October.

SEPT. 30, TUESDAY. . . . Pretty busy this Morning at home having had thirteen young People come to me to be examined against Confirmation next Week. I gave them all Cake and a Glass of Wine. Dinner to day Knuckle of Veal boiled with Pork & Greens and a brace of Partridges rosted &c. In the Afternoon or rather Evening we walked to Hungate Lodge and drank Coffee & Tea with Mr. [and] Mrs. Carbould, Mrs. Corbould's Brother, a Mr. John Warren a Clergyman, and Mr. Girlings eldest Son who had been shooting with Mr. Corbould all the whole morning. We returned home to Supper.

OCT. 7, TUESDAY. We breakfasted, supped & slept
again at home. It being a fine cheery Morning tho'
cool, we got up at 7. o'clock, dressed ourselves, and
about 8. we got into my little Curricle, and I drove
Nancy over to Witchingham to Mr. Jeans's where we
made a second tho late breakfast with Mr. & Mrs.
Jeans, the Bishop of Norwich Dr. Charles Sutton and
his Chaplain, Mr. Thoroton a young Man, and half
Brother to the Bishop who married his Sister. We
had for breakfast, Chocolate, green & brown Tea,
hot Rolls, dried Toast, Bread & Butter, Honey,
Tongue and ham grated very small. The Bishop did
not come to Mr. Jeans's till 10. o'clock having mis-
taken the road. He and his Chaplain came in a Post-
Chariot & four, with three Servants. About a Quarter
before 11., we attended the Bishop to Reepham to
Mr. Priest's, and when the Bishop had robed himself
we attended him to Church in our Gowns, where he
confirmed about 200. People. Mr. Priest, Mr. Jeans
& self were with the Bishop in the Church, arranging
the People in order as they came & the Chaplain
recd. the Tickets at the Church Gates. It was all
finished by two Clock, and the Bishop walked back to
Mr. Priests, we attending him, and after drinking a
Dish of Chocolate, the Bishop with his Chaplain drove
back to Norwich to a late Dinner. A great Many
Clergy attended on the Occasion, in their Canonicals,
who most of them after their return from Church,
went for their respective homes. Mr. Jeans, Nancy &
self dined at Mr. Priests with him, Mrs. Priest, Miss
Mary & Miss Sally Priest, Robt. & Charles Priest.
Dinner to day Leg of Mutton boiled & a Couple of
Ducks rosted, and a baked rice Pudding. About 5.
o'clock we left Reepham and drove to our respective
homes. We left Mr. Jeans at Witchingham, did not

get out being likely for Rain, which it did a little on the road from Mr. Jeans's, and lucky we had not more, for our Umbrella was clung so fast that we had a hard matter to open it when at home. Mr. Priest, Mr. Jeans & self, went to the Kings Arms after the Bishop was gone, to dine with some of the Clergy, as there was a Dinner bespoke, but only meeting with Mr. Atthill of Foulsham there, we returned to Mr. Priests. As we did not dine at the Kings Arms we gave the Landlord, Bell, by way of compensation one Shilling each, with which he was very well satisfied. We got home safe & well, thank God for it before seven o'clock. The Rain that fell Yesterday rose the Water at Foxford & at Eads Mill quite high, Nancy very much alarmed & frightened therewith as it came almost into our little Cart. Every thing however passed over exceeding well to day and all conducted well throughout. Miss Woodforde much pleased with her Excursion and mightily so with the Bishop's very agreeable and affable, as well as polite & sensible behaviour.

OCT. 20, MONDAY. . . . About 10. o'clock this morning I walked to Church and married George Barnard & Mary Girling by Licence, for which I received 1. 1. 0. Had but an indifferent night of Sleep last Night my Ancle being painful most part of the night, and also towards the Morning had a gouty Pain on the great Toe of the other Leg, but not bad. It made me hobble however between both this morning. Dr. Thorne called on me about 1. o'clock and dressed my Leg. No discharge but kind of blood on the Lint appeared, the red precipitate Yesterday did more harm than good I apprehend and which occasioned so much pain in the night. The Doctor dressed it to day with yellow Basilicum only, except a little corner of the Wound where was a little speck of proud flesh on which he put a very small matter of red precipitate Powder, instead of Ointment & that covered with Basilicum Ointment. The red Precipitate Powder gave me much pain for a little time but after being dressed some time, my Ancle much easier. Busy most part of the Afternoon in making some Mead Wine, to fourteen Pound of Honey, I put four Gallons of Water, boiled it more than an hour with Ginger and two handfulls of dried Elder-Flowers in it, and skimmed it well. Then put it into a small Tub to cool, and when almost cold I put in a large gravey-Spoon full of fresh Yeast, keeping it in a warm place, the Kitchen during night. Dinner to day, Breast of Veal rosted &c.

Oct. 26, Sunday. ... We are afraid that our Maid, Molly, is with Child she looks so big, but she denies it very positively.

Oct. 27, Monday. . . . My Ancle still continues very finely, thank God. Dr. Thorne called here about 1. o'clock, and dressed it as he did before. He was surprised to see it so well, it was almost healed. He said that it required but very little more to be done to it. No pain at all to signify. Very dull, wet, melancholy day, but mild. Dinner to day, Cottage Pye, and a Neck of Mutton rosted. Betty, both the Washerwomen as well as ourselves say that our Maid Molly is with Child, but she persists in it that she is not.

Oct. 29, Wednesday. . . . My Ancle rather painful in the Night, having the Cramp a good deal in that Leg last night. At Eleven o'clock this morning I walked to Weston Church and married Joseph

Bowles, Widower, & Sarah Nobbs, Widow, by Banns,
for which I received only o. 2. 6. having had 2ˢ/6ᵈ.
before for publishing them. On my return home from
Church, found Mr. Jeans and Dr. Thorne at my
House, but they did not stay very long; after Mr.
Jeans went, the Doctor dressed my Ancle, he said it
did not look so well as when he saw it last. The
Plaister I apprehend and as Betty said, was removed
from its place. The Dr. dressed it with yellow basili-
cum Ointment and a Turners Cerate upon that.
Whilst Mr. Jeans and Dr. Thorne were with us,
James Pegg, called on me for the Taxes. Paid James
Pegg, this Morn' in the whole 7. 10. 3. That is, Land
Tax 1 Qr. for Rect. & Coll. Land 3. 0. 0. Window &
House Tax, half a Year 2. 15. 0. Male-Servant Tax,
half a Year 1. 5. 0. Horse Tax, half a Year 0. 5. 0.
Ten per Cent on Taxes,[1] half a Year 0. 5. 3. As I went
to Church this Morning, I met Mr. Stoughton of
Sparham, just by our Church, with his Pointers &
Gun, in a Shooting Dress, going over our Parish to
try if he could kill a few Partridges. I pressed him to
take his dinner with us after he had finished, but he
said he could not. If he had Sport, he would call in
the Afternoon and leave us some Birds, which he did,
a Leash, between four & five o'clock, but he would not
come in, drank a Glass of Beer & off directly. He had
a very nice Green Cart at the Heart, for himself and
Dogs &c—Quite a new Carriage, exceeding neat &
convenient.[2] Dinner to day, boiled Beef, with Odds
& Ends.

---

[1] i.e. Ten per cent. on the Assessed Taxes (those touching House-
holders and Establishments). This increase of ten per cent. had first
been made by Pitt in 1791. In the 1793 budget the increased tax was
made permanent.

[2] Mr. James Stoughton was appointed Rector of Sparham on April
19th, 1792, and was Rector for 48 years.

Nov. 2, Sunday. ... I read Prayers & Preached this Aft. at Weston-Church. Had a pretty full Congregation at Church. My Maid Molly has declared herself with Child, more than half gone. Molly is with Child by one Sam. Cudble, a Carpenter of the Parish of Coulton, and he says that he will marry her—The Man bears a fair Character—However, in her Situation, it is necessary for me to part with her as soon as possible. To Morrow therefore I intend at present to dismiss her. She is a very poor, weak Girl, but I believe honest. Dinner to day, Breast of Veal rosted &c.

Nov. 3, Monday. ... After breakfast, I talked with Molly, paid her three Quarters of a Year and one Months Wages, which amounted in the whole to 4. 7. 0 and after packing up her things, about one o'clock she left my House, and walked off for Coulton where she is to be at Cudble's Father's, till such time that they are married. She says that Cudble made not the least objection to marrying her, she foolishly denied being with Child till the middle of last Week, and then obliged to, the Work becoming too much for her present Situation. I don't think that she is far from lying in by her appearance. For my own part, I have long thought her breeding. My Ancle, thank God, is now almost well, I dressed it in the same manner as the Doctor did Yesterday. ...

Nov. 8, Saturday. ... Sent Ben early this Morning to Norwich with ten Coomb of Wheat to Mr. Bloomes at Trowse-Mills. A fine Sunshine Morning, small Frost, and cool. My Ankle so easy to day that I did not dress it. Sent by Ben a fine Cock-Pheasant to Mr. Corbould who with his Wife are at old Mr. Corboulds at Norwich. Ben did not return till after 6. this Evening, he brought back half a Chaldron of

Coals. Mr. Bloome gave for my Wheat 27. Shillings per Coomb, and Ben brought me home in Cash for the same 13. 10. 0. Sally Gunton (a Girl about 20. Years of Age) who is at present in Mr. Townshends Service at Honingham Hall, came this Evening to offer her Service in the Room of my late Maid. The Townshend Family going to London next Week, wants her no longer. She appears to be a Girl that will do, and comes from honest Parents, tho' they are both dead. Dinner to day, Beef-Steak Pudding &c. Not much News on the Papers, only that one Hardy[1] tried this last Week for high Treason was acquitted. It was a very long Trial indeed at the old Bailey, it lasted full seven Days.

NOV. 17, MONDAY. . . . Mr. Maynard Rector of Morton called on me this Morning to ask my Advice, about one of his Parish by name Fisher, doing a kind of Penance next Sunday for calling Mrs. Michael Andrews, a Whore. He shewed me the form issued out of the Bishops Court. It is called a Deed of Retractation. A foolish kind of Affair between the parties, and the expences of which to both must be high. At 2. o'clock this Afternoon I walked to Weston Ch. and buried poor old Natl. Heavers, aged 85. Yrs. Dinner to day, a boiled Fowl & a Neck of Mutton rosted. My Ancle, thank God, continues finely. I still keep a thin Linnen Bandage upon it. Had a fat Pig killed this Morning by Tom Thurston, weight 8 Stone 4. lb.

---

[1] Thomas Hardy (1752–1832), the radical shoemaker and founder in January 1792 of the London Corresponding Society, of which the object was Parliamentary Reform. On May 12th, 1794, Hardy, who was actively promoting a convention of other Reform Societies, was arrested on a charge of high treason. Hardy's trial began on October 28th and ended on November 5th, 1794, with his acquittal. The crowd triumphantly drew him in a coach through the streets of London.

Nov. 18, Tuesday. . . . Sally Gunton, my new Maid, came to my House this Evening, and entered upon her new Service. Sarah Richmond went home to her Friends, having been here to help Betty, just a fortnight. Sally Gunton is to have per Annum 5. 5. 0. Very cold indeed all day with rough wind.

Nov. 24, Monday. . . . To my blacksmith, John Buck, this Morning paid him, his annual Bill, which amounted to 4. 1. 6. being 1. 7. 6. More than the last Bill paid by me, as I have had a good deal of little Jobbs within doors done. Dinner to day, Fillet of Veal rosted &c. Mem.—Cavendo tutus.[1]

Nov. 30, Sunday. . . . Mem. a Primrose in my Garden in full bloom, seen by myself and my Niece.

Dec. 3, Wednesday. . . . Widow Pratt called on me this Morning and paid me for Tithe 2. 8. 0. Barnard Dunnell also paid me for Tithe 2. 14. 0. About 1. o'clock Mr. and Mrs. Foster of Lenewade Bridge called on me, to desire me to write to the Warden of New College, on Account of the Fine set by the Society for this Year, upwards of 500 pd. They stayed till after 2. o'clock. I was obliged to go to Church to bury a Child of James Arthurtons, a little Girl, about 3. Years old which I did, and on my return home, met them on their way to Lenewade Bridge. Mrs. Foster then made use of the following expression that if matters were not easier, there would be no peace in Israel, which had better not have been mentioned—

---

[1] See entries for September 17th and October 12th, 1792, for John Buck, blacksmith and smuggler. The taxation of spirits had been greatly increased by Pitt, and smuggling was, therefore, at once more profitable and more dangerous; hence Parson Woodforde's observation.

I thought it very weak. Dinner to day, Neck of Veal
rosted &c. Mem:—

Paid Mr. Foster for Coll. Land	.	.	16.	0. 0
Paid him also for Flour &c.	.	.	4.	16. 0

	20.	16. 0
Recd. of him for Bark . . .	2.	12. 6

Balance pd. £18. 3. 6

DEC. 5, FRIDAY. . . . One Richd. Kittle, rider to the
Norwich Iron Foundry called on me this Morning
with a Bill for two cast-iron Box Scrapers in July last,
pd. 0. 11. 0. Mr. Foster of Lenewade Bridge brought
me a brace of Pheasants this Morning. Very busy in
writing Letters this Morning to the Warden of New
College and to Caldecot in behalf of Foster, respecting
the very high Fine set him. I wish it may be of Service
to him, but I have little hopes. It has made me very
uneasy since I first heard it. As not knowing scarce
how to act, so as to steer clear of blame from every
Quarter. Mr. Foster appears greatly depressed and
says he shall be ruined. It grieved me to see him and
that determined me to do what I could for him. Mr.
Jeans is so inveterate against him, that he has been
the principal Actor against him in it. Dinner to day,
Codfish, fryed Beef & Potatoes.

DEC. 13, SATURDAY. . . . Busy all the Morning
almost in bottling two tubs of Gin, that came by
Moonshine this Morn' very early. Had a very friendly
Letter from the Warden of New-College Saml. Gauntlett, brought by Ben this Evening from Norwich, concerning myself & Foster. Recd. for butter to day at
1s 0d a Pint 0. 2. 0.

DEC. 16, TUESDAY. . . . Brewed a Barrell of common

Beer to day. Mr. Symonds of Reepham, cleaned both my eight day Clocks to day, almost the whole day after them, he breakfasted & dined with our folks. When he went away, which was in the Evening I paid him a Bill for cleaning Clocks & Watch from October, 1789, to Dec. 1794 1. 0. 6. cleaning my Clocks to day included in it. I did not take any change of him out of a Guinea. Dinner to day, fine Rump of Beef boiled &c.

Dec. 17, Wednesday. . . . Sent Lizzy Arthurton this Morning a fat Chicken fit to dress, she being very ill indeed, many think her in a decline, she very late laid in. . . .

Dec. 22, Monday. . . . Gave to the poor People of Weston against Xmas as usual, 57. in Number at 6ᵈ each 1. 8. 6. Mr. Stoughton of Sparham about 3. o'clock this Afternoon brought us a brace of Partridges, just as we had sat down to dinner, having been shooting at Weston all the Morning, and he dined and spent the Afternoon with us, till near 6. o'clock. We had for dinner to day, a boiled Tongue with Mashed Potatoes and Turnips & a Loin of Veal rosted.

Dec. 25, Thursday, Xmas Day. We breakfasted, dined, &c. again at home. It was very cold indeed this Morning, and the Snow in many Places quite deep, with an E. Wind. About 11. this Morning I walked to Church and read Prayers & administered the Holy Sacrament. Had but few Communicants the Weather so bad. Gave at the Altar for an Offering 0. 2. 6. Immediately after the Morning Service so far as before the administration of the H. Sacrament I was attacked with an Epileptic Fit, and fainted away in my Desk, but thank God! soon recovered and went through the remaining part of my duty. Mr. & Mrs.

Girling, Mr. & Mrs. Howlett, Mr. St. Andrews, Mr. Hardy &c. &c. were much alarmed and were very kind to Me, during the fit and after. The Weather being so severely cold, which I could never escape from feeling its effect at all times, affected me so much this Morning, that made me faint away, what I always was afraid off for some Winters past, having often had many fears. Mr. Howlett after Service, very kindly offered to drive me home in his Cart, but as I was better I declined it, however hope that I shall not forget his civility. After Service was over, I walked into Mr. Stephen Andrew's House, and having warmed myself, I walked home and thank God, got home very well. Mr. Stephen Andrews & Family behaved very kindly. After I got home and had something warm to drink, I soon got tolerably well, but could only eat some plumb Pudding & a few Potatoes. Nancy was much alarmed when she first heard of it. Eliz. Case, Widow, Ned Howes, Thos. Atterton Senr., Christ. Dunnell, Robert Downing, and my Clerk Thos. Thurston, all dined at my House to day being Christmas Day, & each had a Shilling o. 6. o. A very fine Sirloin of Beef rosted and plenty of plumb Puddings for dinner & strong beer after. Took some Rhubarb going to bed.

Dec. 26, Friday. . . . Thank God! had a pretty good Night last Night, and I hope am something better, but rather languid & low. Could eat but very little for dinner to day. Appetite bad. To Weston Ringers, gave o. 2. 6. To Christmas Boxes &c. gave o. 4. o. Dinner to day, Calfs Fry & a Rabbit rosted. I drank plentifully of Port Wine after dinner, instead of one Glass, drank 7. or 8. Wine Glasses, and it seemed to do me much good, being better for it.

1795

JAN. 5, MONDAY. . . . Gave Nancy this Morn' a ten Pound Note 10. 0. 0. Paid my Servants their Wages this Morn', viz: To Ben. Leggatt, a Years Wages due this Day 10. 0. 0. To Bretingham Scurl, ditto 8. 0. 0. To Timothy Tooley, ditto 2. 2. 0. Gave him also extraordinary 0. 2. 6. To Betty Dade, a Years Wages 5. 5. 0. To Sally Gunton, 7. Weeks Wages 0. 15. 0. Mr. Mellish made us a Morning Visit, he was going to Reepham to Mr. Priests to dinner. Dinner to day, boiled Pork & Greens & a Couple of Wigeon. In the Afternoon the Weather seemed likely to alter rather Milder if any thing than it was. The Horison in the West on the going down of the Sun was remarkably red. I thank God! have felt better to day, than lately, tho' much inclined to sleep in the day time. That Sleepiness I cannot account for, unless from cold.

JAN. 8, THURSDAY. . . . Betty returned home this Evening from Mattishall. She brought but a very indifferent account of both Mr. Bodham and Mr. Smith. The former almost blind and has a Person to sit up every night with him. The latter, Mr. Smith, has such a bad humour in his Legs, that almost distracts him, very bad Yesterday.

JAN. 15, THURSDAY. . . . Got up this morning very bad indeed in the Gout in my right foot, could scarce bare to put him on the ground, and so it continued the whole Day and night, not free one Minute from violent pain. The Weather Most piercing, severe frost, with Wind & some Snow, the Wind from the East and very rough. We had some boiled Beef & a Hare rosted for dinner. I could eat but very little indeed for dinner to day. I had my bed warmed to night & a fire in my bed-Room. I never was attacked so severe before in my life. Obliged to put on my great Shoe, lined with flannel. The Weather very much against me besides.

JAN. 20, TUESDAY. . . . Last Night was the severest we have yet had. It froze so sharp within doors, that the milk in the Milk-pans in the Dairy, was froze in a Mass. Something better to day thank God! but still in pain. Dinner to day, Knuckle of Veal boiled &c. I think that this Day has been the coldest that ever I felt in my life, so cold within doors. To poor lame John Spraggs, gave o. o. 6.

JAN. 21, WEDNESDAY. . . . Had a very good Night of rest, better this morning. My foot still painful, and foot & leg much swelled. The last Night, the most severest yet, extreme cold. So cold that the Poultry kept in the Cart-Shed and obliged to be driven out to be fed. . . .

JAN. 23, FRIDAY. We breakfasted, dined, &c. again at home. The Weather more severe than ever, it froze apples within doors, tho' covered with a thick carpet. The cold to day was the severest I ever felt. The Thermometer in my Study, with a fire, down to No. 46. Very lame to day in both feet, but not very painful. Mr. Corbould made us a Morning Visit, very friendly. Dinner to day, odds and ends &c. Mr. Buck the Farmer brought us this Morning as a present an uncommon bird, shot by Mr. Emeris this Morning in Weston, not good to eat, called by what we could find out, a Pippet-Grebe, remarkable for the beautiful Feathers on his breast, like the finest white Sattin, with uncommon feet, about the size of a duck, only much longer Neck with a long sharp pointed bill, something of the Moor-Hen species, a smutty back.

JAN. 25, SUNDAY. We breakfasted, dined, &c. again at home. The Frost this Morning more severe than Yesterday. It froze last Night the Chamber Pots above Stairs. Thermometer in the Study down to No. 40. this Morn. Barometer up high, No. 29 = 16. & very fair. The Cold so severe that it effects me very much. Thank God! however that the Gout is much better. No Service again at Church this day (and which should have been in the Afternoon) owing to the Cold. Dinner to day, a boiled Pike very good (and which Briton brought from Norwich Yesterday) and a nice small Neck of Pork rosted with Apple-Sauce. The French have taken all Holland, and the Stadt-holder the Prince of Orange with his Princess and Family, landed at Yarmouth & Harwich, last Tuesday & Wednesday, and are all gone to London.[1] Dread & terrible times appear to be near at hand. Pray God! deliver us and send us an happy Peace. The Ice in the Pond in the Yard which is broke every Morning for the Horses, froze two Inches in thickness last Night, when broke this morning.

FEB. 4, WEDNESDAY. ... As cold a Night last night almost as we have had yet, it froze very sharp within doors, all the Milk & Cream froze. Extreme cold this Morning with cutting wind, and much Snow besides. Both Barometer & Thermometer very low. Many birds have been found dead, and the Rooks and Crows so tame that they come up to the Kitchen door where I feed my Poultry. Dinner to day, boiled Veal and Pork, &c.

[1] The frost was so intense in Holland that the French Hussars rode over the ice and captured the Dutch fleet in the Texel.

FEB. 5, THURSDAY. . . . Sent Ben this morning after breakfast down to Mr. Girlings with a ten Pound Note for him to dispose of the same to the Poor of Weston as he should think Most to their advantage in this inclement Season. Very soon after I heard that Mr. Custance arrived at Weston House last Night from Bath. As cold and as severe a Frost as Ever, and now not likely to alter, being very fair above. My Pain in my Foot rather worse this Morning. About 2. o'clock Mr. Custance very kindly came on foot (tho' the Snow was deep on the ground) to our House, and spent an Hour with us. Mr. Custance looks thin, but was in high Spirits. Miss Woodforde had a Note from Mrs. Custance. Dinner to day, Leg of Mutton rosted &c.

FEB. 8, SUNDAY. . . . Weather much altered, very foggy and a cold Thawe, with very small Rain, all the whole Day. I hope to God that now We shall no more have any very severe Frosts this Year. Barometer fell, Thermometer rose. No Service this Afternoon at Weston Church. . . .

FEB. 13, FRIDAY. . . . Dinner to day a Couple of Ducks rosted &c. Mr. Corbould called on us this Evening about 5. o'clock. I would have had Mr. Corbould drank Tea with us this Evening, but he promised to return home to Tea. Whilst Mr. Corbould was with us this Evening, Mr. Girling and Mr. Howlett called on me and stayed about an Hour with us, they came to talk about disposing of the Money collected for the Poor. The whole Sum collected, amount to 43. 12. 0. which was very great indeed —Mr. Custance gave 10. Pounds—Mr. Howlett 5.£—Mr. Corbould 3. Guineas—Mr. Girling 3. Guineas—Mr. Emeris 3. Guineas, and many others 1. Guinea apiece.

FEB. 14, SATURDAY. . . . This being Valentine's Day, gave to Children that were under 14. Years & could speak, at one penny each, 56. in Number o. 4. 8. . . .

FEB. 15, SUNDAY. . . . There was no duty at Weston Church to day, tho' I am much better than I have been, yet not quite well enough to go to Church, for fear of a Relapse. Divine Service to day would have been in the Morn'. There was forty Shillings worth of brown bread given to the Poor of Weston on Tuesday last, and fifty Shillings worth of the same given this day, from the late Collection for the poor. Please God! I hope to be able to go to Church next Sunday. Dinner to day, Loin of Veal rosted &c. Britons Father dined with our Folks to day. As Britons Father is a Baker, I spoke for him to the Gentlemen of the Parish, to make part of the bread which is to be given away, and he is to make 50. Shillings worth against next Sunday.

FEB. 18, WEDNESDAY. . . . Very hard Frost with strong Easterly Winds, a black Frost. Every Vegetable seems affected by it. As cold this day almost, as any this Winter. I felt it before I got up this Morning, pain within me. It froze very sharp within doors all the day long. Dinner to day odds and ends, but very good. Had a fire again in My bedchamber to night, tho' I had left it off some time, bitter cold to night.

FEB. 19, THURSDAY. . . . Colder and More severe if any thing than Yesterday with very strong Easterly Wind, and at times some fine Snow, but very little indeed of it, so little as not to make the least appearance of it on the ground. It froze very sharp again within doors all day. The Gout I thank God is better, & I feel better. Dinner to day, boiled Beef &c. Mr.

Herring gave 3. Guineas on Saturday last to the Poor of Weston which now makes the Subscription for the Poor of Weston 46. 15. 0. The Money is to be laid out in Bread and Coal.

FEB. 20, FRIDAY. ... Colder than Yesterday, and a harder Frost, with very strong Easterly Wind & much Snow. It froze amazingly sharp last Night within doors. More severe this Morning than any this Winter. The Wind very piercing indeed all the day long. This Day is said to be the most cutting this Winter. It snowed the whole Day, but small & very drifting. The cold this day affected us this day so much that it gave us pains all over us, within & without and were even cold tho' sitting by a good fire. Dinner to day, a Couple of Rabbits boiled &c.

FEB. 22, SUNDAY. We breakfasted, dined, &c. again at home. Severe, cold Weather still continues, froze again within doors. In the Afternoon some Snow. I am afraid now that we shall have more of it—The New Moon being now three Days old, and no appearance of a change. Gout much better. I fully intended to have gone to Church and done my duty this Afternoon at Weston-Church, but the Weather still continuing so very severe, and much Snow on the Ground, I thought too dangerous for me to venture to go into a damp Church and Walking upon Snow, having not left off my flannel lined second Gouty Shoes, therefore sent word to my Parishioners, that there would be no Service. There was fifty Shillings worth of bread given again this day at 3. in the Aft. to the Poor of Weston. Britons Father baked the bread for this Day. I weighed two of the Loaves. The Sixpenny Loaf weighed—4. Pound, 5. Ounces. The Threepenny Loaf—2. Pound, 2. Ounces. The Bread seemed larger than Doughty's & lighter but not baked so much as Doughtys. Dinner to day Shoulder of Mutton rosted &c.

MARCH 6, FRIDAY. Mr. Girling called on me this Morning and paid Me, for Tithe for Mr. Custance for 1794 18. 18. 6. Mr. Custance, Mr. and Mrs. Corbould, and Mr. Stoughton of Sparham, dined & spent the Afternoon with us and stayed till after 9. o'clock at Weston Parsonage. We gave them for Dinner a Couple of boiled Chicken and Pigs Face, very good Peas Soup, a boiled Rump of Beef very fine, a prodigious fine, large and very fat Cock-Turkey rosted, Maccaroni, Batter Custard Pudding with Jelly, Apple Fritters, Tarts and Raspberry Puffs. Desert, baked Apples, nice Nonpareils, brandy Cherries and Filberts. Wines, Port & Sherries, Malt Liquors, Strong Beer, bottled Porter &c. After Coffee & Tea we got to Cards, limited Loo, at 1^d. per Counter. I won at it abt. 0. 2. 0. It turned out a very indifferent Day of weather as it rained Almost the whole Day, was very sorry for it. All our Dinner was very nicely cooked indeed. Mr. Custance eat very hearty for dinner.

MARCH 7, SATURDAY. . . . Mr. Jeans's Cousin William called on us this Morning, and stayed about half an Hour here. His chief business I find was to enquire about the price of washing things, our Neighbour Downing having washed some things for some French People now at Mr. Jeans's—Mrs. Jeans thinking that she charged too Much, but as we wash all our things at home, could not say anything about it. The whole was but a trifle and not worth making words about, especially also, as the poor Woman had a walk of 6. Miles to carry the things home after washing them. The Woman wanted the money for them when she carried them back, but she was not then paid and has not from thence to this time. . . .

MARCH 8, SUNDAY. . . . Mr. Stoughton of Sparham did duty for me this Aft. at Weston-Church, being unable, tho' very desirous. Mr. Custance at Church and a large Congregation.

MARCH 11, WEDNESDAY. . . . Did not sleep very well last Night, as the Pills I took last night occasioned rumblings within me. . . .

MARCH 13, FRIDAY. . . . Ground covered with Snow this Morning, having a great deal of Snow in the Night. The Morning was fair but Air very cold. A 4th Winter. . . .

MARCH 17, TUESDAY. . . . Very cold & very damp. Water overflows the Ditches all round us. The Yard almost covered with Water. In the Well the Water is almost up to the Top. In the Garden the Water from the Slope Garden runs into the Great Pond. Land Springs about us were scarce ever known to be so full as at present. The Water in the Ditch by the road runs over it into College Pit. Thank God! had a tolerable good Night last Night. . . .

MARCH 22, SUNDAY. We breakfasted, dined, again at home. My Ancle in the Night rather pained me but not much. When I dressed it this morning I did not think that it looked so well as last Night, rather deeper and the Edges of the Sore rather thick, as if proud Flesh was arising. I dressed it however as I did last Night. The Gout (I thank God) was finely, not by any Means swelled so much as it was very lately. I walked to Weston-Church in the Afternoon and there read Prayers & Preached, which I have not been able to do before since Janry. 11th. Had a very large

Congregation at Church to day. Mr. Custance at Church, as was my Niece. Fifty Shillings-worth of Bread given after Service to the Poor of Weston, out of the late Collection. Blessed be God! that I was able to do my Duty at Church again. I performed it with much more ease, than I thought myself able to day— The Day turning out very dry, though cold Air. Dinner to day, boiled Pork and a Turkey rosted. We did not dine till after Divine Service. I wore both of my largest gouty Shoes to Church to day. I think myself obliged to my Parishioners, for their expressions of kindness towards me in seeing me again at Church & performing My Duty there.

MARCH 28, SATURDAY. ... I slept very well (thank God) last night, my Ancle a little painful in the Morning early but not much. It looked in a fair way when dressed this Morning. Sent Briton early this Morning to Norwich with my little old Cart after News & many other things. Mr. Thorne waited on me again this morning and looked at my Ancle, applied a Caustic to it just touching the part with it with a small kind of fine hair Pencil in a Quill-Case. He much recommended again the resting of it. Briton returned between 4. and 5. this Afternoon brought a Letter for me from my Niece J. Pounsett acquainting us that Mr. Pounsett was very bad in the Gout, and not likely to live long, unless he was soon better, intreating me to come into the Country. My Sister Pounsett also very poorly. The Letter greatly distressed me, as in my present Situation respecting my Leg, it would be almost Death to me to undertake such a Journey. Mr. Custance sent us a brace of Snipes this Morning. Dinner to day, boiled Beef &c. My Ancle looked finely this Evening on dressing it.

I took a little Rhubarb this Evening instead of the Pill.

APRIL 4, SATURDAY. ... Charles Cary's People brought my Newspapers this Evening with two Letters for me from Somersett one from my Brother and another from my Niece Jenny Pounsett, both announcing the Death of poor Mr. Pounsett on Tuesday last, March 31st., entreating Me to come into the Country as soon as possible, but in my present Situation with so bad an Ancle, I cannot at present do it, and which I am very sorry for. As they have so many Relations near them is a Satisfaction to me. Am truly sorry for poor Mr. Pounsett, pray God he may be eternally happy. His Sufferings for many Years have been very great. Pray God direct My Sister and Niece for the best under their Loss. I know nothing of Mr. Pounsetts Affairs nor Will. He used to say that he had left my Sister & Niece all that he had, equally between them. It made us both low this Evening on the Occasion.

APRIL 26, SUNDAY. ... Thank God Almighty! got up this Morning very finely indeed, almost totally free from any pain whatever, either from Ancle or Gout. I walked to Church this Afternoon and there read Prayers and Preached. Had a very large Congregation. Mr. Custance at Church. Fifty-Shillings worth of Bread given to the Poor again to Day after Divine Service. Dinner to day, Loin of Veal rosted &c. Mr. Stoughton of Sparham sent us a fine Pike this Evening by his Servant Man John. Gave John for bringing it o. 1. o. I took another Pill again to night.

MAY 1ST, FRIDAY. I breakfasted, supped and slept again at home. Nancy breakfasted, dined &c. again at home. It being a fine Morning I drove to Reepham to the ArchDeacon Yonges Visitation, and there dined and spent the Afternoon at the Kings-Arms Inn there, with the following Clergy and Laity, viz. Clergy, The ArchDeacon, Mr. Johnson Preacher, Mr. Priest Senr., St. John Priest, Reader, Mr. Maynard, Mr. Jeans, Mr. Church, Mr. Stoughton, Mr. Bulwer, A Mr. Munnings and myself; Laity, Mr. Repton, Mr. Addey, Mr. Holley, Mr. Munnings Junr., and Mr. Morphew. Mr. Johnson gave us a very excellent Sermon indeed, very apropos to the times. St. John Priest read Prayers for his Father. Dinner, boiled Leg of Mutton, a Piece of rost Beef, Fillet of Veal rosted, two Fowls and a Pigs Face, and a plumb Pudding &c. Dinner, ordinary and extraordinary, I pd. o. 4. 6. I stayed till 6. o'clock in the Evening and then drove back to Weston and Briton with me. Briton being in Liquor was very saucy in his return home with me. He is treading fast the steps that poor Will. Coleman did before he was obliged to be sent away. I called at Witchingham at Mr. Jeans, but Mrs. Jeans never appeared, which I think was very ungenteel indeed.

MAY 15, FRIDAY. We breakfasted, dined, supped & slept at home. Mr. Wilson, Curate of Ling, who has a Wife and a large Family, being exceeding poor and owing entirely to his own indiscretion & dissipation, called on me this morning to borrow 3. or 4. Shillings of Me. I let him have immediately a Guinea 1. 1. o. Dinner to day—boiled Pork & Greens, Souce, &c. Sent Mr. Custance this Evening some Rasberry Puffs and some small Cakes, having baked to day. Sent Mr. Corbould about 2. Hndrd. of Hay this Even'.

MAY 26, TUESDAY. . . . The Members of the

Purse-Club with a Drum & Fife, made their Annual Perambulation. They called at my House, and I gave them as usual o. 10. 6.

MAY 30, SATURDAY. . . . Recd. a Letter this Evening from Mr. Custance in London, desiring me to send as soon as possible a Copy of the Register of his Son, George, who has got an appointment on the Madrass Establishment in the East Indies, & is going for the Indies soon. Mr. Custance likewise informed me that he had been to Bath and back again since he left Weston. The News & Letter came from Billy Bidewells.

JUNE 1, MONDAY. . . . About half past 8. o'clock this Morning, just as we had breakfasted, who should come to our House in a Kings-Head-Chaise from Norwich but Mr. Custance and his Butler, Rising, and they breakfasted at Weston Parsonage. Mr. Custance with us and Rising in the Kitchen. The Driver also had his breakfast here. Mr. Custance said that he had been near five Hundred [miles], since last Friday se'ennight, he looked much jaded. He made a very good breakfast, had little or no refreshment Yesterday. He stayed with us about an Hour and half and then walked to Weston House by himself. He took Leave of us also, as he sets forth to Morrow Morn' about 8. o'clock, back for London where he stays a short time with his Son George and then both return to Bath, where Mr. Custance remains for some time, after his Son is settled. To the Woman, Lancaster of Tuddenham, having lost some things which [s]he had bought at Norwich, on her way home from a Waggon, gave o. 2. 6. Mr. Custance brought us this Morn' two Maccarel. Dinner to day, Maccarel & a Shoulder of Veal. Mr. & Mrs. Bodham sent over to enquire after

us this Morning from Mattishall—Want to see us.
Mr. Custance sent us this Evening a large Piece of a
fine Wedding Cake sent from London to Mr. C. on
the Marriage of Miss Durrant (Daughter of Lady
Durrants) and Captain Swinfen of Swinfen-Hall in
the County of Stafford, eldest Son of — Swinfen, Esq.
Very curious devices on the Top of the Cake. . . .

JUNE 3, WEDNESDAY. . . . I drove Nancy over to
Mattishal to day about Noon, and we dined & spent
the Afternoon at Mr. Bodhams, with him, Mrs. Bodham, & Miss Anne Donne, Daughter of the late
Revd. Castres Donne who is about thirteen Years of
Age, a very nice Girl. We found Mr. Bodham very
bad indeed, much altered, As helpless almost as an
Infant, being led about and also fed, besides being
almost blind. He looks fresh, and eats and drinks
heartily, he complains at times of violent pains, and
very sleepy by day, but very restless at nights, is had
out of bed often in the Night. Poor Mrs. Bodham does
everything for him, poor Woman I heartily pity her,
she bears it up wonderfully well. We had for Dinner
a few Maccarel, some Veal Cutlets and a small Green-
Goose & Asparagus, and some Gooseberry Tarts. No
Potatoes, Greens &c. Mr. Bodham is very hasty &
often swears at People. He is certainly at times deranged & talks wildly. Tho' he has been so ill & so
long, yet is continually having Workmen about him
& spends great Sums that way, in building up and
pulling down, besides buying Carriages to go out in,
but will get into none of them. We saw a prodigious handsome new full-bodied Coach, sent from
London half a Year ago. He behaved very civil indeed
to us & glad to have us. We stayed till about 7. in
the Evening & then returned home. In our way to

Mattishall, we called on Betty England at Tuddenham & had some Chat with her, but we did not get out of our Carriage. We got home about half past 8. o'clock, & soon after Mr. Corbould with Miss Sutcliffe called at the Gate in their Carriage & we had some Chat with them there.

JUNE 4, THURSDAY. We breakfasted, dined, &c. again at home. About half past 9. this Morning I got into my Curricle and drove over to Norwich, it being the Kings Birth Day. Nancy would not go—So I took Briton. Got there about a Quarter after Eleven. Saw all the Soldiers both Horse & Foot drawn up in the Market Place about one o'clock, and the foot fired three Vollies, and the Cannon on the Castle Hill also fired thrice. Soon after the Soldiers fired, they marched off. And those Soldiers lately returned from the Continent, marched to Coe's late Quantrille's Garden, where a Subscription Dinner was provided for them, of rost Beef & boiled Beef &c. Pies, and plenty of rost Legs of Mutton. I walked thither on purpose to see them at dinnèr, & a pretty Sight it was. They all had Porter to drink. A great deal of Company were in the Gardens to see them. I gave to go into the Gardens o. 1. o. Paid there for refreshment o. o. 3. The Soldiers dined at 3. & at 4. marched off for the Barracks, all things conducted very well. About one Thousand Soldiers were supposed to be there. The Subscription for them was said to be 100. Pound. For some Crabs, Gingerbread &c. paid abt. o. 2. o. Saw all the Norwich Priests at one Place or another. Saw also at Mr. Priests Senr.—the Revd. Mr. Howes of Fordingbridge, son of the late Mr. Howes of Hockering. I bespoke a new grey Coat of Bath Coating. At six o'clock this Evening I left Norwich and got home to Weston by eight and then dined & supped at the same time. I was but very little fatigued considering walking about so much &c. Saw old Mr. Corbould at Norwich to day. My dinner was some Mutton Steaks.

JUNE 16, TUESDAY. ... After breakfast I got into my Curricle and drove to Norwich, taking Briton with me. We got [there] about Noon—And it being Guild-Day when the new Mayor is sworn in, there were great doings, the Court going in Procession to the great Church and from thence to the Guild-Hall, & then to St. Andrews Hall to dinner. Old Mr. Alderman Ives is the new Mayor, and it is the second Time of his succeeding to that Office. Some of the old time doings exhibited to day such as he did the last Time of being Mayor—A fine & curious Triumphal Arch of green Box intersped with many Flowers & variegated Lamps hung in the Centre of the Arch, near Mr. Ives's House and by St. Clements Church near Fye Bridge. At the Mayors Door there was a similar Arch with three golden Crowns on it and the Prince of Wales's Feather in the middle, of Gold, with a continual Firing of Cannon & Guns. Flaggs flying through-out the Mayors Parish &c. A vast Number of People at Norwich to day indeed. At 3 o'clock I went to the Wool-Pocket and eat part of Mutton Chop quietly, but very tough. For a Lobster to carry home 3. lb. 3 Qrs., pd. o. 2. 6. To Gingerbread Nuts &c. &c. paid & gave abt. o. 1. o. For my Dinner paid and gave o. 2. o. About 6. o'clock this Evening I got into my Curricle & drove home to Weston by 8. to Supper. The Main Spring of my Watch being broke I left it at Amyots to be repaired by Saturday next. I fagged about a good deal to day.

JUNE 24, WEDNESDAY. We breakfasted & spent the Morning at Weston P. About 2. o'clock this Afternoon we got into a Norwich Post-Chaise from the Kings Head and got to Norwich about 4. o'clock where we dined & spent the Afternoon and part of the Evening till 9. o'clock. Briton went with us. Paid at the Kings Head for our Dinners and Chaise to Norwich, Driver, Waiter &c. 1. 5. 2. At Bakers for Luggage to London 4 Stone at 1ˢ 9ᵈ per Stone paid 0. 7. 0. About 9. this Evening we got into the London Coach from the Angel Inn & went off for London. Briton went in the outside. We had four inside Passengers besides: one very stout Man of Norwich by name Hix, a Grocer, one Single Lady, and a comical Woman and a little Boy her Son—The Child sick most part of the night as was the single Woman. We dropped the Stout Man at Bury & took up a very agreeable one. We travelled all Night some Rain.

> The Diarist and Nancy spent four nights in London and two at Bath where they dined with the Custances—and reached Sister Pounsett at Cole on July 1st.

JULY 13, MONDAY. We breakfasted & spent the Morning at Cole. Gout almost gone. Leg where I scratched it, indifferent. Nancy paid me this morning the Guinea she borrowed. About Noon, I walked with Nancy, and Miss Pounsett to Castle-Cary, and there we dined & spent the Aft. at Mrs. Richd. Clarke's with her, my Brother and Wife, and my Sister Pounsett. My Sister Pounsett rode there. In the Evening I walked back to Cole with Miss P. and supped, spent the Evening and slept there. My Sister being afraid to ride back, walked home rather late and Mr. Robt. White with her and he supped and spent the Evening at Cole. We left Nancy at Cary to spend a few Days at Mrs. R. Clarkes. Dinner to day a Couple of Chicken boiled & a Pigs face, Peas, a Leg of Mutton rosted and Tarts. Paid my Brother to day for Carriage which he paid for me for our large Trunk from Norfolk 0. 10. 0.

JULY 14, TUESDAY. ... To poor old John Coles of Cary, who used to go on foot to Oxford for me after my Horse gave 0. 1. 0. Dinner to day boiled Beef, fryed Souce &c. I was bad in my Stomach to day & vomited a good deal.

JULY 15, WEDNESDAY. ... My Sister P. complains a good deal, more so than I think she ought. She eats too gross things, too rich for her Stomach.

JULY 20, MONDAY. I supped and slept again at Cole. Leg bravely. At 8. o'clock this Morning I walked with my Niece Pounsett to Castle-Cary, and there we breakfasted at Mrs. R. Clarkes with her, my Brother & Wife, Nancy Woodforde and my Sister Pounsett, who rode on horseback behind Phillip. After breakfast I walked with my Brother to Gall-hampton and spent an hour with Willm. Woodforde and Wife. Saw the Hermitage which Willm. lately [built?] in which he has shewn great Taste. From thence we walked to the Parsonage at Ansford and spent half an Hour with Mr. Frank Woodforde & Wife. Then we walked to Mr. Robt. White's where we dined and spent the Afternoon with him & Wife, Sister White, My Brother's Wife, Mrs. R. Clarke, my Sister Pounsett & Daughter and Nancy Woodforde. In the Afternoon I walked over to my Uncle's and made him & his Wife a Visit, both of whom considering their Age, my Uncle being in his 90th. Year and his Wife in her 84th. were very well. My Uncle can see and walk without a Stick and has all his faculties remarkably well. I stayed about half an Hour with them, & returned to Mr. Whites. I called in at many Places in Cary. We all walked back to Cole after Tea, got home abt. 9. o'clock. My Niece Pounsett was crying, & fretting all the way back to Cole which made it very unpleasant. She never enjoys herself in Company, and does not like to go from Cole, very uncommon in one so young. . . .

JULY 31, FRIDAY. It being a fine Morning and Hay-makers all at work, My Sister ordered a Leg of Pork to be dressed for them, but Rain coming about Noon they were obliged to leave off and go to their respective homes. The Pork had been boiling for them two Hours, we had it taken up and put by for them against another Day. Dinner to day, boiled Salmon & cold rost Beef &c.

AUG. 1ST., SATURDAY. . . . Very wet all the day, but not heavy Rain. My Sister has about 4 acres of Hay, all abroad, good for very little now. She has however made three Ricks very well indeed.

AUG. 6, THURSDAY. . . . My Sister Pounsett is greatly altered to what she used to be, she is vexing, fretting & complaining all the day long. Nothing can please her. The Folks busy in making Cheesecakes &c. to day. To Hannah Arnold & her Sister gave 0. 1. 0.

AUG. 21, FRIDAY. I breakfasted, dined, &c. again at Cole, as did Mrs. Penny. This morning I partly settled Accounts with my Sister Pounsett, of Monies received and paid by her for me during the last two Years—She had received for me in all 95. 15. 6. Paid

in all 44. 3. 8¾. Balance due to me from her 51. 11. 9½.
Recd. of her in Bills & Cash the Sum of 42. 1. 3½.
Remaining due from her to me 9. 10. 5¾. Dinner to
day, Knuckle of Veal boiled, rost Beef &c. At Quadrille this Evening after Tea, lost o. o. 6. We had a very
heavy Storm of Rain with Thunder and Lightning
about dinner Time, but soon over.

Aug. 23, Sunday. I breakfasted, dined, &c. again
at Cole. Mrs. Penny breakfasted, dined & spent the
Aft. at Cole. About 11. o'clock this Morning, Mrs.
Penny's Husband and a Mr. Webb who married
Pennys Sister came to Cole in a one Horse Chaise from
Sherborne and they dined & spent the Afternoon with
us, and in the Evening returned home to Sherbourne
taking Mrs. Penny with them. My Brother, Sister
White, Mr. Robt. White and Wife, and Mr. Saml.
Pounsett also dined & spent the Afternoon with us.
We had for Dinner, some boiled Tripe, a boiled Leg
of Mutton, a Couple of Ducks rosted and a boiled
Orlean-Plumb Pudding. Mr. Penny is a Stationer at
Sherborne and Mr. Webb is a Saddler at Sherborne
& his Wife a Millener. For a Pack of Message Cards,
gilt, pd. Mr. Penny o. 1. 2. Mr. John Dalton, and a
Mr. Ford a Clergyman, called on us just before
Dinner & rather kept us from Dinner. Ford is a
Wiccamist, came off when I was Poser. Mrs. Penny
fell down Stairs this Afternoon, but I hope did not
hurt herself much as she is breeding. All our Company but Sister White left us about 7. o'clock, she
stayed & supped & slept at Cole. Mr. Saml. Pounsett
also returned to us at Supper time and he supped &
spent the Evening with us. My Brother was getting
forward very fast.

Aug. 28, Friday. I breakfasted, dined, supped &

slept again at Gallhampton. After breakfast, I desired Willm. to drive me over in his one horse Phaeton to Sandford-Orcas, where I have a small Estate which I have not seen for many Years, accordingly we took a ride thither and had very fine Weather for it, tho' very rough road and a great way, near eight Miles from Gallhampton. We got thither about 12. o'clock, and viewed all the Premises. Farmer John Downe has taken to it, and has let one of the Tenements to one Thomas Marks, a Husbandman, and the other Tenement to one Saml. Bullen, a Carpenter. The whole has been put in very sufficient repair, and a new blacksmith's Shop erected upon it, all done by the above Farmer John Downe, the Orchards near the Tenements have been dug up and set to Potatoes, which should not have been done. I did not see either the Farmer or his Tenants. I have recd. no Rent for the above Premises since Lady Day, 1787. Last Lady Day therefore had eight Years Rent due from my Estate at Sandford. We returned home about 3. o'clock to dinner. Dinner to day, 3. boiled Chicken and a Pigs Face, a Bullocks Heart rosted & a rich plumb Pudding. After Coffee and Tea this Evening we got to Whist again the same as last Night, won 0. 1. 0. but did not receive the Cash either to night or last Night, so that Mary stands indebted to me 0. 2. 6. I had an exceeding good bed & Room indeed last Night.

Sept. 5, Saturday. ... To a very poor old Man, 85. Years old, and a Native of North America, a very thankfull Man, gave 0. 1. 0. Dinner to day, fryed Soals, very fine indeed 1. pair only near three Pound weight. We had also one of the finest Crabs for Supper I ever saw, it weighed six Pounds. I gave for it 2. Shillings. At Quadrille this Evening with Sister White, Sister Pounsett and Nancy, lost 0. 1. 0.

SEPT. 8, TUESDAY. ... Mr. Frank Woodforde and Wife & Daughter Fanny with her Brother Tom dined and spent the Afternoon with us. ... They came & returned in Captain Johnsons Carriage. Fanny Woodforde was left behind to spend a Day or two with Jane Pounsett. Jane behaved quite rude this Evening, I never saw a Girl in my Life of such a Disposition, she is never easy, & always disturbing other People.

SEPT. 14, MONDAY. ... Farmer John Downe of Sanford Orcas my Tenant came to Cole about 2. o'clock this Afternoon to settle some Matters with me. William Woodforde came with him. He brought me in Bills for repairs for the last four Years, to the Sum of 31. 18. 9¼. Mr. Pounsett let him have the whole for four Guineas a Year, 4. Years due from Downe at last Lady Day, from last Lady Day for the future He is to give five Guineas per Annum, till the whole Expences of the late Repairs are paid. The last four Years being deducted from the above Expences, that is 16. 16. 0, there then remains to be paid 15. 2. 9¼. The Farmer eat some Victuals & had some Cyder. Willm. Woodforde dined & spent the Aft. with us. My Brother spent the Afternoon with us. Soon after he came, Farmer Clements of Wicke and Robin Francis came here to settle about his [and] Robin's taking mine & my Brother's Estate at Ansford. After long talking we closed. He is to give me for mine, forty Guineas a Year and pay all Rates & Taxes, the Land-Tax only excepted. Dinner to day, Cottage Pye, Tripe, a fine Pheasant rosted and an Apple Pudding. My Brother left us about 8—Willm. about 7. o'clock. At Whist this Evening, Mary Woodforde and me against Sister Pounsett & Nancy, lost 0. 3. 0.

SEPT. 15, TUESDAY. . . . Fanny Woodforde & Jenny Pounsett had a little sparring this Afternoon— Fanny in the Wrong.

OCT. 3RD, SATURDAY. . . . Caught a very large Bitch Otter in the Garden to day with a large Gin.

OCT. 7, WEDNESDAY. I breakfasted, dined, &c. again at Cole. Nancy breakfasted, dined, &c. again at Cole. Jenny Pounsett rode up to Ansford this Morning behind Philip to Mr. Frank Woodfordes, she saw only Fan Woodforde & Mary Woodforde of Taunton. Fan was very angry with Nancy W. and said that Nancy was very much like Nann Stride an old Woman who goes about in Errands. Fan never speaks well of any body. She was very mad that she did not go in our Chaise to Cary. Jenny returned home to dinner. Sent a Letter to my Maid Betty at Weston Parsonage. Dinner to day, Mutton Soup, a boiled Rabbit &c. At Quadrille this Evening, neither won or lost.

OCT. 14, WEDNESDAY. I breakfasted, dined, &c. again at Cole. Nancy breakfasted, dined, &c. again at Cole. Saml. Woodforde breakfasted, dined &c. at Cole. Saml. Pounsett spent the Afternoon, supped and spent Evening with us. After Tea we got to Cards limited Loo. Neither won or lost. Dinner to day, rost Beef & a Damson Pudding. Sam. Pounsett told us three very remarkable facts this Evening of some wonderful Men. The first was, that he saw a Man who was a Soldier eat a hind-Quarter of Veal that weighed eighteen Pounds, a sixpenny Loaf of Bread, and drank three Quarts of Beer, at one Meal

for a Wager. The Second was that there were two
Men, that eat a Leg of Beef, bone and all, one eat the
Meat and the other eat the bone. The third was, of
a Man drinking half Pint Tumbler Glass of Beer and
eat the Glass after it.

OCT. 15, THURSDAY. I breakfasted, and spent
Most of the Morn' at Cole. Nancy breakfasted, &
spent the Morn' at Cole. Saml. Woodforde breakfasted & spent the Morn' at Cole. Had a very restless
Night indeed last Night, very little Sleep and fright-
full Dreams but short. Dreamt that I took out three
of my Teeth, and my Sister Pounsett had taken out
two of hers, likewise that my Brother John was terribly
bruised. It was very hot in the Night, with Thunder,
and Lightning and heavy Storms of Rain. To John
Tally Junr. for some Mushrooms, gave 1ˢ 0ᵈ. About
Noon I took a Walk with Saml. Woodforde to Castle-
Cary to Mrs. Richard Clarke's where we dined &
spent the Afternoon with her, my Brother & Wife,
Sister Pounsett & daughter, & Nancy Woodforde.
After Coffee & Tea, Saml. Woodforde took a Walk
to his Brothers at Gallhampton & there he supped &
slept. Sister Pounsett, and Daughter, Nancy and self
supped & slept at Mrs. R. Clarkes. Dinner to day,
Harrico Neck of Mutton, rost Beef a Couple of Chicken
boiled & Pigs Face &c. At Cards, Commerce, this
Evening, lost 0. 0. 6.

OCT. 20, TUESDAY. . . . N.B. We were very busy
Yesterday in packing up our travelling Trunk that
goes by the Waggon to Morrow from C. Cary to
London. . . .

OCT. 22, THURSDAY. . . . Mr. Fooks of Shepton-
Mallett dined, supped and slept at Cole. He brought

over Bank Notes & Cash to my Sister of 300. Pound,
for the Bond she gave him when last at Cole. It was
advanced by one Mrs. Candy near Frome. My Sister
is to give five per Cent. Interest for the same. Mr.
James Woodforde of Allhampton drank Coffee & Tea
with us this Afternoon. Dinner to day, a Leg of Pork
boiled & a Surloin of Beef rosted and an Apple Pudding. At Cards, Commerce, this Evening, lost 0. 1. 0.
Gave Will: Coleman this Evening 0. 1. 0. We spent
a very merry Evening and did not get to bed till after
12. o'clock to night. Mr. Fooks is a very cheerfull,
merry Companion & full of goodnature.

OCT. 23, FRIDAY. I breakfasted, dined, &c. again
at Cole. Sister White, my Brother & Nancy breakfasted, dined &c. again at Cole. Mr. Fooks breakfasted at Cole, and soon after breakfast, he rode off for
Shepton-Mallett. A very fine Morning but a Frost &
cold, there was a great deal of Rain in the Night—
Water high. I paid into Mr. Fooks's Hands this
Morning for my Sister, the Sum of fifty Pounds to pay
to Mrs. Eliz. Penny (late Betsy Guppey) of Sherborne
when next there, being Money left in the late Mr.
Pounsetts hands by her, left her by Mrs. Donne. I
desired him also to pay her the Interest due for the
same and we would pay him again. Also I paid him a
Legacy of thirty Pounds left by the late Mr. Pounsett
to one Anne Robins of Sherborne lately but now of
Bruton, Wife of George Robins, Staymaker, which I
desired him to pay as he went thro' Bruton, to day.
The said Anne Robins was a natural Daughter of
Mr. Pounsetts, by one Bull. I also walked up to Mr.
Sam. Pounsetts this Morn' with my Brother and there
paid Sybil Shears late Servant of Mr. Guppey's, the
Sum of 107. 10. 0. being Principal & Interest, Money

lately lodged in the hands of poor Mr. John Pounsett, deceased. Sent Philip also to Cary to pay Mrs. Gardners Bill for the Funeral of the same, the Sum of 53. 16. 9. My Brother's Wife & Mrs. R. Clarke came to Cole about 2. o'clock in George Pews little Cart & they dined, supped & slept at Sister Pounsetts. Dinner to day, fryed Eels, Ham & 2. boiled Fowls, a very fine Hare rosted & a bread-Pudding. At Cards (Commerce) this Evening, lost 0. 1. 0. Mr. Sam. Pounsett supped & spent the Evening with us.

OCT. 24, SATURDAY. . . . Paid my Sister Pounsetts Man Philip this Morn' for a Years Wages due April 5th. 1795 9. 9. 0.

OCT. 26, MONDAY. I breakfasted & spent part of the Morn' at Cole—As did also Miss Woodforde. Sister White, my Brother & Wife & Mrs. R. Clarke also breakfasted with us at my Sister Pounsetts. About Eleven o'clock this Morning, Nancy and self took leave of our Friends at Cole, and sat off for Bath. Briton went with us on an hired Horse. We had one of Ansford Inn Chaises. Gave to my Sister Pounsetts Servants 1. 1. 0. We went thro' Bruton, Evercreech, Shepton Mallet to old Downe Inn, about 13. Miles from Bruton. We got thither about one o'clock, eat a bit of cold Beef, and then got into a fresh Chaise and Horses and off for Bath. We left our Friends at Cole very low, we were so also. Sent to Sybil (an old Servant Maid of the late Mr. Guppeys & who now lives at Mr. Sam. Pounsetts) by Mr. Sam Pounsett this Morning 0. 2. 6. To some poor Neighbours of my Sister Pounsetts directly opposite their House, by name, Williams & Curtis, gave this Morning 0. 3. 6. Paid for the Ansford Chaise & single Horse from Cole to Old Downe to the Driver 1. 3. 6. To the Driver of

the Ansford Chaise gave o. 2. o. Paid and gave for
Refreshment at Old Down 4. o. We got I thank God!
safe and well to the White Hart Inn, Bath, kept by
Pickwick about 4. o'clock this Afternoon, where we
drank Tea, supped & slept, not fatigued at all to day.
Paid for the Old Downe Chaise & Horse o. 18. 8. To
the Driver, gave 2/0. Tolls, 6, 3/6, o. 5. 6. Sent in
the Evening to enquire for Mr. and Mrs. Custance &
Family at Portland Place, and likewise a fine Cock
Pheasant which my Sister Pounsett gave us to carry to
them. The Family were all very well & much obliged.
To a pair of Elastic Soles for Shoes pd. o. 2. o. To a
Tunbridge Soap Box with Naples Soap pd. o. 3. 6.
To a small Shaving-Brush in an Ivory Case o. 2. o.

OCT. 27, TUESDAY. We breakfasted, supped & slept
at the White-Hart. I took a long Walk early this
Morning about Bath. To a Barber shaving me &
dressing my Wig o. 1. o. After breakfast whilst Nancy
was dressing I walked to Sydney Gardens, very pretty,
gave there &c. o. 1. o. Mr. Custance called on us this
Morning about 11. o'clock and stayed a full hour with
us. He desired us to dine with them to day. As we
were at our Inn Window opposite the Pump Room
this Morn' we saw John Dalton coming from the
Pump-Room way on foot. We did not call to him,
as he was with Company. About 2. o'clock I walked
with Nancy to Portland Place where we dined &
spent the Afternoon with Mr. & Mrs. Custance, their
Children, Willm., Miss Custance, Emily, John, Neville
& Charlotte. Poor Nancy was greatly chagrined &
mortifyed going up to Portland Place which stands
very high & the Wind much Power. The Wind was
unluckily very high with some Rain just before we got
thither, and directly opposite Mr. Custance's Front

Windows, the Wind took Nancy's riding Hat & Feathers with a green Vail entirely off and was blown some little way, and her Hair tho' but just dressed, quite destroyed, the Family at Portland-Place, seeing it all. The Family were extremely glad to see us. A Mrs. La Mair, Governess, dined with us. We had for Dinner, some Soals rather stale, a Saddle of Mutton rosted, Pork Steaks, Soup &c. We returned to our Inn about 8 o'clock & had a better Walk back, tho' Windy & cold.

OCT. 28, WEDNESDAY. We breakfasted and dined at the White Hart. Mr. Custance called on [us] about Noon and spent the best part of an Hour with us, and then took leave of us, as we go for London at 4. this Aft. Paid at the Coach Office at Pickwicks for two inside Places and one outside to London 4. 0. 0. viz: inside each £1. 11^s. 6^d. outside 17^s 0^d. The Coach carries only four insides and goes from Pickwicks at the White Hart. Paid & gave at the White Hart 2. 12. 5. At four we got into the London Coach, and had two Gentlemen with us, one of them was a Counsellor Bragge Member for Monmouth & a Co-temporary of mine at New-College, as he did not acknowledge me, I did not him. It turned out a very fine Afternoon & Evening.

OCT. 29, THURSDAY. I thank God we had fine Weather and a good Moon all last Night, and about 10 o'clock this Morning we got safe & well to London to the Angel Inn at the back of St. Clements Church in the Strand, where we breakfasted, dined, supped & slept. We were not much fatigued with our Journey or otherwise indisposed, tho' travelling all Night. Paid for refreshment on the Road abt. 0. 2. 0. To Coachmen on the Road, gave 0. 4. 0. To Guard near

London, gave 0. 1. 0. To extra Luggage, 50. lb. at 1½d. pd. 0. 6. 0. As we heard when we got to London that the Sessions of Parliament was to be opened this Day—At one o'clock I walked with Nancy to St. James's Park about half a Mile, where at two o'clock or rather after we saw the King go in his State Coach drawn with eight fine Cream-Coloured Horses in red Morrocco-leather Harness, to the House of Lords. The Park was uncommonly crouded indeed, never was known a greater Concourse of People before, and I am very [sorry] to insert that his Majesty was very grossly insulted by some of the Mob, and had a very narrow escape of being killed going to the House, a Ball passing thro' the Windows as he went thro' old Palace-Yard, supposed to be discharged from an air Gun, but very fortunately did not strike the King or Lords. On his return from the House to James's Palace he was very much hissed & hooted at, and on his going from St. James's to the Queens Palace in his private Coach, he had another very lucky Escape, as the Mob surrounded his Coach and one of them was going to open the Door but the Horse Guards coming up very providentially at the Time, prevented any further danger. The State-Coach Windows going from St. James's to the Mews were broke all to Pieces by the Mob, but no other damage done to the Coach. We had very difficult work to get out of the Park, the Croud still increasing, however at about 4. o'clock we got out thro' a narrow Passage between Marlborough House and St. James's Palace into Pall-Mall, and when we got to Charing-Cross in going up the Strand We Met such a Mob of the lowest Class that quite alarmed us, they were going to the Park. We crossed the Street under the Heads of Horses that were in the Coaches which stood quite close one to

another all up the Strand. The Mob was composed
of the most violent & lowest Democrats. Thank God
the King received no Injury whatever, neither did we
as it happened. Every Person attached to his Majesty
was very much alarmed and concerned for him to-day.
It was said that there were near two hundred thousand People in St. James Park about 3 o'clock. I
never was in such a Croud in all my Life. By the
Horse Guards the whole Area of the Parade was
entirely filled up and all the Park quite to the Queens
Palace very much crouded besides. Soon as ever the
King got thro' the Horse Guards the Gates were shut
as he went & as he returned. We were glad to get
back to our Inn safe. Dreadful Work was expected
to be done to night. Three or four of the Rascals that
insulted the King were taken into Custody & had
before Parliament. Both Houses of Parliament were
very busy almost the whole night in consultation
concerning the shameful Insult his Majesty received,[1]
but nothing done as we heard off when we went to bed
which was very late to night. Dinner to day, Whitings
& some Veal Cutlets.

OCT. 30, FRIDAY. We breakfasted, dined, supped
& slept again at the Angel-Inn. Thank God! no bad
work done last night tho' much was expected. Soon

[1] This scene of mob violence on October 29th, 1795, followed on a
mass meeting on October 26th in Copenhagen Fields, organized by the
London Society, to present remonstrances on the state of the country.
Prices had risen steeply and in the autumn and winter reached famine
level (see, for instance, Parson Woodforde's entry for December 26th
following). The King on proceeding to open Parliament was greeted
with cries of 'Give us peace and bread', 'No King!', 'No War!' and so
on. How serious this demonstration was is abundantly illustrated by
the account so vividly given by the Diarist. Following on this disturbance Parliament passed measures for the defence of the King's person,
and to prohibit assemblies of the kind which had given rise to the
tumult of October 29th.

after breakfast I walked with Nancy to Miss Sally Popes in Newgate-Street, and from thence to Miss Webbs in Tudor-Street, but neither Miss Webb or her Brother or Miss Hussey [were at home], but as they were expected soon I left Nancy there and walked back to my Inn. About 3. o'clock I sent Briton after her whilst I was dressing. Nothing talked of to Day but the happy Escape from the danger the King had Yesterday. His Majesty nevertheless with the Royal Family go this Evening to Covent Garden Theatre. Every Well-Wisher to them, is very anxious for their Welfare to night. Pray God! defend them. To 2. pair of Silk Stockings, partly Cotton pd. 17. 0. To 3. pair of white worsted Boot-Stockings, pd. 6. 0. To Cakes & other refreshment in the Morn', pd. 0. 6. Dinner to day, Soals & Pork Stakes. Mr. Webb called on us about 10 o'clock this Night, smoked a Pipe with me & had Brandy & Water.

OCT. 31, SATURDAY. We breakfasted, dined, &c. again at the Angel Inn. Took a long Walk this morning by myself abt. the Court End of the Town long before breakfast. In my Walk for a Pair of Gloves, pd. 0. 2. 0. For a Ladies Pocket Book for 1796, pd. 0. 2. 0. Mr. and Miss Webb drank Coffee and Tea with us this Evening, after which we all got into an Hackney Coach and went to New-Drury-Lane Theatre where we saw performed a very pretty new Comedy called, First-Love. Enter[tainment]: Lottery Ticket. Both pretty things and extremely well performed. Principal Actors & Actresses were Palmer, Bannister Junr., King, Mrs. Jourdan, Miss Farren, Miss Pope, Signiora Storace &c. For 2. Tickets, pd. 0. 7. 0. To Coach hire from the Theatre &c. pd. 0. 2. 0. I walked about with Nancy after breakfast, to Miss Popes Miss Webb &c. Dinner to day fryed Herrings and some Beef Steaks &c. Cyder, Wine & Porter to drink. His Majesty with the Queen and most of the Royal Family were at Covent Garden last Night, and very graciously received, God Save the King was played six Times—Every thing pleasant. Thank God! that they met with nothing disagreeable.

Nov. 1, SUNDAY. We breakfasted, supped & slept again at the Angel. It being a wet Morning, very little going out to day. Had a new Wig brought me this Morning made by one Lambert in St. Clement's Church Yard, made since Thursday Afternoon last. He is Barber to the Inn. Gave to his Man that shaves me 0. 1. 0. I am to pay for my Wig to Lambert one Pound five. About 3. o'clock this Afternoon we went in a Coach to Mr. Webbs in Tudor Street and there dined and drank Tea and spent part of the Evening with Mr. & Miss Webb. We had for Dinner some Salmon, rost Beef &c. We returned to our Inn about 9. in the Evening. For a Coach to and back from Mr. Webbs pd. 2. 0.

Nov. 2, MONDAY. I breakfasted, dined &c. again at the Angel. Nancy breakfasted, supped & slept at the Angel. Soon after breakfast I walked with Nancy to her Mantua Maker, Miss Ryder, Southampton buildings Chancery Lane, from thence went with her to Sally Pope's in Newgate Street and there left her to spend the remaining part of the Day. I then returned to my Inn & wrote a long Letter to my Sister Pounsett & sent it this Evening. About 6. in the Evening I walked to Miss Popes and there drank Tea with her, Mr. Baker & Nancy. Paid this morning to Mr. Stephenson, Landlord, of the Angel Inn for our Dinners &c. since Thursday Morning last to this

Morning, 3. 18. 2. To extra Expences in the City for fruit &c. pd. 0. 1. 0.

Nov. 3, Tuesday. We breakfasted, & spent part of the Morning at the Angel Inn. Paid for my New Wig 1. 5. 0. To 2. new Table Cloths very large of one Jeremy in Tavistock Street near Covent Garden pd. 2. 2. 0. We packed up all our things this Morning, and then paid our Landlord since Sunday Night 1. 19. 6. Our beds & Servants' Bed was charged out of the above one Pound, 1s/6d each Night for Each of us and one Shilling per Night for Briton. Paid & gave to Barber & Servants at the Inn 0. 18. 0. To a black Leather Watch-Chain pd. 0. 1. 0. About 3. o'clock this Afternoon We left the Angel Inn, got into a Coach with our Luggage and drove to the Swan & two Necks in Lad-Lane, where at 4. o'clock we got into one of the Norwich Coaches & set off for Norwich. Paid for the Coach from the Angel 0. 1. 6. To extra Luggage from London to Norwich pd. 0. 7. 0. To refreshment at the Swan & 2 Necks, pd. 0. 2. 0. To a Porter at the Swan, pd. 0. 0. 3.

Nov. 4, Wednesday. We had I thank God! a good night of Weather all last night, good Lights to our Coach the beginning of the Night, and a good Moon early in the Morning. It was very cold in the Night being a smart Frost. We did not breakfast till we got to Tivetshall Ram in Norfolk about 8. o'clock this Morning, and only fifteen Miles from Norwich. Gave to Coachmen & Guard from London 0. 5. 0. For our breakfast this Morn' & on the Road 0. 4. 0. About 11. o'clock this Morn' we got to Norwich safe & well, blessed be God for it. We stayed at Norwich at the Kings Head about an Hour then off in one of their Chaises for Weston and got home to Weston Parsonage between 3. and 4. o'clock in the Afternoon, and found all my Family well & all things in order— accept O Lord my Thanks for the same. Paid for Refreshment at Norwich & Chaise to Weston and Horse for Briton & given to Servants 1. 1. 7. To the Norwich Driver, gave 0. 1. 6. Gave my Barber at Norwich, Frank 0. 1. 0 as he brought me a new Wig to carry home. We drank Tea, supped & slept at our comfortable quiet, happy, thatched Dwelling. Our People had been expecting us some time.

Nov. 6, Friday. We breakfasted, dined &c. again at home. There was a most violent Gale of Wind this Morn' early about 3. o'clock, continued More than an Hour. It waked me. It also shook the House. It greatly frightened our Maids in the Garrett. Some Limbs of Trees blown down in my Garden. Many Windmills blown down, and a good deal of Damage done to Weston House-Tiles. Mr. Girling called on us this Morning. Mr. Maynard, my Curate in my absence, called on me also this Morning. I thanked him for serving my Church and gave him 10. 0. 0. He served Weston from June 24. to Nov^er. 5th. being 19. Sundays. He stayed about half an Hour. Mr. Corbould & the Revd. Mr. John Warren made us also a Morning Visit. Mr. Girling sent us a Leash of Partridges this Even'. Gave to the Servant that brought them 0. 1. 0. Dinner to day a boiled Chicken and a Pigs Face and some beef Steaks.

Nov. 16, Monday. . . . Mr. and Mrs. Corbould made us a late Morning Visit. I engaged Mr. Corbould this Morning to be my Curate for the ensuing six Months, to begin on Sunday next, at the rate of thirty Pounds per Annum with all Surplice Fees. . . .

Nov. 22, Sunday Mem: . . . Mr. Corbould read

Prayers & Preached for me this Morning at Weston
Church, for the first time on being appointed by me
for my Curate. He called on us as he rode to Church.
We did not go to Church this Morning. Dinner to
day, Neck of Veal rosted &c. Mr. Smith of Mattishall
sent over his Servant Lad this Morning to enquire for
us after our Journey. It is somewhat strange, as he
has not sent a Servant to enquire after us for Years—
No Note.

Nov. 24, Tuesday. . . . Mrs. Bodham sent Nancy
a Note this Morning by their Servant Willm. Ward,
to enquire after us. Poor Mr. Bodham rather worse
than better, Senses almost gone. The Servant stayed
some time on Account of the Rain. Soon after the
Servant went, Aldridge who goes abt. with Cottons
&c. called here, and whilst I was dealing with him,
Mr. Mellish of Tuddenham made us a Visit and
stayed about half an Hour with us, I asked him to
dine with us & meet Mr. & Mrs. Corbould but he
said that he expected his Sister from London. To
Aldridge for 14. Yards of Cotton, at 2ˢ/3ᵈ. pd. 1. 11. 6.
which I gave to my two Maids, a Gown each. To
Aldridge also, for 8. Yrds. of Cotton, at 2/6, 1. 0. 0
which I gave to Miss Woodforde. Also for 7. Yards of
Cotton for a Gown for myself, at 2ˢ/2ᵈ. pd. 0. 15. 0.
Pd. him likewise for a Marcella-Waistcoat Piece
Yellow Ground ¾ yrd. square, for Ben 0. 8. 0. To
Aldridge also, for 2. Silk Handkerchiefs from Spittal
Fields, Chocolate Ground & Yellow Spots, pd. 11. 0.
One of which I gave to Ben & the other to Boy, Tim.
Paid Aldridge in the whole 4. 5. 2. It being late
almost dinner time, before I had finished with Al-
dridge, I asked him to dine with our Folks but he
could not stay for that, he eat some cold rost beef and

had some Table-Beer. Before I had quite dressed Mr. & Mrs. Corbould came to dine with us, which they did in a friendly way and stayed till near 8. in the Evening. We gave them for dinner, Hashed-Calfs Head a boiled Chicken & some Bacon, a Leg of Mutton rosted, and a Norfolk batter-Pudding & drippings after that, we had a Duck rosted, Maccaroni & Tarts. By way of Desert, we had white Currants, Pears & Apples, and Filberts. After Coffee & Tea we played one Pool of Quadrille at 2^d. per fish, very little lost, I neither won or lost.

Nov. 25, WEDNESDAY. . . . Our late Journey to Somersett, expences there and back again to Weston, paying Mr. Maynard serving my Church in my Absence, with things bought in London & elsewhere, cost me about 80. 0. 0.

DEC. 1ST., TUESDAY. We breakfasted, dined, &c. again at home. This being my Tithe-Audit Day— The following Farmers &c. paid me their respective Composition and dined at my House afterwards— Stephen Andrews, Thos. Reynolds Junr., J^n_o Norton, John Mann Junr., J^n Buck Senr., Wm. Bidewell, Js. Pegg, J^n Buck Junr., Mary Pratt, Henry Rising, Charles Hardy, John Girling, John Baker, Willm. Howlett, James Herring, Henry Case, Andrew Spraggs, Robt. Emeris, Hugh Bush, John Heavers, and Charles Cary. They all behaved remarkably well, and were all happy & well pleased with the Frolic. Mr. Howlett was very indifferent indeed and went away very early, could neither eat or drink, appeared very feaverish all the time. His usual flow of Spirits quite gone. My Company to day, at least most of them did not leave my House, till after 2. in the Morn' but all parted then in very high Glee—

Stephen Andrews, John Buck Senr., and Hugh Bush, very much disguised in Liquor. Michael Andrews who has taken Mr. Smiths Farm (lately James Herrings) dined with us, as did Js. Jermyn, who has taken the Estate (late John Bucks Senr.). I gave them for Dinner, the best part of a Rump of Beef, a slipMarrow bone of Beef, both boiled, a Leg of Mutton boiled & Capers, a fine Surloin of Beef, Salt Fish, a Couple of Rabbits boiled & Onion Sauce, & plumb & plain Puddings in plenty. Small Beer & strong, Punch & Wine as much as they pleased to make use off—Strong Beer amazingly liked and drank in great Quantity, six Bottles of Rum made into Punch, one Dozen of Lemons, and about five Bottles of Port Wine drank to day. They were all extremely well pleased with their Entertainment and very harmonious. Recd. to day for Tithe about 286. 18. 6. Paid Mr. Emeris to day a poor Rate at 1ˢ/6ᵈ from last Lady Day to Michaelmas 2. 5. 4½. Paid Mr. Bidewell for Carriage of 2. Chldrn of Coal 0. 10. 0. Paid Mr. Mann Junr., for ditto, ditto 0. 10. 0.

DEC. 17, THURSDAY. ... Had a new London Wigg brought home this Morning, made by Lambert, St. Clements Church Yard. A Note came in the box with an Account of it—Viz: for the Wig, £1. 5ˢ 0ᵈ, Box 1ˢ/0ᵈ, which with the Carriage from London to my House was 1ˢ/6ᵈ more, my Wig will stand me in 1. 6. 6. Dinner to day, Rabbits & Onions & a rost Duck.

DEC. 19, SATURDAY. . . . Billy Bidewell's People brought our News &c. Nancy had a Letter this Evening from Js. Woodforde from Allhampton, he lives with his Mother there. Wheat very dear indeed, fifty Shillings per Coomb and Wheat Flour very difficult to get at all. Meal per Stone three Shillings & three pence. . . .

DEC. 21, MONDAY. . . . This being St. Thomas's Day, I gave to 52. poor People of my Parish, against Christmas, 6ᵈ each, 1. 6. 0. Dinner to day, boiled Beef & a Rabbit rosted &c. Nancy wrote a long Letter to Mrs. Custance and sent it this Evening to their Tenant, Mr. Best at their Farm who sends a Parcel to them to Morrow with Turkies &c. against Christmas Day.

DEC. 25, FRIDAY, Christmas Day. We breakfasted, dined, &c. again at home. This being Christmas-Day, the following poor People dined at my House & had each one Shilling apiece given to them by me 0. 6. 0. Old Tom Atterton, Ned Howes, Robin Downing, old Mrs. Case, old Cutty Dunnell, and my Clerk Tom Thurston. They had each a Glass of strong Beer after they had dined. The Holy Sacrament was administered this Morning at Weston Church by Mr. Corbould. It hurt me to think that I could not do it myself, but suffering so much the last Christmas Day by the cold, am afraid since to go to Church during the Winter Season. Nancy might have gone, but did not. It turned out a very fine Day indeed, no frost. Dinner to day, a Surloin of Beef rosted, a fine Fowl boiled & Bacon, & plumb Puddings.

DEC. 26, SATURDAY. We breakfasted, dined, &c. again at home. Sent Ben early this Morning to Norwich with 10. Coomb of Barley to carry to Mr. Bloome. Ben returned about 5. this Evening, all safe & well thank God. He brought a Note of the Barley as he did not see Mr. Bloome, but Ben told me that Barley was at 17ˢ/6ᵈ and 18ˢ/0ᵈ per Coomb. If at

18/0, Mr. Bloome owes me 9. 0. 0. To Charles Wibley, Blacksmiths Man 0. 1. 0. To Tom Short, Wheel-wright's Son 0. 1. 0. To Weston Ringers 0. 2. 6. To Weston Singers 0. 2. 6. Dinner to day, Souce fryed & boiled Beef &c. Recd. for Butter to day at 1^s/1^d 0. 2. 8½. Wheat amazingly dear indeed 3. Pound, & three Guineas, per Coomb given it is said.

1796

1796, JANRY. 1ST., FRIDAY. We breakfasted, dined, &c. again at home. To my Butcher's Lad, Peter Sharman, gave this Morning a Christmas Gift of 0. 1. 0. To my Malster Man, Jos. Edwards, Xmas Gift 0. 1. 0. Dinner to day, boiled Pork, hash Mutton & a Pudding. Gave Nancy this Afternoon being New Years Day her annual Gift of the Sum of 10. 0. 0 but her pleasing me to day I added to it 0. 10. 0 which made it ten Guineas.

JAN. 2, SATURDAY. . . . Billy Bidewell brought our Papers from Norwich. Very little News on the Papers, People rather More peaceable, tho' Wheat still very high.

FEB. 5, FRIDAY. . . . Mr. Custance arrived this Evening at Weston House from Bath. Mrs. Custance &c. left at Bath. We sent to enquire for Mr. Custance this Even' by Briton, who brought back a Letter from Mrs. Custance to Miss Woodforde, all well.

FEB. 6, SATURDAY. . . . Mr. Custance was so kind as to Make us a long Morning Visit. He looked very thin. Received for Butter this Morn' at 1^s/1^d, 0. 3. 3. Dinner to day, Mutton Soup, Beef Steaks &c. Billy Bidewell brought our News from Norwich. On

Monday Night last, their Majesties were insulted on their return from Drury Theatre. A Stone was thrown and broke one of the windows of the Kings Coach, no other damage.

FEB. 9, TUESDAY. ... Widow Greaves Junr. who in the last Summer lost a Cow, waited on me this morning with the Petition that was drawn up for her on the Occasion with the List of the Subscribers. She had collected near Six Pounds, had bought another Cow for four Pounds, so that she was a great Gainer by her loss. I gave her, this Morning (as I happened not to be at home at the time) 0. 5. 0. Dinner to day, fryed Pork & Turnip Green, a Duck rosted and some Apple Fritters being Shrove-Tuesday.

FEB. 15, MONDAY. ... To one John Turner an old decayed Fisherman with a petition, gave 0. 1. 0. He was the Man that brought me once some very indifferent Spratts. I had 70. Children this Morning at my House after Valentine Money, each 1^d, 0. 5. 10. ...

MARCH 8, TUESDAY. ... Very indifferent to day again, especially abt. Noon, very cold & trembled much, had a hard matter to shave myself to day.

MARCH 9, WEDNESDAY. ... Very ill this morning, having had little or no Sleep all last Night, so very cold. A general Fast this Day. Mr. Corbould read Prayers only this morning at Weston-Church. Mr. Custance at Church, we were not. Mr. Corbould called on us as he went to Church. Dinner to day, boiled Veal & Pork &c.

MARCH 12, SATURDAY. ... Thank God! I feel myself more comfortable. Mr. Wilson of Lyng sent me a Note this Morning to desire me to lend him half

a Guinea, which I sent to him, inclosed in paper
0. 10. 6. Dinner to day, boiled Beef, &c.

MARCH 16, WEDNESDAY. . . . Very busy in my
Garden all the Morning pruning up my Trees &
Shrubs. . . .

APRIL 3, SUNDAY. We breakfasted, dined, &c.
again at home. Mr. Corbould called here this Morning in his way to Weston Church. I walked with him
to Church, where Mr. Corbould read Prayers and
administered the Holy Sacrament at which I was present. I gave for an Offering 0. 2. 6. It gave Me Much
pleasure & Satisfaction in my Attendance this day on
Divine Service. It was ever my greatest Pleasure to
pay that homage to our great Creator which even
only from Gratitude, it demands. It gave me also
pleasure to see so many Communicants—25 or 26—
present. Mr. Custance, was not at Church, neither
were Mrs. Corbould or Miss Woodforde. Dinner to
day, Loin of Veal rosted &c. Sent a Note this Afternoon to Mr. Custance to desire the favour of his Company to dinner on Friday next or Thursday, and he
fixed on Friday next.

APRIL 8, FRIDAY. We breakfasted, dined, &c.
again at home. Recd. for Butter this Morning at
1^s $0\frac{1}{2}^d$, o. 4. $8\frac{1}{2}$. Mr. Custance, Mr. and Mrs. Corbould, Mr. Mellish of Tuddenham, and Mr. Stough-
ton of Sparham, dined and spent the Afternoon with
us, and did not leave us, till after 9. in the Evening.
Each Gentleman had a Servant with him. It was
very near 4. o'clock before we sat down to dinner,
Mr. Corbould coming very late to us. Mr. Custance
was with us by half past two. He brought us a brace
of Cucumbers, very fine ones, and the first we have

seen this Year. It was extremely kind of Mr. Custance. We had for Dinner, a fine Cod's Head and Shoulders, boiled, and Oyster Sauce, Peas-Soup, Ham and 2. boiled Chicken, and a fine Saddle of Mutton rosted, Potatoes, Colli-Flower-Brocoli, and Cucumber. 2nd. Course, a rost Duck, Maccaroni, a sweet batter Pudding & Currant Jelly, Blamange, and Rasberry Puffs. Desert, Oranges, Almonds & Raisins, Nutts, & dried Apples, Beefans. Port & Sherry Wines, Porter, strong Beer & small. After Coffee & Tea, we got to Cards, limited Loo, at which I neither won or lost. Nancy lost 5^s 6^d, Mr. Custance won abt. 12^s 0^d. Mr. Mellish having no Silver, lent him 0. 2. 0. Every thing very well conducted to day. My Company seemed well-pleased &c. We spent upon the whole a very agreeable Day.

APRIL 11, MONDAY. . . . Very cold, barren, growless Weather still.

APRIL 13, WEDNESDAY. . . . To Stephen Andrews paid this Morn' a half Years poor Rate from Michaelmas last to the fifth of April last past at 1^s 10^d in the Pound which amounted to the Sum of 2. 15. 5½ as I am charged at 30. 5. 0 for Land in hand. . . .

APRIL 14, THURSDAY. . . . Paid Mr. Corbould £3. 3^s 0^d to day to get three Receipts for the Powder Tax[1] from Norwich on Saturday next, as he goes to Norwich that Day.

APRIL 20, WEDNESDAY. We breakfasted, supped & slept again at home. Mr. Corbould made us a

[1] Pitt first taxed hair-powder in 1786, but the tax was put on a personal basis at a guinea a head in the 1795 Budget. Pitt greatly overestimated the yield of the tax, which caused a revolution in fashion. The Whigs now wore their hair short *à la guillotine*, as it was said, while those Tories who continued to use hair-powder were called *guinea-pigs*.

Morning Visit, soon after, Mr. Thorne, my Doctor, called on me and stayed a considerable time with us after Mr. Corbould was gone. I paid him a Bill of 3. 13. 6. It was after two o'clock before Dr. Thorne left us, and both of us quite undressed, so that we had to dress ourselves (being going to Mr. Mellish's to dinner) and to be at Tuddenham by half past three o'clock, if we could. At 3. o'clock I drove Nancy over in my little Cart to Mr. Mellishs, and did not get there till 4. o'clock, owing to Briton's being on foot. Mr. Corbould overtook us near Mouses House and went with us, he being going to dine there. The Party we met there was Mr. Mellish, Mr. and Mrs. Eaton, Mr. and Mrs. Howman and Mr. Corbould. All the Company met within ten Minutes of each other. Dinner was soon announced after our Arrival, which consisted of the following things, Salmon boiled & Shrimp Sauce, some White Soup, Saddle of Mutton rosted & Cucumber &c., Lambs Fry, Tongue, Breast of Veal ragoued, rice Pudding the best part of a Rump of Beef stewed immediately after the Salmon was removed. 2nd. Course. A Couple of Spring Chicken, rosted Sweetbreads, Jellies, Maccaroni, frill'd Oysters, 2. small Crabs, & made Dish of Eggs. N.B. No kind of Pastrey, no Wheat Flour made use of[1] and even the melted Butter thickened with Wheat-Meal, and the Bread all brown Wheat-Meal with one part in four of Barley Flour. The Bread was well made and eat very well indeed, may we never eat worse. After Coffee & Tea we got to Quadrille, that is, Mr. Mellish, Mr. Corbould, Miss W. and self. Neither Mr. & Mrs. Eaton, nor Mr. & Mrs. Howman played at all at

[1] Probably this was a patriotic effort of Mr. Mellish's. Pitt was said to have suggested that people should eat meat to save bread—which was excessively dear as we have seen.

Cards, but were setters by. About half past eight we all took our Leave of Mr. Mellish and returned to our respective homes as we went, we got home about half past nine, as we went very slowly on Account of Briton's walking, who muttered very much about walking and when he got home was very impudent indeed, but I believe he had been making too free with Mr. Mellishs Beer &c. Mr. & Mrs. Howman are both high and consequential, the Latter remarkably so, if a Dutchess (by which name she is by some called) could not give herself more consequential Airs. Mr. Mellish is a very worthy Man I verily believe. No Affectation or Pride, but seems to have every good Quality that can belong to Man. I neither won or lost at Cards this Evening. Nancy lost 1ˢ 6ᵈ.

MAY 1ST., SUNDAY. We breakfasted, dined, &c. again at home. No Service at Church this morning, being under repair. A Most gracious Rain almost the whole night. Lord make us thankfull for the same. All Vegetation seems at the height of growing. Dinner to day, Leg of Mutton rosted &c. Mrs. Corbould went to Norwich to day to stay there till she is brought to bed.

MAY 6, FRIDAY. . . . Gave my Boy, Tim Tooley, being going to Norwich to Morrow to get some Cloaths 0. 5. 0. Billy Gunton, Brother to my Maid, and who at present lives at Michael Andrews being in a low way—I had some talk with him on it at the desire of Michael's Wife.

MAY 7, SATURDAY. . . . My Boy, Tim, walked to Norwich this Morning and returned in very good time in the Evening. I gave him 2. pair of very good Worsted Stockings to day, which I promised Yesterday, that he might not buy much of that Article. . . .

MAY 8, SUNDAY. We breakfasted, dined, &c. again
at home. By particular desire of Billy Gunton, &
which I promised him on friday last, as this day to
administer the H. Sacrament to him, himself with his
Mistress Mrs. Michael Andrews, came to my House
about 11. o'clock this Morning and I then had them
into the Parlour and there administered the H. Sacrament to them and which I hope will be attended with
due effects both to him, Mrs. Andrews & myself. I
put on my Gown and Band on the Occasion. Mrs.
Andrews appeared to pay as much Attention to Billy
Gunton, tho' her Servant, as if it was really her own
Son—very good of her. It gave me great pleasure,
tho' far from well in doing what I did, as it will ever
give me pleasure to do any thing in my power, that
may give any satisfaction or ease to any person whatever, especially to the distressed. No Service at
Church this Afternoon, the Church not being fit.
Next Sunday I hope there will. Dinner to day,
Leg of Mutton rosted &c.

MAY 10, TUESDAY. We breakfasted, dined, &c.
again at home. I privately baptized a Child of John
Lilly-stone's this morning at My House by name,
Elizabeth. Dinner to day, hashed Mutton & Pudding
&c. Hubbard the Glazier dined with our folks to day.
He finished my Chancel Windows this Aft. On going
to bed to Night, our Boy Tim Tooley who was supposed to have been gone to bed was not to be found—
All his Cloaths gone also. It is thought that he is gone
to Norwich to enlist himself, as his Head has long run
on a Soldiers Life. His being at Norwich last Saturday & then offered ten Guineas if he would go for a
Soldier, determined him.

MAY 11, WEDNESDAY. . . . My Boy Tim Tooley

was supposed to have slept in my Barn last night, and that very early this Morning he marched off for Norwich to enter into his Majesty's Land Service. Richmonds eldest Son is likewise gone. They both agreed last Sunday to leave Weston and enlist. Both our Maids being gone most of the Morning to Church, to clean it against Sunday next, we helped dressing our Dinner which was a piece of rost Beef & a Suet Pudding. Gave Willm. Nelson, my Carpenter this Even' 0. 1. 0.

MAY 12, THURSDAY. . . . Mr. Corbould gave us a Call this Morning, did not stay long—His Wife has made him a present of another Son—Mrs. Corbould finely. Dinner to day, cold rost Beef &c. No Cooking to day, both my Maids being at Church in cleaning of it against Sunday next. Recd. for Butter this Evening at $11\frac{1}{2}$d, 0. 8. $1\frac{3}{4}$. Stormy rather this Afternoon and cold. Gave a little Girl of Bowles's 0. 0. 6. Tim Tooley's Brother, Thomas, entered my Service in his Brothers Place.

MAY 16, MONDAY. . . . My late Servant Lad, Tim Tooley, called on us this Morning. He came from Norwich with a Cockade in his Hat, and says he has entered himself in the thirty third Regiment of Foot. Poor Fellow, he appeared happy & looked well. I paid him what Wages were due to him and half a Crown extraordinary, in all 17. 6. Dinner to day, some more Eels fryed, mince Veal and some boiled Pork &c. Merry doings at the Heart to day being Whit-Monday.

MAY 25, WEDNESDAY. . . . Election of Members for Norwich to day, a strong Contest, one of the Gurneys put up, in opposition to Mr. Wyndham. It is supposed however that Mr. Wyndham will succeed

—Henry Hobart quite secure of being the other Member—Mr. Wyndham very unpopular at present at Norwich amongst the Revolutionists and which are great Numbers at Norwich, especially Dissenters. Knuckle of Veal & boiled Tongue for dinner to day. Mr. Stoughton of Sparham called upon us this Aft. whilst we were at Tea and he joined us. He was just come from Norwich. When he came away it was talked of that the Election would be over about 7. o'clock this Evening, and that Wyndham when he left Norwich, had several head of Gurney. Mr. Stoughton left us about 8. o'clock.

MAY 26, THURSDAY. . . . Mr. Corbould called on us this Morning being just come from Norwich. The Election for Norwich ended last Night in favour of Hobart & Wyndham. Mr. Corbould brought us a Couple of Maccarel, the first we have seen this Season. We took a Walk to Weston House about Noon and spent an Hour with Mr. Custance who is very low on the thoughts of leaving Weston very soon and going to Bath till next Year. Whilst we were walking to Weston House, Mr. Custance walked to our House, as we heard from Mr. Custance who soon came to us at Weston House. We went towards Morton to go to Weston House, or else we should in all probability have met Mr. Custance who came across Weston-great-Field. Mr. Custance very genteelly and very earnestly desired that we would send at any time and the oftner the better for any thing whatever his Garden produced. Next to his Brother, he desired that we might be served. Dinner to day, a Couple of Maccarel boiled and stewed Gooseberries & Leg of Mutton rosted &c. Mr. Corbould called on us again just as we had dined & he drank a few Glasses of Wine with us. Recd. for Butter this Evening at $10\frac{1}{2}$d, o. 7. o. Mr. Wyndham had upwards of 100. Majority above Bertelett Gurney on the Close of the Election.

MAY 27, FRIDAY. ... Tim Tooley, late a Servant of ours, but now a Soldier gave us a Call this Morning, he still continues at Norwich and continues firmly attached to the Army. ...

JUNE 4, SATURDAY. ... Still very rough, tempestuous Weather, not quite so much Rain. We are quite flooded in the Yard. I promised to send for Nancy this Morning from Norwich, but the Weather proving so very bad prevented me, tho' I wish for her home. I told Nancy before Miss Corbould on Thursday last, that I would send for her on Saturday. Miss Corbould was totally silent on the Occasion, did not express the least desire of Nancy's staying any longer. Miss Corbould they say, is like her Father, rather penurious and stingy. Mr. Custance drank Tea with me this Evening and stayed till after 8. o'clock. He came walking. He goes for Bath on Monday next. Mr. Custance quite sorry to leave Weston House. Dinner to day, boiled Beef & a rost Chicken &c.

JUNE 8, WEDNESDAY. ... Sent Ben, to Norwich this Morning early, with my great Cart, to bring home some Wine for me. He returned home by 4. o'clock with the same. Had 3. Dozen of Port Wine 13. to the Dozen this Morning of Johnny Reeves at the Heart for wch. I paid him, at 29^s/o^d per Dozen 4. 7. o. I likewise had of him one Gallon of Rum for which I also paid him o. 16. o. Dinner to day, Rabbit Pudding & a Goose rosted. Finding myself rather poorly to day, I took some Rhubarb this Evening on going to bed.

JUNE 11, SATURDAY. . . . In the room of my last
Boy, I took one John Brand off France Green, this
Morning on trial. . . .

JUNE 12, SUNDAY. . . . No Service at Weston
Church this Morning, as Mr. Corbould had three
Churches to serve this day. Dinner to day, fryed
Souce & a Couple of Chicken rosted and Asparagus,
&c. I was very low to day, being far from well.

JUNE 15, WEDNESDAY. I breakfasted, supped &
slept again at home. Miss Woodforde, breakfasted,
dined &c. again at home. It being a very bright
Morn' I got up early, shaved & dressed myself, and
immediately after breakfast abt. 8. o'clock, I got into
my little Cart and drove off for Norwich, taking
Briton with me. We got thither before ten o'clock.
I got out of my Cart just before we entered the City,
and walked down to Trowse-Mills to speak to Mr.
Bloome, whom I found at home. He promised to call
on me at the Kings Head and settle all Accounts at
3. o'clock this Afternoon. I stayed about half an Hour
with Mr. & Mrs. Bloome and then walked back to
Norwich thro' Kings Street to Tombland, and to my
Taylors, Willm. Forster, to whm. I paid a Bill for the
last Year, of the Sum of 4. 11. 6. From thence Went
to Mrs. Brewster's in Cockey Lane and paid to Miss
Gillman, for Tea &c. 3. 18. 0. From thence went to
Mannings my Brazier in the same Street but nearer
the Market & paid him 3. 6. 4. for a new Washing
Copper. Recd. of him for the old one, 29 lb. at 9^d per
Pd. 1. 1. 3. So that I paid him on the balance 2. 5. 0.
From thence went to Oxley's, Hatter, in the Market
Place and paid him for a New Hatt 1. 1. 0. From
thence went to my Mercers, Smith, almost next Door
to Oxley's, and paid him a Bill 6. 18. 0. From thence

went to my Wine Merchant, Mr. Robt. Priest, and paid him for a Qr. of a Pipe of Port, had last Week, Discount for ready Money included 17. 0. 0. Corks and Cooperage &c. 0. 6. 6. Paid him also for 2. Gallons of Rum, had at the same time, at 16^s 0^d per Gallon 1. 12. 0. So that I paid him in the whole 18. 18. 6. I paid him the above at his Son John's House, who asked me to dine with him at his Sons, which I promised if I could—they dine at 2. o'clock. I then called at Mr. Corboulds, went in, but saw only a Servant, Mrs. Corbould and Miss Corbould were at home but above Stairs, but did not make their appearance, sending word down that they were dressing. Mr. Corbould Junr. was just walked out, it was said. Old Mr. Corbould I knew was at Weston. I never saw any thing at all of them all the time I was at Norwich which was till 5. in the Afternoon. I was obliged to go many times by their Door, my Cart being put up almost directly opposite their House, which is in St. Giles's. At 2. o'clock I went to Mr. John Priests and made a very good dinner on a fore Qr. of Lamb, with him and his Father only, Mrs. J. Priest in the Country. Paid Thos. Burroughs, Breeches Maker in London Lane, for a Pr. of Breeches for Briton &c. 1. 4. 0. At three this afternoon, I went to the Kings Head and there waited till near 4. o'clock before Mr. Bloome came. When he was come we soon settled Accounts. I paid him for Coals 15. 13. 6. And I received of him for Corn 43. 10. 0. So that I received of him on Balance 27. 16. 0. To my Barber, Frank Lofty, for a new Wigg 1. 1. 0. For a Glass of white Wine & Water at Ravens, pd. 0. 6. At Nosworthy's, for 2. Rolls of Pomatum, pd. 2. 0. For three Coombs also there, pd. 1. 8. To my Taylors Men, gave as a free Gift 1. 0. For some Cakes & Porter &c. pd. & gave 0. 6. At 5.

this Evening got into my Cart and went for home. Almost immediately after we got out of the City, we had a very heavy Storm of Rain which made us wet thro' but it [did] not last long, having a new Hat on, it did it no benefit or good. We had very little or none after till we got home, which was about 7. o'clock, thank God safe & well.

JUNE 17, FRIDAY. . . . All kinds of Meat very high indeed at present. My Butcher charged me to Day for Beef 6½ᵈ per lb. For Mutton also 6ᵈ ditto. For Lamb, also 6ᵈ ditto. For Veal, also 5ᵈ ditto. Recd. for Butter to day, at 9½ᵈ, o. 4. 4¼. Dinner to day, Neck of Mutton boiled & a Goose.

JUNE 25, SATURDAY. We breakfasted, dined, &c. again at home. This Morning about 9. o'clock, got into my Cart and drove to Mattishall to attend at the funeral of Mr. Bodham, an old acquaintance. I got thither about half past ten o'clock, and there stayed at the House till near half past two in the Afternoon before the Corpse was carried to Church. It was a very handsome Funeral indeed. Two mourning Coaches and four, one Mourning Chariot and pair, two Post Chaises, besides other Carriages. The Pall-bearers, were Mr. Smith, Vicar of Mattishall, Mr. Edwards, Rector of Hethersett, myself; Mr. Shelford, Rector of N. Tuddenham, Mr. St. John Priest, of Scarning, and Mr. Howman Rector of Hockering. We each of us had a rich black Silk Scarf & Hatband, and a pr. of Beaver Gloves. Poor Mr. Bodham was fifty five Years of Age. Mr. George Smith, Curate of Mattishall, buried him. A great Number of People attended indeed. Chocolate, cold Ham, Veal &c. at the side Tables in the Room we were in, the best Parlour. We returned back to the House after the interment, took some little refreshment, and then each went to their respective homes. I did not get home to Weston to dinner till 5. o'clock this Afternoon. I took Briton with me. He had a black Silk Hatband and a pair of Gloves. I brought Nancy a pair of the best white Kid Gloves which was orderd by Mrs. Bodham. Nancy had saved me for Dinner a few green Peas & Bacon, and some rost Chicken. I was quite jaded when I got home and very hungry. I was very glad when I got home, for I much dreaded the Day, my Spirits being but indifferent, thank God however, I got thro' it extremely well.

JULY 9, SATURDAY. . . . We were very busy all the Morning in our Garden in raking Gravel about our Walks. . . .

JULY 14, THURSDAY. We breakfasted, dined, &c. again at home. It being a fine Morning I drove Nancy over to Mattishall and made Mrs. Bodham a Morning Visit, being the first since the Death of poor Mr. Bodham. We found her at home, her Sister Mrs. Balls, Miss Johnson and little Miss Donne, Niece to Mrs. Bodham. Old Mr. Hewitt called there also whilst we were there. We stayed about an Hour, and then returned home to dinner. Called at Betty Englands at E. Tuddenham late a Servant to poor Mr. Du Quesne. When at Tuddenham we went to the Church and saw the Monument put up lately by Mr. Townshend for his Friend & Relation Mr. Du Quesne. It was the plainnest I ever saw, it is Marble, but nothing more than a mere Slab, only wrote on. The Character given of him is very great. We got home before 3. o'clock. Had for dinner a large Piece of Beef boiled &c.

JULY 17, SUNDAY. ... Mr. Corbould served Weston Church this Aft. at 2. o'clock. I did not go being unwell. Miss Woodforde went with Mr. & Mrs. Corbould in their new Chariot, which is very handsome. We did not dine to day till after 3. o'clock. We had some Peas and a Fillett of Veal rosted &c. for dinner to day.

JULY 18, MONDAY. ... Drew my great Bason in the Garden this Morn' after breakfast, and caught one very fine Silver Eel, which weighed two Pounds, drew out also several small Carp all which I threw back again. Not one Tench seen. In all probability The Eel eat the Tench. ...

JULY 19, TUESDAY. ... Willm. Bidewell & James Pegg called on me this morning, concerning the Dog-Tax,[1] to know how many Dogs I intend to pay for, two only.

JULY 20, WEDNESDAY. ... To a poor dumb Man, who sells Matches, gave 0. 6.—a short Man rather but strongly made, very much tanned with the Sun, & without any kind of Shirt.

AUG. 7, SUNDAY. We breakfasted, dined, &c. again at home. Mr. Corbould read Prayers & Preached this Morning at Weston Church. Mrs. Corbould at Church as were Miss Woodforde & self. Mrs. Corbould was so frightened at Church by a Bat flying about the Church, that she was obliged to leave the

---

[1] Pitt taxed dogs in this year in order to make up the loss of revenue consequent upon the rejection of a proposal to increase the duty on printed calicoes and linen. The tax was in respect of sporting dogs only, or where more than one dog was kept. The tax, as usual, excited the caricaturist, and Gillray depicted Fox and his friends hanged 'as dogs not worth a tax'; on the other hand, Burke, as a friend of the Government, was drawn—together with other Government supporters—as a well-fed dog, 'paid for' with 'G.R.' on his collar.

Church. Nancy went out also to attend her. They went to the Parsonage where Mrs. Corbould stayed till we returned. Mrs. Howlett was at Church and exhibited for the first time, a black Vail over her Face. Mem. Times must be good for Farmers when their Wives can dress in such stile. Dinner to day Loin of Veal rosted &c. Very fine and pleasant Day. Mr. & Mrs. Corbould with young Longdale, Miss Woodforde & self took a Walk this Evening after Tea, to Farmer John Buck's. Himself & Wife behaved very hearty & generous, we staid abt. half an Hour there, & returned home.

AUG. 8TH, MONDAY. . . . It being a fine Morning, I drove down to Lyng and made the Revd. Mr. Anson[1] Rector of that Place my first Visit. He is but very lately come to reside. He is quite a young Man, very fair, of great Family. He has at present two younger Brothers with him. I stayed about half an Hour with them. Dinner to day, rost Beef &c. In the Evening between Tea & Supper we took a Walk to Hungate Lodge, found Mrs. Corbould at home but not Mr. Corbould, he was gone a fishing.

AUG. 31, WEDNESDAY. . . . We dined & spent the Afternoon at Hungate with Mr. and Mrs. Corbould, as did Mr. Mellish, Mr. and Mrs. Shelford, Mr. Howman, Mrs. Jeans, and with her Mr. Robt. Francis & his eldest Sister. Mrs. Jeans appeared more affected than ever. We have not been in Company before with her for near eighteen Months—much altered since. We had for Dinner, Peas Soup, Pigeon Pye, best part of a Rump of Beef rosted, Ham & two boiled Chicken, Broad Beans, and Patties. 2nd. Course. Fricaseed

---

[1] The Rev. Charles Anson, Rector of Lyng with Whitwell, 1794–1827.

Rabbitts, baked Currant Pudding, Couple Ducks rosted, Blamange, Pickled Salmon, French Beans and Tarts. Desert, a fine Melon and some Plumbs. Soon after Coffee & Tea, we all returned to our respective homes, all in two Wheel Carriages—five in all. Mrs. Jeans had three in hers, and a little grey Horse in it about the Size of a Calf. We got home in our little Cart in about ten Minutes.

SEPT. 1ST., THURSDAY. . . . Harvest rather at a Stand at present, it being rather indifferent Weather for the same. We had twenty-eight Pound of exceeding good Honey from Nanny Spraggs to day, we are to give sixpence a Pound for it, quite cheap. . . .

SEPT. 10, SATURDAY. . . . We finished Harvest this Afternoon, and thank God! had a fine Time for it, & all well. Sent a Note this Morning early by Briton to Mr. Anson at Lyng, to desire his and Brothers Company to dinner on Wednesday next, had a genteel Answer back, but they are engaged. Bidewell's Folks, got the Newspapers for us. The Austrians have beaten the French smartly of late, killed 5000, and taken 2000. Serious apprehensions are entertained by many in high rank of the French invading England some time this Autumn. Preparations are making.

SEPT. 12, MONDAY. We breakfasted, dined, &c. again at home. I dreamt last Night that I was at an Entertainment given by Mr. Coke at his House, amongst other Dishes there was a Faun rosted but cold, and plenty of Hares rosted, and cold also, &c. Mr. Coke very civil to me, on coming away I lost my Hat, some one had taken it, & I thought a Soldier. I thought however that I bought a second hand one of old Mr. Corbould, with many other things, all forgot.

A Raven fled over my House this Morning. All which tokens are said to bode no good. To Largesses to day, gave 0. 2. 0. Dinner to day, boiled Beef &c. We drank Tea this Evening with Mr. and Mrs. Corbould at Hungate-Lodge, and played one Pool at Quadrille. I lost 0. 1. 6. [Opposite the dream there is drawn the little pointing hand which Parson Woodforde uses only rarely for entries containing accounts of dreams, &c.]

SEPT. 24, SATURDAY. We breakfasted, dined &c. again at home. The Morning was cool. Afternoon fair. Evening cold with a kind of Scotch Mist. Dinner to day, Bullocks Cheek stewed, and a Neck of Mutton rosted &c. James Pegg brought our News for us to day, & likewise two Letters, One for me from my Niece Jane Pounsett, and one for Nancy from her Brother Saml. now at Stourhead. Miss Pounsett informs me that she and Mother had been lately at Weymouth for six Weeks, during the Time of the Royal Family being there, and that my Sister Pounsett was much better by going. And also she acquainted me that during her stay at Weymouth, a Mr. Grove a young Man & a Clergyman (and a quondam Admirer of Janes) had again paid his Addresses to her, and that she accepted of him & hope it will meet my Approbation. Nancy's Letter from her Brother informs her that he is at Sr. Colt Hoares at Stourhead with a full House of Company, Lord & Lady Bruce, Lady Hoare &c.

OCT. 6, THURSDAY. I breakfasted, dined, &c. again at home. Had very broken Sleep all night, very restless. I sent Briton after my Niece this Morning soon after breakfast, with a Note to Mrs. Bodham and a small Melon with half a Dozen Figs. Mr. Maynard made me a Morning Visit. Nancy returned home just at dinner time, and was lucky in escaping Rain, being a Showery Morn'. She was quite well and in high Spirits, never spent her time more agreeable than at Mattishall with her Friend Mrs. Bodham, who study to make everything pleasant to her Company. Her House full all the time that Nancy was there. Many Strangers she saw there, more particularly two Miss Hewits, Nieces to old Mr. Hewits, the eldest of them, the prettiest and most agreeable young Lady that Nancy ever saw, but alas! It is very much feared that she is very far gone in a consumptive State—Oh! what Pity. Dinner to day, Neck of Mutton boiled &c. Thank God! was much better this Afternoon and Made a good dinner, much easier in my Bowels. One Glass of red Wine only after dinner to day. Mr. Stoughton of Sparham gave a short call on us this Evening. Came to ask me to dinner on Saturday, to meet Mr. Anson & Brother.

OCT. 10, MONDAY. . . . My Boy, John Brand, left my Service to day, as he had proper Notice so to do, being the most saucy swearing Lad that ever we had, and am afraid that if he does not soon do better, he will bring his poor Mother with sorrow to her Grave. He can do his Work well if he pleases, but cannot be trusted out of Sight, but the worst is, he is profligate. Ben paid him his Wages due to him for four Months Service, due this Michaelmas at the Rate of two Guineas per Annum. He went before Dinner, and in the Evening my new Boy of this Parish by name Barnabas Woodcock between 11. and 12. Years of age, succeeded him. Dinner to day, Hash-Mutton &c. Pudding and a Goose rosted, being old Michaelmas Day.

OCT. 14, FRIDAY. We breakfasted, dined, &c. again at home. We made Mr. & Mrs. Corbould a

Morning Visit, Miss Corbould and Mr. Willins [a young Divine from Norwich] at Hungate Lodge, returned home to dinner on a Hare &c. Recd. for Butter to day, at 1ˢ/0ᵈ, 0. 3. 0. Just as we had dined Mr. Girling with one of the Chief Constables by name Copeman called on me to subscribe my name to an agreement, to prevent Riots or any publick disturbances that may happen by being active in suppressing such. I told them that I heartily concurred in it, and would do all in my power, but did not think it consistent with the Character of a Clergyman to put his name to it, therefore I did not.

OCT. 15, SATURDAY. . . . Mr. and Mrs. Jeans and Family have left their House at Witchingham & gone to reside in London. They left Witchingham we heard this day. They have let their House ready furnished to a Revd. Mr. Beevor, Son of Mr. James Beevor of Norwich.

OCT. 27, THURSDAY. . . . Paid my Blacksmith (John Buck)[1] this Morn' his annual Bill for Work done 4. 8. 7. . . .

OCT. 28, FRIDAY. . . . Gathered in my keeping Apples this Morn' had but very few Nonpareils or Pearmains but a good many large Russetts, and seven Bushel-Baskits of the old true Beefans, so peculiar to the County of Norfolk. Willm. Thorogold, Gardner, here to day, to trim up, my Fig Trees & Vines, against rough Winds. Dinner to day, rost Breast of Mutton &c. Had one of my little Pigs killed, to have it rosted. Quite a cheery Day but Air cool.

NOV. 5, SATURDAY. . . . Sent Briton over to Matti-

---

[1] The Smuggler, *alias* Moonshine Buck.

shall this morning to Mrs. Bodhams with a present of a nice rosting Pig from us to her. . . .

Nov. 6, Sunday. We breakfasted, dined, &c. again at home. Mr. Corbould read Prayers & Preached this Aft. at Weston Church. He called on us as he Went to Church & young Longdale with him. They each eat a Cake and drank a Glass of Wine. We did not go to Church, Nancy having a bad Cold, and myself but poorly, and it being very cold, there being a smart Frost this Morning. The general talk is now concerning an Invasion from the French—Mr. Pitt having Mentioned in the House of Commons that he had substantial reasons for believing it, but such as at present improper to mention. As Mr. Pitt is prime Minister, it is much credited throughout the whole Country, and creates a general alarm. The Militia are to be doubled, and new Cavalry to be raised. Dinner to day, Skaite & a fine Hare rosted.

Nov. 7, Monday. We breakfasted, dined &c. again at home. There being a Justice Meeting to day at Reepham, respecting Militia Men, and those inrolled concerning this Hundred in defence of it, against any Riots or disturbances that might happen—I sent my two Men, Ben and Briton (whose Names were put down some time back) this Morning to Reepham & there they stayed all Day but returned in good Time in the Evening abt. six o'clock, with two black Staves in their Hands with a black Leather-Guard for the Hand, and on the Staff were painted these Letters in white and figures 58, 59. E. H. L. A., viz: Eynesford Hundred Loyal Association.

Nov. 12, Saturday. . . . We gathered some white Currants from a tree in the walled Garden this Day

about Noon. Dinner to day, Giblet-Soup, with odds
& ends. Bidewell's People brought our Newspapers.
Admiral Elphinston's Squadron off the Cape of Good
Hope had fell in with a Dutch Squadron and captured
every Ship without firing a single Gun—9. Ships,
342 Guns, 1972 Men. Admiral Elphinstone's Fleet
consisted of 14. Ships, too great a Match for the
Dutch. The Dutch Admirals Name is Lucas. They
took our Fleet for the French Fleet, Admiral Richery's,
which were to have joined them there and to have
retaken the Cape of good Hope.[1]

Nov. 19, SATURDAY. . . . James Pegg brought our
News from Norwich. No good News upon the Papers
but rather the contrary on Account of the late Act for
augmenting the Militia—Riots talked of very much
about it—Rebellion said to be in Ireland, & the
French at the bottom of it.[2]

Nov. 28, MONDAY. . . . I bought a small Colt with a
white face going into his fourth Year, abt. 14. Hands,
of one Neale near Lenewade Bridge a very civil Man,
an Husbandman, I soon agreed with him, and paid

[1] Following the offensive alliance concluded between the Dutch and
the French against England in the spring of 1795, the English Fleet had
proceeded to capture the Dutch colonies. The Cape of Good Hope and
Ceylon had been taken in that year (1795) by Admiral George Elphinstone (1747–1823), better known by his later title of Admiral Viscount
Keith. Elphinstone's subsequent victory here described by Parson
Woodforde took place in August of this year, but the news had only
just arrived. It was to be Lord Keith's destiny nineteen years later
(1815) to receive the surrender of Napoleon at Plymouth—the Admiral
was in command of the Channel Fleet—and to dispatch him to St.
Helena.
[2] There was no actual rebellion in Ireland at this time, but the
country, specially Ulster, was seething with discontent. The stronghold
of the United Irishmen was Belfast, and the hatred of England was as
strong or stronger among Presbyterians than among Catholics. Wolfe
Tone, who was assisting the organization of the French expedition of
invasion at Brest, was a Protestant.

him for the same 6. 6. 0. It is a Mare, and very poor at present. Dinner to day, boiled Pork and Cottage Pye. Washing Week.[1]

DEC. 17, SATURDAY. . . . Bidewells People brought our Newspapers & a Letter for Miss W. from her Br. William of Gallhampton near Castle-Cary, Somersett. N.B. Compts being forgot in the Letter, Willm. put them on a very small strip of Paper and fixed it between the Seal & one Side of the Letter in the folding down of the same which made it a double Letter & I am to pay for it as such. I think it rather too dear to pay for Compts & should have been thought of by him. Williams' Wife wrote the Letter, therefore I should have inserted as such. Willm. only added the *very expensive* Compts. Very little News on the Papers, no bad.

DEC. 21, WEDNESDAY. . . . This being St. Thomas's Day, I gave to the Poor of Weston at 6d. apiece 1. 7. 0. Mr. Mellish made us a Morning Visit. Dinner to day, Hash Mutton & a Rabbit rosted &c. It was a cheery Day for the Poor People, tho' cold, it being good walking & dry over head.

DEC. 24, SATURDAY. We breakfasted, dined, &c. again at home. Very hard Frost indeed, last Night, froze above Stairs in the Stair-Case window quite hard. It froze the whole day within doors in a few Minutes—very severe Weather indeed—So cold last Night that it was a long time before I could get any sleep at all. I am much afraid that the Turnips will

[1] The last entry of 'Washing Week' was on October 24th. After November 28th the next entry is made on January 2nd, 1797, and the next on February 6th. Presumably this indicates that the washing of personal linen, &c., was a five-weekly event in the late eighteenth century.

suffer greatly by the present severe Weather, being almost entirely uncovered—We want Snow. Dinner to day, Neck of Mutton boiled & a Fowl rosted. Betty Cary went to Norwich to day and brought our News &c. She brought a Letter for me from my Brother and another for Nancy from Jenny Pounsett now at Cole Place, Somersett. We were obliged to have Hulver-branches without berries to dress up our Windows &c. against Christmas, the Weather having been so severe all this Month, that the poor Birds have entirely already stript the Bushes.

DEC. 25, XMAS DAY, SUNDAY. We breakfasted, dined, &c. again at home. This Day the coldest we have had yet and Frost more severe. It froze all the Day long and within Doors, the last Night intensely cold. Mr. Corbould read Prayers & administered the H. Sacrament this Morning at Weston Church. He called on us as he went and also on his return from Church. He said the cold at Church was so great as to make him tremble again. We did not go, the Weather being so severe. This being Christmas Day, the following People had their Dinner at my House, Widow Case, old Thos. Atterton, Christ. Dunnell, Edwd. Howes. Robt. Downing and my Clerk, Thos. Thurston. Dinner to day, Surloin of Beef rosted, plumb Puddings and mince Pies. My Appetite this very cold Weather very bad. The Cold pierces me thro' almost on going to bed, cannot get to sleep for a long time, We however do not have our beds warmed. Gave the People that dined here to day before they went, to each of them 1. Shilling o. 6. o. After they had dined they had some strong Beer.

DEC. 31, SATURDAY. We breakfasted, dined, &c. again at home. Very Mild but dark and damp.

Dinner to day, a boiled Rabbit & Onion Sauce, Peas-Soup and a breast of Mutton rosted &c. To John Shorten, Miller's Man, by J^n_o Lillistone 1. 0. Mrs. Bidewell brought our Newspapers to day and likewise a Letter for Miss Woodforde from her Brother Saml., now at Sr. Thos. Champneys at his Seat at Orcherly near Frome in Somersett giving her some Description of a late Masquerade Ball, given at the House, upwards of one Hundred & fifty genteel People at it. It was said on the Papers, that it was of the first Degree of Taste. Saml. was at it, being there to paint some Portraits. The Treaty on Peace, between England & France, which has been some time transacting, broke off very suddenly last Week by the French & our Negociator, Ld. Malmesbury ordered to leave Paris in 48 Hours—bad News indeed. The French in short, are afraid of making Peace, for fear of the Consequences which might arise from their dismembering their great Armies. Tho' very unfavourable the present aspect of public Affairs throughout Europe, at the Conclusion of the Year 1796—May God so direct the Minds of Men before the Conclusion of the ensuing Year, that a general Peace and every blessing attending it, may be felt in every Nation of Europe & over the whole World and whenever such Blessings arrive, May we all with one Heart & one Mind give our Most hearty thanks to that God for the same, and not unmindful of him Now or for ever.[1]

[1] Lord Malmesbury (Sir James Harris 1746–1820) had proceeded to Paris, following on the promise contained in the King's Speech to Parliament on October 6th. Pitt was forced to seek peace by the unfavourable position of affairs. One by one our allies had dropped away, and two of them, the Dutch and the Spaniards, had become our enemies—Spain declaring war in October. Italy, through the victories of Bonaparte, was rapidly becoming a French dominion. Ireland was seething with disaffection, and the heavy taxation made the war unpopular in England. In the negotiations England stipulated for the

1797

JAN. 4, WEDNESDAY. ... Sent Briton with my little
Cart to Norwich this morning after Fish &c. having
Company to dine with us on Friday next. I privately
named a Child of Henry Briggs this morning at my
House, by name Susannah. Sent by Briton a very fine
fat Turkey-Cock in his Feathers to Mr. Webb—
Tudor Street No. 5 Black Friars—London—to be put
into one of the London Coaches this afternoon for
London which will get there to morrow by noon. The
Turkey weighed twelve Pounds. Briton returned in
the evening about 5. o'clock, and brought a Letter for
Nancy from J^s Woodforde of Allhampton in Somersetshire. To my Carpenters Willm Nelson & Tom
Allen, who are sawing out a very large Oak Tree for
me—0. 1. 0. Dinner to day fryed Souse & a Goose
rosted &c. Poor old Mrs. Brewster is dead, died
yesterday. My poor old Mare Jenny, was shot this
morning. She was so old as not able to eat Hay, therefore thought it greater Charity to have her killed—
Mr. Townshends Gamekeeper John Hutchins shot
her. Mr. Girling Junr brought us a Leash of Partridges this morning.

JAN. 15, SUNDAY. We breakfasted, dined, &c. again
at home. Mr. Corbould read Prayers & Preached
this afternoon at Weston-Church, he called on us as
he went, and told us that one of his Pointer Dogs, by
name Tony, was gone mad and had got out in the

restoration of Belgium to Austria, otherwise France was to retain her
conquests and to receive back her colonies in the East and West Indies,
which our fleets had enabled us to conquer. The captured Dutch
colonies we would retain. These terms were rejected by the victorious
Directory on December 19th, and Lord Malmesbury was summarily
dismissed from France.

Night when confined by making a Hole in the door, after loosening his Chain, and went over great part of the Parish & the Parish of Ling, biting many dogs, Pigs, &c. But was killed this Morning at Mr. Corboulds, as he returned home. Mr. Corbould hung all his Greyhounds & other Dogs immediately, except a favourite Pointer by name Juno, which is close confined & Antidotes given her, and is to be removed to Bracon, soon. The mischief done by the Dog, as known, is this, 2. Piggs of Mr. Howletts, Michael Andrews Yard Dog, Mr. Girlings ditto. 2. Pigs of Cases, and what is worse than all, is, that Jermyn's Son was bit in the hand—so far known, but what other Mischief has been done, God knows. I hope we shall not hear of much more. Mr. Corbould is very uneasy about it. We did not go to Church, being rather dirty &c. Dinner to day, rost Beef & a Rabbit boiled &c.

FEB. 3, FRIDAY. We breakfasted, dined, &c. again at home. To a poor French emigrant Woman, very short, who came to my House this Morning to ask Charity, being in very great distress—gave 0. 1. 0. and also a Mince Pye & some Beer. She told me as far as I understood her (as she talked but little English) that her Husband with 2. or 3. Children were killed in the late Bloody Commotions in France. Dinner to day, boiled Leg of Mutton & Capers &c.

FEB. 24, FRIDAY. . . . The old Apparitor's Son, Roberson, called here this Morning on me, concerning a public Fast on Wednesday March 8. His Father he tells me is 85. Years of Age and hearty but lame having a bad Leg—The Son is past 60. I asked him to eat and drink at my House which he did very hearty, & was welcome.

FEB. 25, SATURDAY. . . . Nancy rather better than worse this Morning. Sent Ben early this Morn' to Norwich with 10. Coomb of Barley to Mr. Bloome's. My Maid, Sally Gunton went to Norwich with Ben, to see her Brother if she can find him. He is spending his Money and Time there in a very idle Manner— has been to London &c. Ben & Sally returned about 5. o'clock this Afternoon. Barley sold for little or nothing. I did not receive Cash from Mr. Bloome but only a Note for the Sum of three Pounds, which is only six Shillings per Coomb for my Barley, which was the lowest Price for Barley I ever knew. The Corn Merchants said that it was at present such a glut that they had almost as soon not have it as have it. Very little Corn indeed at Market to day. Mr. Maynard just called on us this Morning but did not come within doors. Dinner to day, Rost Beef & Water-Cresses &c.

FEB. 26, SUNDAY. We breakfasted, dined, &c. again at home. Nancy near the same as Yesterday. Sent Ben this Morning to Dr. Thorne's at Mattishall to desire the Dr. to come to Morrow Morn to see Nancy. The Dr. sent Word that he would call this Afternoon. Dr. Thorne came to see Nancy this Afternoon about three o'clock, stayed near an Hour with us, I asked him to dine with us, but he could not. He said, that her complaint proceeded from a feverish kind, and had affected a weak part. He told her to live as usual, by no means lower, to poultice her Knee by Night with a Milk Poultice, and to keep a bandage on it by Day. Not to walk on it but little, no cold Water whatever to be applied. To take some Camphor &c. Pills some of which he left with her, 10. of them to be taken at 2. different times between 5. o'clock this Evening and before she went to bed. To Morrow he said he

should send something for the Knee to be bathed with.
He said he did not think it of any great consequence.
Mr. Willins did duty again at Weston Church for Mr.
Corbould. Mr. Custance not there. I did not go,
being very damp, Nancy could not. Mrs. Corbould
was not at Church either. Mr. Corbould sent us this
morning a small Codling about half a Pound—Value
about 3. pence. We did not dine to day till after 4.
o'clock. Dinner to day, the Codling boiled and a very
fat Turkey Hen rosted &c.

MARCH 1, WEDNESDAY. We breakfasted, dined,
&c. again at home. Mr. Custance with his Son Willm.
made us a Morning Visit, informed us, that a Proclamation from the Privy Council had been issued, to
stop paying in Cash at the Bank of England for some
time, fearing that if not stopped, there would not be
soon enough to transact necessary & urgent business.
On that Account, All Country Banks have done the
same, and are at present shut up.[1] Nancy much better
(thank God) this Morning. Dinner to day, Salt Fish
& Breast of Mutton rosted.

MAR. 4, SATURDAY. . . . Sent Briton early this

---

[1] The banking crisis of February 1797 was due to a variety of causes:
large advances to finance the war, made by the Bank of England to the
Government, the critical state of affairs at home and abroad—on
February 4th news reached Pitt of Napoleon's victory at Rivoli—the
fear of invasion, which caused farmers and others in different parts of
the country, specially on the coasts, to withdraw their money from the
banks and hoard it. There was a run on the Newcastle banks; they
suspended payment in specie, and endeavoured to obtain cash from
London. The panic spread to other parts of the country, and finally on
February 26th Pitt caused an Order in Council to be issued authorizing
the Directors of the Bank of England to refuse cash payments till
Parliament gave further orders. As the Bank's position was actually
exceedingly sound the panic passed pretty quickly. The Bank, moreover, was authorized to issue notes for £2 and £1 (hitherto notes for
less than £5 had not been issued). The new paper currency was soon
found to be convenient, and the discretionary power to refuse cash
payments was continued as a safety-valve.

morning to Norwich with the little Cart after News &
other little Jobbs. He returned home by four o'clock
this Afternoon bringing great News with him, of
Admiral Sʳ John Jervis, having had an Engagement
with the Spanish Fleet (who were going to join the
French Fleet) and had obtained a complete & glorious
Victory over them. Four very large Men of War
taken &c. two of them 110. Guns.[1]

MAR. 16, THURSDAY. . . . Mrs. Corbould called
on us about Noon and took out Miss Woodforde an
Airing in her Chariot. Dinner to day, boiled Neck of
Veal & Pork &c. There being little or no Cash stirring and the Country Bank Notes being refused to be
taken, create great uneasiness in almost all People—
fearful what Consequences may follow. Excise Officers refuse taking Country Notes for the payment of
the several Duties. Many do not know what to do on
the present Occasion having but very little Cash by
them.

MAR. 22, WEDNESDAY. . . . Nancy continues still
to get better by drinking plentifully of Port Wine, at
least 1. Pint in a day. Busy in brewing of strong Beer
Yesterday & to day. Mr. & Mrs. Corbould made us
a late Morning Visit. . . .

MAR. 29, WEDNESDAY. . . . Mr. Corbould called
on us this Morning, as did Mr. Stoughton of Sparham.

---

[1] Sir John Jervis (1735–1823) had been appointed to the command of
the Mediterranean Fleet in 1795. The French victories in Italy in 1796
and the combination of the French and Spanish fleets compelled him
to withdraw from the Mediterranean, and it now became essential to
prevent any junction of the Mediterranean French and Spanish fleets
with the French fleet at Brest. Accordingly Jervis stationed himself off
Cape St. Vincent early in February, 1797, and on St. Valentine's day
he and Nelson, with fifteen ships, attacked the Spanish fleet of twenty-
seven. The Spaniards were completely defeated and four of their ships
were captured.

Mr. Thorne came to see Nancy this Morning. He strongly recommends Port Wine and to drink rather More than less. She drank to day between a Pint & a Quart without having the lest effect upon the Brain. She has not drank less than a Pint for many Days. Dinner to day, Tripe boiled & cold Beef &c. Mr. Stoughton brought us some good news. That we had taken the Island of Trinidad in the West Indies from the Spaniards, had taken some of their Ships &c. Admiral Harvey's Fleet gained the above Victory. Nancy continues near the same as Yesterday.

APRIL 10, MONDAY. ... Very cold, strong E. Wind & cloudy—colder a great deal than Yesterday, the Wind being high. Last night I had but indifferent Night of Sleep, having very hurrying & frightful Dreams at times. Dinner to day, Peas Soup & some Beef Steaks.

APRIL 24, MONDAY. We breakfasted, dined &c. again at home. Paid James Pegg this Morning 1. Q^{rs} Land-Tax and half a Years other Taxes. In all Pd. 8. 15. 4¾. Mem: It was ^{s}2/6^d too much. It should have been no more [than] 8. 12. 10¾. Soon after Js. Pegg was gone, John Girling Junr. called on me for the Poor Rate at ^{s}1/4^d in the Pd. for half a Year, from Michlms. last to Lady Day last past, for which I paid him 2. 0. 4. I am charged to the Rate at £30 ^{s}5 0^d. Just before Dinner, Sudbury of Norwich also called on me for Orders, but I gave him none. He did not stay long, drank a Glass of Wine &c. Dinner to day, boiled Calfs Head & Pork &c. In the Afternoon Mr. Custance and Son Willm. came to our House & drank Coffee & Tea with us in a friendly, neighbourly way, and stayed with us till after 8. in the Evening. Rather disagreeable News at present going abt. of a Mutiny of the Seamen on board his Majesty's Fleet now at Spithead.[1]

APRIL 27, THURSDAY. We breakfasted, dined, &c. again at home. About Noon, Mr. Suckling of Aylsham with his Brother Horace[2] from London, came to my House in a Post-Chaise and a Servant on Horseback and they stayed and dined & spent the Afternoon with us. They came to see Hungate-Lodge and to treat with Mr. Custance about the same. I went with them in the Chaise to Hungate and immediately after to Weston House, but Mr. Custance was gone to his Brothers at Lyng.- We saw Mr. Willm. Custance who shewed them some of the Rooms. I left Compts. for

[1] The mutiny in the Channel Fleet at Spithead first broke out on April 15th. It was due to the disgraceful conditions under which sailors then served. Their pay had remained unchanged since the time of Charles II, despite the great increase in prices—specially since the outbreak of the Revolutionary Wars. Their food was insufficient and bad, and the discipline inordinately brutal. The Admiralty were forced to concede the Fleet's demands, and after an interval of nearly ten days the sailors returned to their allegiance. But a second mutiny broke out on May 7th, the Fleet refused to sail against the French who were said to have left Brest, and a number of unpopular officers were sent ashore. This second mutiny was finally settled by Admiral Howe on May 14th, certain officers being superseded. Meanwhile another and more dangerous mutiny broke out in the ships at Sheerness, and spread to those at the Nore. This mutiny was almost purely revolutionary, moreover it spread to the northern fleet at sea under Admiral Duncan, then blockading the Dutch Fleet in the Texel. The mutiny lasted over a month—till June 14th, when it was finally stamped out through the energetic measures taken by the Government and Parliament. The mutinous ships were cut off from supplies, all intercourse with the land was stopped, and the leading mutineer Parker was at length arrested and hanged. Meanwhile Admiral Duncan with two loyal ships deceived the Dutch by signalling to an imaginary force in support. As Lord Rosebery says in his *Pitt*, this year, 1797, was 'the darkest and most desperate that any British minister has ever had to face'. England's main and almost last ally, Austria, had made peace with France in the preliminary treaty of Leoben (April 7th), and Pitt himself a little later in the year was impelled to seek for peace—in vain.

[2] The Sucklings were first cousins to Nelson.

Mr. C. and should be glad to see him in the Afternoon. We returned home by 3. o'clock to dinner. Dinner a Piece of rost Beef, hashed Calfs Head, a plain Pudding, Rasberry Puffs &c. About 5. o'clock Mr. Custance came to us and drank Coffee and Tea with us. A little after 6. Mr. Suckling & Brother went for Aylsham having settled all Matters with Mr. Custance to the Satisfaction of all Parties. Mr. C. stayed with us afterwards till after 8. o'clock. He approves much of the Messrs. Sucklings. They are fashionable young Men, and Horace who is to be my Curate, appears to be a good natured, sensible, easy Man—rather fat & short. He is to enter on my Curacy & Hungate Lodge at Michlms. Mr. Custance sent us half a dozen young Pigeons by Knights. Gave him 0. 1. 0.

MAY 12, FRIDAY. We breakfasted, dined, &c. again at home. Had but an indifferent night of Sleep last Night. My cold being very troublesome wi^ch made me cough. Very ill indeed towards bed-time &c.

Memorandum

Being taken extremely ill on 12th May 1797 declined entering any thing in this Book. [The diarist, however, continued his diary on loose sheets.]

MAY 13, SATURDAY. Had a very indifferent Night last night. This Morning taken very ill, could scarce get down Stairs. Sent for Mr. Thorne, who ordered me immediately to bed, having had a fit in the last Night and there I laid all night in a very bad State scarce sensible all the Night long. In the Night had a Blister put between my Shoulders which discharged very much indeed in the night and which made me soon better. But before that was put on was all but dead quite senseless. Nancy & Betty up with me most part of the night.

MAY 20, SATURDAY. Had a good Night again last night thank God and got up very early. N.B. Sally a bad Sitter up at Nights. My Brother & Wife from Somersett, came to us just before Dinner to day, and they dined, supped & slept there. They were much fatigued indeed. I was very glad to see them. Nancy had very properly informed them of my Illness. Dr. Thorne called on me again to day, found me better. Briton & Betty sat up with me to night.

MAY 21, SUNDAY. Had a good Night again last Night. Got up this Morning much better thank God —was below stairs very early. My Brother & Wife breakfasted, dined &c. here again. About 11. o'clock this Morning Willm. Woodforde of Gallhampton came in a Post Chaise to my House from Somersett having heard of my being ill—and he dined &c. here. Ben & Sally sat up with me to Night but an indifferent night.

MAY 22, MONDAY. We breakfasted &c. again at home. My Brother & Wife breakfasted, dined &c. &c. here again. Somewhat better to day thank God had a tolerable night.

Memorandum. Ben Leggatt & Sally Gunton sat up with me last Night.

The next four lines are crossed out but are just decipherable and read as follows: 'N.B. I have a particular reason for making this remark[1] which made me uneasy—not to sit up with me on any account. Time will shew the cause of my Uneasiness and Suspicion.' The last line of the day's entry is not scored through and simply reads: 'Slept but very indifferent all the night long—rather uneasy.'

[1] i.e. presumably the remark about Ben and Sally.

MAY 31, WEDNESDAY. We breakfasted, dined, &c. again at home. My Brother & Wife, & Willm. Woodforde breakfasted, dined &c. here again. Somewhat better, thank God this Morning, but very weak yet. I find by my Niece that I have been very dangerously ill indeed, quite senseless some times. I have been blistered and I do not know what I have suffered. Quite senseless at times, and in very great danger indeed. Dr. Thorne with me very often indeed & did me great Service.

JUNE 13, TUESDAY. ... Mr. & Mrs. Custance with all their Family from Bath arrived at Weston-House about 5. o'clock this Afternoon. They went by our House in a new Coach & four Horses and a Post-Chaise with Servants attending on the same. Great Rejoicings on their Return to Weston made on the occasion. Mr. Maynard called on us about Noon & stayed about an Hour with us. He brought me & Nancy a Couple of Books which we subscribed to some time back of Newtons Poems a young man of Norwich Son to Newton, Minor Canon of Norwich C. a small affair—Mr. Maynard is Curate to his Father at Attlebridge. I would have paid for both Books but Mr. Maynard would not take for Nancys Book as he intended to give it to her. So that I paid him only for one Book & that was 0. 3. 0. Paid him also, for paying for me at the late Generals etc 0. 1. 0. Mr. Corbould gave us a Call this Morning but did not stay long. During his stay with us, we recd. a Letter each of us from Revd. Ben. Suckling of Aylsham, respecting Furniture at Hungate Lodge, what his Brother would chuse to take at Michaelmas &c.

JUNE 19, MONDAY. We breakfasted, dined &c. again at home. My Brother & Wife & My Nephew

Willm. breakfasted &c. here again. Had a tolerable good Night last Night. After breakfast between 11. and 12. My Brother's Wife & Nancy went in my little Curricle or taxed Cart to Weston House, My Brother & Willm. walked with me thither, we stayed there till near 2. o'clock. We returned as we went—saw all the Family but Mr. George who is in the E. Indies. All the young Folks much grown and much altered but Emily who is just the same but much grown. On our return home found Mrs. Thorne & daughter Mary Anne at my House, had been there some time. They stayed & dined with us & spent the Afternoon. They came in a one horse Chaise a Servant Boy driving them. A Mantua Maker from Mattishall Burgh by name Burroughs came here early this Morning, and she breakfasted, dined & stayed the Afternoon at Weston Parsonage. Miss W. by desire of her Aunt sent 3. Maccarel to Weston-House (having bought 1 doz. this Morning before we went out) before our return home—Mrs. Custance wishing the Man had called there also. I was quite tired out almost by the time that Dinner came in. Very much vexed indeed on going up to Weston H. to see a Clay Pit of mine in the Field in the path thro which we go thither (occupied at present by J^n_o Baker) so much Clay having been of late taken from thence by him & carried away, as to make the foot path very dangerous indeed for Passengers, in some places the foot path entirely taken away. I sent to him directly to leave that Glebe at Michelmas next—It greatly hurt me. In Parlour & Kitchen to day we had 14 People at Dinner. I was quite tired out almost before I got to bed to Night. Dinner to day, Maccarel & fore Qr. of Lamb rosted &c.

JULY 20, THURSDAY. We breakfasted, dined, &c,

again at home. My Brother and Wife breakfasted, dined &c. here again. I find myself rather getting strength but very slow indeed. Have at times uncommon sinkings within me—tho' I constantly take Cake and a Glass of Port Wine every Morn' about 11. o'clock and strengthening Cordial twice a Day the first thing before breakfast and at 2. in the Afternoon being an Hour before Dinner—which I have constantly been taken for the last Month if not longer. Finished my last Dose this Afternoon and now am to drop it. Dinner to day, fryed Soals and boiled Beef &c.

JULY 21, FRIDAY. We breakfasted, dined, &c. again at home. My Brother & Wife breakfasted, dined &c. here again. A Mr. Cotman a young Man & a Clergyman (Son also of a Mr. Cotman well known by late Mr. Du Quesne) called on me this Morning concerning the Curacy of Weston in case Mr. Suckling does not take it after Mr. Corbould at Michelmas next & I cannot get a resident Curate. He did not stay long with me, would not walk in. Dinner to day Leg of Mutton rosted &c. Sent a Letter to Mr. Fookes in answer to his lately recd. directed to him at Shepton Mallet, Somersett. I sent it by Briton this Evening to Billy Bidewell, to be carried by some of them to Morrow to Norwich who go to Norwich Market.

AUGUST 12, SATURDAY. We breakfasted, dined, &c. again at home. My Brother & wife breakfasted, dined &c. here again. Sent Ben to Norwich this Morning after Coal &c. Holland the Chimney Sweeper, swept my Study Chimney, Parlour ditto— and their Chamber Chimneys, with Kitchen and Back-Kitchen ditto—in all six. He had a new Boy with him who had likely to have lost his Life this Morning at Weston House in sticking in one [of] their Chimnies. I gave the poor Boy a Shilling. Dinner Shoulder of Lamb rosted &c.

Aug. 14, Monday. . . . Begun Shearing Wheat to day. I was taking very poorly this Evening soon after walking out.

Aug. 16, Wednesday. . . . Mr. Stoughton of Sparham sent us a Leveret this Morning—very kind of him. Sent his Servant for bringing it 1. 0. . . .

Sep. 3, Sunday. We breakfasted, dined, &c. again at home. My Brother & Wife breakfasted, dined &c. here again. My Brother had a Letter from our Sister Pounsett this Morn'. It came by a Norwich Carrier to Taylor Cary's. All Friends tolerably well in Somersett—upon the whole a pleasing Letter. Mr. Corbould read Prayers & Preached at Weston Ch. this Afternoon. Mrs. Woodforde and Nancy were at Church to day. Dinner to day, fryed Soals again and Pigs Fry &c. Not quite so well again to day—very much blown up.

Sep. 20, Wednesday. I breakfasted, dined, &c. again at home. My Brother breakfasted, dined, &c. here again. Soon after breakfast this Morning, I made my Brother a Present of a twenty Pound Bank of England Note 20. 0. 0. I also desired him to accept of a ten Pound Bank of England note for Mrs. Woodforde to spend in Town 10. 0. 0. Sent Briton as soon as he had breakfasted after our Ladies at Mattishall to bring them home. They returned home to dinner highly pleased with Mrs. Bodham, for her very kind attention towards them. Dinner to day, boiled Leg of Mutton & Capers &c. I put on a flannel Waistcoat

under my other, for the first time during my Life—
and hope it will do me good.

SEP. 22, FRIDAY. We breakfasted, dined, &c. again
at home. My Brother & Wife breakfasted, dined, &c.
here again. Mr. Stoughton of Sparham sent us a
Leash of Partridges. Mr. Cotman, called on me this
Afternoon soon after dinner to talk with me about
being my Curate—I soon settled with him—That is,
he is to have it and enter upon it when Mr. Corbould
leaves it which will be in November. He did not stay
long with me having 2. Ladies with him at ye Gate.
Dinner to day, fryed Eels, Calfs Pluck or Fry &c.

SEPBR. 23, SATURDAY. We breakfasted, dined,
&c. again at home. My Brother & Wife breakfasted,
dined &c. here again. Bidewells People brought our
News-papers—No Letters. Dinner to day, a Couple
of Chicken boiled & Pork, & Leg Mutton rosted. My
Brother but indifferent, Inflammation in one of his
Eyes and much of the flying Gout in his Constitution.
Since I have taken to the Flannel Waistcoat, think
myself better & stronger for so doing. No good News.
Less appearance of Peace than ever. Lord Malmesbury sent home in a hurry from France.[1]

OCTOBER 5, THURSDAY. We breakfasted, dined

---

[1] In the middle of June the Cabinet, under Pitt's influence, decided
that a further effort must be made to obtain peace. From early in
July to the middle of September Lord Malmesbury negotiated at Lille
with the representatives of the Directory. Pitt was prepared to recog-
nize all the French conquests in Europe, including Belgium, while
French dominance in Holland and Italy was acknowledged. Out of
the naval conquests from France and her allies only the Cape, Ceylon,
and Trinidad would be retained. But finally the French Directory,
from which the moderate elements were expelled by the *coup d'état* of
the 18th Fructidor (Sept. 4), insisted on an absolute restoration of all
the English conquests whatsoever: on Lord Malmesbury's refusal he
was ordered, September 17th, to quit France within 24 hours.

&c. again at home. My Brother & Wife breakfasted with us and about 10. o'clock set off in one of the Kings Head Chaises from Norwich (wh. came here about 8. o'clock this Morning) for their return into Somersett. About 4. this Afternoon they take one of the Mail Coaches from Norwich and set off for London. Pray God! they may have a good and safe Journey to Castle-Cary. They are to spend a few days in Town with Mrs. Goujon in Newgate Street whose Maiden Name was Pope of Shepton Mallett. It made us very low indeed on leaving them. Dinner to day, Neck of Mutton boiled &c.

OCTOBER 9, MONDAY. ... Mrs. Beevor of Witchingham with a Mrs. Whalley an agreeable Married Lady from Colchester made us a Morning Visit—very pleasing agreeable Ladies. They eat some Cake and drank a Glass of our Mead. Dinner to day fryed Eels and heatups—in short odds. Very weak and poorly to day. Appetite very bad.

OCTOBER 10, TUESDAY. We breakfasted, dined, &c. again at home. Dinner to day boiled Fowl & Pork &c. Brewed a Barrel of Table Beer to day. Very weak indeed to day. No Appetite whatever. Unless I get better soon I cannot long survive it. Pray God! have mercy on me a poor, weak Creature. Lent Mr. Corbould my common Cart with harness for 2. Horses, Waggon Line &c. to go to Norwich with Goods.

OCTOBER 11, WEDNESDAY. We breakfasted, dined, &c. again at home. Mr. Mellish sent us about 12. lb. of Honey—rather old. Paid young Mr. Girling for his Father for a half yrs. poor Rate at 11^d. 1. 13. 2½. Dinner to day, Leg of Mutton boiled & Capers &c.

Very poorly & very weak all the whole day. Mr. Corbould sent home the Cart &c. this Afternoon. Mr. Corbould carried away every thing from Hungate Lodge that could be, every Nail & every Vegetable in the Garden.

OCTOBER 15, SUNDAY. We breakfasted, dined, &c. again at home. Weaker this Morning than I have been yet. Scarce able to make a Walk of it to day. No Appetite still. Mr. Corbould did duty this Afternoon at Weston Church. He made us a Visit on his return from Church. He went to Norwich afterwards, they having left Hungate-Lodge. Dinner to day, rost Beef & Plumb Pudding &c. I eat some plumb Pudding for Dinner but nothing else. In the Evening thought Myself a little better. The Medicine that Mr. Thorne sent me seem to do good. For the last two days I have been very bad indeed not able to put on some of my Cloaths or pull them off. Great News on the public Papers, Admiral Duncan having completely beaten a large Fleet of the Dutch.[1]

OCTBR. 24, TUESDAY. . . . Thank God! I had a good Night of rest last Night and found myself pretty strong & hearty this Morning without any Assistance or Attendance whatever I got up. Dinner to day fryed Beef & Potatoes & a rost Chicken.

---

[1] From the beginning of July all had been in readiness for a renewed invasion of Ireland by the French convoyed by the Dutch fleet in the Texel. The Dutch fleet at that time was superior in power to Duncan's —which moreover had only just passed through the Nore mutiny. But the Dutch fleet could only move with favourable wind and tide, and both were contrary for six weeks on end. Meanwhile Duncan's fleet was reinforced. At last, on October 8th, the Dutch fleet put out to sea under Admiral de Winter. On October 11th was fought the stubborn battle of Camperdown between equal English and Dutch forces. Finally Duncan shattered the Dutch fleet, capturing nine ships of the line.

NOVBR. 17, FRIDAY. We breakfasted, dined, &c. again at home. Thank God! found myself rather better this Morn' not so bewildered or so weak as Yesterday, Senses better & stronger—still however very, very poorly. Appetite better, made a very good Dinner considering what I have done of late. Eat pretty hearty of a fresh boiled Tongue & mash Potatoes. Smoaked my Pipe this Afternoon better than of late. Paid my Blacksmith John Buck his Annual Bill—3. 8. 6.

NOVBR. 26, SUNDAY. ... Quite mild this Morning with some Rain. Found myself better to day, but still cannot gain strength. Dinner to day, a Loin of Pork boiled & a Hare rosted &c. My Appetite is pretty good, Made a very good dinner. Mr. Cotman entered upon the Curacy of Weston this day and therefore read Prayers & Preached here this Afternoon. None of Mr. Custance's Family at Church to day being wet. Mr. Custance's People have taken up some Poachers that were found in ipso facto on his Premises.

DECBR. 3, SUNDAY. ... Mr. Cotman did duty this Morning at Weston Church. Mr. Custance and his eldest Son, called on us this Morn' after Divine Service—They had been at Church. A smart Frost this Morning which rather affected me, but upon the whole think myself rather stronger than of late. Dinner to day, Neck of Veal rosted &c. The present times seem to prognosticate e'er long very alarming circumstances. No appearance of Peace, but on the contrary the French reject every Proposition of it and so inveterate are they against our Government, that they are determined to make a descent on England & the Taxes therefore on the above account are talked of being raised trebly to what they were last Year.[1]

DECMBR. 17, SUNDAY. We breakfasted, dined, &c.
again at home. I found myself rather weaker to day
than of late; but very little. I can eat pretty well and
thank God sleep very well. Mr. Cotman did duty
this Afternoon at Weston Church. It grieves me much
that I am rendered unable to do it myself or to attend
at Church being so very infirm. Dinner to day, Shoulder of Veal rosted &c. Very windy all the Day,
obliged to be in the Parlour as our Study smoaked so
very much. Wind W.N.W. Ben went to Crownthorp
on my Horse to day, returned in very good time in
the Evening.

1798

JANRY. 4, THURSDAY. . . . Weather altered, no
Frost, but cold and hazy & unpleasant. Mr. Stoughton of Sparham sent Miss Woodforde to day a Skep
of Bees by his farming Man J^{no} Springle who brought
them all the Way on foot and upon his Head tyed up
in a Cloth. He was 4. Hours almost coming from
Sparham. I gave the Man a good Dinner, some strong
Beer, and made him a Present besides of half a Guinea
in Gold. 10. 6. Dinner to day, rost Beef, Tripe &c.
Pd. Briton 0. 15. 1.

JANRY. 15, MONDAY. We breakfasted, dined, &c.

---

[1] On October 26th, 1797, the Directory had named 'Citizen General
Bonaparte' commander-in-chief of the 'Army of England', and the
troops already assembled on the western coasts of France were to be
supplemented by reinforcements from the Army of Italy. Admiral
Duncan's victory had, in fact, rendered an invasion impracticable for
the time being, but the Directory did not relax their preparatory efforts,
and far into the spring of 1798 appeared to be concentrating all attention on England when, in reality, they were latterly preparing for
Bonaparte's Egyptian expedition.

again at home. After breakfast I paid my Servants their Year's Wages due Janry. 5th. 1798 as follows.

To Benj. Leggatt, my farming Man pd. 10. 0. 0.
To Bretingham Scurl my Footman pd. 8. 0. 0.
To Betty Dade, my House-Maid pd. 5. 5. 0.
To Sally Gunton, my Cook & Dairy Maid pd. 5.5.0.
To Barnabas Woodcock my Yard-Boy pd. 2. 2. 0.

Dinner to day, a boiled Fowl & Pork, & Beef-Steaks &c. To a poor Man, lately a Marine, by name Cleveland, gave 1. 0. Sally Gunton's Brother, Billy Gunton, a Grenadier and Corporal in the Norfolk Militia, a very fine looking young Man, called here in the Evening to take leave of his Sister to join his Regiment at Colchester on Wednesday next or Thursday without fail having been absent near 3. Weeks. I gave him on his going away 0. 2. 6. Nancy sent a Letter by him to Norwich, to Miss Pounsett.

FEBRY. 3, SATURDAY. We breakfasted, dined, &c. again at home. Sent Briton this Morning to Norwich in my old Cart after many things. He returned home about 4. in the After. brought a Letter to Nancy from her Aunt Jno Woodforde announcing the Marriage between my Niece Jane Pounsett and the Revd. Frederick Grove to have taken place on Thursday the 25th. Day of January last past, at Pitcomb Church in Somersett. Immediately after the Ceremony they set off for Bath with my Sister Pounsett and Mary Woodforde of Taunton who was bride-Maid where they are to spend some Days. Mrs. Woodforde's Letter also mentions that the Settlement on Jane Pounsett is a very bad one & a very cunning one for in case she dies without Issue, every thing whatever goes to Grove immediately on her demise. Dinner to day, rost Pork &c.

FEBRY. 14, WEDNESDAY. . . . This being Valentine's Day, gave to Children in my Parish under the Age of 14 one penny each 0. 7. 6. Made Nancy this Morning a Present of 10. 0. 0. Old Robertson, the Apparitor, brought a form of Prayer for a general Fast to be observed on Wednesday the 7th. of March next in all Churches & Chapels. Dinner to day, fryed Haddocks & cold Beef Steaks &c. Still weak and poorly. Appetite still very bad.

FEBRY. 16, FRIDAY. We breakfasted, dined, &c. again at home. Paid John Reeve for 2. doz. of Port Wine 3. 6. 0. 13. Quart Bottles to the Dozen—an amazing Price indeed, 33ˢ/0ᵈ per Dozen.[1] In the Year 1774 we had Port Wine at New-College at 1ˢ/6ᵈ per Qt. Bottle. A Pipe of Wine then to be had at about £30. pr. Pipe. Now it cannot be had under near £70. Dinner to day boiled Pork & a rost Rabbit &c.

FEBRY. 19, MONDAY. . . . Michael Andrew's Wife called on me this Morning upon Mrs. Mann's Account she being dangerously ill and informed me that she was desirous of having the Sacrament administered to her on Wednesday next. I sent to Mr. Maynard directly to desire him to do it. A more officious, busy-bodied, Woman in all Cases relating to other People's Concerns I know not. More particularly when ill—a true Jobish Friend. Dinner to day, fryed Pork & Potatoes &c. Sent Mrs. Mann to day, she having Company at her house a Couple of ready trussed Chicken, a nice Duck and three Mince Pies—by my Maid Betty. Poor Woman she now keeps her bed I am afraid she cannot last long. The only Company I hear that is at Mrs. Manns is only Johnny Rose's

---

[1] In 1795 and 1796 Pitt more than doubled the wine duties, so that the increased price is easily accounted for.

Wife, late Miss Temple, whose Father marry'd Johnny Rose's Mother who formerly lived here.

FEBRY. 21, ASH-WEDNESDAY. . . . Mr. Maynard dined & spent the Afternoon with us, he administered the Sacrament this Morning to poor Mrs. Mann of my Parish who is now very dangerously ill and keeps her Bed. Mrs. Mann has been in a declining state ever since the Death of her late Husband, having lived so happy together. Pray God! comfort and assist her in her present distress. She keeps her bed, is exceeding weak, very much emaciated and at times much deranged in mind. Dinner to day, Salt-fish, a Turkey rosted & fritters. Mr. Maynard left us soon after Tea this Evening.

FEBRY. 28, WEDNESDAY. . . . Hambleton Custance made us a short Morning Visit. Dinner to day, Knuckle of Veal boiled & Pork &c. My poor Dog Rover, a Most sagacious & sensible Dog as I ever had, was found dead this Morning near his kennel, supposed to be poisoned, as at this time of the Year, Farmers lay Poison, on Account of their Lambs. It vexed me much, he being a favourite of my Dairy Maid, Sally Gunton, she could not help crying for him—she was very fond of him. He was as sensible a Dog if not more so, than I ever had.

MARCH 13, TUESDAY. . . . I made a very good dinner to day considering my State. Poor Mrs. Mann, is very near departing this Life, being scarce able to move or eat any thing whatever, she is reduced (I hear) almost to nothing—yet has her Senses. Pray God! give her an easy transition from this world to one more happy and eternal. She died this Aft.

MARCH 14, WEDNESDAY. We breakfasted, dined,

&c. again at home. Rather better to day & stronger I think than of late, my Appetite somewhat better, but still remain very weak. Mr. Mellish made us a Morning Visit—looked at my Roller. Dinner to day, odds and ends &c. Js. Pegg called on me this Morning and left me an account of the new additional Taxes per annum exclusive of the old, which amount to my Share 25. 5. 6. Very heavy indeed are the new Taxes on the Clergy in short. How the new taxes will go down with the People in general I know not, I hope they will not create more new Taxes after these, tho' at present are talked of.

MARCH 27, TUESDAY. . . . Gave my Maid, Sally Gunton, for sitting up with me when ill, 2. Yards of black Silk, being a hatband sent me by John Mann on the Death of his Mother. Dinner to day, Neck of Veal rosted &c. Mr. Hambleton Custance drank Tea with us this Evening.

APRIL 1, SUNDAY. We breakfasted, dined, &c. again at home. Mr. Cotman read Prayers & Preached this Morn' at Weston C. Mr. Hambleton Custance called on us this Morning after Divine Service and spent near an Hour with us. Dinner to day, Fillett of Veal rosted &c. Very cold indeed to day & severe Frost—very unusual. By the publick Papers, every thing in them appears very distressing & alarming. French Invasion daily expected.[1] Made a very good dinner to day, but cannot gain Strength.

[1] The entries for this date, for April 12th, 23rd, 25th, 26th, and 27th bring out vividly how deep was the anxiety in England in the spring of 1798. Preparations for an invasion were being pushed on with great activity in France, and an English spy met Bonaparte between Furnes and Dunkirk on February 13th 'going to Ostend to inspect the port, and make contracts for building flat-bottom boats for the descent'. Though the Directory had for the moment abandoned the idea of an immediate invasion of England, and were preparing for Bonaparte's

APRIL 6, GOOD-FRIDAY. We breakfasted, dined, &c. again at home. My Parishioners were much disappointed in not having Divine Service this Morning at Church as usual on G. Friday. Mr. Cotman promised me that he would attend this Day and declared the same last Sunday at Church. Mr. Custance with most of the Family with a great many of my Parishioners were at Church, and much displeased. It vexed me a great deal, as I told him of having Divine Service in the Morning of Good-Friday as usual on this Day. It hurt me very much to hear of it in my Weak State. Young Mr. Girling brought us a small Pike this Morning. Dinner to day, Salt Fish, Eggs, & Fritters &c. Between one thing and another was made very uneasy.

APRIL 12, THURSDAY. . . . Mr. Ham. Custance called on us this Morning. Bottled off my last Mead this Morning, it filled twenty six Quart-Bottles—not so clear as I could wish. We were rather too late this Year in bottling it off. Dinner to day, Neck of Pork rosted, &c. By the publick Papers every thing appears on them most alarming not only respecting Great Briton but every other State in Europe, and beyond it—Oh Tempora oh Mores. I hope my Strength is increasing as I feel better to day.

APRIL 16, MONDAY. . . . My oldest Sow had 16. young Piggs this Morning. . . .

APRIL 17, TUESDAY. . . . My youngest Sow, had 11. young Pigs. My Cow Polly had a Bull-Calf. To

expedition to Egypt, they never lost sight of the original plan and, in fact, an attempt on Ireland was made later in the year. Moreover, the English Ministry were quite in the dark as to the intention of the French preparations at Toulon right up to the date of Bonaparte's departure with his armament for Egypt on May 19th, and it was supposed that either England or Ireland was the real objective.

John Mann this Morning paid 1. 10. 5¾. being a Poor Rate at 11ᵈ in the Pound from Michaelmas last past to Lady Day last at 33. 5. 0. per Annum. Dinner to day, boiled Beef &c. Mr. Custance with his eldest Son called on us this Even' & drank Tea with us. Mrs. C. and Daughters gone to Sr. Ed. Bacons.

APRIL 23, MONDAY. We breakfasted, dined, &c. again at home. Washing Week—Richmond & Downing, Washers. Very fine Weather indeed to day. A great Meeting at Reepham to day, respecting all People arming themselves &c. against an Invasion of this Country from the French &c. which is much talked of at present by all kinds of People especially the poor. Pray God preserve us from our private Enemies at home. Dinner to day, a Fillett of Veal rosted &c. The Apparitors Son called on me this Morning to let me know that Arch-Deacons Visitation will be held at Reepham on Friday the 11th of May next. His old Father is still alive but now too old to do it. The Son had both Victuals and drink.

APRIL 25, WEDNESDAY. . . . Nothing talked of at present but an Invasion of England by the French. Great Preparations making all over England &c. against the said intended Invasion, especially all along the Sea Coasts every where.

APRIL 26, THURSDAY. . . . Js. Pegg called on me again this Morning with more Papers respecting an Invasion, the Names of all People in the Parish between 15. and 63. Years of Age &c. &c. Dinner to day—Leg of Mutton rosted &c. Mr. Hambleton Custance drank Tea with us this Aft.

APRIL 27, FRIDAY. We breakfasted, dined &c. again at home. Dinner to day, hash Mutton and a

Suet Pudding, I made a very great Dinner to day indeed, was rather afraid I had eat too much but I recd. no Inconvenience from it. A Meeting of the Parish this Afternoon at the Heart, respecting a sudden Invasion from the French &c. what was necessary and proper to be done on a sudden attack. Mr. Custance attended as did most of the Parish—I could not.

MAY 14, MONDAY. ... Sent a very nice rosting Pig this Morning to Weston-House. Sent another also to Mr. Stoughton of Sparham. I hope that I am now getting more strength—Appetite good. ...

JUNE 28, THURSDAY. ... Busy finishing carrying Hay my People have been at all day long. Finished this Evening and very fine Weather we have had for the last ten Days, and very hot indeed to day. Our Hay has been little or nothing at all hurt by the Rain which fell on it one Day when we had some Thunder with it. ...

JULY 1, SUNDAY. We breakfasted, dined, &c. again at home. Danl. Breeze brought a very fine Leveret to my House this Morning, desiring my acceptance of it, but I declined it, having some time back been made uneasy, by receiving such from Bowles of this Parish, who hires Mr. Townshends Rabbitts in Honingham & Ringland &c. My Name having been mentioned to Mr. Townshend (as I have been informed by Bowles himself) by some Person or Persons unknown. I gave Breeze however for his trouble and after 0. 1. 0. There was no Service at Weston-Church to day, Mr. Cotman being gone to a Living of his in Kent which he has scarce seen yet. Dinner to day, hind Qr. of Lamb, not good tho' so lately recd.

JULY 4, WEDNESDAY. . . . I measured a Scotch Fir Tree of my Planting in the Shrubbery near the Pond by me about twenty Years ago, and it was fifty four inches in Circumference at the largest Girt. Dinner to day, a fore-Quarter of a small Pig rosted &c. Busy in plowing and sowing Turnip-Seed.

JULY 15, SUNDAY. . . . Briton went to see his Friends at Reepham, came home drunk. Mr. Cotman neglected doing duty at Weston-Church this Aft. Many People displeased at it & it made me quite uneasy. . . .

JULY 20, FRIDAY. We breakfasted, dined, &c. again at home. Mrs. Custance with her two Daughters & Son John called here this Morning and stayed near an Hour with us. They took Miss Woodforde back with them to Weston-House to spend the Day with them. The young Ladies looked but poorly as did Master John—they have been too free with fruit I shd. suspect. They looked dull and pale—by no means Well. Dinner to day, Shoulder of Mutton rosted &c. I made a tolerable good Dinner tho' by myself. Miss W. returned home about 8. o'clock this Evening. She was brought back in their Coach. A Mr. Whitbread from Suffolk & Mr. Press Custance dined there. Mr. Whitbread is a very old Acquaintance of Mr. Custance. It rained again to day and so it has more or less on the Day of St. Swithin and every day since.

AUG. 7, TUESDAY. . . . My poor Cow is a good deal better to day, Put her in my Garden. The old Gander very weak and lame and very poor indeed, had him into the Garden and gave him plenty of Barley. . . .

SEPBR. 3, MONDAY. . . . Mrs. Beeston of Tuddenham made us a Present Yesterday Morn of a frizzled

Cock and Hen, and we returned her Present by our sending her a Pheasant Cock & Hen, which pleased her much.

SEPR. 4, TUESDAY. We breakfasted, dined, &c. again at home. Paid my Butcher, Wm. Stoughton this Morning a Bill for Meat from April 12, 1798 to Sepbr. 1st. 1798. 12. 15. 6. Wm. Stoughton also paid me for Pigs 6. 4. 5. On balance of accounts paid him in Cash 6. 11. 0. Paid Miss Woodforde for a Pig she sold to my Butcher some time back & wh. I recd. of him now for the same 1. 6. 0. Dinner to day, boiled Beef, Apple-Dumplins &c. There was some small Rain this Afternoon, but did not last long. Never was known scarce ever so fine a Harvest Season. Lord! make us truly thankful & grateful for the same.

SEPBR. 14, FRIDAY. . . . Mr. Custance made us a Morning Visit, he came on foot. To one Largess to day, Emeris's Men gave 0. 1. 0. Dinner to day, Pigs Fry & Pork Steaks &c. I fancy myself rather stronger of a few days past than of late tho' at times I feel myself rather hurried and alarmed. Mr. Willm. Custance sent us a brace of Partridges, which was very kind of him, this being the first Day of shooting Partridges. Great News said to be recd. from London, concerning Ireland; viz. that the French who had landed there, had been defeated, and that the Irish were in a fair Way, of being made quiet.

SEP. 15, SATURDAY. . . . Briton went to Norwich this Morn' with Mrs. Bidewell. Dinner to day, Neck of Pork rosted &c. Briton returned home from Norwich about 6. this Evening. The Rebellion in Ireland much abated. The French that have landed there have been defeated and the rest surrendered. The rebel Irish have most of them surrendered, and great discoveries made respecting the Rebellion there. It has been plotting & planning Schemes with the French for the last five Years, the Irish having so long been under French Principles.

Oct. 25. Thursday. We breakfasted, dined, &c. again at home. To James Pegg this Morning paid him the new assessed Taxes for six Weeks the Sum of 4. 4. 3. Had a very good Night of Sleep last Night. Dinner to day, hash Mutton & a Suet-Pudding &c. Mr. Emeris sent us a nice Hare to day. Great News almost every Week from the signal Victories of our Fleets over the French, Spaniards, and Dutch Fleets of the first Degree. Admiral Sr. James Borlace Warren have taken and destroyed the whole of the Brest-Fleet that were going to Ireland with Troops to assist the rebellious Irish & invade England. Thanks to the Almighty for this and all other of his blessings to us, and may he continue his goodness to us, and make us all truly thankful for the same. The French seem now to lose Ground. May we e'er long once more enjoy Peace.[1]

Nov. 8, Thursday. . . . Very poorly and very weak this Morning as I was taken in a kind of fainting Fit, getting into bed, last Night. I had just time to

---

[1] Parson Woodforde's reference to 'signal victories' is doubtless mainly to Nelson's destruction of the French fleet in the battle of the Nile on August 1st. The news of this victory did not reach London till October 2nd, and unfortunately the loss of the Diary for the early part of October prevents our knowing exactly how the first triumphant tidings re-acted on the Rectory. However, the entry for November 29th (see footnote thereto) still thrills with the name of Nelson. The Diarist's addition of victories over the Spanish and Dutch fleets is not strictly accurate, unless his memory is going back to the preceding year—the victories of Cape St. Vincent and Camperdown. In 1798 the Spanish fleet was cooped up in Cadiz, and the Dutch fleet in the Texel.

open my Bed-Room Door before I fell down, wch.
Miss Woodforde hearing, came to my assistance and
our Betty also came soon after. I fell down and being
so extremely weak could not get off my Breeches or
get on my Legs. Dinner to day, rost Beef &c. Mr.
Custance made us a Morning Visit, he had been to
Mr. Townshend, alias, Lrd. Baynings.

Nov. 11, SUNDAY. We breakfasted, dined, &c.
again at home. Getting up this Morning I was taken
very ill, with a giddiness in my Head, could not get
down Stairs without Assistance (after some little time
I got better)—owing to great Weakness & relaxation.
Mr. Cotman being gone into Kent to a Living that he
has got there, Weston Church was not served this
Morn' as it ought to have been. Mr Cotman should
have got a Substitute. It is not using me well by
neglecting it. Dinner to day, the other fore Qr. of
Pork rosted &c. Miss Woodforde had a Letter last
Night from her Aunt John Woodforde from Bath,
informing us that they had left Castle-Cary and had
gone to Bath to live, himself and Wife—Her Sister
Patty Clarke having married Jean's. They left Castle-
Cary, the third of October. They have hired Lodgings in Chatham-Row No. 8—at a Widows House
with only a Servant. They carried with them, a Girl
only as a servant. I cannot say that I approve of their
living there.

Nov. 12, MONDAY. We breakfasted, dined, &c.
again at home. Very poorly, very giddy & weak
again this Morn'. Mrs. Bodham sent a Note by her
Man, Willm. Ward, to enquire after us, and also
respecting the Curacy of Weston for a Young Man by
name Dade, Nephew of the Dean of Norwich, but tho'
I had partly promised him before, but recollecting

that Dr. Baker's Son of Cawston had applied prior to him, in case one by name Brown of Norwich refuses it—wch I had entirely forgot to mention to her here— I desired Nancy to acquaint her of the same. Mr. Maynard also called this Morning, and he had scarce left us, before Mrs. Custance and her two Daughters called on us in a Walk and stayed upwards of an Hour with us. Dinner to day, boiled Leg of Mutton & Capers &c.

NOVBR. 29, THURSDAY. We breakfasted, dined, &c. again at home. Great Rejoicings at Norwich to day on Lord Nelsons late great & noble Victory over the French near Alexandria in Egypt. An Ox rosted whole in the Market-Place &c. This being a day of general Thanksgiving Mr. Cotman read Prayers this Morning at Weston-Church, proper on the Occasion. Dinner to day, Leg of Mutton rosted &c. I gave my Servants this Evening after Supper some strong-Beer and some Punch to drink Admiral Lord Nelson's Health on his late grand Victory and also all the other Officers with him and all the brave Sailors with them, and also all those brave Admirals, Officers and Sailors that have gained such great & noble Victories of late over the French &c. &c.¹ Miss Woodforde recd. a

¹ It was natural that Norwich and Norfolk men generally should rejoice specially over the Battle of the Nile. Nelson had been born in 1758 at Burnham Thorpe of which his father was still Rector, and had been educated at Norwich Grammar School and at North Walsham. Moreover between December 1787 and January 1793, when he was on half pay, he and his wife had spent nearly the whole time at Burnham Thorpe Parsonage. Nelson had thrown himself into country pursuits with the same ardour that he fought his battles: he coursed with Coke of Norfolk's harriers, birds-nested with his wife, and shot partridges by himself being too dangerous for his companions as 'he let fly, without ever putting the fowling-piece to his shoulder'. The completeness of his victory—only four ships escaped out of seventeen—took the world by storm. Gold and diamond presents from the Emperor of Russia and the Sultan of Turkey, pensions from Parliament, and £10,000 from

Letter this Morning from Richardson & Goodluck in London, informing her of her having a Prize in the Irish Lottery which was entirely done unknown to me. It was a 16th. Share in the Irish Lottery of a nine Pound Prize. She paid for the Share elevn Shillings & sixpence and she will receive for her Share only 11. Shillings and 3. pence, by which Prize, she will be out of Pocket 3^d. if not more when it is received. No rejoicings at all at Weston. I should have been very glad to have contributed towards some, if Mr. Custance had come forward.

DECBR. 12, WEDNESDAY. We breakfasted, dined, &c. again at home. The first thing I heard this Morning when I came down Stairs, was the Death of my poor Clerk Thos. Thurston, He was out and at Work on Monday at Mr. Custances. His Death was occasioned by a sudden & rapid Swelling in his Throat which suffocated him, something of the Quinsey. His Death was very sudden indeed. Poor Tom Thurston was at Church on Sunday and did his Duty as Clerk as usual. He was an harmless, industrious working Man as any in the Parish and very serviceable. Dinner to day a fresh Tongue boiled & a Duck &c. Bitter cold indeed to day with rough NEE Wind which pinches me in the extreme. Willm. Large applied for the Clerkship this Morning & I appointed him to the same.

DEC. 16, SUNDAY. We breakfasted, dined, &c.

the East India Company, gold boxes and swords of honour poured in upon him. He was made Baron Nelson of the Nile and of Burnham Thorpe, and when this honour was criticized as inadequate Pitt made the memorable answer 'Admiral Nelson's fame would be co-equal with the British name; and it would be remembered that he had obtained the greatest naval victory on record, when no man would think of asking whether he had been created a baron, a viscount, or an earl'.

again at home. Nancy had two Letters this Morning brought from Weston House by Briton, which they brought Yesterday from Norwich, some of the Family being at Norwich then. Both very melancholy ones indeed, One was from Cole from Mrs. Grove at Cole, the other from Nancys Brother William. The former giving us the dismal Account of the Death of my dear Sister Pounsett on Tuesday last in the Afternoon of a putrid Fever at her House at Ansford. Nancys Brother did not mention her Death only that she was very dangerously ill. The melancholy News of the Death of poor dear Sister Pounsett made me very miserable indeed. It is our great Loss—but to her I hope great Gain. We thought her quite well and happy at her little Palace at Ansford—and we were informed in a late Letter from Miss Hussey, that her Aunt Mrs Webb had been very lately into Somersett and at my Sister Pounsett's—and that my Sister Pounsett with her Aunt talked of going to Bath and also to London together very soon. I don't know after all things considered whether it is not happier for her, her Son in Law, Grove, having of late behaved to her rather unkind on all accounts—Oh! Tempora quo modo mutantur!—In his Temporibus, Quid desiderandum! Dinner to day, a Turkey rosted etc.

DECBR. 22, SATURDAY. We breakfasted, dined, &c. again at home. Betty Dades Father called here this Morning. Dinner to day, a boiled Rabbit & Beef Steaks &c. Nancy had a Letter this Evening from her Brother William at Gallhampton confirming the bad News of my dear Sister Pounsetts Death and the unfeeling behaviour of her Son in Law, Grove respecting the burial of my poor Sister, none of her Relations invited to attend her to her last home. No Pall-

Bearers & also even a Pall partly refused. From such unfeeling & base Hearts which Grove hath shewn to so deserving a Woman may we never more hear of such. What a miserable Prospect has my Niece his Wife before her! She would have him, and every device from her Friends respecting a proper Marriage-Settlement was thrown away upon her, So that Grove had everything not only all Jane's but her Mothers also—which now comes to him, every thing of my late poor Sister Pounsetts.

Decbr. 28, Friday. We breakfasted, dined, &c. again at home. Frost last Night & this Morning & all the Day intense—it froze in every part of the House even in the Kitchen. Milk & Cream tho' kept in the Kitchen all froze. Meat like blocks of Wood. It froze in the Kitchen even by the fire in a very few Minutes. So severe Weather I think I never felt before. Even the Meat in our Pantry all froze & also our Bread. I think the Cold was never more severe in my Life. Giblett Soup & Piggs Fry for Dinner to day &c. This Evening, if anything, Frost more severe.

1799

Janry. 19, Saturday. We breakfasted, dined, &c. again at home. Cold, dark & raw Thawe this Morning. Briton walked to Reepham to see his Friends this Morning and had my leave to stay out all Night but to come home by dinner time to Morrow. Dinner to day, Calf's Fry &c. Bidewells People brought our News to day. Recd. a Letter this Evening from my Nephew Willm. Woodforde of Gallhampton in Somersett brought from Norwich by Mr. Custance's Servant. The Contents were mostly concerning the

Cole Family, of the ill treatment of Grove to my late dear Sister Pounsett, but that she had made a Will and had given all she could give to her Sister White and her Family. It grieved me to hear so very indifferent a Character of Grove who married my Niece Jane Pounsett, and more so as he is a Clergyman— very unbecoming one. I was extremely sorry to hear he was such a Man.

JANRY. 29, TUESDAY. ... Very intensely cold, & a very hard Frost last Night and this Morning. It froze sharply within doors last Night and also this Morning. Nevertheless tho' the Weather has been & is still severely cold we have not had our beds warmed at all during the whole Winter as yet, neither do we intend to. Dinner to day, a Turkey rosted &c.

JANRY. 31, THURSDAY. We breakfasted, dined, &c. again at home. Paid Js. Pegg this Morning a Qrs. Land-Tax 3. 0. 0. John Norton was Yesterday committed to Aylesham Bridewell for a Breach of the Peace. Dinner to day, boiled Veal & Pork &c. Many People are glad that J_o^n Norton is sent to Bridewell as he was so unruly. His Wife & Daughter, as well as Neighbours were afraid almost to go to bed at Nights afraid of being burnt in their beds, as he took so little care of fire—scarce ever went to bed, and his behaviour to a poor-bed-ridden Wife and a good Daughter, was almost beyond example, distressing. Bitter cold again to day with some Snow. Frost very severe, froze sharp within doors.

FEBRY. 1, FRIDAY. We breakfasted, dined, &c. again at home. Very hard Frost with much Snow and very rough Easterly Wind. By much the coldest & most severe cold Day, we have had as yet during the

Winter—very distressing to a poor Invalide. Dinner to day, boiled Pork and Duck rosted. This Day the most severe we have had all the whole Winter. It froze sharp within doors. I don't know that I ever felt a more severe Day. The Turnips all froze to blocks, obliged to split them with Beetle[1] & Wedges, and some difficulty to get at them on account of the Snow —their Tops entirely gone and they lay as Apples on the Ground—No Tops. This Day has been, I apprehend, the most severe that we have had this Winter. The Snow has in many Places rendered the Road impassable. Morn' very hard Frost with Snow & Wind. The most severe Morn' we have had this Winter. Afternoon much Snow & more severe. Frost sharp even within doors. Never scarce a more severe Day known. The Dairy Window quite darkened. The present severe cold Weather pinches me almost to death.

FEBRY. 2, SATURDAY. We breakfasted, dined, &c. again at home. Still very severe Weather, much Snow & hard Frost. The Turnips have lost all their Tops and now look like so many large Bowls or foot-Balls. I was taken very ill last Night on going to bed fell down in a fit, but Nancy hearing me fall came kindly to my Assistance with Betty. The cold quite overpowered me, going from a warm Room to a cold Room above without fire, and after walking round below in seeing all things safe—the cold was too much for me. The Snow so drifted in some Places as to make the Roads almost impassable. Scarce ever known such severe Weather for the last forty Years and still likely to continue. It affects me extremely indeed, have scarce any feeling, am almost benumbed

---

[1] A Beetle is a heavy wooden mallet (see Wright's *Dialect Dictionary*).

both in Mind & Body. Bidewells People brought our
Norwich Paper, the Ipswich Paper not come to Nor-
wich owing to the Severity of the Weather—The
Roads being impassable almost to any Place on
Account of the Snow being drifted in almost every
Road. Such severe Weather has not been known for
the last 60. Years till the present. Snow drifted in
some places uncommonly high. Dinner to day, boiled
Pork and a roast Duck &c.

FEBRY. 3, SUNDAY. We breakfasted, dined, &c.
again at home. The Weather more severe than ever
with continued Snow all last Night and continued
snowing all this whole Day with a good deal of Wind
which have drifted the Snow in some Places so very
deep as to make almost every road impassable—in
many roads 15 feet deep. No Service at Weston
Church to day. Such Weather with so much Snow
I never knew before—not able to go to Jericho.
Dreadful Weather for the poor People and likewise for
all kinds of Cattle &c. &c. It is dangerous almost for
any person to be out. Dinner to day a boiled Rabbit
and Onion Sauce and a very fine Goose rosted &c.
Briton walked to Weston-House this Morning with
the News but had a hard matter to get there—obliged
to get over hedges &c. I would not have had him go,
but he liked it. He however got thro' it pretty well.
If the present severe Weather continues long, God
only knows what we shall all do &c. The Turnips
being all froze is very bad for Stock. There having
been such a severe Winter with so much Snow and of
so long continuance for the last 60. Years, in the hard
Winter of 1740—The Year that I was born—It held
then 13. Weeks.

FEBRY. 7, THURSDAY. We breakfasted, dined, &c.

again at home. The same cold Weather prevails with very severe Frost accompanied with some Snow. Water froze in the back-house quite hard within, in less than four hours after it had been brought in from the Well to day abt. Noon. Such severe Frost to day, as scarce was known. Mr. Custance obliged to send to Norwich to day after Coal being quite out. Two Waggons went this Morning after some and obliged to come by my House to France-Green and so on to Honingham to get to the Turnpike Road there, and three or four Men went with the Teams. It is also even thought that when they get there, that they could [not] get any, as no Coals can come from Yarmouth, No Barges stirring—all bound fast by the Frost on the River. This very severe Weather almost kills me. I am much affected by it for the worse. Dinner to day, boiled Leg of Pork &c.

FEBRY. 8, FRIDAY. We breakfasted, dined, &c. again at home. The very severe cold Weather that have so long prevailed, is to day if any thing, more piercing. I have felt it more to day, than any yet. Dinner to day, rost Beef &c. We want many things from Norwich, but am afraid to send any Servant in such bad Weather. Within these last few days have been afraid to go out of Doors by myself. Fear seems to have got great Power over me of late Days. Very fearful of being out of doors by myself having of late been very much afraid of having an Epileptic or falling fit—My Head inclining I have thought of late that way. It makes me very low indeed on that account. Mr. Custances Waggons returned home last Night in very good time, but had a most terrible Journey of it, but got home safe. They were four Hours in getting to the Turnpike Road at Honingham—The Road so deep. I am very glad that they got back all safe.

FEBRY. 9, SATURDAY. We breakfasted, dined, &c, again at home. The most severe Morning of Weather we have had this Winter, the hardest Frost yet known with very driving Snow, attended with Wind. It is remarked that this Morning of Weather was as severe as any ever felt in England.[1] Mr. Custance had another Waggon go to Norwich this Morning after Coal again. They went by my House again with two other Waggons with them belonging to others. In the Afternoon (thank God) came on a gentle Thawe all of a sudden which made us rejoice. Dinner to day, fryed Pork & Potatoes &c. No Newspapers from Norwich to day.

FEBRY. 10, SUNDAY. We breakfasted, dined, &c. again at home. Fair & fine but a Frost & very cold withall. The Snow decreased very little indeed, tho' sunck. No Divine Service at Church this afternoon, the Weather such and Roads impassable some Places. Road impassable from the Church to Odnam-Green by Car-Cross. Dinner to day, Part of a Loin of Veal rosted &c.

FEBRY. 11, MONDAY. We breakfasted, dined, &c. again at home. I got up this Morning, in high Spirits, after having a very good Night of Sleep, owing I take it to my drinking Coffee in the Afternoon, Yesterday. I had Coffee also this Morning for breakfast but about Noon was taken very flighty & giddy, which I cannot but partly attribute to Coffee. Paid Ben, this Morn' for divers things 0. 14. 1½. Paid Briton, ditto for ditto

[1] In the chronicle of the *Annual Register* for 1799, under date February 9th, it is stated that 'The mail-guards, who arrived in town, declare they never experienced so severe a night as that of February 8th'.

o. 8. 1. Paid Betty, ditto for ditto 1. 4. 10. Recd. of Betty, for Butter 0. 7. 3¾. Captn. Hambleton Custance called on us this Morn'. Dinner to day, boiled Pork & a rosted Hare &c. A great Thawe all Day, but nevertheless very cold.

FEB. 15, FRIDAY. . . . A fine cheary Morning with a rapid Thawe but nevertheless cold and very bad walking indeed. It is a happy change for all things I hope. Dinner to day, boiled Beef & Apple Dumplins &c. The Thawe will I hope now continue. My Butcher, for the future, is to bring my News &c. from Norwich every Week to my House.

FEB. 16, SATURDAY. . . . Early in the Morn' there was a small Frost but it thawed again fast about 8. o'clock after. I felt pretty well & strong this Morning. Dinner to day, Shoulder of Mutton rosted &c. No News Papers &c. came to hand to day, Tho' my Butcher promised me faithfully to bring them which very much disconcerted me.

FEB. 17, SUNDAY. We breakfasted, dined, &c. again at home. Our Newspapers &c. we received this Morning by Sarah Grant of the Poor House on Hungate Common. My Butcher having left them there last Night. Had a Letter from Mrs. Grove in Somersett. No Duty at Weston Church this Morning, Mr. Cotman attended but it was late when he got there. Dinner to day, boiled Pork & a Turkey rosted &c. My Strength rather better, Spirits also, and my Appetite very good but feel however feverish. I eat five times a day—at breakfast, abt. Noon, Dinner, Afternoon at Tea, and at Supper—and at all times with a proper relish. Mr. William Custance called on us this Morning. Very dismal Accounts on the Papers respecting the last severe Weather—many, many People having lost their Lives thro' the inclemency of the same. Mail Coaches &c. unable to travel. The Roads in very, very many Places impassable. The long continuance of so severe cold Weather having scarce been ever known for the last Century. It has lasted now (with scarce any intermission) from the 17th of December last past & still likely.

FEBRY. 26, TUESDAY. We breakfasted, dined, &c. again at home. Sent Ben, this Morning, to Norwich, on purpose to pay off two Bills for me, having been wrote to by the People, here mentioned. Messrs. Smith, Woolen-Drapers, and Forster, Taylor. I told Ben to take a stamp Receipt of each of them in full of all Demands having done with them. Dinner to day, a boiled Fowl & Pork & Beef-Steaks. Ben returned about 4. o'clock this Afternoon with proper Receipts on paying the said Bills. It pleased me much on the said Bills being paid but the remembrance of their being sent me by them, will not be by me so soon forgot having dealt with them for at least 23 Years. Smith the Mercer is a Presbyterian and I suppose, Forster, the Taylor, is of the same Persuasion. I have now done with them for ever for their late shabby, ungentleman-like behaviour. Fish at Norwich very scarce and very dear.

MARCH 8, FRIDAY. . . . Mr. Palmer (my Malster) called on me this Morning respecting some London-Newspapers that I had of Mr. Custances as he is making a Collection of all he can get, to send to his Son[1] in the East-Indies. Dinner to day, a boiled Pike & Cottage-Pye. Very indifferent indeed all the Day long.

[1] George Custance, who eventually became a Lt.-Col. in the East India Company's service: he died in 1814.

MARCH 22, G. FRIDAY. ... Mr. Cotman called on me this Morning before he went to Weston Church to read Prayers being Good-Friday. He also wished to leave the Curacy of Weston at the expiration of the present Quarter. I cannot say that I was displeased at it, as he has been rather too inattentive to duty. Dinner to day, Salt Fish, Eggs & Fritters. I was rather a little giddy in my Head to day a little before dinner —but only a few minutes.

MARCH 23, SATURDAY. We breakfasted, dined, &c. again at home. Sent Ben early this Morning to Norwich to settle Accounts for me with Mr. Bloome. I sent him also a State of the Accounts between us and Mr. Bloome's Corn-Notes & his Bill for Coal due from me to him—38. 4. 6. Due from Mr. Bloome to me for Corn 65. 8. 6. Balance due to me from D. Bloome 27. 4. 0. Nancy sent a Letter to her Aunt J^n_o Woodforde by him. I sent Ben on horseback. Ben returned from Norwich about 4. this Aft. and brought me in Cash from Mr. Bloome on balance of

Accounts between us	27.	4.	0.
that is, for Corn due from him to me	65.	8.	6.
Due from me to him for Coal	38.	4.	6.
Balance therefore as above	27.	4.	0.

Ben brought a Letter for Nancy from her Brother Willm. of Gallhampton, informing her of her Mother's Death &c. and that Admiral Squire & Lady had made them a Visit lately. Dinner to day, Neck of Pork rosted &c. Ben Recd. at Norwich to day for himself a 16th Share of a Prize in the present English Lottery of twenty Pounds

The sum of	1.	4.	6.
The Share cost him	0.	19.	6.
So that he got clear, only	0.	5.	0.

MARCH 31, SUNDAY. We breakfasted, dined &c.
again at home. Mr. Cotman read Prayers and administered the H. Sacrament this Morn' at Weston
Church. Nancy had a Letter from her Brother
William this Morning brought Yesterday from Norwich by Mr. Custance Servant—a most melancholy
one indeed to us, as it announced to us the Death of
our dear Friend my dear Brother John Woodforde,
who died very suddenly at Mrs. Patty Clarkes at
Castle-Cary on Saturday last, having come from Bath.
He came from Bath with Ralph Woodforde on the
Sunday before, Ralph coming from Allhampton on
the Death of his Mother—Ralph being executor. I
sincerely pity poor Mrs. Woodforde my poor Brothers
Wife for so dreadful a shock & not being with him at
the time.

APRIL 2, TUESDAY. . . . Bitter cold again to day,
hard Frost, but less Wind. There being but few sound
Turnips, the poor Stock such as Bullocks, Cows, Sheep
&c. are shockingly distressed, few Farmers have
scarce anything to give them. Scarce ever known such
distressed times for Stock of all kinds, nothing growing, no vegetation, every thing almost dead in the
gardens, Beans & Peas &c. almost all gone dead. It
is grievous to behold how every Vegetable is hurt—
Not even a Daisy or any kind of flower seen. What
dismal, dreary Aspect have we at present.

APRIL 3, WEDNESDAY. . . . Very severe Frosts still
continue, bitter cold indeed. Every kind of Vegetable
almost destroyed by the Frost. Turnips all froze—alas
poor Stock. Peas & Beans, sown in Gardens, almost
all gone. Such severe, cold Weather of so long continuance was scarce known in the Memory of Man.
Dinner to day, boiled Veal & Pork & a rosted Duck.

APRIL 18, THURSDAY. . . . Nancy had a Letter
from her Cousin, Jane Grove, dated from Shrewton
in Dorsetshire, to which Place, they have very lately
removed, having let Cole Place to one James of
Bruton on a Lease of twenty one Years—Farewell!
adieu—S:—. My Nephew Willm. Woodforde will I
hope thrive & prosper & his Family—Pray God! bless
them. Dinner to day, broiled breast of Veal & Apple
Dumplins.

APRIL 19, FRIDAY. . . . To a poor old Sailor gave
this Morning o. o. 6. I delivered this Morning my
Income Tax-Paper to Js. Pegg in which I have
charged myself 20£ per Ann.[1] Dinner to day, a
boiled Fowl & a Tongue &c. Very wet all the day
long, but not very cold. Thank God! am not quite so
nervous or fearfull as I was some time back but Spirits
poorly.

APRIL 22, MONDAY. We breakfasted, dined, &c.
again at h[ome]. Betty Dade, my head Maid, went
early this Morning in Johnny Reeves Cart to Melton
to meet her Father there, and from thence she is to go
with her Father into Suffolk to see a Mr. Donne,
Farmer, at Tattington near Ipswich whose Son was
to have married Betty, but he dying before it took
Place, the Father have always taken great Notice of
her & Family. He having been of late very bad and
but little hopes of his ever getting well again, is very
desirous of seeing Betty once more. She is to be from
home three Nights & four Days. Sally's Brother,

---

[1] Pitt's preliminary income-tax attempt having failed to produce the
expected results, he repealed the Triple Assessment, and in January of
this year (1799) introduced a direct tax on income from all sources.
Incomes under £60 were exempt, between £60 and £200 charged at
various rates, and at £200 upwards at the full charge of 10 per cent.
The actual yield for 1799 was just over £6,000,000.

Willm. Gunton, called on her this Morn'. He is still
in the Norfolk Militia. He looked very well indeed,
he is now a Serjeant. Dinner to day, boiled Calfs
Head &c. Nancy busy to day in answering her Brother
Willm. Woodfordes Letter. Rather low-spirited to
day, all Family Affairs in the Country contrary to my
desire or wish and those People which ought to be
Friends by blood turn out the greatest Enemies on
Earth.

MAY 6, MONDAY. . . . Sold to Mr. Girling, sixteen
Hundred of Hay, he being greatly distressed for Food
[for] his Sheep and Cattle, the Season continuing on
so very cold and wet, that Nothing grows scarce yet.
No Hay almost to be got for Love or Money. Mr.
Girling is to give me 4ˢ/6ᵈ per Hundred so that he
owes me for the above Hay 3. 12. 0. Dinner to day,
Leg of Mutton boiled & Capers &c. I was finely to
day and made an excellent Dinner on the Mutton.
Saw the first Swallow.

MAY 26, SUNDAY. We breakfasted, dined, &c.
again at home. Mr. Cotman read Prayers & Preached
this Afternoon at Weston Church for the last time as
he leaves the Curacy this Day of Weston. He called
on me (by my desire) this Afternoon and I paid him
for his last half Year's Curacy, before Miss Woodforde
the sum of 15. 0. 0. in full of every demand from me
to him. He drank a Glass of Port Wine and soon left
us. Young Mr. Dade (who is to succeed Mr. Cotman
in the Curacy of Weston) called on me also this Afternoon, and informed me that he would enter upon the
Curacy of Weston by my desire on Sunday next, and
therefore will read Prayers and Preach at Weston-
Church on Sunday morning next—to begin at a Qr.
before Eleven. When Duty in the Afternoon at Qr.

before three. Mr. Dade drank a Glass of Port Wine whilst here. Dinner to day a Calfs Head boiled & Pork &c. I was pretty well to day, not so very nervous. Young Baker of Cawston was to have succeeded Cotman in my Church as Curate, but was very lately preferred to a Readers Place at Bury. I cannot say that I am very sorry for it, as of late I heard that Dr. Baker and whole Family are very violent Democrats indeed.

MAY 31, FRIDAY. . . . I was but poorly to day, a great weakness inwardly which I take proceeds from too great depression of Spirits from many divers Family Losses and the unpleasant Prospect of things on that Account. Dinner to day, Part of a Rump of Beef boiled &c.

JUNE 2, SUNDAY. We breakfasted, dined, &c. again at home. Mr. Dade entered upon the Curacy of Weston this Morning, and he read Prayers & Preached & christened a Child at Weston-Church and he was much esteemed by all that heard him. Mr. Custance was at Church as was my Niece and spoke much in his favour indeed. I am very glad that he gives such Satisfaction. Dinner to day, a Bullocks Heart rosted &c. I was very poorly indeed all the Morning, got rather better towards the Evening.

JUNE 8, SATURDAY. . . . I was finely to day, thank God, than what I have been for some days past. Appetite much better. Dinner to day, a boiled Codling & hashed B. Heart &c. A most heavenly Day, all Vegetation in the quickest growth and in the most flourishing State. Our News Papers did not come to day at all.

JUNE 10, MONDAY. We breakfasted, dined &c.

again at home. Mr. Maynard called on us this Morning. To a Man of Shearingham by name Hull for six small Crabs paid him 0. 1. 0. Dinner to day, a small Leg of Mutton rosted and remarkably fine flavoured —Scotch Mutton. Mr. Custance called on us in his Evenings Walk about 7. o'clock & spent an Hour with us. Michael Andrews Wife has met with a very bad Fall and very dangerously strained her Ancle. Washing Week with us this Week. We wash every five Weeks. Our present Washerwomen are Anne Downing and Anne Richmond. Washing and Ironing generally take us four Days. The Washerwomen breakfast and dine the Monday and Tuesday, and have each one Shilling on their going away in the Evening of Tuesday. Mr. Custance brought us great News, that the French had been entirely driven out of Italy by the Austrians & vast Numbers of them had been killed and taken Prisoners in the late battles.[1]

JUNE 19, WEDNESDAY. We breakfasted, dined, &c. again at home. Paid Js. Pegg this Morning 2. Months Income Tax at 20. Pounds per Annum 3. 6. 8. Mrs. Custance & Son Neville called on us this Morn'. I may say Afternoon for they did not come till near two o'clock in the Afternoon. It made it rather late for our Dinner to day. Dinner to day, hash'd Calfs Head &c. Very cold indeed again to day, so cold that Mrs. Custance came walking in her Spenser[2] with a Bosom-

---

[1] The reference is to the victorious campaign of the Austrian and Russian forces in Northern Italy. The Allies entered Milan on April 28th, and Turin on May 27th, and shut up the French in Genoa. The French were not, however, entirely expelled from Italy till November, the decisive battles being Suvorov's victory at Novi (Aug. 15th) and Melas' at Genoa (Nov. 4th).

[2] A spencer—so named from Earl Spencer (1758–1834), Pitt's eminent First Lord of the Admiralty—is described in the *N.E.D.* as regards men as 'a short double-breasted overcoat without tails worn by men in the latter part of the eighteenth century and the beginning of the

Friend.[1] Neville Custance is a very chuff Boy indeed as I ever saw, seem displeased & cross with every thing—would not eat a bit of Cake when brought to him. Says little or nothing to any body and when he does speak, it is in a bluff and very rough & bluff way. He is not at all like his Brother or Sister in Temper.

JULY 16, TUESDAY. . . . Rather more nervous and timorous to day. A Pigs Chop with Beans and Peas for Dinner. Fine Day for our Hay, almost all cocked.

JULY 25, THURSDAY. We breakfasted, dined, &c. again at home. Very casualty Weather for the Hay, fine Rain most of the Morning, Afternoon, mostly fair. The Trial relating to Tom Bakers Servant Man stealing Corn from Mr. Girling finished to day the Man pleaded guilty, and is to go a Soldier. Nothing reflecting on Tom Baker was advanced. Dinner to day, a boiled Fowl & Ham & Leg of Mutton rosted with a Cucumber &c.

AUG. 30, FRIDAY. . . . Busy in carrying Oats to day, being a dry Day. A very late Harvest this Year indeed, we dont begin cutting Wheat till Monday next, if then. Last Year we cut Wheat on Monday Aug. 6th.

nineteenth', also, later, as 'a short coat or jacket', and as regards women as 'a kind of close-fitting jacket or bodice commonly worn by women and children early in the nineteenth century, and since revived'. The earliest reference to a woman's spencer given in the *N.E.D.* is dated 1803, and thus Parson Woodforde's Diary now carries this particular 'Spencer' pedigree back another four years.

[1] A bosom friend is described in the *N.E.D.* as 'an article of wearing apparel to protect the bosom from cold', and the earliest reference quoted is from the *Hull Packet* for September 28th, 1802: 'Handkerchiefs, tippets, bosom friends and other articles peculiarly adapted to the ensuing season.' It must be remembered that the fashions of 1799 tended to 'expose the person' not a little: indeed it was said that it required the aid of the north wind to enforce a return to modesty in women's dress (see Wright's *Caricature History*, ch. xiv, on the contemporary fashions).

Sepbr. 3, Tuesday. We breakfasted, dined, &c. again at home. Our Wheat remarkably fine & heavy but very much beat down by the late Winds & Rain which makes it very bad for shearing. I hired, Yesterday, one Henry Daines, a Boy of 13. Years old, in the place of Barnard Woodcock, who leaves me at Michaelmas next being too old for his Place & can better himself. I liked the Boy very well, having an open, honest countenance to all appearances, his Mother who came with him, seemed to be a good kind of Woman & very Motherly. I gave the Boy, on hiring him 0. 1. 0. Dinner to day, rost Beef & Plumb Pudding as our People are busy, in shearing of Wheat. I was but indifferent all day, very weak, tho' I made a very good Dinner on the Beef.

Sepbr. 11, Wednesday. . . . Very fine Day again for the Harvest &c. 'Lord make us all truly thankful for the same and give us gratefull Hearts in return.' Dinner to day, Beans & Bacon & Partridges. Thank God! I was very finely to day & eat hearty. All my Wheat but a very few Sheaves carried and put into Barn without any Rain at all upon it during the whole time of cutting, &c. Uncommonly fine Weather indeed have we had for the last 6. Weeks past.

Sep. 25, Wednesday. We breakfasted, dined, &c. again at home. Mr. Maynard called here this Morning. Just before Dinner, Nancy's Brother William from Somersett came riding into our Yard, and he dined, supped & slept here. His coming upon us so sudden affected us at first, but after dinner we were better. William slept in his usual Room. We had for Dinner to day boiled Eels &c.

Octbr. 6, Sunday. We breakfasted, dined, &c. again at home. Andrew Spraggs brought a Box for me this Morning to my House, which he brought Yesterday from Norwich, in which was a fine large Somersett Cheese, a present from my Nephew now with me, from a Relation of his Wife's at Mew near Stowton by name James Jules, a great Dealer in Cheese and employed for Government in that way and is getting a good fortune by it. It was a very kind Present from my Nephew. The Cheese was about a Qr. of a Hundred Wht. with the Kings Arms on the side of it. The Cheese was made near Wells in Somersett, Mr. Dade read Prayers & Preached this Morn' at Weston-Church. It being rather damp & inclined to wet Nancy & Brother did not go. Dinner to day, Breast of Veal rosted &c.

DECBR. 1, SUNDAY. We breakfasted, dined, &c. again at home, Mr. Dade (my Curate) called on me this Morning before Divine Service, and I paid him, half a Years serving Weston Church for me, due about this time 15. 6. 0. Nancy & her Brother went to Church this Morn'. Mr. Custance was at Church and he brought them home in his Coach but he did not come in. Dinner to day, Cod-Fish & a Co. Ducks rosted. Bread given to the Poor at Church to day. Wheat being very dear 50. Shillings per Coomb.

DECBR. 10, TUESDAY. We breakfasted, dined, &c. again at home. This being my Tithe Audit-Day, the following People paid me their respective Compositions for Tithe &c. for the last Year to Michaelmas last. Stephen Andrews Senr., John Pegg for his Father, Michael Andrews, Willm. Bidewell, John Baker, Thos. Reynolds Junr., Js. Jermyn, J_o^n Norton, John Girling Junr., Willm. Howlett, Barnard Dunnell, John Mann, J_o^n Culley, Thos. Baker, Mary Pratt, Charles Cary, Henry Case, John Buck Junr., An.

Spraggs, Charles Hardy, John Hubbard, & J$^{n}_{o}$ Heavers. I recd. of them upon the whole about ———. They dined & stayed at my House, till abt. 11 at Night & went away then highly pleased. I did not see any of them the lest disguised. Dinner, two Legs of Mutton boiled & Capers, Salt-Fish, a Sur-Loin of Beef rosted, with plenty of plumb & plain Puddings &c. Only two Bowls of Punch, four Bottles of Wine four Bottles of Rum—eight Lemons, about three Pounds of Sugar, and at lest six Gallons of strong Beer besides small. My Nephew gave them a Song. It was the pleasantest & most agreeable Tithe-Audit, I ever experienced. Every thing harmonious & agreeable.

DECBR. 23, MONDAY. ... The Poor of Weston went about to day for their Christmas Gifts, instead of St. Thos. Day on Saturday last, it being more convenient for them. I gave to 51 of them at my House this Morn' at 6^{d}. each 1. 5. 6. Mr. Hambleton Custance called on us this Morning as he was out a Shooting and during the time of the Poor People being here. Dinner to day, Fish & a Leg of Mutton rosted.

1800

JANUARY 24, FRIDAY. We breakfasted, dined, &c. again at home. Very busy all the Morning in looking over Family Accounts & Goods relating to Somersett that my Nephew Willm. Woodforde might take a Copy of the same with him into Somersett. After which I made him a Present of a Bank of England Note of 5. 0. 0. Also two Guineas, to be laid out in Town for things in remembrance of me to his Wife and Children —2. 2. 0. Dinnèr to day, Leg of Mutton rosted &c.

JANRY. 26, SUNDAY. ... Mr. Dade read Prayers &

Preached this Morn' at Weston Church. Few People there. It was a dark wet Morning and mild. Dinner to day, Shoulder of Mutton rosted &c. We were rather dull and flat to day, as to Morrow Nancy's Brother Willm. Woodforde leaves Weston Parsonage for Somersett.

JANRY. 27, MONDAY. ... We got up very early this Morning on Account of my Nephew setting out for Somersett, we breakfasted about seven o'clock and at eight my nephew mounted his Mare and set off for Somersett by the Newmarket Road by Attleborough, Thetford, &c. He purposed reaching Barton Mills this Evening. Pray God! send him a good & safe Journey. It made us very low on parting. Sent Briton this Morning early to Norwich with his Trunk to go by one of the London Coaches this Afternoon. Dinner to day, Shoulder of Veal rosted &c. Briton returned home about 5. this Aft. A very fine and mild Day for the Season.

FEBRY. 25, TUESDAY. ... Paid Ben, this Morning for divers things 3. 5. 3. Aldridge called here this Morning with divers things in the Muslin & Cotton Goods, I paid him a Bill for goods sent me some time back from Norwich, for Thick Set for Briton 1. 7. 0. The Price of Wheat being so very dear at present occasions very great grumbling amongst the Poor at this time, and makes them talk loudly. Three Pounds per Coomb[1] for Wheat on Saturday last was said to be asked at Norwich Market. Dinner to day, Leg of Mutton rosted & Fritters. Very piercing cold indeed to day, a smart Frost, with a strong ENE Wind—It pinches me sorely.

---

[1] This means the enormous price of £6 a quarter (a coomb = half a quarter). Even this price was exceeded in the ensuing winter.

MARCH 10, MONDAY.... The same cold Weather still prevails, tho' fair. I made a bet with Nancy this Evening of 1. Shilling that it rained before to Morrow Night.

MARCH 11, TUESDAY. . . . It rained softly a good part of the Day, so that I got my bet with my Niece, but not recd. it. Taylor Cary, named Robert, called on me this Morn' and measured me for a Pair of Breeches of black Velverett which he had of me 2 Yrds ½. We heard to day that there was a bad fever at Easton, some People of that Parish having very lately died there of the same. The common People talk much of it, & call it the Yellow-Fever which was so fatal the last Year in America. A Farmer & his Wife, by name Vincent with their Maid, died at Easton within 10. Days of each other in the last Week —They were much respected. Am truly sorry, it proved so fatal—may they be happy.

MARCH 24, MONDAY. We breakfasted, &c. again at home. Nancy dined & spent the Afternoon and great part of the Evening at Weston-House, with Mr. & Mrs. Custance & their two Daughters, with their Sons Hambleton and William Custance, Lady Bacon with her Daughters Anne, and Maria Bacon, Miss Mary Anne Bacon from Devonshire, and Edmund Bacon eldest Son of Sr. Edmund & Lady Bacon. Nancy did not return till after 9. o'clock this Evening as the young folks at Weston House had something of a Masquerade-Ball this Evening. Dramatis Personae, Miss Custance in the Character of an old Woman, Emily Custance a flower Girl, Devonshire Miss Bacon a Fortune-Teller alias Gipsy, Miss Bacon in the Character of a Fool, Miss Maria Bacon, a Ghost[1]—None of

---

[1] Of these 'Characters' it may be interesting to state that Miss Custance (Frances Ann) married on June 26th, 1804, Robert Marsham

the young Gentlemen acted at all or were dressed. I had for my Dinner to day a boiled Chicken &c.

APRIL 15, TUESDAY. We breakfasted, dined, &c. again at home. Paid James Hardy, Landlord of Weston-Heart, this Morning, for Liquors 2. 13. 0.

viz, to two Gallons of Rum at 16^s/0^d.   1. 12. 0.

To one Gallon of Brandy at 21^s/0^d.   1. 1. 0.

Dinner to day, Leg of Pork boiled &c. I eat very hearty for Dinner to day & feel stronger inwardly, but right hand very weak & swelled wch. I attribute to Gout. It is with great Pain that I write this. [The writing here is shaky, but not markedly so.]

APRIL 16, WEDNESDAY. ... Taylor Cary measured Briton for a new Frock of brown Velveret which I had by me. My right hand rather better but still swelled, & painful and weak.

MAY 9, FRIDAY. We breakfasted, dined, &c. again at home. Finely again this Morning before & at breakfast but being made uneasy soon after, was made quite ill again and very nervous &c. Poor Mr. John Buck was buried in Weston Church about Noon by Mr. Maynard. That added to my uneasiness also. My Maid Sally was invited to the Funeral as was also, my Man Ben Leggatt, both went. Ben was a near Relation to poor John Buck. Mr. Maynard called on me before the Funeral. Dr. Thorne called on us this Afternoon in his return from the Funeral & spent near

of Stratton Strawless, and died March 20th, 1874; Miss Emily Custance married the Rev. Bartholomew Edwards, Rector of Ashill, and died in 1864; Miss Bacon (Anne Frances, d. of Sir Edmund Bacon) married in 1803 Edward Thos. Hussey of Galtrim, Co. Meath, while her sister Maria married Edward Hodge, Major in the 7th Hussars, who fell at Genappe on June 16th (Waterloo was fought on the 18th), 1815. The Devonshire Miss Bacon—Mary Anne, the Fortune-Teller—married her cousin Edmund Bacon.

an Hour with us, he came about 4. o'clock. Mr. Buck
was 58 Years of Age. I had a Hatband & pair of
Gloves sent me. Betty went also to see him buried.
Dinner to day, Soup & a Co. Ducks rosted &c. I told
Mr. Maynard that he was to take 1. 1. 0. of the
Undertaker, it being the usual Fee for burying a
Person in the Church not living in the Parish, and
that could be well afforded.

MAY 12, MONDAY. We breakfasted, dined, &c.
again at home. Very cold indeed, to day—Wind
ENE. Gave Nancy to day before Dinner a ten Pound
Note of Kerrisons of Norwich, for the last Year due in
January 1800 to her but did not give before, for
Reasons of pertness. Dinner to day, rost Beef & Sallad
&c. I was tolerably well to day, rather pinched by
the cold, it being very cold indeed. Money paid to
day 10. 0. 0. Very busy all the Morning about
Weston Register. James Peggs Son called here this
Morning to leave some Tax-Papers with me.

JUNE 2, MONDAY. We breakfasted, dined, &c.
again at home. Our Maid (Betty Dade) taken very
ill in the Night in her old Complaint, Hysteric-Wind
Cholic. Very ill all the whole Day long—a little
matter better in the Evening. We gave her Port-Wine
and Water, Rum & Water, Lavender Drops &c. Mr.
Emeris very ill indeed, sent to me to borrow some
Lisbon-Wine. I sent him almost a Bottle and thought
it was all I had, but searching about afterwards, did
find one Bottle more. Dinner to day, fore Qr. of
Lamb rosted &c.

JUNE 22, SUNDAY. We breakfasted, dined, &c.
again at home. Mr. Dade read Prayers & Preached
this Afternoon at Weston-Church. Stormy Weather

about Noon with Thunder & Hail and Rain, but we had not much of it. Dinner to day, boiled Leg of Lamb & Loin fryed. Betty continues but poorly & weak still. Nancy thinks that it is owing to a Love Affair with my farming Man & Servant, Ben. Leggatt who hath for a long time taken notice of her. They have a long time been talked of. Whether he now slights her or not, I cannot say. I hope he hath not been too intimate with her. Thank God! I felt myself pretty well to day.

JUNE 27, FRIDAY. We breakfasted, dined, &c. again at home. I was finely to day thank God for it! and this Day I entered my sixtieth Year being born (old Stile) the sixteenth of June in the Year, 1740. Dinner to day, Shoulder of Mutton rosted &c. Accept my thanks O! Almighty God! for thy great Goodness to me in enabling me (after my Late great Illness) to return my grateful thanks for the same.

JUNE 29, SUNDAY. We breakfasted, dined, &c. again at home. Mr. Dade read Prayers & Preached this Morning at Weston Church—None of Weston-House there. Nancy intended to be there, but prevented by Rain. Dinner to day, a Sculphling of Lamb rosted (viz.) a Breast and Neck joined together. The Weather being Muggy with gentle soft Rain made me rather dull and spiritless to day. Delightful Weather however for all kinds of Vegetables, particularly so for all kinds of Grain. Thanks to the Almighty Creator for the same.

JULY 9, WEDNESDAY. . . . Nancy, very busy most part of the Morning, in Ironing her Cloths in our Kitchen.

JULY 12, SATURDAY. . . . Nancy had another

Swarm of Bees about Noon from the same old Hive which the last Swarm came from. It should have been mentioned Yesterday instead of to day as Yesterday it happened unknown to me and our Maids hived them. They settled in our Wall-Garden on one of the Sticks put into the Ground to prop up and for Peas to twist round & keep from the Ground. The Swarm of Bees happened very suddenly. Our Maids hived them very well indeed and they seemed to settle very well this Morn'. I think Nancy very lucky with her Bees. Dinner to day, Peas & Bacon &c.

AUGUST 27, WEDNESDAY. . . . Our tame Hawk that we had so long in the Walled Garden fled away Yesterday and hath not been heard of since. The Lapwing also we had so long, have not been heard of some Days. Harvest quite at a Stand at present. Mr. Hambleton Custance drank Tea with us in the Evening. He came riding, stayed till near 8. Mr. Foster sent us some Eels this Morning. Dinner to day, fryed Eels, boiled Pork & Greens &c. I was but poorly to day, weak, giddy & faint.

OCTOBER 10, FRIDAY. We breakfasted, dined, &c. again at home. This being old Michaelmas Day, I paid my Servant Boy, Henry Daines, three Quarters of a Years Wages due this Day at two Guineas per Annum. 1. 11. 6. and dismissed him from my Service not behaving in a manner that I expected from him, as he could not be trusted to do any thing if not overlooked, and also a very saucy, foul-mouthed Lad. Mr. Custance made us a Morning Visit he came walking & had been to Hungate-Lodge where his Brother is coming to reside this Day. Dinner to day, Mutton Soup & a rost Goose &c.

NOV. 18, TUESDAY. We breakfasted, dined, &c.

again at home. Mrs. Custance with her Daughters called on us this Morning in their way to Lord Baynings and stayed with us about half an Hour. They were very fashionably dressed. Mrs. Custance & eldest Daughter were dressed in brown Silk Pellices, alias great-Coats. Emily Custance was dressed in white. Dinner to day, Part of a Rump of a Beef Boiled &c. Thank God! I was tolerably well to day. Had a small Pig killed this Morning. Betty Dade's Father here again this Morn'. The Afternoon rather dark, damp & cold.

NOVBR. 27, THURSDAY. We breakfasted, dined, &c. again at home. Dinner to day, fryed Pork & a Rabbit rosted &c. Mr. and Mrs. Shrimpton (late Betsy Davy) who are on a Visit at Mr. Thornes of Mattishall made us a Morning Visit and stayed with us upwards of an Hour, Mrs. Shrimpton looked remarkably well & of good Spirits. They live in a genteel Way in Suffolk and have one Child; a little Boy, by name Joseph, his Father's Name, about 2. Years old. Mr. Shrimpton is a Dissenter, I believe a Presbyterian, he is rather plain and I should take him to be about 35. Yrs. old. They came in a genteel Whiskey and had a Servant to attend them. They stayed with us upwards of an Hour, had some refreshment & returned back to Mattishall. They leave Mattishall to Morrow and return home to Walpole in Suffolk not a great many Miles from Beccles, where Mr. Shrimpton's Father (who is lately dead) lived, and the Estate now comes to his Son. Mr. Maynard called on us this Morning whilst Mrs. Shrimpton was here—and during the time that Mr. Shrimpton went in his Whiskey to see Weston-House. Mr. Shrimpton had a Gun & a Pointer with him. I was rather hurried at first seeing them. I sent Ben, round this Morn' to my Farmers to meet at Parsonage on Tuesday next to pay me their Composition for Tithe for 1800 & dine here. Ben returned about 9. o'clock quite drunk which made me rather uneasy being rather ill.

DECBR. 11, THURSDAY. We breakfasted, dined, &c. again at home. A cold, raw, foggy, and dark day. Dinner to day, Giblet-Soup & a rost Rabbit. A Man called here this Evening about 5. o'clock had Trowsers on and had he said been a Sailor. He walked as if he was lame, he asked Charity. He appeared rather a suspicious Character & that he had other things in view than mere asking Charity, this time of the Day. I rather suspect of his being after Poultry. As he might however be in want, gave him 0. 1. I was finely this Morning when I came down Stairs, but being soon after made rather uneasy discomposed me the whole day after.

DECBR. 22, MONDAY. We breakfasted, dined, &c. again at home. Yesterday being Sunday & St. Thomas's Day the Poor deferred going after their Christmas Gifts till this Morning, I had at my House fifty five, gave only to 53, the other two not living in the Parish. Gave in the Whole this Morn' at 6^d each in Number 53. 1. 6. 6. Dinner to day, boiled Beef & a rost Chicken. I was but poorly to day after dinner, giddy &c. Sitting too long to day at one time I think. The Poor to day behaved extremely well indeed tho' times were extremely hard for them—They all appeared very patient & submissive. Mr. Press Custance sent us a Pheasant this Even'. Very fine and open Weather for the Season. I cannot remember a finer day (I think) for St. Thomas's Day, than this Day proved. Pray God! make us all thankfull for the same.

DECBR. 24, WEDNESDAY. We breakfasted, dined
&c. again at home. Recd. of Betty for Butter to day—
½ Pint o. 8½. Dinner to day, Skaite & broiled Mutton
&c. This being Christmas Eve we dressed up our
Windows with Hulver Branches as usual.

DECBR. 25, THURSDAY AND CHRISTMAS DAY.
We breakfasted, dined, &c. again at home. Mr. Dade
read Prayers, Preached and administered the Holy-
Sacrament this Morning at Weston-Church. Mrs.
Custance was there and after Divine Service she made
us a Visit & stayed near an Hour with us. This being
Christmas Day, the following poor People, dined at
my House, Eliz: Case, Thos. Atterton Senr., Robt.
Downing, Roger Sherwood and my Clerk Willm.
Large. Old Mary Heavers not being able to come I
sent her some rost Beef and plumb Pudding and o. 1. o.
I gave to those that dined at my House after Dinner
some strong Beer and when they went away, gave
each of them 1. Shilling o. 5. o. I lighted my great
Wax-Candle as usual on this High-day, but it is almost
burnt up. The poor People went away about 5.
o'clock happy and well pleased with their fare.

1801

JANRY. 19, MONDAY. . . . Dearness of Bread &c.
rather advances. Bread now very high—a formerly
6ᵈ. penny Loaf is now sold at the high Price of seven-
teen-pence.

JANUARY 31, SATURDAY. We breakfasted, dined,
&c. again at home. Sent Ben this Morning to Norwich with eight Coomb of Wheat to Mr. Bloome.
Thank God! I was finely to day. Dinner to day, Pork
and Peas &c. Ben returned home from Norwich

about 5. o'clock this Evening, safe & well (thanks to
God for it) and brought me Cash for my Wheat from
Mr. Bloome at 3. 15. 0. pr Coomb. 30. 0. 0. an
enormous Price I must confess indeed and sincerely
wish that it might be cheaper e'er long for the benefit
of the Poor who are distressed on that Account—tho'
much alleviated by the liberal Allowance to them of
every Parish.[1] Pray God! send us better Times and
all People better. Fine mild Weather for the Season,
thank God for it.

FEBRUARY 5, THURSDAY. . . . Very fine Weather
indeed for the Season. Bees quite brisk. Crocus's &
Snow Drops out in full blossom. Gooseberry Trees
coming into Leaf very fast indeed.

FEBRUARY 6, FRIDAY. We breakfasted, dined, &c.
again at home. Had my Study, Kitchen, and Back-
Kitchen Chimnies swept by Holland & his Boy, Hunt.
To a Man of Sparham having lately lost a Cow, gave
him 0. 1. 0. Received of Betty this Morning for 4.
Pints and half of Butter at ^{s}1/5^d pr. Pt. 0. 6. 4½.
Nancy got up early this Morning and walked to
Weston-House before I was down Stairs, and there
breakfasted, and soon after went with Mr. & Mrs.

[1] The steady rise in prices, reaching famine levels in the year 1795,
and again in 1800–1, had been countered as far as possible by a variety
of measures. Of these the most important was the extensive provision
of out-relief from the rates in supplement of wages introduced by the
famous Speenhamland decision of the Berkshire magistrates in May
1795, and later in the same year endorsed by an Act of Parliament.
Whether the precise Speenhamland scheme which regulated relief in
accordance with the price of bread was actually adopted in Weston is
not clear, but the Diarist's entries for Dec. 22nd, 1800, and for the
present date, indicate that the relief given was pretty extensive. Where-
as Parson Woodforde's half-year's poor-rate from Lady Day to Michaelmas, 1794, was £1 10s. 3d., in 1796 for the same six months it was
£2 5s. 4½d., while in 1800 the corresponding figure is £5 8s. 0¾d., which
rises to £6 13s. for the six months from Michaelmas 1800 to Lady Day
1801.

Custance & Daughters to Norwich and did not return till after 5. this Evening about which time they brought her home. The Weather rather unfavourable, as it rained most part of the Day tho' not a heavy Rain. She was well pleased however with her Jaunt. Bought a new Pair of Stays &c. Dinner to day, a Leg of Mutton rosted &c. Miss W: did not dine till after return home. Thank God! they all went & returned home safe.

FEBRY. 20, FRIDAY. We breakfasted, dined, &c. again at home. Briton was out all Night last Night at Js. Peggs but not without my consent, Js. Pegg had a few Friends of his to spend the Evening. Dinner to day, Knuckle of Veal, Bacon & Greens &c. Meat, by my Butchers Account this Day, was at the following high Price—Beef at 7^d Pr. lb, Mutton at 7^{d}½., Veal at 7^d. per lb.[1] Briton returned home early in the Morning.

MARCH 10, TUESDAY. We breakfasted, dined, &c. again at home. Gave my Niece this Morning 10. 0. 0. Mr. Aldridge called here this Morning with Cottons of different Patterns &c. &c. I paid him for divers things as under 3. 10. 11. Viz, 8. Yards of Purple and White Cotton for a Morning Gown for myself at ^{s}2/3^d 0. 18. 0. To 6. Yrds and ¾ Callico-Lining at ^{s}1/4^d. 0. 9. 0. To 2. Coloured Handkerchiefs for my two Washerwomen, Downing & Richmond 4. 8. To 2. Waistcoat Pieces for my two Men, Benj: Leggatt & Bretingham Scurl, of Woolen but of pretty Pattern, red, green & brown in stripes about one Yard in

---

[1] These prices for home-grown meat seem cheap enough compared with modern prices. When, however, they are compared with the prices paid by Parson Woodforde in, for instance, 1765 (beef steaks 3d. per lb.), he had cause for lament. Moreover it is clear from the Diary what a great part meat played in the eighteenth-century diet, at any rate of those who were better to do.

length, each pd. 0. 14. 0. To a Waistcoat-Piece for my boy Robt. Case also, about a Yard also of Woollen 0. 4. 0. So that I paid Aldridge in toto 3. 10. 11. He had also besides, both Victuals & Drink. So that upon the whole, he did not make a bad-Calling here this Morning and his obliging behaviour merited it also. Paid also to Alldridge (omitted before) for 2. Cotton Gowns for my two Maids of Pink & White 17. Yards at ˢ2/6ᵈ. 2. 2. 6. Dinner to day, Leg of Pork boiled & Peas.

APRIL 16, THURSDAY. We breakfasted, dined &c. again at home. Mrs. Custance with her two Daughters made us a Morning Visit & stayed upwards of an Hour. Brought us great News, that Lord Nelson had taken several Men of War from the Danes, had demolished Copenhagen, a great Part of it at least. The Danes defied him. They have of late behaved very shabby towards us. The Emperor of Russia also is said to be dead supposed to have been put to death. He had long behaved bad towards England.[1] Dinner to day, Breast of Mutton rosted &c.

MAY 9, SATURDAY. We breakfasted, dined &c. again at home. Dinner to day, 2. blade-bones of Pork rosted &c. I was rather better to day than Yesterday. Our Kitchen &c. White-washed to day by Js. Hardy

---

[1] The Battle of Copenhagen on April 2nd, and the assassination of the Emperor Paul on March 24th—though this event was not known till after the battle—brought the 'armed neutrality' of Russia, Prussia, Denmark, and Sweden to an end, and reopened the Baltic to British trade. The fleet, with Sir Hyde Parker in command, and Nelson under him, left Yarmouth on March 12th. Nelson urged the importance of instant action as soon as it was clear that the Danes were in no pacific mood, and despite the paralysing caution of Parker, the shoals in the Sound, the fears of the pilots, and the embattled Danish fleet, protected by numerous shore and floating batteries, he won his astounding victory.

Junr. but neither Parlour or Study. Mr. Jeans of Whichingham, who has been gone from thence from the Year 1795 is reported to have been at Wichingham for many days and is still there—Mr. Beevor being in the Kings-Bench-Prison and is to continue there for some little time yet for challenging Capt. Pain.[1]

MAY 29, FRIDAY. We breakfasted, dined, &c. again at home. Nancy got up this Morning quite ill and much Fever about her of the low kind. After however taking a Glass or two of Port Wine She felt herself much better and made a tolerable good Dinner after on a boiled Leg of Lamb. I was very poorly myself all Day. I dare say the full Moon much affected us. Dinner to day, boiled Leg of Lamb and Spinage.

JUNE 10, WEDNESDAY. . . . Andrew Spraggs of this Parish, a Married Man with a Wife and a large Family of Children, having lately lost a Cow gave him this Morn' o. 10. 6. He bears a good Character and is very industrious. His Wife came about with a Brief for them. Dinner to day, green Peas for the first time &c. Thank God! was finely to day, think myself much better by what I have taken lately.

JUNE 26, FRIDAY. . . . It being a fine Day, I had all my Hay carried, only five Cart Load from four acres, very well made indeed & without a drop of Rain. It makes but little Show but smells like a Violet.

JULY 14, TUESDAY. We breakfasted, dined &c. again at home. Sent Briton this Morn' to Mr. Ansons

[1] The 'Revd. Mr. Beevor, son of Mr. James Beevor of Norwich', had apparently been doing duty for the now non-resident Rev. Dr. Jeans. The war-like Beevor did not long remain in prison, for he nearly did duty at Weston on Sunday, July 19th. It is certainly startling to find a clergyman challenging to a duel as late as 1801, though duels were still fought by prime ministers, e.g. Pitt with Tierney in 1798, and the Duke of Wellington with Lord Winchelsea in 1829.

of Ling after a Puppey promised me by him, and a very nice little bitch he sent me back of a reddish Colour, all over—quite of the Fairy Size, therefore we named her Mab. Mrs. Custance with Lady Bacon made us a Morning Visit, they came walking and were much frightened by a Cow coming across the Field. They appeared much agitated, they had each a Glass of Port Wine & other refreshment. They came about 2. o'clock and stayed till 3. as they stayed till we could send to Weston House after the Coach. Briton went to order it directly. It came in about an Hour after it was ordered. They were pretty well composed when they went. Mr. Maynard dined & spent the Afternoon with us. Mrs. Custance and Lady Bacon met him as they came near my House and he appeared to them disguised in Liquor; which I heard afterwards was the Case—he having been to Mr. Mann's to name a Child, they perhaps urging him to drink. To James Rope of Ringland, losing Stock 0. 2. 6. Dinner to day, a Couple of boiled Chicken and a Chop, rost Beef & a Currant Pudding &c. Mr. Maynard left us about 7. this Evening and perfectly sober & well. I would not by no means push the Glass on fast as I was uneasy about his drinking too much this Morn' at Manns he having been there to name Mann's Child.

AUGUST 2, SUNDAY. . . . I waked this Morning in kind of a Fit in a very violent Perspiration & depression of Spirits. It was very hot all the Night long, and my Bed Curtains too close drawn, and also too much Cloaths upon my Bed in such hot Weather. Mr. Dade read Prayers & Preached this Morn' at Weston-Church. Mr. & Mrs. Custance there. Nancy was also at Church to day. . . .

AUGUST 8, SATURDAY. . . . Begun Harvest this Morn' in cutting Oats. Dinner to day, Calfs Fry & Heart rosted &c. Great Feats done again by Admiral Nelson over the French and also the Spaniards, also of besieging Bologne in France &c.[1]

AUGUST 10, MONDAY. . . . Begun cutting Peas this Morn' in the Field. A Parish Meeting held this Evening at the Heart to take into consideration the Papers lately recd. concerning what is to be done in case of an Invasion of the French on this Country. Dinner to day, Beans and Bacon &c. I was very nervous and weak to day, much agitated not knowing what to do at the present Crisis & wanting Health & Strength am scarce able to do even the most trivial action.

AUGUST 25, TUESDAY. . . . Mr. Maynard called on us early this Morning during the time we were at breakfast, We asked him to drink a dish of Tea with us, but he declined it, having breakfasted. He looked very sadly I thought. He said that he had been much

[1] After the naval campaign in the Baltic Nelson had been appointed (July 24th) to command coastal operations from Orfordness in Suffolk to Beachy Head in Sussex. Through the Spring and Summer of 1801 England expected an invasion of the French, great preparations of flat-bottomed boats and gun-boats having been set in hand on the French coast under Napoleon's direction. On July 21st, a secret circular was issued to all District Commanders warning them of the probability of an immediate descent and giving orders for 'the utmost vigilance to be observed throughout your district. . . .' Actually—at least after Copenhagen—Napoleon does not seem to have contemplated such an attempt, but he desired to keep us in a state of alarm. Nelson thought an attack likely at first, but subsequently pronounced it 'almost impracticable'. On August 4th he bombarded Boulogne, but despite Parson Woodforde's belief that 'great feats' had been accomplished, little damage seems to have been done. Nor did any greater success attend the attempted night-attack on Boulogne of August 15th. This was the occasion when a French officer called out in English: 'You can do nothing here, and it is only useless shedding the blood of brave men to make the attempt.'

hurried & fatigued concerning the Papers he lately
recd. in case of an Invasion by the French and Dutch
on this Coast which is talked of at present. Dinner to
day, Pork and Greens &c. Busy in carrying Barley
all day again.

AUGUST 31, MONDAY. We breakfasted, dined, &c.
again at home. We finished Harvest to day before
Dinner, cut, dried and in Barn without any Rain at
all. Never known finer Weather during any Harvest.
Make us gratefull to thee O Lord for the same. Dinner
to day, Loin of Veal rosted &c. Mr. Emeris sent us a
fine Leveret this Evening. We carried 1. Load of our
second Crop of Clover Grass this Afternoon from
Alder-Close, 4 Acres near Greengate. The Weather
having been so very dry we were obliged to feed our
Stock with some of our second Crop of Clover.

SEPBR. 27, SUNDAY. We breakfasted, dined, &c.
again at home. Mr. Dade read Prayers & Preached
this Morning at Weston-Church. Mr. Dade read the
new Thanks giving Prayer to Almighty God! for his
late blessing to us in a fine & plentiful Harvest. Mr.
and Mrs. Custance at Church to day. Miss Woodforde also at Church. Dinner to day, Loin of Veal
rosted & a Pudding. Ben abused Betty this evening
on his hearing that she had accepted his Cousin Thos.
Leggatt of Ringland for a Paramour.

OCTOBER 3, SATURDAY. We breakfasted, dined,
&c. again at home. Recd. of Betty for Butter this
Week 6 Pints made, 3½ sold at ˢ1/5½ᵈ per Pint
o. 5. 2¼. Dinner to day, Pork & Greens & a Pheasant
rosted &c. Great Rejoicings we heard this day at
Norwich on a report of there being Peace proclaimed

in London. Briton heard of it this Morning at Mr.
Press Custance's. I hope it is a true report.[1]

OCTBR. 21, WEDNESDAY. We breakfasted, dined,
&c. again at home. Great Rejoicings to be to day on
Account of Peace. A bullock to be rosted in the
Market-Place &c. It raining all the Morning rather
against them. About 6. in the Afternoon it cleared up
and many went from Weston. Ben went about that
time and had my Mare, Jenny, to go thither. Dinner
to day, Ham & 2. Fowls boiled &c. Whilst we were
at Dinner to day, there was a large flash of Lightning
and one loud Clap of Thunder. The Lightning shone
on Nancy's Plate. It rained hard for about an Hour
afterwards. N.B. No Bullock rosted at Norwich as
talked of.

OCTBR. 22, THURSDAY. We breakfasted, dined,
&c. again at home. Ben did not return from Norwich
I heard this Morn' till near 3. o'clock in the Morning.
Dinner to day, Giblet-Soup & rost Loin of Mutton.
Afternoon, cold NW Wind & some Rain. Dereham
Ball this Evening and Illuminations on Account of
Peace with other Rejoicings. Mrs. Custance and
Daughters are said to be there as were also, Lord &
Lady Bayning & Daughters.

NOVBR. 8, SUNDAY. We breakfasted, dined, &c.
again at home. Mr. Dade read Prayers and Preached
this Morning at Weston Church, Mrs. Custance with

---

[1] The preliminaries of peace were signed in London on Thursday,
Oct. 1st, 1801, were confirmed by Bonaparte on Oct. 5th, and finally
incorporated in the definitive Peace of Amiens on March 27th, 1802.
The public relief and joy in those early October days was enormous,
as the mail coaches, gay with laurels, and bearing banners proclaiming
'Peace with France', sped from London to the principal provincial
towns. No one could foresee that the peace would last for only a year
and a half.

her two Daughters, and with them, a Mrs. Hobart with her Sister, Miss Harriet Beauchamp, Daughters of Sr. Thomas Beauchamp of Langley-Park, near Sr Edmund Bacon's at Raveningham, were at Weston-Church this Morning & made us a Morning Visit after Divine Service and stayed with us near an Hour. They all eat some of our small Cakes, Mrs. Hobart and Sister, very handsome indeed, but not very talkative. I was very poorly all Day, so very low-spirited. N.B. Mrs. Custance brought us a fine Hen-Pheasant. Miss Woodforde had a Letter from Mrs. Bodham this Afternoon soon after Dinner by Betty's Nephew, Billy Dade, apologizing for her not answering, my Niece's last Letter before now. Nancy something better to day than Yesterday.

NOVBR. 24, TUESDAY. We breakfasted, dined, &c. again at home. This being my Tithe-Audit Day, the following Farmers of my Parish waited on me and paid me their respective dues for Tithe and Rent, & dined here afterwards—Stephen Andrews Senr., Willm. Bidewell, James Pegg, Henry Case, Mary Pratt, Mich. Andrews, John Buck, Robt. Emeris, Henry Rising, John Norton, Jn̄o Baker, Thos. Baker, Willm. Howlett, John Girling, Andrew Spraggs, Charles Hardy, Jn̄o Mann, Thos. Reynolds, Charles Cary, Jn̄o Hubbard, Willm. Large. Dinner to day, Salt Fish, two boiled Legs of Mutton, Surloin of Beef rosted, plumb Pudding boiled &c. &c. Port Wine, and Punch, with plenty of strong Beer. Thos. Salisbury paid for John Buck [who] was sent for home from my House, Mrs. Buck being very ill. They all went away abt. 11 o'clock this Night and very well indeed. Briton behaved not so well as I could wish, exposing himself and behaving rather impudently in making a great noise in Kitchen by singing in an impudent & loud & bold Manner in the Kitchen, tho' not very tipsy.

DECBR. 7, MONDAY. . . . I was very indifferent & very unwell indeed to day so blown up with gouty Wind & strange feelings. Dinner to day, boiled Beef &c. Towards the evening I got something better. Cow, Beauty had a Cow-Calf.

DECBR. 17, THURSDAY. . . . Had a Letter this Morning (by Mr. Custance's Servant) from Robt Clarke of Castle-Cary, concerning some Money lent by him to my late Brother Heighes of 12-£—dated March 24, 1783—unknown of by any of the family before now. Dinner to day, Giblet-Soup & cold rost Turkey. N.B. The above Robt. Clarke (tho' very ingenious) hath greatly injured himself by following too Many Schemes one after the other to better himself. Mr. Maynard buried poor old Widow Case this Afternoon at Weston-Church aged 78. Years.

DECBR. 25, FRIDAY. We breakfasted, dined, &c. again at home. Mr. Dade read Prayers, Preached and administered the H. Sacrament this Morn' at Weston Church, being Christmas-Day. None from Weston-House at Church to day. Old Thos Atterton, Robt Downing, Roger Sherwood, Eliz. Ward Widow and the Clerk Willm Large, dined at Weston-Parsonage to day, being Christmas Day and had each in Money ^{s}1/o^d—5. 0. Poor old Mary Heavers, Widow, very old & infirm I sent her Dinner to her and likewise— 0. 1. 0. Dinner to day, Surloin of Beef rosted & plumb Puddings boiled for both Parlour & Kitchen. We had also in Parlour some Mince-Pies.

1802

JANRY. 1, FRIDAY. We breakfasted, dined, &c. again at home. The New Year came in with Frost & Snow and with it very cold Weather indeed, which pinched me much—being an invalid. Dinner to day, Peas Soup & a Breast of Mutton. Our Servants being invited to Weston-House to Dinner to day, Briton & Sally went, but returned in good time about 10. o'clock at Night Much fatigued & tired, it being very bad & cold walking—The Snow in places quite high and No Moon. I hope they will not be ill after it.

FEBRY. 1, MONDAY. We breakfasted, dined, &c. again at home. Mr. Maynard called on us this Morning and stayed with us near an Hour. Paid Ben this Morning for divers things—3. 7. 11. Paid Taylor Cary this Morning for a great Coat for my Servant, Bretingham Scurl, of a brown-Drab narrow Cloth at $^s5/o^d$ per Yard, 7. Yards—1. 5. 0.—Making &c— 12/6½—1. 17. 6½. Dinner to day, Neck of Mutton, boiled &c. Being hurried a good deal this Morning, disconcerted me & made me very nervous. Lent my little Cart to Mr. Ham. Custance to go to Lord Wodehouse's at Kimberley for a Day or two.

FEBRY. 20, SATURDAY. We breakfasted, dined, &c. again at home. Mr. Thorne (alias Dr.) called about Noon and stayed about an Hour with us. He says Nancy's Complaint is an internal one. The Dr. drank a small Tumbler of Brandy & Cold Water he having a bad Cold. The Dr. says that it will take a little time to set her right by a due course of Medicine. Sent Ben to Norwich this Morning with ten Coomb of Barley to Mr. Bloome's. Dinner to day, a Breast of Veal rosted

&c. Ben returned from Norwich this Evening between five and six o'clock, he brought me Cash for the Barley—at 19/0—9. 10. 0. Nancy had a Letter from Mrs. Jane Grove from Melbury in Dorsetshire. Very low, faint and very unwell all the Morn'. I dont know that I ever felt myself so depressed and so spiritless as this very day. Nancy out of Temper all the Whole day, very saucy.

March 18, Thursday. We breakfasted, dined, &c. again at home. I was taken very giddy this Morning before I came down Stairs whilst I was washing my Face & Hands in the Passage next my Room and afraid to go down Stairs without help. After breakfast I got something better. Betty's Father (Willm. Dade of Mattishall) came here this Morning ab^t breakfast time to see his Daughter. Briton's Father from Reepham by Name Robert Scurl, Baker, called here this Morning to see his Son and inform him, that his poor weak consumptive Brother was released from his Misery—died on Thursday. His name was John, only 20 years of Age. Dinner to day, boiled Neck of Mutton &c. Nancy not liking boiled Neck of Mutton, had a Mutton Stake taken from the Neck before it was boiled—on wch she dined. I continued but poorly all the day, tho' better in the Afternoon and Evening—About Noon time almost every Day I feel poorly.

April 7, Wednesday. We breakfasted, dined, &c. again at home. Mr. Maynard called on us this Morning. I was rather faint & weak to day. Dinner to day, a Pike rosted &c. Sent my poor Neighbour Will: Richmond to day a Bottle (and the last I had) of very old strong Beer 10 y^rs old, he being dropsically inclined.

APRIL 11, SUNDAY. We breakfasted, dined, &c. again at home. I slept but very little last Night, there being a strong and rough North-Westerly Wind all the whole Night almost making the doors & Windows above & below continually ratling—No service at Weston Church to day, Mr. Dade not being returned from Cambridge as yet, and Mr. Stoughton of Sparham (to whom I applied) being so very ill that he was unable to do duty at his own Church—in short, so ill, as to be carried to Norwich to be under Doctor Beevor's continual direction & advice. Dinner to day, Breast of Veal rosted &c.

APRIL 13, TUESDAY. We breakfasted, dined, &c. again at home. To James Pegg this Morn' by Betty, pd. 3. 6. 8. being two Months Income Tax—at twenty Pounds Pr Annum—Valued at 200£ p^r Annum N.B.—The above Tax to be repealed this Month—is now pretty generally believed if not already done—it being universally disliked.[1] Very cold to day with Hail, Snow and Rain at times. Dinner to day, Leg of Mutton rosted &c. Had a Note this Evening from Mr. Press Custance of Hungate-Lodge, informing us that Mr. Stoughton of Sparham who is now at Norwich under Dr. Beevor is better and declared out of danger—Mr. P. Custance having been at Norwich to day. I was very indifferent all day, the Weather being severely & bitterly cold to day. To Will: Richmond being very ill sent—o. 2. 6.

MAY 20, THURSDAY. We breakfasted, dined, &c. again at home. Paid Robert Cary, Taylor, for a new

[1] Pitt's Income Tax was repealed in this year by 42 Geo. III, c. 42. In 1801 it had produced £5,600,000. The repeal was short-lived. War broke out again in May, 1803, and the tax was reimposed in a modified form by Addington.

Pair of brown striped Velveret Breeches for Briton,
every thing included whatever 1. 1. 6. I came down
Stairs this Morn' very weak but more giddy, and
obliged to have some Assistance, therefore had Betty
to help me down the Stairs. Brewed a Barrell of
common Beer to day. About Noon and after Dinner
somewhat better I felt myself, and Spirits better than
in the Morn'. Brewed a Barrel of Table-Beer.

MAY 30, SUNDAY. . . . Mr. Dade read Prayers &
Preached this Afternoon at Weston Church—Mrs.
Custance there. There was Bread given to the Poor at
Church this Afternoon by Briton from Money which
he had received for that Purpose from some Person
who desired that it may not be known from whom it
came in value abt. 1. 5. 0. Dinner to day a brace of
Trout & a Fillet of Veal &c.

JUNE 1, TUESDAY. We breakfasted, dined, &c. again
at home. This Day being appointed for a general
Thanksgiving for Peace, Mr. Dade read Prayers and
Preached this Morning at Weston-Church. Mr. and
Mrs. Custance at Church, Miss Woodforde also there.
I was rather poorly this Morning, so very cold &
giddy & weak. It was very cold this Morn'. Many
complained of it. Dinner to day, Knuckle of Veal,
Pork and Greens & a large boiled plumb-Pudding.
Mem. great Doings in many Places to day. At Weston
nothing at all—Mr. Custance against it.[1]

[1] Though the Peace of Amiens was popular with the mass of people
it was strongly criticized by individuals, and notably by Windham,
who profoundly distrusted Napoleon. Mr. Custance evidently sympa-
thized with Windham's views. Windham had gone so far as to move
an address to the Crown opposing the peace on May 13th, and his
hostile attitude cost him his seat at the general election. Windham was
afterwards magnanimous enough to acknowledge that he was wrong,
and that Addington had been right to make peace, a breathing-space
being absolutely essential to the country.

June 2, Wednesday. We breakfasted, dined, &c. again at home. Rather odd feelings about me immediately after breakfast this Morning, just as was going to shave, attended with the Cramp in my right hand, thank God! it did not last long, but alarmed me. Mrs. Custance by herself called on us this Morning and made us a long Visit. Miss Woodforde shewed her a new Bonnett (by name Pick-Nick) which she had sent her from London by Miss Rider and came home by Mrs. Stephen Andrews Junior who (with her Husband) returned from London on Saturday. Mrs. Custance said it was very handsome and had seen nothing like it at Norwich as yet, tho' only at Norwich last Week to see the new Fashions. Dinner to day, boiled Beef &c. Very unwell and giddy & weak to walk. But still tolerable to what I have been.

June 18, Friday. We breakfasted, dined, &c. again at home. Recd. of Betty this Morning for Butter sold to Betty Cary at $^s1/0\frac{1}{2}{}^d$ per Pint 0. 8. 10$\frac{1}{4}$. This Morn a Person by name Richard Page, dressed as a Clergyman, walked up boldly to our Front Door through the Garden and knocked. I went and let him in, and walked into my Study and there informed me before Nancy, that he was a reduced Clergyman from Oxfordshire, was born at Bath in Somersetshire, had read Prayers &c. at the Abbey Church there for 12. Years. That a Dr. Lawrence of Doctors Commons was his great Friend &c. He seemed well acquainted with Oxford and with many of my old Contemporaries there, was formerly of Baliol College or at St. Edmund Hall, a short Man and thin, talked rather fast and made a plausible Story. Shewed me his Letters of Orders, signed by the late Dr. Lowthe when Bishop of Oxford &c. He stayed about half an Hour with us,

drank a Glass of Table Beer and then walked away.
I gave him before he went, half a Guinea o. 10. 6.
After he was gone we heard by Ben, that he had a
Companion who talked with Ben all the time the
other Man was with me, and that he saw the Man
that was with me give the other the Money that I had
given to him. That Man asked Ben many Questions
about me. I do not know what to make of them. I
saw Mr. Maynard's Name on his Petition. Marquiss
Townsend's Name was also on the same.

JULY 16, FRIDAY. We breakfasted, dined &c. again
at home. A Dr. Ogilvie from Norwich came post
haste in a Post Chaise after me to go back with him to
Norwich to vote for Colonel Wodehouse. Sr. Jacob
Astley is running him hard—but I was too ill to go
any where at present therefore was obliged to decline
going. He stayed about half an Hour, came here
about five o'clock in the Afternoon. It hurried me a
great deal indeed. Dinner to day, Leg of Mutton
rosted &c.

JULY 17, SATURDAY. We breakfasted, dined &c.
again at home. Neville Custance called here this
Morning. Dinner to day Beans & Pork & Beef Steaks.
I was quite low & ill to day respecting the Election.
Astley gaining on Wodehouse.

Three manuscript pages have at this point been
torn from the Diary containing the entries for July
18th to August 28th. It is clear from the entries
which begin again on August 29th that the Diarist
has been very ill in the interval with some violent
throat 'affection'. But that the Diary was regularly
kept on each of the missing days is clear from the
fact that fragments of the missing pages remain—

they were clumsily torn out. Moreover between each manuscript sheet of the booklets there is a sheet of grey paper of different texture. It was the Diarist's custom to enter in the grey paper sheets the weather of each day, thus 'Morn cloudy with some Rain—Afternoon more dry'. The carefully ruled divisions of each day are normally carried over to the opposite grey sheet. These sheets for the period July 18th to August 28th have not been torn out, and the weather of each day is duly noted.

AUGUST 29, SUNDAY. We breakfasted, dined, &c. again at home. I felt finely this Morning thank God! & stronger. Very hot indeed to day, especially at Noon. Dr. Thorne was with us to day between 12 and 1 o'clock. He stayed some little time with us. My Throat is daily getting better he says. Mr. Dade read Prayers & Preached this Afternoon at Weston-Church —Nancy at Church to day. Dinner to day, rost Beef & Plumb Pudding &c. Mrs. Custance and Daughters at Church to day.

SEPBR. 2, THURSDAY. We breakfasted, dined &c. again at home. Fine Weather still continues (thank God for it), finer Harvest Weather scarce ever known. As our Folks were carrying a Cart-Load of Barley into the Barn this Morning before Dinner, with the Boy (Bob Case) upon it, the Load or great Part of it slipt off and fell into the Pond almost close to the Barn. The Barley being so very dry it slipt all at once and fell off but thank God! no great damage at all sustained, but a little Barley wetted. The Boy not hurt at all. Dr. Thorne here again near the same time as Yesterday. Dinner to day, boiled Beef & a Partridge rosted &c.

SEPBR. 8, WEDNESDAY. We breakfasted, dined, &c. again at home. Very weak & indifferent again to day & all day. So depressed in Spirits to day made me miserable. I was assisted down Stairs & up to day. Dinner to day, Leg of Mutton rosted &c. The lest Uneasiness affects me very much.

SEPBR. 12, SUNDAY. We breakfasted, dined, &c. again at home. Very weak still, if not weaker, had a hard Matter to get down Stairs this Morn' tho' help'd. So tired after I got down, that I panted for breath. Mr. Dade read Prayers & Preached this Afternoon at Weston-Church. Miss Woodforde at Church. Mr. Custance at Church this Afternoon but none of the rest of the Family. Mrs. Custance with her daughters & Hambleton Custance, being gone this Morning for Sr. Edmund Bacons at Rainingham. Dinner to day, Calfs-Head boiled, Pork & Greens &c.

SEPBR. 17, FRIDAY. We breakfasted, dined, &c. again at home. Thank God! that I rather think, I am somewhat better than I felt myself Yesterday, and I hope stronger. Mr. Stoughton of Sparham called on us this Morn' since his return from Cromer, having been there some time for his Health, it being close to the Sea. To a travelling Woman by Name (Falling), a married Woman, who sold divers things, for a Pound of different kinds of Thread for the use of the Family —paid 0. 7. 0. Dinner to day, Shoulder Mutton rosted &c. Mr. Salisbury brought us a brace of Partridges this Evening—very weak towards bed-time. Briton still sleeps in my Room upon the Sofa, and a Candle burning all Night in the Chamber.

OCTBR. 2, SATURDAY. We breakfasted, dined, &c. again at home. I was rather better this Morning when I got up I think, than I was Yesterday Morning. Mr. Custance sent us a brace of Partridges. Dry Weather still continues to prevail. Dr. Thorne called here about 4. o'clock this Aft. Dinner to day, boiled Calfs Head, Pork & Greens and a Pigeon-Pye hot. My Legs & Thighs still continue much swelled, if any thing rather more and higher. Spirits much depressed to day upon that Account.

OCTBR. 4, MONDAY. We breakfasted, dined, &c. again at home. Mr. Maynard called on us this Morning and I paid him for my not attending the Generals at Reepham on Friday last as usual. o. 2. o. Dinner to day, hash'd Calfs Head & Partridges.

Two manuscript pages of the Diary containing the entries for October 5th to October 16th have been torn out. The interleaved pages on which the Diarist entered his weather record remain, and on these one or two supplementary notes have been carried over from the main entries. Thus on October 11th: 'Our New Boy J^n_o Lane about 13 Years old, came to his Place to Night and slept here. I continue very indifferent indeed. Pain so great scarce able to walk.' On October 15th: 'Mr. Emeris brought us some Damson Plumbs.' On October 16th: 'Eliz. Grey (an Infant) was buried this Afternoon by Mr. Maynard, aged 12 Years. Rather weaker & full of Pain all over me.' Then follows the last entry in the Diary.

OCTOBER 17, SUNDAY. We breakfasted, dined,

Very weak this Morning, scarce able to put on my Cloaths and with great difficulty, get down Stairs with help. Mr. Dade read Prayers & Preached this Morn-

ing at Weston Church—Nancy at Church. Mr. &
Mrs. Custance & Lady Bacon at Church. Dinner to
day, Rost Beef &c.

The rest of the page is blank. The Diary has
come to an end. On New Year's Day, 1803, Parson
Woodforde died.

APPENDIX

Notes relating to the death of Parson Woodforde, with some particulars of Nancy Woodforde, as supplied by Dr. R. E. H. Woodforde, the Diarist's great-great-great nephew.

Extract from Nancy's Diary for 1803:[1]

'January 1. Saturday. Weston. Norfolk. This morning about a quarter after Ten o'clock died my ever dear Uncle James Woodforde whose loss I shall lament all the days of my life. Mrs. Custance came to me about 12 o'clock.'

'Su(nday) Mrs. Custance called on me this morning. Mrs. Bodham came to stay with me just before Mrs. Custance left me.'

Extract from the Weston Register by the Rector, the Rev. Edward Clark:

'James Woodforde, single man, was buried Jan. 5th, aged 63—Rector.' The entry is in the hand of Mr. Maynard but there is nothing to show who performed the ceremony. The Register is signed at the foot by John Dell, who followed James Woodforde as Rector.

A note in the handwriting of Nephew Bill:

'Wednesday the 5th of January 1803 set off in the Taunton coach from Castle Cary about half past 1 o'clock at noon for Norfolk, got to London the next day about 1 o'clock, set off in the Mail Coach the same evening and got to Norwich the day being the 7th of the month, got to the House of mourning about 4 after noon, running in that short time a distance of 238 miles without 1 minutes sleep.'

There is no reference in Nancy's Diary to the funeral on January 5th. On January 22nd 'Brother W'm and self

---

[1] Nancy's Diary for 1802 is missing.

went to Norwich and administered to my Uncles Will'. The Will is dated 29th April, 1799. The Diarist left £5 to the poor of Weston and the rest of his estate equally between Bill and Nancy.

'A True and Perfect Inventory of all Goods Chattels, Wares and Merchandises, as well moveable as not moveable, and other Personal Estate and effects of the Rev^d Ja. Woodforde, Late of the parish of Weston in the County of Norfolk in the Diocese Norwich Deceased, Made by us whose names are hereunto Subscribed the 27th Day of January in the Year of our Lord 1803

	£	s
Purse and Wearing Apparel	120	0
Plate and Household Furniture	171	0
Library	30	0
Horses and Harness	26	0
3 Cows and 1 Heifer	20	0
2 Swine	4	0
Hay	22	0
Corn	20	0
Plough Carts and other implements of Husbandry	18	0
Turnips	5	0
Poultry	1	0
Sum Total	£437	0

Debts owing by the Deceased £250
  Appraised by us the Day and Year above Written

Stepn Andrews
Wm Dade'[1]

Extract from Nancy's Diary for 1803:
  January 31st 'Brother Wm and self went to church for the first Time since my poor Uncle was buried, very low to-day. Greatly affected at seeing my dear Uncles Grave to-day.'

---

[1] The sale of the Diarist's effects, both inside and out, took place on April 19th, 20th, and 21st. Everything, including books and pictures, seems to have been sold. The auctioneer was W. Parson of Norwich.

February 26th 'Had a new Black Silk Sarst Gown from Miss Ryder in London £5 6 0.'

March 20th 'The Miss Custances came for me this morning and took me Home with them, left Weston Parsonage this morning where I had lived with my late dear and worthy Uncle 24 years.'

April 24th 'Went to Church with Mrs. Custance etc, saw Mr. Dell [the new Rector] there for the first time. Mr. Dell dined with us at Weston House.'

Some time in May Nancy left Weston House and stayed with the Thornes until May 28th, when she went to Mrs. Bodham's. On August 11th Nancy arrived in London to live with her Brother Samuel. She finally left London on July 5th, 1805, for Castle Cary, where she lived with Mr. and Mrs. Jeans (not to be confused with the Jeans of Witchingham) for the rest of her life. She became known as Great Aunt Anne to a crowd of relatives young and old, who lived in the neighbourhood. She died at Cary January 6th, 1830, and was buried at Ansford on January 15th.

Some volumes of her Diary have survived, but several of these have only a few entries. The last volume is dated 1813.

There is nothing to show that she revisited Weston. She often wrote to the Custances and to Briton. A great number of letters from Mrs. Custance were accidentally destroyed, many were dated from Bath, and it is likely that Nancy met her there, Bath being the shopping centre for Cary.

William Woodforde died July 23rd, 1844, aged 86. Samuel died at Ferrara from 'Fever' July 27th, 1817, on his homeward journey from Rome.